D1519036

CAMBRIDGE CLASSICAL STUDIES

General editors: M.I.Finley, E.J.Kenney, G.E.L.Owen

THE AUTHENTICITY OF *PROMETHEUS BOUND*

The authenticity of 'Prometheus Bound'

MARK GRIFFITH
Assistant Professor of the Classics
Harvard University

CAMBRIDGE UNIVERSITY PRESS
Cambridge
London : New York : Melbourne

Published by the Syndics of the Cambridge University Press
The Pitt Building, Trumpington Street, Cambridge CB2 1RP
Bentley House, 200 Euston Road, London NW1 2DB
32 East 57th Street, New York, NY 10022, USA
296 Beaconsfield Parade, Middle Park, Melbourne 3206, Australia

First published 1977

Printed in Great Britain by
Redwood Burn Limited
Trowbridge and Esher

Library of Congress Cataloguing in Publication Data

Griffith, Mark.
The authenticity of Prometheus bound.

(Cambridge classical studies)
Bibliography: p.

1. Aeschylus. Prometheus vinctus. I. Title.
II. Series.
PA3825.P8G68 882'.01 76-14031

ISBN 0 521 21099 2

To my parents, Guy and Marjorie Griffith

CONTENTS

TABLES

PREFACE

From time to time, people have tried to show that the works of Shakespeare were written by somebody else. Few have believed them, or even taken them seriously. So too, a book which revives the argument that Aeschylus may not have composed *Prometheus Bound* is liable to be greeted by students of Greek tragedy, and by the world at large, with misgivings bordering on derision, and a young scholar who challenges prevailing opinion on a popular subject may be suspected of wantonly and perversely trying to make a stir. I should therefore say a word about the way this book developed.

When Professor D.L. Page suggested to me that I write my doctoral thesis on this topic, I had few doubts about the play's authenticity, and expected that my task would be simply to lay those last few doubts to rest. I found, however, over the next three years, that the evidence which I was assembling showed *Prom.* consistently behaving quite differently from the six undisputed plays of Aeschylus, and I was driven to believe that another hand was probably at work. This is still my belief; but I should stress that the discovery tomorrow of a scrap of papyrus, confirming Aeschylus as author, would in no way astonish me. We know too little to be certain about anything: I am concerned here merely with argument from probability.

In collecting and assessing the evidence, I tried to remain as objective and impartial as possible, and to suppress the natural tendency to look for unexpected and sensational results. In my dissertation (presented to the University of Cambridge in the summer of 1973), I limited my conclusions to a page and a half of equivocation; here I have committed myself a little more strongly in the last chapter to the view that the play is spurious, but I hope that my presentation of the evidence in the earlier chapters has not been distorted by this. I trust that those who come to read this book will likewise suspend their disbelief for an hour or two, and that those who do disbelieve will at least find some of the discussion of tragic style interesting in its own right.

Many sections of the book will be rather heavy going for the non-specialist, as they depend on technical and detailed analysis of the practice of the three major tragedians. I have generally tried to summarize the main points at the end of each section in a more digestible form. (It so happens, for example, that some of the most striking arguments against Aeschylean authorship are to be found in the lyric metres, an area in which most undergraduates are rather at sea. For them, and for other more casual readers, it may be helpful in chapter 2 to read only the summaries (on pp. 32-3, 37, 39, 46-7, 49, 53, 55-6, and 60), and then the broader treatment on pp.60-7.) But in the last resort, of course, it is on the details, and the laborious collection of parallels, that the case for or against authenticity must rest, and I make no further apology for producing such an unreadable book. If it helps others to make up their minds, or merely provides them with information which they can use more effectively for themselves, it will have served its purpose.

I am grateful to many scholars and friends for their criticisms and help, in particular to Professor W.S. Allen, Mr H. Griffith, Professor A. Henrichs, Professor H. Lloyd-Jones, Professor A.N. Michelini, and Mr T.C.W. Stinton. I am especially indebted to Dr R.D. Dawe, whose encouragement and opinions, on matters large and small, have at every stage been generous and salutary; and, above all, to Professor Page, who has unstintingly placed at my disposal the full range of his learning, judgement, and patience, since I first began work on this subject. I should also like to thank the Master and Fellows of Peterhouse, where I was a Research Fellow during 1972-3; the Department of the Classics at Harvard University, which met the cost of preparing the final typescript; the Faculty of Classics in the University of Cambridge, which is underwriting the publication of a book destined surely to find few readers; and the staff of the Cambridge University Press, whose attention to the details of production has been both friendly and scrupulous. Finally, to my wife, Cheryl, I offer my apologies for the time spent on this book, and my gratitude for her unfailing encouragement and support: ταύτηι γέγηθα κἀπιλήθομαι κακῶν.

Cambridge, Mass. M.G.
1976

Chapter 1
THE PROBLEM

The play known to us as Προμηθεὺς Δεσμώτης is one of seven which are preserved by the Medicean codex[1] as the work of Aeschylus, and one of the three which were frequently copied during the thirteenth and fourteenth centuries (the so-called 'Byzantine triad'). The tradition records no doubt but that Aeschylus was the author, and no suspicion is voiced by the scholia or ancient lexicons; so we may take it that the ascription to Aeschylus goes back at least two thousand years.

The first discordant voice was raised by R. Westphal in 1869.[2] In his study of Greek metre, and of Aeschylus in particular, he noticed that *Prom.* displayed several peculiarities, both in its lyric metres and in the spoken trimeters, which led him to conclude that the play had suffered revision at the hands of a later writer. It was by this time quite widely accepted that *Seven against Thebes* had undergone just such a revision,[3] and Westphal's theory won several adherents; over the next forty years further studies of the language, structure, style, staging, and metre led more scholars to accept his conclusions,[4] though the majority remained unconvinced.

The nineteenth century witnessed many attempts to prove widespread interpolation, wholesale revision, multiple authorship, or outright spuriousness of a wide range of classical works. In retrospect, some of these attempts seem pedantic, some wild; others have been accepted and have become canonical. But it was not until 1911 that Aeschylean authorship of the whole *Prom.* was first denied. By then it was becoming clear that the linguistic and stylistic peculiarities of the play were not confined to any particular passages:[5] thus those who found themselves unable to accept Aeschylean authorship of the peculiarities were forced to deny him the whole play. Faced with such an awkward choice, most scholars understandably preferred to accept the peculiarities in an author whose style is in any case strange, whose originality is undeniable, and whose surviving works represent a mere fraction of his total output.

The first to deny Aeschylean authorship outright was A. Gercke.[6] His pupil F. Niedzballa found solid evidence in the play's vocabulary to support his case, but much of Gercke's argument was based on apparent contradictions between *Prom.* and the surviving fragments of Προμηθεὺς Λυόμενος, generally regarded[7] as a companion-piece from the same Aeschylean trilogy; he concluded that the two plays could not belong to the same trilogy; that Λυόμενος was Aeschylean, that the third play, Προμηθεὺς Πυρφόρος, which most scholars regarded as the third member of the trilogy, was in fact the same as Προμηθεὺς Πυρκαεύς (a satyr-play produced in 472 B.C. with A. *Pers.*); and that Δεσμώτης was composed not earlier than the 430s, but before 424, when it was parodied by Aristophanes in his *Knights*.[8]

Gercke's arguments were opposed by Wilamowitz and Körte,[9] and his theory seemed at first to have won few supporters. Yet the defenders of Aeschylean authorship were often driven to rather desperate arguments of their own; Körte even admitted that 'if nothing else stood in the way, one would certainly place *Prom.* ten or twenty years later than the *Oresteia*', on the basis of the linguistic and stylistic evidence, but went on to argue from the structure and geographical details that an early date, soon after 475 B.C., was to be preferred: Aeschylus' connection with Sicily might explain the peculiarities. This suggestion was developed further by F. Focke, who argued for a Sicilian dilogy (Δεσμώτης and Λυόμενος), produced by Aeschylus for an audience with rather different expectations from those of the Athenians.[10]

But meanwhile another voice had entered the discussion on the other side. Wilhelm Schmid was a figure not lightly to be dismissed. In 1912 he had merely concluded that *Prom.* had undergone extensive revision;[11] but in the second volume of his monumental history of Greek literature, he omitted the play completely from his treatment of Aeschylus, and it appeared instead in the third volume, under the heading 'Die Tragödie unter dem Einfluss von Sophistik und Rhetorik'. Schmid gave his reasons in full in a separate monograph,[12] which remains in many respects the most thorough and detailed statement of the case against Aeschylean authorship. Apart from the linguistic and stylistic peculiarities noted by his predecessors, and others added by himself, Schmid dwelt at some length on the treatment of the myth and on the general tone of the drama, which he thought displayed unmistakable signs of sophistic influence and religious views incompatible with those of Aeschylus.

Schmid's overconfident tone, and the uneven quality of his arguments, which range from the feeble to the devastating, have often discouraged scholars from taking him as seriously as he deserves, and relatively few have been convinced. The opinion of the majority (particularly in England) is clearly that the play's peculiarities, though real and puzzling, are not weighty enough to cause serious doubt, when we possess only about one tenth of Aeschylus' works. Over the last forty years or so the tendency has been to ascribe *Prom.* to Aeschylus' last years, perhaps after the *Oresteia*, and to explain its peculiarities as being due to the influence of the young Sophocles, of the changes in Athenian society, or of Aeschylus' final visit to Sicily.[13]

Yet the problem has not been by any means fully explored. The defenders of Aeschylean authorship have relied heavily on the weight of tradition, and on the sense of outrage naturally felt at the denial to one of the world's greatest tragedians of one of the world's greatest tragedies. But a number of technical studies, not specifically directed towards the authorship problem but incidentally revealing further unaeschylean details unknown to Schmid, have continued to cause concern among those who recognized that a problem existed.[14] Many scholars now feel that, although no conclusive proof of spuriousness has hitherto been produced, no sure decision either way is really justified.[15]

It seems then that the time has come to try to set the problem on a sounder factual basis, and thus enable us to assess more accurately the similarities and dissimilarities between *Prom.* and the extant work of Aeschylus. This can only be done if we can discover and apply truly objective criteria to the available material, and this has been my main concern throughout this study. As far as possible my approach has been impartial, and in particular I have taken care to compare *Prom.* with the work, not only of Aeschylus, but also of Sophocles and Euripides, so as to provide an adequate check on the evidence and ensure that it can be seen in the correct perspective.

All authorship problems are bedevilled by the subjective nature of the judgements that have to be made; and ultimately, of course, the decision whether or not Aeschylus wrote all (or part) of *Prom.* must remain subjective. But we should try to explore all the possibilities of objective observation and measurement before we make that decision. It may be felt that the *prima facie* case for Aeschylean authorship is so strong that we should demand overwhelming proof before we give up the traditional ascription - and proof in such matters is rarely to be obtained. It seems to me, however, that we should try to assess, more or less independently, first this *prima facie* case (see chapter 2), and then the stylistic evidence of the play itself: only then should we put the two together and see what they add up to.

In looking for objective criteria, I have concentrated on those details of style in which we can observe a consistent and distinctive difference between Aeschylus and one or both of the other tragedians. In this way we can measure where *Prom.* stands in relation to all three. Most previous studies have been hampered by the vagueness of their criteria; and if *Prom.* is examined in relation to Aeschylus alone, it is impossible to estimate the true extent of its divergence or concurrence, in the absence of comparative material from any other author.

Modern stylistic studies may be said to have really started with the work of Lewis Campbell and A. Lutoslawski on the dating of Plato's dialogues.[16] Their work has been supplemented, and new methods developed, by several scholars over the last seventy years; as a result, we can now ascribe most of Plato's works with some confidence to his early, middle, or late period. But beyond that it has not been possible to go. Studies of particles, of vocabulary, of sentence length, and other aspects of his style, have not been conclusive. Thus, for example, it has not been proven whether or not Plato composed such important and substantial works as the *Seventh Letter* or *Hippias A*. 'The conventional methods of statistical measurement are of little use with an author such as Plato, who constantly and deliberately changes his style from passage to passage and from work to work.'[17] Similarly inconclusive results have attended the investigation of the *Corpus Lysiacum*, and of the works of Isokrates and Demosthenes.[18]

If stylometrists have been relatively unsuccessful with Plato, a prose author whose work survives in considerable bulk, it might be felt that any attempt to measure a single tragedy against Aeschylus' small and varied remains is doomed to failure. Even in the case of *Rhesos*, where eighteen undisputedly Euripidean plays are available for comparison, objective stylometry has not been decisive: most scholars appeared to be swayed at least as much by *Gefühl* as by measurable evidence, and the question of authenticity still remains open.[19] But stylometrists have rarely claimed to be able to prove a case one way or the other: usually they talk in terms of probabilities; and the twentieth century has, I think, made some progress towards a more systematic and thorough investigation of problems of authenticity, not least in the classics.

Modern advances in statistics and computer technology have also proven valuable in some authorship disputes.[20] My decision not to employ a computer was due, not simply to conservatism or ignorance, but to an awareness that, for the moment at least, its capabilities in dealing with Greek poetry are extremely limited, and that the corpus of Aeschylus' works, even of extant Greek tragedy, is small enough to allow most operations of collecting and counting to be done by hand. So too, I have only rarely had occasion to use the methods and terminology of true statisticians, as I have rarely found myself dealing with numbers and samples large enough to justify them. The result may seem unscientific or amateurish to a professional statistician, but I think it will be seen that I have not sacrificed all standards of objective measurement: instead I have tried to adapt them to the specific requirements of this study.

Perhaps the most satisfactory and genuinely objective criteria are to be found in the study of metre. Here the peculiar demands of the subject matter can be more or less discounted, and we are entitled to regard differences of technique as being truly characteristic of their author. We possess quite a substantial sample of lyrics from the three major tragedians, enough to identify quite distinct patterns in each. The anapaests too offer interesting information about their different practices. In chapters 3 and 4 I examine *Prom.* in relation to these differences; and in chapter 5 I consider various technical features of the iambic trimeters which seem also to be helpful.

Less reliable as stylometric criteria are details of structure and dramatic technique, since these are more liable to be affected by the particular requirements of the subject matter of each play. Nevertheless we can identify certain individual preferences and aversions which we may regard as characteristic of each tragedian, and in chapter 6 I measure *Prom.* against these.

Much weight has sometimes been given to the alleged problems of staging presented by *Prom.* Although this is a field in which opinion necessarily rules over knowledge, in chapter 7 I consider some of the questions which do seem capable of resolution and which may bear upon the problem of authenticity.

In my vocabulary tests (chapter 8), I have taken care to avoid the mistakes of method displayed by my predecessors, and to use as much comparative material as possible from all three tragedians. Certain statistical methods which have proven successful in distinguishing between the vocabularies of some prose authors in various languages turned out to be unhelpful in the case of Greek tragedy (the same is true of the study of sentence-length: in each case I have explained briefly why these criteria are unhelpful, and shown that the results are inconclusive).[21]

Finally I study details of syntax and style which seem to be characteristic of *Prom.*, and measure them against the practices of Aeschylus, Sophocles, and Euripides. Here it is particularly difficult to remain objective, in that one inevitably tends to *look* for oddities, but in chapter 9 I have again tried to check this tendency by the use of Sophocles and Euripides for comparison.

Other areas of investigation naturally present themselves, which I have rejected, at any rate for the present study. The whole dramatic 'meaning' of the play has been interpreted by some as being entirely characteristic of Aeschylus, by others as being incompatible with his style and beliefs: it seems clear to me that any interpretation of the play is liable to be affected by our decisions as to its author and its possible place in a trilogy;[22] I therefore prefer to consider first those arguments which are more capable of objective analysis and evaluation. So this study is no more than a prelude to the interpretation of the play. Such important and fascinating topics as the play's religious and political content, and even its patterns of imagery, have been excluded from consideration, simply because they are too hard to pin down. This emphasis on objective criteria inevitably involves closing the eyes to much that is beautiful and important in the play; we end up treating it as a problem rather than a drama. But we have no choice. Although many of the most interesting and challenging questions about *Prom.* ultimately concern its interpretation as a play, this is not the place to try to answer them.[23]

Chapter 2
EXTERNAL EVIDENCE

AUTHENTICITY

The earliest explicit reference to a Prometheus-play is found in Aristotle (*Poet.* 18.1456a2f); we have no idea whether it refers to *Prom.*, to a Prometheus trilogy, or to another play, and there is no real reason to suppose that Aristotle considered Aeschylus to be the author.[1] So for our purposes this reference is useless.

The earliest attestation of Aeschylean authorship of *Prom.* is implicitly that of the Alexandrian tradition. This is not unusual for a Greek tragedy, though it so happens that of Aeschylus' six undisputed extant plays, four are attested as his by Aristophanes.[2] *Prom.*'s *hypothesis* does not record the occasion of its first performance. This too is not in itself remarkable (for only two of Sophocles' surviving plays do the *hypotheses* give us this information), though we are given didaskalic information about *Persians*, *Seven against Thebes*, and *Oresteia*, and we now have Pap. Oxy. 2256.3 to tell us about *Suppliants*.

The fact that we have no evidence from the 200 years after Aeschylus' death to connect him with *Prom.* does not amount to a positive indication that he did not write the play. An Aristophanic citation would be an unexpected bonus to a modern scholar, and there are few other likely sources of reference. Plato quotes nine times from lost Aeschylean plays, but only from *Th.* of his extant works (*Rep.* 2.361b-362a, cf. 8.550c); no dramatic source is suggested for Protagoras' story of Prometheus (*Prot.* 320c-323a), nor for the brief reference in the *Second Letter* (311b). Aristotle rarely mentions any fifth-century tragedians apart from Sophocles, Euripides, and Agathon: of Aeschylus' extant plays, he only refers to *Cho.* (*Poet.* 16.1455a4).[3]

It is clear that the scholiasts of *Prom.* are in no doubt that Aeschylus was its author, and that the play was at one time bound with Λυόμενος (cf. Σ513, 524 τὸ ἑξῆς δρᾶμα); the list of τὰ τοῦ δράματος πρόσωπα includes the names of Ge and Herakles, who very probably took part in Λυόμενος. The Medicean Catalogue records three Prometheus-plays among its seventy-three titles, Δεσμώτης, Λυόμενος, Πυρφόρος. And if we conclude from this that the Alexandrians accepted *Prom.* as the work of Aeschylus (as Cicero accepted Λυόμενος, cf. fr. 193), we should be unwise to ignore their judgement. Their material for comparison was extensive, far greater than ours,[4] and their critical powers seem in some cases to have been keen. They are known to have expressed doubts as to the authenticity of certain dramas, to have speculated about possible cases of dramatic plagiarism, and to have pointed to occasions on which sons of tragedians produced their fathers' plays.[5]

On the other hand, it seems pretty clear that the 'minor' tragedians of the fifth century were poorly represented with the Alexandrians and their scholarly successors, in comparison to Aeschylus, Sophocles, and Euripides.[6] The Suda appears to know very little about most of them, and we hear almost nothing from other ancient sources; even the most successful tragedians are rarely quoted. Aristophanes of Byzantium and his successors often wrote as if there were only three tragedians, and apparently had little interest in the work of their rivals. Our own knowledge of the history of the tragic texts from their first performance to their arrival in Alexandria is minimal:[7] theirs may not always have been much greater. In short, it would be unwise to rest much weight on the Alexandrian ascription of our play to Aeschylus.[8]

THE DATE

The latest firm *terminus post quem* for the composition of *Prom.* is provided by 351ff, which undoubtedly refers, by *vaticinium ex eventu*, to the eruption of Etna, which can be fixed in 475 (Thuc. 3.116) or 479 B.C. (Marmor Parium 52).[9] This passage and Pindar *P.* 1.15-28 (of 470 B.C.) are obviously not independent descriptions of the eruption; either one has borrowed from the other, or both have borrowed from a common (epic?) source.[10] There is no need to conclude that *Prom.* must have been composed very soon after the eruption, or that this suggests a connection with Sicily. The Typhos incident is an important part of Zeus' *aristeia* in Hesiod's *Theogony*, and its inclusion in a play dealing with Zeus' new tyranny is therefore apt;[11] and to any dramatist writing after 470 about Typhos, Pindar's description would be an obvious source to draw from.

The echo between Pindar *O.* 4.8 (452 B.C.) ἶπον ἀνεμόεσσαν ἑκατογκεφάλα Τυφῶνος ὀβρίμου and *Prom.* 365 ἰπούμενος ῥίζαισιν Αἰτναίαις ὕπο, both concerning Etna, is unlikely to be mere coincidence: ἶπος, ἰποῦν are extremely rare words (confined mostly to comedy and medicine). But we can do no more than conclude that either *Prom.* imitated Pindar *P.* 1, and was in turn imitated by Pindar *O.* 4, or all three passages draw from a common source, or the author of *Prom.* had both Pindaric passages in mind when he wrote his Typhos-episode, in which case he was writing after 452.[12] Further Pindaric influence may perhaps be traced in the whole idea of the Thetis-secret, first found in *Isthmian* 8.30ff, of 478 B.C.

For a *terminus ante quem* we must look for passages in other works of known date which are unmistakably influenced by *Prom.* These are not easy to find. Echoes of individual phrases are common, indeed inevitable in the stylized *Kunstsprache* of tragic dialogue; they need not indicate any borrowing, conscious or unconscious, of one play from another, but may often be due to chance or to common borrowing from a source unknown to us (for example, the lost 'Homeric' epics). Thus of the seventy or so examples which Niedzballa cites of echoes between *Prom.* and the extant work of Sophocles, only about ten seem to me to be worth a second thought, and none of them are by any means certain.[13] Even more frustrating for our purposes is the fact that, even when two passages seem to be interdependent, it is rarely possible to be sure which is the original.

The same is true of *Prom.* and Euripides: we cannot point to a single passage where imitation is certain.[14] Attempts to show conscious echoes between *Prom.* and E. *Hks*, or S. *Ant.*,[15] merely establish certain similarities of theme and treatment inherent in the basic elements of the plot. An interesting but inconclusive list of possible echoes can be drawn up for *Prom.* and the *Peirithous* and *Sisyphos* of Kritias or Euripides;[16] but again this does not really help us.[17] They merely balance the possible Aeschylean echoes in *Prom.* (which are similarly uncertain),[18] and serve to remind us that *Prom.* is not noticeably more archaic, or more Aeschylean, in its allusions than we might expect any play of (say)

430 B.C. to be.

It is not surprising that we find so little to help us in fifth-century tragedy. There was no reason for tragedians obviously to copy one another, or to repeat themselves; they preferred variation and adaptation, and this process was often more or less unconscious. But in the case of Aristophanes all is different. He is eager to remind us of familiar tragic passages, for his own comic purposes. He produced *Knights* in 424, and this has usually been accepted as a *terminus ante quem* for *Prom.*, on the strength of the echoes *Prom.* 613/*Knights* 836; *Prom.* 59, 308/*Knights* 758f.[19] Even here we cannot be quite sure.

The similarity between *Prom.* 59 δεινὸς γὰρ εὑρεῖν κἀξ ἀμηχάνων πόρον and *Knights* 758f ποικίλος γὰρ ἀνὴρ κἀκ τῶν ἀμηχάνων πόρους εὐμήχανος πορίζειν is obvious enough, and *Prom.* 308 ποικίλωι, though separated by 250 lines, might be felt to be decisive. But we can point to other passages with similar phraseology, where no conscious allusion is being made, e.g. Dion. Hal. *AR* 7.36 δεινὸς ἀνὴρ τά τε ἄλλα καὶ πόρους εὑρεῖν ἐν ἀπόροις, cf. E. *IA* 356, Plato *Symp.* 203d; also Hesychius ἀμήχανον · ἄπορον · πρὸς ὃν μηχανὴν οὐκ ἔστιν εὑρεῖν. And ποικίλος is quite common in this sense (cf. ποικιλόμητις etc., and especially Hesiod *Th.* 511, 521). Perhaps more significant is the resemblance between *Prom.* 613 ὦ κοινὸν ὠφέλημα θνητοῖσιν φανείς and *Knights* 836 ὦ πᾶσιν ἀνθρώποις φανεὶς μέγιστον ὠφέλημα, which, if accidental, would be a remarkable coincidence. The phraseology ὦ ... φανείς is not unparalleled, but is unusual (cf. S. *Ph.* 1445f); the same is true of ὠφέλημα describing a person (cf. E. *Tro.* 702f). The combination of the two, and the appropriateness of the parallel (Sausage-seller/ Prometheus) in this context, are perhaps enough to lead us to accept that this is an allusion to *Prom.* which we are expected to notice. And if we accept this allusion, it is easier to accept the first, where again the context is appropriate.

If we are convinced that *Knights* parodies *Prom.*, our play is to be dated between 479 and 424 B.C. If not, the later limit may be shifted to perhaps 414, when *Birds* was produced. *Prom.* 975 ἁπλῶι λόγωι τοὺς πάντας ἐχθαίρω θεούς seems to be echoed in *Birds* 1547 (also spoken by Prometheus) μισῶ δ'ἅπαντας τοὺς θεούς, ὡς οἶσθα σύ, and *Prom.* 547ff τίς ἐφαμερίων ἄρηξις; οὐδ'ἐδέρχθης ὀλιγοδρανίαν ἄκικυν ἰσόνειρον may be a source of *Birds* 685ff ἄνδρες ... ὀλιγοδρανέες, πλάσματα πηλοῦ, σκιοειδέα φῦλ' ἀμενηνά, ἀπτῆνες ἐφημέριοι ταλαοὶ βροτοὶ ἀνέρες εἰκελόνειροι (where πλάσματα πηλοῦ reminds us of Prometheus, though not the Prometheus of our play). The whole Prometheus-scene in *Birds* (1494-1552), with the threats to Zeus' τυραννίς (1605, 1643; cf. too 1673, 1708), has some broad similarities to the situation in *Prom.*[20] It is unlikely that all these similarities are due to coincidence alone: it seems that Aristophanes at least by this date was familiar with our play.

This range of dates tells us nothing that we could not decide for ourselves from reading the play.[21] There is a fair body of evidence that *Prom.*, if Aeschylean, may date from the last years of his life,[22] and we will come across several details in our investigation which seem to be characteristic of later tragedy.

Nor does the pictorial art of the fifth century help us much. Certainly the treatment of Io underwent a change:[23] early in the fifth century she is shown as a cow, while by 450 or so she is a βούκερως παρθένος. This change may be due to a particular dramatic performance, in which she obviously could not enter as a cow. But A. *Supp.* 568ff already describes a part-human Io (cf. the horse-headed Demeter, bull-headed minotaur, and Egyptian Hathor and Isis), and Beazley points out that in *ARV* 1689 Hermes appears to be chasing Io, while in 1122 on one side Zeus touches Io (a scene not shown on the stage in *Prom.*), and on the other Hermes talks to Hera (which has nothing to do with *Prom.*). We know that Sophocles produced an *Inachos*, which included the Io-story; he too may have put her on the stage.[24]

As for Prometheus himself, the representations of his punishment that survive from the archaic age show him bound to a pillar or post, with the eagle, and sometimes Herakles, in attendance.[25] Later we find him chained to a rock, or newly released from it, with the eagle (alive or dead) and Herakles, plus from time to time Apollo, Kastor, Asklepios, or Athene, and sometimes a crown. The change from pillar to rockface may be due to the influence of Λυόμενος, but these fifth- and fourth-century representations comprise merely three Etruscan mirrors, and some gems;[26] none comes from Attica, their dates are very uncertain, and the attendant figures do not correspond to anything known about *Prom.* or Λυόμενος, although the crown does.[27] There is no certain representation of any scene from *Prom.* before the Christian era, despite the excellent opportunities it offered with its extensive use of unusual spectacle.

In Attica the only Prometheus-subject popular in fifth-century art was the bringing of fire.[28] After 440 B.C. satyrs are in attendance: they might remind us of Πυρκαεύς, yet this was first produced in 472. Again, we are left in the dark as to the painters' inspiration.

All in all, we must conclude that the external evidence as to *Prom.*'s date is of no real use to us, beyond confirming what we already believe from reading the play: it was written between 479 and 415 B.C., probably before 424.

THE TRILOGY[29]

The scholiast to *Prom.* 513 says that Prometheus is released 'in the next play'. It is generally inferred that this means Λυόμενος, and that the scholiast regards that play as the sequel to Δεσμώτης. In fact τὸ ἑξῆς δρᾶμα need mean no more than the next play in the scholiast's collection, which would probably be alphabetical,[30] and there is no evidence that the ancients knew anything of a Prometheus-trilogy. (The first suggestion seems to have been made by Welcker in 1824.) But the *prima facie* case for a connection between Δεσμώτης and Λυόμενος is fairly strong.

The list of characters for *Prom.* contains the names of Ge and Herakles. Fragments ascribed to Aeschylus suggest that Λυόμενος contained a scene in which Herakles killed the eagle, and Prometheus described to him his future travels.[31] This is confirmed by later accounts which combine Herakles' killing of the eagle and Prometheus' release with Prometheus' revelation of the Thetis-secret;[32] these may well be based on Λυόμενος. Thus the broad outlines of the plot seem to fit well with *Prom.*

Similarities of detail can also be seen even from our limited material: in particular, compare fr. 190/*Prom.* 141ff, 298ff; fr. 195, 196, 199/*Prom.* 707-41, 790-818 (but also S. *Triptolemos* fr. 541),[33] with Herakles' journey west complementing Io's wanderings east (cf. too Atlas), and perhaps Ge's appearance balancing that of Okeanos.[34] In some other respects the two plays seem to fit less well. In *Prometheus* the Titan is chained in the far north-west, in

Λυόμενος in the Caucasus (as in most other versions of the myth):[35] but the geography of *Prom.* is too vague for us to rest much weight on this (cf. the confused descriptions of Io's travels).[36] Fr. 194 appears to be part of an account like that of *Prom.* 462ff, which would scarcely bear repetition in successive plays. So, too, some of the verbal echoes[37] seem so obvious as to be clumsy, e.g. *Prom.* 619/fr. 193.6; *Prom.* 141ff/fr. 193.1-3, unless Cicero is conflating the two plays.[38]

But in the last resort it is on the basis of *Prom.* itself that we must decide whether we are to think in terms of a trilogy. Is it conceivable that no sequel was intended? Can the Titan's defiant words of 1093 mark the end of the author's treatment of this subject? Unterberger's study has shown most effectively how the tension is increased throughout the play by the references to the future; and there is no doubt that by the end we are keenly interested in the solution to the puzzle, *how* will Zeus and Prometheus come εἰς ἀρθμὸν ... καὶ φιλότητα ... σπεύδων σπεύδοντι (191f)? We have heard that someone will release Prometheus after twelve generations (771-4), and we understand that this must be Herakles. We have heard Prometheus claim that he will only reveal his secret if he is released (770); this secret we understand to be that of Thetis (cf. Pindar *I.* 8.30ff). If the secret is not revealed, Zeus will go the way of his father and grandfather. We have heard Hermes tell Prometheus what he will suffer: first Tartaros, then the eagle, with no release until another god agrees to go down into Hades. As the play ends, we witness the start of the first stage of that suffering (1080ff), with Prometheus unrepentant, and the chorus terrified but sympathetic. The tyrant Zeus[39] is temporarily victorious; yet we know that quite soon he must either be reconciled with Prometheus, or fall from power.

The constant references to the newness of Zeus' tyranny have built up a strong feeling that change is possible, and it may be that the story of Prometheus' release was already familiar enough to be taken for granted at Athens.[40] The annual λαμπαδηδρομία, the altar of Prometheus and Hephaistos in the Akademeia,[41] Prometheus' symbolic crown and ring,[42] Pindar's eighth *Isthmian* and Hesiod's *Theogony*, were all well known.[43] But most scholars feel that *Prom.* leaves too many questions unresolved, too much hanging in the air, for the audience to be satisfied with it as an independent monodrama. How *will* Zeus and Prometheus be reconciled? They want to know, and perhaps they expect to see ἐν τῶι ἑξῆς δράματι.[44]

It seems fair to say that, had we no prejudice as to the author of *Prom.*, and no ancient reference to other plays by the same author on the same theme, we would think it quite likely that Δεσμώτης had a sequel. When we find in Λυόμενος a play which appears to fit very neatly with *Prom.*, it seems reasonable to conclude, with due reservations, that they may well form two parts of a connected trilogy.[45] The Medicean Catalogue lists Πυρφόρος among Aeschylus' plays, as well as Δεσμώτης and Λυόμενος. Here we seem to have an obvious candidate for our third play, but the existence of Πυρφόρος as a tragedy, distinct from the satyric Πυρκαεύς, has been questioned. Πυρκαεύς is not listed in the Catalogue, yet it is cited twice by name by Pollux.[46] There is an almost total lack of ancient references to Πυρφόρος: we find only Σ *Prom.* 94 and Gellius 13.19.4. This is in marked contrast to Λυόμενος.

If we identify Πυρφόρος with the satyric Πυρκαεύς, we may have difficulty in finding an appropriate Aeschylean play to make up a monothematic Prometheus trilogy.[47] If we accept *Prom.* as part of a trilogy, Λυόμενος and Πυρφόρος are much the most likely candidates, out of the titles known to us, for the other two plays. We must then decide whether Πυρφόρος came first or third, again largely by inference from what we know about the other two plays.

If Πυρφόρος came first, with Prometheus the 'bringer of fire',[48] it is hard to account for the lengthy enquiries and explanations of the causes of Prometheus' punishment in *Prom.* (7-11, 107-13, 199-258, 613-21). But if it came third, the problems are even greater: we are simply at a loss to suggest any plausible action for the play. By the end of Λυόμενος the eagle is dead, Prometheus is free, and some sort of celebratory customs already instituted.[49] A whole play can hardly have been devoted to the reconciliation of Prometheus and Zeus, which must already have been at least partially achieved in Λυόμενος.[50] Furthermore, if Σ *Prom.* 94 is right in saying ἐν γὰρ τῶι Πυρφόρωι τρεῖς μυριάδας φησὶ δεδέσθαι, it is hard to see how Prometheus can speak of being bound for 30,000 years when he has already been released after only 500 years or so. (If Πυρφόρος is the first play, he can be *sentenced* to 30,000 years' punishment, and speak of this quite naturally.)[51]

On the face of it, the case for a Prometheus-trilogy seems quite strong: the pieces fit pretty neatly together, as far as we can distinguish them. It seems perhaps more likely that Δεσμώτης and Λυόμενος were part of the same trilogy than that they were independent compositions. This is generally taken as a strong argument in favour of Aeschylean authorship, in that he is known to have composed several monothematic trilogies (*Oresteia*, the Theban trilogy, a *Lykourgeia*, probably a Danaid trilogy),[52] unlike Sophocles and Euripides. It is certainly fair to say that a Prometheus-trilogy would fit well with what we know of Aeschylus; but it is impossible to generalize with any confidence about the practice of other mid-fifth-century tragedians. Sophocles wrote a *Telepheia*, Euripides may have composed a connected trilogy *Chrysippos*, *Oinomaos*, *Phoinissai* in 411; cf. too his *Alexandros*, *Palamedes*, *Troiades* of 415.[53] Polyphrasmon produced a *Lykourgeia* tetralogy in 468;[54] Philokles wrote a *Pandionis*,[55] Meletos an *Oedipodeia*.[56]

Neither the *Life* of Aeschylus nor the *Life* of Sophocles, nor Aristotle in his brief account of the development of tragic conventions (*Poet*. 4.1449a9-13) gives us any good reason for concluding that connected trilogies were especially associated with Aeschylus. We simply do not know how common they were in other authors. The Suda remarks on Sophocles, καὶ αὐτὸς ἤρξεν τοῦ δρᾶμα πρὸς δρᾶμα ἀγωνίζεσθαι ἀλλὰ μὴ τετραλογίαν [Meursius for στρατολογίαν]. If this means that Sophocles was the first not to write connected tetralogies, we know that the Suda is mistaken: in 472 B.C. Aeschylus produced *Phineus*, *Persians*, *Glaukos*, *Prometheus*.[57]

THE MYTH

No tragedian except Aeschylus is known to have dealt at length with the Prometheus-myth before the fourth century, and this is often taken as further evidence for Aeschylean authorship of *Prom*.[58] The *hypothesis* to *Prom*. informs us that the subject (μυθοποιία) occurs in S. *Kolchides* ἐν παρεκβάσει, but nowhere in Euripides. Nothing is said about any other fifth-century tragedian, perhaps because nothing was known. We know that Sophocles wrote Πανδώρα ἢ

Σφυροκόποι, which may well have given a major role to Prometheus.[59] Fr. *adesp.* 470 contains an obvious echo of *Prom.* 459, and clearly comes from a speech in which someone claims to have raised Hellas from barbarism to civilization (cf. Gorgias *Palam.* 30; A. *Palamedes*? fr. 182; also Σ *Prom.* 457). The Io story was also dealt with at some length by Sophocles in *Inachos*.

In view of the many different strands and variations of the Prometheus-myth which we can trace, it is likely that several works of literature now lost to us formed part of the archaic and fifth-century tradition. We possess only Hesiod and *Prom.*, plus little pieces (or references) from Πυρκαεύς, Epicharmos' Προμαθεύς, Protagoras (if Plato's account at *Prot.* 320ff has an authentic origin, at least in outline), and Pherekydes (*FGH* 3 fr. 17),[60] apart from Λυόμενος and Πυρφόρος. Prometheus meant many things: creator of man from clay; potter-god of the Keramikos; trickster and stealer of fire; associate of Hephaistos; companion, or violator, of Athene; father of Deukalion, and thus of the human race. However original the author of *Prom.* may have been in his adaptation of the tradition,[61] we cannot deny that he was drawing on more than just Hesiod. And of all the cities of Greece, Athens was uniquely interested in Prometheus: nowhere else was he given such public prominence and personal respect, with an altar, a torchrace, and a festival.[62]

For the Dionysian competitions at Athens between 470 and 420 B.C. we have the titles of at most 75 of the 400 or more plays produced by tragedians other than Aeschylus, Sophocles, and Euripides. We have no idea how many of the others may have dealt with some aspect of the Prometheus-myth: Aristophanes certainly seems to know different versions (cf. *Birds* 686 and 1545ff, etc.). Thus, while it is fair to say that interest in Prometheus fits with what we know about Aeschylus, it is dangerous to use this as a basis of argument for Aeschylean authorship of our play.

SUMMARY

Our external evidence is at all points inconclusive, and we constantly find that we know less than we thought. What evidence we have does not contradict the hypothesis that *Prom.* is part of a trilogy, with Πυρφόρος and Λυόμενος, composed by Aeschylus between

479 and 456 B.C. But a conservative faith in the tradition, which presents us with *Prom.* as one of Aeschylus' seven extant plays, is not really a solid foundation on which to build an argument about its authenticity; nor are the scraps of information that we possess about a possible trilogy. There is a fair case to be made that Λυόμενος (and Πυρφόρος) stand or fall with *Prom.*; but this is, at best, merely circumstantial evidence for Aeschylean authorship.

It is clear that any attempt to determine the authenticity of *Prom.* one way or the other must be based primarily on internal evidence. Only when we have found out all that we can about the play itself can we return to our unresolved questions as to its date and circumstances of composition. If the internal evidence of *Prom.* fits reasonably well with the extant work of Aeschylus, we need worry no more. If it conflicts to the point where we feel genuinely uneasy about Aeschylean authorship, then we may legitimately throw the external evidence into the scales on Aeschylus' side, where its weight will not be negligible. If the internal evidence presents us with such a mass of apparently unaeschylean material that we find it hard to see how Aeschylus can be the author of *Prom.*, then we will recognize that the external evidence is too small and too uncertain to count for much against it.

Chapter 3

THE LYRIC METRES

No systematic study of the lyrics of *Prom.* in relation to those of Aeschylus has been made, and few scholars have touched seriously on this aspect of the authorship problem since the revolution in modern theories of Greek metre led by Wilamowitz, Schroeder, Maas, and Fraenkel. (The older studies of e.g. Rossbach-Westphal, and Heidler, while often coming to similar general conclusions to mine, were based on principles of metrical analysis which are now discredited, and have perhaps for this reason been virtually ignored. Schmid, for example, strangely places almost no emphasis on the peculiarities of *Prom.*'s lyric metres: nor does Herington.)

On the face of it, we would seem to have here one of the most promising areas of investigation in our authorship problem. In their lyric metres Aeschylus, Sophocles and Euripides all display distinctive and characteristic habits, which are to a large extent capable of objective measurement and comparison. My method has been first to discuss each lyric stanza or strophic pair separately, with an analysis of its metrical components, and a comparative assessment of its similarity to the work of Aeschylus and to the other tragedians. I then give a survey of the author's treatment of the different types of metres (iambic, dochmiac, dactylic, etc.), as compared with that of Aeschylus, Sophocles, and Euripides, and a brief summary of my conclusions.

(A key to my abbreviations and a description of the metrical units which they describe are to be found in Appendix A.)

88-127

There are no metrical problems until we come to 114-19:

114 ἆ ἆ ἔα ἔα
115 ⏑– – ⏑– – ⏑– – ⏑– – 4 ba.
116 ⏑⏑⏑⏑– ⏑–⏑– ⏑–⏑– 3 ia.
117 –⏑⏑–⏑⏑⏑ ⏑⏑⏑– do. cr.
118 ⏑–⏑– ⏑–⏑– ⏑–⏑– ia. trim.

119 ⏑–⏑– ⏑–⏑– ⏑–⏑– ia. trim.

Whether, and if so how, the exclamations[1] (114) should be included in the metrical system, we cannot be sure. MSS are notoriously unreliable and arbitrary in their treatment of exclamations, though here the tradition is unanimous. They certainly could be *extra metrum*, as often in all three tragedians; or if they are included, we could scan them several ways, as hiatus and correption both seem to be common in tragic exclamations (e.g. A. *Ag*. 1485, S. *Tr*. 1034). Either –‸– ⏑–⏑– cr‸.ia., or ⏑⏑⏑–⏑– do. (cf. S. *Tr*. 1025 = 1043), or ⏑–⏑⏑⏑– do., would seem the most plausible. Our decision as to which, if any, to adopt depends partly on the reading of 117.

The MSS give ἵκετο τερμόνιον ἐπὶ πάγον πόνων ἐμῶν θεωρὸς ἢ τί δὴ θέλων; this gives perfect sense, but was emended by Headlam and Wilamowitz[2] because of the metre.[3] The sense is obviously unaltered by the transposition, which gives –⏑⏑⏑– ⏑⏑⏑⏑– 2 ia., and is adopted by Murray and Page. But Wilamowitz's objection, that a dochmiac does not belong in this context, seems to apply also, if to a lesser degree, to his emendation, which gives us one doubly resolved iambic dimeter among unsyncopated and largely unresolved[4] trimeters. Where we divide 117-18 with his reading is a matter of taste; Wilamowitz after ἐμῶν, Murray after πάγον. In either case we have the single dimeter isolated among trimeters.[5] For this the best parallels that I can find[6] are:

A. *Cho*. 423ff = 444ff (3 ia. 2 ia. 3 ia. 3 ia. 3 ia. 3 ia., where we observe (a) the context is unmistakably lyric (in strophic responsion, and heavily resolved), (b) each time the dimeter is followed by punctuation).

E. *Or*. 1474ff (3 ia. 3 ia. 2 ia. 3 ia. 2 ia. 2 ia. lek. ba. etc., by Murray's colometry). (We could perhaps take ὃ δὲ ξίφος with the previous line, to give 3 ia. 3 ia. 3 ia. 2 ia. 2 ia., but we are then faced with a rather inadequate caesura in 1476 ὃ δ'// ἀγκύλας.)

?*Pho*. 1714ff (2 ia. 3 ia. 5 ia.(2+3) (Murray), but here the text is suspect, the change of speaker interrupts the flow, and we note that 1710ff were irregular, 3 ia. 2 ia. 2 ia. ba.)

Further more or less close parallels occur at:

A. *Supp*. 776ff = 784ff (ba. lek. 3 ia. 3 ia. ia. cr. 2 ia. 3 ia.)

Ag. 406ff = 423ff (3 ia. ba. cr. 3 ia.)

Cho. 66ff = 71ff (3 ia. 3 ia. ba. sp. cr.? 3 ia. where the text is very uncertain, as it is at *Cho.* 80ff)

S. *Aj.* 869ff (3 ia. ia. lek.//(change of speaker) 3 ia.)

Ant. 1272ff = 1295ff (3 ia. 3 cr. much resolved, 3 ia.)

E. *And.* 1197ff = 1213ff (3 ia. ba. cr. ba. 3 ia. ba. cr. ba. 3 ia., with changes of speaker)

Pho. 337ff (2 ia. 3 ia. 2 ia. 2 ia. 4 ia. ia. ba.)

El. 1206ff = 1214ff (3 ia. 2 ia. ba. ba. cr. 3 ia.)

Or. 960ff = 971ff (3 ia. 3 ia. cr. ba. 3 ia.)

fr. 52 (*Alexandros*): (Snell[7] prints as 5 ia. 5 ia. 6 ia. 4 ia. 3 ia.).

On the whole question of the possibility of iambic dimeters among non-lyric iambic trimeters, Fraenkel on *Ag.* 1216 and 1256 concludes (p. 558), 'there is not the remotest parallel for the interposition between trimeters of any chance piece of a statement of fact in the form of a dimeter (or monometer)', though later (p. 580) he considers it 'possible that Wilamowitz in his early article (*Hermes* (1883) 246 n. 2) propounded the right solution for 1256f, though his treatment of *Ag.* 1214ff was not happy'. We notice that *Ag.* 1256f are the opening words of a long rhesis, and syntactically independent of their surroundings. Even if we accept them as iambic dimeters, they are scarcely more than exclamations.

On this evidence, in *Prom.* 117f, Headlam and Wilamowitz have merely substituted one metrical anomaly for another. If we keep the MSS reading we have –⏑⏑–⏑⏑⏑⏑⏑⏑– ⏑–⏑– ⏑–⏑– ⏑–⏑– do. cr. 3 ia. The dochmiac form –⏑⏑–⏑⏑⏑ does not occur in Aeschylus,[8] but comes twice in Sophocles, five or six times in Euripides.[9] Sikes and Willson suggest ἵκετο, giving ⏑⏑⏑–⏑⏑⏑ do., paralleled in A. only at *Eum.* 838, but twenty-two times in E; but the omission of the temporal augment is rare (cf. *Prom.* 181 and Murray *ad loc.*). It is tempting to remove ἐμῶν (though ἡμῶν M is presumably just a phonetic mistake), a common sort of gloss word, to give us

ἵκετο τερμόνιον ἐπὶ πάγον πόνων 2 do.
θεωρός, ἤ τί δὴ θέλων; 2 ia.

but in any case it is difficult to dodge the dochmiac.[10]

As for the lack of company for the dochmiac, it is perhaps

worth considering that the exclamations at 114 could be taken as dochmiac too (see above), and that, as we shall see, runs of bacchiacs like 115 occur most frequently in dochmiac contexts.

The four bacchiacs (115) are arresting and effective.[11] Similar outbursts occur, in comparable metrical surroundings, at: A. *Th.* 104-5; *Eum.* 788-9; E. *Ion* 1445-7; *Hks* 906; *Rhesos* 706ff = 724ff.

In Aeschylus see further, for repeated bacchiacs, *Ag.* 1100-4 = 1107-11; *Cho.* 345ff = 363ff, 386ff = 410ff.

In Sophocles we frequently find 2 ba. in iambic context, and cf. also S. *Ph.* 395-9 = 510-15 and fr. 376. Isolated interjections and exclamations among iambic trimeters often take the form of one or two bacchiacs, e.g. *OT* 1468ff, *Tr.* 890ff, *Ph.* 785ff, *OK* 1271. In Euripides we find *Tro.* 587-90 = 591-4; *Hel.* 639ff; *Pho.* 293ff, 1535ff; *Or.* 1434ff; *Ba.* 991ff = 1011ff; and *Hik.* 990ff = 1012ff, where the strophe offers an interesting echo of *Prom.* 115,

τί φέγγος, τίν' αἴγλαν ...   2 ba. etc.

In several of these examples, the similarity of the repeated bacchiacs ⏑–– ⏑–– to the dochmiac ⏑––⏑– makes analysis difficult or impossible (cf. *Prom.* 578).

Prom. 115 is particularly striking because the bacchiacs are the first colon of the brief lyric section: they may well have been preceded by something of a pause. E. *Tro.* 587ff also opens with bacchiacs, but the passages closest to *Prom.* 115ff are, I think, *Ion* 1445ff, where Kreousa is just starting her wild ἀπολελυμένα,[12] and *Hks* 906, where Herakles' voice is unexpectedly heard from within.

It appears then that the use of repeated bacchiacs is common to all three tragedians, particularly, as in *Prom.* 115, for the expression of apprehension or dismay.[13] Whether this effect was felt to be conveyed by the similarity to dochmiac, amongst which the bacchiacs often occur, or by the violent syncopation of iambic rhythm, or whether the bacchiac itself was thought of as a metrical element in its own right, we are not really in a position to decide, or even to guess. We observe though that the bacchiacs almost invariably occur in an iambic and dochmiac context, so that Wilamowitz's remark on the unsuitability of a dochmiac at 117 is scarcely justified.

Much more peculiar, indeed completely unique, is the whole metrical structure of 88-127. We are faced with a run of iambic trimeters, then anapaests, again iambic trimeters, this brief lyric iambic (+dochmiac?) interruption, and more anapaests, all without a single change of speaker. We even find (119-20) the transition from iambics to anapaests within a sentence: there is no question of the slightest pause between the two.

There is nothing remotely similar to this sequence in Aeschylus, or indeed in the whole of Greek tragedy. The nearest parallels that can be drawn only emphasize the differences.

A. *Cho.* 855ff: the chorus' anapaests are suddenly interrupted by Aigisthos' shriek (ἒ ἒ ὀτοτοτοῖ either *extra metrum* or ? ∪–∪∪∪– dochmiac); then follows ἔα ἔα μάλα· πῶς ἔχει, πῶς κέκρανται δόμοις; (do.?) 3 cr. from the chorus, who then resume in iambic trimeters.

Pers. 950-61 = 962-73 (cf. 974-86 = 987-1001): [Xerxes] anap. (or ionics? + anap.) [chorus] 2 do? (anap?), 2 chor., 2 lek., anap.

Th. 848-74: [chorus] (strophic?) lyric ia., then anap. (but 861-74 almost certainly spurious), then kommos, with alternate lyric ia. (including a few trimeters) and anapaests. But the changes of metre are accompanied by change of speaker in the antistrophic structure.

Ag. 1407ff: the chorus' largely lyric iambic strophes are each followed by Klytaimestra, first in iambic trimeters, then (1462ff) in anapaests.

S. *OT* 1297-1321: first chorus, then Oedipus, in anapaests; then one iambic trimeter before the strophic lyrics. Again, though, the changes of metre go with change of speaker.

Ph. 1400ff: iambic trimeter dialogue gives way to trochaic tetrameter dialogue; then Herakles opens with anapaests, and soon changes to iambic trimeters (1418). But his change is clearly marked by a rhetorical pause: his anapaests are merely introductory, and perhaps accompany the movement of his 'machine'.

E. *Hipp.* 1370ff: Hippolytos' lyric anapaests pass with only a slight pause (1378) into lyric iambics, before the iambic trimeter dialogue.

Hek. 59-97: Hekabe twice interrupts her anapaests with a pair of dactylic hexameters, the first of which is syntactically dependent on the preceding lines, so cannot be separated from them by any appreciable pause.

Hik. 1072-9: in the middle of a long passage of iambic trimeters the chorus breaks into a brief succession of dochmiacs, punctuated by Iphis' replies in single iambic trimeters. The interesting feature of this passage is its brevity: as with *Prom.* 114ff the lyrics are hardly more than a series of exclamations. But, unlike *Prom.*, they are here interruptions from another speaker.

Ion 881ff: Kreousa's spondaic anapaests contain apparently (apart from 889 which can possibly be contorted into some form of resolved anapaests, rather than iambics) two unexpected dochmiacs 894-5 (and see Dale 60f).

Or. 1369ff: the Phrygian's monody comprises a mixture of anapaests, dactyls, iambics, and dochmiacs in a bizarre medley far removed from *Prom.*; cf. Iphigenia's monody *IA* 1279ff.

There is no parallel (a) for so many changes of basic metre in the space of so few lines, (b) for so many changes within one speech by the same character, or even the chorus, (c) for the syntactical connection over the transition from iambics to anapaests, or vice versa.[14]

The fact that Prometheus is unable to move hand or foot to convey any emotion by gesture might be thought an explanation of the rapid changes:[15] yet recitative anapaests are not intrinsically more expressive of emotion than iambics. One would expect rather a mixture of iambics and dochmiacs, as in e.g. *Th.* 78-107, if that were the aim.

If the variety of metres employed is wholly alien to Aeschylus' usual style, the form in which they are combined is equally dissimilar to the ἀπολελυμένα of Euripides.[16] The really striking and startling point for the audience was probably 114-15, rather than the change from iambic to anapaestic and back again. In view of our limited acquaintance with Aeschylus' work (we possess somewhat less than a tenth), we are obviously in no position to say that he could not have written *Prom.* 88-127 on metrical grounds. We can say, however, that this differs considerably from his observed practice in the six undisputed plays (and from that of Sophocles and Euripides). Whether we ascribe this difference to chance (there may be parallels in the lost plays), conscious experiment on Aeschylus' part (just because a feature is unique, it is not necessarily spurious), or the hand of another author, will depend on our assessment of the whole body of evidence.

128-135 = 144-151

Either (A) (Wilamowitz; cf. Page)

128 = 144	––⏑– –⏑⏑–	ia. chor.
	⏑–⏑– –⏑⏑–	ia. chor.
130 = 145	⏑–⏑– –⏑⏑–	ia. chor.
	–⏑⏑– ⏑––	arist.
131 = 146	⏑–⏑– –⏑⏑–	ia. chor.
132 = 147	–⏑⏑–⏑⏑– ⏑––‖	alc. dec.
133 = 148	⏑–⏑– –⏑⏑–	ia. chor.
	⏑–⏑– –⏑⏑–	ia. chor.
134 = 150	⏑–⏑– –⏑⏑– ⏑––	ia. arist.
135 = 151	⏑–⏑⏑–⏑⏑– ⏑––‖	⏑ alc. dec.

or (B) (Murray, Dale)

128 = 144	––⏑–– ⏑⏑–⏑–⏑––	––⏑–– anac. ion.
	⏑⏑–⏑ –⏑––	anac. ion.
	⏑⏑–– ⏑⏑–⏑[––	(anac. ion.)
	––]⏑–⏑– –⏑⏑–	(anac. ion.) [ia. chor.]
132 = 147	–⏑⏑–⏑⏑– ⏑––‖	alc. dec.
	⏑–⏑–– ⏑⏑–⏑–⏑––	⏑–⏑–– anac. ion.
	⏑⏑–⏑ –⏑––	anac. ion.
	⏑⏑– ⏑––	anac. ‸ion.
135 = 151	⏑–⏑⏑–⏑⏑– ⏑––‖	⏑ alc. dec.

The colometry of this ode, and that of 397ff, has been the object of considerable disagreement, though surprisingly little discussion.[17] To summarize briefly the main advantages and disadvantages of each:

(A) *For* (i) Uniformity of metre (all choriambic and iambic elements).

(ii) No metrical peculiarities.

Against (i) Lack of coincidence of word-end and colon-end.

(ii) Failure to take account of strong punctuation in 128, 144 (and word-end in 133, 406) after × –⏑––.

(B) *For* (i) The break after × – ∪ – – (128 = 144) is recognized.

(ii) Slightly more coincidence of word-end and colon-end.

(iii) The resemblance to 397ff, where the case for ionics is perhaps stronger.

Against (i) The interpretation of × – ∪ – – (128 = 144). This cannot be what it appears, i.e. anceps cretic anceps, for we then have anceps followed by short. In any case, it seems a bit out of place here.

(ii) Some very peculiar forms of ionic have to be accepted: 130f either (Murray) ∪∪ – – ∪∪ – ∪ | – – ∪ – ∪ – – ∪∪ – ∧ |, which defies belief, or (Dale) ∪∪ – – ∪∪ – ∧ ∪ – – | ∪ – ∪ – – ∪∪ – |, which appears to admit a choriambic colon, but is rather optimistically defended by Dale, 'μόγις παρειποῦσα φρένας has the effect less of an iambochoriambic dimeter than of a catalectic ionic colon ∪ – ∪ – – | ∪∪ –'; 134 = 150 ∪∪ – ∪ – –, which Dale and Fraenkel interpret as ∪∪ – ∪ – ∧∧ – or ∪∪ – ∧ ∪ ∧ – – (cf. Anak. *PMG* 346; Korinna *PMG* 654; Ar. *Wasps* 302; A. *Pers*. 662; E. *Alk*. 910, *Ba*. 385, 536, *Hipp*. 733, etc.).

(iii) The clausulae (132 = 148, 135 = 151) are of a different character from the preceding cola.

Some of these considerations are of comparatively minor importance. The number of coincidences of word-end and colon-end is only marginally greater in (B), nine as opposed to eight (though more markedly so in 397ff). And for the alcaic decasyllable as clausula to ionics we can compare A. *Th*. 726 = 733, S. *El*. 1069 = 1081 (and see below).

The real crux is the 'iambic penthemimer' which Dale and Fraenkel postulate as an independent colon. As × – ∪ – × it is a standard element of dactylo-epitrite. Its possible presence in dochmiac context must be considered later with regard to *Prom*. 580=599. But it clearly cannot be followed without pause by a short syllable unless we consider the fifth syllable to be a genuine long. If we regularly encountered – – ∪ – – in this sort of context, we might explain it as – ∧ – ∪ – – spondee (= cretic) + bacchiac, and this passage would appear at first glance to allow that interpretation. But *Prom.* 133 = 149, 397 = 406, A. *Th.* 720 = 727, all offer ⏑ – ⏑ – – ⏑ ⏑ – with *short* first syllable.

But, most important of all, although the strong punctuation in both strophe and antistrophe (127 = 143) after × – ⏑ – – is indeed remarkable, at *Prom.* 148, 397 and *Th.* 720 there is not even word-end at that point. Dale[18] cites S. *Ant.* 839 = 857 to support her hypothesis: but the evidence of the antistrophe at least balances that of the strophe, and reminds us that punctuation is by no means an infallible guide to colometry. In fact, Dale[19] prints *Prom.* 128 = 144 as a single line (unlike Murray), which rather compromises the status of – – ⏑ – –.[20] It might be preferable to take that line as × – ⏑ – – ⏑ ⏑ – ⏑ – ⏑ – – ia. dodrans ba. (dodrans + ba. = Barrett's 'hipponactean a').[21] Certainly, that seems the only way to take S. *Ant.* 839ff – – ⏑ – – ⏑ ⏑ – ⏑ – ⏑ – – ia. hipp. a, – – ⏑ ⏑ – ⏑ – – – ⏑ ⏑ – – tel. reiz. There is no place for isolated anaclastic ionics there. Similarly, at A. *Th.* 720ff, *pace* Fraenkel, I would take Murray's first line as ⏑ – ⏑ – – ⏑ ⏑ – – ia. adon., followed by ionics. For similar single choriambic cola introducing ionics, cf. Anakreon *PMG* 346, 398?, 416, A. *Ag.* 448ff?, *Pers.* 648ff, E. *Ba.* 72ff (and see Fraenkel *Ag.* pp. 184-5).

But if we did treat the first line of *Prom.* 128ff in this way, we would already have sacrificed most of the advantages of the ionic interpretation, and there would be little point in adopting it for the rest of the stanza. But we should perhaps bear it in mind for our treatment of 397ff.

In fact, the strongest arguments for taking 128ff as ionic seem to me to be external, rather than internal: (i) the resemblance to 397ff, (ii) the resemblance to A. *Th.* 720ff, which I think must be taken as ionic (though Wilamowitz divides as choriambic, thus giving eleven consecutive metra without word-end and colon-end coinciding, an unlikely πνῖγος). But the ionics of *Th.* 720ff are much more straightforward than those produced by Murray's, or even Dale's, colometry of *Prom.* 128ff. The analysis of this stanza as choriambic cola is rhetorically almost as easy, and metrically far more satisfactory than any supposed alternative.

It would seem best to deal with 397ff here, in view of its obvious similarities to this ode, before looking for parallels to them both.

397-405 = 406-414[22]

Either (A)

397 = 406 ⏑–⏑– –⏑⏑– ia. chor.

398 = 407 ⏑–⏑– –⏑⏑– ia. chor.

399 = 408 –⏑⏑– –⏑⏑– [–⏑⏑–] 2 chor.

400 = 409 ⏑–⏑– –⏑⏑– ia. chor.

401 = 410 ⏑–⏑– –⏑⏑– ia. chor.

402 = 411 ⏑–⏑– –⏑⏑– ia. chor.

403 = 412 ⏑–⏑– –⏑⏑– ⏑–⏑– ia. chor. ia.

405 = 414 –⏑⏑– ––⏑––‖ chor. ia. – [alc. dec.?]

Or (B)

397 = 406 ⏑–⏑– –⏑⏑–⏑– ⏑–– ia. dodrans ba.

399 = 408 ⏑⏑–– ⏑⏑–– 2 ion.

400 = 409 ⏑⏑–[–⏑⏑–]⏑ –⏑–– anac. ion.

401 = 410 ⏑⏑–⏑ –⏑–– anac. ion.

402 = 411 ⏑⏑–⏑ –⏑–– anac. ion.

403 = 412 ⏑⏑–⏑ –⏑–– anac. ion.

404 = 413 ⏑⏑–⏑ –⏑–– anac. ion.

405 = 414 ⏑⏑–– –⏑––‖ 2 (anac.?) ion.

Here the disparity between the two interpretations in word-end and colon-end is much more marked. In the ionic analysis, too, colon-end coincides with punctuation in both strophe and antistrophe at the end of the first colon (light) and again 401 = 410 (heavy). Even so, the choriambic analysis does not produce more than six metra without diaeresis, and so does not break Maas' law (*GM* §65) that not more than eight metra may normally occur in πνῖγος.

Both interpretations are perfectly acceptable metrically: again the choriambic one is more consistent, as (B) demands a transition in the first and second cola from aeolic to ionic. In both, the most unusual feature (apart from the possible freedom of responsion ⏔ 399 = 408) is the final clausula. Wilamowitz describes it in his edition as 'clausula Alcaicus decasyllabus, sed contracto "dactylo" altero tardatus', i.e. –⏑⏑–⏕–⏑––, presumably with the clausulae of 128ff in mind. But elsewhere (*GV* 250) he mentions *Prom.* 405 as an example of –⏑⏑–⏓–⏑––, along with A. *Pers.* 648,

977, *Ag.* 687; S. *Aj.* 698, 701; E. *IA* 761, *Hks* 881. But whereas –⏑⏑–⏑–⏑–– is the sort of aeolic colon that we expect to meet (cf. above on *Prom.* 128), the dragged –⏑⏑–––⏑–– is rather different. The only examples, apart from *Prom.* 405, cited by Wilamowitz are A. *Pers.* 977, in a metrically very obscure context, and E. *IA* 761. It might be easier to take the clausula as –⏑⏑– ×–⏑–× chor. ia. × (cf. S. *Ph.* 1180 after aeolics –⏑⏑––⏑––), but the long anceps in both strophe and antistrophe is slightly suspicious, as is the final syllable. We expect, after –⏑⏑–⏑–⏑– etc., an aristophanean (as at *Prom.* 130), i.e. syncopation rather than extension. If we do think of it as 'contraction' of an alcaic decasyllabic, we might point to A. *Supp.* 867 = 877 –––⏑⏑–⏑––, which could be similarly explained, or might simply be hipponactean.

In the ionic analysis, the clausula is again rather unusual, ⏑⏑–⏑–⏑–‸. Dale (*LM* 121) claims that this is 'not uncommon' (cf. A. *Supp.* 1021 = 1029, *Th.* 723??, *Prom.* 399?? Aristophanes has a succession of free responsions ⏑⏑––⏑̱⏑–– at *Frogs* 323-36 = 340-53). Alternatively, one could divide after θεοῖς ⏑⏑–⏑–⏑–‸| –⏑⏑–––⏑–– anac. ion‸. plus (alc. dec.); this would both give word- and colon-end together, and make the final line self-contained in sense, as the poet seems to prefer elsewhere (132, 135, 151, cf. A. *Th.* 726). The colon ⏑⏑–⏑–⏑–‸ would have near parallels in such passages as *Th.* 725ff ⏑⏑–– ⏑⏑–– ⏑⏑–‸|–⏑⏑–⏑⏑– ⏑––‖ and *Pers.* 93ff, which ends ⏑⏑––⏑⏑–‸|–⏑⏑–⏑⏑–⏑–⏑– i.e. either 2 ion., ion‸., anac. ion‸., or 2 ion‸. plus –⏑⏑–⏑⏑–⏑–⏑– (expanded alc. dec.).

We cannot be sure which analysis is correct for 397ff, or how far the ambiguity may have been intentional,[23] and appreciated by the audience, or even whether it makes any difference at all, since we lack all knowledge of the musical and choreographical accompaniment. The elements (–)⏑⏑–⏑–⏑––⏑⏑–⏑–⏑–(–) and (–)⏑⏑––⏑⏑––⏑⏑–(–) etc. are in ἐπιπλοκή, and a certain amount of ambiguity is almost inevitable. What is of interest to us is whether similarly constructed odes from other plays can be found to show us if this pattern can be identified as common or rare, Aeschylean or unaeschylean. We are looking for parallels to cola that comprise *either* choriambs and iambics, with word-end regularly overlapping colon-end by one syllable (an effect comparable to Euripides' glyconic /

hipponactean ambiguities[24] – × – ⏑⏑ – ⏑ – – { × – ⏑⏑ – ⏑ – – { etc.), *or* anaclastic ionics introduced by an aeolic colon which itself resembles them.

The most commonly cited parallels are A. *Th.* 720ff and *Ag.* 447 ff. In *Th.* 720ff, like *Prom.* 397ff and 128ff, the whole stanza is metrically of uniform character, and like them it is introduced by × – ⏑ – – – ⏑⏑ – before, in this case, resolving itself into unmistakable ionics, which only occur twice in their anaclastic form. The clausula too is an alcaic decasyllable.[25] In *Ag.* 447ff = 466ff, Fraenkel's analysis (p. 185) seems good: – – ⏑ – ⏑ – ⏑ – – ⏑⏑ – ⏑ – ⏑ – –, followed by anac. ionics (cf. analysis B of *Prom.* 397ff).

Other comparable passages can easily be found in Aeschylus: *Pers.* 646ff, 657ff; *Supp.* 524ff; *Ag.* 686ff, 742ff; *Cho.* 324ff.

We may conclude, then, that *Prom.* 128ff, 397ff show definite affinities with the practice of Aeschylus as observed in his extant plays. But, as we have seen, the nature of the relationship between choriambic and ionic tends to encourage the sort of ambiguity or transition between the two that we have seen frequently in Aeschylus, and we are not surprised to find it in other authors too.

Anakreon himself, the eponymous practitioner of anaclastic ionics, contains similar ambiguities. The metrical scholion to *Prom.* 128 compares the metre to *PMG* 412; we might add *PMG* 346, 386, 397, 398, 399, 413 (cf. Hephaistion *ench.* 12.4 p. 39).[26]

In the tragedians too we find similar passages, where editors disagree as to the correct colometry and analysis, though A. *Th.* 720ff is the only other stanza in the surviving plays of the three major tragedians composed solely in such a metre:[27]

S. *El.* 1058ff

⏑ – ⏑ – – ⏑⏑ – ⏑ – ⏑ –	ia. chor. ia.
– ⏑⏑ – ⏑ – ⏑ –	chor. ia.
– ⏑⏑ – ⏑ – ⏑ –	chor. ia.
– ⏑⏑ – ⏑ – ⏑ –	chor. ia.
– ⏑⏑ – ⏑⏑ – ⏑ – – ‖	alc. dec.
– – – ⏑⏑ – ⏑ –	glyc.
– – – ⏑⏑ – ⏑ –	glyc.
– ⏓ – ⏑⏑ – – ‖	pher.
– ⏑⏑ – ⏑ – ⏑ –	chor. ia.
– ⏑⏑ – ⏑ – ⏑ –	chor. ia.

–⏑⏑– ⏑–⏑– chor. ia.

–⏑⏑–⏑⏑– ⏑––‖ alc. dec.

Here the choriambic interpretation definitely seems preferable, particularly with the unmistakably aeolic cola in the middle. But we note (a) the 'trimeter' 1058 ⏑–⏑– –⏑⏑– ⏑–⏑– (cf. *Prom.* 403) where the diaeresis after ⏑–⏑–– might again tempt some into analysing as penthemimer plus ionics, thus leaving us with the unlikely clausula (for ionics) ⏑⏑–⏑⏑–⏑–– (hipp., or ion$_{\wedge}$. anac.$_{\wedge}$ ion.); (b) the regular overlap by one syllable of the colon-end (1066ff); (c) the clausular alcaic decasyllables.

(The glyconic middle section is not as far removed in character from its surroundings as the description might suggest. × –⏑––⏑⏑ –⏑–⏑– etc. is in ἐπιπλοκή with the glyconic form ⏑––⏑⏑–⏑–, and we are familiar with Euripides', and less frequently Sophocles' use of the choriambic dimeter – × – × –⏑⏑– in association with, and even responsion to, the glyconic – × –⏑⏑– × –.)

We may compare further *Ph.* 680ff, *Aj.* 1199ff, *OT* 483ff, *Ant.* 604ff, 839ff, and should bear in mind the statement by Σ Prom. 130, that 'Sophocles used the same rhythm in his *Tyro* B'.

In Euripides we may point to *Hks* 677-80, *Hipp.* 732ff, *Ba.* 73ff, fr. 429 (and cf. *Pho.* 1514, *IA* 171ff) for similarly ambiguous choriambic/ionic passages. *Rhesos* 360ff reminds us in places of *Prom.*:

–⏑⏑– ⏑–⏑– –⏑⏑– chor. ia. chor.

–⏑⏑– ⏑–⏑– –⏑⏑– ⏑–– chor. ia. arist.

––⏑–⏑⏑– –⏑⏑– –⏑⏑– ⏑–⏑– –⏑⏑–⏑⏑–– – dodrans [= tel.] 2 chor. ia. hem. –

–––⏑⏑– –⏑⏑–⏑–– –– chor. [= hem?] arist.

–⏑⏑–⏑– –⏑⏑– –⏑⏑– –⏑⏑–⏑––‖ dodrans 2 chor. arist.

Even closer, in some respects, is a fragment preserved from Satyros[28] and in part from Plutarch.[29] The metre is uncertain, often for the same reasons that *Prom.* 397ff is uncertain,[30] but it involves choriambic + iambic with overlap, or anaclastic ionic, and contains a clausula (–⏑⏑–⏑⏑–⏑–⏑––) reminiscent of alc. dec.

Another fragment[31] (which apparently[32] the actor Neoptolemos recited to Philip at his wedding, and which Wilamowitz (*GV* 328) considered 'ein Lied wohl aus junger Tragödie', though Burges[33] suggested it might be attributed to Aeschylus) is printed by Nauck to give the following metre:

1 ⏑–⏑– –⏑⏑– –⏑⏑– ia. 2 chor.

2 –⏑⏑–⏑⏑– ⏑–– alc. dec.

3 ⏑–⏑– –⏑⏑– ia. chor.

4 ⏑–⏑– –⏑⏑– ia. chor.

5 ⏑–⏑⏑– ⏓–⏑⏑–‖ × chor. × chor.

6 ⏑–⏑– –⏑⏑– ia. chor.

7 ⏑–⏑– –⏑⏑– ia. chor.

8 ⏑–⏑– –⏑⏑– ia. chor.

9 ⏑–⏑– –⏑⏑–⏑– ? ia. dodrans

10 ––⏑⏑– ⏑––‖ ? enop. (perhaps better ia. chor. ba. chor. ba.?)

The text is uncertain, and the last two lines are particularly unsatisfactory, but the resemblances to the *Prom.* stanzas are unmistakable:

(a) the alcaic decasyllable in the second line;

(b) the ambiguous nature of 6ff. The metre must here be chor. + ia., in view of what has preceded, and what appears to succeed it, but we notice that word-end would equally suggest ⏑–⏑––| ⏑⏑–⏑–⏑––|⏑⏑–⏑–⏑––|⏑⏑–⏑–⏑––| ⏑⏑–⏑–‸––|⏑⏑–⏑––‖ (or, better for these last three cola, ⏑⏑–⏑–⏑–‸|–⏑⏑–⏑––|–⏑⏑–⏑––‖ anac. ion‸. 2 arist.). Again the word-end after ⏑–⏑–– proves misleading.

Summary

The practice of Anakreon, of Sophocles and Euripides, and of at least one[34] anonymous tragedian of uncertain date, shows that the ambiguity between choriambic-iambic and anaclastic ionic in *Prom.* 397ff, and to a less extent 128ff, while it is consistent with the style of Aeschylus, is by no means peculiar to it. Parallel passages occur relatively most frequently in Aeschylus, and *Th.* 720ff remains perhaps the closest: but the presence of several quite close parallels in the only two other tragedians whose work survives in any bulk, and in one or more unknown authors of unknown date, suggests that there is nothing distinctively Aeschylean about the metre of these odes. The only passages which remain metrically as uniform in character as *Prom.* 128ff, 397ff (i.e. not admitting any 'glyconic' elements, which would interrupt the succession ⏑ – ⏑ – – ⏑ ⏑ – ⏑ – ⏑ – etc.) are A. *Th.* 720ff and fr. *adesp.* 127, though *Rhesos* 360ff is almost as 'pure'. Aeschylus, Sophocles and Euripides all tend to have a passage of this nature as one part only, perhaps one or two periods, of a stanza that contains other elements as well. There is no parallel for two strophic odes wholly, or even largely, of this type in the same play. On the other hand, all three surviving tragedians seem often to aim for some metrical unity within a play: e.g. A. *Pers.* (ionics); S. *El.* (ia./tro.), *Ph.* (aeolic); E. *Med.* (dac.-ep.), *Hik.* (ia.), *Hkd.* (aeolic), *Ba.* (ionic).

160-167 = 178-185

160 = 178	⏑–⏑– ⏑–⏑–	2 ia.
161 = 179	⏑–⏑– ⏑⏑⏑⏑–	2 ia.
162 = 180	⏑–⏑– ⏑–⏑–	2 ia
163 = 182	⏑–⏑⏑⏑ ⏒⏑⏑⏑⏑⏑ ⏑–⏑–	3 ia.
164 = 182	⏑⏑⏑– ⏑̄–⏑–	cr. ia.
164 = 183	–⏑⏑–⏑⏑–	(hem.) (3 dac.)
165 = 184	–⏑– ⏑–– ⏑⏑–⏑⏑–⏑⏑–⏑⏑–⏑⏑	(cr. ba. ⏑⏑ 4 dac.) (ia. 5 dac.)
167 = 185	–⏑⏑–⏑⏑– ⏑––‖	(alc. dec.)

At 164 = 182 the MSS read θέμενος ἄγναμπτον νόον cr. ia. in responsion to δέδια γὰρ ἀμφὶ σαῖς τύχαις ia. ia. Wilamowitz claims (*GV* 293-4) that such responsion of cr. ~ ia. is possible, but only in plays earlier than the *Oresteia*. He gives as examples

A. *Th.* 170 = 178 ἑτεροφώνωι στράτωι (⏑⏑⏑– –⏑–)
μελόμενοι δ'ἀρήξατε (⏑⏑⏑– ⏑–⏑–) (ἄλξατε Maas)

Th. 330 = 342 δ' ἐκκενουμένα πόλις (–⏑– ⏑–⏑–)
δὲ χραίνεται πόλισμ' ἅπαν (⏑–⏑– ⏑–⏑–) (δέ *del.* Brunck).

Triclinius made the responsion exact by replacing γάρ with δ', 'zum Schaden des Sinnes' in Wilamowitz's view. (Others have suggested τιθέμενος.) γάρ for δέ is a common enough substitution by scribes who could not understand δέ as anything but adversative.

Even if we do believe in the possibility of this responsion, Denniston[35] gives several examples from Euripides which are harder to emend than the two in Aeschylus, e.g. *And.* 140 = 146, *El.* 1185 =

1203 (cf. 1177 = 1190), *Tro.* 523 = 543. The freedom of responsion, then, is (a) probably the result of a faulty text, (b) even if true, of no significance to us with our limited knowledge of Greek metre, as far as authorship is concerned.

The most difficult feature of this ode is the colometry of 165, where most editors and Dale divide –⏑–⏑––|⏑⏑–⏑⏑–⏑⏑–⏑⏑–⏑⏑. The lack of word-end and pause after the 'ithyphallic' clausula (cretic + bacchiac) is very unusual, but no satisfactory alternative colometry is to be found.[36] There is no parallel in tragedy for an ithyphallic following dactyls and leading straight into more dactyls (here of the 'rising' kind).

As for the other features of this stanza, the occurrence of –⏑⏑–⏑⏑– (hemiepes) in iambics is not unusual in any of the three extant tragedians (e.g. A. *Pers.* 131, *Supp.* 541, *Ag.* 1022f; S. *Tr.* 885, *OK* 1082; E. *Alk.* 876, *Hik.* 598f, 835, *Tro.* 1069), and the interruption of iambics by a run of dactyls, 'rising' or otherwise, is likewise not peculiar. But Aeschylus seems usually to have the dactyls as *penultimate* colon and relapse into iambics for the final clausula (*Ag.* 163ff lek. lek. 5 dac. lek.//; 1001ff ends 6 lek. 8 dac. lek.//; *Cho.* 27ff 2 ia. 2 ia. 5 dac. lek.//, 588ff 3 lek. 5 dac. lek.//, cf. *Supp.* 538ff, *Eum.* 956ff). He never ends an iambic strophe with a run of dactyls (though once, *Th.* 860, with an alcaic decasyllable); at *Eum.* 996 he opens an otherwise iambic strophe –⏑⏑–⏑⏑–⏑⏑–⏑––. His usual non-iambic end to an iambic strophe is –⏑⏑–⏑–– (aristophanean). After dactyls, he sometimes ends with an alcaic decasyllable (e.g. *Th.* 485 = 525, *Cho.* 811), but he never has a long run of dactyls with this ⏑⏑–⏑⏑–⏑–– ending: the longest is *Eum.* 996 –⏑⏑–⏑⏑–⏑⏑–⏑––, one degree longer than the alc. dec. He has nothing like *Prom.* 166ff as clausula, (–)⏑⏑–⏑⏑–⏑⏑–⏑⏑–⏑⏑–⏑⏑–⏑⏑–⏑––‖.

Sophocles also often has penultimate dactylic cola in iambics (e.g. *El.* 153ff, 221ff, *OT* 168ff). Like Aeschylus he avoids alc. dec. after iambics (*El.* 1062, 1069, *OK* 1214, 1244 after aeolic, *Ant.* 585 after dactylo-epitrite), but *El.* 856f is closer to *Prom.* 166ff, ⏑–⏑–⏑–⏑⏑–⏑⏑– –⏑⏑–⏑–– as clausula.

Euripides is much more fond than the other two of cola of the 'expanded alcaic decasyllable' type, i.e. dactyls with this pendant –⏑–– ending. (He is also more fond of alc. dec. after iambics, e.g. *Tro*. 1070, *El*. 1226, cf. *Hik*. 599.) We may compare:

Ion 1505ff hem. ⏑ hem. 2 ia. ⏑⏑–⏑⏑–⏑⏑–⏑⏑–⏑⏑–⏑⏑–⏑–⏑–––‖

And. 863, after ia., then do. etc., ––––⏑⏑–⏑⏑–⏑⏑–⏑⏑–⏑––
–⏑⏑–⏑–‖

And. 835 = 838 do. ? do. cr. –⏑⏑–⏑⏑–⏑⏑–⏑–⏓–‖

Tro. 1070 = 1080, after ia. lek. 2 ia. hem. cr.–⏑⏑–⏑⏑–⏑⏑–⏑––‖
(cf. *Hks* 1206 ⏑⏑–⏑⏑–⏑⏑–⏑⏑–⏒–‖, *Ion* 716 ⏑⏑–⏑⏑–⏑⏑–
⏑⏑–––‖, *Med*. 432 –⏑⏑–⏑⏑–⏑⏑–⏑⏑–⏑––, *Ion* 1075
–⏑⏑–⏑⏑–⏑⏑–⏑––).

Or. 1299f –⏑⏑–⏑⏑–⏑⏑–⏑⏑–⏑⏑–⏑⏑–⏑⏑–⏑––

Hik. 598 = 608f hem. cr. ba.|–⏑⏑–⏑⏑–⏔–⏑––; n.b. too Ar.
Thesm. 1158f –⏑⏑–⏑⏑–⏑⏑–⏑⏑–⏑⏑–⏑⏑–⏑––.

Particularly close to *Prom*. 164ff, with hemiepes, iambic metron of some sort, and final dactylic ending –⏑––, are *Tro*. 1068ff (also after iambic strophe), *Ion* 1505ff, *Hik*. 598f, and also *Rhesos* 535ff = 554ff, hem. cr. ––⏑⏑–⏑⏑–⏑––‖.

As for the *form* of the iambics of *Prom*. 160ff, we notice that of the five purely iambic cola (not counting 165 = 184) only one, the last, is syncopated. There are five resolutions in the eleven metra, all with exact responsion; indeed the responsion of the whole stanza is exact apart from two anceps, if we follow Triclinius in 182.

Denniston[37] says that more than half tragic dimeters are syncopated, and about two-thirds of the trimeters. Syncopation is most common in Sophocles, least in Euripides. He also observes[38] that resolution is more common in Euripides than in Aeschylus or Sophocles.

It is noticeable how few of the many Aeschylean iambic strophes are unsyncopated. *Pers*. 1038ff, 1054ff, 1066ff (first half); *Th*. 989ff (first half); *Supp*. 112ff, 134ff (first half), 776ff (after first line), 792ff (first half), 808ff; *Cho*. 22ff (first half), 66ff, 423ff are wholly or largely unsyncopated. In these, the proportion of resolutions to metra is as follows: 2/14, 4/12, 0/10, 2/12, 6/8, 1/8, 0/14, 0/10, 6/10, 5/19, 0/10, 5/17. *Prom*. 160ff has 5/11, 901ff (see below) has 8/12.

The only passages to exceed *Prom*. 160ff's proportion are *Supp*. 112ff (6/8) and 808ff (6/10), though *Pers*. 1054ff (4/12) is not far off. But Aeschylus' practice is clearly not consistent, either from play to play or within the same play. His responsion of resolutions is in all these passages exact.

Sophocles does not have many wholly iambic strophes: of these only *OK* 1724ff (first half) is unsyncopated. In thirteen metra (on my analysis), there is one responding resolution, and two not-responding; i.e. an average of 2/13.

In Euripides, wholly or largely iambic strophes are comparatively rarer than in Aeschylus, but not absolutely. Of them, the following are wholly or largely unsyncopated: *And.* 465ff (first half); *Hik.* 1123ff, 1153ff; *Tro.* 551ff; *Pho.* 1710ff (first half); *Or.* 960ff (first half); *El.* 1165ff (first half), 1177ff, 1206ff, 1221ff.[39] In these the rate of resolution is 2½/8, 6½/15, 6/28, 5/18, 3/11, 0/8, 7½/36, 3/17, 2/15, 2½/11.

Nothing very significant seems to emerge from comparison of these figures with those for Aeschylus. Euripides too is not consistent, though we note that he tends to have inexact responsion (× ⏖ ⏑ ⏔) more often than Aeschylus. In that respect *Prom.* 160 ff is closer to Aeschylus. Euripides does not have a passage proportionally so resolved as A. *Supp.* 112ff (6/8); but E. *Hik.* 1153 ff (6½/15) shows a similar rate to the *Prom.* passage (5/11).

For the whole stanza, with ingredients of iambic, hemiepes, ?iambic, dactylic (plus alc. dec.), the closest parallels are perhaps:

A. *Th.* 778ff do. 2 ia. (resolved), 2 ia. hem. do? hem. chor. cr. ba.
Supp. 538ff ba. cr. ba. alc. dec., ia. cr. ba. hem//hem. 4 dac. 5 chor. arist.
Eum. 956ff 2 cr. 2 lek. 5 dac., ba. cr.‸, 2 hem. 6 dac. lek.// cr.‸ lek.
Ag. 1001ff 2 cr. pher? anap.//2 hem. alc. dec.//6 lek. 8 dac. lek.

S. *Tr.* 881ff 2 ia. lek. glyc. 2 ia.//hem.//paroem.//cr. ba.//ia. ba. cr.? ia. etc.
El. 854ff cr. ia. cr., 2 ia., 2 anap. arist.//
Ant. 582ff – hem. x tro. cr. paroem., tro., alc. dec.//2 ia.// lek. 3 ia. etc.

E. *Tro.* 1060ff 2 glyc. pher.//2 glyc. pher.//ia. lek. 2 ia. hem. cr. –⏑⏑ alc. dec.
Ion 1497ff 3 ia. 2 do. 2 ia. ba.//ba. do. ibyc. ba.//hem. x hem. 2 ia.//'6 anap.' ⏑–⏑–––

Tro. 820ff dac.-ep. + dac. runs, ending '2 anap.' ia., '2 anap.' 4 ia., 4 dac. ia. ba.

Hik. 598ff hem. cr. ba. –⏑⏑–⏑⏑–⏒–⏑––, ba. cr. ia. etc., in ia.

El. 476ff 6 dac. ba. cr. ia., 2 ia. lek. ia. ia.$_\wedge$, × hem. glyc. ia. cr. alc. dec.

Hipp. 161ff ia. cr. ba. arist. alc. dec. –– hem., 12 anap. 3 tro., cr. ba.

Med. 204ff ––– 4 ia., ia. reiz., 2 tro. ×e×D×D 2 ia. pher.

To go further, and try to say which of these is closest to *Prom.* 160ff, is, I think, too subjective to be profitable.

Summary

Obviously we do not expect exact parallels to every detail from the limited remains of the tragedians. But, apart from the anomalous lines 184-5, we can say:

(a) there is no parallel in tragedy for a stanza starting in pure iambics (i.e. unmixed with non-iambic elements), and ending in dactyls;[40]

(b) there is no example in Aeschylus of a comparable run of lyric dactyls ending ⏑⏑–⏑⏑–⏑––,[41] whereas Euripides has several.

415-419 = 420-424

415 = 420	⏒⏑–⏑ –⏑––	2 tro.
416 = 421	–⏑–⏑ –⏑–⏑̄	2 tro.
417 = 422	–⏑–⏑ –⏑––	2 tro.
418 = 423	–⏑–⏑⏑–⏑– –⏑⏑–⏑––‖	glyc. arist.

In 421, whether or not we read θ' makes no difference to the metre, as the syllable is in any case anceps.

The metre is extremely simple: trochaic dimeters, unsyncopated and unresolved (except for the proper name 420), with aeolic clausula. Dale (*LM* 91-2) rightly distinguishes true trochaics from ia./tro. and tro./cret. (i.e. lekythia etc.), and remarks 'in Aeschylus the only continuous trochaic passage is *Prom.* 415ff'.

The nearest to continuous trochaics in Aeschylus are:

Th. 832f –⏑–⏑–⏑––⏑⏑⏑–⏓–⏑–, then iambics. This could be either tro. tetr. cat., or lek. 2 ia. Word-end favours the former, metrical consistency the latter.

Th. 352: again tro. tetr. cat. among lekythia.

Eum. 918 sp. 2 tro. lek., then leks.

Elsewhere, Aeschylus prefers even more heavily syncopated tro./cret., especially lek. (cf. *Pers.* 115ff; *Supp.* 1062ff; *Ag.* 160ff, 176ff, 681ff, 1008ff; *Cho.* 585ff, 602ff; *Eum.* 490ff, 508ff, 997ff). Often he has lekythia in iambic context: they do not with Aeschylus tend to imply trochaic rhythm as they often do with Euripides. –⏑–⏑–⏑– can just as easily be ‸–⏑– ⏑–⏑– as –⏑–⏑–⏑–‸. Aeschylus never has more than –⏑–⏑–⏑– × –⏑–⏑–⏑–(×), i.e. one trochaic tetrameter (sometimes catalectic), though if followed by a lekythion this can give 5 tro. cr. Even these few passages are all embedded in longer series of syncopated ia./tro. cola: there is nothing approaching the simplicity of *Prom.* 415ff.

In Sophocles we find:

El. 1281ff after ia., 3 tro. cr., 2 tro. cr. tro.//4 tro. lek. ba.//

Ant. 880ff 4 tro.//ia. ba.//

OK 1219ff after aeolics, 2 ia. 3 tro. 4 tro. (resolved) cr. ba.//

OK 1730ff 4 tro. 4 tro.

(and cf. *OT* 894ff, *OK* 1679ff)

There are few examples of trochaics in early Euripides: they become more frequent in his later plays, often alternating with iambics in the same stanza or major period. He tends to admit extensive resolution, and violent syncopation, e.g. –‸–⏑ –‸–⏑ ('palimbacchiac'), more readily than Aeschylus or Sophocles, cf. *Hel.* 167ff, 205ff, 237ff, 345ff; *Hks* 380ff, 408ff; *Pho.* 638ff, 1732ff; *IA* 1305ff.

Wilamowitz (*GV* 266-7), after describing the simple trochaics of comedy, continues, 'Neben diesen leichten Trochaen hat Aischylos eine ganz andere Art. Zwar ganz fehlen auch jene nicht, *Prom.* 415 und am Schluss der *Hiketiden*, aber wie anders klingen sie schon *Hik.* 154 und erst recht *Pers.* 117, 547, *Sept.* 357 und in den zahlreichen Liedern der *Orestie*.' His parallel to *Prom.* 415ff, i.e. *Supp.* 1062ff, seems wholly inappropriate: the passage goes, 2 lek.//arist.//lek. cr. lek. lek.//, i.e. very like those in the *Oresteia*, completely unlike *Prom.* 415ff. In fact, there is no comparable stanza in extant Greek tragedy to this trio of unresolved and unsyncopated trochaic dimeters.

The clausula, glyconic plus aristophanean with word-overlap –⏑–⏑⏑–⏑–|–⏑⏑–⏑––‖ ('priapean'), is not very common in this precise form: we are more accustomed to –⏑⏑–⏑–⏑–|–⏑⏑–⏑––‖, or –⏑–⏑⏑–⏑–|–⏑–⏑⏑––‖. Exact parallels to it occur at:

A. *Pers.* 571 after dacs., with similar overlap
Cho. 315ff, after aeolics
?*Ag.* 696f, after aeolic/ionic (see Fraenkel's note on 714)
S. *OK* 186f, after aeolics (in the form ⏑⏑⏑⏑⏑⏑⏑–⏑–|–⏑⏑–⏑––)
E. *Alk.* 402 (corrupt?) after ia. + do.
Alk. 970f, after aeolics
Hkd. 353ff, 378ff, both with overlap, after aeolics
El. 709f, after aeolics

Aeschylus is more fond of ending iambic strophes with a non-iambic clausula (usually –⏑⏑–⏑–– 'aristophanean') than Sophocles and Euripides, who usually prefer (×)–⏑– ⏑––. But for such an aeolic 'dicolon' clausula to iambics, there are not many parallels in any of the three:

A. *Supp.* 96ff, 524ff, 808ff, *Ag.* 725ff, 763ff.
S. *OK* 1695f, *Tr.* 529f.
E. *Alk.* 403ff, *Ba.* 1156f, *Tro.* 322ff, 566f, 1069f.

Summary

The simple trochaics of this strophic pair are completely unique in tragedy. They are wholly unlike the iambic/cretic/trochaic strophes of Aeschylus, and comparable trochaics only occur in Sophocles and Euripides as subsidiary parts of a longer major period. The clausula is also rather unusual in its context.

425-430 = ?431-435

It is disputed (a) whether μόνον ... ὑποστενάζει should be here at all, or whether the stanza is interpolated, (b) whether, if it was written by the same author, it is supposed to be answered by 431-435 in responsion.

If the two stanzas are supposed to correspond, they are hopelessly corrupt, and we should not waste too much time trying to construct hypothetical metrical analyses; we might improve our Greek verse composition, but we are hardly likely to arrive at objective judgements as to the original author.

As they stand, the stanzas scan as follows:

425 ⏑–– –⏑– ⏑–⏑– ba. lek.
426 ⏑–⏑⏑–⏑⏑– ––⏑–– ⏑ D – e –
427 –⏑⏑–⏑⏑⏓–⏑–⏑⏑⏑⏑–⏑–⏑–⏑ D e ⏑ e ⏑ e ⏑ ??
429 –⏑⏑–⏑⏑– ––⏑–?⏑––‖ D – e ba.//
431 ⏑–⏑– ⏑–⏑– 2 ia.
432 –⏑– ⏑–⏑– lek.
433 ⏑–– –⏑⏑⏓ ⏑ – ⏑ – ?̱ ?ba. cr. ia. –
434 –––⏑⏑–⏑⏑– – – D
435 ⏑–⏑– ⏑––‖ ia. ba.//

Even much of this is necessarily guesswork: we have no check as to the required metrical length of θεόν (⏑ or ⏑⏑), 'Ᾰ̄τλ-, ὑπŏ̄βρέμει, nor as to whether κραταιόν is followed by pause, to give ⏑––‖.

A quick glance at the analysis above, which is all it deserves, suggests, as Wilamowitz (*ad loc.* in *ed.*) remarked, '425–9 videntur fuisse dactylo epitriti'. Deeming them spurious anyway, he was free to interpret 431–5 as 'periodus iambica, tetram. dac. cat., dim. ia.'. If we think they originally corresponded, we may see 434 as a relic of a dactylo-epitritic element, the hemiepes. But all we can safely say is that the stanzas contained elements that were (a) cretic-iambic, (b) dactylic, probably –⏑⏑–⏑⏑–.

From what we can see there is nothing remarkable or distinctive about the metre: we may have had an 'impure', partly dactylo-epitritic strophic pair (cf. e.g. S. *OT* 1086ff, *Tr.* 821ff, E. *And.* 789ff, 1027ff) or perhaps just iambics with the occasional dactylic element thrown in (cf. e.g. A. *Pers.* 126ff, *Th.* 345ff; S. *Aj.* 879ff, *El.* 1082ff, *OT* 190ff; E. *Alk.* 872ff, *Hek.* 649ff, *Hik.* 598ff, *Med.* 204ff).

Further speculation seems idle.

526–535 = 536–544

526 = 536 –⏑⏑–⏑⏑– D
527 = 537 –⏑–– –⏑⏑–⏑⏑–– e – D –
529 = 539 –⏑–– –⏑⏑–⏑⏑– e – D
530 = 540 ––⏑⏑–⏑⏑– – D
531 = 541 –⏑–⏓ –⏑⏑–⏑⏑– ––⏑– e ⏓ D – e
533 = 542 –⏑⏑–⏑⏑– D
534 = 543 ⏒⏑– ⏓–⏑– (e) ⏓ e

535 = 544   – – ⏑ – ⏑ – – ‖   – e ba.

Straightforward dactylo-epitrite:[42] the arrangement above gives agreement of word-end with colon-end. The metre is pure dac. -ep. (i.e. contains nothing except for – ⏑⏑ – ⏑⏑ –, – ⏑ – and ⏓) apart from the ithyphallic clausula, which is more common than not in tragic dactylo-epitrite.[43]

The six undisputed plays of Aeschylus do not contain any dactylo-epitritic stanzas at all. This could be a matter of chance: if all we possessed of Euripides was *Hipp.*, *Hkd.*, *Hik.*, *Hks*, *Ion* and *IT*, we could say the same. Purely dactylo-epitritic[44] strophes like *Prom.* 526ff and 887ff are not particularly common in surviving tragedy: S. *Tr.* 94ff, E. *And.* 766ff, *Med.* 410ff, 627ff, 976ff. But there are many more which one would describe as predominantly or substantially dac.-ep., though they also contain other, often related, elements: e.g. S. *Aj.* 172ff, *OT* 1086ff, *Ant.* 582ff, *Tr.* 497ff, 821ff, fr. 435, fr. 533, fr. 535-6; E. *Alk.* 588ff, *And.* 789ff, 1009ff, *Hks* 1185ff, *Tro.* 799ff, 820ff, *Med.* 824ff, *Hek.* 943ff, *El.* 859ff, *Hel.* 1137ff, *Rh.* 224ff, 243ff, 895ff. It is noticeable that, where the dates of these plays are known or surmised, apart from *Helen* (412 B.C.), they are comparatively early. S. *Ph.* and *OK*, E. *Pho.*, *Or.*, *IA*, *Ba.*[45] contain almost no dac.-ep. elements.

In Aeschylus, not only do we not find any wholly or even substantially dactylo-epitrite stanzas in six plays and the fragments: we do not even find a single period of it. Both Sophocles and Euripides have numerous stanzas in which individual dac.-ep. periods occur only briefly, usually in the form of the 'iambelegos' × – ⏑ – × – ⏑⏑ – ⏑⏑ –, though the rest of the stanza is of a different metrical nature: e.g. S. *Aj.* 881ff, *OT* 195, *Tr.* 520ff, 635f, 648; E. *Alk.* 438f, *And.* 135ff, 1027f, *Hek.* 649f, 906ff, *Hipp.* 1268ff, *Hik.* 598ff, 835f, *Hks* 1185ff, 1199ff, *Ion* 1048f, 768ff, 1503ff, *Tro.* 255ff, 275f, 285f, *IT* 1234f, *Hel.* 1107f.

Aeschylus does use the hemiepes – ⏑⏑ – ⏑⏑ –, occasionally in iambic context, but never combined, and with the distinctive anceps, × – ⏑ – × – ⏑⏑ – ⏑⏑ – or – ⏑⏑ – ⏑⏑ – × – ⏑⏑ – ⏑⏑ – (cf. *Pers.* 584ff, *Supp.* 541f, *Ag.* 720ff. A. fr. 74 (*Herakleidai*) is analysed by Wilamowitz (*GV* 460-1): ... ⏑ – – ‖ – ⏑ ⏑ – ⏑ ⏑ – – – ⏑⏑ – ⏑⏑ – | – – – ⏑⏑ – ⏑ – – – ⏑ – – – ⏑ – | ⏑ – – ⏑⏑ – ⏑ – – – ⏑ – ⏑ – ⏑ – etc. as hem.-hem., glyc. 2 ia., glyc. 2 ia. The first line might really just be 6 dac. In any case, there does not seem to be any dac.-ep. here either). There is no reason why Aeschylus should not have written dactylo-epitrite. The metre had been in use some time (cf. e.g. Stesichoros *PMG* 210, 212, Pindar etc.), and even if it had not been used in earlier tragedy (which of course we have no means of knowing), Aeschylus was not afraid of innovations in matters other than metrical, and is even credited with the invention of the dochmiac.[46] But the fact remains, that whereas Sophocles and Euripides, in all their tragedies except their very latest (S. *Ph.*, *OK*; E. *Pho.*, *Or.*, *IA*) employ at least some dac.-ep. periods,[47] and in several plays employ the metre extensively, Aeschylus does not provide us with a single example of a dac.-ep. period. We gather from the *Frogs* that Aeschylus' favourite mixture of dactylic and iambic elements was of a very different nature,[48] and we must conclude that at least in his later plays (into which category all the six that survive fall) he used the dactylo-epitrite metre sparingly or not at all.

545-552 = 553-560

545 = 553 ⏑⏑–⏑⏑–⏑⏑–⏑⏑–⏑–⏑––

547 = 555 ⏑⏑–⏑⏑–⏑–⏑–⏑––

549 = 557 ⏑⏑–⏑⏑–⏑–⏑–⏑–⏑–⏑––

550 = 559 ⏑⏑–⏑⏑–⏑⏑–⏑⏑–⏑⏑[––]

551 = 560 –⏑⏑–⏑⏑–⏑̄–⏑–⏑–⏑––‖

In 549 = 558 ἰσόνειρον corresponds to καὶ λέχος σόν. Rather than suppose a highly irregular responsion ⏑̱⏑–⏑ we must assume that the first iota of ἰσόνειρον is here long. Such lengthening is regular with ἰσόθεος in tragic lyrics (not in dialogue, see L-S-J *s.v.*), presumably in imitation of epic, where several ἰσο- compounds are found with long first syllable from metrical necessity (cf. ἀθάνατος, and also *Prom.* 185 ἀπαράμυθον). But the lengthening in a word like ἰσόνειρον, which does not contain more than two consecutive shorts and so can fit into a dactylic line without modification, is decidedly irregular. The only comparable example seems to be Pindar *N.*4.84 ἰσοδαίμονα. Murray (*ad loc.*) refers to *Cho.* 319, where the MSS are confused between ἰσόμοιρον and ἀντίμοιρον: but I think it is better to assume a licence in prosody in our passage than to emend to ἀντόνειρον, a word that does not otherwise occur.

Line 559 is longer by a spondee than 550: several suggestions[49] have been made, either as to how to fill out 550, or (more plausibly, I think) what to remove in 559. The simplest answer seems to me to remove ἕδνοις (as Lachmann apparently thought), and make no further change. (The schol. is: πείθων δάμαρτα · ἕδνοις πείθων τὴν ἐσομένην σοι δάμαρτα κοινόλεκτρον.) In either case the basic metre is not affected.

Wilamowitz states on this pair of strophes (*GV* 388): 'Ich nun richtiger verstehe als in der Ausgabe', and analyses as follows. 'Hier ist das Enoplion viermal erstes Glied eines Dikolon, an letzter Stelle steht dafür ein Klingendes Hemiepes, wenn man so sagen darf: es fehlt ihm also nur vorn eine Silbe, um ein Enoplion zu sein ... Die zweiten Glieder wechseln (Ithyph., troch. Metron, troch. Dim., Adon.). Das seltenste ist, dass das Enoplion nicht nur, wie öfter, mit zwei Kürzen anhebt ... sondern auch so schliesst'. So by his reckoning we have:

enop. cr. ba. ⏑⏑–⏑⏑–⏑⏑–⏕ –⏑– ⏑––
enop. tro. ⏑⏑–⏑⏑–⏑–⏑ –⏑––‖
enop. 2 tro. ⏑⏑–⏑⏑–⏑⏑–⏑ –⏑–⏑ –⏑––‖
enop. adon. ⏑⏑–⏑⏑–⏑⏑–⏕ –⏑⏑––‖

If we believe that all Greek metrical periods are reducible to such short, conveniently labelled units, then we must adopt some such analysis: and, to be fair, Wilamowitz himself points to the peculiarities, and talks of a series of 'Dicola'. The further step, taken by Dale, of refusing to break down these long cola into artificial, shorter units, is less neat, in that names cannot be found so easily to make us feel familiar with the sequence of long and short syllables before us, but more objective, in that it records what form these longs and shorts are taking, rather than struggling to explain them in terms of more familiar, shorter cola.

When Dale (*LM* 193) describes S. *Tr.* 497 ⏑⏑–⏑⏑–⏑⏑–⏑⏑–⏑–⏑– as 'a compound of anapaestic enoplion plus iambic metron', she is using the same sort of terminology as Wilamowitz. The difference is that hers is a description, his an analysis: Dale does not believe in the separate existence here of the two elements, enoplion and iambic, whereas Wilamowitz on *Prom.* 545ff does.

The metrical nature of 545ff is immediately apparent when one looks at it as a whole. We have a series of long, aeolic cola which open with double shorts, change to single shorts, and have 'pendant' close. 550 = 559 might be considered pure, 'rising' dactyls. The only slight uncertainty is 551 = 560 which could, if thought of in aeolic terms, be –⏑⏑–⏑⏑– × –|⏑–⏑– ⏑––‖ ibycean, ia. ba. But if we read πιθών in 560, as all modern editors do, we have the responsion –⏑⏑–⏑⏑–⏒– which, while possible,[50] is very rare. So the alternative analysis, –⏑⏑–⏑⏑– × –⏑– ⏑–⏑––‖ D × e × e ×, in view of the dactylo-epitritic stanzas that preceded these, seems preferable. The freedom of responsion now occurs in a *syllaba anceps*.

Dale (*LM* 159) remarks, 'Though prosodiacs and enoplions taken altogether do not bulk very large in the drama, yet their variety of form is so great, and their associations with other kinds of metre so multifarious, that it is difficult to get any clear impression of them; there are not enough of any one sort for their habits to be observed very closely.'[51] Theoretically, there is no reason why any combination of single longs with double and single shorts should not have been used: in practice we find, in our limited acquaintance with three tragedians, that certain forms seem to be avoided (e.g. the change from double short to single and back, or vice versa, such as ⏑⏑–⏑⏑–⏑–⏑–⏑⏑– or ⏑–⏑–⏑⏑–⏑–⏑⏑– etc.[52]), while of the rest, some seem more popular than others (e.g. more start with double shorts and end with single, than vice versa, just as in 'glyconic' verse the central –⏑⏑–⏑– is more common than –⏑–⏑⏑–).

In our state of ignorance, partial as to metre, total as to music and dance, we can do no more than observe unusual phenomena such as *Prom.* 545ff, and look around for comparable phenomena in other plays. The nearest parallels that I can find are:

S. *Tr.* 647ff ⏑⏑–⏑⏑–⏑–––⏑⏑–⏑⏑–⏑–⏑–– followed by iambics
497ff ⏑⏑–⏑⏑–⏑⏑–⏑⏑–––⏑–––⏑––
⏑⏑–⏑⏑–⏑⏑–⏑⏑–⏑–⏑–‖ followed by dactylo-epitrite
633ff ⏒–⏑⏑–⏑–⏓–⏑–⏑–⏑–
––⏑⏑–⏑⏑–⏑–⏑––
El. 857 ⏑⏑–⏑⏑––⏑⏑–⏑–– after aeolics and iambics
OT 870ff ⏑–⏑–⏑–⏑⏑––⏑⏑–––
⏑⏑–––⏑⏑–⏑–––‖

885ff ⏓–⏑⏑–⏑–⏑–⏑–⏑–⏑– twice (tel. + 2 ia.)
OK 117ff ⏑–⏑⏑––⏑––⏑⏑–⏑⏑–⏑–⏑––‖ then aeolics

One could compare too *Aj*. 629ff, 699ff; *Ant*. 134ff, 582ff; *Tr*. 112ff, 960f; *Ph*. 135ff, 855ff; *OK* 220ff.

E. *Alk*. 435ff –⏑⏑–⏑⏑–– –⏑⏑–⏑⏑–⏑⏑–⏑⏑–⏑⏑–⏑–⏑––
––⏑⏑–⏑⏑– ––⏑⏑–⏑⏑– ––⏑⏑–⏑⏑– –⏑– ⏑––
⏑⏑–⏑⏑–⏑–⏑–– ––⏑⏑–⏑–⏑– –⏑⏑–⏑––‖

where the kinship of the long cola to dactylo-epitrite is clear.

568ff –⏑–– –⏑⏑–⏑⏑–⏑⏑–⏑––‖
⏑–⏑⏑–⏑⏑–⏑–⏑– ––⏑– ⏑––
⏑–⏑–⏑–⏑⏑– –⏑– ⏑––‖

903ff ⏑–⏑– –⏑⏑–⏑⏑–⏑⏑– ⏑–⏑– ⏑––‖

Hkd. 356ff after aeolics, ⏑⏑–⏑⏑–⏑⏑–⏑⏑–⏑–– then 3 glyc. arist.

Hek. 649ff ia. ⏑ hem. –– ia. ⏑ hem. –– 3 ia., ⏑⏑–⏑⏑–⏑– –⏑– ⏑––
⏑⏑–⏑⏑–⏑– ⏑––‖ 2 ia. ba. ‖

923ff 2 ia. 2 ia. ––⏑––––⏑–⏑⏑–––‖⏑⏑–⏑⏑–⏑–⏑––

Ion. 1445ff 2 do. 4 ba., ⏑⏑–⏑⏑–⏑–⏑–, 1465ff 2 ia. ba., 2 ba.
⏑⏑–⏑⏑–⏑⏑–⏑⏑–⏑–⏑–‖

IT 400ff after 2 pher. 3 ia., ⏑–⏑–––– –⏑⏑–⏑–– ⏑–⏑⏑–⏑⏑–⏑–
⏑–⏑––‖

Med. 643ff –⏑⏑– –⏑⏑– –⏑⏑–⏑––|⏑⏑–⏑⏑–⏑–⏑–⏑–⏑–| ––⏑⏑⏑⏑–|
⏑⏑–⏑⏑–⏑–⏑––‖ then aeolics

991ff ⏑–⏑⏑–⏑⏑– ⏑–⏑– ⏑–– –⏑– ⏑––|⏑⏑–⏑⏑–
⏑⏑–⏑⏑– ⏑–⏑⏑–⏑⏑–|––⏑– –⏑– ⏑––‖

Hipp. 755ff, after 2 glyc., pher. ⏑⏑–⏑⏑–⏑–⏑–⏑–⏑––‖ ⏑⏑–⏑⏑
–⏑–⏑–⏑⏑–⏑⏑– then iambics

Pho. 330f among ia. + do., ⏑⏑–⏑⏑–⏑⏑–⏑⏑–⏑–⏑–⏑–

Rhes. 250 ⏑⏑–⏑⏑–⏑–⏑–⏑– etc. (see Ritchie p. 303, who remarks that the enoplion ⏑⏑–⏑⏑–⏑–⏑ 'makes a transition from dactylo-epitrite to choriambic, having a rhythmical affinity with both').

Fr. 369 according to Wilamowitz (*GV* 388, immediately after *Prom*. 545ff) is rather similar to our passage:

––⏑⏑–⏑⏑– –⏑– ⏑–– 'Prosodiakon + ithyphall.
⏑⏑–⏑⏑–⏑⏑– ––⏑––– enop. + ithyph. (cf. *OT* 1199)
––⏑–⏑⏑– ⏑–⏑⏑–⏑⏑–– enop. + "3 Daktyl"
–⏑⏑–– –⏑⏑–– 2 adon.
⏑⏑–⏑⏑– ⏑⏑–⏑⏑– ––⏑– ––⏑– ⏑–⏑– ⏑––‖ anap. dim., 4 ia.'

But in Austin's[53] text the metre is more straightforward

⏔–⏑⏑–⏑⏑–⏕–⏑–– (twice)

––⏑⏑–⏑⏑–⏑⏑–⏑⏑––

–⏑⏑–––⏑––

5 ⏑⏑–⏑⏑–⏑⏑–⏑⏑–

––⏑– ––⏑– ⏑–⏑– ⏑–– ‖

'Numeri: 1-5 dac. (saepe ab "anap." incip. et cum clausula –⏑––)
6-7 ia. ba.'

(Other passages of interest are: *Alk.* 224f, 252f, 455ff; *Hkd.* 774ff; *And.* 124f, 279, 293ff, 1014ff, 1034f; *Hek.* 905ff, 1100f; *Hks.* 382f, 1016ff; *Ion* 1503ff; *El.* 585ff, 698ff; *Tro.* 833f; *IT* 1244ff; *Pho.* 146; *Or.* 1369ff, 1398f; fr. 781.)

Several of these Euripidean examples can be interpreted as anapaests plus iambics, but the effect of 'uncontracted' anapaests, plus invariably short anceps in the iambics (i.e. ⏑⏑–⏑⏑–⏑–⏑– etc.) often in aeolic contexts, reminds us very strongly of familiar aeolic cola, e.g. ⏑⏑–⏑⏑–⏑– (tel. or glyc.). So when we find other passages of similar appearance, like *Prom.* 545ff and E. *Pho.* 330f, where the supposed 'anapaests' and 'iambics' do not in fact fall into pairs and are not separated by diaeresis, we have reason to suspect the 'anapaesto-iambic' description as being no more than a name; it is not an analysis or explanation.

Summary

Whether we regard *Prom.* 545ff as aeolic and iambic, as Wilamowitz did, with a remarkable consistency of double-short openings to enoplia and of short anceps in the iambic metra; or as 'anapaesto-iambics', again with regularly short anceps, and with awkward division; or as single indivisible cola which have associations with aeolic and with dactylo-epitrite (cf. Pindar's expanded hemiepe –⏑⏑–⏑⏑–⏑⏑– in dactylo-epitrite, and his acephalous ‸⏑⏑–⏑⏑–), the most significant thing for our purposes is that we find nothing remotely comparable in Aeschylus. In his use of aeolic metres, Aeschylus rarely uses the open double-short start, and never intermingles iambic elements in such a way that they can be considered part of the same colon.[54] *Supp.* 86ff; *Ag.* 1481ff, 1489ff; *Cho.* 315ff, 345ff, 380ff are perhaps the nearest he offers to a parallel: all are more remarkable for their differences than their similarities. They are all *either* dactylic *or* simple aeolic, and these elements are never combined or confused, as they are in *Prom.* 545ff.

Dale (*LM* 194) concludes, 'The general similarity of *Prom.* 545ff to this group of Euripidean iambo-anapaestic odes is in fact one more puzzling element in the riddle of this play's choral lyric'. We saw too, to a less extent, similar passages in Sophocles, especially in *Trachiniai*. But neither Sophocles nor Euripides offers whole stanzas with quite this flavour: the examples listed above are mainly isolated among more easily identifiable cola. *Prom.* 545ff falls completely outside the known Aeschylean pattern, and only partly inside that of Sophocles and Euripides.

566-573

	⏑–⏑– or ⏑⏑⏑– (ἀ ἀ ἐ ἐ)	(cr.?)
566	⏑–⏑– ⏑–⏑– ⏑––‖	2 ia. ba.//
567	––⏑– ––⏑–† ⏑–⏓– ⏑––†	2 ia.? ba.?
568	––⏑– ⏑–⏑– ⏑––‖	2 ia. ba.//
569	⏑⏑⏑–⏑– ⏑⏑⏑–⏑–	2 do.
570	⏑–⏑– ⏑–⏑– ⏑––‖	2 ia. ba.//
571	–⏑⏑– ⏑–⏑	(?arist.?)
572	–⏑⏑–⏑– ⏑–⏑–⏑– ⏑–⏑⏑⏑– ⏑⏑⏑–––‖	4 do.

For 567 the various breathings, accents, divisions and apostrophes for ΑΛΕΥΑΔΑ in the MSS show that the scribes had no more idea than we have what the word(s) was supposed to mean. Ya omits φοβοῦμαι which Dindorf independently rejected as a gloss: Dawe[55] is inclined to believe that Ya here is right. Certainly, as he says, φοβοῦμαι would be a likely gloss word, and it renders the metre very much more obscure. Wilamowitz's ἀλεῦμαι is ingenious, and metrically simple, as it gives another catalectic iambic trimeter. Other attempts to make the line both intelligible and metrically possible yield 2 ia., ia. ba. (with ἄλευε δᾶ, φοβοῦμαι), or 3 ia. (same, without φοβοῦμαι). Dale (*LM* 100 n.1) implies that if we accept ἀλεῦμαι and thus print three consecutive ia. trim. cat., we would 'add yet another technical reason for doubting Aeschylean authorship':[56] she is 'reluctant' to do so, and finishes the sentence with an amused exclamation mark. Clearly certainty in a passage such as this is unattainable, and Wilamowitz's emendation is far from sure.

Otherwise, the metre is straightforward until we come to 571ff. These lines are analysed more fully in Appendix C. Here we may simply observe that no analysis fails to produce at least one peculiarity. If 571 is aristophanean, its isolated situation, preceded and succeeded by pause, is very unusual.[57] If the MSS tradition in 572 is correct, we also have an irregular 'hexasyllabic' dochmiac ⏑–⏑–⏑–, for which there is no likely Aeschylean parallel, though Sophocles and Euripides offer certain examples.[58]

The iambics of 566-70 provide more solid evidence. Denniston[59] states that, of the lyric iambic trimeters in tragedy, 388 are syncopated, 196 unsyncopated. Of those syncopated in only one metron, the most common form is × – ⏑ – × – ⏑ – ⏑ – – 2 ia. ba. (sixty-five times); next come × – ⏑ – – ⏑ – × – ⏑ – ia. cr. ia. (forty-two times, twenty-seven in Aeschylus) and × – ⏑ – × – ⏑ – – ⏑ – 2 ia. cr. (thirteen times, ten in Euripides). The others are rare.

He does not analyse the sixty-five occurrences of 2 ia. ba. My figures, which seem roughly to agree with his (more than this, with alternative readings and colometries, is not to be expected), give the following occurrences:[60]

Aeschylus four times in responsion[61] = eight.

Sophocles ten times in responsion, twice not = twenty-two.

Euripides eight times in responsion, thirteen not = twenty-nine (certain), plus (probable) once in responsion, four times not = six: (total thirty-five?).

Prom. four times not in responsion (certain) = four, plus (possible) three times not in responsion: (total seven?).

In view of the very considerable number of lyric iambic trimeters that we possess from Aeschylus' pen, we are entitled to conclude that his preference was for *either* ia. cr. ia., *or* more than one syncopation. According to Denniston, ia. cr. ba. occurs seventy-seven times in the three tragedians, ba. cr. ia. twenty-seven times; ia. 2 cr. occurs sixteen times (twelve in Aeschylus); triple syncopation is particularly characteristic of Aeschylus. On ba. cr. ba. Denniston comments, 'Some of Aeschylus' most impressive lyric iambics are in this rhythm'. 2 cr. ba. and 3 ba., are also not uncommon.

2 ia. ba. never occurs twice in one stanza in Aeschylus' six undisputed plays.

Summary

The combination of metres is not unusual; syncopated iambics and dochmiac, cf. e.g. A. *Th.* 109ff, *Ag.* 1136ff; S. *El.* 1232ff; E. *Hkd.* 75ff, *Hks* 875ff.

Possible curiosities of detail are:

(i) Three consecutive 2 ia. ba. trimeters (566-8)

(ii) Hexasyllabic dochmiac in 572

(iii) Isolated aristophanean sandwiched between pauses and before dochmiacs (571).

The iambics are of a type rare in Aeschylus, but comparatively common in both Sophocles and Euripides.

574-588 = 593-608

574 = 593	⏑⏑⏑–⏑– ⏑⏑⏑–⏑– –⏑– ⏓⏑⏑–⏑⏓‖	2 do. cr. do.//
576 = 594	⏑⏑⏑–⏑– ⏒⏑⏑–⏑–? ⏑⏕–⏑–	3 do.
578 = 596	⏑⏑⏑–⏑⏑⏑–⏑⏑⏑–⏑––⏑––⏑––⏑––⏑–⏑	(ἐ ἐ)//
580 = 599	––⏑–⏑–⏑⏑–––	?
582 = 600	⏑⏑⏑⏑– ⏑––‖	ia. ba.//
583 = 601	⏑⏕–⏑– ⏑⏑⏑–⏑– –⏑– ⏑⏑⏑–⏑–	2 do. cr. do.
584 = 603	–⏑– ⏑–⏒‖	cr. ba.
	–⏑–⏑–	hyp.
585 = 605	⏑–⏑⏑⏑ ⏑–⏑–	2 ia.
586 = 606	⏑–⏑– ⏑–⏑– ⏑–⏑–	3 ia.
587 = 607	–⏑– ⏑––‖	cr. ba.//
588 = 608	⏑––⏑– –⏑– –⏑–‖	do. 2 cr.//

In 600 Ἥρας (Hermann) is metrically suitable (we lack ––) and the scholiast looks as if he may have read it.[62]

For 576 = 594 the tradition gives –⏑–⏑– in responsion to –⏑––⏑–, each preceded and followed by a dochmiac. Wilamowitz emended 594 to τὰν τάλαιναν ὧδ', which gives two hypodochmiacs –⏑–⏑– in responsion, which is possible, though not common. Murray omits τὰν (after Hartung), to give hypodochmiac in strophe answered by ⏑––⏑– dochmiac: this clearly cannot be right. Page's addition of δέ after ποῖ in 576 gives –⏑⏑–⏑– = dochmiac (δέ could easily have dropped out through the reluctance of scribes to include a particle that they believed adversative and connective, after an exclamation). In the antistrophe, the omission of the article gives us ⏑––⏑–, another dochmiac. The only drawback of this solution is that it involves altering both strophe and antistrophe for solely metrical reasons. Of the alternatives, Wilamowitz's τὰν τάλαιναν, despite the comparison Murray makes with 566, is clumsy immediately after τάλας, while attempts to fill out 576 to give, like 594, do. 2 cr. do., have not so far been very convincing (e.g. Mazon ποῖ μ' ἄγουσ' αἴδε τηλ-).

At 582, the desirability of με depends on our view of the author's practice with respect to short vowels before mute and liquid in dochmiacs (and before *initial* mute and liquid in lyrics in general). According to Conomis,[63] such lengthening 'is very rare in dochmiacs'. Apart from *Prom.* 593 πόθεν ἐμοῦ σὺ πᾱτρός, he finds no examples in Aeschylus, three certain in Sophocles, five in Euripides, plus more possible in each. In view of 593, we cannot say on these grounds that πυρὶ φλέξον ἢ should be altered. But in 582 we have the further problem, unlike 593, that the lengthening is before *initial* mute and liquid.[64] Elmsley's is an easy emendation, which is generally accepted. It might not be, if the canon of Sophocles and Euripides, rather than Aeschylus, were applied. If we retain the MSS reading, we have two unaeschylean points of prosody in these lines; even if we do not, we still have one.

As Dale remarks (*LM* 108), this strophe is a good example of the difficulties of colometry and analysis presented by dochmiacs in combination with other metres, because of their multifarious possible forms. Thus 578-80 = 596-9 allow of several interpretations. In the first two lines, the various possible analyses do not disturb us: do. 6 cr. x; or 3 cr. do. 3 cr. x; or 3 cr. 5 ba.; or do. ia. 5 ba.; or do. ia. do. 3 cr. x; or 8 ba.; or others yet more outlandish, are all theoretically possible. Dale includes ἒ ἕ in the metrical system, to give 3 cr. 4 ba. plus ⏑–⏑––. But if we did want to include the exclamation, (a) it is debatable whether, as Dale asserts,[65] 'ἒ ἕ in Aeschylus has full spondaic value, like αἰαῖ'; cf. for example *Pers.* 977 = 991; (b) it would in any case surely be preferable to take the lines as 3 cr. do. 3 cr. ba., to avoid cr. followed by ba. without pause. Which of these analyses we accept does not matter much, unless we see τί ποτέ μ' ὦ Κρόνιε = θεόσυτόν τε νόσον as ⏑⏑⏑–⏑⏑⏑ dochmiac. This form only occurs in Aeschylus at *Eum.* 838, twice in Sophocles, twenty-two times in Euripides. In its favour is the diaeresis in strophe and antistrophe after it: against it, the possibility of alternative interpretations.

For a discussion of 580 = 599 and the problems of analysis which it presents, see Appendix D. The question of exclamations that arose with respect to 578f = 596f (and earlier on 114) returns with greater urgency in 583 = 602, where we have the responsion:

583 ποντίοις δάκεσι δὸς βοράν cr. do.

602 (δυσ)δαιμόνων δὲ τίνες οἳ ἒ ἕ ...

The overwhelmingly greater frequency of ⏑⏑⏑–⏑– than ⏑⏑⏑––– in Aeschylus and Sophocles (A. 194 to 12, S. 57 to 2), plus the scansion of the strophe, demand that ἒ ἕ be here scanned ⏑–. The poet can obviously choose what quantity an exclamation shall have; the letters he puts down on the page, even if they are accurately transmitted to us, may well bear little resemblance to the shriek or groan uttered on stage.

But of more interest than the scansion of ἒ ἕ here is its unusual usage, as part of a metrical colon in *responsion* to ordinary, non-exclamatory words. There are several examples of such a responsion at the beginning of a period or colon, often dochmiac in Aeschylus: *Th.* 780 = 787, *Pers.* 977 = 991, 974 = 987 (1004 = 1010), *Ag.* 1485 = 1509,(1114 = 1125). The only examples that I have found in Aeschylus where the exclamation is in the middle or at the end of a colon are: *Th.* 481 = 521 ἰὼ ~ ἔχοντ' (where we could analyse ia. do./ia. cr. do., which puts the exclamation at the start of the colon); *Pers.* 257 καὶ δαΐ'· ἀιαῖ διαιν- = 264 αἰὼν ἐφάνθη γεραι- ia. cr. (also cf. *Pers.* 283 = 289); *Cho.* 434 οἴμοι ~439 εἰδῇς (in these last three cases the punctuation and syntax render the exclamation much less unexpected and remarkable than *Prom.* 602); and *Ag.* 1143 ἀκόρετος βοᾶς φεῦ φιλοίκτοις φρεσίν (so Fraenkel) = 1153 μελοτυπεῖς ὁμοῦ τ' ὀρθίοις ἐν νόμοις. M's φεῦ is omitted by F Tr, but retained by modern editors for the responsion. The MSS are very confused over the next word(s) too: F φιλοίκτοις ταλαίναις φρεσίν, Tr. φιλοίκτοισι ταλαίναις φρεσίν, M ταλαιναῖς (α above) φρεσίν. Hermann, Wilamowitz and Fraenkel all view φεῦ with great suspicion, but Fraenkel shares Wilamowitz's reluctance to alter the antistrophe.[66]

Pers. 977 seems to be the only example in Aeschylus of ἒ ἕ responding to a non-exclamatory word (and even there βοαῖ βοαῖ has much of the force of an exclamation): but we should perhaps not make too fine a distinction between ἰή, ἰώ, αἰαῖ, ἒ ἔ etc. They were peculiarly liable to phonetic error in the course of transmission.

In Sophocles and Euripides we can compare: S. *Ant.* 1261 = 1284, 1265f = 1288f, 1306 = 1328; *El.* 133 = 149; *Tr.* 1034; and especially *Tr.* 1025 = 1043, *OK* 117 = 150; *OT* 154 = 163 and *Ant.* 1310 = 1331 (as printed by Pearson, after Erfurdt, with αἰαῖ ~ ἴτω).

E. *Or.* 145 = 157; *El.* 1185 = 1201, and especially *Hik.* 77-8 = 85-6 (the text, which is dubious,[67] has αἱματοῦτε χρῶτά τε φόνιον answered by ἐς γόους πέφυκε πάθος ἒ ἔ); cf. too *Hks* 1051, *Ion* 1445, *Tro.* 1216.

Of these, only S. *Ant.* 1310?, *OT* 163; E. *Hik.* 85? have an exclamation corresponding to an ordinary word at colon-end (and *OT* 154 is almost an exclamation). We do however have similar examples of exclamation at colon end, not in responsion, at S. *Tr.* 1034, E. *Hks* 1051.

Prom. 602 is indeed extraordinary. We have no real grounds for suspecting corruption, in that strophe and antistrophe correspond exactly, and the sense in both is satisfactory, even if the construction, δυσδαιμόνων δὲ τίνες[sc. εἰσὶν] οἳ οἷα ἐγὼ [sc. μογῶ] μογοῦσιν; is rather harsh. Even if we did feel misgivings about the construction and point to ΟΙΟΙΕΓΩ as a possible source of confusion, it is highly unlikely that a scribe would insert ἒ ἔ, unless he were aware of the lack of ⏑– for the metre; and the exclamation is not out of place as far as the sense is concerned.

In 584 = 603, Dale (*LM* 108f) prints μηδέ μοι φθονήσῃς εὐγμάτων ἄναξ as one line, although in the antistrophe the short last syllable of μογοῦσιν, as well as the clausular nature of the ithyphallic, demand pause after –⏑–⏑–⏓‖. The remainder –⏑–⏑– can be thought of either as an hypodochmiac or as an iambic pentasyllable: in this context either is appropriate, though its isolation here, between pause and unsyncopated iambics, is I think unique. We could take 584 as one line comprising two such cola divided by anceps –⏑–⏑– × –⏑–⏑–, but there is no parallel for such an anceps, and the diaeresis after the anceps would be unlikely.

The last line is difficult to analyse for certain, but the difficulties are trivial: do. 2 cr., ba. do. cr., 2 ba. do. are all possible. This sort of ambiguity is most common in Aeschylus (e.g.

Supp. 738, *Ag*. 1103, *Cho*. 944), but not unusual in all three tragedians in such dochmiac and iambic contexts (e.g. E. *Hkd*. 91, *Med*. 1281, *Hks* 921).

Summary

The general character of the ode is, as Dale says, typical, at any rate of Aeschylus and Euripides (Sophocles is less inclined to mix iambics with dochmiacs; the two elements tend to remain more clearly distinguished). It is in the details that we become less certain, partly no doubt because of the usual ambiguities of dochmiacs with their various possible permutations, partly too at times because of textual uncertainty. But still some features stand out which strike us as unusual, even with our limited knowledge of Greek tragic lyric, drawn from a few plays of only three authors:

(i) πᾱτρός 593. There is no probable parallel in Aeschylus for lengthening before mute and liquid in dochmiacs. Sophocles and Euripides each have four certain examples. (582 πυρῑ φλέξον, if right, is additionally remarkable as offering an unaeschylean lengthening before *initial* mute and liquid in lyrics.)

(ii) 580 = 599f offer *either* the unique trimeter – – ‸ – ⏑⏑⏑⏑ – ⏑ – – with unaeschylean molossus, *or* a rare, contracted iambelegos – – ⏑ – ⏑ – ⏑⏑ – – –.[68] Only Euripides (who has several) has any parallel for such an element among dochmiacs and iambics.

(iii) 583 = 602 the responsion of exclamatory ἒ ἔ to ordinary words at the end of a colon, almost unparalleled in tragedy.

(iv) 584 = 604 – ⏑ – ⏑ – after – ⏑ – ⏑ – ⏒ (without sense-pause in strophe). The only certain example of – ⏑ – ⏑ – in Aeschylus is next to a dochmiac. There are certain examples at S. *El*. 246-7 (two); E. *Or*. 140 = 153, 1382, 1385; *Hipp*. 879 (two) etc.[69] (and cf. *Prom*. 688. Here it seems to be iambic, and to be akin to the preceding metron).

Some of these details might seem less odd if we possessed more of Aeschylus' lyrics: in that case we would learn not to read too much into comparatively minor and shadowy details. Or they might seem less odd if we possessed lyrics by other roughly contemporary tragedians: in that case we would be more certain that we discerned unaeschylean features. But, as things are, they still seem odd.

687-695

687 ∪∪∪–‖∪∪∪– (exclam.) 2 cr.
688 †–∪– ∪––∪– cr. do. (?)
689 ∪––∪– ∪∪∪–∪– 2 do.
690 ––∪– ∪–∪– ∪––‖ 2 ia. ba.
691 †–∪∪–∪∪–∪– ––––– –––∪– ?
694 ∪∪∪– –∪–∪ ‖ (cr.) tro.
695 ∪–⏓ ∪–∪– ∪––‖ ba. ia. ba., or tel. ba.

At 688 most MSS have οὔποτ' οὔποτ' ηὐχόμην ξένους. ΣM preserves ηὔχουν, which must be right. V has οὐπώποτε for οὔποτ' οὔποτ'. Dawe[70] points out that οὐπώποτε might be possible here; but in either case the metre is straightforward, either –∪– ∪––∪– cr. do., or ––∪– –∪– ia. cr. But many editors have felt the need for an adverb expressing the idea 'like this', 'as in fact they are coming', such as is commonly used with αὐχέω.[71] So Wecklein inserted ὧδ' between the two οὔποτ's, giving 3 cr., Wilamowitz ὧδε after ηὔχουν giving –∪–∪– –––∪– which he explained as hyp. + do. I am not convinced that ὧδε is required here, especially as we have it anyway in the next clause (690); at E. *Hkd.* 931 we have a similar construction without the demonstrative, οὐ γάρ ποτ' ηὔχει χεῖρας ἵξεσθαι σέθεν, cf. *Hel.* 1619. The adjective ξένους may be felt to make a difference at *Prom.* 688: it is in any case a peculiar epithet,[72] and ξύννους (Pγρ), though itself even more improbable, suggests that there may be something wrong here. If we do insert ὧδε or some such word, I think it is unwise to create an unnecessary (and unaeschylean) hypodochmiac. Wecklein's emendation (adopted by Page), or possibly οὐπώποθ' ὧδ' ηὔχουν ξένους (2 ia.), would seem better.

Much less tractable is 691, which is discussed in Appendix E. The passage is certainly corrupt, and we cannot be sure whether the various metrical anomalies which present themselves are the work of the author or of the tradition.

In 695 the MSS are divided: QKBHNO εἰσιδοῦσα, MCPΔIVYa ἐσιδοῦσα. Both are possible metrically, either ∪–– ∪–∪– ∪––‖ ba. ia. ba.// or ∪–∪∪–∪– ∪––‖ tel. ba.//. Most editors have assumed that εἰσ- is more likely (Murray does not even mention ἐσ-), presumably for metrical reasons.

In fact, it is curious that ba. ia. ba. (according to Denniston a fairly rare form of syncopated iambic trimeter) very seldom occurs as a clausula: only, I think, at E. *Pho.* 298 (after 2 do.).

Exact parallels for ⏑–⏑⏑–⏑–⏑––‖ after ia./do. are lacking, but very close to it is E. *Hks* 1080 after 4 do. ⏑⏑–⏑⏑–⏑–⏑––‖ (glyc. ba.); cf. too A. *Supp.* 353 2 do. ⏑––⏑⏑–⏑––‖ (hipp.), *Ag.* 1411 2 do. –⏑–⏑⏑––‖ (pher.), both as final clausula to the stanza, S. *Aj.* 409 ⏑–⏑⏑–– (reiz. or do.?), E. *Ion* 1494 ⏑⏑–⏑⏑–⏑–––.

A third possibility, of taking the clausula as ⏑––⏑– ⏑–⏑––‖ = do. ia.-// is not to be ignored: cf. A. *Ag.* 1123?, S. *Tr.* 893ff ⏑⏑⏑⏑⏑⏑ ⏑––⏑– ⏑–⏑– –⏑– ⏑–⏑––‖ ?ia. do., ia. cr. ia.-// E. *Hek.* 692? 2 do. ⏑–⏑–––, *Hik.* 376 ⏑––⏑–⏑––⏑––‖ after 374 ⏑–⏑––⏑––‖, 804, 836; *Pho.* 187ff 3 do. –⏑––| 3 do. (or 3 do. 3 cr. do.) etc.

It is impossible to tell how ambiguous ⏑––⏑––... etc., occurring in ia./do. context, would have been to the fifth-century audience. To us, the difficulties of division, with possible dochmiac or bacchiac + cretic interpretation, are sometimes insuperable. But the difference of delivery between the two may have been considerable: ⏑–– ⏑–– ⏑–– (3 ba.) may not have sounded at all like ×––×– –⏑–× (do. tro.). So, however we scan and interpret 695, it is an unusual, but not an incredible clausula.

694 too is unusual: μοῖρα μοῖρα apparently comprises an isolated trochaic metron (cf. ?A. *Ag.* 1123, E. *Pho.* 187 etc.) among ia./do. ἰὼ ἰὼ μοῖρα μοῖρα can be either ⏑⏑⏑– –⏑–⏑ (cr. tro.) or ⏑–⏑– –⏑–⏑ (ia. tro.) or just –⏑–⏑ (exclamation *extra metrum*). Weil (followed by Wilamowitz) omitted the first ἰώ to give ⏑––⏑–⏓‖ = 2 ba. Others omit the second μοῖρα to give ⏑⏑⏑––⏓‖ = do. In view of the unpredictable and inconsistent behaviour of exclamations, often doubtless distorted by puzzled scribes, we should probably not attach too much importance to this apparently anomalous detail, especially as the phrase is syntactically, as well as metrically, isolated from its surroundings.

Summary

In fact, in our examination of these few lines 687-95, we have found several apparently strange features, some more credible than others, but none sufficiently certain to withstand close individual scrutiny. We have decided that 687 and 694 do not really count, as exclamations are a law to themselves: 688, 691-3, 695 are too uncertain textually for us to be sure of the metre; so we are left with the meagre prospect of 689 and 690, two impeccable dochmiacs and an undistinguished iambic trimeter cetalectic. We might be so bold as to remark that, unless 691-4 have suffered a succession of accidents so bizarre as to render them wholly unrecognisable, we seem to discern either dochmiacs of an unaeschylean nature (–––––, –––⏑–) or a dactylic-anapaestic-spondaic period wholly foreign to the practice of both Aeschylus and Sophocles in iambic-dochmiac contexts,[73] but common in Euripides.[74] But a severe judge of this case would probably rule such a remark out of court, based as it is on the most unreliable and imprecise evidence.

887-893 = 894-900

887 = 894	–⏑⏑–⏑⏑–	D
888 = 895	––⏑–– –⏑⏑–⏑⏑–– –⏑⏑–⏑⏑–⏒	– e – D – D –
890 = 897	–⏑–– –⏑⏑–⏑⏑– ––⏑–‖	e – D – e
891 = 898	––⏑–– –⏑⏑–⏑⏑–	– e – D
892 = 899	–⏑–– –⏑⏑–⏑⏑–	e – D
893 = 900	–⏑–– –⏑–– –⏑–‖	e – e – e //

This is the only 'pure' example of dactylo-epitrite in drama, though several are flawed only by the presence of ithyphallic clausulae (see on 526ff), or one or two related cola, such as dactyls or lyric iambics. We note here the exact responsion[75] (except for ⏒ at colon end 889 = 896) and the exclusively long anceps: this is quite usual in dactylo-epitrite, cf. e.g. E. *Med.* 410ff (2 anc. not responding), 627ff (one anc.), S. *OT* 1088ff etc., and Pindar *passim.*

The metrical unity of this ode reminds us that of the choral strophic songs in this play, most are remarkably homogeneous in their choice of metres: e.g. 128ff = 144ff (choriambic), 397ff = 406ff (choriambic/anakreontic), 415ff = 420ff (trochaic, with aeolic clausula), 526ff = 536ff (dactylo-epitrite), 545ff = 553ff ('anapaesto-iambic'), 887 = 894ff (dactylo-epitrite), and furthermore, that the play shows consistency in choice of metre: 128ff cf. 397ff, 526ff cf. 887ff. We should bear this in mind in our final assessment of the metres of the play.

We pointed out on 526ff that the dactylo-epitritic metre does not occur in the extant works of Aeschylus, but is quite common in

Sophocles and Euripides.

901-907 (EPODE)

901	⏑–⏑⏑⏑ ⏑⏑⏑⏑⏑⏑	2 ia.
902	⏑⏑⏑–⏑⏑⏑–[⏑]–⏑–[⏑–] ⏑–⏑– ⏑–⏑– ⏑–⏓‖	? 2 ia. ba.//
904	⏑⏑⏑⏑⏑⏑ ⏑⏑⏑⏑⏑⏑ ⏑⏑⏑⏑– ⏑–⏑– ⏑––‖	4 ia. ba.//
906	–⏑– ⏑–⏑–	lek.
907	–⏑⏑– ⏑––‖	arist.//

902 does not, as it stands in the MSS, provide possible Greek: nor does Headlam's emendation, adopted by Murray. ἄφοβος οὐ δέδια cannot be right: but if either is to be rejected outright, I think it must be (οὐ) δέδια, which is lacking from BH, and occurs as a gloss word in M at *Pers*. 702.[76] But if we just read ἄφοβος · μηδέ, the metre becomes impossible, unless we take 901 + ἄφοβος as ⏑–⏑⏑⏑⏑⏑ ⏑⏑⏑⏑⏑⏑–, two mathematically feasible but wholly unpersuasive dochmiacs. Furthermore, the presence in BH of οὐ is strange, if the lack of δέδια is genuinely original, and ἄφοβος would hardly need a gloss.

In the face of two unobjectionable iambics in the first line, which we have no reason to suspect of corruption, it seems perverse, as some do, to try to turn 901 ⏑–⏑⏑⏑⏑ into a dochmiac that would only have two possible fellows in the whole of tragedy (S. *Ant*. 1273, E. ?*Hks* 1061). 902 however has yet to receive a convincing emendation. θεῶν has rightly been viewed with the greatest mistrust (Wilamowitz 'Glossam delevi. nulli nobilitatis gradus in deis, nec deas loqui curamus'). Page reads ἄφοβος ἔφυ · δέδια δὲ μή etc., which gives straightforward metre (with 901 ia. trim. ⏑–⏑⏑⏑ ⏑⏑⏑⏑⏑⏑ ⏑⏑⏑⏑–, 902 [omitting θεῶν] ia. dim. ⏑⏑⏑⏑– –⏑–, and 903 ia. trim. cat. ⏑–⏑– ⏑–⏑– ⏑–⏓‖), and excellent sense.[77] Palaeographically the changes may be thought too great, but if ἔφυ became οὐ later scribes might, indeed must, reverse the order of δὲ μή to try to make the sentence ἄφοβος οὐ δέδια δὲ μή ... into possible sense.

Whatever reading we adopt for 902, and even if we still reserve our final approval of any, it seems highly probable that the metre remains iambic, and either side of the disaster area we can see perfectly presentable metrical cola, viz. 901 2 ia., 903 2 ia. ba.//. 904ff is probably iambic, though it could be explained as ⏑⏑⏑⏑⏑⏑⏑⏑|⏑⏑⏑⏑⏑⏑⏑⏑ (2 do.) followed by tro. tetram. cat., arist., or as

∪∪∪∪∪ ∪∪∪∪∪∪|∪∪∪∪∪ (lek. cr.) etc. The dochmiacs are not likely: Conomis gives three examples in Aeschylus (all surrounded by other dochmiacs) of this fully resolved form. It is commoner in Euripides (*Hel*. 695 has two running), but again always in unmistakably dochmiac context. The trochaic analysis has the advantage of diaeresis after πόριμος to coincide with punctuation, but the objection that the first colon (lek. cr.) is unsatisfactory, especially in that trochaic metres tend not to move in trimeters.

As iambics, the lines are remarkable in having no word-end at colon-end: it is impossible to divide for certain either as 2 ia., 2 ia. ba., or as 3 ia., ia. ba. We might compare A. *Th*. 767ff, 838f, 877f, *Pers*. 118ff, *Ag*. 378f, 442ff., *Eum*. 382ff; S. *Aj*. 351f, *El*. 1086f, etc.; E. *And*. 287f, *Hik*. 826f, 605f, 923f, *Tro*. 1092, etc. But most of these examples are of four metra: we might consider the iambic tetrameter as a colon in its own right. Much rarer are series of five iambic metra without diaeresis:

A.	(*Pers*. 117ff	–∪– ∪–∪– –∪– ∪–∪– –∪– –∪– ∪–∪–	2 lek. cr. lek.)
	Ag. 378f	∪–∪– –∪– –∪– –∪– ∪––	ia. 3 cr. ba.
	Ag. 241	∪–∪– –∪– –∪– ∪–∪– ∪––	ia. cr. lek. ba.[78]
	Cho. 825f	∪∪∪– –∪– ∪–∪– –∪– ∪–∪–	cr. 2 lek.
	Eum. 382f	∪–∪– –∪– ∪–∪– –∪– ∪–∪–	ia. 2 lek. (though Wilamowitz and Murray arrange it another way)
E.	*Hik*. 923f	∪–∪– ∪–∪– ∪–∪– –∪– ∪––	3 ia. cr. ba. (and perhaps 605f ? corrupt.)
	Hik. 826f	∪∪∪∪– ∪–∪– ∪–∪– ∪–∪– ∪–∪–	5 ia. (the diaeresis after ἀμφὶ δέ scarcely counts)
	Tro. 1092f	–∪– –∪– –∪– –∪– –∪∪∪ ∪–∪–	5 cr. ia.
	Tro. 1315f	∪–∪– ∪∪∪∪– ∪∪∪∪∪∪ ∪∪∪∪– ∪––	4 ia. ba.

Or. 1412ff 5 ia. (then among its other museum pieces, it contains a run of 7 ia. + spondee without diaeresis (1444ff), and lek. 2 ia. ba. (1468ff), cf. *El.* 1179ff).

The difference between the overlapping cola of Aeschylus and those of Euripides is marked: Aeschylus' are all syncopated and unresolved, with the lekythion much in evidence: Euripides' (though he has some examples of that kind, e.g. *Tro.* 1092f) are usually unsyncopated, and sometimes highly resolved. So whether *Prom.* 904 is dochmiac, trochaic, or iambic, it has no near parallel in Aeschylus or Sophocles.

(If we have to divide the five metra (if only for printing convenience), I think Wilamowitz's ∪∪∪∪∪∪ ∪∪∪∪∪∪|∪∪∪∪– ∪–∪– ∪––‖ is to be preferred. Murray's trimeter ∪∪∪∪∪∪ ∪∪∪∪∪∪ ∪∪∪∪– seems rather outlandish, with οὐδ' thus isolated.)

The final clausula, lekythion + aristophanean, surprisingly only occurs twice in extant tragedy, as far as I can discover. It would seem an obvious enough dicolon, and there are frequent examples in all three tragedians of –∪∪– ∪–∪– –∪∪– ∪––‖ or ∪–∪– –∪∪– ∪––‖ . Aeschylus uses the aristophanean much more often than the other two, particularly as a clausula to iambics or dochmiacs. But it is common in all three in various clausulae, some close to this (e.g. A. *Pers.* 1044f, *Th.* 303, *Supp.* 116, 580, *Cho.* 459, *Eum.* 535; S. *Aj.* 353, *El.* 479, *Ant.* 1119, *Tr.* 505; E. *Alk.* 218, *Hek.* 950ff, *Or.* 994, *Hipp.* 533). The exact parallels are A. *Cho.* 792, where lek. arist. are in overlap, and E. *Hipp.* 1149f, after iambics + dactyls. We might count too A. *Supp.* 1062, where aristophanean follows lekythion, but with pause in between.

In view of the rarity of this precise phenomenon, but abundance of near parallels, I do not think we are justified in considering the clausula as useful evidence for or against Aeschylean authorship. If we pointed on the one hand to Aeschylus' preference for the aristophanean as clausula to iambics, we could equally reply that it is perhaps remarkable that in his frequent usage of it, he did not favour this particular formula. Wilamowitz is not strictly right when he comments 'clausula e more Aeschyli tetrameter'.

Despite uncertainties as to 902, the general character of the metre of this epode seems quite clear: iambics, largely unsyncopated and very extensively resolved, exaggerating the tendencies already observed in 160ff. Here the 'rate of resolutions'[79] (omitting 902) is eight in twelve metra, producing some very striking lines: 901 ⏑–⏑⏑⏑ ⏑⏑⏑⏑⏑⏑, 904 ⏑⏑⏑⏑⏑⏑ ⏑⏑⏑⏑⏑⏑; cf. A. *Pers*. 256 = 262 ⏖⏑⏑⏑ ⏑⏑⏑⏑⏑⏑ or (Broadhead) –⏔⏑⏑⏑ ⏑⏑⏑⏑–, 269 = 275, 1057; *Th*. 961ff, *Supp*. 112-13 = 123-4 ⏒–⏑⏑⏑ ⏑⏑⏑⏑⏑⏑ ⏑–⏑– ⏑⏑⏑⏑⏑⏑ ⏑⏑⏑⏑–, 810f; *Ag*. 769 ⏑⏑⏑⏑⏑⏑ ⏑⏑⏑⏑–, 485; *Cho*. 152 ⏑⏑⏑⏑⏑⏑ ⏑⏑⏑⏑⏑⏑|⏑⏑⏑– –⏑– ⏑⏑⏑⏑⏑⏑ ⏑–⏑–|⏑⏑⏑⏑⏑⏑ ⏑–⏑–, then dochmiacs.

Sophocles never has more than two resolutions in iambic dimeters, though he does in trochaics; cf. *El*. 154ff, 229f; *OT* 190ff; *Ant*. 876, 1273 = 1296 ⏔⏑⏖ ⏑⏑⏑⏑⏑ ⏔⏑–; *Tr*. 947f, 1009; *OK* 537, 1221f, 1447, 1732f.

E. *Hek*. 950; *Ion* 138; *Tro*. 316, 518, 520 = 540 ⏓⏔⏑⏔|⏑⏑⏑⏑⏑⏑, 525 = 545 ⏑⏑⏑⏑⏑⏑ ⏑–⏑⏖, 1085, 1316; *Hel*. 1117ff, 1148, 1485; *Pho*. 1567ff, 1751f; *Or*. 329, 986, 1413ff, 1500 ⏑⏑⏑⏑⏑⏑ ⏑⏑⏑⏑⏑⏑; *IA* 1477 ⏑⏑⏑⏑⏑⏑ ⏑⏑⏑⏑⏑⏑ ⏑⏑⏑⏑⏑ ⏑–⏑–.

Summary

The general character of this epode is unremarkable (iambic), but the frequency of resolution and lack of syncopation, while not unparalleled in Aeschylus, are in contrast to his usual style of lyric iambics, and more similar to those of Euripides.

We are now in a position to put together the information we have collected in our study of the individual lyric stanzas of *Prom*., and to survey the author's treatment of the various types of metre (iambic, dochmiac, dactylic, aeolic, trochaic, dactylo-epitritic), in comparison with that of Aeschylus, Sophocles, and Euripides.

IAMBIC

'The mention of lyric iambics suggests to the mind, before all else, the great choruses of Aeschylus.'[80] Reversing the mental process, we might say, 'The mention of the choruses of Aeschylus suggests to the mind, before all else, lyric iambics.' This is not purely a matter of quantity. 'The lyric iambics of Sophocles ... are ... in total bulk, only some 25% less than those of Aeschylus. But one notices their presence far less, because they rarely constitute the prevailing rhythm of a strophe, being usually interwoven with other metres.'[81]

Following this up, I have made a list of the purely iambic

lyric stanzas in the three tragedians.[82] (See Table 1.)

TABLE 1. *Purely iambic stanzas*

	Play	Iambic stanzas		Total	
A.	*Pers.*	15	stanzas out of a total of	56	
	Th.	21		62	
	Supp.	20		89	
	Ag.	17		70	
	Cho.	26		53	
	Eum.	14		39	
TOTAL		113		369	(about 31%)
	Prom.	2	stanzas out of a total of	20	(10%)
S.	*Aj.*	1	stanza out of a total of	28	
	El.	1		29	
	OT	2		28	
	Ant.	0		33	
	Tr.	4		29	
	Ph.	0		23	
	OK	6		39	
TOTAL		14		209	(about 7%)
E.	*Alk.*	0	stanzas out of a total of	28	
	Med.	0		24	
	Hipp.	1		33	
	Hkd.	0		15	
	And.	4		30	
	Hek.[83]	0		21+	
	Hik.	16		32	
	Hks	5		30+	
	Ion	2		30+	
	Tro.	7		30+	
	IT	0		15+	
	El.	6		29	
	Hel.	6		30+	
	Pho.	9		30+	
	Or.	4		19+	
	IA	5		22+	
	Ba.	0		30	
	Rhesos	0		21	
TOTAL		65		450+	(roughly 14%)

It should be made clear that the criteria by which these figures were obtained are somewhat arbitrary (see the previous two notes); but they were, I think, consistently applied, and the figures may be taken as more or less accurate indications (which in the nature of the case are all we can hope for) of each author's habits.

In *Prom.*, it is not easy to decide what to do about 425-35; I prefer to leave them out: if they were included, we should be in the anomalous position of counting one stanza as purely iambic (431ff), and the other as not, although many scholars believe they should respond. It is also hard to decide whether 114ff should count as a stanza, and if so, whether it is purely iambic. I have included it as an iambic stanza, despite my suspicion that one or more dochmiacs lie within, and despite its shortness and unusual character.

So we find in *Prom.* that two stanzas out of twenty are purely iambic, i.e. 10% (three out of twenty-two, i.e. 14%, if 425-35 are included). This proportion is clearly much lower than that of any of Aeschylus' plays. The two iambic stanzas of *Prom.* are both very short: 114-19 (Prometheus' outburst) and 901-7 (epode). There are no strophic iambic odes.[84] Thus in the most distinctively Aeschylean feature *Prom.* is largely lacking.

So much for purely quantitative comparison. When we come to consider the *nature* of these lyric iambics, it is obviously difficult to avoid a greater element of subjectivity. But we saw earlier, in dealing with the individual lyric passages, that *Prom.* does display some remarkable differences from what we believe to be the characteristic Aeschylean style. We must remember that in his extensive use of lyric iambics, even within the space of six plays, Aeschylus shows a considerable range of variety. Thus, for instance, *Cho.* 423ff and *Ag.* 176ff are of completely different characters. On the other hand, we would say quite confidently, on the evidence available, that *Ag.* 176ff was much closer to Aeschylus' usual style - or rather an exaggeration of it; and we would point out that the rest of *Cho.*'s lyric iambics are closer to that style.

We observed that most of the iambics in *Prom.* are unsyncopated, unlike most of Aeschylus'.[85] Where they are syncopated, *Prom.*'s trimeters favour the form of syncopation (2 ia. ba.) which is most popular with both Sophocles and Euripides, but rare in Aeschylus.[86] We also observed the high rate of resolutions in

160ff = 178ff, and 901ff; this rate is paralleled occasionally in Aeschylus, but is in contrast to his usual technique.[87]

A further detail should perhaps be mentioned, the predominance of short anceps in *Prom.*'s lyric iambics. Denniston remarks[88] that 'spondees' (i.e. long anceps – – ⏑ –) are less common in lyric than in spoken iambic, and gives the following figures, as the proportion of 'spondees' to metra:

	Dimeters	*Trimeters*
Aeschylus	21.4%	23.8%
Sophocles	37.5%	28.8%
Euripides	16.4%	11.4%
Aristophanes	68%	45%

(If we leave *Prom.* out of Aeschylus' figures, I calculate that they should be: dimeters about 22.5%, trimeters about 24.5%.)[89]

In *Prom.* there are ten unsyncopated dimeters = twenty metra, all with short anceps: i.e. the proportion of 'spondees' to metra is 0%.

There are also five unsyncopated trimeters, = fifteen metra, with one long anceps, i.e. 6.7%.[90]

Obviously *Prom.*'s samples are too small to provide a reliable basis for argument, but such evidence as they do give puts *Prom.*. well below Aeschylus' and even Euripides' figures.[91]

The combination in *Prom.*'s lyric iambics of lack of syncopation, short anceps, and frequent resolution gives a light, free-flowing effect that contrasts with the heavier, more halting periods for which Aeschylus is best known. (The trochaic stanzas 415ff = 420ff have a similar effect.)

DOCHMIAC

With its conveniently Protean aspect (⏓⏖⏖⏓⏖), the dochmiac is constantly abused by harassed editors, struggling to fit an unlikely series of long and short syllables into a terminological strait-jacket. It is often impossible to decide whether a colon is dochmiac or iambic, and when (as in *Prom.*) the two are mixed, there are no really distinctive differences in the techniques of the three tragedians, until we come to the extravagant astropha of late Euripides.

Between thirty and forty dochmiac metra occur in *Prom.* (In some cases we do not know if the metre is dochmiac, in others we know that it is dochmiac, but cannot be certain which form a particular metron offers, because of textual problems.) The actual forms which we find in *Prom.* are given below, with an indication (often very tentative) as to their frequency.[92]

Form	*Occurrences*	in *Prom.*	in A.	in S.	in E.
⏑⏑⏑–⏑–		17	194	57	403
⏑––⏑–	(573?,576,588=608,688?,689)	6	114	128	281
–⏑⏑–⏑–	(572,594) [691?]	2	127	33	73
⏑–⏑⏑⏑–	(573) [114?]	1	14	2	14
⏑⏑⏑–––	(573)	1	12	2	98
–––⏑–	(693?)	(1?)	?3	9	38
–––––	(693?)	(1?)	?4	1	19
–⏑⏑–⏑⏑⏑	(117)	1?	0	2	6
–⏑⏑–––	(580+599?)	2?	?5	12	33
⏑⏑⏑–⏑⏑⏑	(578=596?,902?)	(3?)	1	2	22

We are not really sure enough of any of the forms (⏑⏑⏑–⏑⏑⏑, –⏑⏑–––, –––––, –––⏑– and especially –⏑⏑–⏑⏑⏑) which are rare or non-existent in Aeschylus but more common in Sophocles and/or Euripides; in every case in *Prom.* a possible alternative - often equally unusual in itself - can be found. Our suspicions that some unaeschylean dochmiacs are at large do not amount to a solid argument.[93]

The total number of dochmiacs in *Prom.* is of course too small for any reliable conclusions to be drawn as to the relative frequency of the various forms, especially when so much is uncertain. We observe though that –⏑⏑–⏑–, which comprises almost a quarter of Aeschylus' total (127 out of 527), about one ninth of Sophocles' (33 out of 291), and only about one sixteenth of Euripides' (73 out of 1166), only occurs twice in *Prom.* for certain (though emendations at 576, 691 can produce two more), out of thirty or more dochmiacs.

The hexasyllabic dochmiac is very rare in all tragedy, and usually admits alternative interpretations.[94] If *Prom.* 572 (κυνηγετεῖ πλαναῖ) were to be accepted,[95] it would be paralleled nowhere in Aeschylus for certain (and the possible parallels[96] are all heavily resolved, not the simple ⏑–⏑–⏑–), only twice for certain in Sophocles and a few times in Euripides.[97]

The hypodochmiacs –⏑–⏑– in responsion at *Prom.* 584 = 604 have one certain Aeschylean parallel[98] (*Th.* 566 = 629), and a dubious one at *Pers.* 961 = 973: Sophocles gives one probable pair, Euripides seven certain, six dubious pairs. *Prom.* 688, as printed by most editors, gives an hypodochmiac in astrophic lyrics; there is no Aeschylean parallel for this (perhaps two in Sophocles, several in Euripides), but it is not certain that it really occurs here.[99] Three hypodochmiacs would be a remarkably high proportion of such a small dochmiac total (A. *Th.* of course is very rich in dochmiacs).

Less uncertain, and more peculiar, is the prosody of 593: there is no Aeschylean parallel to such a lengthening before mute and liquid in dochmiacs;[100] cf. too 582.

We can point to several apparently suspicious details in *Prom.*'s dochmiacs; but we cannot really put our finger on any of them. Each suspect has an alibi (some more convincing than others). Perhaps the circumstantial evidence should be ignored completely, and no judgement made.

DACTYLIC

There is no trace in *Prom.* of the style which Aristophanes chose to parody in the *Frogs* as being characteristically Aeschylean, the mixture of iambics and dactyls.[101] But since only *Persians* and *Agamemnon* of our extant plays contain such a mixture,[102] this argument from silence is palpably weak.

We observed[103] that neither the run of dactyls at *Prom.* 166f = 184f as the final colon of a stanza, nor the ending of such a run ⏑⏑–⏑⏑–⏑⏑–⏑––‖, has any parallel in Aeschylus; we find several parallels to both in Euripides.

AEOLIC

Here the argument from silence is on the other side. There is no passage in *Prom.* which continuously employs the aeolic metres of the –×–⏑⏑–×– (glyconic) or –×–×–⏑⏑– (choriambic dimeter) type. Every extant play of Euripides has at least one ode composed largely in this metre (though *Rhesos* does not have a wholly aeolic strophe). E. *Alk.*, *And.*, *Hek.*, *Tro.* are more restricted in their use of aeolic than the other plays, but it is not surprising that

Aeschylus' parody of Euripides' lyrics in the *Frogs* comprises largely glyconics and choriambic dimeters. But this in itself suggests that these were thought of as being characteristically Euripidean, and we are not suggesting that Euripides wrote *Prom.* We simply do not know the habits of tragedians other than Aeschylus, Sophocles, and Euripides with regard to aeolic metres. Aeschylus very rarely has a wholly aeolic strophe,[104] though quite often has an ephymnion of the form pher., pher., glyc., pher.//, after a non-aeolic strophe.[105]

If we take Aeschylus and Euripides as the two extremes in the frequency of aeolic strophes, Sophocles is our sole surviving author for comparison, and his plays vary considerably. *Aj.* 596ff, 624ff, 693ff, 1199ff are all predominantly 'glyconic' (cf. too 192ff, 1185ff), whereas *El.* only has part of one stanza in aeolics (1063ff); so too *Ant.*, *Ph.* and *OK* use aeolics extensively, *Tr.* and *OT* rarely.[106]

I have spoken so far only of 'glyconic' aeolics, whose rarity in *Prom.* is just about matched by S. *El.* and *Tr.* But *Prom.* has a large number of 'iambo-choriambic' and of 'anapaesto-iambic' aeolics. 128ff, 397ff both employ almost exclusively a sort of choriambic dimeter (× – ∪ – – ∪∪ –), though the iambic half is clearly very different from the 'aeolic base' – × – × of Euripidean choriambic dimeters. This type of metre we saw to be fairly common in all three tragedians, and even in fragments of unknown authorship.[107] 545ff too must be counted as 'aeolic', of the 'anapaestic' or 'enoplion' kind. There is nothing remotely like this pair of stanzas in Aeschylus, though we find more or less close parallels, usually of just two or three cola, scattered throughout Sophocles and Euripides.

TROCHAIC

On 415ff we commented on the rarity of continuous trochaic metre in Aeschylus, and found no parallel in extant tragedy to the simplicity of this purely trochaic strophic pair (with aeolic clausula).

DACTYLO-EPITRITE

526ff = 536ff, 887ff = 894ff are straightforward dactylo-epitrite, a metre found in almost every play of Sophocles and Euripides, and sometimes employed by them very extensively, but conspicuously and totally absent from Aeschylus' surviving plays, even in its shortest elements.

CONCLUSIONS

The lyric metres of *Prom.* diverge consistently and strikingly from the Aeschylean pattern, as far as it is known to us from six undisputed plays. They fail to exhibit the characteristics, common to those six plays, which we think of as peculiarly Aeschylean. They reveal, both in many points of detail, and in the overall choice and treatment of the basic metres, differences from Aeschylus' normal style which far exceed the individual and minor oddities of each of his extant plays. Were the choral lyrics of *Prom.* all that we possessed of an anonymous tragedy, we would on metrical grounds reject absolutely the idea that Aeschylus could be their author. As it is, we can merely observe that the weight of the evidence, largely objective and measurable as it is, comes down solidly against Aeschylean authorship of these lyrics.

Chapter 4

THE RECITATIVE ANAPAESTS

Little work seems to have been done by way of a comparative study of the anapaestic systems of the three extant tragedians. Broadhead[1] gives some useful information about Aeschylus; Dale makes the generalization, 'On the whole, Aeschylus has the least regular anapaestic systems of all the dramatists',[2] but does not go into details.

In this survey, it is easiest to deal with the 'metron' as the basic unit. The following forms of the anapaestic metron are regular in the non-lyric anapaests of tragedy:[3]

– – ∪ ∪ –	'spondee anapaest'	(SA)
– ∪ ∪ – –	'dactyl spondee'	(DS)
∪ ∪ – ∪ ∪ –	'anapaest anapaest'	(AA)
∪ ∪ – – –	'anapaest spondee'	(AS)
– – – –	'spondee spondee'	(SS)

Less common are:[4]

– ∪ ∪ – ∪ ∪	'dactyl dactyl'	(DD)
– – – ∪ ∪	'spondee dactyl'	(SD)
∪ ∪ – – ∪ ∪	'anapaest dactyl'	(AD)

METRON FREQUENCY

A comparison of the relative frequencies of these various forms in the three major tragedians is, I think, interesting and informative. Table 2 shows the percentage frequencies of each form in A. *Pers.*, *Supp.*, *Ag.*, *Cho.*, *Eum.*; S. *Aj.*, *Ant.*, *Tr.*, *El.*, *Ph.*, *OK*; E. *Alk.*, *Med.*, *Hipp.*, *Hek.*, *Ion*, *Tro.*, *El.*, *Rhesos*. (A. *Th.* is not included, as only twelve anapaestic metra are attributable to Aeschylus with any great likelihood (822ff) and a sample of this size is obviously useless. Similarly S. *OT* offers too few metra to be worth including.) We should bear in mind throughout that the value of these percentage figures depends on the size of the total sample. In some cases, it is difficult to be certain whether anapaests are 'recitative' or lyric *Klaganapäste*, e.g. S. *Tr.* 974ff, which I take as recitative, despite undeniable irregularities. In E. *Ion* I have included 81-111, 862-80, 1244-9, in E. *Hek*. 98-153 (not 59-72, 92-7 which must be considered lyric), 1293-5. The metra of the clausular paroemiacs are not included, and will be considered later.

TABLE 2. *Anapaestic metra: percentage of each type*

	SA	*DS*	*SS*	*AS*	*AA*	*DD*	*SD*	*AD*	*TOTAL SAMPLE*
A. *Pers.*	31%	31%	10%	9%	18%	1%	1%	0%	173
Supp.	25	30	6	16	19	3	0	1	85
Ag.	21	34	6	11	23	3	1	1	255
Cho.	18	44	8	12	18	0	0	1	99
Eum.	25	33	1	17	18	4	1	1	88
Prom.	32	26	16	14	11	1	0	0	236
S. *Aj.*	28	21	9	19	22	1	0	0	163
Ant.	28	26	14	15	16	0	1	0	130
Tr.	22	13	18	22	22	1	1	0	77
El.	33	24	14	12	16	1	0	0	58
Ph.	35	23	15	9	16	1	1	0	105
OK	28	29	10	15	12	3	2	0	78
E. *Alk.*	27	29	10	19	14	1	1	0	154
Med.	32	32	8	13	13	3	0	0	273
Hipp.	32	26	4	19	18	2	0	0	240
Hek.	42	24	3	18	13	0	0	0	100
Ion	36	19	8	10	19	2	1	3	88
Tro.	31	22	8	13	21	4	0	0	106
El.	36	24	7	15	14	3	2	0	136
Rhesos	38	19	5	22	14	1	0	0	111

Prom. contains 236 anapaestic metra, plus fifteen paroemiacs. This is a large enough sample to give us some confidence in the figures which they yield as evidence of the author's technique.

From Table 2 the following observations may be made:

(i) Aeschylus favours DS –⏑⏑–– rather than SA ––⏑⏑– as the most common metron (see Broadhead); the preponderance seems most marked in the latest plays. Sophocles prefers SA in all except *OK*, where the total sample (78) is rather small. Euripides appears to use them equally in his early plays, but increasingly to prefer SA in his later. *Prom.*'s marked preference for SA (32% as against 26%) is thus unaeschylean. Only *Pers.* with 31% comes nearly as high for SA as *Prom.* None of Aeschylus' plays comes as low as 26% for DS: the nearest is *Supp.* (30%): 26% is however typical of Sophocles or Euripides.

(ii) SS –––– is much more common in *Prom.* (16%) than in any of the plays of Aeschylus or Euripides; Sophocles has similar figures in *Ant.*, *El.*, *Ph.*, and exceeds them in *Tr.* (if we accept the heavily spondaic 974ff as recitative). Aeschylus and Euripides never exceed 10%;[5] Sophocles never has less than 9%.

(iii) AA ⏑⏑–⏑⏑– in Aeschylus is consistently the third most common form of metron, after DS and SA (see Broadhead): the proportion is never less than 18%. *Prom.*'s proportion of AA (11%) is the fifth most common, after SA, DS, SS, AS. Sophocles' rate is usually similar to Aeschylus' (the lowest is *OK* 12%; again n.b. the small sample); Euripides comes nearest with *Med.*, *Hek.* 13%, *Alk.*, *El.*, *Rhesos* 14%.

OVERLAP

The frequency with which diaeresis between metra is not observed, whether through overlap or elision, does not seem to help us, since the authors themselves are inconsistent in their admission of this licence. L. Parker[6] remarks that overlap by one short syllable is commonest in Aeschylus (twenty-one times), less so in Sophocles (ten), and that Euripides contains 'very few'. But as she also points out that thirteen of the twenty-one Aeschylean examples occur in *Ag.*, four in *Cho.*, i.e. only four other examples in *Pers.*, *Supp.*, *Th.*, *Eum.* and *Prom.*, we can hardly describe the licence as characteristic or otherwise of Aeschylus.

More problematical are the more considerable overlaps, of which the most striking is *Prom.* 172 καί μ'οὔτι μελι/γλώσσοις πειθοῦς. Fraenkel (on *Ag.* 52) gives Aeschylean examples of single-syllable overlap, and cites, as his only parallel to *Prom.* 172, S. *Tr.* 985 κεῖμαι πεπονη/μένος ἀλλήκτοις. As we have already remarked, this passage has distinct elements of lyric *Klaganapästen*, and this is not really a satisfactory parallel.[7] A. fr. 192.4 (from Π. Λυόμενος) has come down to us in the form λίμναν παντο/τρόφον

Αἰθιόπων, with a similar overlap. Wilamowitz emended, stating flatly 'duae breves metrum nusquam excedunt', and Fraenkel remarks 'it must be owned that the expression in the form in which we have it seems doubtful on stylistic grounds'.[8] It is probably best to leave it out of the argument. Other odd overlaps occur:

Prom.	287	στομίων/ἄτερ
	293	γνώσηι δὲ τάδ' ὡς/ἔτυμ' οὐδὲ μάτην
	295	ὅ τι χρή/σοι συμπράσσειν (long syllable overlaps)
A. *Pers.*	47	δίρρυμά τε καὶ/τρίρρυμα τέλη
Ag.	800	Ἑλένης ἕνεκ' οὐ/γάρ σ' ἐπικεύσω
	1555	ἀλλ' Ἰφιγένει/ά νιν ἀσπασίως
S. *Ph.*	162	δῆλον ἔμοιγ' ὡς/φορβῆς χρείαι
	196	οὐκ ἔστιν ὅπως/οὐ θεῶν μελέτηι
E. *Hks*	443	τοὺς τοῦ μεγάλου/δή ποτε παῖδας
	449	δακρύων ὡς οὐ/δύναμαι
El.	1295	κἀμοὶ μύθου/μέτα, Τυνδαρίδαι
	1355	μηδ' ἐπιόρκων/μέτα συμπλείτω

(cf. *Rhesos* 17?, *Alk.* 81f?, 94?)

Prom. with four such examples is thus exceptional, and 172 μελι/γλώσσοις remains the most violent infraction of metron-diaeresis in all tragedy. Even A. fr. 192 παντο/τρόφον, with its overlap of two short syllables (comparable to e.g. A. *Ag.* 1555), is not as striking as this: the division of metra is completely straddled and obliterated. The other three examples are less startling in that they do have word-division between metra, even if that division is of a very unnatural kind. It is slightly curious, though, that they all occur in the passage 284–97.

LENGTH OF PERIODS

The end of each metrical period in recitative anapaests is marked by a clausular paroemiac. In general we find that Aeschylus has shorter periods (i.e. more paroemiacs) than Sophocles[9] and Euripides. The ratios of metra to each paroemiac are as follows:

A. *Pers.* 8.7, *Supp.* 6.1, *Ag.* 8.1, *Cho.* 5.0, *Eum.* 8.0.
S. *Aj.* 11.0, *Ant.* 8.1, *Tr.* 7.5, *El.* 8.3, *Ph.* 15.0, *OK* 11.1.
E. *Alk.* 11.0, *Med.* 16.0, *Hipp.* 20.0, *Hek.* 16.6, *Ion* 12.6, *Tro.* 11.8, *El.* 19.4, *Rhesos* 6.2.
Prom. 13.9.

Prom.'s ratio is thus far higher than Aeschylus', but typical of Euripides. It might be objected that the ratio depends on the exigencies of the drama, that e.g. short anapaestic passages of only half-a-dozen or so metra plus their paroemiac might be required in some plays, not in others, and thus lower the ratio for those plays. Certainly this principle applies e.g. to A. *Cho.*, S. *Ant.*, E. *Alk.*; but we need only look at the parodoi of A. *Pers.* and *Ag.*, and also *Ag.* 782ff, *Cho.* 855ff, *Eum.* 307ff, etc. to see that Aeschylus prefers much shorter periods than Sophocles and Euripides.

These figures are conclusively confirmed by those for the longest sequences of metra without a clausular paroemiac:

A. *Pers.* 17, *Supp.* 14, *Ag.* 18, *Cho.* 14, *Eum.* 18.
S. *Aj.* 27, *Ant.* 18, *Tr.* 19, *El.* 24, *Ph.* 32, *OK* 25.
E. *Alk.* 25, *Med.* 47, *Hipp.* 57, *Hek.* 25, *Ion* 18, *Tro.* 20, *El.* 41, *Rhesos* 12.
Prom. 26.

In Aeschylus the longest periods are: eighteen metra (*Ag.* 72ff, *Eum.* 927ff), seventeen metra (*Pers.* 49ff, *Ag.* 1567ff). Otherwise he never has more than sixteen, rarely more than fourteen, before a paroemiac. In *Prom.* we find twenty-six metra (1040ff), twenty-five (284ff, 1080ff), twenty (167ff), to confirm that the high ratio is totally uncharacteristic of Aeschylus.

We notice in Sophocles thirty-two (*Ph.* 1452ff), twenty-seven (*Aj.* 1402ff), twenty-five (*OK* 1754ff), twenty-four (*El.* 90ff), twenty-three (*El.* 107ff), twenty-one (*Aj.* 233ff), nineteen (*Tr.* 1264ff), eighteen (*Ant.* 929ff, *Ph.* 191ff, *Aj.* 154ff), and in Euripides fifty-seven (*Hipp.* 208ff), forty-seven (*Med.* 1389ff), forty-one (*El.* 1331ff), thirty-nine (*El.* 1308ff), thirty-seven (*Med.* 184 ff), thirty (*Med.* 114ff), twenty-five (*Alk.* 911ff), etc.

PAROEMIACS

The clausular paroemiacs also yield interesting information. The smallness of the actual numbers involved makes it dangerous to attribute much significance to the preference for one or other form of paroemiac within one play or one author, but Table 3 does suggest some general differences in the technique of the three tragedians. This table gives, in the first six columns, the percentage frequency in each play of each form of the paroemiac;[10]

then the total number of paroemiacs, followed by the proportion of that total containing diaeresis[11] after the first metron.

TABLE 3. *Clausular paroemiacs: percentage of each type*

	A	B	C	D	E	*OTHERS*	*TOTAL*	*% DIAERESIS*
A. *Pers.*	5%	20%	15%	30%	20%	10%	20	75%
Supp.	22	22	22	14	14	7	14	64
Ag.	32	29	16	3	16	3	31	68
Cho.	15	35	20	5	25	0	20	65
Eum.	18	27	27	9	18	0	11	82
Prom.	7	46	7	40	0	0	15	20
S. *Aj.*	7	20	13	53	7	0	15	40
Ant.	13	50	6	25	6	0	16	63
Tr.	33	22	11	33	0	0	9	57
El.	0	0	0	57	0	43	7	14
Ph.	0	43	29	29	0	0	7	57
OK	0	14	0	71	14	0	7	71
E. *Alk.*	7	43	21	14	14	0	14	93
Med.	12	47	0	23	18	0	17	83
Hipp.	8	33	0	42	8	8	12	75
Hek.	0	33	17	50	0	0	6	67
Ion	0	57	0	14	29	0	7	86
Tro.	22	55	0	22	0	0	9	67
El.	0	14	14	71	0	0	7	57
Rhesos	6	22	6	67	0	0	18	72

A = ∪∪–∪∪–∪∪––‖ B = ––∪∪–∪∪––‖ C = ∪∪–––∪∪––‖
D = ––––∪∪––‖ E = –∪∪––∪∪––‖

From the table we observe:

(i) B is the most common form in Aeschylus and Euripides and in *Prom.*, second most common in Sophocles. But whereas in Aeschylus A, C and E are equally common, and D rather less so (total numbers for each of the first three 19, 18, 18, for D

11), in Sophocles and Euripides D tends to be decidedly more common than any of the other three. In *Prom.* D is easily second most common (six times = 40%): of Aeschylus' plays only *Pers.* (six = 30%) comes near this frequency; none of his late plays has more than one example of this form. *Prom.* is correspondingly lacking in three forms common in Aeschylus, less so in Sophocles and Euripides, A (once), C (once), E (never).

(ii) *Prom.* clearly favours overlap or elision in the paroemiac, rather than diaeresis. Both Aeschylus and Euripides consistently prefer diaeresis (Aeschylus never less than 64%, Euripides than 57%). Sophocles varies, but is regularly lower than the other two. *Prom.* 3/15 = 20% diaeresis seems to be based on a sufficiently large sample for it to be legitimate to talk of a decided preference for no diaeresis. Nine of the twelve examples without diaeresis have overlap. This apparent avoidance of diaeresis differs from the practice of all three tragedians.[12]

SUMMARY

In this examination of the anapaestic systems of the three tragedians in relation to *Prom.*, we have found that in almost every respect in which a divergence of technique can be traced between Aeschylus and either one or both of the others, *Prom.* is to be placed on the opposite side to Aeschylus. The most remarkable divergences of *Prom.* from Aeschylus' practice seem to be:

(i) The high proportion of spondaic metra (SS) in *Prom.*, and the (to some extent corresponding) low proportion of the purely anapaestic AA form, and of DS.

(ii) The overlap of more than a short syllable from one metron to the next, most strikingly at *Prom.* 172, but also in three other places.

(iii) The high ratio of metra to paroemiacs and the long sequences of metra before their clausular paroemiac (four times twenty metra or more).

(iv) The avoidance of metron-diaeresis in the paroemiac.

Furthermore we have seen that *Prom.* is rather closer to *Pers.* than to late Aeschylus in several respects; this obviously rules out any theory of a development in Aeschylus' anapaestic technique such as has been postulated for his iambic trimeters - even supposing that there was much likelihood of such a development in the short time between the *Oresteia* and his death.

The facts, for what they are worth, point unmistakably away from Aeschylean authorship of the anapaests of *Prom.*: and some of the facts in this case seem to be worth quite a lot.

Chapter 5

THE IAMBIC TRIMETERS

RESOLUTIONS[1]

We can trace a steady, if unspectacular, decrease in the number of resolutions within the iambic trimeter which Aeschylus allows himself, from the *Persians* onwards. Leaving aside resolutions caused by proper names,[2] the rate per 100 trimeters in each play is: A. *Pers*. 11.0, *Th*. 9.3, *Supp*. 8.4, *Ag*. 4.8, *Cho*. 5.2, *Eum*. 5.0. It is natural to infer that these figures reflect a gradual development in Aeschylus' technique, particularly in view of the remarkable uniformity of development that we see in Euripides.[3] We must remember of course that the material available for study in the case of Aeschylus is much more limited, and the figures for Sophocles serve to remind us that a tragedian was not necessarily consistent in his practice: S. *Aj*. 6.2, *Ant*. 3.9, *OT* 6.0, *Tr*. 5.9, *El*. 3.4, *Ph*. 11.0, *OK* 5.2. But the uniformity of the figures for the three plays of the *Oresteia* suggests that we do have here a useful criterion for dating Aeschylus' plays.

Prom.'s figure is 4.8. Thus if *Prom*. is Aeschylean, we would tend to place it among his latest plays; but the figure also fits well with Sophocles and with early Euripides (e.g. *Hipp*. 4.3, *Hkd*. 5.7, *Alk*. 6.9). Our knowledge of the other tragedians of the mid-fifth century is far too scanty for us to draw any conclusions about their technique (though there is evidence to suggest that some of them may have been much freer with their resolutions[4]), and we may merely remark that *Prom*. would seem to be typical of tragedy written between 460 and 425, regardless of author.

Resolutions occur in the following lines of *Prom*. (I have bracketed those due to proper names): 2, 6, (18), 52, 54, 64, 76, 89, 116, 210, 239, 273, (351), 353, 354?, 366, 368, (369), 371, 464, 487, 666, 680?, 709, (715), 717, 720, 721, 722, 729, (730), (735), 746, 762, 788, 793, 796, (805), 809, 811, (840), 847, 849, (851), 993, 994, 1009, 1027 = 37 + 2? (plus 9).[5] Descroix states (p. 235) that Aeschylus never has more than two consecutive lines containing resolutions, whereas all the plays of Sophocles and Euripides have at least one passage of three such lines (in Euripides often more than three). But he has not noticed A. *Supp.* 319ff, *Eum.* 455ff. Thus *Prom.* 720-2 is not too unusual by Aeschylus' standards, even though both Aeschylean parallels, unlike *Prom.* 720ff, owe at least one of their resolutions to a proper name.

At least as important as the quantity of resolutions is their nature, i.e. the relative frequency of the various kinds. Here *Prom.* is, in one very obvious respect, extraordinary. As Garvie remarks,[6] in his analysis of the distribution of resolutions within the line in Aeschylus, 'the most striking peculiarity ... concerns ... the *Prometheus* with its very large number of first foot anapaests'. This distinctive feature of *Prom.* has often been remarked upon,[7] though it is sometimes obscured by the inclusion of proper names, which disguise the peculiar nature of *Prom.*'s usage.[8]

Prom. has twelve first foot anapaests (plus one proper name); in Aeschylus we find *Pers.* 2, *Th.* 1, *Supp.* 1, *Ag.* 5 (7?), *Cho.* 1, *Eum.* 3 (plus 6? in his tragic fragments). Furthermore, not only does *Prom.* contain markedly more than any of these six plays, but it also appears, from the limited evidence, that a difference of technique may be observed between the first foot anapaests of *Prom.* and those of Aeschylus. In Aeschylus' tragedies we rarely find diaeresis after ⏑⏑–; it usually comes after ⏑⏑–⏑ or even later. The only examples of ⏑⏑–{ are *Pers.* 343 ἑκατὸν δίς (virtually ⏑⏑–{), *Ag.* 1257?, and *Eum.* 92, 474, 577 (all ἱκέτης etc.), plus fr. 144, fr. 253?, fr. 301 (fr. 50.21 L.-J.?, fr. 251?) and fr. 199.7 from Π. Λυόμενος;[9] we find seven examples of ⏑⏑–⏑{ (*Pers.* 184; *Th.* 268; *Ag.* 28, (30?), 337, 504, 509, 595) plus two of longer words (*Supp.* 713, *Cho.* 275). By contrast, six of *Prom.*'s twelve examples are of ⏑⏑–{ (366, 368, 721, 722, 849, 994), only three of ⏑⏑–⏑{(89, 796, 811; cf. proper name 805), plus three of longer words (6, 64, 353). *Prom.* thus agrees with the practice of Euripides in his earlier plays,[10] where ⏑⏑–{ accounts for roughly half the occurrences (though the numbers involved are again very small: *Alk.* ⏑⏑–{ four, others four; *Hkd.* ⏑⏑–{ seven, others none; *Med.* ⏑⏑–{ one, others one (two); *And.* ⏑⏑–{ one (two), others three). The same seems to be true of Sophocles: (*Aj.* ⏑⏑–{ three?, others one; *OT* ⏑⏑–{ three, others four (six); *Ph.* ⏑⏑–{ seven, others nine).

No satisfactory explanation presents itself for *Prom.*'s divergence from Aeschylean practice, if the play is by Aeschylus; we must attribute it to chance.[11] The alternative is that we have here a small but distinctive piece of evidence that another hand is at work. The curious thing is that it is only in this one licence that *Prom.* is so free; in its resolutions elsewhere in the line, as we have seen, it is very strict.

We find from a study of Descroix and others that in general the three major tragedians observe similar 'rules' in their admission of resolutions (until Euripides' increasing freedom sets him apart, from *And.* onwards). In all three, the commonest form of resolved line is the so-called 'third-foot dactyl' × – ⏑ – – ⏑ ⏑ ⏑ – × – ⏑ – . Garvie's chart (p. 35), which excludes proper names, shows that in Aeschylus the proportion of third-foot dactyls to total resolutions is: A. *Pers.* 42.6%, *Th.* 57.7%, *Supp.* 62.5%, *Ag.* 43.9%, *Cho.* 40.6%, *Eum.* 43.8%: thus *Prom.* with 37.8% is slightly lower. But when proper names are included (see Descroix p. 112) this discrepancy disappears (A. *Cho.* 37%, *Prom.* 40%; cf. S. *Aj.* 40%, *OT* 42%, *Ant.* 24%; E. *Alk.* 28%, *Med*, 45%, *Hipp.* 42%) and we can attribute *Prom.*'s low figure directly to its high proportion of first-foot anapaests.

One or two other minor details are worth mentioning, though none of them carries much weight: every play will show little variations from an author's norm, and we should not exaggerate their significance. Zielinski's tenth Law (p. 152) reads: 'Solutio non admittitur nisi in vocabulis ex tribus vel pluribus syllabis compositis'. Aeschylus seems to be less strict in observing this 'law' than early Euripides, where *Alk.* has five exceptions, *Med.* two, *Hkd.* three, *Hipp.* three (*Rhesos* none), almost all of the 'easy' kind (e.g. preposition plus noun) where the diaeresis is scarcely felt. In Aeschylus we find six exceptions in *Pers.* (181, 682, 782, 793, 403, 330), all of them fairly harsh; as in other respects, his technique is stricter in the later plays, but we still find *Th.* 433, 513, 593 (easy); *Supp.* 193, 241, 390, 416, 475 (easy), 214, 303, 516 (harsh); *Ag.* 600, 1584 (easy), 1312 (harsh); *Cho.* 171, 569 (easy), 130, 489, 885 (harsh); *Eum.* 64, 232, 485, 586 (easy), 446, 602, 892 (harsh).

Prom. has only one, easy, exception, 273 διὰ τέλους. It is thus apparently rather stricter in this respect than Aeschylus; but the totals are too small to be really reliable.

Zielinski's ninth Law states (p. 150): 'Utramque solutae arseos syllabam natura brevem esse oportet, positione debili non admissa'. There are few exceptions in early Euripides: *Alk.* 0, *Med.* 1, *Hkd.* 1, *Hipp.* 4 (*Rhesos* 0). Kopp[12] finds in Aeschylus: *Pers.* 5 (203, 382, 403, 500, 693); *Th.* 7 (59, 191, 198, 495, 704, 710, 806 - plus proper name 6, 39, (458), 1007); *Supp.* 2 (334, 354 - plus 282); *Ag.* 1 (270, plus 309); *Cho.* 4 (207, 209, 697, 912); *Eum.* 1 (806), i.e. 20 instances, plus 6 proper names. Sophocles only has 11 instances;[13] none in *Aj.* or *Ant.*; *OT* 3 (641, 825, 844); *Tr.* 1 (362); *El.* 2 (425, 1231); *Ph.* 3 (222?, 751, 815); *OK* 2 (428, 1251).

Unfortunately we cannot be sure how many exceptions there are in *Prom.*: 762 κενοφρόνων is certain; 2 ἄβροτον is likely; 680 ἀφνίδιος is improbable. This does not really help us, as the total is anyway unremarkable.

The irrational resolution of anceps other than at the beginning of the line (i.e. 'anapaest' within the trimeter) is extremely rare in extant tragedy before E. *And.*, even when we include proper names. Descroix's chart (p. 112) gives only one example from Aeschylus, *Th.* 569: even here, it is possible that Ἀμφιάρεω should be taken as –∪–.[14] In Sophocles he finds, *Aj.* 1, *Ant.* 4, *OT* 2, *Tr.* 3, *El.* 0, *Ph.* 1, *OK* 7; in Euripides, *Alk.* 0, *Med.* 0, *Hkd.* 0, *Hipp.* 2, *And.* 9.

Descroix does not mention *Prom.* 840 σαφῶς ἐπίστασ' Ἰόνιος κεκλήσεται (which presumably he classes as 'third-foot tribrach'). The first iota of Ἰόνιος is invariably long,[15] and the derivation here from Ἰώ makes it certain that Descroix is mistaken. This 'fourth-foot anapaest' has no certain parallel in Aeschylus, and it is clear that he went to some lengths to avoid irrational resolution of this kind.[16] *Prom.* 840 is therefore an oddity, by Aeschylean standards: but we cannot really put it higher than that, as proper names are always something of a law to themselves, and one isolated example is worth very little.

VERSEWEIGHT[17]

Ritchie gives a table (p. 282) which shows that, generally speaking, the three tragedians do not differ radically in their preference for long or short syllables in the three 'anceps' positions of the iambic trimeter.[18] One or two minor details are attributable to chance,[19] but we may be justified in concluding that the *Oresteia* is rather 'lighter' (i.e. has a higher proportion of short anceps) than Aeschylus' other extant works: A. *Ag.* 44.6%, *Cho.* 44.9%, *Eum.* 43.9%; cf. *Supp.* 40.1%[20] (and S. *Aj.* 40.8%). *Prom.* 41.9% is slightly lower than the *Oresteia* (whose uniformity is very striking), but clearly compatible with Aeschylus in general, and also with Sophocles. Further investigations of the occurrences of short and long anceps in *Prom.*, and in the three major tragedians, produce little of real substance, unless we are impressed by the slightly higher figure in *Prom.* for long anceps in both the last two positions in the line[21] than is usual for Aeschylus: *Prom.* 29.2%; cf. A. *Pers.* 25.7%, *Th.* 27.8%, *Supp.* 27.7%, *Ag.* 25.2%, *Cho.* 23.3%, *Eum.* 25.6%. (These figures do not include resolved lines: from them the same pattern emerges, that *Prom.* tends to have more long anceps in these two positions, i.e. long final anceps after 'third-foot dactyl':[22] A. *Pers.* 7 long, 13 short; *Th.* 15 long, 12 short; *Supp.* 11 long, 11 short; *Ag.* 9 long, 12 short; *Cho.* 4 long, 8 short; *Eum.* 2 long, 11 short: *Prom.* 11 long, 6 short.)

But it must be acknowledged that this tendency of *Prom.* towards a 'heavier' second half of the line is too slight, in comparison with A. *Th.* and *Supp.* in particular, to provide the basis of an argument against Aeschylean authorship.

POSITIO DEBILIS[23]

Kopp and von Mess give the following figures for lengthening before mute and liquid ('weak position') in iambic trimeters:

A. *Pers.* 15 (+ 3 in tro. tetr.); *Th.* 3, *Supp.* 4, *Ag.* 9, *Cho.* 7, *Eum.* 6.

Prom. 18.

S. *Aj.* 28, *Ant.* 14, *OT* 19, *Tr.* 20, *El.* 33, *Ph.* 47, *OK* 29.

early E. *Alk.* 17, *Med.* 36, *Hkd.* 25, *Hipp.* 34 (*Rhesos* 15).

Two things stand out here: (1) the difference between *Pers.* and the rest of Aeschylus' plays; (2) the greater overall frequency of such lengthening in Sophocles and Euripides as compared with Aeschylus' later plays.

(1) It appears that Aeschylus' technique grew stricter after

Pers. (as it did with regard to resolutions, though not so abruptly). *Prom.* clearly comes closer to *Pers.* than to Aeschylus' other five plays. (*Prom.* once in 43 trimeters on average; cf. *Pers.* once in 28; *Th.* 165; *Supp.* 119; *Ag.* 95; *Cho.* 88; *Eum.* 107.)

(2) Though the plays of Sophocles and Euripides contain more trimeters overall, it is nevertheless clear that they admit such lengthening more freely than Aeschylus in his later plays (e.g. S. *Aj.* once in 37 trimeters, *Tr.* in 48; E. *Hkd.* 36, *Alk.* 47 etc.). Much of this increase is due to their usage of a few common words, most notably πατήρ (πᾱ̆τρ-) and τέκνον (τε̄̆κν-).[24] We find πᾱ̆τρ- lengthened only three times in Aeschylus' trimeters (*Pers.* 609, *Th.* 70, *Cho.* 14), but forty-seven times in Sophocles (*Aj.* four, *Ant.* four, *OT* three, *Tr.* four, *El.* seventeen, *Ph.* nine, *OK* six) and quite often in early Euripides (*Alk.* one, *Med.* four, *Hkd.* six, *Hipp.* six; never in *Rhesos*). Similarly the first syllable of τέκνον is never long in Aeschylus, but is so in e.g. S. *OK* thirteen times, E. *Med.* seven, *Hipp.* eight.

πᾰ̄τρός/πᾰ̄τρί is anceps at *Prom.* 40, 910; short at 17, 636, 653, 656, 768; long at 969 (i.e. one long to five short, plus two anceps).

For Aeschylus the figures are:[25] 3 long, 46 short, 7 anceps; for Sophocles, 47 long, 65 short, 18 anceps; for Euripides, 71 long, 126 short, 37 anceps.

(τέκνα is short at *Prom.* 205, anceps at 815. This tells us nothing.)

The other examples of lengthening in *Prom.* are: 358 ᾱ̓γρυπνος, 368 ᾱ̓γριαις, 492 συνε̄δριαι, 968 λᾱ̆τρευειν, 366 ᾱ̓κραις, 803 ᾱ̓κραγεις, 1016 ὀκριδα, 24 ἀπο̄̆κρυψει, 659 θεο̄̆προπους, 263 ἐλᾱ̆φρον, 459 ἀρῑ̆θμον, 5 ὀ̄χμασαι, 644 σχε̄̆τλιαι, 91 κῡ̆κλον, 67 κατο̄̆κνεις, 795 κῡ̆κνομορφοι, 32 ἀῡ̆πνος. They seem to be unremarkable except for their number.

Although the figures for *Prom.*'s treatment of πᾱ̆τρ- are too small to help us much (n.b. the lengthening πᾱ̆τρ- in *dochmiacs* at *Prom.* 593, unparalleled in Aeschylus), the overall picture is one in which *Prom.* seems to fit with Sophocles, Euripides, and A. *Pers.*, rather than with the bulk of Aeschylus' plays.

PROSODY

There are probably no true parallels in all extant tragedy to the two examples in *Prom.* of a vowel remaining short before initial ῥ.

Prom. 713 χρίμπτουσᾰ ῥαχίαισιν, and 992 πρὸς ταῦτᾰ ῥιπτέσθω are, it seems, unique.[26] The only possible parallel in Aeschylus' trimeters is *Eum.* 232: but A. *Th.* 93, S. *OT* 72, E. *Hik.* 380, *Ba.* 1338 lead us to accept Maas' suggestion that we should read ἐρυ- in each case (or regard ῥύομαι as a freak). A. *Th.* 105, *Cho.* 315, *Eum.* 789, all in lyrics, all involve τί ῥεξ-: none of them is remotely comparable.

Nor do Sophocles and Euripides provide a certain parallel: S. *OT* 1289 may simply be an infringement of Porson's Law (as may A. *Eum.* 232); E. *Ba.* 59 may be a 'first-foot anapaest' τύπανᾱ 'Ρέας.[27] Only E. *Ba.* 128 seems unavoidable, and this again is in lyrics.

Ar. *Wasps* 1067 offers a genuine parallel. At such an isolated peculiarity we merely shrug our shoulders; but when we find two or possibly three of them within one play, as at *Prom.* 713, 992 and ?89 we feel we are entitled to an explanation. It seems that our author simply does not observe the same rules as the three major tragedians. Herington is right: 'Whatever the explanation, the clear fact remains that the passages are unique in tragedy'.[28]

There are a few other curious details of prosody in *Prom.*, though none of them is nearly as striking as 713 and 992.

In *Prom.* 1023 we find an orthodox, but still rare, occurrence of initial ῥ making position, μεγᾱ ῥάκος.[29] The only parallel in Aeschylus is *Eum.* 190 ὑπō ῥάχιν (ὑπορράχιν codd.)[30] Sophocles and Euripides are slightly freer with such usages: cf. S. *Ant.* 318, 712; *OT* 847; *OK* 900; fr. 873; E. *Hipp.* 459, *Hik.* 94, *El.* 772, *Hel.* 492, 1090, *Rhesos* 919.

Prom. 935 ὁ δ' οὖν πŏείτω is not paralleled in Aeschylus, who never used this form of ποιέω,[31] which occurs about thirty-five times in Sophocles, but only three times in Euripides (*Alk.* 1108, *Pho.* 516, *Ba.* 301). But this apparently remarkable peculiarity of *Prom.* loses most of its force when we observe that Aeschylus only uses ποιέω about five times anyway (see Italie *s.v.*).

Much more striking is *Prom.* 821 ἡμῐν, where we are faced either with a major infraction of Porson's Law, or a short iota. On A. *Eum.* 347 (in lyrics) Wilamowitz comments, 'unus Sophocles ionicam pronominis formam admisit' (and emends accordingly). This is confirmed by Dindorf, who gives ἡμῐν as follows: S. *Aj.* twice; *Ant.* once; *OT* seven times; *Tr.* twice; *El.* nine times; *Ph.* twice; *OK* five times; but adds 'Euripides nusquam'. Only if we are prejudiced by a belief in Aeschylean authorship will we take ἡμιν at *Prom.* 821 as long. It is natural to assume that it is short, and that we have here an unaeschylean detail.[32]

Prom. 997 ὅρα νῦν εἴ σοι presents us with another prosody unparalleled in Aeschylus, who uses νῦν some eighteen times (see Italie *s.v.*), but never as a short syllable in iambics. In Sophocles νυν is certainly short at *Aj.* 87, *Ant.* 524, *Tr.* 92. But Aeschylus admits νῦν in lyrics (*Pers.* 1040, *Th.* 417, *Cho.* 332), and its absence from iambics may simply be due to chance.

Prom. contains two strange Ionic contractions: 122 εἰσοιχνεῦσιν, 645 πωλεύμεναι. There are no parallels in Aeschylus (*Th.* 78 θρεῦμαι is unnecessary); elsewhere in tragedy we find only E. *Med.* 423, *Hipp.* 167, *IA* 789. There is no apparent explanation for these occasional occurrences. Equally odd is *Prom.* 992 αἰθαλοῦσσα (and ? 235 τολμῇς; see Page's app. crit.), which seems only to be paralleled by S. *Ph.* 984, E. *Tro.* 440, and ? S. *OT* 1279. Otherwise tragedy avoids adjectives in -οεις, -αεις, -ηεις, whether or not they are contracted.[33]

We have already seen *Prom.*'s scansion of Ἰόνιος with long initial iota, in contrast to Aeschylus' practice at *Pers.* 178, 563, 949, 1011, 1025, 898, and *Supp.* 69, where we find Ἰ̆ᾱονες etc. But the etymological play with Ἰώ may be enough to account for this. So too, metrical necessity explains such occurrences in *Prom.* as 90 ἀνήριθμον (185 ᾱ̄παραμυθον, 548 ῑ̄σονειρον in lyric) and 333 εὐπιθής; such licences are not uncommon in tragedy.[34]

CAESURA

Descroix's chart (p. 263) gives absolute figures and percentage occurrences for the various possible mid-line 'caesurae': (1) × – ᴗ –' ‖, (2) × – ᴗ – × ‖ (penthemimeral), (3) × – ᴗ – ×' ‖ (penth. plus elision), (4) × – ᴗ – × –' ‖, (5) × – ᴗ – × – ᴗ ‖ (hephthemimeral), (6) × – ᴗ – × – ᴗ' ‖ (hephth. plus elision), (7) × – ᴗ – × – ‖, etc. In many respects the practice of the three major tragedians cannot be distinguished, but there are some details which may help us.

(1) is too rare to be any use. *Prom.* has no instance.

(2) × – ᴗ – × ‖ (penth.) is much the most common.[35] 72.2% of *Prom.*'s trimeters contain this caesura. This figure fits equally

well with Aeschylus, Sophocles, and Euripides (though early Euripides tends to be slightly higher, e.g. *Alk.* 77.4%, *Med.* 78.2%, *Hkd.* 74.9%: cf. e.g. *Tro.* 71.4%, *Ion* 72.9%. *Rhesos* is unusual with 84.5%).

(3) × – ∪ – × ’‖ (penth. + elision):

A. *Pers.* 4.2%, *Th.* 5.3%, *Supp.* 5.2%, *Ag.* 3.7%, *Cho.* 4.7%, *Eum.* 4.3%, (frs. 3.8%).

S. *Aj.* 3.5%, *Ant.* 5.1%, *Tr.* 5.6%, *OT* 7.8%, *El.* 5.1%, *Ph.* 5.2%, *OK* 5.1%, (frs. 2.0%).

early E. *Alk.* 6.9%, *Med.* 7.1%, *Hkd.* 8%, *Hipp.* 8.2%, *And.* 7.6%, *Hik.* 6.7%, (*Rhesos* 5.8%).

Prom. 6.4% (50 out of 773 trimeters).

Aeschylus is regularly the lowest of the three, Euripides the highest. (Sophocles is variable, with *OT* a useful warning that individual figures may be misleading.)

Prom.'s 6.4% is higher than any of Aeschylus' six plays (in which we may observe the consistency of *Oresteia*'s figures around 4%), slightly lower than Euripides' (though n.b. *Alk.*, *Hik.*). This figure represents fifty occurrences, so that it may be thought to bear some weight as an indication of the author's style.

(4) × – ∪ – × –’‖ (the so-called 'false' caesura). This is rarer in *Prom.* than in any extant play except *Rhesos*. All Aeschylus' plays have at least five instances (*Pers.* six, *Th.* six, *Supp.* five, *Ag.* seventeen, *Cho.* nine, *Eum.* six); Sophocles' range is similar (from *OK* six to *Ant.* thirteen), though the proportion is rather lower as Aeschylus has less trimeters overall; Euripides' figures in his early plays are slightly lower (from *Hkd.* three to *Alk.* eight; cf. *Tro.* fourteen); *Rhesos* has only one instance.

Prom. has two instances (612, 710). We should of course not attach too much significance to an occurrence that is so rare, but we may observe that in Aeschylus the rate is never lower than one in 107 lines (*Eum.*), whereas in *Prom.* it is one in 386 lines.

(5) × – ∪ – × – ∪‖ (hephth.): the second most common. The figures are naturally complementary to those of (2); there is nothing of interest to add.

(6) × – ∪ – × – ∪’‖ (hephth. + elision)

A. *Pers.* 2, *Th.* 1, *Supp.* 4, *Ag.* 4, *Cho.* 2, *Eum.* 4 (3).[36]

S. *Aj.* 10, *Ant.* 2, *OT* 11, *Tr.* 2, *El.* 9, *Ph.* 11, *OK* 10.

E. *Alk.* 4, *Med.* 2, *Hkd.* 6, *Hipp.* 5 (*Rhesos* 1; commoner in later plays, e.g. *Ion* 14, *Hel.* 20).

Prom. 8 (245, 357, 610, 703, 734, 805, 977, 1035).[37]

There is no consistently observed difference between Aeschylus, Sophocles, and Euripides. *Prom.*'s figure is rather higher than we find in Aeschylus, and we might add it to *Prom.*'s similar preference (see (3) above) for elision at the penthemimeral caesura, as a possibly distinctive detail. The smallness of our figures, and the inconsistent practice of Sophocles, will prevent us from putting too much weight on such a detail.

(7) No proper caesura: usually × – ⏑ – × – ‖. This is pretty rare in all the tragedies: A. *Pers.* is highest with nine examples, then A. *Supp.* with five; the other plays of Aeschylus, Sophocles, and Euripides range between none and three.

Prom. has (probably) two instances (17, 113?), and is thus unremarkable.

But on pp. 282f Descroix lists occurrences of proclitic monosyllables followed by caesura. In some cases, another form of caesura or 'false' caesura occurs in the same line, so that the absence of a true division is not strongly felt (e.g. S. *Ant.* 997, *Aj.* 312); but in a few cases, the effect is totally to obliterate the caesura.

(a) the article: there is no instance in Aeschylus;[38] *Prom.* has two (589, 797); (cf. S. *Aj.* 71, *Ant.* 503, *Tr.* 725, *Ph.* 778[39]).

(b) adverbs, οὐ, μή: not in Aeschylus; Sophocles four times; Euripides seven times; not in *Prom.*

(c) prepositions: again, not in Aeschylus; once in *Prom.* (6; though here it is preceded by a 'false' caesura at mid-line); Sophocles has five examples, Euripides ?six.

(d) conjunctions, ὡς, εἰ: not in Aeschylus; εἰ once in *Prom.* (345); Sophocles twice, Euripides twice.

But Aeschylus does have one instance of καί preceding the only possible caesura, at *Cho.* 558,[40] as does Sophocles four times, and Euripides four times. (It is worth pointing out that at *Cho.* 558 καί is not connective, so that the caesura can be felt after it.)

It seems that Sophocles and even Euripides to a lesser extent, are freer with these proclitic monosyllables which virtually ignore the caesura than Aeschylus is; and it seems that *Prom.* with four examples, three of them of a most striking kind (589, 797, 345), does diverge from Aeschylus' normal practice, though again our figures are too small for us to be sure.

(Descroix's figures for caesura followed by enclitic monosyllable are unremarkable; all three tragedians show similar habits, and *Prom.* fits with them all.)[41]

PORSON'S LAW[42]

Aeschylus has word-end at × – ⏑ – × – ⏑ – × ‖ less often than Sophocles and slightly less often than Euripides:[43]

A. *Pers.* 15.8%, *Th.* 10.6%, *Supp.* 10.4%, *Ag.* 9.5%, *Cho.* 12%, *Eum.* 12.4%.

S. *Aj.* 20.2%, *Ant.* 17.4%, *OT* 26.7%, *Tr.* 22.1%, *El.* 23%, *Ph.* 23.9%, *OK* 23.9%.

E. *Alk.* 20.4%, *Med.* 13.4%, *Hkd.* 17%, *Hipp.* 14.8%, *And.* 18.6%, *Hik.* 14.1%, (*Rhesos* 15.7%).

Prom. 13% is thus well below Sophocles,[44] but fits easily with Aeschylus (usually lower, but *Pers.* higher), and is compatible with early Euripides (e.g. *Med.*, *Hipp.*). The relatively low figure for *Prom.* may simply be attributable to its low average number of words per line, as compared with Sophocles and (to a lesser degree) Euripides.[45]

Of the lines with this word-end, 86% in *Prom.* follow Porson's Law (i.e. have short anceps). This proportion is typical of all three tragedians.

Major infractions of Porson's Law are very rare in tragedy. The only possible example in Aeschylus is *Pers.* 321, which should be viewed with suspicion.[46] Descroix tentatively suggests that *Prom.* 821 is a major infraction; but we have already seen that it is preferable to accept the unaeschylean form ἡμῐν, which gives us a short anceps. Thus *Prom.*, like most tragedies, has no example of a major infraction.

There is little to be said about the minor infractions, of which Descroix records (pp. 326ff) 59 in Aeschylus, 13 in *Prom.*[47] (cf. S. *Aj.* 26, *Ant.* 20, *OT* 52 in more trimeters). Of Aeschylus' 59, 29 are accounted for by the definite article; in Sophocles the proportion is rather less; in *Prom.* only two of the thirteen instances involve the article (313, 1027), which we might take as an indication that the author was slightly freer than Aeschylus; but there is too little here to go on.

The tragedians tend to avoid placing a word of more than one syllable before a 'minor infraction'.[48] The only examples in Aeschylus of polysyllable plus (quasi-) enclitic in this position are *Ag.* 1052[49] and *Cho.* 903 (cf. *Supp.* 785, in a lyric trimeter), whereas they are slightly more common in Sophocles (*OT* 142; *Tr.* 718, 932; *El.* 357, 413; *Ph.* 422, 466, 596, 801; *OK* 982, 1543) and Euripides (*Hkd.* 303, 640; *And.* 93, 1184; *Hek.* 507; *El.* 1119; *IT* 678, 942; *Ion* 633; *Tro.* 1182; *Hel.* 471, 1552; *Pho.* 885, 1619, 1626; *IA* 1212; *Kyk.* 331; *Rhesos* 715, 868).

Prom. has two instances (107, 648), which again seems slightly to exceed Aeschylus' normal restraint, but is not sufficiently striking to bear much weight.

FINAL MONOSYLLABLES

All the extant tragedies of the major tragedians contain several examples of monosyllabic enclitics and quasi-enclitics (μέν, γάρ etc.) at the end of the line, and such phrases as τὰ νῦν, τὸ πρίν, σὺ δέ, etc. But on looking at the non-enclitic final monosyllables of *Prom.*, as compared with those of Aeschylus, we find that some remarkable facts emerge.[50]

Final monosyllables occur in Aeschylus in the following places:

Pers. 338, 341 ἦν; 802 οὐ; 496 πᾶν/ῥέεθρον; 486 κόλπον, οὗ/Σπερχειός = five (plus enclitics[51] at 180, 403, 418, 430, 457, 470, 497, 506, 824, 834).

Th. 491, 663 ἦν, 605 ὧν; 267 σύ; 385 δὲ τῶι? (δ' ἐσῶ?); 535 ἀντέλλουσα θρίξ; [1005 χρή, 1050 ἦν] = six (plus 665 enclitic).

Supp. 244, 296, 344 ἦν = three (plus enclitics 290, 331, 391, 509, 729, 772, 995, 999).

Ag. 1352, 1608 ὧν; 928 χρή; 1194, 1354 ὥς; [7? τῶν] = five (six?) (plus enclitics 340, 556, 601, 615, 650, 672, 674, 819, 1199, 1239, 1249, 1256, 1270, 1327, 1375, 1378, 1396, 1421).

Cho. 91 τί φῶ; 882 τί δρᾶι; 879 δεῖ; 1016 γένος τε πᾶν; 1005 μή/γένοιτ' = five (plus enclitics 116, 172, 185, 223, 245, 559, 584, 668, 702, 880, 999, 1010, 1057).

Eum. 848 εἶ; 678 ὦ; 94 δεῖ; 708 χρή; 893 σύ; 137 ἐπουρίσασα τῶι; 238 πρὸς/ἄλλοισιν = seven (plus enclitics 38, 87, 140, 147,

203, 442, 594, 609, 755, 914).

fr. 62 ἦν; fr. 199.2, fr. 289 ὧν; fr. 276.4 (L-J.) εἶ; fr. 199.8 σύ; fr. 261 ὥς; fr. 393 οἶνος δὲ νοῦ = seven.

Of these thirty-eight examples, sixteen comprise part of εἰμί, four χρή/δεῖ, two or three ὥς looking back,[52] three σύ, two τῶι, all of which are felt to be more or less inseparable from the preceding word: the same applies to *Pers*. 802 τὰ δ' οὐ, *Cho*. 91 τί φῶ, and *Cho*. 882 τί δρᾶι.

Of the remaining seven or eight examples, three or four lead into the next line in a striking enjambement (*Pers*. 486, [*Ag*. 1354], *Cho*. 1005, *Eum*. 238).[53] The only truly independent monosyllables at the end of the line are *Th*. 535 ἀντέλλουσα θρίξ, *Cho*. 1016 γένος τε πᾶν, *Pers*. 496 πᾶν, and fr. 393 (an unknown play) οἶνος δὲ νοῦ. (Even *Pers*. 496 should almost be classed as an example of enjambement.)

In *Prom*. we find the following occurrences:

697 πλέα τις εἶ

103 τὴν πεπρωμένην δὲ χρή, 485 ἃ χρή, 640 με χρή, 659 τὶ χρή, 715 σε χρή, 721 ἀστρογείτονας δὲ χρή, 730 σε χρή

915 πρὸς ταῦτα νῦν

502 χρυσόν τε, τίς/φήσειεν

90 παμμῆτόρ τε γῆ

619 Ἡφαίστου δὲ χείρ

807 τηλουρὸν δὲ γῆν

18 αἰπυμῆτα παῖ

392 τὸν παρόντα νοῦν

992 αἰθαλοῦσσα φλόξ

= sixteen examples (more than twice the number in any of Aeschylus' six plays).

Of these sixteen, one is a part of εἰμί, seven are χρή; these may be classed as semi-enclitic: similarly νῦν (915). *Prom*. 502 is an example of enjambement, parallel to A. *Pers*. 486, S. *Ant*. 171 etc.

We are left with six striking, independent monosyllables (18, 90, 392, 619, 807, 992), all of them nouns (for which the only parallels in Aeschylus are *Th*. 535, and fr. 393).

Thus both in the total of non-enclitic final monosyllables, and in their type, *Prom*. diverges sharply from Aeschylus' normal practice.

In Sophocles we find that the frequency is consistently higher than Aeschylus', similar to *Prom.*'s, and that nouns are found in this position in all plays except *Aj.*

The occurrences in Sophocles are as follows:

Aj. seventeen examples (44, 77, 269, 281, 284, 288, 371, 545, 725, 970, 1000, 1087, 1117, 1301, 1348, 1355, 1373), of which eight are parts of εἰμί, two are χρή. The rest are 269 ἀτώμεσθα νῦν; 1373 ἃ χρῆις (χρή?); 545 ταρβήσει γὰρ οὐ; 725 οὔτις ἔσθ' ὃς οὐ; 970 οὐ κείνοισιν, οὔ; 288 τί χρῆμα δρᾶις; 371 φρόνησον εὖ.

Ant. twenty-three examples (5, 35, 42, 89, 96, 171, 247, 249, 250, 252, 255, 320, 324, 403, 409, 410, 448, 460, 578, 662, 909, 1004, 1334), eight with εἰμι, four χρή, five οὐ/μή. The rest are: 35 τί δρᾶι, 403 ἃ φής, 410 γυμνώσαντες εὖ, 171 παίσαντές τε καὶ/πληγέντες, 409 κατεῖχε τὸν/νέκυν, 250* στύφλος δὲ γῆ.[54]

OT forty-four examples (47, 133, 236, 267, 278, 298, 308, 320, 332, 371, 372, 379, 393, 415, 575, 585, 635, 645, 655, 659, 747, 752, 803, 819, 825, 919, 931, 976, 1008, 1036, 1068, 1117, 1122, 1126, 1177, 1180, 1183, 1233, 1234, 1266, 1327, 1386, 1427, 1460), fifteen part of εἰμί; six part of σύ; two δεῖ; five looking forward (267, 298, 332, 585, 1234). Of the others, 308 μαθόντες εὖ, 575 σὺ νῦν, 645 με δρᾶν, 655, 1233 τί φής, 803 σὺ φής, 1008 τί δρᾶις, 1183 προσβλέψαιμι νῦν, 1460 ὥστε μή are 'easy'; more remarkable are 47* ἥδε γῆ, 659* τῆσδε γῆς, 1266* ἐπεὶ δὲ γῆι, 1427* τὸ μήτε γῆ, 635* ἐπαισχύνεσθε γῆς, (and 236* ὅστις ἐστί, γῆς/(τῆσδ'), 1327* τοιαῦτα σὰ /(ὄψεις), both of which look forward[55] to some extent).

El. twenty-five examples (27, 44, 71, 317, 336, 339, 368, 411, 652, 671, 873, 930, 1033, 1036, 1037, 1038, 1123, 1215, 1309, 1355, 1422, 1440, 1466, 1470, 1491), four εἰμί; two δεῖ; two σύ; two νῦν; 336 δὲ μή, 1038 σὺ νῶιν, 317 τί φής; 1466 μὲν οὐ; 1491 γὰρ οὐ; four look forward (873, 1123, 1309, 1440). 368* φίλους προδοῦσα σούς, 1033* μητρί ... ἔξειπε σῆι, 1215* τοῦτο δ' οὐχὶ σόν, 1470* ἀλλὰ σόν, 1422* φοινία δὲ χείρ, 71* ἀποστείλητε γῆς.

Tr. twenty-five examples (19, 22, 143, 258, 285, 316, 321, 337, 362, 411, 416, 462, 578, 617, 745, 799, 801, 819, 878, 1107, 1162, 1169, 1137, 1200, 1254), eleven εἰμί, three looking forward (362?, 462, 819); 337 ἃ δεῖ; 1169 παρόντι νῦν; 745 με φής, 878 σφε φῄς; 799 με θές, 1254 με θῆις; 285* πόσις τε σός; 617* περισσὰ δρᾶν; 801* τῆσδε γῆς; 1137* χρῆστ' ... πατέρα σὸν κτείνασα δρᾶι; 19* Ἀλκμήνης τε παῖς.

Ph. thirty-three examples (11, 21, 54, 115, 133, 238, 240, 263, 312, 361, 362, 377, 442, 485, 528, 545, 577, 759, 803, 888, 912, 915, 949, 958, 972, 974, 982, 1068, 1225, 1312, 1367, 1397, 1428), nine εἰμί, four δεῖ; 115, 759, 1367, 133 συ, νῶιν etc.; 958 νῦν; 545 οὐ, 912 μή; two look forward (263, 312). Also 915 σε πλεῖν, 949 με δρᾶν, 974 τί δρᾶις, 888 ἐμοί τε δρᾶν, 1428 μέλαθρα σά, 21* ἐστὶ σῶν, 528*, 577* τῆσδε γῆς, 972* ἄλλοισι δοῦς, 803* ἐπηξίωσα δρᾶν, 240* αὐδῶμαι δὲ παῖς/ (Ἀχιλλέως).

OK twenty-nine examples (14, 24, 28, 48, 75, 294, 317, 351, 462, 476, 494, 495, 565, 573, 642, 654, 932, 937, 940, 954, 973, 993, 1130, 1175, 1202, 1307, 1312, 1335, 1656), three εἰμί, two νῦν; 24 οὐ; 1335 δὲ σύ; 476 με χρή; nine looking forward (14, 351, 495, 573, 954, 993, 1130, 1175, 1202). Also 48 τί δρᾶις, 317 τί φῶ, 654 με δρᾶν, 28 οἴομαι δὲ δεῖν, 940 σὺ φῄς, 1656 οὐδ' ἂν εἷς/(θνητῶν), 294*, 462* τῆσδε γῆς, 642* τοιούτοισιν εὖ, 494* πρόστασσε δρᾶν, 1312 ἀμφεστᾶσι πᾶν, 1307* ἐκβάλοιμι γῆς.

I have only checked two early plays of Euripides plus *Rhesos*, but they indicate that Euripides too is freer than Aeschylus with final monosyllables, and similar to *Prom.*

The occurrences in Euripides are:

Med. twenty-four examples, six εἰμί; five χρή or δεῖ; three times participle plus εὐ; 589 νῦν, 1230 οὐ. One looks forward (1053). The rest are: 955 ἐκγόνοισιν οἷς; 578* δίκαια δρᾶν; 1149* πόσις δὲ σός; 764* ἡλίου τε φῶς; 1207* ὦ δύστηνε παῖ; 269* ἄνακτα γῆς; 27* ἀπαλλάσσουσα γῆς.

Hipp. twenty-five examples, five εἰμί; six δεῖ or χρή; three σύ or σέ; two verb + εὖ; 519 δειμαίνεις δὲ τί;. One looks forward (305). The rest are: 662* δέσποινα σή; 893*, 1199* τῆσδε γῆς; 495* ἡδονῆς τε σῆς; 1056* ἐκβαλεῖς με γῆς; 1065* τάχιστα γῆς; 920* ἔνεστι νοῦς.

Rhesos fifteen examples, n.b. 81* τοσόνδε φῶς, 277* τῆιδε γῆι, 408* Παιόνων τε γῆν, 421 ὄμμα σόν, 525* ἐστὶ σῶς, 762* Ἑκτόρεια χείρ (cf. too e.g. E. *Alk.* 758* ἀμφιβᾶσα φλόξ; *Hek.* 668* βλέπουσα φῶς, 1278* τοσόνδε παῖς; *Hkd.* 192, 431, 551, 557, 325).

Further proof that Aeschylus' avoidance of final non-enclitic monosyllables is real, and not merely accidental, can be found if we look at the occurrences of the two commonest monosyllabic nouns in tragedy, γῆ and παῖς.

γῆ (in one form or another) occurs forty-four times in the iambics of Aeschylus' tragedies (plus three times in the fragments, and *Th.* 1008). Never is it the last word of the line.

In Sophocles γῆ occurs about eighty-six times in iambics, thirteen times as last word (fourteen including *OT* 236).

In the three plays I have examined of Euripides (*Med.*, *Hipp.*, *Rhesos*), we find γῆ as last word eight times (cf. too *Hkd.* 192, 431).

Similarly παῖς (or παῖ) occurs seventeen times in Aeschylus' iambics, never as last word. In Sophocles we find it at *Tr.* 19, *Ph.* 240; in Euripides at *Med.* 1207, *Hek.* 1278, at the end of the line.

In *Prom.* γῆ occurs five times (90, 666, 682, 807, 924), twice as last word; παῖς occurs four times (18, 651, 773, 987), once as last word in the line.

It seems clear, then, that the author of *Prom.*, like Sophocles and Euripides, consistently shows himself freer than Aeschylus in his use of non-enclitic final monosyllables. Both in quantity, and in type, he appears to display quite a different technique: indeed, the six final nouns observed in *Prom.* suggest that he is freer even than Sophocles and Euripides.

THREE-WORD TRIMETERS[56]

Characteristic of Aeschylean ὄγκος is the iambic trimeter formed simply by three massive words. That the fifth-century Athenians felt this too is shown by Aristophanes' grotesque parodies, which even introduce two-word trimeters unparalleled in the extant words of Aeschylus.

The figures for the three tragedians, together with proportional frequencies are as follows:

A. *Pers.* 3 = 0.0069, *Th.* 13 = 0.0238, *Supp.* 4 = 0.0083, *Ag.* 4 = 0.0045, *Cho.* 5 = 0.0078, *Eum.* 6 = 0.0093 (plus frs. 2, 160, 180, 304, 326, 330).

S. *Aj.* 4 = 0.004, *Ant.* 2 = 0.0027, *OT* 3 = 0.0025, *Tr.* 1 = 0.001, *El.* 3 = 0.0026, *Ph.* 1 = 0.0009, *OK* 3 = 0.0024 (plus frs. 306, 355, 432, 447, 494, 605, 702, 1025).

E. *Pho.* 8 = 0.0067, *Ba.* 5 = 0.0054, *Rhesos* 3 = 0.0045: the rest have 4 or less (*Hek.* none), average 0.0028.

Prom. 9 = 0.0116 is thus second only to A. *Th.*, and markedly higher than any of the plays of Sophocles or Euripides. But it is striking how much the authors vary: as we might expect from the grand, heroic subject matter, A. *Th.* and E. *Pho.* offer many more such lines than the others. Hence the frequency of such lines, for impressive description or narrative, in *Prom.*, a play of superhuman cast and theme, is not surprising. That this is an obvious stylistic device for an author seeking grandeur and solemnity is confirmed by its occurrence no less than sixty times in the 1474 lines of Lykophron's *Alexandra.*[57] We find three more examples in 118 lines of Semonides.

So we may describe this feature of *Prom.* as Aeschylean, but as exactly the sort of feature most liable to be imitated by other authors, where appropriate. It has often been remarked that *Prom.*'s language and style seem less dense and majestic than Aeschylus: its ὄγκος seems to be only skin-deep.

WORD DIVISION

S.L. Schein[58] is mainly concerned with analysing the different positions in the line where word-end occurs in the plays of Aeschylus and Sophocles. It is a pity that Euripides is not included, as we are often left with no idea whether Aeschylus or Sophocles represents the more orthodox technique in a particular detail. But his study is useful for our purposes in distinguishing between the practices of two tragedians in details which are probably outside their conscious control, and therefore likely to be genuinely characteristic.

One major point should be observed at once.[59] Sophocles consistently has more words per trimeter than Aeschylus. The averages per play are:

A. *Pers.* 5.4, *Th.* 5.4, *Supp.* 5.6, *Ag.* 5.4, *Cho.* 5.5, *Eum.* 5.5.
S. *Aj.* 5.9, *Ant.* 5.9, *OT* 6.0, *Tr.* 5.8, *El.* 5.8, *Ph.* 6.1, *OK* 6.0.
Prom. with 5.4, is thus typical of Aeschylus and incompatible with Sophocles. It is clear from Schein's chart (p. 165) that most of this difference is accounted for by the greater number of monosyllables in Sophocles.

But despite the overall consistency of Aeschylus' and Sophocles' plays, they each vary quite markedly even with the same play, as we might expect. I took a few specimen samples of fifty lines from passages of continuous rhesis, with the following results:

A. *Pers.* 353-402	286 words
Th. 375-416 + 422-9	306
631-80	284
Supp. 234-83	283
Ag. 281-330	273
810-59	277
551-600	293
Cho. 535-84	306
Eum. 1-50	294
Prom. 197-246	281
298-347	302
436-85	281
635-84	289
823-72	291
700-39 + 801-10	290
S. *Aj.* 430-79	316
815-65 (minus one)	309
Ant. 162-211	304
639-88	318
Tr. 672-723 (minus two)	301
OT 774-823	325
Ph. 254-303	310
E. *Med.* 1136-85	296
Hkd. 134-83	318
Hipp. 1-50	295
983-1032	321
1173-1222	290
Hik. 673-722	304
Tro. 726-75	318
1-52 (minus two)	292
Pho. 1141-93 (minus three)	291
1372-1421	291
Rhesos 105-21 + 284-316	293
393-442	310
756-805	298

We see that, although it is confirmed that Sophocles regularly uses more words than Aeschylus, and also more than Euripides, the range of an author can apparently be quite wide. Thus in the two E. *Pho.* passages, a similar rate is found to that of Aeschylus and *Prom.* (We remember that *Pho.* also contained an exceptional number of three-word trimeters; clearly its heroic atmosphere is responsible for both.) And the first twenty-two lines of E. *Tro.* (minus two spurious lines) yield only 111 words, a rate that would give 278 words in fifty lines. So it seems that an author can vary his style quite considerably, to obtain the tone he wants: an author aiming to compose an elevated, grandiose drama on the scale of *Prom.* would naturally try to maintain such a tone throughout.

Nevertheless, if we leave aside what an author might or might not choose to do, of the plays we have actually looked at, *Prom.* seems to resemble those of Aeschylus rather than those of Sophocles in this respect.

This simple fact (that Sophocles has more words per line than Aeschylus) accounts for most of the differences between the two observed by Schein, in that they largely involve higher figures for Sophocles (i.e. more diaereses, because more words): this is especially true of word-end after the first syllable (Aeschylus 23%, Sophocles 37%-41%).[60]

In general there are few points in the line at which significant differences can be observed from one play to another, apart from Sophocles' overall higher figures. But in two places *Prom.* diverges remarkably from Aeschylus' norm. The first is at 'position 2' (i.e. word-end after two syllables × –{⏑– etc.): A. *Pers.* 62%, *Th.* 61%, *Supp.* 65%, *Ag.* 63%, *Cho.* 64%, *Eum.* 64%; *Prom.* 55%. As *Prom.* is not remarkable for its number of initial monosyllables, this means that *Prom.* has less disyllables starting the line than is normal for Aeschylus. (Sophocles' figures range from 50%-62%.) The second is at 'position 11' (i.e. × –⏑– × –⏑– × –⏑{–) where we have already observed *Prom.*'s unaeschylean fondness for final monosyllables: A. *Pers.* 2%, *Th.* 1%, *Supp.* 2%, *Ag.* 2%, *Cho.* 2%, *Eum.* 2%; *Prom.* 4%. (Sophocles ranges from 4% to 7%.)[61]

Other smaller details emerge from the study of the frequency with which words of particular shapes precede particular diaereses. Inevitably, from time to time one play or another produces a figure outside the normal span of its author. But it is clear from Schein that *Prom.* is the odd man out by Aeschylean standards far more often than any of the other plays. In particular we may note:

(a) preceding position 3 (× – ⏑ { – ....),[62] '*Prom.* has far fewer monosyllables, noticeably more trisyllabic words' than the other six plays: (monosyllables A. *Pers.* 41%, *Th.* 47%, *Supp.* 42%, *Ag.* 41%, *Cho.* 41%, *Eum.* 41%; *Prom.* 32%; cf. Sophocles, highest *OT* 44%, lowest *Tr.* 30%, average about 37%).

(b) preceding position 9 (× – ⏑ – × – ⏑ – × { – ⏑ –),[63] '*Prom.* is ... similar to *Persai*, and unlike the other plays of Aeschylus' in having a low proportion of monosyllables: A. *Pers.* 34%, *Th.* 52%, *Supp.* 51%, *Ag.* 47%, *Cho.* 55%, *Eum.* 48%; *Prom.* 26%; cf. Sophocles' highest *OK* 49%, lowest *Tr.* 32%.

(c) 'The figures for word-end at position 10 show that, as at positions 2, 3, 4 and 9, *Prom.* is somewhat different from the other plays ... it is the only play with as many words of disyllabic as of trisyllabic shape ending at that position.'[64] (A. *Pers.* 47% trisyllabic, 28% disyllabic; *Th.* 45%/36%; *Supp.* 43%/28%; *Ag.* 41%/34%; *Cho.* 41%/29%; *Eum.* 37%/29%; *Prom.* 36%/36%; cf. S. *Aj.* 35%/35%, but *Ant.* 39%/32%.) *Prom.* also has an unusually high number of words of five syllables ending in that position: Aeschylus 2%-4%; *Prom.* 7%.

(d) At the end of the line,[65] disyllabic endings are always the most common, but they are less so in *Prom.* than in Aeschylus: *Pers.* 64%, *Th.* 60%, *Supp.* 64%, *Ag.* 63%, *Cho.* 62%, *Eum.* 63%; *Prom.* 58%. (Sophocles ranges from *Tr.* 61% to *Aj.* 67%.)

On the other hand, in its large number of final four-syllable words *Prom.*, with 24%, fits with Aeschylus (19%-27%) rather than Sophocles (14%-18%).

It is difficult to draw any firm conclusions from Schein's study,[66] but it appears that *Prom.* does not fit easily with the six undisputed plays of Aeschylus. The discrepancies are often in small details, but these may be the sort of details which are not subject to imitation or conscious modification by an author (unlike e.g. three-word trimeters or the overall number of words per line) and hence genuinely characteristic of that author.

ENJAMBEMENT

(1) Sophoclean Enjambement

This feature of *Prom.* has been quite fully discussed,[67] and a summary should here suffice: the main facts are not in dispute. Aeschylus has few examples of the favourite Sophoclean device, of placing at the end of a trimeter a word (or two) which does not allow the slightest pause in the sense and belongs strictly to what follows (in its most extreme form, it is preceded by punctuation). A. *Pers.* 486; *Ag.* 556, (601), 1354; *Cho.* (702), 1005; *Eum.* 98, 131, 238, 914; (*Supp.* 772); i.e. eleven examples at the most. Of these, only four (if we count *Supp.* 772, *Ag.* 601, *Cho.* 702 as well as *Ag.* 556; but *Pers.* 486, *Ag.* 1354, *Cho.* 1005 are rather different) are preceded by strong punctuation.

By contrast, *Prom.* has instances as follows: 61, 725, 793, 830 (ἵνα); 104, 259, 323, 328, 377, 951 (ὅτι); 384 (ἐπεὶ); 463 (ὅπως); 470, 989 (ὅτωι), 683 (ὅ τι), 341 (ἀτὰρ), 865 (τὸ μὴ), 918 (τὸ μὴ οὐ), i.e. eighteen examples, according to Yorke, to which we might add 43, 961, 1033 (σὺ δέ), 83 (τί σοι), 264 (τοὺς κακῶς/πράσσοντας) and 743 (τί που/δράσεις), making twenty-four in all. Of these, twelve are preceded by strong punctuation.

Many of those who believe that Aeschylus wrote *Prom.* suggest that he was influenced by Sophocles in this respect, and that the occurrences in the *Oresteia* reflect the first signs of that influence.[68] They conclude that *Prom.* is to be dated after the *Oresteia*.

In Sophocles the rate of such enjambements is about one per 50 lines; Aeschylus' highest rate is that of *Eum.*, one per 160 lines. Euripides has only about thirty instances in nineteen plays, but it seems to be not unknown in the minor tragedians, as far as can be judged.[69] In *Prom.* the rate is about one per 35 lines.

It is hard to see why Aeschylus (who had been exposed to Sophoclean influence since 468) should suddenly transform his technique between 458 and his death two years later. It seems rather that we are here face to face with a distinctly different technique from that of Aeschylus.

(2) Other Enjambements

In overall numbers of enjambements, *Prom.* slightly exceeds the figures for Aeschylus' plays:[70] A. *Pers.* 7.7%, *Th.* 4.6%, *Supp.* 8.5%, *Ag.* 7.3%, *Cho.* 6.6%, *Eum.* 4.9%; *Prom.* 9.7%.[71] In this respect again, *Prom.* seems to be less 'stichic' in its structure than Aeschylus, though the difference is small.

(3) Rhetorical Pauses Within the Line

J.D. Denniston[72] gives figures for the occurrences of major stops and of commas, (a) up to the end of the first metron following a line without end-stop, (b) from the end of the second metron onwards in a line which is not end-stopped. I reproduce most of his figures in Table 4 below.[73]

It is clear from the table that *Prom.* contains more of these pauses than any of Aeschylus' six plays: A. *Pers.* 49 pauses in 429 trimeters,[74] *Th.* 37 in 457, *Supp.* 46 in 399, *Ag.* 70 in 780, *Cho.* 51 in 532, *Eum.* 44 in 573; *Prom.* 101 in 672. Aeschylus' highest rate is *Pers.* one per 8.6 lines; *Prom.*'s rate is one per 6.7 lines.

For Sophocles the figures are *Aj.* 84, *Ant.* 100, *Tr.* 108, *OT* 154, *El.* 126, *Ph.* 111, *OK* 160.

For early Euripides, *Alk.* 76, *Med.* 96, *Hkd.* 77, *Hipp.* 76, *And.* 63 (cf. *Hek.* 91, *Rhesos* 61). It appears that *Prom.* fits with Sophocles rather than with Aeschylus or Euripides.

Not only are the overall numbers in *Prom.* higher than we would expect for an Aeschylean play, but their distribution is also highly distinctive.

(a) Position 1: pause here is 'noticeably rare in Aeschylus'.[75] Most plays of Sophocles and Euripides have between one and five instances. *Prom.* 821, a major stop, is unusual by Aeschylean standards.

(b) Position 2: pause here accounts for roughly half of all Aeschylus' instances: *Pers.* 57%, *Th.* 54%, *Supp.* 39%, *Ag.* 57%, *Cho.* 47%, *Eum.* 55%, but only 33% of *Prom.*'s. For Sophocles the figures are: *Aj.* 23%, *Ant.* 25%, *OT* 16%, *Tr.* 27%, *El.* 24%, *Ph.* 19%, *OK* 18%; for Euripides, *Alk.* 54%, *Med.* 34%, *Hkd.* 43%, *Hipp.* 41%, *And.* 38%, *Hek.* 46%, *Rhesos* 39%.

Prom.'s figure is markedly lower than Aeschylus', slightly lower than Euripides', rather higher than Sophocles'. It is thus apparent that *Prom.*'s large number (by Aeschylean standards) of mid-line pauses is not concentrated in Aeschylus' favourite position.

(c) Position 4: 'This stop is particularly common in the *PV*.'[76] Aeschylus has 12 pauses (only 3 major) in six plays, Sophocles 15 (8 major) in seven longer plays, Euripides only 4 (3 major) in seven

plays. *Prom.* with 10 pauses (I make it 11, 7 major and 4 minor[77]) is thus quite unique in tragedy.

(d) Position 8: *Prom.* is again higher than Aeschylus here (though in terms of distribution *Prom.* with 10 out of 101 is matched by A. *Pers.* 5 out of 49, i.e. both about 10%).

(e) Position 10: Common in Sophocles and *Prom.*, rare in Aeschylus, even rarer in Euripides. This accounts for 17% of *Prom.*'s pauses: the highest proportion in Aeschylus is *Eum.* 11% (cf. S. *Aj.* 19%, *Ph.* 15% etc.). Many of these occurrences will be accounted for by 'Sophoclean' enjambement.

Thus at positions 1, 2, 4, 8, 10 - the *only* positions where it is possible to see a real difference between the techniques of the three tragedians[78] - *Prom.* is found to diverge from the Aeschylean pattern. None of Aeschylus' undisputed plays shows anything approaching this degree of irregularity.[79] Most striking of all is *Prom.*'s high figure for stop after position 4, a curious stylistic quirk which gives rather an unusual rhythm to the lines in which it occurs.

It is therefore interesting to note that in another similar detail *Prom.* is again distinctive. Denniston's figures for pauses at position 4 following a stop at the end of the previous line[80] reveal that *Prom.* and Sophocles behave differently from Aeschylus and Euripides. Aeschylus has only two instances (*Ag.* one major, *Cho.* one minor); Euripides also has two in seven plays (*Kyk.* one major, and one minor); Sophocles has fifty, and *Prom.* five (S. *Aj.* 6 major, 2 minor, *Ant.* 1 + 3, *OT* 4 + 8, *Tr.* 5 + 1, *El.* 4 + 3, *Ph.* 7 + 1, *OK* 5 + 0; *Prom.* 3 + 2, at 46, 74, 259, 274, 763). This of course is not enjambement; but it seems to confirm the existence of one peculiar detail of *Prom.*'s style, fondness for punctuation at position 4.

(4) End-stops

As far as I know, it has not been pointed out that an unusually large proportion of *Prom.*'s lines have no end-stop, in the form of punctuation,[81] as compared with Aeschylus. In A. *Pers.* 136 out of 429 trimeters have no end-stop; *Th.* 153 out of 543; *Supp.* 138 out of 475; *Ag.* 287 out of 859; *Cho.* 167 out of 618; *Eum.* 190 out of 640 (none of them as much as one in three lines). For *Prom.* the proportion is 312 out of 773 (about one in 2.5 lines); cf. S. *Tr.*

TABLE 4. *Rhetorical pauses within the trimeter*

	1A	*1B*	*Total*	*2A*	*2B*	*Total*	*3A*	*3B*	*Total*	*4A*	*4B*	*Total*	*8A*	*8B*	*Total*	*9A*	*9B*	*Total*	*10A*	*10B*	*Total*	*11A*	*11B*	*Total*
A. *Pers.*		1	1	7	21	28	4	5	9		2	2	3	2	5	2	2	4			0		1	1
Th.			0	7	13	20	1	7	8		1	1	2	1	3		1	1		4	4			0
Supp.		1	1	12	6	18	9	8	17		4	4		1	1			0	2	3	5			0
Ag.			0	18	22	40	5	13	18	1	2	3	1	1	2			0	1	6	7			0
Cho.			0	7	17	24	8	10	18	2		2	1	3	4			0	1	2	3			0
Eum.			0	6	18	24	2	9	11			0	1	2	3		1	1	1	4	5			0
Prom.	1		1	13	20	33	6	23	29	7	3	10	6	4	10		1	1	6	11	17			0
S. *Aj.*		2	2	8	11	19	7	20	27		2	2	2	9	11		7	7	2	14	16			0
Ant.	1	2	3	12	13	25	11	19	30	1		1	5	12	17		4	4	3	17	20			0
OT	2	5	7	5	20	25	5	17	22	3		3	9	30	39	5	17	22	11	25	36		2	2
Tr.			0	2	27	29	7	26	33	1	1	2	2	11	13	1	5	6	6	19	25			0
El.		2	2	8	22	30	16	19	35		1	1	8	14	22	3	10	13	7	16	23			0
Ph.	1	4	5	8	13	21	13	14	27	3	3	6	12	16	28	1	6	7	2	15	17			0
OK		1	1	9	19	28	9	26	35			0	20	38	58	1	7	8	6	23	29		1	1
E. *Alk.*	2		2	22	19	41	11	12	23		1	1	4	4	8	1		1			0			0
Med.	2	3	5	16	17	33	17	24	41			0	10	6	16			0		1	1			0
Hkd.	2		2	18	15	33	13	12	25	1		1	6	4	10	1	2	3		3	3			0
Hipp.	1	2	3	15	16	31	10	21	31	1		1	3	4	7	1	1	2		1	1			0
And.	1	1	2	13	11	24	9	15	24			0	10	1	11			0		2	2			0
Rhesos		1	1	13	11	24	12	12	24			0	5	5	10		1	1			0		1	1
Kyk.			0	4	5	9	5	8	13	1		1	6	2	8		1	1		2	2			0

Key: A = 'major stop'; B = 'minor stop'.

(Thus e.g. 1A means 'major stop after position 1', × ·–∪– ×–∪– ×–∪–,

9B means 'minor stop after position 9', ×–∪–×–∪–×, –∪– etc.)

371 out of 962, *Ph.* 366 out of 1078; E. *Alk.* 239 out of 802, *Med.* 312 out of 1037, *Hkd.* 322 out of 888, *Rhesos* 245 out of 682.

Prom.'s proportion is substantially higher than any of Aeschylus': this is all the more remarkable in that *Prom.* has a comparatively large amount of stichomythia, in which end-stop is unavoidable. It seems that we have here further evidence that *Prom.* is less 'stichic' than Aeschylus.

We may conclude, then, that *Prom.*, as compared with Aeschylus, is both freer overall in its use of enjambement and the breakdown of the strict, stichic structure, and also unorthodox in detail, in its fondness for Sophoclean enjambement and its unusual number of pauses other than at the normal places (i.e. end of the line, penthemimeral and hephthemimeral caesurae, and position 2). In many respects *Prom.* is similar to the technique of Sophocles. If Aeschylus was the author, it is very hard to explain his change of style; if he was not, we have here identified some characteristic details of our unknown author's individual technique. It is difficult to deny that this amounts to some solid evidence against Aeschylean authorship.

INTERLINEAR HIATUS

E. Harrison pointed out,[82] without trying to explain, a unique feature of *Prom.* among extant tragedies. Of its 773 trimeters, 326 start with vowels, 447 with consonants; 342 end with vowels, 431 with consonants. 130 times a trimeter ending with a vowel is followed by a trimeter starting with a vowel: this is roughly equal to the figure we would expect from a random arrangement of the lines. Of those 130 instances of hiatus, 78 coincide with punctuation, 52 do not: this again roughly corresponds to the chance figure. Harrison concluded that the author of *Prom.* appears to have made no effort to avoid interlinear hiatus.

In all other tragedies, hiatus with stop is markedly more common than hiatus without stop: the most striking examples are: S. *Tr.* 150 hiatus, 133 with stop, 17 without; E. *Med.* 165 hiatus, 151 with stop, 14 without.

Herington gives figures for non-stop hiatus in Aeschylus:[83] A. *Pers.* 19, *Th.* 15, *Supp.* 12, *Ag.* 31, *Cho.* 17, *Eum.* 24; *Prom.* 53.

Part of this discrepancy may be explained by *Prom.*'s greater number of lines without end-stop overall,[84] but it is still clear that *Prom.* is the only play in which the rate of hiatus *with* stop and hiatus *without* stop is the same.

Aeschylus' highest rate of non-stop hiatus is in *Eum.*, 24 times in 190 unstopped lines = 13%, as compared with *Prom.*, 53 times in 312 unstopped lines = 17%. The rates for Aeschylus' other plays are: *Pers.* 13%, *Th.* 10%, *Supp.* 9%, *Ag.* 11%, *Cho.* 10%. Sophocles ranges from *Tr.* 5% to *Ph.* 10%; Euripides from *Med.* 5% to *Hel.* 15%.

I have checked A. *Eum.* (the play with Aeschylus' highest rate), and noted those places in which no rhetorical pause at all is possible, and hiatus occurs:[85] there are only ten such places (13, 30, 98, 193, 213, 439, 451, 576, 758, 795). In *Prom.* I find thirty-seven places (8, 23, 83, 103, 216, 221, 226, 229, 230, 244, 259, 263, 300, 301, 351, 366, 377, 381, 442, 457, 485, 490, 493, 498, 508, 656, 673, 735, 747, 793, 796, 851, 860, 875, 920, 972, 1015). In A. *Ag.* there are only twenty.

It seems that we have here another distinctive detail of our author's style, suggesting perhaps a less sensitive ear than that of the three great tragedians.[86]

SUMMARY

Some of the details of the iambic trimeters which I have investigated (at first or second hand) prove inconclusive, often because we cannot really differentiate between the styles of Aeschylus and his successors. If *Prom.* agrees with all three, this tells us nothing about its authenticity. In two striking features *Prom.* comes out clearly with Aeschylus, in contrast to Sophocles and Euripides: three-word trimeters, and the number of words per line. But in other respects, *Prom.* diverges quite sharply from Aeschylus' normal practice: first foot anapaests, details of prosody, final monosyllables, enjambement, and interlinear hiatus. (Other minor discrepancies are found in *Prom.*'s treatment of *positio debilis*, word-division in the trimeter, and caesura, but these are too uncertain to bear much weight.)

In evaluating this evidence, we should keep two principles in mind, which may appear contradictory: (a) individual details can fluctuate from play to play for no apparent reason, and are often based on figures too small to support a solid argument; (b) on the other hand, such details can often be an invaluable guide to an author's *unconscious* stylistic mannerisms, as opposed to the larger features which he may vary consciously for specific effect (e.g. satyr/tragedy), and they may be of considerable cumulative weight.

All Aeschylus' plays contain some peculiarities, and we only have six to compare with *Prom.* But it is abundantly clear[87] that the peculiarities in the iambic trimeters of *Prom.* are incomparably greater in number and stranger in nature than those of any of the six undisputed plays. Many of them were unknown to Schmid (who wrote before Descroix, Denniston, Yorke, and Harrison). We seem in some respects to be faced with a distinctly different technique from that of Aeschylus.

Chapter 6

STRUCTURE AND DRAMATIC TECHNIQUE

THE PROLOGUE (1-87)

Lines 1-87 form a self-contained unit which we may conveniently call the prologue. Four figures enter together, of whom one is a κωφὸν πρόσωπον (Bia), and another (Prometheus) makes no sound until the others have gone.[1] The dialogue between Kratos and Hephaistos is 'utterly unlike the opening of any other extant Aeschylean play'.[2] We have of course only six plays with which to compare it, and these are by no means uniform in their opening; nevertheless we must agree that *Prom.* 1-87 shows much closer resemblances to Sophocles than to Aeschylus.[3]

There is no reason why a tragedian should have felt himself bound consistently to employ the same form of opening scene. In the earliest plays which come down to us, Aeschylus felt free to choose between a spoken prologue (*Th.*) and an anapaestic introduction to the parodos by the chorus (*Pers.*), and his later plays used both forms (anapaests *Supp.*, cf. *Myrmidons* - also Π. Λυόμενος; spoken prologue *Ag.*, *Cho.*, *Eum.*). Scholars disagree as to which, if either, of these forms is original to tragedy. The objections to Nestle's plausible and well-argued case for the early existence of the iambic prologue have been considerably weakened by the late dating of A. *Supp.*; but for our purposes it is not very important.[4] Even if the prologue was a comparatively late addition to the 'original' tragic structure,[5] it was certainly current by the mid-470s.

It is quite possible that more than one form may have existed side by side from the earliest times.[6] If we believe that the largely expository, undramatic prologue was an old, established convention which Euripides merely continued,[7] then we may feel that Aeschylus and Sophocles were to some extent exceptional in their attempts to achieve greater dramatic effect in their opening scene. Thus the dramatic opening to *Prom.* may be thought Aeschylean in so far as it is uneuripidean, i.e. it shares with the plays of Aeschylus (and Sophocles) a reluctance to employ the traditional prologue form.[8] But with our lack of comparative material, we are in no position to say with any confidence whether the detachable 'Euripidean' prologue was normal or exceptional in the mid-fifth century. Apart from Aeschylus and Sophocles, and Phrynichos' *Phoinissai*, we have no knowledge of how tragedians other than Euripides opened their plays. (Even in the case of Euripides, we do not know how many plays may have opened with anapaests.[9]) The scholiasts frequently contrast Sophocles' technique (favourably) with that of Euripides,[10] but they give no indication as to which was the more typical of tragedy.

So we cannot say what we would expect a non-Aeschylean play to offer as an opening scene. But it seems likely that whenever the spoken iambic prologue was introduced it was originally undramatic in nature, and delivered by a minor character, and that the integration of this prologue into the drama, and the use of dialogue, represent 'advances' on the more primitive form. In these terms, A. *Ag.* and *Eum.* are less 'advanced' than *Cho.* and *Th.*, where the προλογίζων is in each case the main character, so that the plot unfolds naturally from the opening situation (though *Cho.*'s prologue does not seem to have been really integrated into the rest). Sophocles advances further, in presenting an opening dialogue which allows the exposition and the action to proceed simultaneously, and disguises the exposition in a more naturalistic garb. The openings of S. *Aj.*, *Ant.*, *Ph.*, *OK* are all more 'advanced' than anything in Aeschylus. So, it appears, is the opening of *Prom.*

Nestle[11] considered the following elements of the opening scene of *Prom.* to be Aeschylean:

(i) the symmetry of the stichomythia (archaic, non-Sophoclean);
(ii) the express description of the place and Prometheus' physical discomfort;
(iii) the presence of a πρόσωπον προτατικόν representing a leading character (Kratos for Zeus);
(iv) the lack of connection between the dialogue and Prometheus' monologue;
(v) Prometheus' inactivity in the opening scene;
(vi) the entrance of the hero before the parodos;
(vii) the dramatic nature of all three parts (prologue, monologue, parodos).

He considered as later and Sophoclean:

(a) the fully developed dialogue opening;

(b) the speeches aimed at characterization, not exposition;

(c) the contrast of the dialogue characters (cf. e.g. S. *Ph.*, *Ant.*).

To take the 'Aeschylean' elements first:

(i) The 2:1 symmetry of the stichomythia may be archaic and unsophoclean, but it is also apparently unaeschylean.[12]

(ii) The references to the physical location are striking (1f, 4f, 15, 20ff) and similar to those of A. *Ag.* (4ff, 12), but they are equally comparable to S. *Ph.* 1f, 20ff; *OK* 14ff; *Aj.* 3. So too, the descriptions of Prometheus' position and suffering (31ff) may be compared to A. *Ag.* 3 etc., *Eum.* 36ff,[13] but also to S. *Aj.* 9f; *Ph.* 6ff; *OK* 9ff, 19ff (and cf. E. *Or.* 34ff).

(iii) The dialogue in *Prom.* 1-87 is in effect between two πρόσωπα προτατικά (Kratos representing Zeus, Hephaistos representing Prometheus), who play no further part in the drama, though Hephaistos does address Prometheus directly (18, 66), and so does Kratos as he departs (82ff). The choice of such subordinate extra-dramatic characters as προλογίζοντες could be taken as a sign of a less advanced technique than that of Sophocles. We may compare it to that of the watchman of A. *Ag.*, or the priestess of *Eum.*, and of Apollo and Thanatos in E. *Alk.*, Aphrodite in *Hipp.*, the ghost of Polydoros in *Hek.*: Athene in S. *Aj.* is the nearest Sophocles comes to such a choice; cf. too Phrynichos' *Phoinissai*.

(iv) There is no Sophoclean parallel for a break like *Prom.* 87 between two scenes before the parodos; A. *Eum.* (63 and 93) has two such breaks.[14] In effect then, we may say that the prologue of *Prom.* is more easily detachable than those of Sophocles. Euripides' prologues are notoriously detachable, though he tends to disguise the lack of dramatic connection by having the προλογίζων announce the approach of the characters of the next scene (e.g. *Hipp.* 51ff, *Hek.* 52ff) before retiring. In our play, the figure of Prometheus himself acts as a similar link, physical rather than chronological as in Euripides, between the prologue and what follows.

(v) The famous silences of A. *Niobe* and *Phrygians*[15] (and also of

Klytaimestra in A. *Ag.*, though it is uncertain when she enters or leaves the stage between 39 and 680[16]) have no certain parallels in Sophocles or Euripides, though in E. *Or.* it seems that Orestes is visible from the start. The opening of S. *Aj.*, with the descriptions of Ajax's antics within, has a similar effect of creating suspense and anticipation for his first utterance. The silence of Prometheus seems more natural than that of Niobe or Achilles: there is nothing for him to say, and Hephaistos is virtually speaking for him.[17]

(vi) The presence of the hero before the parodos seems no more characteristic of Aeschylus than it is of Sophocles or Euripides; e.g. S. *Aj.*, E. *Hipp.* both have an opening scene ('prologue'), followed by a scene in which the hero participates, and then the parodos, a similar structure to *Prom.* In any case, given the story that he wanted to dramatize, the author had little choice but to bring Prometheus on at the start (cf. E. *Andromeda*).

(vii) *Prom.* 1-87 is 'dramatic' to a limited extent. The dialogue form is more naturalistic than the Euripidean monologue; the chaining of Prometheus is obviously an essential part, or prerequisite, of the drama, like e.g. the news contained in the watchman's speech in A. *Ag.* At the same time, the function of this scene is perhaps more obviously expository than is usual in Aeschylus: the first two speeches are largely concerned with informing us of the immediate cause of Prometheus' punishment.[18] To a certain extent we feel at 87, with the departure of Hephaistos, Kratos, and Bia, that the scene is now set, and the play proper can begin. We have little idea as to how the drama will develop, whereas the dark hints of A. *Ag.*, the contrast of *Eum.* 1-33 with 34-63, point the direction of the play from the start (cf. the parodoi of *Supp.* and *Pers.*). But such impressions are too subjective to be of much value to us.

We turn now to those elements which Nestle held to be later and Sophoclean.

(a) The fully developed dialogue opening may have been partially paralleled by Aeschylus in *Phrygians*,[19] but this was clearly of minor proportions, whatever its nature. Otherwise the nearest to an Aeschylean parallel is *Th.*; here the prologue is divided between two speakers, but the arrival of the messenger represents a step forward in the action, and there is nothing that we could call a dialogue, let alone stichomythia. The dialogue opening allows the exposition of the situation to be integrated more naturalistically into the drama, and is employed by Sophocles in *Aj.*, *Ant.*, *Ph.*, *OK.* Euripides never has stichomythic dialogue in the actual prologue, but quite frequently uses it before the parodos in an intermediate scene (e.g. *Alk.* 38ff, *Med.* 49ff, *Hipp.* 73ff).

(b) The speeches aimed at characterization, rather than exposition, remind us of the Antigone/Ismene, or Hippolytos/Servant confrontations. The ἐπιστολαί mentioned in line 3 have still not begun to be carried out by line 36. The lines between have served to arouse in us attitudes towards Zeus (10f, 34f, through the character of Kratos his wholehearted retainer) and Prometheus (11, 28ff, through the character of Hephaistos, who expresses his powerless sympathy and pity), which put us already firmly on the side of the Titan. In A. *Th.* the opening speech of Eteokles does establish for us some of the characteristics of the ruler and protector of the city; the watchman's speech in *Ag.* tells us something of his different attitudes to Klytaimestra (10f, 18f) and Agamemnon (34f). But generally Aeschylus' aim is to create a mood in the prologue, to begin the buildup of tension and expectancy. The introduction of ἦθος where it is not strictly necessary might be felt to be unaeschylean.

(c) The contrast of the dialogue characters is virtually included in (b). S. *Ph.*, *Ant.*, E. *Hipp.* and *El.* show the same tendency as *Prom.*

Just as the 'Euripidean' prologue differs in its undramatic nature from the prologue of Aeschylus and Sophocles, so too does his technique of exposition of 'the story so far'. Gollwitzer[20] points out that Aeschylus' prologues tend to deal with the immediate past, not the whole situation and sequence of events leading up to it: these details are usually introduced into the play later, when they are dramatically significant. Euripides prefers to narrate events in chronological order, dealing first with the distant past.

Sophocles shows a similar technique to Aeschylus (e.g. S. *Ant.*, where we learn only of the immediate past in the prologue and have to wait until the parodos for the story of the seven against Thebes, and until 162ff, 289ff, 486 for further details[21]). *Prom.* is also similar, in that we only learn some of the essential background at 199ff and 442ff.

Although this carries us outside the prologue, we might here observe that the technique of exposition at *Prom.* 199ff, 442ff (i.e. iambic narrative) contrasts with the less formal, more dramatic technique of the *Oresteia*, where past events are subtly, and often ambiguously, introduced, largely in the choral lyrics. (So too past events in A. *Pers.* are described in the parodos.) Gollwitzer does not point this out, but the *Prom.* passages of exposition do show resemblances to the undramatic, narrative prologues of Euripides.

To sum up: the prologue of *Prom.*, though generally closer to the technique of Aeschylus than to that of Euripides, is still quite different in form from any of Aeschylus' surviving plays, and is closer to Sophocles. Nestle's list of 'Aeschylean' and 'unaeschylean' elements does not prove to be very accurate or helpful beyond this central fact.

PROMETHEUS' SOLILOQUY (88-127)

Herington remarks,[22] 'The actor-monodies in *Prom.* 114-117 and 566-608, not in lyric interchange with the Chorus, are unique in Aeschylus. Such monodies are fairly frequent in post-Aeschylean tragedy, especially Euripidean.' He does not elsewhere mention Prometheus' soliloquy 88-127, and I feel that it is hardly accurate to place it, or any part of it, in the same category as Io's monody, or to claim that 'such monodies are fairly frequent'. 114-17 is merely one small section of an extraordinary succession of changes of metre within the same speech, even once (119) within the same sentence. The succession iambic-anapaestic-iambic-lyric-iambic-anapaestic, without change of speaker and within such a short space, is very peculiar.[23] It is often suggested that the changes of metre reflect the changing mood of Prometheus;[24] certainly the iambics of 101ff are more restrained than the preceding anapaests; and at 114ff the bacchiacs express Prometheus' excitement and apprehension at the unexpected arrival of the Okeanids: both these changes of metre would seem to follow appreciable pauses. But no such explanation seems possible for 92-3ff, or 119-20ff, which are strikingly parallel in their form (92 ἴδεσθε /119 ὁρᾶτε, 98/124 φεῦ φεῦ, and cf. the general tone of the anapaests).

Wilamowitz remarks[25] that the anapaest-iambic transition is 'nichts unerhörtes' and compares Artemis in E. *Hipp.*, Herakles in S. *Ph.*; similarly iambic-anapaestic at the end of E. *Med.* and *El.* 'Beides ist von dem Bau der Prometheusrede verschieden; aber es zeigt doch die Richtung auf der er nur weiter geschritten ist.' But in these examples the single change has an obvious point: the entry in anapaests may have had a particularly solemn effect (or been for some reason suitable for entries on or over the roof of the skene,[26] cf. Okeanos' entry ?), while the playwright wanted to return to the more normal spoken iambics for the ensuing scene: so too in E. *Med.* and *El.* the change to anapaests seems merely to mark the start of the *exodos*, in the literal sense of 'departure' of the characters from the stage (or rather above it). I do not feel that these passages are pointing in the same 'Richtung' as *Prom.* 88ff at all.[27]

Even if we agreed that the changes of metre from 88ff do at least in part reflect changes of mood, we would still have to confess that they are unlike anything in Aeschylus, Sophocles, or Euripides. Wilamowitz suggests[28] that Euripides would have written a true monody here (anapaests and lyrics), as in *And.* and *Ion*; instead 'Aeschylus ... die Anapäste als Steigerung der Trimeter so anwandte wie sie sonst durch Tanzrhythmen gesteigert werden'. We can only ask, *Why ?* Anapaests are not particularly suitable for self-pity unless they are sung *Klaganapäste*, which these are not. And if Prometheus is prevented from expressing himself in lyrics by his physical immobility, how does he come to sing the lyrics of 114-17? We cannot maintain that lyrics were *inevitably* accompanied by dance: did Herakles dance at S. *Tr.* 1004ff, or Hippolytos at E. *Hipp.* 1370ff? And we have no comparable example anywhere of changes of mood being accompanied by such changes of metre within one speech: yet we do find abrupt and striking changes of mood that might be expected, on this analogy, to be accompanied by such metrical changes in Aeschylus, e.g. *Ag.* 22ff, *Cho.* 1048ff, *Eum.* 34ff;

in each case Aeschylus is perfectly content to employ iambic trimeters throughout, as is Euripides at *Med.* 364ff and Sophocles at *El.* 804ff (and cf. S. *El.* 86ff anapaests throughout, with no change at 110 or elsewhere).[29]

(The structure of 88-127 is not actually strophic or perfectly symmetrical; it is nevertheless highly formalized and balanced. We have: five iambic trimeters; thirteen anapaestic metra plus paroemiac; then thirteen trimeters, followed perhaps by a pause; then five cola of lyrics and trimeters; and finally fourteen anapaestic metra plus paroemiac. Nestle argues that such formalistic alternation must be archaic.[30] A. *Th.* 375-676 also displays a massive formalism of construction; but e.g. the artificial formalism of the strophic lamentation of Alkestis' son at E. *Alk.* 393-415 seems equally relevant, and equally distant from *Prom.*)

In sum, we must confess that the structure of Prometheus' soliloquy is utterly unlike anything in Aeschylus, or indeed Sophocles or Euripides. Its formal symmetry is curious, but not characteristic of any particular author.

THE PARODOS (128-192)

The simple epirrhematic structure of the parodos, with the strophic lyrics of the chorus answered by the anapaests of Prometheus, is unlike the parodoi of the surviving Aeschylean plays, none of which is epirrhematic. Epirrhematic parodoi are found in S. *Aj.*, *Ant.*, *Ph.*, *OK*; E. *Alk.*, *Med.*, and *Rhesos*; but in none of these except S. *Ant.* is the structure as formal and simple as *Prom.*; in the others the anapaests are divided between more than one speaker (in E. *Alk.* amongst the chorus), and S. *Ph.* and *OK* in particular are much less regular and more 'dramatic', i.e. closer to dialogue, than *Prom.*

It is generally agreed that an epirrhematic structure, whether of lyrics and iambics or lyrics and anapaests, is characteristic of early tragedy, despite its presence in Sophocles' last two plays.[31] This conclusion is based on the presence of such scenes at A. *Pers.* 256ff; *Th.* 203ff, (397ff), 683ff; *Supp.* 348ff, 873ff; *Ag.* 1072ff, 1407ff; *Eum.* 778ff, 916ff; in early Sophocles at *Aj.* 201ff, 866ff; *Ant.* 100ff, 802ff, 1261ff; (later at *Ph.* 135ff; *OK* 117ff, 1447ff); in early Euripides at *Alk.* 86ff, 244ff, 861ff; *Med.* 131ff; *And.* 501ff; also *Rhesos* 1ff, 527ff, 675ff; (in later Euripides only at

El. 859ff).[32]

Unterberger remarks on *Prom.*'s parodos,[33] 'Die Form der Parodos ist ungewöhnlich, weil die szenische Situation und der Chor selbst gleichermassen ungewöhnlich sind. Die Okeaniden kommen nicht auf eine leere Szene, ja, sie kommen eigens zu dem dort Angeschmiedeten.' We may observe however that Aeschylus did not employ this form for the parodos of *Th.*, where Eteokles is already on stage when the chorus enter; presumably, too, Danaos entered with his daughters at the beginning of *Supp.* We obviously cannot be certain that the structure is 'ungewöhnlich' with our incomplete knowledge of Aeschylus' parodoi; but it appears that Aeschylus preferred to introduce the parodos with anapaests from the chorus leader (*Pers.*, *Supp.*, *Ag.*, fr. 131; cf. fr. 190?), though *Th.*, *Cho.*, and *Eum.* are all sufficiently different to discourage us from overconfident generalization.[34]

In short, the parodos of *Prom.* is of a form not known to be used by Aeschylus, but quite frequently used in the early plays of Sophocles and Euripides. Its formal and symmetrical structure give it a slightly more archaic air than those of Sophocles and Euripides, except S. *Ant.*

ACTORS' ANAPAESTS[35]

Prom. 284ff: Okeanos enters, unannounced, with anapaests; Prometheus addresses him in iambics, and the dialogue continues, and concludes, in iambics.

561ff: Io enters, unannounced, with anapaests; after her monody and the long iambic epeisodion, broken only by the astrophic lyrics of the chorus (687-95), she falls into anapaests as the madness comes over her again and she is driven from the stage (877-86).

1040ff: After a lengthy dialogue in iambics (944-1039) the chorus, Hermes, and Prometheus end the play in anapaests; the final words are Prometheus' anapaestic call to the elements to witness his unfair punishment (cf. his first words 88ff).

(1) The only place in Aeschylus where an actor enters with anapaests, as Okeanos and Io do, is *Pers.* 908ff: here Xerxes' anapaests are answered by the chorus' anapaests, which turn into lyric *Klaganapäste* (922ff), and the scene develops into a fully epirrhe-

matic lyric kommos (931ff). No iambic trimeters are spoken after the entry of Xerxes.

In Sophocles, actors enter with anapaests at *Aj*. 201ff, like A. *Pers*. introducing an epirrhematic scene; *Tr*. 974ff, where Herakles' anapaests are at least in part lyric (983-8), and he continues in a lyric monody (1003ff, 1024ff), before finally falling into iambic trimeters; *El*. 86ff, Elektra's anapaests followed by lyric exchange; *Ph*. 1409ff, where Herakles appears with anapaests, and then (1418ff) continues in iambics.

In Euripides, we find *Alk*. 29ff, the entry of Thanatos; *Hipp*. 176ff, the Nurse and Phaidra in anapaestic dialogue; *Hipp*. 1283ff, entry of Artemis; also *Rhesos* 733ff, the entry of the Charioteer (mostly in anapaests), answered by the chorus in iambics: in each of these four passages the scene continues in iambic trimeters. At *Hek*. 59ff, *Ion* 82ff, *Tro*. 98ff, *IA* 1ff,[36] an actor enters with anapaests, and continues in lyrics, either in a monody or in *Klaganapäste.*

(It is remarkable that the three closest parallels to Okeanos' entry are all theophanies[37] (Herakles, Thanatos, Artemis), and that at E. *And*. 1226ff and *El*. 1233ff the *deus ex machina* (or ἐπὶ θεολογείωι ?) is again heralded by anapaests, this time from the chorus. It seems that anapaests were suitable for the appearance of a god above the stage; and although Okeanos is far from performing the customary role of a *deus ex machina*, his anapaests may be performing the same function, as he flies in on his πτερυγωκῆς οἰωνός.[38])

(2) Nowhere in Aeschylus does an actor leave the stage with anapaests, as Io does (877-86). Indeed only three times in Aeschylus do actors deliver recitative anapaests at all; *Pers*. 908ff (mentioned above); and *Ag*. 1462ff and *Eum*. 927ff, both epirrhematic, in alternation with choral lyrics.

Sophocles has nine passages in all where actors deliver recitative anapaests.[39] Of these, only two are epirrhematic. Four plays are ended by actors' anapaests, to accompany their departure (*Aj*., *Tr*., *Ph*., *OK*, though only *Tr*.(?) does not have a final little choral appendage). A close parallel to Io's departure with anapaests during the course of the play is *Ant*. 937ff.[40]

Euripides has about twenty passages of actors' recitative anapaests: they are markedly commoner in his earlier plays.[41] Only three are epirrhematic. Four plays end with actors' anapaests (*Med.*, *El.*, *Or.*, *Ba.*), apart from the short final comment of the chorus (πολλαὶ μορφαί etc.), by now apparently of little more significance than 'God Save the Queen'. Only I think at *Med.* 184ff (Nurse) and *IA* 155ff (Agamemnon) does a character leave the stage with anapaests other than at the end of a play, and in both cases they have been speaking in anapaests throughout the preceding scene, and do not, as in the *Prom.* and S. *Ant.* passages, adopt anapaests only for their final speech.

(3) In extant tragedy, there are few plays which do not end with choral anapaests, however brief. But we are of course on dangerous ground here, as a short anapaestic coda would be particularly liable to accidental omission, or intentional replacement, or insertion where none previously existed, according to the taste of the actors and producer. We have no idea how reliable our tradition is here.

The plays are: A. *Pers.*, *Supp.*, *Ag.*, *Eum.*, (*Th.* uncertain); S. *OT* (?), *Tr.* (?); E. *Ion*, *Tro.*, (*IA* uncertain); and *Prom.*

Of these A. *Pers.*, *Supp.*, *Eum.*, (and *Th.* ?), E. *Tro.* (and *IA* ?) end with choral lyrics in the form of a kommos or processional song; S. *OT* (?) and E. *Ion* end with trochaic tetrameters from the chorus.[42]

Only A. *Ag.*, (S. *Tr.* ? and *OT* ?), and *Prom.* end with the words of an actor; Klytaimestra in trochaic tetrameters (cf. S. *OT* ? , E. *Ion*), Prometheus (and ?Hyllos) in anapaests.[43] Thus, although Aeschylus seems to use the anapaestic coda much less regularly than Sophocles and especially Euripides, he does, like them, appear to favour a final utterance of some sort by the chorus:[44] it seems that by Euripides' time the coda had become an empty convention (and cf. S. *Ant.*).

Apart from the lack of such a coda, the end of *Prom.* is similar to S. *Aj.*, *Tr.*, *Ph.*; E. *Med.*, *El.*, *Or.*, *Ba.*, in that the characters involved in the final iambic scene pass over into anapaests for no particular internal reason, but rather, it seems, to signify the approach of the end, and to accompany their movement off the stage. Usually the chorus would be the last to leave, and would have furthest to go to the *parodoi*; they would therefore be given the last few anapaests (or occasionally lyrics). In *Prom.* the attention of the audience is inevitably concentrated on the motionless figure of Prometheus, who cannot move from the stage.[45] There is therefore no opportunity for the chorus to deliver their usual last words over the empty stage, as they too are involved in the final disaster.[46]

It seems, then, that the anapaestic final scene of *Prom.* has much more in common with some of the plays of Sophocles and Euripides than with any of the surviving plays of Aeschylus. But Aeschylus' flexibility in the structure of his final scenes is apparent from just five plays: if he could end *Ag.* with a trochaic tetrameter dialogue, we cannot put the anapaestic dialogue of *Prom.* beyond him. We can merely observe, first, that he does not so end any of his surviving plays, while Sophocles and Euripides do so repeatedly, whereas the end of A. *Ag.* is only paralleled at E. *Ion* and (?) S. *OT*; cf. E. *Pho.*; and secondly that his use of actors' anapaests is very much more sparing than that of Sophocles and Euripides, and is restricted in his extant plays to pre- or inter-lyric passages.

If we put together what we have observed of the use of actors' anapaests in tragedy, we may draw the following conclusions. Aeschylus very rarely uses actors' anapaests (three times in all, never more than once in a play). *Prom.* with five separate passages (93ff, 284ff, 561ff, 877ff, 1040ff) exceeds the number of any extant Greek tragedy (E. *Alk.* and *Hipp.* three; so too S. *Ph.*). Sophocles and Euripides usually have one or two such passages per play.

The entry of Okeanos, with anapaests, leading into an iambic scene, has no Aeschylean parallel, but several in Sophocles and Euripides.

The entry of Io, with anapaests followed by the actor's lyrics, is paralleled closely by S. *Tr.* 974ff; E. *Hek.* 59ff, *Ion* 82ff, *Tro.* 98ff; less closely by A. *Pers.* 908ff; S. *Aj.* 200ff, *El.* 86ff.

The departure of Io with anapaests is paralleled by S. *Ant.* 938ff, and less closely by E. *Med.* 184ff, (*IA* 155ff), and the final scenes of S. *Aj.*, *Tr.*, *Ph.*, *OK*; E. *Med.*, *El.*, *Or.*, *Ba.* There is nothing comparable in Aeschylus.

The final scene, with the chorus, Hermes, and Prometheus in anapaests, is paralleled by the anapaestic final scenes of S. *Aj.*, *Tr.*, *Ph.*; E. *Med.*, *El.*, *Or.*, *Ba.* There are no such final scenes in Aeschylus. The lack of a final coda from the chorus sets *Prom.*

apart from the plays of Euripides; but it still does not resemble any of the extant plays of Aeschylus, and this lack may well be due to the dramatic situation.

THE OKEANOS-SCENE (284-396)

Σ *Prom.* 287 καιρὸν δίδωσι τῶι χορῶι καθῆκασθαι τῆς μηχανῆς 'Ωκεανὸς ἐλθών. It appears that ancient commentators were as uncomfortable as modern about this scene, which displays several peculiarities.

Some of these peculiarities must be attributed, it seems, to the problems of staging.[47] The lack of announcement of Okeanos' arrival (which interrupts Prometheus when he is about to tell the chorus about the future), and the failure of the chorus to speak to him or participate in any way in the scene, or to comment on it after his departure (even though they are his daughters, and have referred to him in unnecessary detail earlier on, 131ff; cf. 136 ff),[48] are both best explained on the assumption that the chorus are no longer present.[49] They are dismounting from their aerial transport offstage.

But there is no such justification for the arrival of Okeanos on a τετρασκελὴς οἰωνός: it has no mythological authority, and no apparent dramatic point, save that of distracting the audience's attention from the departing chorus. Nor is there any very satisfactory motive given for his arrival,[50] beyond his relationship to Prometheus, and friendship (289, 297). We are not told the basis for that friendship. (331 may once have contained an answer? But the reference is still obscure, unless we agree with Wilamowitz that the poet is following a story of the Titanomachy already well known to his audience. Yet 217ff does not leave much room for Okeanos' cooperation with Prometheus in that struggle.[51])

Okeanos accomplishes nothing,[52] but the scene serves two functions, *Retardierung* of the plot,[53] to stop Prometheus revealing too much too soon, and the demonstration of ἦθος, in the contrast of personality between Okeanos and Prometheus, and in the opportunity it gives for Prometheus' character to be developed. Of these, the first may seem rather clumsy,[54] in that we could, I think, cut from 270 to 439 without losing anything of real dramatic substance,[55] and the second seems more characteristic of Sophocles than of Aeschylus (e.g. Chrysothemis/Elektra, Ismene/Antigone). Although Aeschylus does sometimes characterize through contrast (e.g. Dareios/ Xerxes), his figures always have some dramatic significance of their own (e.g. the watchman in *Ag.*, the nurse in *Cho.*); 'Dieser Okeanos dagegen ist dramatisch müssig wie keine andere Figur des Aeschylus.'[56]

Even Okeanos' final remarks seem feebler than we would expect from Aeschylus. 387 alone would make a reasonable and satisfactory explanation for his departure; the description of the antics of his winged beast seems rather out of place, if γάρ (394) is intended as any sort of motivation. Generally Aeschylus allows a character, when he has fulfilled his function, to depart without explanation (e.g. *Supp.* 951; *Pers.* 514, 839; *Th.* 652; *Eum.* 93, 139, 777).

All in all, we may feel that the Okeanos-scene, in its enthusiasm for τὸ τερατῶδες, has involved the dramatist in some rather clumsy manoeuvres, which do little to further the development of the play, and little to increase the tension or arouse the audience's expectations. This is ultimately, of course, a subjective judgement - and strictly it is of limited relevance to our authorship problem: we must beware of the false equations, 'good = Aeschylus, bad = somebody else'. But I do agree with Schmid that in dramatic terms there is no single scene in Aeschylus as weak as this.

PROMETHEUS' SILENCE[57]

σιγᾶν με (437) has caused some embarrassment and provoked several different explanations among scholars. Schmid was so uncomfortable about it that he suggested[58] that σιγᾶν is not absolute, but means 'nicht sagen, was erwartet wird', and refers to Prometheus' failure to carry out his intentions of 271ff. This idea seems fantastic, and σιγᾶν cannot mean all that Schmid would like it to mean. But he was right to draw attention to the strangeness of σιγᾶν here,[59] in that Prometheus was talking to Okeanos up to the moment of his departure, and now, after the stasimon (in which by convention he cannot speak), starts speaking without being addressed.

There seem to me to be only two possible explanations, and both are rather peculiar. The first[60] is, that as the chorus enter the orchestra before 397, neither they nor Prometheus speak, although it would take some time for them to assume their positions for the stasimon, and Prometheus is referring to this silence at 437. The objections to this are however considerable. (a) Why does Prometheus refer now to a silence which is over and done with, and best ignored or forgotten? By doing so, he merely reminds us of the peculiar staging arrangements for the chorus. (b) Why does he use the present infinitive rather than the aorist? (c) Why in any case did the author not give the chorus or Prometheus something to say between 396 and 397? Choral anapaests, or another monologue by Prometheus, to cover the chorus' entry, would be perfectly natural at that point. For Prometheus now to apologize for such an unnecessary and pointless silence would be very clumsy. (d) The conventions of the theatre would surely allow the chorus to enter in silence and then start singing, without need of an apology from a bystander. (So e.g. at E. *Hks* 107 the chorus enter and sing, without anapaests to cover their movement into the orchestra, while Megara and Amphitryon stand by.[61])

The alternative, which is accepted by Wilamowitz and most commentators, is that after 435 there is an appreciable pause.[62] Other pauses have been postulated, with varying degrees of confidence, after 87[63] and 114.[64] These are sometimes taken, together with Prometheus' silence throughout 1-87 and the apparent silence at 435, to reflect the Aeschylean technique mocked in Aristophanes *Frogs* 911ff.[65] But we should distinguish between the different silences in *Prom.* On Prometheus' silence from 1-87 Thomson rightly remarks, 'The device is as old as Homer: perhaps the most famous example is the silence of Achilles after the news of the death of Patroclus (*Il.* 18.15-77).' Here the Titan's silence in the presence of his tormentors, and his eventual eruption into speech, are effective and dramatically successful:[66] we can compare A. *Ag.* 810-1072 (Kassandra) (and also *Niobe* and *Phrygians*) for this technique of keeping the audience in suspense for a major character's first utterance. We find a similar build-up in S. *Aj.* 1-91, and E. *Or.* 1-211 (where Orestes, like Prometheus, is visible on stage throughout[67]); cf. too Phaidra's silence at E. *Hipp.* 601-68.

Very different would be the silence of a character who is alone on stage, as Prometheus is at 87 and 114. We have no means of knowing whether a pause was made at those points or not. Similarly after e.g. S. *Aj.* 814, or E. *Med.* 1020 there may have been a pause: in the absence of ancient stage directions we simply cannot tell. The pauses at *Prom.* 87 and 114 might represent the passing of ages: but the dramatic effect of such pauses would tend to wane with repetition. A pause after 435 would seem pointless and feeble, and not a very effective way of demonstrating χλιδῇ, αὐθαδίᾳ or σύννοια, which Prometheus gives as the possible reasons for it. The apology for silence is thus utterly different from A. *Pers.* 290ff,[68] where it has motivation and dramatic point. Aeschylus was certainly famous among his successors for his silences; perhaps they were the object of imitation. Perhaps that is the explanation of this clumsy and pointless device at *Prom.* 435.

THE ARRIVAL OF A NEW CHARACTER

We have already observed[69] that the chorus make no reference to Okeanos as he arrives, and that this must be because they are not present to see him. Deckinger and Schmid[70] point out, however, that nowhere in *Prom.* do the chorus announce an incoming character, and suggest that this is unaeschylean; they point out further that Prometheus' announcement of Hermes' arrival (941ff) is an example, without a true parallel in Aeschylus, of an actor performing this function, as at e.g. S. *OT* 78ff, E. *Med.* 1118ff.

The lack of a conventional announcement by the chorus of an incoming character is by no means rare in Aeschylus: indeed we only find such announcements nine times or so in the six undisputed plays (*Pers.* 150ff, 246ff; *Th.* 369ff, 372ff;[71] *Supp.* 180ff; *Ag.* 489ff, 782ff; *Cho.* 10ff, 731ff; also cf. *Pers.* 623ff, *Th.* 36ff, *Supp.* 713ff, *Eum.* 39ff. All of these are delivered by the chorus, except for *Supp.* 180ff, which is more elaborate and dramatic than a conventional announcement, and *Cho.* 10ff, where the chorus have not yet arrived; cf. *Prom.* 114ff). It is quite possible that the lack of a parallel in Aeschylus to *Prom.* 941ff, where the chorus are available to perform this function, but neglected in favour of Prometheus, is due to chance: the number of occasions in Aeschylus on which a character is present on stage to observe the approach of another is after all relatively small (about fifteen, of which six have announcements by the chorus).

The expression by an incoming character of his/her reason for coming in simple and explicit terms is characteristic of Aeschylus;[72]

Sophocles tends to be more subtle.[73] So *Prom.* 1ff, 128ff, 284ff (and also the departures 81ff, 393ff) are similar to Aeschylus.[74] But parallels in Sophocles and Euripides are numerous,[75] and *Prom.* is in this respect unremarkable.

IO'S MONODY (561ff)

Herington states the position briefly:[76]

> 'The actor monodies in *Prom.* 114-119[77] and 566-608, not in lyric interchange with the chorus, are unique in Aeschylus. Such monodies are fairly frequent in post-Aeschylean tragedy, especially Euripidean.[78] The passages are collected by Owen.[79] I would add that the closest formal parallels to Io's monody (long strophe - four trimeters spoken by the calmer Prometheus - antistrophe) that I have noticed are as follows: S. *Aj.* 394-427 ..., E. *Alk.* 393-415 ..., *And.* 1173-1196 ..., *Hik.* 990-1030 ... But none of these passages is preceded, as the *Prom.* passage is, by astrophic monody.'

But surely E. *Hipp.* 817-51, and *Rhesos* 895-914 are much closer than S. *Aj.* 394ff, which is merely the last of three pairs of strophes, or E. *And.* 1173ff, which continues in a lyric kommos?

The form of Euripidean actor's monody up to the time of *Hik.* is usually that of strophe and antistrophe separated by two or three iambic trimeters.[80] Later his monodies are less formally and symmetrically organized. None of Sophocles' actor's lyrics are quite so simple as early Euripides' in form. A. *Ant.* 806-82 is the most formal, an epirrhematic arrangement of two strophes and antistrophes from Antigone, each followed by choral anapaests, with a final lyric epode from Antigone. Elsewhere, even in *Aj.* 348ff, Sophocles tends to construct the actors' lyrics more loosely, interrupting them with iambic trimeters or choral lyrics, with an effect close to dialogue.[81]

Prom. 561ff, with its symmetrical formal arrangement, seems to belong to a period not later than early Sophocles and Euripides, though the astrophic 567-73, a sort of pro-ode, is unusual and less formal. The metre of Io's monody is dochmiac and lyric iambic (apart from a few peculiarities[82]), which may have been easier to sing than some of the other lyric metres.[83] E. *Hipp.* 817-51 is even simpler metrically (pure dochmiac plus iambic trimeters); the other monodies cited above are rather more varied, though none of them is very complicated, in contrast to the later virtuoso arias of Euripides.

Only three times in the extant works of Aeschylus do actors deliver lyrics.[84] At *Pers.* 931ff, Xerxes and the chorus exchange lyrics in a kommos. The metre is complicated, or at any rate difficult for us to understand, and the solo singing part long and demanding. *Ag.* 1072ff is epirrhematic, with Kassandra's fairly simple iambic + dochmiac answered by the chorus' iambic trimeters and lyrics. At *Cho.* 315ff, the kommos makes considerable demands on the actors playing Orestes and Elektra. It is clear that Aeschylus was not afraid to give his actors quite large singing parts; and the kommos of *Cho.* is clearly a bold experiment on a grand scale: but it is noticeable that he only gives them such parts in kommos or epirrhema, in contrast to Euripides, in whom Ritchie[85] counts eighteen examples of actor's monody. Sophocles did not apparently favour the formal 'solo' either, but he is much freer with actor's lyrics in general than Aeschylus: I count[86] fourteen passages (of varying lengths) in the seven plays.

So *Prom.*, with two actors' parts requiring singing, one of them in a full-scale monody, is apparently in this respect unaeschylean, but not unlike early Euripides. Io's song and dance makes an effective contrast to the statuesque figure of Prometheus.[87]

ADDRESS FORMULAE[88]

In *Prom.*, out of a total (by my calculation) of thirty address formulae, we find no less than eighteen times an address comprising the bare proper name (thirteen times Προμηθεῦ, three times 'Ιοῖ, once Κράτος Βία τε, once Ἥφαιστε), whereas in all Aeschylus the proper name only so occurs eight times (never more than twice in one play). In Sophocles and Euripides such a form of address is common; it varies in Sophocles from once in *Ant.* to thirteen times in *Aj.*[89]

Herington argues[90] (a) that of Aeschylus' examples, four are from the *Oresteia*, and one from fr. 190 Π. Λυόμενος; (b) 'the very frequent recurrence of a noun in the vocative is not at all unique in Aeschylus. The vocative πάτερ is found six times in *Supp.*, twelve times in *Cho.* (both, it should be noted, plays of the "later group"), but nowhere else in the corpus.' He suggests that *Prom.*, in this as in other features, is merely further advanced along the path already begun in *Supp.* and *Oresteia*, and that the repetition of Prometheus' name is of a similar significance to that of πάτερ in *Supp.* and *Cho.*

There are however serious objections to his argument. (a) We can hardly talk of an advance of this technique in Aeschylus, when the occurrences are *Pers.* 1, *Th.* 0, *Supp.* 0, *Ag.* 2, *Cho.* 2, *Eum.* 1. (b) The examples of πάτερ in *Cho.* are not address formulae (in Wendel's terms anyway): they are invocations, and in a prayer some form of address is necessary to make any sense, whereas in dialogue it is discretionary. *Supp.* is the only Aeschylean play in which characters have to address their father; hence the lack of πάτερ in the other plays. (τέκνον, παῖ/παῖδες etc. are commoner in A. *Supp.* and *Cho.* for the same reason.) In any case, 'a noun in the vocative' like πάτερ is very different from the proper names, Προμηθεῦ, Ἰοῖ etc. We might agree that the repetition of Προμηθεῦ was an intentional 'artistic' use,[91] and hence in line with Aeschylus' 'economy and deliberation', were it not for the other occurrences (Ἰοῖ, Ἥφαιστε, Κράτος Βία τε[92]), which even by themselves would be extraordinary for Aeschylus, and together with the hero's name suggest that this form of address was simply felt by the author to be normal and natural.

Another detail of *Prom.*'s address formulae, which Wendel regarded as peculiar and unaeschylean, is ignored by Herington: five times the proper name alone is used in lyrics. For this there is no Aeschylean parallel (though πάτερ does occur in lyric, once in *Supp.*, twice - in prayer - in *Cho.*).[93]

(Schmid's argument that *Prom.* 18, 137-40, 647, 705 are unaeschylean in their elaboration is not supported by Wendel, and Herington rightly rejects it, comparing A. *Th.* 39, 203, 792; *Ag.* 1295f; *Eum.* 1032f (and cf. esp. *Pers.* 155f; fr. 384). ὦ φίλος (*Prom.* 546) was also considered by Schmid[94] to be unaeschylean. Wendel gives no Aeschylean parallel;[95] but, as Herington points out, *Diktyoulkoi* 807 has ὦ φίλος, and although this is a satyr-play, it seems a good enough parallel, since there is nothing to suggest that the nominative form was low or comic in tone. Other peculiarities of detail in *Prom.*'s address formulae are minor, and comparable to those inevitably displayed by all of the plays of Aeschylus, Sophocles and

Euripides alike.[96])

Strangely, Herington makes no use of Wendel's figures[97] for the relative frequency of address formulae in the different poets, beyond remarking,[98] 'On the whole, Aeschylus is very restrained in his use of address expressions, by comparison with any other epic or dramatic poet.' The figures (proportion of total lines containing an address) are: *Iliad* 4.5%, *Od.* 5%, *Hom. Hymns* 4.25%, Aeschylus 2.25%, Sophocles 6.1%, Euripides 6%, Aristophanes 6%.

Prom. with thirty address formulae in 1093 lines gives roughly 2.7% and is thus close to Aeschylus' average, well below Sophocles and Euripides (and Aristophanes). The biggest single difference in technique is probably Aeschylus' avoidance of the conventional use of e.g. τέκνον, πατήρ, ξένος, φίλος, γέρων etc., which Sophocles and Euripides tend to include sometimes almost as padding for a line. *Prom.*, with only 651 ὦ παῖ (in reported speech) and 546 ὦ φίλος (in lyrics), is in this respect Aeschylean.[99]

The rate of frequency naturally varies within one author, even one play, according to the context.[100] Much of the difference between Aeschylus on the one hand, and Sophocles and Euripides on the other, can be explained by the increase in three-actor dialogue,[101] where it is necessary to make it clear who is being addressed; whereas in Aeschylus' dialogue this is usually obvious, as it is in *Prom.* Thus, if we look at E. *Med.*, we find that the Aigeus-scene (663-759) is similar to the technique of *Prom.*: each character greets the other by name (663 proper name alone,[102] as often in *Prom.*, very rarely in Aeschylus); then no more address formulae until the striking line 690 Αἰγεῦ, κάκιστός ἐστί μοι πάντων πόσις. The only detail that is really different from *Prom.* (and Aeschylus) is 720 γύναι. Throughout the scene the two actors talk to each other quite easily without any need for address formulae. Conversely, in A. *Ag.* 1612-end, as Klytaimestra, Aigisthos, and the chorus argue amongst themselves in rapid dialogue, we find five address formulae in sixty-one lines.

We may conclude then, that in its address formulae *Prom.* diverges both from the usual practice of Aeschylus, in its repeated use of the bare proper name, and from that of Sophocles and Euripides, in its low overall rate of address.

THE CHORUS

(1) Proportion of choral lyric

The small amount of choral lyric in *Prom.* was one of the features which first led scholars to question Aeschylean authorship,[103] but in recent years it has not been given much weight in the argument. Table 5 gives a general picture of the facts.[104]

TABLE 5. *Proportion of choral lyric*

PLAY	*TOTAL NO. LINES*	*CHORAL LYRIC + ANAP.*	*CHORAL IA. TRIMETERS (+ TRO.TETR.)*	*CHORAL TOTAL*
A. *Pers.*	1076	457=43%	35(+28)	520=49%
Th.	1077	468=43%	33	501=46%
Supp.	1072	594=55%	67	661=61%
Ag.	1673	682=41%	152(+9)	843=50%
Cho.	1076	380=35%	72	452=42%
Eum.	1047	354=34%	103	457=43%
Prom.	1093	147=13%	54	201=18%
S. *Aj.*	1419	266=19%	83	349=24%
Ant.	1352	304=22.5%	45	349=26%
OT	1530	256=16%	57(+7)	320=20%
Tr.	1278	205=16%	42	247=19%
El.	1510	174=11%	40	214=14%
Ph.	1471	206=14%	15	221=15%
OK	1779	323=19%	74	397=22%
E. *Alk.*	1163	251=22%	51	302=26%
Med.	1419	267=19%	26	293=21%

It is clear that Aeschylus regularly has a far higher proportion of choral lyrics and anapaests than Sophocles or Euripides, even when we allow for the considerable variation from play to play within the same author (Aeschylus 34%-55%,[105] Sophocles 11%-22.5%). It is also clear that *Prom.*'s figure of 13% is lower than much of Sophocles and Euripides, and lies far below the Aeschylean range.

Here, apparently, we have an easily measured stylometric criterion, which holds good for all the extant plays, and reflects a really significant difference between the practice of Aeschylus on the one hand, Sophocles and Euripides on the other. How are we to explain *Prom.*'s presence on the opposite side to Aeschylus?

The usual explanation, accepted even by Schmid, the arch-exponent of spuriousness,[106] is that the presence of Prometheus on stage from start to finish of the play, prominent and immobile, dictates to the author that he employ only the minimum of choral lyric. This explanation (often coupled with reminders of Aeschylus' flexibility and adaptability to the context) has apparently been generally accepted as satisfactory. Yet it clearly is not.

Why should Prometheus' presence on the stage affect the length of the choral lyrics? I can only think of two possible reasons that might be put forward: (a) because Greek tragedy was reluctant to leave a character inactive on stage while the chorus sang and danced in the orchestra, (b) because the action and plot of *Prom.* were already rather static, and lengthy choral odes might be felt to be a further hindrance to the development of the *Handlung*. Neither reason will bear scrutiny.

(a) We are of course severely hampered by our lack of stage directions, and by our ignorance of the techniques and conventions of acting and production. But it seems quite clear that characters were not infrequently visible on stage while choral odes were sung: e.g. A. *Pers.* 623-80 (Atossa); *Th.* 78-180 (Eteokles); *Supp.* 1-175, 625-709 (Danaos); *Ag.* 40-257? 355-487? 681-809? (Klytaimestra),[107] 975-1035 (Kassandra); *Cho.* 22-83 (Elektra); *Eum.* 307-96 (Orestes and Apollo);[108] S. *Aj.* 1185-1222 (Eurysakes); *Ant.* 582-625, 944-87 (Kreon); *Tr.* 94-140 (Deianeira), etc.; E. *Med.* 410-45, 627-62, 824-65 (Medea); *Hek.* 444-83, 905-52 (Hekabe), etc.

There is no apparent reduction in the length of these odes; nor would it have been difficult to motivate the departure of e.g. Medea at E. *Med.* 409, Eteokles at A. *Th.* 77, to delay the arrival of Elektra until A. *Cho.* 83, and to dispense with Eurysakes at S. *Aj.* 1185ff completely, had there been any constraint on the tragedians to avoid the presence of a silent character on stage during choral lyrics.

On some occasions such a presence is of considerable dramatic force (e.g. Kassandra, Atossa, Kreon), and where it is suitably motivated, it is a natural and effective device. The tormented Prometheus, fettered to his remote rock, makes a striking backdrop for the chorus' lyrics, and obviously requires no explicit motivation for his presence - and it was presumably *this* feeling, that some sort of motivation was required, i.e. that the character alone on the stage should have some reason for being there, which encouraged the dramatists on the whole to leave the stage empty during the odes.

(b) Very little actually happens in *Prom.* between lines 87 and 1040ff. Okeanos, Io, and Hermes enter in turn and talk to the motionless hero. Apart from the aerobatics of the chorus and Okeanos, the eye has little to entertain it. There is not even very much immediate excitement or tension in the conversations until Hermes and Prometheus begin to argue: Prometheus' release and Zeus' possible downfall are apparently set far in the future. It might be felt that lengthy choral odes would slow the pace down still further.

Against this we need merely remark that by any standards the parodos of e.g. A. *Ag.* creates more tension, and carries the *Handlung* further, if not always explicitly or in a straight line, than any of the long iambic episodes of *Prom.* It is hard to deny that the exposition of past and future events could have been more dramatically and emotively accomplished in lyrics of the type and quality of A. *Ag.*, and thus the dangers of monotony which the poet seems anxious to avoid in *Prom.* by rapid changes of time-reference and order of narration could be obviated. No Aeschylean choral lyrics are as slow to develop *Handlung* or *Stimmung* as the formal and rather laboured narrative of *Prom.*'s episodes. In terms too of visual effect, choral odes, with their accompanying dance, would provide contrast to (and relief from) the static situation on stage, where the figures at times almost freeze into a tableau of speaker and audience. The constant presence of Prometheus would seem to invite contrast, in the form of physical movement: who better to provide it than the chorus?[109]

I do not see, therefore, in what sense Prometheus' enforced presence on stage throughout the play is supposed to explain the scarcity of choral lyric. In fact, we would expect, if anything, the opposite.

We must acknowledge that this scarcity is a result of choice, not dramatic necessity. The poet has decided that he only wants a limited amount of choral lyric. His reasons are not clear to us.

If the poet was Aeschylus (writing within a year or two of the *Oresteia*?), his decision marks a very striking divergence from his normal style, and we might expect such a divergence to have good reasons.[110] If the poet was not Aeschylus, we require no further explanation for the proportion of choral lyric, as it coincides with what we would expect from other playwrights.

(2) External form of choral lyric

I have shown already[111] that the metres of the choral lyrics differ strikingly from the usual Aeschylean patterns. So too the structure of the odes is remarkable, even apart from the epirrhematic parodos:[112] the overall shortage of lyrics as compared with Aeschylus' norm, discussed in the previous section, is reflected in the number of stanzas in each ode. Table 6[113] shows the number of strophic pairs in the parodoi and stasima of tragedy.

Two striking facts are immediately apparent:

(a) Aeschylus has less than three strophic pairs on only one occasion for certain, viz. *Ag.* 975ff. (*Th.* 78ff might offer astropha plus two pairs, but it seems quite probable that 109-49 originally gave another responding pair, as e.g. Murray believed. *Th.* 832ff is best left out of the reckoning: even as it stands, it is not clear whether one or two pairs occur, and the ode is surrounded by suspicious and probably spurious passages. *Cho.* 935ff should not be counted either, as two pairs plus mesodes give 1½ + 1½ = three altogether.)

Sophocles and Euripides, on the other hand, regularly have two pairs (Sophocles seventeen, Euripides thirty-five times, excluding epirrhematic passages), and quite often 1½ (Sophocles five, Euripides about eighteen times[114]). Only rarely do they have more than two pairs (S. *OT* parodos three, *Tr.* parodos 2½, *Ph.* parodos three in epirrhema, *El.* parodos two plus epirrhema, cf. *OK* parodos; E. *IA* parodos four (?), *Ba.* parodos 2½ plus astropha, *Hks* 348ff three, *Hik.* parodos three, plus five times 2½).

Prom. twice has two pairs (if we count the epirrhematic parodos) and once 1½ (887ff). The first stasimon is problematical in that we have no idea what has happened to 425-35. If we have there the remains of two responding stanzas, then this stasimon comprises three pairs (rare in Sophocles and Euripides, regular in Aeschylus); if the whole passage is genuine, but not divided into respond-

TABLE 6. *External form of choral lyric*

	PARODOS	STAS.1	STAS.2	STAS.3	STAS.4	STAS.5
A. *Pers.*	5½	3	3½	3½	-	-
Th.	1? +2	3	5	2? (or 1+a)	-	-
Supp.	8	5	4	3	-	-
Ag.	6½	3½	4	2	-	-
Cho.	3½	4	3	2+1	-	-
Eum.	3	4	4	-	-	-
Prom.	2(e)	2½? (3?)	2	1½	-	-
S. *Aj.*	1½	2	1	a+1	2	-
Ant.	2	2	2	1	2	2
OT	3	2	2	1	2	-
Tr.	2½	1½	2	2	2	-
El.	2+e	1½	2(e)	2	1	-
Ph.	3(e)	2	1½(e)	2(e)	-	-
OK	2(e)+a	2	2	1½	1	-
E. *Alk.*	2	(1)	2	2	2	-
Med.	1½(e)	2	2	2	2	2
Hkd.	1(e)	1½	1	2	2	-
Hipp.	2½	2	2	2½	a	-
And.	2	2	2	1½	2	-
Hek.	(anap.)	2	1½	2½	a	-
Hik.	3	2	(2)	1	1½	-
Hks	1½	3	2	2	a	a
Tro.	2(e)	1½	2	2	-	-
IT	a	2	a(e)	2	1	-
El.	1(e)	2½	2	1(e)	1½	-
Hel.	1(e)	a(e)	a	2	2	2
Ion	2(e)	1½	1½	2	a	-
Pho.	2½	1½	1½	1	1	-
Or.	2(e)	1	1½	1(e)	(1)	-
Ba.	a+2½	2	1½	1½	1½	a
IA	4? (1½+2½)	1½	1½	1½	a(e)	-
Rhes.	1(e)	2	2	1	(1½)	-

[Kranz adds: *Phaethon* parodos 2½, *Hypsipyle* parodos 1½(e)]

a = astrophic lyrics; e = lyrics in epirrhema

ing halves (i.e. an epode), then we have 2½ pairs (once in Sophocles, five times in Euripides, never in Aeschylus[115]); again, if 425-30 is interpolated, we still have 2½ pairs. In all, I think it is best to leave the stasimon out of the reckoning completely.[116] The other three strophic choral odes of *Prom.* all contain less than three pairs of stanzas. The short triadic structure of 887ff (strophe, antistrophe, epode) has no parallel in Aeschylus, four in Sophocles,[117] eighteen in Euripides. All Aeschylus' extant plays contain at least two choral odes longer than three strophic pairs, and some reach far greater proportions.[118]

(b) It appears at first glance that Aeschylus differs from Sophocles and Euripides in the number of stasima he has in his plays. According to the table, Aeschylus never has more than three (apart from the parodos), while Sophocles and Euripides regularly have four, sometimes five: only S. *Ph.*, E. *Tro.* have as few as three. Thus when *Prom.* appears with only three stasima in the table, we seem to have a sign of Aeschylean authorship. Of course, it should not surprise us that Sophocles and Euripides regularly seem to have more stasima than Aeschylus: their plays seem regularly to have been longer than his. But in any case Kranz in compiling the table does not seem to have applied his criteria consistently. He calls the table 'Übersicht über die vom Gesamtchor vorgetragenen strophisch gegliederten Lieder', yet includes several *astrophic* passages in Euripides 'soweit sie die Stelle einer Parodos oder eines Stasimon einnehmen'. But I do not understand why e.g. E. *Hipp.* 1268ff, *Hek.* 1024ff, *IT* 643ff, *Ion* 1229ff, *Hel.* 515 ff, *Ba.* 1153ff are considered to be 'taking the place of a stasimon', whereas *Prom.* 687ff is not, nor are A. *Cho.* 152ff, E. *El.* 585ff. Again, it is difficult to see why S. *El.* 823ff and *Ph.* 1081ff are included, but not *Ag.* 1114ff or *Cho.* 315ff. If *Prom.* 687ff is included, then *Prom.* with four stasima is typical of Sophocles and Euripides, and paralleled by A. *Cho.* (if 152ff is similarly included). If it is not, then to E. *Tro.* we should add *Hipp.*, *Hek.*, *Ion* as parallels.[119]

In sum, there is nothing remarkable about the number of stasima in *Prom.* But the overall lack of choral lyrics is reflected in the external form of the individual odes; they are all shorter than Aeschylus', similar to those of Sophocles and Euripides.

(3) The content and function of the choral lyrics

It is easy to be too schematic in analysing the choral lyrics of a single play, let alone of an author over several plays, and we cannot produce a neat and satisfactory description of this aspect of Aeschylus' style.[120] But scholars since Westphal have rejected various of the choral lyrics of *Prom.* on grounds of metre or content or both, and in general nobody could fail to observe that they are far less significant for the central issues of the play and for the development of dramatic tension than those of Aeschylus.

Prom.'s choral lyrics do not really expand or develop the

meaning of the drama, but are largely dependent on the preceding epeisodia, and subordinate to them. They contain little new material for consideration, no new interpretation of the situation: they merely reinforce the prevailing mood, at times with rather irrelevant application by the chorus to themselves of ideas arising from the predicament of those characters actually involved in the action, e.g. the third stasimon.[121] In this respect they resemble the chorus in early Euripides much more than Aeschylus: their connection to the drama is more 'external', in their personal expressions of sympathy for Prometheus and anxiety for themselves, than it is integral to the themes of the play.

There is no parallel in Aeschylus for the direct address to Prometheus at 397ff,[122] though Aeschylus' choruses have plenty of opportunities for such an address to a character on the stage,[123] or off it.[124] The device is common in early Euripides (especially in *Med.*; cf. too *OT* 1193-5 and *Tr.* parodos), and occurs again in *Prom.*'s second stasimon (544, 554).

Although the chorus of *Prom.* by their nature are inevitably far less involved in the action than those of A. *Supp.* and *Eum.* (and to a lesser extent *Th.* and *Cho.*), they do not seem to be *necessarily* much less involved than the old men of *Pers.* or *Ag.* I see no reason why Aeschylus, if he were writing *Prom.*, should not have allowed the Okeanids to display a wider knowledge of the nature of Prometheus' dispute with Zeus, and a far more imaginative interest in the interpretation of past events and their possible outcome. If the old men of *Ag.* could be given such an enormous and vital dramatic role in their lyrics, why should not the young nymphs of *Prom.*? Yet when critics discuss the meaning of *Prom.*, how often do they cite passages from the choral lyrics to show what the poet intended? What a contrast to *Suppliants* and the *Oresteia*!

Prom.'s choral lyrics are not without Aeschylean elements: for example, the catalogue of names at 412ff reminds us of A. *Pers.* 863ff. But the differences in technique from Aeschylus' choral lyrics in the other six plays seem to me much greater than can be accounted for in terms of dramatic necessity or expediency. Suggestions that some of the lyrics may have been inserted later are not convincing:[125] they seem to show a unity of technique and manner, even if they differ from the technique and manner of Aeschylus.[126] It must be all, or nothing.[127] And overall, one consistently finds in reading *Prom.* that the choral lyrics remind one of early Euripides far more than of Aeschylus. This judgement is to some extent subjective: but I think few would seriously dispute it.

(4) The iambic utterances of the chorus

As we saw from Table 5, Aeschylus generally gives his chorus rather more spoken iambics (or trochaic tetrameters) than do Sophocles and Euripides, whose plays are mostly somewhat longer. *Prom.* falls in between, and is compatible with either.[128] Though the number of choral trimeters is slightly higher than most of Sophocles and Euripides, it is lower than we might expect from Aeschylus when we bear in mind that the chorus leader is often Prometheus' sole interlocutor (193-283, 436-525, 907-43). Aeschylus appears to use the chorus in dialogue more in his later plays.

But while these overall figures are inconclusive, the form in which the chorus deliver their iambic utterances is extremely interesting. Herington has drawn attention[129] to the remarkable preference shown by the author of *Prom.* for quatrains spoken by the chorus, to the virtual exclusion of utterances of two, three, five or more lines. The chorus in *Prom.* in fact speak the following iambic lines: 193-6 (4), 242ff (4, 1, 1, 1, 1, 1, 1, 4), 472-5 (4), 507ff (4, 1, 1, 1, 1), 631-4 (4), 698-9 (2), 745 (1), 782-5 (4), 819-22 (4), 928ff (1, 1, 1, 1, 1), 1036-9 (4), a total of fifty-four lines, of which thirty-six occur in quatrains. Even the couplet 698f follows a couplet of Prometheus, and is followed by a long speech, so that it almost has the effect of an introductory quatrain. All the quatrains fall into one of three categories of formal, conventional arrangement:

(i) introduction to a long speech by an actor (193ff, 819ff);
(ii) comment on a long speech (242ff, 472ff, 507ff, 1036ff);
(iii) the conclusion of stichomythia (259ff, 631ff, 782ff).

Herington[130] gives the parallels in tragedy for such quatrains, and also lists for Aeschylus alone the other iambic (and trochaic tetrameter) utterances of the chorus.

A. *Pers.* No quatrains (but we should surely count 155-8 tro. tetr.); couplets at 515f, 798f, 843f; three lines 787ff, 173ff, 246ff; eleven lines 215ff; single lines 793, 795,

232ff.

Th. No quatrains: six lines 677ff, and single lines in stichomythia.

Supp. One quatrain 1014-17: seven couplets, four triplets; five lines 328ff; seven single lines in stichomythia.

Ag. Five quatrains 351ff, 583ff, 1198ff, 1242ff, 1295ff: also, of the conventional type defined above, couplet 1399f, triplets 317ff, 1047ff; and of non-conventional type, several single lines and couplets, three triplets, two five-line, two six-line, one fourteen-line(?) speech.[131]

Cho. Four quatrains 931ff, 1044ff (conventional), and 510ff, 770ff (non-conventional): also one couplet 181f, one triplet 551ff (conventional); and seven couplets, three triplets, two five-line speeches, several single lines in stichomythia (non-conventional).

Eum. One quatrain 640ff (non-conventional);[132] ten couplets, six triplets, one five-line, one eight-line, one ten-line speech, several single lines.

S. *Aj.*[133] Two quatrains 481ff, 1040ff, twelve couplets, one triplet (conventional), twelve couplets, one triplet, several single lines (non-conventional).

Ant. Two quatrains 211ff, 1091ff, four couplets, one triplet (conventional); eight couplets, several single lines (non-conventional).

OT Two quatrains 276ff, 404ff (conventional).

Tr. No quatrains.

El. One quatrain 324ff.

Ph. One quatrain 1218ff (non-conventional).

OK Three quatrains 254ff, 292ff, 461ff (conventional).

E. *Alk.* One quatrain 416ff, seven couplets, one triplet, one five-line speech 136ff (conventional); three couplets, one triplet, several single lines (non-conventional).

Med. One quatrain 267ff, two couplets, one triplet, one five-line speech 1231ff (conventional), one couplet, one triplet, several single lines (non-conventional).

Hkd. Three quatrains 232ff, 329ff, 535ff, four couplets, one triplet (conventional), three couplets, three triplets, single lines (non-conventional).

Hipp. Three quatrains, 482ff (conventional) and 267ff, 782ff (non-conventional).

And. One quatrain 421ff.

Hek. Three quatrains, 846ff, 1183ff(?) (conventional), and 722ff (non-conventional).

Hik. No quatrains.

Hks One quatrain 312ff, *Ion* one 832ff, *Tro.* one 462ff (non-conventional), *El.* one 1051ff.

IT, *Hel.*, *Pho.*, *Or.*, *Ba.*, *IA* have no quatrains.

Kyk. One quatrain 437ff.

Rhesos One quatrain 804ff.

No play of Sophocles or Euripides has more than three choric quatrains, 'and it may be added that in them couplets or triplets are at least equally frequent in contexts similar to those where quatrains are found in the *Prom.*'[134] (i.e. what I have termed 'conventional'). No play of Euripides after 413 B.C. contains a choric quatrain.

Herington argues that here (as elsewhere) we can trace a development in Aeschylus from *Pers.*, through *Oresteia*, to *Prom.* By the time of *Prom.* the preference for quatrains 'is a rigid rule to be observed on occasion, even at the cost of poetic quality', adding the note 'Most of the choric quatrains in the play are flat by Aeschylean standards.'[135]

Certain points in Herington's argument should be supplemented or corrected; other points that he ignores should perhaps be mentioned:

(a) Although A. *Ag.* with five examples of choric quatrains comes closer than any other play to *Prom.*'s figure of nine, of the four *Cho.* examples two are of a different (i.e. non-conventional) character, and the single *Eum.* example is also non-conventional. We note further that *Ag.*, with 159 (or 147) lines of spoken choric dialogue, far exceeds any other tragedy, so that the higher number of quatrains is not quite so remarkable as at first appears. If Herington's table is right to suggest that the five quatrains in *Ag.* represent almost all the 'conventional' choric utterances in the play, then the figure is indeed striking. But it seems to me that we should include 615ff (five lines), 1612ff (five lines), perhaps 489ff (fourteen lines), as well as the couplet 1399f, and triplets 317ff, 1047ff, as 'conventional'. Since *Cho.* offers only two conventional quatrains, plus one couplet and one triplet, and *Eum.* none at all, we can hardly talk of a 'development' in Aeschylus. *Ag.* is certainly much closer to *Prom.* than is any other play of Aeschylus. But is it closer than E. *Hkd.*, where we find three conventional quatrains (plus four couplets and a triplet), and, of a non-conventional type, only three couplets, three triplets and single lines in stichomythia, with no speeches of five lines or more, and far less choral involvement in the dialogue than A. *Ag.*? This brings us to our second and third points:

(b) The content of the choric iambic utterances in *Prom.* is largely conventional, and corresponds to their formal arrangement. Not only do they tend to be feeble in sense, but they are sometimes inserted only to mark a temporary, formal break between two speeches, e.g. 472ff, 819ff, 1036ff (and cf. 631ff, 782ff). The fact that every single utterance of more than one line is of the conventional type finds no parallel in tragedy. We find that Sophocles and Euripides are *more* formal and conventional than Aeschylus in their treatment of the chorus in dialogue (though they prefer the couplet to the quatrain for conventional use, i.e. dividing, introducing, or commenting on long speeches), and that Aeschylus in his later plays involves the chorus more and more in non-conventional dialogue. *Prom.*'s restriction of the chorus in dialogue to a formal and conventional function seems thus to exaggerate tendencies visible in Sophocles and Euripides in contrast to the practice of Aeschylus, particularly in his later plays.[136] This again leads us to our third point:

(c) All Aeschylus' plays contain at least one iambic or trochaic speech longer than four lines from the chorus (*Pers.* eleven lines 215ff; *Th.* six lines 677ff; *Supp.* five lines 328ff; *Ag.* fourteen lines 489ff?, six lines twice, five lines twice; *Cho.* five lines twice; *Eum.* ten lines 244ff, eight lines 299ff, and five lines 652ff), whereas Sophocles never gives the chorus more than four lines, and Euripides offers only seven examples in nineteen plays (*Alk.* 136ff five lines, *Med.* 1231ff five, *And.* 820ff five, *Hel.* 317ff thirteen, *Pho.* 280ff eight, *Or.* 1549ff five, and *Hks* 252ff twenty-three). In *Prom.* the chorus never speaks more than four consecutive lines, in its obedience to the self-imposed 'rigid rule' noticed by Herington. This is the more remarkable in view of the scarcity of other characters to converse with Prometheus. We might expect Aeschylus to give the chorus a rather greater share in the dialogue than this.

(d) Herington offers no explanation as to why Aeschylus should suddenly feel inclined to apply this rigid rule, whose limitations are obvious enough, and whose advantages seem artificial and rather pointless.[137] We saw that it was hard to trace any development in Aeschylus' extant plays (we merely find *Ag.* in a slightly exceptional position); there is certainly nothing to prepare us for the extraordinary formalism and stiffness of *Prom.*'s chorus in the dialogue.

(5) The chorus as characters in the drama

The chorus of *Prom.* are less well integrated into the drama than we would expect from Aeschylus: this much we have already seen. They have an adequate external motivation, in their connection with Prometheus through Hesione, their pre-Olympian background, and Prometheus' geographical position by the sea, so their expressions of sympathy and fear are not out of place. Yet the author seems to have chosen to allow them neither to contribute much to the drama in their lyrics,[138] nor to involve themselves at all closely with Prometheus in dialogue.[139] At the same time, he has created for himself what appear to be quite unnecessary problems, in his treatment of the chorus as characters in the drama.

(a) Why do they arrive by air? Sea nymphs would not be expected to change their environment except for a good reason. Prometheus is clearly in sight of the sea;[140] Io manages to visit him without wings ἀνὰ τὰν παραλίαν ψάμμον (573). If the chorus enter and sing their first ode above Prometheus' head,[141] this can only be because the author considered that this would make an effective spectacle. He seems in fact to have judged that the ἔκπληξις thereby achieved is worth the awkwardness of an aerial transport for marine dwellers, and of the chorus' enforced absence from the Okeanos-scene as they dismount and prepare to re-enter for the first stasimon.

(b) The chorus remain in their vehicle(s) throughout the parodos, on the *theologeion*, and are thus unable to accompany their song with dance. There is no likely parallel to this in tragedy.[142]

(c) The maidens, though they are the immortal daughters of the venerable Okeanos, seem almost human in their timorousness, and in their sympathy for Io (especially 887ff). They are fearful and ignorant, though curious to know of Prometheus and Io, their past and future. This curiosity is of course dramatically necessary, as the chorus must provide the audience for much of Prometheus' and Io's narration. So too their sympathy for the victims of Zeus' anger and apparent cruelty, tempered with criticism for Prometheus' past actions and present attitudes, is dramatically appropriate. But we are wholly unprepared for their abrupt decision (made between 1039 and 1063) voluntarily to share Prometheus' ensuing punishment. This sudden injection of courage and defiance is presumably intended to rouse the audience's sympathy still more strongly in favour of Prometheus, against Hermes and his master. But this desire for dramatic, even sensational effect, not only destroys the continuity and credibility of the chorus as characters,[143] but also plunges the author into problems of staging.[144]

(d) There is the further problem: not only does the character of the chorus as hitherto portrayed render this defiant gesture wholly unexpected and inexplicable, but the mythological tradition (and the demands of the next play?) does not allow the audience really to believe that the Okeanids suffered the fate of Prometheus. Their place is in the ἄντρων μυχός of their father, and we do not expect to hear or see anything more of them in the ensuing stages of Prometheus' quarrel with Zeus. It is hard to see *why* the author has felt it more effective to link their fate so closely with the hero's, when it would be so much simpler to disengage them, and leave Prometheus to his lonely torment, as at 88ff.

Conclusions

In sum, we find that the author seems far from consistent or confident in his treatment of the chorus. Their lyrics are short, and contain little of dramatic significance. His attempts to integrate those lyrics with the surrounding scenes are superficial and sometimes incongruous (887ff). He makes little use of the chorus in the dialogue, apart from curiously formal and conventional fill-ins, although interlocutors for Prometheus are much in demand. He seems to have tried to compensate for this overall feebleness and irrelevance of the chorus by extraordinary and unexpected twists at the beginning and end of the play (aerial entry, final defiance). We get the impression that the author had almost completed his planning and construction of the play before he considered the question of the nature and function of the chorus: they are not an integral part of his conception of the drama.

It is difficult to reconcile either this basic lack of concern for the chorus as an essential part of the drama, or the technical clumsiness of the attempts to give the chorus something to do and say to disguise their irrelevance, with our knowledge of Aeschylus' masterly use of the chorus as an integral and vital part of the dramatic whole. The treatment of the chorus in *Prom.* reminds us much more of early Euripides.

STICHOMYTHIA

The two major studies of stichomythia in tragedy[145] both find that *Prom.* diverges from Aeschylus' pattern of development[146] to a striking extent. Jens, with the precedent of Gercke, Niedzballa, Schmid etc., concluded,[147] 'Dies alles lässt den Schluss zu, dass der *Prometheus* kaum von Dichter der *Hiketiden* und der *Orestie* stammen kann.' Gross, at the beginning of the century, was more reserved in his judgement, and reminded us of Wilamowitz's warning,[148] 'Übrigens bietet jedes Drama des Aischylos Singularitäten.'

The singularities of *Prom.*'s stichomythia appear to be the following:

(1) The 2:1 arrangement of 40-81[149] has no parallel in Aeschylus or Euripides.[150] Only Sophocles employs this technique in extant tragedy, most notably at *Aj.* 791-802,[151] where the character speaking the single lines is under greater emotional stress than the other, with an effect similar to the *Prom.* passage. But all Sophocles' examples are much shorter, often occurring in the middle of more normal stichomythia; *Prom.* 40-81 is unique in its strict formal structure.

Strictness and formalism in stichomythia are characteristic of Aeschylus above all. Sophocles tends to aim at increasingly free and naturalistic dialogue. Euripides lies in between, with a tendency towards more mannered formalism in his later plays. On the rare occasions when Aeschylus abandons the strict 1:1 or 2:2 arrangement, he usually still preserves a symmetrical structure (e.g. *Pers.* 787ff; *Cho.* 479ff; *Eum.* 582ff). Only I think at *Ag.* 1307 (where Kassandra's φεῦ φεῦ has the function of a whole line), *Cho.* 766ff, 892ff (which scarcely qualifies as stichomythia), and *Eum.* 674ff[152] do we find irregular patterns. By contrast, Sophocles frequently moves from one- to two- or three-line stichomythia, without any concern for symmetry,[153] and Euripides is not always much more regular or symmetrical.[154]

Thus, although the 2:1 arrangement is uncharacteristic of Aeschylus, the strictness of its observance in *Prom.* 40-81, and the special effect thereby achieved, make it difficult to assert that the stichomythia is unaeschylean. It is really only when we observe the other irregularities of *Prom.*'s stichomythia that we feel inclined to view the technique of this passage with suspicion.

(2) The transition from two-line to one-line stichomythia, within one passage of dialogue, without interruption, is quite common in Sophocles and Euripides,[155] but not found in Aeschylus. (The nearest in Aeschylus are *Pers.* 787ff 3311122, *Cho.* 479ff 22331111 etc., and *Eum.* 582ff 331111 etc.)[156] *Prom.* 377ff 22212111 etc. and 964ff 22211212111 etc. (or perhaps 2222 1212 1111)[157] both therefore seem to be unaeschylean. Not only do we have the two-line to one-line transition in both, but we also have an irregular (and in at least one of the cases asymmetrical) pattern. *Prom.* 377ff is less regular than the usual Sophoclean or Euripidean arrangement (22221111 etc.), but similar e.g. to S. *Tr.* 383ff 22211222 1111 etc., E. *Hek.* 754ff 22121111 etc. (For *Prom.* 964ff cf. S. *Ant.* 78ff, *OT* 99ff.)[158]

The only passage in Aeschylus which we might compare to the irregularity of *Prom.* 377ff and 964ff is *Cho.* 892ff 1123135111 etc., which on paper looks an even more startling breakdown of the customary 1:1 or 2:2 responsion of stichomythia. But the peculiarities of this passage are easily accounted for by the context. From 885 to 910 no less than four characters speak, one of them (in defiance of known convention) the κωφὸν πρόσωπον Pylades: the stage is full of movement, violent action is being threatened. It is only at 908ff that true stichomythia begins. For what precedes, we may compare e.g. *Prom.* 742ff (exclamation, 211551111 etc.) or S. *El.* 1466ff (4221½½1½1½211½ 7½ 2222 etc., in almost identical context). By contrast, the two *Prom.* passages involve only two interlocutors; nothing is happening on stage; and there is no apparent reason for the unusual switches from two- to one-line utterances. We can only conclude that the author did not feel obliged to obey the rules of conventional symmetry as strictly as Aeschylus did in his extant plays.

(3) The interruption of one-line stichomythia by a two-line utterance at *Prom.* 622f is remarkable. (We may compare S. *Aj.* 74ff (twice), *Ant.* 401, *OT* 356ff, *OK* 579ff; E. *Alk.* 1126ff, *IT* 805ff, *Ba.* 1263ff.) The interruption here marks the introduction of a new topic into the debate, which is considered unaeschylean by Jens.[159]

As to the external form (111121111 etc.), we find in Aeschylus the striking passage *Cho.* 766ff 11114111 etc. (cf. E. *Hkd.* 656ff 111141111 etc.), where the chorus abandons the single-line pattern to give its vital instructions.[160] Otherwise, Aeschylus never interrupts strict one-line stichomythia.[161]

(4) *Prom.* 256. Gross remarks[162] on the not uncommon occurrence in strict single-line stichomythia of a line which interrupts the grammatical and rhetorical continuity of the previous speaker's statement, which may be resumed and completed in the next line. The interruption is generally little more than a formal observance of the 1:1 line arrangement in a context where one speaker requires two lines to express himself satisfactorily, though sometimes (especially in the less formalistic Sophocles) it also conveys a sense of impatience, excitement, or other form of πάθος in the other interlocutor.

Gross' list of examples is as follows (I bracket those I do not consider to be true examples):

A. *Pers.* (731), 735; *Th.* (806), 810;[163] (*Cho.* 530); *Eum.* 209. We should add *Cho.* 118 (not 110 or 120), 175; and *Supp.* 460, 462.

S. *Ant.* 1049; *OT* (326), 559, 1009, 1129; *Ph.* 918, 1227, 1231, 1233; *OK* 815.

E. (*Alk.* 1088); (*Med.* 337, 929); *Hipp.* 338, 340; *Hkd.* (676), 737, (795); *Hks* 714, 716; *Ion* 320, 1012, 1430; (*Tro.* 714); *IT* 1036; *El.* 564, 624, 972; *Hel.* 836, 1242, (1256); (*Or.* 439); *IA* (517), 728, (1439f). We should add *Med.* 680, *Hel.* 1238, and perhaps *Tro.* 722, 724.

It seems to me that *Prom.* 255f is of a different kind from the Aeschylus examples, and indeed from most of those of Sophocles and

Euripides. In Aeschylus the interruptions are of a delaying nature (though they may express the speaker's impatience), in that they postpone the completion of the first speaker's sentence. In the *Prom.* example on the other hand, Prometheus himself rounds off the chorus leader's sentence: he takes the words out of her mouth. His impatience leads him to accelerate the progress of the stichomythia, whereas generally Aeschylus seems to retard it in his determination to observe strict alternation of speakers. S. *Ph.* 1233, E. *Hipp.* 338 seem to me to be the nearest parallels in tragedy, in that both make a positive contribution to the sense of the previous speaker's last line; but both are still interrogative, and demand that the first speaker explain himself/herself more completely.[164]

(5) *Prom.* 980 is usually taken to be the only example of ἀντιλαβή (the sharing of one iambic trimeter or trochaic tetrameter between two or more speakers) to be found in Aeschylus.[165]

Sophocles does not use ἀντιλαβή in *Ant.* It is fairly rare in *Aj.* and *Tr.*, but occurs with increasing frequency in his later plays.[166] Euripides does not use ἀντιλαβή in *Hkd.* or *Tro.*; *Rhesos* has it only in trochaic tetrameters (where it seems always more common, in Sophocles, Euripides, and Aristophanes). In his other plays, the occurrences range from one to twenty-four.[167]

Most of the examples from the earlier plays of Sophocles and Euripides have the change of speaker at one of the two regular caesurae (more often the penthemimeral). *Prom.* 980 has therefore been suspected, and it is suggested that Prometheus may merely groan, while Hermes speaks the whole line (cf. A. *Ag.* 1306ff). But this will not do: Hermes' line (as printed e.g. in Murray) is very unnatural; τόδε is superfluous - and in what sort of voice is Hermes supposed to repeat Prometheus' groan? There are perfectly good parallels for ἀντιλαβή at this point in the line (S. *OT* 1176; E. *Hik.* 291, the latter very similar; cf. too E. *Hks* 1421, *El.* 693). I think nobody would have questioned the MSS tradition at *Prom.* 980 but for the lack of an Aeschylean parallel for ἀντιλαβή.

(6) We have already noted[168] the strict limitation of the chorus' share in the dialogue to single lines and quatrains, apart from the couplet 698f (= half a quatrain). This we found to be unparalleled in tragedy. The tendency to formalism of the chorus leader's iambic utterances is characteristic rather of Sophocles

and Euripides than of Aeschylus in his extant plays.

(One or two other points raised by Gross and Jens do not seem to amount to much. Gross[169] considered the technique of presenting narrations in stichomythia as typical of Aeschylus: he cited A. *Pers.* 232-45; *Supp.* 294-323; *Ag.* 620-35, 1202-13; *Cho.* 526-34; fr. 6. Of this kind are *Prom.* 246-58 and 757-79. But although Sophocles apparently avoids this rather artificial and formalistic mode of exposition, Gross gives as examples in Euripides *Hik.* 115-60; *Ion* 264-369, 934-70 etc., to which we could add, from early Euripides, e.g. *Med.* 663-707. Jens considered *Prom.* 246-58 unaeschylean in its further development of the subject of the previous rhesis, though he found 757-79 more regular. I do not think that there is anything very remarkable about these two passages. The author of *Prom.* was faced with a problem anyway, as to how to provide the necessary exposition and narration without monotony, and the use of stichomythia was an obvious means to this end.)

Gross gives a table[170] in which the occurrences of four different categories of stichomythia are recorded for every extant tragedy. His four categories are:

a = uninterrupted, one-line stichomythia.

b = uninterrupted, two-line stichomythia.

c = ἀντιλαβή, with regular half-lines in exchange.

d = interrupted (i.e. irregular) stichomythia.

He includes under 'a' stichomythia that is only interrupted once (so presumably A. *Cho.* 766ff; *Prom.* 615ff etc.):

A. *Pers.* 3a; *Th.* 3a; *Supp.* 6a; *Ag.* 8a 2b; *Cho.* 7a 1b; *Eum.* 6a 1b.

S. *Aj.* 5a 1b 6d; *Ant.* 9a 2b/a 3d; *OT* 2a 2a/c 1c 14d; *Tr.* 3a 1b 1b/a 6d; *El.* 4a 2b 1a/c 7d; *Ph.* 3a 1c 14d; *OK* 1a 1a/c 13d.

E. *Alk.* 7a 1d; *Med.* 4a 1b 3d; *Hkd.* 7a 1d; *Hipp.* 8a 2b 1d; *And.* 3a 3b/a; *Hek.* 5a 1b 1b/a 1a/c 2d; *Hik.* 4a 1c/a 1d; *Hks* 7a 1a/c 1d; *Ion* 6a 1b/a 3a/c 1d; *Tro.* 2a 1b 1b/a; *El.* 6a 2d; *IT* 7a 1a/c 4d; *Hel.* 7a 1b 1a/c 2d; *Pho.* 4a 2a/c 1c 3d; *Or.* 7a 2b 3a/c 2d; *Ba.* 5a 2b/a 1b 1c; *IA* 6a 1b/a 1a/c 1c 2d.[171]

Prom. 5a 3d.[172]

These figures show us at a glance what we have already noted in detail, that is the extent to which *Prom.* diverges from the strict Aeschylean norm. Whereas Aeschylus only admits 'a' and 'b' (i.e. 1:1 and 2:2 stich.), *Prom.* three times has the irregular 'd', so common in Sophocles, and not rare in Euripides. (Alternatively *Prom.* has 'd' twice, and 'b/a' once, i.e. the transition from two- to one-line stichomythia, found in two Sophocles plays, five Euripides.)

We may summarize *Prom.*'s singularities again:

(1) the 2:1 arrangement of *Prom.* 40-81; (2) the transition or alternation from two-line to one-line stichomythia at 377ff, 964ff; (3) the interruption of one-line stichomythia by a two-line utterance at 622f; (4) *Prom.* 256, with Prometheus' completion of the chorus leader's sentence; (5) ἀντιλαβή at 980; (6) the chorus' restriction to conventional quatrains and one-line stichomythia.

Of these, (1) is extraordinary, but only argues against Aeschylean authorship when taken in combination with (2) and (3), which undeniably diverge from Aeschylus' observed practice. (4) is a curious, though minor, apparently unaeschylean detail; (5) is, I feel, a weightier detail; and we have already seen that it is difficult to account for (6) from what we know of Aeschylus' style.

It seems fair to conclude that the author of *Prom.* does not observe such strict and regular patterns as Aeschylus. On the rare occasions when we see Aeschylus abandon strict single- or double-line stichomythia, it is for a purpose: but in *Prom.* the movement from one to the other has no particular dramatic point, but represents, it seems, a more naturalistic form of dialogue than we expect from Aeschylus. (2), (3), (4) and (5) may all be thought to reflect this same tendency. In that respect *Prom.*'s stichomythia has been called 'Sophoclean'. Though stricter and more formalistic generally than Sophocles, it goes quite a long way beyond the limits normally observed by Aeschylus.

At the same time, (6) represents a very artificial formalism in the treatment of the chorus in dialogue. And here we should bear in mind that in both Sophocles and Euripides, in contrast to Aeschylus, the increased flexibility of the stichomythia is accompanied by a growing conventionality in the treatment of the chorus, and a tendency to limit its role to the routine marking of the end of one character's speech, or introduction of another's, and to single-line stichomythia. Aeschylus tends to involve the chorus leader more freely in the dialogue.[173]

We may take (6) with (1) as indications of archaic formalism;

yet it is hard to deny that even these do not fit what we take to be the Aeschylean pattern. Overall, the stichomythia of *Prom.* shows distinct signs that another syle may be in evidence.

Chapter 7

STAGING

We have no stage directions for Greek tragedy, and only a very sketchy knowledge of the fifth-century conventions at Athens. It is generally agreed nowadays that the theatre of Aeschylus and Sophocles was closer to that of the Elizabethans than that of the Victorians, in requiring the audience to use its imagination rather than presenting lavish naturalistic devices. Thus when we hear Kratos' instructions to Hephaistos as to how to fetter Prometheus, we do not need to see it done; and when we hear the description of the final earthquake, we do not expect to see Prometheus sink out of sight below the ground. A few stylized gestures and offstage noises would suffice.

The two main problems of the staging of *Prom.* concern the entry and departure of (1) the chorus, and (2) Okeanos.

(1) The chorus seem to have entered above Prometheus' head, and to have remained there until he advises them to descend (272ff). The frequent references to flight (124, 128, 135, 279f), and Prometheus' ability to hear their approach (115ff) some time before he can see who they are (cf. 124ff), make this a natural assumption;[1] this is strongly confirmed by the apparent disappearance of the chorus during the Okeanos-scene,[2] whose only explanation seems to be that they are dismounting offstage.

Whether they travelled in a single huge car or on individual winged seats,[3] it is highly unlikely that any mechanism known to the fifth-century Athenian theatre could have suspended all the members of the chorus simultaneously.[4] The chorus must presumably have entered on to the *theologeion* (= the roof of the skene ?), and remained there until 283. Yet it would seem to follow from this that they cannot have danced to their lyrics (128-85): there was probably not room for much movement there, and the place for dancing was, as far as we know, the orchestra.[5] It seems to me that for a chorus to sing lyrics without dancing to the music that accompanied them would strike an Athenian audience as most irregular.

The Okeanos-scene covers the movement of the chorus from the roof, so that they can reassemble at ground level and enter the orchestra at 397. We have seen already that the Okeanos-scene is dramatically rather weak, and we cannot but ask ourselves *why* the author manoeuvres himself into a position (at 283) where such a scene is necessary, to divert the audience's attention and give Prometheus someone to talk to. The aerial entry of the Okeanids has no obvious point save that of ἔκπληξις of Prometheus and the audience. Prometheus' rock is near the sea (cf. 89, 1048ff; also 573, 583), and the Okeanids have heard the ring of the hammer (133f) from their father's home. Kratos, Bia, Hephaistos, Io, and Hermes all make their way to Prometheus without using wings; why do the sea-nymphs take to the air? It seems that the author has simply created unnecessary problems for himself through his desire to achieve a spectacular effect.

At the end of the play, too, the chorus' behaviour is strange. After their timorous expressions of sympathy (and muted criticism) for Prometheus during the play, they suddenly take up a stance of defiance against Hermes, and (1063ff) announce that they will stay by Prometheus' side and suffer his torments. Whereas it would be quite natural and normal for the chorus to look on with horror, fear and pity, as Prometheus' new punishment begins, and then to leave the orchestra (with anapaests or a lyric lament) in the usual ἔξοδος, it is difficult to see how the chorus in our play are moved from the orchestra at all, once they have announced their intention of remaining μετὰ τοῦδε (1067), and have been taken at their word by Hermes (1071ff). No *ekkuklema* could possibly withdraw both Prometheus *and* the chorus; nor do we expect the sea-nymphs actually to descend to Tartaros. So either the chorus must rush to cluster round Prometheus at the end, presenting a final tableau for the audience (after which the chorus - and the Titan? - simply walk off to prepare for the next play),[6] or their intentions are thwarted by the fury of the earthquake: they remain in the orchestra, and merely observe Prometheus' fate from nearby. In the latter case, it is hard to see why they are given 1067 to say.

(2) The chorus are still above Prometheus' head, and probably out of his sight, when they speak 277ff. His instruction to them (272) to come down to ground level, which they eagerly accept, is

followed, not by their arrival in the orchestra to 'hear the approaching fortunes' of Prometheus (272f), but by the entry of Okeanos on a 'wing-swift bird' (286), later described as 'four-legged'.[7] Were the chorus present, they would be required to greet their father (whose permission to come and visit Prometheus they had only gained with difficulty, cf. 131), and fulfil the conventional duties of a chorus in dialogue. But it is clear that the chorus do not see him.

Okeanos' references to his tame griffon would be pointless, indeed grotesque, if he were really on the ground throughout: he must be up in the air somewhere.[8] If he entered on the *theologeion*[9] (where the audience are already looking), it would be difficult for the chorus not to see him. Much more probable is the interpretation accepted by most commentators, that he was swung into view on the γέρανος. His unexpected arrival, from a different quarter and *above* the chorus, would thus distract attention from his departing daughters. (Similarly, as he flies away, he will not come into contact with the chorus as they enter by one or both *parodoi*.) The use of anapaests may be felt to support this view: they often accompany movement of a god above the stage in Euripides.

We are told (Pollux 4.130) that the γέρανος was used in Aeschylus' *Psychostasia* for Eos to collect the body of Memnon. We do not know if this is true, and if so how Pollux knew about it. If it is true, it is the only example known to us of Aeschylus' use of a μηχανή.[10] It is difficult to decide how often it was used in post-Aeschylean tragedy. Sophocles seems to have employed it little, if at all, and even in Euripides many supposed instances may merely have used the *theologeion*.[11] The Aristophanic parodies (*Peace* 1-178, *Thesm*. 1097-1134) of E. *Bellerophon* and *Andromeda* suggest that Euripides was notorious for his use of the μηχανή, but we have no idea whether other dramatists were equally free with it.[12] The rebuilding of the theatre with stone foundations may have encouraged its use.

We may conclude tentatively that the use of the μηχανή for Okeanos would be unusual for Aeschylus, though not for Euripides. Beyond this we should not go. Yet even this is interesting, in that (as with the Okeanids) there seems no real point in an aerial entry, except for sensational visual effect.[13] We know of Aeschylus' love of spectacle, even from his extant plays (e.g. the end of *Eum*., the foreign costumes of *Pers.* and *Supp.*): but it is hard to escape the feeling that in *Prom.* the spectacle is less grand, less dramatic, and that it is irrelevant to the essential action and rather self-consciously and obtrusively introduced. But this is a subjective opinion, and others may feel differently. It is probably safest to leave this aspect of *Prom.* out of our final judgement, and try to concentrate on criteria whose objective validity is more surely guaranteed.[14]

One further detail of possible significance remains to be discussed, but this too cannot be reliably interpreted. At no point in *Prom.* are more than two speaking actors required, and it is interesting that Prometheus does not utter a word as long as Kratos and Hephaistos are on stage.[15] It is often inferred from this that only two actors were in fact used, and that the play therefore must precede the institution of the third actor.[16] Yet the evidence is again insufficient for any confident conclusion to be drawn. Prometheus' opening silence may be due to dramatic preference rather than practical necessity, and the use of only two actors in the rest of the play is paralleled by Aeschylus during most of the *Oresteia*,[17] and by Euripides throughout *Medea* and *Alkestis*.[18] In general, the tragedians seem to have been fairly sparing with scenes involving all three actors fully in the dialogue, at least before 430 B.C.[19]

Unless we feel certain that *Prom.* employed only two actors, and that it should therefore be placed in the years before the third actor was introduced (probably in the 460s), we are not entitled to draw any firm conclusions about its authenticity. The avoidance of three-actor dialogue is not peculiarly Aeschylean; we may merely say that it represents another slightly archaic feature of *Prom.*'s dramatic technique.

Chapter 8

VOCABULARY

The analysis of an author's vocabulary is no straightforward task.[1] The very term 'vocabulary' is itself ambiguous and often misleading. If it is taken to denote simply the words which an author uses with various frequencies in his extant works, then we can in that sense talk of 'Aeschylus' vocabulary'. Yet nobody would claim that this vocabulary represented the total sum of words known to Aeschylus, and many words not found in his extant works must have been used in his lost plays. Indeed the whole idea of a finite, definable 'vocabulary' for any individual is mistaken, and in Greek tragedy the problem is made all the more complicated by the freedom with which the poets invented new words (usually adjectives or verbs) by combining or modifying more familiar words to suit a particular context.

Much of a playwright's vocabulary is more or less dictated to him by his subject matter. So we would expect every play to exhibit peculiarities corresponding to its content. Our aim is to distinguish between these and the truly individual peculiarities of the author, and to isolate the latter. Every play is made up of a large number of words which are used only once or a few times, and a small number which are used frequently; the occurrence, or non-occurrence, of the former is likely to be due to chance and the requirements of the subject matter. Indeed the significance of any single word is always difficult to assess, and we must take care only to pay much attention to those which are repeatedly and regularly used, and with which we can observe a definite pattern in an author's use, as measured against other authors. Douglas Young[2] has shown the inadequacies of an analysis which concentrates too narrowly on individual words; only if we have good reason to suppose that Aeschylus would not have used a particular word with great frequency will we attach any significance to its repeated occurrence in a work ascribed to him, and only if we can identify distinctive differences between Aeschylus, Sophocles, and Euripides in a particular usage will we think it profitable to see how *Prom.* fits in.

In this study I have approached the problem in three different ways.

(1) I have isolated particular types of words (i.e. different parts of speech, word-forms etc.) which Aeschylus uses more (or less) than Sophocles and/or Euripides, and I have treated these as objective criteria by which to measure *Prom.* We can thus see whether it fits with Aeschylus' pattern of preferences any better than it does with Sophocles' or Euripides'.

(2) I have drawn up figures for those words which occur in one play but not elsewhere in Aeschylus, to establish what number we might expect to find in an Aeschylean play; for comparison I also examine a play of Sophocles. This again gives us an objective criterion for judging *Prom.*, without consideration of individual words. I then go on to analyse these words in the attempt to identify those which are to be regarded as possibly significant and indicative of an individual preference on the author's part. The emphasis throughout is on numbers, not on the actual words.

(3) Only then do I look at individual words whose usage in Aeschylus is distinctively different from Sophocles and Euripides, or whose occurrence in *Prom.*, when measured against the three great tragedians, seems to be significant for our purposes.

In this way I hope that I have succeeded, as far as possible, in maintaining objective standards, which are free from the workings of chance or the subject matter of a particular play.

TYPES OF WORDS[3]

Clay's lists allow us to see at a glance if there are particular types of word which seem to be more (or less) common in one of the tragedians than in the others. In categories which include only a few words such differences are not likely to be of much use to us.[4] We should concentrate therefore on the larger categories, where it is clear that different habits can be identified in the three tragedians as to their preference for certain types of word.

The advantage of this approach is that it largely eliminates the element of chance due to the subject matter. Any study which considers individual words cannot escape this problem, i.e. the limits imposed on an author in his choice of words by the context. But a study which considers only types of word, which are seen to be used with consistently differing frequencies by the three tragedians, is likely to be a more or less objective and reliable criterion of authorship.

It is important to remember that the seven plays generally attributed to Aeschylus comprise a markedly smaller sample than the seven plays of Sophocles,[5] and far smaller than the nineteen of Euripides. When we make these necessary adjustments, we find that many of Clay's lists are, as we might expect, unhelpful: there is no apparent difference between the three tragedians.

Those lists which on a preliminary examination seemed to show significant differences were: (a) compound adjectives,[6] (b) adverbs, (c) neuter nouns with -μα suffix. In all three categories Aeschylus seemed to be represented by proportionately more words than the others, considering the smaller bulk of his work. Further investigation of my own showed this was in each case true: Aeschylus regularly uses more words of these three types than Sophocles or Euripides.[7] It seems that we have here an objective confirmation of any reader's subjective *Stilgefühl*, that Aeschylus is the leading exponent of 'high' tragic diction. Compound adjectives, adverbs, and -μα nouns (often apparently *ad hoc* creations from more familiar verbs) are all characteristic of an elevated style far removed from ordinary speech. All three of these categories are large enough to be statistically significant, and in all of them the individual plays of each author are sufficiently consistent with each other for valid conclusions to be drawn as to what is 'characteristic' of that author.

Some other categories seem to show differences between the tragedians, but are less easy to evaluate: (d) adjectives in -μων; (e) adjectives in -τεος; (f) adjectives in -ηριος; (g) verbs in -ευω; (h) *nomina agentis*. These are also studied below, together with one or two small categories which seemed possibly to be of particular interest for *Prom*.

Let us start with the three main categories in which significant differences could be observed between the tragedians.

(a) Compound Adjectives[8]

The totals of words of this category in tragedy are:

A. *Pers.* 271, *Th.* 309, *Supp.* 339, *Ag.* 455, *Cho.* 269, *Eum.* 260.
S. *Aj.* 245, *Ant.* 271, *OT* 233, *Tr.* 193, *El.* 204, *Ph.* 186, *OK* 306.
E. *Alk.* 139, *Med.* 191, *Hkd.* 110, *Hipp.* 210, *And.* 166, *Hek.* 165, *Hik.* 146, *Hks* 237, *Ion* 258, *Tro.* 173, *El.* 180, *IT* 237, *Hel.* 270, *Pho.* 306, *Or.* 252, *Ba.* 198, *IA* 213, *Kyk.* 83, *Rhesos* 159.
Prom. 276.

The figures speak for themselves (provided we continue to bear in mind the different lengths of the plays).

The lowest rate in Aeschylus is *Eum.*, 248 per 1000 lines, the highest *Supp.*, 316 per 1000.

The lowest rate in Sophocles is *Ph.*, 126 per 1000 lines, the highest *Ant.*, 200 per 1000.

The lowest rate in Euripides is *Hkd.*, 104 per 1000 lines, the highest *Pho.*, 173 per 1000.

Prom.'s rate is 247 per 1000 lines, almost level with A. *Eum.* (and cf. *Cho.* 250 per 1000, *Pers.* 252 per 1000), but significantly higher than any of the plays of Sophocles or Euripides.[9]

(b) Adverbs

There are two main categories in Clay which are of use to us: (i) adverbs in -ως (much the most common, of course); (ii) adverbs in -δα, -δην, -δον.[10] Here it is worth distinguishing between the number of occurrences and the number of separate words actually used in a play. We will see, for example, that Euripides consistently uses a smaller number of separate words than Aeschylus, but yields almost the same number of occurrences.

(i) *Adverbs in -ως: occurrences*

A. *Pers.* 40, *Th.* 35, *Supp.* 48, *Ag.* 84, *Cho.* 61, *Eum.* 59.
S. *Aj.* 43, *Ant.* 60, *OT* 85, *Tr.* 55, *El.* 75, *Ph.* 64, *OK* 59.
E. *Alk.* 48, *Med.* 86, *Hkd.* 63, *Hipp.* 54, *And.* 45, *Hek.* 59, *Hik.* 39, *Hks* 49, *Ion* 54, *Tro.* 57, *El.* 54, *IT* 50, *Hel.* 68, *Pho.* 33, *Or.* 67, *Ba.* 52, *IA* 86, *Kyk.* 23, *Rhesos* 42.
Prom. 61.

Separate adverbs

A. *Pers.* 27, *Th.* 25, *Supp.* 33, *Ag.* 50, *Cho.* 32, *Eum.* 36.
S. *Aj.* 24, *Ant.* 22, *OT* 30, *Tr.* 21, *El.* 35, *Ph.* 26, *OK* 28.
E. *Alk.* 27, *Med.* 31, *Hkd.* 24, *Hipp.* 23, *And.* 21, *Hek.* 19, *Hik.* 18, *Hks* 25, *Ion* 24, *Tro.* 28, *El.* 23, *IT* 18, *Hel.* 24, *Pho.* 18, *Or.* 27, *Ba.* 24, *IA* 37, *Kyk.* 15, *Rhesos* 29.

Prom. 37.

Aeschylus' figures are consistently higher, though there is some overlap between the lowest of Aeschylus and the highest of Sophocles and Euripides. The figures for separate adverbs seem to be of more use to us: clearly Euripides owes his highest figures for occurrences to repeated use of a few common words (e.g. E. *Med.*); the same is true to a certain extent of Sophocles (e.g. *OT*).[11] Aeschylus therefore may be said to employ a wider range of adverbs, especially when we remember the shortness of five of his plays.

The highest rate of adverbs in Sophocles is in *El.*, 23 per 1000 lines; the highest in Euripides is *Alk.*, 23 per 1000 (but n.b. *Rhesos*, 29 per 1000).

Prom. with 37 adverbs in 1093 lines, i.e. 34 per 1000, is significantly higher than Sophocles or Euripides,[12] but fits well with the Aeschylean pattern, which ranges from *Pers.*, and *Th.*, both 25 per 1000, to *Eum.*, 34 per 1000.

(ii) *Adverbs with suffix* -δα, -δην, -δον. Here again, on a much smaller scale, Aeschylus' range is greater than that of Sophocles or Euripides.

Occurrences

A. *Pers.* 9, *Th.* 1, *Supp.* 3, *Ag.* 1, *Cho.* 3, *Eum.* 2.

S. *Aj.* 2, *Ant.* 2, *OT* 2, *Tr.* 2, *El.* 1, *Ph.* 1, *OK* 1.

E. *Alk.* 1, *Med.* 0, *Hkd.* 0, *Hipp.* 0, *And.* 2, *Hek.* 1, *Hik.* 0, *Hks* 1, *Ion* 2, *Tro.* 2, *El.* 0, *IT* 0, *Hel.* 2, *Pho.* 4, *Or.* 0, *Ba.* 0, *IA* 1, *Kyk.* 0, *Rhesos* 3.

Prom. 5.

Of Euripides' nineteen occurrences, twelve are accounted for by three words (ἄρδην, ἄδην, σχεδόν); these same three also account for six of Sophocles' eleven occurrences, but only one of Aeschylus' nineteen. Aeschylus rarely uses any adverbs of this type more than once in his extant work: some of them may well be of his own invention.

In *Prom.* ἄρδην and ἄδην occur once each.[13] For what these small figures are worth, they suggest that *Prom.* again shows a wider range of adverbs than Sophocles or Euripides but similar to that of Aeschylus. But the remarkable figure for A. *Pers.* reminds us that figures of this size are liable to chance fluctuation, and should not carry much weight.

Overall, we may conclude that *Prom.* in both categories of adverbs fits squarely with Aeschylus, and exceeds the highest figures for Sophocles and Euripides.

(c) Neuter nouns with -μα suffix[14]

Occurrences

A. *Pers.* 56, *Th.* 79, *Supp.* 56, *Ag.* 107, *Cho.* 67, *Eum.* 69.

S. *Aj.* 48, *Ant.* 73, *OT* 64, *Tr.* 49, *El.* 47, *Ph.* 60, *OK* 71.

E. *Alk.* 25, *Med.* 66, *Hkd.* 40, *Hipp.* 69, *And.* 51, *Hek.* 76, *Hik.* 88, *Hks* 83, *Ion* 113, *Tro.* 63, *El.* 71, *IT* 100, *Hel.* 97, *Pho.* 114, *Or.* 104, *Ba.* 68, *IA* 92, *Kyk.* 50, *Rhesos* 37.

Prom. 86.

Separate words

A. *Pers.* 37, *Th.* 45, *Supp.* 34, *Ag.* 65, *Cho.* 45, *Eum.* 43.

S. *Aj.* 32, *Ant.* 47, *OT* 42, *Tr.* 32, *El.* 33, *Ph.* 37, *OK* 39.

E. *Alk.* 16, *Med.* 28, *Hkd.* 27, *Hipp.* 38, *And.* 33, *Hek.* 39, *Hik.* 52, *Hks* 48, *Ion* 62, *Tro.* 49, *El.* 47, *IT* 51, *Hel.* 52, *Pho.* 64, *Or.* 60, *Ba.* 44, *IA* 50, *Kyk.* 27, *Rhesos* 23.

Prom. 49.

Here the pattern is not so simple as in the first two categories. Each tragedian ranges quite widely, and they overlap with each other much more. In general, we may say that Aeschylus and Euripides regularly have rather higher figures than Sophocles.

In occurrences, Aeschylus ranges from 52 per 1000 lines (*Supp.*, *Pers.*) to 79 per 1000 (*Th.*);[15] Sophocles ranges from 31 (*El.*) to 54 per 1000 (*Ant.*); Euripides ranges from 21 (*Alk.*) to 71 per 1000 (*Kyk.*, cf. *Ion* 70);[16] *Prom.* with 79 per 1000 thus equals Aeschylus' highest, and is slightly higher than Euripides' highest, much higher than Sophocles'.

In separate words, Aeschylus ranges from 32 (*Supp.*) to 45 (*Th.*) per 1000; Sophocles ranges from 22 (*El.*) to 34 (*Ant.*) per 1000; Euripides ranges from 14 (*Alk.*) to 42 (*Hik.*) per 1000.[17] *Prom.* with 44 per 1000 again is similar to Aeschylus' highest, slightly higher than Euripides', much higher than Sophocles'.

In view of the closeness of some of Euripides' figures to those of Aeschylus, and the wide range shown by all three, we should not place too much weight on *Prom.*'s high figure; but it seems fair to conclude that in its use of suffixed -μα nouns *Prom.* fits best with Aeschylus.

From these three large categories, which contain enough occurrences to ensure that our conclusions are reasonably solidly based, we move now to other classes which are less fully represented, but which still seem to show differences between the techniques of the three tragedians.

(d) Adjectives Suffixed with -μων[18]

All the adjectives suffixed with -μων which we find in tragedy are compound, with the exceptions of τλήμων and μνήμων. Particularly in Sophocles and Euripides τλήμων is very common, its occurrences far outnumbering those for all other -μων adjectives combined. So it seems most helpful to study the figures of occurrences of compounds only, and here Aeschylus again stands out as the most frequent employer of these essentially 'poetic' adjectives.

Occurrences

A. *Pers.* 6, *Th.* 4, *Supp.* 2, *Ag.* 10, *Cho.* 2, *Eum.* 4.

S. *Aj.* 0, *Ant.* 1, *OT* 1, *Tr.* 2, *El.* 1, *Ph.* 0, *OK* 1.

E. *Alk.* 0, *Med.* 3, *Hipp.* 0, *Hkd.* 2, *And.* 2, *Hek.* 3, *Hik.* 1, *Hks* 1, *Ion* 1, *Tro.* 4, *El.* 1, *IT* 2, *Hel.* 3, *Pho.* 4, *Or.* 2, *Ba.* 0, *IA* 2, *Kyk.* 0, *Rhesos* 1.

Prom. 5.

Prom. thus has more than any play of Sophocles or Euripides.[19] Confirmation of the 'poetic' nature of these words in *Prom.* can be found if we compare the actual words of *Prom.* with those found in Sophocles. In *Prom.* we have ἱπποβάμων, νεκροδέγμων, μεγαλοσχήμων, ποικιλείμων, μαλακογνώμων; in Sophocles we find only ἱπποβάμων (*Tr.*), παντλήμων (*OT*, *El.*), πολυκτήμων (*Ant.*), ἀγνώμων (*Tr.*, *OK*), of which only the first is at all striking or original. Similarly in Euripides nine out of the thirty-two occurrences are merely ἀ-prefixed compounds. So it is difficult to know whether to class this as an indication that Aeschylus and *Prom.* used more adjectives in -μων (apart from τλήμων) than Sophocles or Euripides, or merely to conclude that here again their predilection for any compound adjectives of a striking kind is in evidence. In either case, *Prom.* again fits with Aeschylus.

(e) Adjectives in -τεος[20]

These are more common in Sophocles than in Aeschylus or Euripides:

A. *Th.* 2, *Cho.* 1, *Ag.* 1.

S. *Aj.* 8, *Ant.* 7, *OT* 6, *Tr.* 2, *El.* 4, *Ph.* 4, *OK* 4.

E. *Alk.* 1, *Med.* 2, *Hkd.* 3, *Hipp.* 3, *And.* 1, *Hek.* 1, *Hik.* 1, *Hks* 8, *Ion* 3, *Tro.* 0, *El.* 2, *IT* 6, *Hel.* 5, *Pho.* 5, *Or.* 3, *Ba.* 3, *IA* 5, *Kyk.* 2, *Rhesos* 2.

Prom. 1.

Euripides' figures should perhaps warn us against using this category at all, with their range from none to eight. We may merely conclude that *Prom.*'s single instance (συγκαλυπτέος) fits with Aeschylus and Euripides, not Sophocles.

(f) Adjectives in -ηριος[21]

Again the numbers are too small to be wholly reliable:

A. *Pers.* 2, *Th.* 7, *Supp.* 11, *Ag.* 5, *Cho.* 7, *Eum.* 6.

S. *Aj.* 2, *Ant.* 0, *OT* 4, *Tr.* 2, *El.* 6, *Ph.* 0, *OK* 3.

E. *Alk.* 1, *Med.* 1, *Hkd.* 3, *Hipp.* 2, *And.* 1, *Hek.* 2, *Hik.* 0, *Hks* 1, *Ion* 4, *Tro.* 1, *El.* 0, *IT* 1, *Hel.* 2, *Pho.* 3, *Or.* 4, *Ba.* 1, *IA* 0, *Kyk.* 0, *Rhesos* 1.

Prom. 1.

These adjectives are definitely commoner in Aeschylus than in either of the other two. *Prom.* has less than any of Aeschylus' plays (only λυμαντήριος once); but *Pers.* only has two instances. We might say merely that we would expect a few more words of this class if *Prom.* were a late play of Aeschylus.

(g) Verbs in -ευω[22]

These verbs are commoner in Euripides than in Aeschylus or Sophocles: the totals of separate words are: Aeschylus 48, Sophocles 60, Euripides 130.[23] The figures for occurrences in Aeschylus are: *Pers.* 9, *Th.* 10, *Supp.* 5, *Ag.* 15, *Cho.* 15, *Eum.* 9; cf. *Prom.* 19; and for separate words: A. *Pers.* 9, *Th.* 7, *Supp.* 4, *Ag.* 9, *Cho.* 10, *Eum.* 6; cf. *Prom.* 14.

We may feel that A. *Cho.* is close enough to *Prom.*'s figure, both for occurrences and for separate words; but the fact remains that *Prom.*'s figure is definitely higher than Aeschylus' highest. Again, though, the figures are too small to be really significant.

(h) Nomina agentis in -της, -τωρ, -τηρ[24]

According to Ernst Fraenkel, -τωρ and -τηρ forms die out during the classical period (though they survive in Doric) and leave -της as the prevalent Attic form. Tragedy, however, uses more of the -τωρ and -τηρ forms than comedy, history, oratory or inscriptions, perhaps partly because of the influence of Doric, and of epic in e.g. messenger speeches, but also 'von den Bestreben nach altertümlicher Redeweise'.

It is therefore not surprising to find that Aeschylus seems to use more of the -τωρ and -τηρ forms than Sophocles or Euripides.

Occurrences of -τηρ *(and* -τειρα*)*

A. *Pers.* 7, *Th.* 17, *Supp.* 13, *Ag.* 13, *Cho.* 12, *Eum.* 5.

S. *Aj.* 7, *Ant.* 2, *OT* 13 (only 3 separate words), *Tr.* 9, *El.* 3, *Ph.* 3, *OK* 11.

E. *Alk.* 3, *Med.* 4, *Hkd.* 9, *Hipp.* 0, *And.* 2, *Hek.* 2, *Hik.* 1, *Hks* 7, *Ion* 5, *Tro.* 3, *El.* 9, *IT* 3, *Hel.* 6, *Pho.* 2, *Or.* 1, *Ba.* 6, *IA* 5, *Kyk.* 5, *Rhesos* 3.

Prom. 6.

Occurrences of -τωρ

A. *Pers.* 6, *Th.* 6, *Supp.* 16, *Ag.* 9, *Cho.* 3, *Eum.* 11.

S. *Aj.* 3, *Ant.* 1, *OT* 2, *Tr.* 7, *El.* 6, *Ph.* 4, *OK* 3.

E. *Alk.* 0, *Med.* 6, *Hkd.* 0, *Hipp.* 4, *And.* 6, *Hek.* 3, *Hik.* 3, *Hks* 4, *Ion* 8, *Tro.* 5, *El.* 5, *IT* 4, *Hel.* 0, *Pho.* 3, *Or.* 7, *Ba.* 1, *IA* 3, *Kyk.* 0, *Rhesos* 1.

Prom. 1.

Combined totals

A. *Pers.* 13, *Th.* 23, *Supp.* 29, *Ag.* 22, *Cho.* 15, *Eum.* 16.

S. *Aj.* 10, *Ant.* 3, *OT* 15, *Tr.* 16, *El.* 9, *Ph.* 7, *OK* 14.

E. *Alk.* 3, *Med.* 10, *Hkd.* 9, *Hipp.* 4, *And.* 8, *Hek.* 5, *Hik.* 4, *Hks* 11, *Ion* 13, *Tro.* 8, *El.* 14, *IT* 7, *Hel.* 6, *Pho.* 5, *Or.* 8, *Ba.* 7, *IA* 8, *Kyk.* 5, *Rhesos* 4.

Prom. 7.

Prom.'s figures are markedly lower than Aeschylus'. We find only one -τωρ noun (οἰκήτωρ), found once in Aeschylus, five times in Sophocles, four times in Euripides, and the combined total (seven) is well below Aeschylus' lowest (*Pers.* thirteen), but typical of Sophocles or Euripides.

There does not seem to be any appreciable difference between the three tragedians in their use of -της nouns: the figures for separate words are: Aeschylus 90, Sophocles 113, Euripides 146.[25] *Prom.* with eighteen occurrences is unremarkable (cf. A. *Pers.* 21, *Th.* 34, *Supp.* 17, *Ag.* 25, *Cho.* 13, *Eum.* 29). But it is interesting to compare the ratios of the 'poetic' -τωρ, -τηρ forms to the standard Attic -της: A. *Pers.* 13:21, *Th.* 23:34, *Supp.* 29:17, *Ag.* 22:25, *Cho.* 15:13; *Eum.* 16:29. *Prom.* 7:18 stands out in its preference for the more orthodox forms: only *Pers.* and *Eum.* come anywhere near this ratio.

This discrepancy cannot be explained simply by the proportion of lyric in each play.[26] Of A. *Supp.*'s sixteen -τωρ occurrences, only seven are in lyrics; of *Eum.*'s eleven, only three; and of *Th.*'s seventeen -τηρ and -τειρα occurrences, only seven are in lyrics.

It seems, then, that whereas Aeschylus is the leading exponent of the archaizing tendency which prefers the -τωρ and -τηρ forms to the standard Attic -της, *Prom.* fits instead with the practice of Sophocles and Euripides.[27]

(j) Feminine Nouns in -συνη[28]

This category is really too small to be worth much, but it is interesting to observe that we find in Aeschylus' six plays only one such noun, in Sophocles six, in Euripides eighteen. (Aeschylus' instance is δουλοσύνη in *Th.*) *Prom.* with two examples (πημοσύνη, εὐφροσύνη once each) is thus slightly unusual.

Conclusions

We have been able to identify certain types of words which are significantly commoner in Aeschylus than in Sophocles or Euripides: the high rate of their occurrence we may describe as 'characteristic' of Aeschylus' vocabulary. In two of the largest categories (compound adjectives, adverbs) we have seen that *Prom.* fits pretty squarely with Aeschylus, and falls right outside the limits of Sophocles and Euripides; in a third large category (nouns in -μα) *Prom.* again fits with Aeschylus, and is barely compatible with Euripides, not with Sophocles. In two other small (and hence very unreliable) classes, *Prom.* again seems to fit with Aeschylus (adjectives in -μων, adjectives in -τεος), without strongly contradicting the practice of Sophocles or Euripides.

Three small categories have shown *Prom.* fitting more easily with (one or) both the other tragedians than with Aeschylus (adjectives in -ηριος, verbs in -ευω, nouns in -συνη). In one more sizeable and significant class (*nomina agentis*) *Prom.* seems to diverge quite distinctly from Aeschylus' norm, and to fit with Sophocles and Euripides.

We may feel that the broad categories 'compound adjectives', 'adverbs', are too crude to measure truly individual stylistic preferences: we have merely seen that the author of *Prom.*, like Aeschylus, in his desire for elevated and grandiose diction uses the words most effective for that purpose. The minor discrepancies between *Prom.* and Aeschylus may therefore reflect a genuine difference of style. But the correspondence between *Prom.* and Aeschylus in the three large categories is striking (and with compound adjectives we found that in the one class in which Sophocles predominated[29] *Prom.* gave a low figure, along with Aeschylus and Euripides).

We still need, of course, to investigate further the details of the vocabulary of *Prom.*, i.e. the actual words used in relation to those used by Aeschylus in his six undisputed plays. But the indications so far are that in broad outlines, where the vocabulary of *Prom.* can be measured objectively, it is to be classed as 'Aeschylean'.

EIGENWÖRTER

Some of the most impressive material assembled by Schmid concerns the vocabulary of *Prom.*, in particular those words which are found in *Prom.* but not in any of the undisputed plays of Aeschylus.[30] These he terms '*Eigenwörter*', and it is convenient to retain the term, for want of a satisfactory English equivalent.

According to Schmid,[31] *Prom.* has a much larger number of *Eigenwörter* than any of Aeschylus' six plays, in relation to their length:

A.	*Pers.*	has	474	in	1077	lines	= 44%
	Th.	"	444	"	1078	"	= 41.1%
	Supp.	"	461	"	1074	"	= 42.7%
	Ag.	"	782	"	1673	"	= 46.7%
	Cho.	"	387	"	1076	"	= 35.2%
	Eum.	"	329	"	1048	"	= 31.4%
	Prom.	"	631	"	1094	"	= 57.6%[32]

This is indeed a remarkable discrepancy. Aeschylus' figures are fairly consistent (we expect *Ag.* to be highest, since it is by far the longest play, so that the six plays which comprise the comparative 'Aeschylean' vocabulary against which to measure *Ag.* for *Eigenwörter* make up a smaller 'corpus' than do any five plays plus

Ag. itself: thus there is a greater chance that any particular word in *Ag.* will not be found in that 'corpus'. *Cho.* and *Eum.* may owe their low figures to the continuity of theme within the *Oresteia*): *Prom.* falls right outside their range.

When Schmid goes further, and claims to remove the element of chance in the occurrence of rare or specialized words, by giving figures for what he regards as *charakteristische Eigenwörter*, his figures are worthless, for his choice of 'characteristic' words (as distinct from words whose occurrence is due to chance), is far too subjective: many of his words occur only once in the play in question.

More important is his table of repeated *Eigenwörter* (which he terms *Schlagwörter*), in which *Prom.* again scores markedly higher.[33] I have revised his figures for those plays which I have studied myself, where I can see important omissions or errors:[34]

No. of Occurrences	*Pers.*	*Th.*	*Supp.*	*Ag.*	*Cho.*	*Eum.*	*Prom.*
1	430	414	433	703	371	303	554
2	33	23	17	63	12	18	47
3	4	6	6	12	4	6	18
4	5	2	3	3	0	2	8
5	0	0	0	1	0	0	2
6	1	0	0	0	0	0	1
7	0	0	0	0	0	0	2

Here again *Prom.* stands out most strikingly.

Schmid analyses the rarer of *Prom.*'s *Eigenwörter*, and distinguishes seven categories: (a) Homeric/Hesiodic words, (b) Pindaric, (c) Ionic, (d) Attic, (e) Doric, (f) Empedoklean, (g) invented words. These categories are obviously far from satisfactory (Schmid excludes from (a), for instance, words common in epic but also frequent in later Greek; and his selection of 'Ionic' words is, as we shall see, rather arbitrary), but he tries to use them to compare the *Eigenwörter* of *Prom.* with those of the other six plays. He finds that categories (b), (d), (e) and (f) reveal little to distinguish one play from another, but argues that (a), (c) and (g) all furnish significant evidence that *Prom.* is exceptional. Let us examine that evidence.

(a) Schmid finds that *Prom.* has twice as many rare epic words among its *Eigenwörter* as all the other six plays together.[35] He gives as words of Homeric/Hesiodic origin in *Prom.*:[36] ἄκικυς, απλατος, ἀτέραμνος, ἄψορρον, γαμφηλή, γέγωνα, γνάμπτω, εἰσοιχνέω, ἐπαυρίσκομαι, ἠχέτης, θήν, ἰότης, κραδαίνω, μήδεα, μήνη, μνηστήρ, νωθής, σμερδνός, στρόμβος, φλοῖσβος, φοῖβος, χερνήτης, (plus εἴβομαι, οἴω which probably do not occur in *Prom.*, and ζεύγλη, λευρός, which both are found in Aeschylus, cf. *Th.* 75?, *Supp.* 508). His total should thus be twenty-two.

We might ask, why does Schmid not include ἀκίχητος (*Il.* 17.75; *Prom.* 184), ἀλίγκιος (*Il.* 6.401, *Od.* 8.174; *Prom.* 449), γαμψῶνυξ (*Il.* 16.428, *Od.* 22.302; *Prom.* 488), πωλέομαι (Homer frequently; *Prom.* 645)? And we note that Niedzballa gives 162 *Eigenwörter* of epic origin in *Prom.* It is clear that Schmid's method of selection is individual, to say the least.

When he looks for such words in Aeschylus he finds only: A. *Pers.* δίεμαι; *Th.* κατόπτης, κόναβος, ὄτοβος; *Supp.* γανάω, ἐνώπιον, ὀπτήρ, πόρτις, ἀγός, αἶψα; *Ag.* ὀρφναῖος, ψῦχος; *Cho.* οὖθαρ; *Eum.* none, i.e. a total of thirteen.[37] Snell adds A. *Supp.* πτεροείς; *Ag.* φάσγανον; *Cho.* πλημμυρίς.[38] and it is clear that the list is far too small. I looked through the first 200 lines of A. *Th.* and found the following: βρόμος, ἀγάστονος, δουλοσύνη, γένυς, ἀγήνωρ, ἄξων, ἀμφιβαίνω, αὔω, μελάνδετος, πάταγος, ὠκύς, all of which are epic, and *Eigenwörter*. Of these eleven words, γένυς, ἄξων, ἀμφιβαίνω, ὠκύς would be regarded as too common outside Homer to be classed as 'Homeric' by Schmid - though he includes γέγωνα, κραδαίνω, στρόμβος for *Prom.* - but the other seven seem to me to have a good claim.

We must conclude, then, that Schmid's belief that there are significantly more rare epic words among *Prom.*'s *Eigenwörter* than among those of Aeschylus' plays is false. He only finds more because he looks harder for them in *Prom.*

(c) What about his third category, words which he classes as Ionic? Here again he claims that *Prom.* has an unusual number among its *Eigenwörter*: ἄρδις, δῆθεν, ἐλινύω, ἐργάτις, μασχαλιστήρ, ῥαχία, σκεθρός, ψαίρω, ψάμμος, λεωργός, διαρταμέω, ἀκρατής, ἀιστόω, ἀσχάλλω, ἀχρεῖος, δυσπετής, ἤπιος, θακέω, κομπέω, λῦμα, ὑπέροχος.[39]

(Again Schmid does not enquire how many Ionicisms occur overall: he is concerned only with *Eigenwörter*. This makes for a very limited and arbitary category.) In Aeschylus he finds only *Th.* κατοπτήρ; *Supp.* γόμος, στρέβλη; *Ag.* ἄγγαρος, σίνος, ἀτημέλητος?; *Cho.* ἔμμοτον, λίβος, ἰηλεμίστριος.

But his category of 'Ionic' seems to be too imprecise to be helpful. He counts any word which occurs in Herodotos, Hippokrates, the Presocratics etc., without further definition, and without concern for its occurrence in other, non-Ionic authors. (It is hard to see, for example, why δῆθεν is counted as 'Ionic', or ἐργάτις, ψάμμος, ῥαχία etc.) Again we must conclude that Schmid was misled by his own preconceptions into finding what simply is not there.

(g) The other category which Schmid considered interesting was that of invented words, in which he reckoned *Prom.* was glaringly deficient. Yet his own figures belie this claim (*Pers.* 14, *Th.* 22, *Supp.* 37, *Ag.* 49, *Cho.* 17, *Eum.* 23; *Prom.* 17), and in any case his definition is quite inadequate: he selects θωύσσω, τρόχις, ὀκρίς, for instance, as 'invented' words, yet omits e.g. μυδροκτυπέω, μύκημα, ἀδαμαντόδετος, δύσπλανος, συνασχαλάω. Again we are forced to conclude that his principles are unsound.

So it appears that Schmid's analysis of *Prom.*'s *Eigenwörter* is worthless. Where it tries to establish what sorts of words account for *Prom.*'s high figure, and to point to idiosyncratic preferences that contrast with Aeschylus', it falls down completely. But we have seen enough in his overall figures to encourage us to investigate for ourselves, to see, first, whether *Prom.* really *is* as remarkable for its number of *Eigenwörter* as Schmid maintains, and, secondly, if it is, whether we can find anything distinctive about the individual words or types of words that occur only in this play and not in Aeschylus, as compared with Aeschylus' normal practice.

Schmid's figures and details of *Eigenwörter* are apparently based in part on the work of Niedzballa and Peretti; but each of these has limitations inherent in his method, and they do not provide a reliable basis of evidence on which to build.[40] Both are useful, within their limits, for checking my own investigations, and for providing us with information on certain matters which I have not gone into fully. But it is clear that, if we want to establish the basic facts about *Eigenwörter*, we must investigate for ourselves, with all the advantages that Italie and more than forty years of classical scholarship have provided.

I have been through A. *Pers.* and *Th.*, *Prom.*, and S. *Aj.* 1-1090, recording all the words which do not occur in the other six plays.[41] (For A. *Pers.* and *Th.*, 'the other six plays' include *Prom.*, to give an equivalent amount of material to that available in *Prom.*'s case. The effect, of course, if *Prom.* is not Aeschylean, would be if anything to raise the number of *Eigenwörter* in those plays, since part of the corpus against which they are being measured would not itself be the product of their author. Thus the shortcomings of this method will tend to disguise any discrepancy that might exist between *Prom.* and the other plays. In the case of S. *Aj.* 1-1090, I simply took Aeschylus' six undisputed plays as the 'corpus'.)[42]

I have recorded both proper names and ordinary words, but have taken care to give the figures both with and without proper names, and it will be seen (especially with regard to A. *Pers.*) that this distinction is important and necessary.

In my lists, if an *Eigenwort* occurs more than once in its play (= Schmid's *Schlagwort*), I have recorded the number of its occurrences in parentheses next to it: thus I have been able to give figures both for separate words and for occurrences.[43]

We must be clear in our minds as to what we are investigating. There is no question of our being able to define 'Aeschylus' vocabulary', in any useful sense. Nobody has a particular 'vocabulary' of words which he knows: we all have a wide range of words which are stored in the front or back of our memory, which are likely to occur to us in particular contexts or from particular associations, or which (if we are Attic tragedians) we may invent for a suitable meaning and metrical shape. All we can measure is, which words a particular author in fact uses, in what forms, and how often. We cannot pretend that this is his 'vocabulary': we can, however, compare it with the words, forms, and frequencies of other authors, or we can analyse the range of words within his own works, to try to determine which words seem to be more prominent in his mind than in the mind of another author, or which words he does *not* seem to use much, or at all, in contrast to other authors. At every step we have to remember that a large proportion of the words an author uses are not really his choice, but are more or less dictated to him by the meaning he wants to convey. Only if consistent patterns emerge from within one author's work, as compared with that of another author, will we be confident that a trait of his 'vocabulary' has been identified.

For our purposes, we want to see how many words in a genuinely Aeschylean play do not occur in the other extant Aeschylean plays. The study of S. *Aj.* will help us to see whether this aspect of a play is a valid criterion of Aeschylean authorship, and to evaluate the figures for *Prom.* in relation to the other plays. If possible, we would like to know about the repeated occurrence of these *Eigenwörter* in a particular play: here we might have evidence of a characteristic preference for a particular word, in contrast to its absence from Aeschylus' 'corpus'. Again, the comparison of each of Aeschylus' plays with S. *Aj.* 1-1090 will give us some idea of how much is likely to be due to chance and the exigencies of context, and how much to individual preference.

From my lists I added up: (a) the total number of *Eigenwörter*, subdivided into proper names and ordinary words; (b) the numbers of occurrences of *Eigenwörter* (again subdivided); (c) the number of *Eigenwörter* which occur more than once in their play.[44] At this point, when all three categories revealed markedly higher figures for *Prom.* than for Aeschylus' two plays, it seemed well worth trying to analyse category (c) as systematically as possible, in an attempt to separate those words whose occurrence we might regard as due to chance and the context (i.e. to the fact that a particular context would demand a particular word, and this context would not be expected to crop up elsewhere, so that the word's absence from the other six plays is not remarkable) from words whose repeated occurrence we might regard as 'significant', i.e. as reflecting a stylistic preference of the author. Here, of course, our chief concern is to find genuinely objective criteria: to a reasonable degree, I believe that this has been possible.

I listed the repeated *Eigenwörter* in alphabetical order for each play,[45] together with the number of their occurrences. There was obviously no point in considering any of the *Eigenwörter* which merely occur once as 'significant': for this reason too I marked those words which are merely repeated in refrain or ritual anaphora, and therefore not to be regarded as truly repeated, let alone 'significant'.

In selecting 'significant' words, it seemed best to exclude: (i) the words mentioned above (repeated in refrain, etc.); (ii) all proper names,[46] since their confinement to one play is due largely to the particular demands of the plot, not the author's personal preference; (iii) words which are only repeated within 100 lines of one play, and do not occur anywhere else in that play or Aeschylus' work. It is a commonly observable (and observed)[47] feature of any author's style that, once a word has been used, it is quite likely to be used again soon. The word remains in the front of his mind, and once it has occurred to him, he may well use it two or three times close together, even with different meanings. He may then never use the word again, or not for a long time: the word returns to a more remote corner of his mind, whence perhaps it will only be recalled in a particular context. This tendency is noticeably strong in the Greek tragedians, and it is exaggerated by such a technique as stichomythia, where one speaker will echo the other's words intentionally. I therefore set aside those repeated words which only occur within 100 lines of each other. This is of course an arbitrary and unsatisfactory criterion, since the process at work (the tendency to repeat words close together) is much more imprecise and unpredictable. But I have applied the criterion consistently to all the plays, and I think it removes many words whose repeated occurrence is in no way 'significant'.[48]

(iv) It is also necessary to remove those words whose occurrence is due solely to their specialized sense, and which would only ever be used in a particular context: these too are not characteristic of an author's style, but depend on the situation. Here the element of subjectivity becomes dangerous. My criterion for exclusion is fairly crude: if the peculiar sense of an *Eigenwort* is such that, in my view, not more than one of the other six plays provides a context in which that word could be thought at all likely to occur, then I do not count that word as 'significant'. (Here the extreme examples are easy to isolate: e.g. ἐμβολή found four times in A. *Pers.*, not in the other six plays; its special sense, a 'ramming' of two ships, limits its possible occurrence - we find it twice in Thucydides, in the description of the battle in Syracuse harbour (7.36, 7.70); others are less straightforward, e.g. ἐπεγγελάω and ἐπιχαίρω in S. *Aj.*; how often does a context occur in Aeschylus where these words could be used?) Because the selection here is so subjective, I have taken care to list all the words included and excluded on this criterion (sometimes with my special reasons), so that the reader may compare my selection with his own, and modify his judgement accordingly. I am confident, again, that I have been consistent, and, if anything, over-cautious in omitting possibly 'significant' words from *Prom.*'s list.[49] Although individual selections would vary slightly, I do not think that the final figures for each play would be materially affected.

After excluding all words to which any of these criteria apply, we are left with our lists of what I have termed 'significant' words. By this I mean words which occur at least twice, in widely separated passages, in one play, but nowhere in the other six plays; which are not of narrowly limited and specialized sense; and which therefore may be thought to reflect a personal preference of the author of that play which appears to diverge from that of Aeschylus. Obviously, for an Aeschylean play, 'significant' words turn out to be insignificant, in that their occurrence does *not*, in fact, reveal that another mind is at work: what we want to know is, whether the plays of Aeschylus produce similar figures for this category,[50] and, if so, how *Prom.* and S. *Aj.* 1-1090 compare with them.

Let us see, then, what results this method produces. Table 7 gives the figures for (a) numbers of *Eigenwörter*, (b) occurrences of *Eigenwörter*, (c) repeated *Eigenwörter*.

TABLE 7. *Eigenwörter*

	A. *Pers.*	*Th.*[51]	*Prom.*	S. *Aj.* 1-1090
(a) *Number of words*				
all words	610	516	690	506
proper names	127	47	37	27
ordinary words	483	469	653	479
(b) *Total of occurrences*				
all words	827(801)[52]	625	871	618
proper names	256	94	63	54
ordinary words	571(545)	531	808	564

(c) *Number of repeated words*

all words	96(86)	66	105	64
proper names	36	14	9	8
ordinary words	60(50)	52	96	56

We see from this table that (as we suspected from our preliminary examination) *Prom.*'s figures are markedly higher than those of A. *Pers.* and *Th.* - and we remember that these two plays appear from Schmid's figures to be higher than Aeschylus' average.

The enormous number of proper names in A. *Pers.* inflates its figures for 'all words', so that they are not much smaller than *Prom.*'s. But when we look at 'ordinary words', we find that *Pers.* and *Th.* tally quite well, while *Prom.* stands alone. (S. *Aj.* 1-1090 stands with A. *Pers.* and *Th.*: this is interesting and reminds us that we do not here have an infallible indication of authorship, in that its vocabulary is not demonstrably unaeschylean on these criteria.) For ordinary words alone, the figures speak for themselves: (a) number of words A. *Pers.* 483, *Th.* 469, S. *Aj.* 479, *Prom.* 653; (b) occurrences A. *Pers.* 571 (545),[53] *Th.* 531, S. *Aj.* 564, *Prom.* 808; (c) repeated words A. *Pers.* 60 (50), *Th.* 52, S. *Aj.* 56, *Prom.* 96.

Prom.'s vocabulary seems by these criteria to be unusual. Whether we can describe it as unaeschylean is a different matter. A. *Pers.* also has an unusual vocabulary, with its exceptionally large number of proper names. But whereas we are constantly aware of the occurrence of these impressive names in *Pers.*, and can appreciate the imaginative and dramatic point of their inclusion, with *Prom.* the case is different. The ordinary reader of *Prom.* does not notice an unusual number of strange words, or words which he feels to be 'foreign' to Aeschylus (anymore than he does in reading S. *Aj.*). Yet the figures clearly indicate that *Prom.* does contain many more words which Aeschylus does not use in his extant plays than the other plays we have examined.

We have seen in our earlier section on 'types of words' that *Prom.* contains a large number of compound adjectives, many of them rarely found elsewhere in Greek literature. We might expect a high proportion of any play's *Eigenwörter* to be taken up by compound adjectives: does this account for *Prom.*'s high numbers of *Eigen-*

wörter? Checking through the lists, I found that *Prom.* contained 180 compound adjectives among its 653 'ordinary' *Eigenwörter*, A. *Pers.* 170 out of 483, *Th.* 181 out of 469,[54] S. *Aj.* 134 out of 479. *Prom.*'s proportion of compound adjectives is in fact lower than *Pers.* or *Th.*, similar to S. *Aj.*: A. *Pers.* 35%, *Th.* 38%,[55] *Prom.* 28%, S. *Aj.* 28%. Clearly *Prom.*'s high figures are not simply due to a greater preference for unusual 'poetic' adjectives. Nor in fact would we expect them to be. Almost every reader of *Prom.* who is at all familiar with Aeschylus tends to feel that the language of this play is less high-flown and 'poetic'.

We may conclude then that *Prom.*'s vocabulary appears to be unaeschylean in containing so many words which do not occur in Aeschylus' extant plays, and that there is no obvious explanation for this anomaly.[56] The extent of the divergence from Aeschylus' norm suggests that the figures may be really significant.

To find out whether this divergence is significant, and reflects a difference between our author's preferences and those of Aeschylus, or whether it merely results from chance and the demands of the plot, our best policy seems now to be to analyse (c), ('repeated *Eigenwörter*'), and to try to determine whether *Prom.* and S. *Aj.* are in any way unusual by Aeschylean standards. Here we are dealing with words that are used more than once, where an author's own preferences are likely to begin to reveal themselves. I have already outlined my method of analysis: the results are tabulated in Table 8.

TABLE 8. *Repeated Eigenwörter*

	A. *Pers.*	*Th.*[57]	*Prom.*	S. *Aj.* 1-1090
All words	96(86)	66	105	64
proper names	36	14	9	8
ordinary words	60(50)	52	96	56
'Significant' words[58]	20	14	67	40
'Significant' words occurring more than twice	5[59]	2	28	11

From the table we see at once that *Prom.* and S. *Aj.* 1-1090 contain far more words which I class as 'significant' than do A. *Pers.* and *Th.*: *Prom.* 67, S. *Aj.* 40, A. *Pers.* 20, *Th.* 14.

It is essential that we check as carefully as possible that our criteria are genuinely fair and objective, and have been consistently applied. The complete lists of repeated *Eigenwörter* are given for all four plays in Appendix J below; those words whose repetitions are due to refrain, etc. are bracketed; those which occur only within 100 lines of each other are marked with an asterisk.

To select the 'significant' words out of these lists, I removed: (i) those words due to refrain etc. (10 in *Pers.*, 3 in *Th.*, 1 in *Prom.*, 0 in *Aj.*); (ii) all proper names[60] (36 in *Pers.*, 14 in *Th.*, 9 in *Prom.*, 8 in *Aj.*); (iii) words only repeated within 100 lines (19 in *Pers.*, 15 in *Th.*, 15 in *Prom.*, 7 in *Aj.*).

This leaves us with the following figures: A. *Pers.* 31, *Th.* 34, *Prom.* 80, S. *Aj.* 49.

At this point we may refer to Peretti's lists for A. *Supp.*, *Cho.*, and *Eum.* (His figures for A. *Pers.* and *Prom.* do not coincide exactly with mine, and, as I have pointed out,[61] his method has serious faults; but his figures are not so misleading as to be useless.)[62] I therefore include in Appendix K the lists of repeated *Eigenwörter* which I have compiled for A. *Supp.*, *Cho.* and *Eum.* from Peretti. (He does not give proper names. I omit words listed by Peretti but occurring in *Prom.*, and repetitions from refrain etc.) When we deduct the words repeated only within 100 lines (marked with an asterisk), the figures for these plays are: A. *Supp.* 18, *Cho.* 15, *Eum.* 17.

It may well be that, by my criteria, a few more words would be found for these three plays. But it seems that we were right to concentrate on A. *Pers.* and *Th.*, as representing Aeschylus' highest figures. (*Ag.*, as we have noted, is difficult because of its length, but does not seem to be exceptional.)

Up to this point our criteria of selection for 'significant' words have been purely objective; but we now come to the final process, (iv) the removal of those words whose specialized sense renders them unlikely to be used elsewhere.[63] Here an element of subjectivity is inescapable. I have been through the lists of Appendices J and K many times, trying to guarantee a fair approach: even so, I am conscious that no two investigators would make exactly the same choice in every case. Nevertheless, I am sure that the overall figures would not differ very much, certainly not enough to explain the high figures of *Prom.* and S. *Aj.* 1-1090.

The words which I decided were too specialized in sense to be 'significant' are:

A. *Pers.* ἀντίδουπος, ἐμβολή, ἰσόθεος, κόρυμβος, πάμμεικτος, πεζός, περίκλυστος, στῖφος, τοξοδάμας, τοξουλκός, τρίσκαλμος,[64] i.e. eleven words out of thirty-one.

Th. ἀντηρέτης, ἀντιτάσσω, αὐτοκτόνος, δορίπονος, ἔξοδος, ἐπακτός, ἱππικός, κατόπτης, κοιλογάστωρ, κυκλόω, ὁπλίτης, πάταγος, πρόβλημα, προσμηχανάομαι, πύλωμα, πυργηρέομαι, πύργωμα, συνίσταμαι, φρύαγμα, χνόη,[65] i.e. twenty words out of thirty-four.

Prom. ἀδαμαντόδετος, αὐθάδης, αὐθαδία, δύσπλανος, ἐνζεύγνυμι, μαλθακίζω, ὀχμάζω, πλανάω, πλάνη, προὐξεπίσταμαι, σφάκελος, φάραγξ, φλογωπός,[66] i.e. thirteen words out of eighty.

S. *Aj.* 1-1090 ἄδωρος, ἐπεγγελάω, ἐπιχαίρω, εὔκερως, κίων, λειά, νεόρραντος, νεοσφαγής, σύνδετος,[67] i.e. nine words out of forty-nine.

And for the other plays:

A. *Supp.* διωγμός, ἐφάπτωρ, λευκοστεφής, πόρτις, πρόξενος,[68] i.e. five words out of eighteen.

Cho. ἀνταποκτείνω, μαστός,[69] i.e. two words out of fifteen.

Eum. ἄοινος, βουλευτήριον, διαιρέω, μητροκτονέω, μητρῷος, πρεσβῦτις,[70] i.e. six words out of seventeen.

When these are deducted from their respective plays, we are left with our 'significant' words, for which the figures are: A. *Pers.* 20 or 18,[71] *Th.* 14, *Supp.* 13, *Cho.* 13, *Eum.* 11; *Prom.* 67 (66); S. *Aj.* 40.

These 'significant' words are:

A. *Pers.* Ἀθῆναι (8), ἄρδω (2), διαίνω (4), δύσθροος (3), ἐκπρεπής (2), ἐκφθίνω (2), ἐνύπνιον (2), εὐτυχῶς (2), ἐφέπω (2), θησαυρός (2), καταφθείρω (4), λόγχη (3), πραΰνω (2), προσπίτνω (2), στυφελός (2), ὑπαντιάζω (3), σαφηνής (2), πρόσφθογγος (2), [? ἄνιος (6), ὀᾶ (6)].[72]

Th. ἀψυχία (2), βρόμος (2), ἔξωθεν (2), ἐπαλαλάζω (2), εὔεδρος (2), θύραθεν (2), κάκη (3), καχλάζω (2), πανδάκρυτος (2), πόμπιμος (2), πρόδρομος (2), πρυμνόθεν (2), σπουδή (3), συνάγω (2).

Supp. ἀγός (2), ἀφίκτωρ (2), βούλαρχος (2), βοῦνις (3), ἐπίπνοια (4), ἐσμός (3), ἐκδίδωμι (4), ἐξοπλίζω (3), ἐπιχώριος (2), κινητήριος (2), πίναξ (2), σχολάζω (2), ὑψόθεν (2).
Cho. ἀπεύχετος (2), ἀφίστημι (3), γέλως (2), ἔγκοτος (3), ἐξαυδάομαι (2), θρεπτήριος (2), καρανόω (2), κήδειος (3), λυγρός (2), μάομαι (2), προσφέρω (2), σκοτεινός (2), συγγίγνομαι (3).
Eum. ἀδικέω (3), ἄμομφος (3), ἀντίκεντρον (2), ἐπικτάομαι (2), ἐφέρπω (3), καθιππάζομαι (4), νεβρός (2), ὅρκωμα (2), ποιμαίνω (2), προσέρχομαι (2), προσίκτωρ (2).
Prom. ἀεικής (4), ἆθλος (6), αἰκεία (3), αἰνικτηρίως (2), ἀίσσω (2), ἀσθενής (3), ἀτέραμνος (2), γεγωνῶ (7), γύης (2), ? δάμαρ (3), δαρόν (2), δῆθεν (2), διάδοχος (2), δουλεύω (2), δωρεά (2), δωρέομαι (2), εἰκῆι (2), εἱλίσσω (3), ἐκδιδάσκω (2), ἐκπίπτω (5), ἐλαφρός (3), ἐλινύω (2), ἐμπλέκω (2), ἐξαρτύω (2), ἐξευρίσκω (4), ἐπαναγκάζω (2), ἐπιθωύσσω (2), ἐρεθίζω (2), ἔσχατος (3), ἐφήμερος (3), ζητέω (3), θέαμα (2), θεόσυτος (3), ἴδιος (2), καίτοι (4), λίαν (2), λιπαρέω (2), λωφάω (3), μισέω (2), νοσέω (4), νόσημα (3), οἶμος (2), ὀξύστομος (2), παντελῶς (2), παπταίνω (2), πέρα (3), πορεία (3), προθυμέομαι (3), προσέρπω (2), προσλαμβάνω (2), προσπέτομαι (3), προσχρηίζω (2), σκεθρῶς (2), σόφισμα (3), σοφιστής (2), συγκάμνω (2), συνασχαλάω (3), ταλαίπωρος (3), ταπεινός (2), τεκμαίρω (2), τηλουρός (2), ὑποπτήσσω (2), χειμάζομαι (2), χόλος (4), χρίω (4), χροία (2), ὠφέλημα (3).

S. *Aj.* 1-1090 αἰκίζω (4), ἀίσσω (3), ἀνιάω (3), ἀνόητος (2), ἄρρητος (2), ἀρτίως (6), δειλία (2), δῆλος (2), δορίληπτος (2), δρασείω (2), δύσμορος (6), ἐγκονέω (2), εἰσακούω (2), ἐναλλάσσω (2), ἐξανύω (2), ἐξίστημι (2), ἕσπερος (3), ζητέω (2), ἥδομαι (2), ἡνίκα (3), θακέω (2), καίτοι (5), καταμελέω (2), κοιμίζω (2), λυπέω (5), λώβη (2), μισέω (2), μῶρος (2), νοσέω (6), νύκτωρ (2), ὁθούνεκα (3), πάνδημος (2), περίφαντος (2), προσλεύσσω (2), προσμολεῖν (2), σύναιμος (2), σύντροφος (2), ὑποστενάζω (2), φαεννός (2), χόλος (2).

It seems clear that Aeschylus' five plays produce quite consistent figures for their 'significant' words, ranging between eleven and twenty (or eighteen). *Prom.* and S. *Aj.* 1-1090 fall far outside this range. It appears that not only does *Prom.* have markedly more *Eigenwörter* overall than Aeschylus' plays, but this discrepancy is greatly increased when we narrow the field down to those words we feel to be most significant, i.e. those indicating possible personal preferences of the author. Particularly striking is the fact that S. *Aj.* 1-1090, which in terms of total *Eigenwörter* fitted with Aeschylus' plays, really emerges here as being unaeschylean, with more than twice as many significant words as any Aeschylean play. This gives us quite strong grounds for interpreting *Prom.*'s even larger figures as unmistakable evidence that its vocabulary is in some respects unlike the vocabulary of Aeschylus' surviving plays.

There does not seem to be much to be gained by an individual examination of all the repeated *Eigenwörter* or 'significant' words.[73] But it is worth looking briefly at those 'significant' words which occur more than twice:

A. *Pers.* Ἀθῆναι (8), δύσθροος (3), καταφθείρω (4), λόγχη (3), ὑπαντιάζω (3).
Th. κάκη (3), σπουδή (3).
Supp. βοῦνις (3), ἐπίπνοια (4), ἑσμός (3), ἐκδίδωμι (4), ἐξοπλίζω (3).
Cho. ἀφίστημι (3), ἔγκοτος (3), κήδειος (3), συγγίγνομαι (3).
Eum. ἀδικέω (3), ἄμομφος (3), ἐφέρπω (3), καθιππάζομαι (4).
Prom. ἀεικής (4), ἆθλος (6), αἰκεία (3), ἀσθενής (3), γεγωνέω etc. (7), ? δάμαρ (3), εἱλίσσω (3), ἐκπίπτω (5), ἐλαφρός (3), ἐξευρίσκω (4), ἔσχατος (3), ἐφήμερος (3), ζητέω (3), θεόσυτος (3), καίτοι (4), λωφάω (3), νοσέω (4), νόσημα (3), πέρα (3), πορεία (3), προθυμέομαι (3), προσπέτομαι (3), σόφισμα (3), συναχαλάω (3), ταλαίπωρος (3), χόλος (4), χρίω (4), ὠφέλημα (3).
S. *Aj.* αἰκίζω (4), ἀίσσω (3), ἀνιάω (3), ἀρτίως (6), δύσμορος (6), ἕσπερος (3), ἡνίκα (3), καίτοι (5), λυπέω (5), νοσέω (6), ὁθούνεκα (3).

The totals are: A. *Pers.* 5, *Th.* 2, *Supp.* 5, *Cho.* 4, *Eum.* 4; *Prom.* 28 (27); S. *Aj.* 11.

A few of these words are found in the fragments of Aeschylus:[74] of *Prom.*'s twenty-eight words, four are found there. This does not surprise us, and does not demand any reconsideration of our conclusions. It would be absurd to argue that e.g. ἐκπίπτω was 'not in Aeschylus' vocabulary', simply because it is not found in his extant work. We merely observe that he does not seem to use it much.

The same applies to ἆθλος, which we find once in Aeschylus' fragments; we know that Aeschylus could have used it at any time. But in six plays he never does, whereas Sophocles uses it four times in seven plays, and the author of *Prom.* six times in one play. We must always think in terms of frequencies and probabilities, not a finite, determined 'vocabulary'.

What most strikes us in this list of words, apart from *Prom.*'s very much larger number, is the high proportion in *Prom.* and S. *Aj.* of quite ordinary words. Many of Aeschylus' words only just escape exclusion for being too specialized in meaning (e.g. ὑπαντιάζω, δύσθροος, ἑσμός, βοῦνις, ἐπίπνοια, ἐξοπλίζω, ἔγκοτος, ἄμομφος, καθιππάζομαι, i.e. nine out of twenty): only ἀδικέω, σπουδή, ἐκδίδωμι, ἀφίστημι and συγγίγνομαι seem as 'ordinary' as *Prom.*'s ἀσθενής, ἐκπίπτω, ἐλαφρός, ἐξευρίσκω, ἔσχατος, ζητέω, καίτοι, νοσέω, νόσημα, προθυμέομαι, χόλος; or S. *Aj.* ἀίσσω, ἀρτίως, ἕσπερος, ἡνίκα, ὁθούνεκα, λυπέω (and καίτοι, νοσέω).

This impression is confirmed if we consult Ellendt's *Lexicon Sophocleum*. Of the twenty words from Aeschylus' five plays, only eight occur in Sophocles (Ἀθῆναι, ἀφίστημι, ἀδικέω, ἐκδίδωμι, καταφθείρω, λόγχη, σπουδή, συγγίγνομαι), and only one in S. *Aj.* 1-1090 (σπουδή). Of *Prom.*'s twenty-eight words, nineteen occur in Sophocles, nine in S. *Aj.* 1-1090. Similarly, of S. *Aj.*'s eleven words, six occur in *Prom.* (αἰκίζω, ἀίσσω, ἕσπερος, καίτοι, νοσέω, ὁθούνεκα), four of them more than once.

One final check confirms that *Prom.* seems to have no more in common with Aeschylus' vocabulary than with S. *Aj.* 1-1090. I have recorded those words which occur only in *Prom.* and one other play (*Pers.*, *Th.*, or S. *Aj.*) and nowhere else in Aeschylus.[75] The figures are: A. *Pers.* 52 (plus four proper names), *Th.* 33 (plus one proper name), S. *Aj.* (1-1090) 62. There is no sign here that the Aeschylean plays have any affinity with *Prom.*; in fact S. *Aj.* seems to coincide more often, especially when we remember that A. *Pers.* has more *Eigenwörter* for its size than the other Aeschylean plays, which probably come nearer to *Th.*'s figure.

Conclusions

(a) We have seen that Schmid was right to maintain that *Prom.* contains markedly more *Eigenwörter* than we would expect from a play of

Aeschylus.

(b) Of these words *Prom.* also contains a much larger number of occurrences, if we exclude proper names.[76]

(c) *Prom.* also contains a much larger number of repeated *Eigenwörter*. Even more striking are the figures for words which are to be classed, by my criteria, as 'significant'. Here A. *Pers.* and *Th.* are shown to be higher than the Aeschylean norm, but to be far outstripped both by *Prom.* and by S. *Aj.* 1-1090.

In assessing the validity and importance of these conclusions, we must of course make what use we can of our comparative model, S. *Aj.* 1-1090. Here we have a play certainly not written by Aeschylus: how does it compare with one of his plays in its relation to the Aeschylean 'corpus' of vocabulary? How does it compare with *Prom.*? The answer, as we saw, is not as clear as we might like; in numbers and occurrences of *Eigenwörter*, S. *Aj.*, while yielding figures as high as any in Aeschylus, does not exceed his limits (and is markedly lower than *Prom.*). Only when we come to repeated *Eigenwörter*, and above all 'significant' words, does S. *Aj.* emerge as being quite different from Aeschylus' plays, though still less different than *Prom.*

We noted further that there is, if anything, a closer link between *Prom.* and S. *Aj.* than between *Prom.* and any one play of Aeschylus. Both *Prom.* and S. *Aj.* contain several words which are used more than twice, and which occur quite frequently in Sophocles and elsewhere, but never occur in Aeschylus, words of quite an ordinary nature. This is not true of any of Aeschylus' plays.[77]

All in all, it does seem that the author of *Prom.* displays certain preferences in his vocabulary which do not coincide with those we are accustomed to finding in Aeschylus. The evidence is impressive: the direction in which it points is unmistakable. The vocabulary of *Prom.* appears by this criterion to be unaeschylean.

INDIVIDUAL WORDS

We have looked at some of the types of words used in *Prom.*, and at the overall numbers of words peculiar to it (*Eigenwörter*). It remains now to look at individual words of interest which may help us to see how far *Prom.* resembles the six undisputed plays of Aeschylus in its choice and usage of words.

Isolated occurrences in *Prom.* of words not found in Aeschylus are unlikely to be of use to us, unless they are in some way extraordinary in their own right. What we are looking for above all are words which are distinctively Aeschylean or unaeschylean. An ordinary word, of non-specialized sense, occurring much more frequently in Sophocles and Euripides than in Aeschylus, can be said to be distinctive: we can then see how it is used, if at all, in *Prom.* A word favoured by Aeschylus but more or less neglected by Sophocles and Euripides is of equal interest. But we must always remember that the language of Greek tragedy is highly stylized, and the vocabulary shared to a surprising degree by all three tragedians; that every play of every author will contain words which its author does not use elsewhere in his extant work; that the context may sometimes virtually dictate to an author his choice or usage of words; and that the surviving works of Greek tragedy are a meagre, and possibly unrepresentative, sample of the total corpus: in particular, we have no comparative material for authors contemporary with Aeschylus.

Nevertheless, some very interesting details emerge from this study.[78] I have divided them into three broad categories: in the first I place details of sufficient independent weight to affect our judgement as to the authenticity of *Prom.*; in the second, details which may well reflect a distinctive preference of the author of *Prom.*, but which are not certain enough to bear much weight; and in the third details which are not really striking enough to affect our judgement, but which, if we were sure that Aeschylus was not the author of *Prom.*, we might describe as distinctly unaeschylean in a minor degree; then I list a few details which we might describe as Aeschylean if we were sure that Aeschylus *was* the author.

In the first category we should consider the following:

(a) χόλος

Prom. 29, 199, 370, 376; not in Aeschylus; Sophocles five times; Euripides twelve times.

We find ὀργή as 'anger, rage' seven times in Aeschylus,[79] never in *Prom.*; κότος twenty-four times in Aeschylus, μῆνις nine times; neither occurs in *Prom.*

(b) αἰκεία *etc.*

αἰκεία *Prom.* 93, 177, 601; not in Aeschylus; Sophocles four times; Euripides once.

ἀεικής *Prom.* 97, 472, 525, 1042; Aeschylus ? fr. 279 L-J (Pap. Oxy. 2164.1.9); Sophocles twice; Euripides once.

αἴκισμα *Prom.* 989; not in Aeschylus or Sophocles; once in Euripides.

αἰκιζομαι *Prom.* 168, 195, 227, 256; Aeschylus only fr. 286.15 L-J; Sophocles nine times; Euripides twice.

These words are obviously suited to Prometheus' particular situation, but they could easily be used in other plays (cf. S. *El.*): there may be a legalistic ring from the Athenian courts.[80]

(c) νόσος *etc.*

Disease imagery is quite common in Aeschylus,[81] as in Sophocles and Euripides. But it is curious that *Prom.* has so many explicit uses of the word νόσος and its derivatives, as opposed to the more allusive, metaphorical language generally used by Aeschylus:

νόσος *Prom.* 249, 384, 473, 478, 483, 597, 606, 632, 924, 977, 1069 (= eleven times); the word occurs in Aeschylus fourteen times; in Sophocles forty-seven (seventeen in *Ph.*); in Euripides over fifty times.

νοσέω *Prom.* 378, 384, 698, 978 (= four times); not in Aeschylus; twenty-nine times in Sophocles; about fifty times in Euripides.

νόσημα *Prom.* 225, 685, 978 (= three times); not in Aeschylus; five times in Sophocles; five times in Euripides.

(d) ζητέω

Prom. 262, 316, 776; not in Aeschylus; nine times in Sophocles; thirty-one in Euripides.

This seems to be rather a prosaic little word;[82] it occurs about fifty times in Aristophanes, but seems to be beneath Aeschylus' dignity.

(e) προθυμέομαι

Prom. 381, 630, 786; not in Aeschylus; once in Sophocles (*Tr.* 1119); twice in Euripides (*Hek.* 564, *Pho.* 1709); Thucydides fourteen times; Herodotos nine. And n.b. προθυμία *Prom.* 341; not in Aeschylus (but cf. προθύμως *Ag.* 1591); four times in Sophocles; twenty-three times in Euripides; fifteen in Herodotos; twenty in Thucydides.

(πρόθυμος occurs twice in Sophocles, about thirty times in Euripides, and often in Herodotos and Thucydides.)

Again, perhaps, these words were felt to be rather prosaic?

(f) ταλαίπωρος

Prom. 231, 315, 596, 623; not in Aeschylus; seven times in Sophocles; thirty-three times in Euripides. (τάλας occurs twenty-seven times in Aeschylus; six times in *Prom.*; about eighty times in Sophocles; and about 225 times in Euripides.) A word obviously suited to many tragic contexts, but not used by Aeschylus in six plays.

(g) λίαν

Prom. 123, 1031; not in Aeschylus; twice in Sophocles; thirty-three times or more in Euripides.[83] Aeschylus has κάρτα thirty-one times; Sophocles eighteen times; Euripides fifteen (not later than *Tro.*): it does not occur in *Prom.* It seems that κάρτα is the 'higher', more poetic word; it is rare in comedy and Attic prose.

(h) χρῄζω

Prom. 233, 245, 374, 609, 701, 738, 928, 984 (= eight times); Aeschylus four times (*Pers.* 283; *Cho.* 340, 530, 815); Sophocles thirty-seven; Euripides seventy-five. *Prom.* also has προσχρῄζω twice (641, 787): not in Aeschylus, six times in Sophocles. This word is thus common in Sophocles and Euripides, rare in Aeschylus, and in view of its unspecialized sense may be regarded as distinctive.

(i) Particles

As Herington says, 'the classical Greek particle, in any hands, is the most delicate of all linguistic phenomena'. He argues from this that 'one would almost predict that an Aeschylean tragedy of eccentric content and tone, such as *Prom.*, would show a correspondingly eccentric choice and deployment of particles'.[84] This seems to me to be true only to a limited degree. We might expect a few 'eccentric' usages to suit the context of a particular play, but in general I think we would find that for any one author, the choice and deployment of particles are pretty consistent, though they may differ markedly from those of another author. The particles, because they are so delicate, are a valuable criterion for measuring an author's style, for the very reason that they are *not* dictated by the context, but reflect the author's own more or less unconscious preferences.[85]

Before we examine individual particles in *Prom.*, it is worth looking at the whole range of particles, to see whether an Aeschylean pattern can be identified, against which *Prom.* can be measured.

Herington and Musurillo are both concerned solely with the use in *Prom.* of particles and combinations of particles which are rare or non-existent in Aeschylus. Some of these will be dealt with below. But neither examines the more common particles: Musurillo indeed misleadingly remarks that 'the statistics of Aeschylus' use of ἀλλά, ἄρα, ἆρα, γάρ, γε, δή, μέν, νῦν, οὕτως reveal nothing of significance for our investigation', without giving any figures. If he had given them, he would have given the lie to this statement, and saved me a lot of time and trouble.

Both Herington and Musurillo include in their studies[86] words which clearly should not qualify as particles. I have limited myself to such words as are dealt with by Denniston as particles, and have made no distinction between different usages of the same particle in compiling my table. This method, though crude, gives consistent results. It was sometimes difficult to decide whether to count a particle-combination as one or two words (e.g. καίτοι, τοίνυν). I have usually treated it as a single word if it is normally written as such, but I have not been able to be wholly consistent (καίπερ is particularly awkward, as the περ is sometimes separate).

Particles are particularly vulnerable to omission, corruption, or insertion in the tradition; about half the entry for γε in Italie is in square brackets. But it is surprising how seldom genuine doubt exists as to an occurrence, certainly not often enough to affect the overall figures significantly. I have simply followed Italie: where his entry is in square brackets I do not count it; where it is followed by a question mark my decision to include or exclude depends on Murray's text, an arbitrary but consistently applied criterion.

The figures for S. *Aj.* 1-1090, *OT* 1-1085, E. *Med*, 1-1080, *Hek.* 1-1108 and *Rhesos* were obtained by going through those plays and recording all the particles which occur: Ellendt's *Lexicon* and Allen and Italie's *Concordance* are unfortunately not so complete as Italie's *Index Aeschyleus*. But even Italie does not record all the occurrences of δέ and καί in Aeschylus, so here too I had to compile my own figures.[87]

TABLE 9. *Particles*

	Aesch.							Soph.		Eur.		
	Pers.	*Th.*[88]	*Supp.*	*Ag.* (1-1090)	*Cho.*	*Eum.*	*Prom.*	*Aj.*	*OT*	*Med.*	*Hek.*	*Rhes.*
ἀλλά	25	15	18	27(8)	26	22	33	51	60	54	39	31
ἄρα	5	3	0	1(1)	3	0	2	7	0	3	2	2
ἆρα	2	1	0	1(0)	3	3	1	6	7	1	5	3
ἀτάρ	1	0	0	0(0)	0	0	2	0	1	3	2	0
γάρ	59	40	34	92(59)	63	64	76	82	105	92	58	72
γε	16	10	12	21(10)	15	5	34	26	62	25	23	16
γοῦν	0	0	0	2(1)	0	0	0	1	2	1	0	1
δέ	195	201	188	323(218)	206	194	167	126	175	190	181	180
δή	16	8	9	13(6)	14	9	21	17	10	13	16	10
δῆδεν	0	0	0	0(0)	0	0	2	0	0	0	0	1
δήποτε	0	0	0	1(1)	0	0	0	1	0	0	0	0
δήπου	0	0	0	0(0)	0	0	1	0	1	0	0	0
δῆτα	2	8	4	4(1)	3	2	5	12	17	7	11	6
ἦ	6	8	2	13(5)	6	8	13	11	13	5	3	9
ἠδέ	12	1	0	1(1)	0	2	0	0	0	0	1	0
θήν	0	0	0	0(0)	0	0	1	0	0	0	0	0
καί	140	128	122	159(103)	142	159	121	184	187	182	122	150
καίπερ	0	1	0	1(0)	0	3	5	2	0	0	1	2
καίτοι	0	0	0	0(0)	0	0	4	5	2	3	0	4
μέν	43	20	31	63(46)	35	29	34	41	52	52	44	32
μέντοι	1	3	1	4(4)	0	1	5	3	2	4	3	1
μήν	5	7	3	9(3)	5	4	9	5	9	1	5	15
μῶν	0	0	1	1(0)	1	0	0	1	0	4	2	3
οὔκουν	0	0	1	0(0)	0	1	5	2	5	1	3	0
οὐκοῦν	0	2	1	0(0)	0	0	0	0	1	0	0	1
οὖν	3	5	9	16(12)	13	8	7	10	21	7	11	11
περ	1	1	2	3(2)	1	0	0	0	1	1	0	0
που	2	1	1	3(3)	0	0	5	9	2	1	0	0
τε	85	43	55	66(49)	55	50	70	56	75	76	107	48
τοι	9	10	13	16(13)	9	9	8	12	3	5	3	5
τοίγαρ	3	1	3	0(0)	1	2	0	2	0	3	0	0
τοίνυν	0	1	1	0(0)	1	0	1	1	2	0	0	0
TOTAL	631	518	511	840(546)	602	575	632	673	815	734	642	603

The results of my investigation are presented in Table 9. The figures for Sophocles and Euripides are directly comparable with

Prom., as they are taken from the first 1100 or so lines of each play. *Rhesos* is slightly shorter, with only 996 lines. Only in the case of A. *Ag.* do we have to make allowances for the size of the sample, as the play is half as long again as the other Aeschylean plays and *Prom.*; so I give in brackets the figures for *Ag.* 1-1090 too.

From the table it is immediately obvious that the occurrence of particles in Aeschylus is generally rather lower than in Sophocles and Euripides. When we look a little closer, we see that the discrepancy is much more clearly revealed if we leave out of the reckoning the three particles which are most common and colourless, δέ, καί and τε. In particular, Aeschylus' fondness for δέ tends to disguise his relative lack of the more uncommon particles. If we discount those three, we are left with the following figures:

A. *Pers.* 211, *Th.* 146, *Supp.* 146, *Ag.* 292 (176), *Cho.* 199, *Eum.* 172.
S. *Aj.* 307, *OT* 378.
E. *Med.* 286, *Hek.* 232; *Rhesos* 225.
Prom. 276.

The message is clear: Sophocles, and to a lesser extent Euripides, employ particles more freely than Aeschylus; and *Prom.* fits squarely with Euripides, almost with Sophocles, rather than with Aeschylus. Before we go on to examine these figures in detail, we should pause to look at the three most commonplace particles, to see how *Prom.* compares with Aeschylus, in the light of his predilection for δέ. In its figures for τε and καί *Prom.* is unremarkable, fitting with all three tragedians. But in the case of δέ its figure is rather smaller than that of any of Aeschylus' plays, fitting better with Sophocles and Euripides. It might be argued that Aeschylus' low figures for particles in general, but high figures for δέ in particular, are due to the relatively large proportion of lyric in his plays. In lyrics δέ is frequently used with no real force beyond that of connection. Thus *Prom.*'s higher overall figure, and low figure for δέ, could be taken as being due to the relative lack of lyric in the play. But in fact the figures for δέ in lyric (including anapaests) and in dialogue do not bear this out: A. *Pers.* 63 in anapaests and lyric, as against 133 in dialogue, *Th.* 91 and 110, *Supp.* 104 and 84, *Ag.* (1-1090) 107 and 111, *Cho.* 94 and 112, *Eum.* 60 and 134; for *Prom.* the ratio is 42 to 125. Thus the proportion of occurrences more or less corresponds to the proportion of lyrics in each case. The rate of δέ in Aeschylean dialogue ranges from one per 4.1 lines (*Pers.*) to one per 5.7 (*Supp.*); in *Prom.* it is one per 6.2 lines: cf. S. *Aj.* one per 7.5, *OT* one per 5.5.

Much more striking and distinctive, however, are *Prom.*'s figures for the less commonplace particles, ἀλλά, γάρ, γε, δή, δῆθεν, ἦ, καίπερ, καίτοι, μέντοι, μήν, οὔκουν and που: in each case *Prom.* exceeds Aeschylus' highest figure. The most remarkable detail of all is the occurrence of γε:[89] *Prom.* with thirty-four instances gives a rate more than twice as high as Aeschylus' highest (*Pers.* sixteen). Sophocles' range (*Aj.* twenty-six, *OT* sixty-two) warns us not to expect absolute consistency within one author, though *OT*'s figure may be due in part to the abundance of subtle stichomythia in that play. But Aeschylus appears to be fairly consistent, and *Prom.* falls far outside his range, much further than can be explained by its greater proportion of spoken dialogue.

Some of the other particles are discussed by Schmid, Musurillo and Herington.[90] Especially worthy of note are:

καίτοι: *Prom.* four times; not in Aeschylus; S. *Aj.* five times, *Ant.* four, *OT* twice etc.; E. *Alk.* twice, *Med.* three times, *Rhesos* four times etc.

που (not local): *Prom.* five times; seven times in all Aeschylus; S. *Aj.* 1-1090 nine, *Ant.* three times, *OT* twice; not very common in Euripides, e.g. *Med.* 1-1080 once (cf. 1171, 1308); *Hek.* twice (1124, 1285); *Rhesos* never.

οὔκουν: *Prom.* five times; only twice in Aeschylus; S. *Aj.* twice, *Ant.* four times, *OT* five times etc.; E. *Alk.* three times, *Med.* once, *Hek.* three times. οὔκουν ... γε occurs three times in *Prom.*, never in Aeschylus, eight times in Sophocles, thirteen in Euripides.

οὐ/μὴ δῆτα: *Prom.* three times; not in Aeschylus; fourteen times in Sophocles; about thirty times in Euripides.

δῆθεν: *Prom.* twice; not in Aeschylus; once in Sophocles; seven times in Euripides.

θήν: *Prom.* once; never again in tragedy: apparently an epic or Doric word.

ἀτάρ: *Prom.* twice; once in Aeschylus; three times in Sophocles; thirty-four times in Euripides.

But equally impressive are some of the figures for the commoner particles, which previous scholars appear to have ignored:

ἀλλά: *Prom.* thirty-three times; Aeschylus' highest rate is *Cho.* twenty-six; Sophocles and Euripides range from thirty-nine to sixty, cf. *Rhesos* thirty-one.

γάρ: *Prom.* seventy-six times: Aeschylus ranges from thirty-four to sixty-four times in samples of this size; cf. S. *Aj.* 82, *OT* 105; E. *Med.* 92, *Hek.* 58, *Rhesos* 72.

δή: *Prom.* twenty-one times; Aeschylus' highest is *Pers.* sixteen; cf. S. *Aj.* 1-1090 seventeen times, *OT* 1-1085 ten times; E. *Med.* 1-1080 thirteen, *Hek.* 1-1108 sixteen times.

ἦ: *Prom.* thirteen times; A. *Ag.* has thirteen instances in more lines, otherwise his highest is eight (*Th.* and *Cho.*); cf. S. *Aj.* 1-1090 eleven, *OT* 1-1085 thirteen times; E. *Med.* 1-1080 five, *Alk.* eleven, *Hek.* three times; *Rhesos* nine times.

μήν: *Prom.* nine times; A. *Ag.* nine times (only three in the first 1090 lines), otherwise between three and seven; S. *OT* nine times; cf. E. *Alk.* fourteen times; *Rhesos* fifteen.

In general, then, we may conclude that *Prom.* exceeds Aeschylus' figures in just those areas where one or both of the other tragedians also exceed them. By contrast, the particles which are remarkable in one only of Aeschylus' six plays are *not* common outside Aeschylus. There are not many of them: Herington's list[91] of particles found in one play of Aeschylus but not in the others, and of particles markedly more frequent in one, is very short:

A. *Ag.* γοῦν two or three times; otherwise in Aeschylus only fr. 266?; eleven times in Sophocles; once in E. *Alk.*, twice in E. *Med.*, not in *Hek.*, once in *Rhesos* etc.

δήποτε once; nowhere else in Aeschylus; S. *Aj.* once, not in *OT*; not in E. *Med.*, *Hek.*, or *Rhesos*.

Pers. ἠδέ twelve times; four times elsewhere in Aeschylus, once or twice in Sophocles;[92] three times in all Euripides. We should add here *Pers.*'s remarkable figure of eighty-five for τε. These two particles alone account for *Pers.*' slightly higher total figure for particles than the rest of Aeschylus, and the reason is not far to seek. The long catalogues of places and heroes, strung together with these simple connective particles, have an almost epic flavour, and perform a special dramatic function. No such obvious explanation is at hand for *Prom.*'s consistently higher figures for the subtler particles

Herington admits that his evidence is 'somewhat random;[93] but it is eloquent enough in its absence to indicate that no play of Aeschylus displays any collection of discrepancies comparable to that of *Prom.*[94] As we saw, Aeschylus' practice is pretty consistent for the more common particles, and even in minor details he rarely does anything to surprise us in just one play. It seems that *Prom.* simply presents us with another style, in which particles in general are more freely used than in Aeschylus, and in which individual details reveal a different range of preferences.

We come now to our second category of interesting details, those not decisive enough to bear much weight, but still indicative of a distinctive preference on the author's part.

(a) κέαρ *etc.*

Prom. 165, 184, 245, 379, 390, 437, 590 (i.e. seven times); in Aeschylus only seven times (*Th.* 287; *Supp.* 784; *Ag.* 11, 592, 997; *Cho.* 26, 410); in Sophocles five times; in Euripides three; three times in Pindar; cf. Ar. *Ach.* 5: κῆρ is common in Homer.

Aeschylus has καρδία thirty-two times, *Prom.* only once; Sophocles five times; Euripides about thirty-five times.

Aeschylus has φρήν about 100 times, *Prom.* thirteen; Sophocles about sixty; Euripides about 150.

In *Prom.* κέαρ is usually limiting, and separated from the person (e.g. an internal accusative): so 245, 437; 165, 184, 379, 590.

Of Aeschylus' seven instances, between four and six have κέαρ as subject, so that it virtually stands for the person (*Th.* 287; *Supp.* 784; *Ag.* 11; *Cho.* 26; plus perhaps *Ag.* 592, 997); only *Cho.* 410 seems similar to the *Prom.* examples, and even here it is subject of a passive verb.

(b) γεγωνέω/γεγωνίσκω

Prom. 193, 523, 627, 657, 784, 787, 820, 990 (i.e. eight times); not in Aeschylus;[95] twice in Sophocles (*Ph.* 238, *OK* 213); six times in Euripides. This *Lieblingswort* of *Prom.* is obviously appropriate to Prometheus' position, set apart and remote from the chorus and the other characters. γεγων- always retains a sense of loudness (though 657 only means 'speaks out'), and is rare in Sophocles and Euripides, as in Aeschylus. Thus its frequency in *Prom.* could be due simply to the context; yet it is hard not to feel the author's preference at work too.

(c) σήμαινε, *etc. = 'tell, inform'*

Prom. 295, 564, 618, 684, 763 (no further occurrences of σημαίνω). Aeschylus uses σημαίνω eight times; of these, five or six mean 'show by signs' (*Pers.* 819; *Ag.* 26?, 293, 497, 969; *Cho.* 667); only *Pers.* 479 and *Supp.* 245 have it as 'tell, inform'. None of Aeschylus' examples are imperative.[96] Sophocles has 'tell' sixteen times, eight in imperative (*Aj.* 688; *OT* 1050; *Tr.* 345, 598; *El.* 1294; *Ph.* 22; *OK* 51, 1532; cf. fr. 91.2); only twice as 'show by signs'. Euripides frequently has 'tell', seventeen times in the imperative. Again *Prom.*'s context helps to explain this usage; but the evidence from Sophocles and Euripides suggests that a detail of style is also to be identified here.

(d) μάτην

Prom. 36, 44, 293, 342, 447, 504, 824, 1001, 1007 (i.e. nine times); twelve times in Aeschylus (*Pers.* two, *Ag.* three, *Cho.* five, *Eum.* two); twenty-four in Sophocles; about forty-five in Euripides. There is no parallel in Aeschylus or Sophocles for *Prom.* 44 μή πόνει μάτην, 342 μάτην ... ἐμοὶ πονήσεις; but cf. E. *Med.* 1261; *Hkd.* 448, 616; *Hks* 501, 576; *Tro.* 760; *Hel.* 603; *Ba.* 626; *IA* 353.

(e) τραχύς

Prom. 35, 186, 311, 324, 726, 1048 (i.e. six times); only twice in Aeschylus (*Ag.* 1421; Pap. Oxy. 2164.1.27?; cf. *Th.* 1044); in Sophocles only fr. 278; in Euripides only *Med.* 447, frs. 702, 1083.

The word occurs ten times in Pindar, and quite often in prose. It is of course particularly appropriate to the context; but its repeated occurrence is still interesting.

(f) χειμάζομαι

Prom. 563, 838; not in Aeschylus; four times in Sophocles (three of them metaphorical, as in *Prom.*); three times in Euripides (all metaphorical). χειμών, χειμάζομαι were technical medical terms,[97] and their metaphorical usage in *Prom.* is quite striking.

(g) ἵνα = *'where'*

Prom. 21, 725, 793, 830 (i.e. four times); in Aeschylus only *Th.* 754, *Supp.* 351 (plus frs. 192.5, 195.2, 196.3, from Π. Λυόμενος); thirty times in Sophocles; sixty-eight times in Euripides.

(h) πέρα *etc.*

Prom. 30, 507 πέρα; 247 περαιτέρω; neither occurs in Aeschylus; Sophocles has πέρα nineteen times, περαιτέρω twice; Euripides eleven and four times, respectively. (For *Prom.* 30, 507, cf. S. *El.* 521; E. *Hik.* 745.)

(i) ἔστε

Prom. 376, 457, 656, 697, 792 (i.e. five times); in Aeschylus only once (*Eum.* 449); five times each in Sophocles and Euripides.

The context (i.e. Prometheus' references to the future), helps to explain this unusual detail; but 457, 656 refer to the past, and 697 is very conventional.

(j) παντελῶς, πάντως *etc.*

πάντως *Prom.* 16, 333, 636, 943, 1053 (i.e. five times, three of them with οὐ); in Aeschylus four times (*Pers.* 689; *Th.* 117; *Eum.* 726, 995; never with οὐ); in Sophocles twice (*Aj.* 1068; *OK* 1779); in Euripides about thirteen times (once with οὐ, *Hipp.* 1062).

παντελῶς *Prom.* 440, 911; not in Aeschylus; twice in Sophocles (*OT* 669; fr. 572); not in Euripides. Aeschylus seems to prefer other words or phrases:

πάνυ: Aeschylus three times; Sophocles twice; Euripides once; *Prom.* never.

τὸ πᾶν, εἰς τὸ πᾶν: Aeschylus eighteen times; Sophocles once (*El.* 1009); Euripides three times; *Prom.* once (215).

εἰς τὰ πάντα: Aeschylus twice? (see Italie); Sophocles twelve times; Euripides about six; *Prom.* never.

Prom. fits much better with Sophocles and Euripides overall than with the distinctive preferences of Aeschylus.

We come now to our third category, those details which are not really striking enough to affect our judgement on *Prom.*'s authenticity, but which may nevertheless be regarded as interesting:

(a) φέρε: *Prom.* 294, 544; not in Aeschylus; eleven times in Sophocles; about twenty-five in Euripides. Aeschylus has ἄγε five times, Sophocles four, Euripides fourteen times.

(b) ἐνταῦθα, ἐνθένδε *etc.*

ἐνταῦθα: *Prom.* 82, 203, 638, 848 (i.e. four times); twice in Aeschylus; Sophocles seventeen; Euripides twenty-eight.

ἐνθένδε: *Prom.* 707; not in Aeschylus; seven times in Sophocles; twenty-one in Euripides.

On the other hand n.b. ἐνθάδε, not in *Prom.*, only four times in Aeschylus, but twenty-nine times in Sophocles, about seventy-five times in Euripides.

ἐντεῦθεν: *Prom.* 836; three times in Aeschylus; four in Sophocles; thirteen in Euripides.

ἔνθα: *Prom.* four times; about fourteen in Aeschylus;[98] thirty-seven in Sophocles; about sixty-five in Euripides.

ἔνθεν: *Prom.* once; six times in Aeschylus; eight in Sophocles; nineteen in Euripides.

Little of real substance emerges. If ἐνταῦθα, ἐνθένδε and ἔνθα are unaeschylean, the absence of ἐνθάδε is Aeschylean.

(c) δεῖ: *Prom.* four times; Aeschylus fifteen times, never in *Pers.* or *Th.*; Sophocles about seventy; Euripides about 250. Herington suggests that this is evidence for a late Aeschylean date for *Prom.*, but it does not help us in our authorship problem.

(d) ἄκων: *Prom.* six times; Aeschylus four times (three in *Supp.*); Sophocles sixteen; Euripides nineteen times.

(e) νῦν δέ = *'but as it is'*: *Prom.* 157, 755; Aeschylus only *Ag.* 1030.

(f) ἀίσσω *etc.*: *Prom.* 676, 837 ἀίσσω; 134 διαίσσω; 146 προσαίσσω (i.e. four instances in all); only three times in Aeschylus; fourteen in Sophocles; thirty-four in Euripides.

(g) ὅμως: twenty times in Aeschylus, not in *Prom.*

(h) οὔτοι: twenty-six times in Aeschylus (sixteen in *Oresteia*, not in *Pers.*); not in *Prom.*

(i) θωΰσσω *etc.*: *Prom.* 73, 277 ἐπιθωΰσσω; *Prom.* 393, 1041 θωΰσσω (i.e. four instances); in Aeschylus only once (*Ag.* 893); three times in Sophocles; six in Euripides. Again a word used of loud noises; perhaps the context is responsible.

(j) δάμαρ: *Prom.* 560, 767, 834; in Aeschylus the word is only found in fr. 383 and ? *Ag.* 1495=1519 (with special point, cf. δαμάζω); nine times in Sophocles; about a hundred in Euripides.

(k) δέρκομαι *etc.*: δέρκομαι *Prom.* 54, 93, 140, 304, 539, 546, 679, 843 (i.e. eight times); προσδέρκομαι *Prom.* 53, 796, 903; προδέρκομαι *Prom.* 248 (i.e. another four instances); in Aeschylus only thirteen times in any form; in Sophocles sixteen; in Euripides about forty-five.

The context obviously emphasizes Prometheus' humiliating position, exposed to view (cf. εἰσοράω, θεωρία, θέαμα etc.). But *Prom.* 53, 54, 248, 546, 679, 796, 843, 903 do not refer to Prometheus' position: it seems that the author just likes the words.

Furthermore, Aeschylus seems never to have a direct external object after δέρκομαι: *Prom.* has one five times (53, 93, 140, 248, 546).[99]

Prom. four times has the aorist form ἐδέρχθην, which is not found in Aeschylus (ἔδρακον three times), in Sophocles three times, in Euripides never.

(ℓ) πρὸς βίαν: *Prom.* 208, 353, 592, 672 (i.e. four times); in Aeschylus only once (*Ag.* 876, cf. *Ag.* 130); ten times in Sophocles; fifteen in Euripides (four in *Hkd.*). βίαι is not uncommon in Aeschylus and Euripides; three times in *Prom.*; only once in Sophocles.

(m) αὖτε: at least once in every Aeschylean play (*Ag.* five times); not in *Prom.*; only twice in Sophocles; not in Euripides.[100]

(n) ταύτηι: *Prom.* 189, 511; not in Aeschylus.

(o) παρών *etc. (de rebus praesentibus)*: *Prom.* 26, 47, 98, 271, 314, 321, 375, 392, 471, 971, 1000 (i.e. eleven times); only twice in Aeschylus (*Pers.* 330, 843; cf. *Pers.* 825; *Cho.* 699; *Eum.* 864); twenty-two times in Sophocles; about twenty-five in Euripides. In *Prom.* the high figure is partly due to the context; but n.b. Sophocles' figures (e.g. *Ph.* five, *El.* seven).

(p) Several more words owe their repeated occurrence in *Prom.* to the unusual requirements of the context (e.g. πλάνη, τύραννος, ὠφελέω).[101] Others seem less easily accounted for in this way; they are worth recording even though their frequency may in many cases not be due to the author's own choice:

ἆθλος: *Prom.* six times; Aeschylus twice; Sophocles and Euripides four times each.

εἰσοράω: *Prom.* thirteen times; Aeschylus eight, Sophocles sixty-five, Euripides about 170 times.

ἐκμανθάνω: *Prom.* five times; Aeschylus twice?, Sophocles twenty-one, Euripides seventeen times.

ἐξευρίσκω: *Prom.* four times; not in Aeschylus; Sophocles eight, Euripides about twenty times.

μορφή: *Prom.* six times; Aeschylus four, Sophocles seven, Euripides about thirty times.

πημονή: *Prom.* ten times; Aeschylus six, Sophocles eight, Euripides six times.

σόφισμα: *Prom.* three times; not in Aeschylus; once in Sophocles, eleven times in Euripides.

In all these cases, the word is common enough in Sophocles and/or Euripides to show that *Prom.*'s context is by no means unique. N.b. too:

θάλπω (+ compounds): *Prom.* four times; not in Aeschylus; five times in Sophocles, once in Euripides.

φυγγάνω (+ compound): *Prom.* twice; not in Aeschylus or Euripides, once in Sophocles.

μαλθακίζω: *Prom.* twice; not in Aeschylus or Sophocles, once in Euripides.

σοφιστής: *Prom.* twice; once in Aeschylus in a different sense (fr. 314); Sophocles once or twice in fragments; Euripides six times.

σκεθρῶς: *Prom.* twice; not in Aeschylus or Sophocles; Euripides only fr. 87.

From a study of the individual adverbs of Aeschylus and *Prom.* we find that the numbers are too small for any reliable conclusions to be drawn: each of the plays naturally has its minor peculiarities. We might observe (apart from πάντως, παντελῶς, λίαν, μάτην, αὖτε, ταύτηι, mentioned above), that ὅμως never occurs in *Prom.*, whereas its occurrence in Aeschylus ranges from twice in *Supp.* and *Eum.* to six times in *Pers.*; that ῥαιδίως and ἀκριβῶς occur in *Prom.*, but not in Aeschylus. But we need only compare, for instance, A. *Ag.* with the other plays to find similar discrepancies: φίλως four times in *Ag.*, not elsewhere in Aeschylus; βεβαίως, καιρίως (each twice), εὐμενῶς and δυστυχῶς do not occur elsewhere. Similarly, only *Supp.* does not have any instance of κακῶς, only *Th.* no instance of τορῶς. So too in Sophocles, καλῶς occurs only once in *Ph.*, four times in *Aj.*, otherwise never less than nine times; κακῶς occurs twenty-two times in E. *Med.*, only twice in *Ion*.

Words which only occur once in *Prom.* are unlikely to be significant, as the element of chance is so strong; but one or two are remarkable enough (like θήν) to command our attention. We might note:

ὀλέκω: *Prom.* 564, an epic word, found in tragedy only at S. *Ant.* 1285, *Tr.* 1013.

λεωργός: *Prom.* 5; ionic, vulgar?, not elsewhere in tragedy.[102]

πέργαμα: *Prom.* 956; not in Aeschylus; four times in Sophocles (always of Troy); fifteen times in Euripides (mostly of Troy).

εὐηθία: *Prom.* 383; not in Aeschylus or Sophocles; E. *Hipp.* 639, fr. 904; sophistic? cf. Thucydides.

ὁθούνεκα: *Prom.* 330; not in Aeschylus; Sophocles seventeen, Euripides six times.

But each play of Aeschylus doubtless contains similar little peculiarities; the same applies to Sophocles and Euripides. We could balance these *Prom.* examples with a few minor 'Aeschyleanisms', e.g. τορῶς four times; Aeschylus nine times; not in Sophocles; Euripides only *Ion* 696, and *Rhesos* three times; ματάω *Prom.* 57; Aeschylus twice; not in Sophocles or Euripides; three times in Homer.

In its use of verbs meaning 'to do' etc., *Prom.* fits with Aeschylus:

ποιέω: once in *Prom.*; four times in Aeschylus; forty-seven in Sophocles; thirty-seven in Euripides (e.g. *Med.* twice, *Hipp.* never).

δράω: *Prom.* four times; Aeschylus twenty-two;[103] Sophocles fifty-two (e.g. *Aj.* eight, *Ant.* five); Euripides over 300.

πράσσω: *Prom.* seven times; Aeschylus fifty-nine times; Sophocles about eighty; Euripides slightly less often than δράω. But for each of these *Prom.* is paralleled either in Sophocles or in Euripides.

The observation[104] that πλῆθος occurs eleven times in A. *Pers.*, and only once elsewhere in Aeschylus, has frequently been seized on by scholars who have been embarrassed by *Prom.*'s apparently unaeschylean vocabulary. Undoubtedly there are other quite ordinary words with markedly greater (or smaller) frequency in one play than in the other five, just as there are in Sophocles and Euripides; we saw a few examples in our study of repeated *Eigenwörter*,[105] but there we noticed that very few really ordinary words were peculiar to one play of Aeschylus, unlike *Prom.* (and S. *Aj.*). Our best guide to the 'ordinariness' of a word is its occurrences in other authors, and we should attach more significance to the repeated occurrence of a word unused by Aeschylus but common in Sophocles and Euripides, than we would if the word were rare in all three.

In the case of πλῆθος, we may observe first, that its sense limits its usage to contexts where masses (probably of people) are being referred to; in Aeschylus only *Pers.* and *Supp.* are very likely candidates,[106] plus perhaps *Th.* 1-250; and secondly, that the word is rare in tragedy anyway (eight times in Sophocles, twenty in Euripides, i.e. about once per play).

Some of the words I have listed above may be felt to fall into the same category as πλῆθος: e.g. γεγωνέω, τραχύς, θωΰσσω. But most of them strike us particularly because they are so ordinary: we are slightly surprised to find that Aeschylus seems not to have used them; e.g. in the first category (a) χόλος, (c) νόσος etc., (d) ζητέω, (e) προθυμέομαι, (f) ταλαίπωρος, (g) λίαν, (h) χρῄζω, (i) καίτοι, οὔκουν, δῆθεν, οὐ ... δῆτα, cf. the fondness for γε; in the second (a) κέαρ, (c) σήμαινε, (d) μάτην, (g) ἵνα = 'where',

(h) πέρα, (i) ἔστε, (j) πάντως, παντελῶς; and in the third (k) δέρκομαι, (ℓ) πρὸς βίαν, (n) ταύτηι, (o) παρῶν etc., (p) εἰσοράω.

All in all, it is clear that *Prom.* offers very many more serious discrepancies in its choice and usage of individual words than we would expect from a play of Aeschylus. Some of these discrepancies seem to reflect such a fundamental difference of natural style, apart from the demands of the context, that one is reluctant, on this evidence, to accept Aeschylus as the author. In particular, the particles and the prosaic usages fall right outside the patterns we find in his work.[107]

Chapter 9

STYLE AND SYNTAX

DETAILS OF SYNTAX AND PHRASEOLOGY

Details of syntax and phraseology are unlikely to be decisive for our enquiry, as the conventional tragic *Kunstsprache* serves to disguise individual mannerisms, and it is only when we find an unusual detail frequently repeated that we can be confident that we have distinguished a characteristic feature of an author's style. This chapter inevitably includes all sorts of details, large and small, which have little in common save that they occur in *Prom.*, and there is inevitably some overlap with the preceding chapter.

Sometimes it is possible to trace a historical development in a particular construction, or phrase, or idea; in other cases, it is possible to distinguish a difference between the practice of Aeschylus and that of Sophocles and/or Euripides, which seems to be due to individual preference. We can use these criteria to see where *Prom.* fits into the pattern. But in this chapter, even more than the others perhaps, we must beware of attributing too much significance to individual details. A point of syntax is often dependent on the context of its use; the overall numbers of occurrences for comparison are likely to be small. Nevertheless it does seem that some at least of the features discussed below are of some significance for our investigation.

It seems best again to divide these features roughly into two categories: first, those which are distinctly unusual, and seem to reflect the author's personal taste; and then those which may be significant, but are too uncertain or rare to bear much weight. I will then consider some larger features of the overall style which seem remarkable.

In the first category, of details striking enough to be really significant, we should place the following:

(a) πρίν[1]

Aeschylus has πρίν + infinitive seventeen times (three times after a negative main clause); Sophocles has πρίν + inf. nineteen times (three times after a negative); Euripides has it sixty-eight times (seven after a negative).

Aeschylus never has πρίν + indicative; Sophocles once (*OT* 776); Euripides seven times.

Aeschylus never has πρὶν ἄν + subjunctive; Sophocles twenty-two times (occasionally without ἄν); Euripides nineteen times (all these after a negative main clause).

Sophocles also has πρίν + optative five times (after negative); Aeschylus and Euripides never.

Prom. has πρὶν ἄν + subjunctive six times (165, 175, 719, 756, 991, 1027), all after a negative. The only possible parallel in Aeschylus is fr. 327.

Prom. 481 has πρίν + indicative and *Prom.* 825 πρίν + infinitive, after affirmative main clauses.

The growing frequency of constructions other than the infinitive after πρίν is a traceable historical process.[2] πρὶν ἄν was a development from the basic construction; and Aeschylus, in six plays, uses nothing but the basic infinitive, even after negative main clauses. *Prom.* on the other hand uses the infinitive only once in eight instances. The context may account for the frequency of πρὶν ἄν ('Zeus won't ... until' etc.), but the indicative example indicates that *Prom.* may simply be more 'advanced' than Aeschylus.

(b) φαίνομαι + *infinitive (= videor)*

Prom. 217, 317, 1036 (cf. 997); not in Aeschylus; nor, I think, in Sophocles or Euripides. Quite common in Homer and Herodotos, this seems by the fifth century to have belonged rather to prose than to high poetry.

(c) οἷός τε + *infinitive*

Prom. 41, 84, 107; not in Aeschylus; eight times in Sophocles; in Euripides e.g. *Hek.* 15, *Or.* 674, *Ba.* 266, 1245. Another seemingly prosaic feature; this phrase is common in Herodotos.

(d) ἐπεὶ τάχιστα *Prom.* 199, ὅπως τάχιστα *Prom.* 228 (= 'as soon as')

No parallel in Aeschylus, nor, as far as I know, in Sophocles or Euripides; again rather a prosaic, narrative turn of phrase.

(e) ὅτι *after verb of saying/thinking*

Prom. 104, 186, 259, 323, 328, 377, 951 (= seven times): only once in Aeschylus (*Eum.* 98); thirty-one times in Sophocles; twelve times in Euripides.

All of Sophocles' thirty-one examples, and six of *Prom.*'s seven, are last word in the line; so too is A. *Eum.* 98:[3] this is a form of 'Sophoclean' enjambement. So *Prom.*'s frequent use of ὅτι = 'that' seems to be connected with its use of such enjambement. Unlike e.g. ἵνα, where the final syllable can be elided, ὅτι can only be fitted into iambics through crasis, resolution, lengthening by position, or σχῆμα Σοφόκλεῖον. It seems that Aeschylus chose not to use the word,[4] whereas *Prom.* uses it with Sophoclean frequency and style.

(f) Prepositions

T. Mommsen's study[5] shows that μετά + genitive grows more common from Homer onwards; the ratios of σύν:μετά + gen. are: Homer 35:1, Pindar 19:1, Aeschylus 8:1, Sophocles 4:1, Euripides 2:1.

Aeschylus has μετά + gen. seven times (*Pers.* twice, *Supp.* three times, *Ag.* twice). Mommsen points out that *Prom.* 1067 μετά τοῦδ' ὅ τι χρὴ πάσχειν is unparalleled in Homer, Pindar, or Aeschylus, in that μετά occurs with a genitive singular. In early Greek it keeps a sense of 'among', as do Aeschylus' seven examples.

Equally remarkable is the complete absence from *Prom.* of σύν, a word used by Aeschylus sixty-seven times in six plays.[6] Sophocles has μετά + gen. twenty-three times, σύν ninety-one; Euripides μετά + gen. 101 times, σύν 197.[7]

The combined occurrence of all prepositions grows from early to late fifth-century tragedy:[8] the extremes are A. *Pers.* one per 6.5 lines and E. *Ba.* one per 3.8 lines. But this progress is not steady or uniform enough to help us. *Prom.*, with one per 5.9 lines, fits with Aeschylus (whose other plays range between 5.3 and 5.0), and is rather lower than Sophocles (5.4 to 4.7), but similar to early Euripides (e.g. *Med.* 5.9, *Hkd.* 5.4). Aristophanes ranges from 6.3 to 4.0, without any apparent chronological development.

More helpful to us is the general rule established by Mommsen[9] that preference for preposition + dative is old and poetical, prep. + accusative later and prosaic (while prep. + genitive is rhetorical /philosophical?). In epic and early lyric dative prepositions predominate. In A. *Th.*, *Cho.*, *Eum.* dative predominates; in *Supp.* and *Ag.* genitive; in *Pers.* all three are roughly equal. In Sophocles the genitive predominates, as it does in Euripides' earliest plays, closely followed by the accusative, which predominates in his twelve latest plays. Aristophanes and prose authors favour the accusative, with the dative least common.

In *Prom.* accusative prepositions predominate, as in later Euripides, prose, and comedy.[10] The incidence of εἰς and πρός + accusative in *Prom.* resembles Euripides rather than Aeschylus:[11]

εἰς *Prom.* thirty times (+ two if we count εἰσαεί, εἰσάπαξ); A. *Pers.* twenty-one, *Th.* fifteen, *Supp.* eleven, *Ag.* twenty-two, *Cho.* seventeen, *Eum.* nineteen (+ εἰσαεί once).

πρός (and ποτί) + acc. *Prom.* twenty-nine times; A. *Pers.* seven, *Th.* eleven, *Supp.* fourteen, *Ag.* twenty-eight, *Cho.* fifteen, *Eum.* fifteen.

When we bear in mind *Ag.*'s greater length, *Prom.*'s figures really stand out. In view of the historical and generic factors which Mommsen shows to be at work in determining the relative frequency of the different prepositions in Greek, it seems to me unlikely that *Prom.*'s unaeschylean characteristics are due solely to chance or to the context (e.g. Prometheus' geographical instructions telling Io where to go).

The complete avoidance of σύν, the 'late' usage of μετά + genitive singular, and the predominence of prepositions governing the accusative, all suggest a fundamental difference of style between the author of *Prom.* and Aeschylus.

(g) Compound verb + same preposition[12]

Prom. 276, 321, 381, 578, 909, 956, 1074 (i.e. seven times); Aeschylus eight times (*Pers.* 531; *Th.* 461; *Ag.* 156, 284, 500; *Cho.* 149, 404, 1012);[13] Sophocles seventeen times; Euripides over 100; Aristophanes 130; Thucydides over 300 times.

Prom.'s examples (the highest number for any tragedy outside Euripides), are all simple and obvious, and give a rather prosaic ring to the lines in which they occur.[14]

(h) Ellipse of second person of εἰμί[15]

Prom. 42, 178, 320, 373, 475, 987 (i.e. six times); there is no parallel in Aeschylus to this technique, which the author of *Prom.* seems to consider quite normal.

(i) Similes: ὅπως, δίκην, ὡς *etc. in comparison*[16]

ὅπως *Prom.* 1001; not in Aeschylus;[17] seven times in Sophocles, four in Euripides.

δίκην + genitive; not in *Prom.*; Aeschylus twenty-seven times (mostly in *Oresteia*); Sophocles twice? (fr. 587.1, fr. *inc.* 941); not in Euripides.

ὡς:[18] Aeschylus thirty-two times; Sophocles about twenty-two; Euripides fifteen (cf. ὡσεί, ὥστε); not in *Prom.*

ὥσπερ (in comparison): Aeschylus four times; Sophocles once (*Tr.* 118); not in *Prom.* or Euripides. *Prom.* 449 ἀλίγκιοι is unparalleled in Aeschylus, Sophocles or Euripides (cf. Homer). Again *Prom.*'s technique seems quite different from Aeschylus'.

(j) τοῦ παντὸς δέω (*Prom.* 1006), πολλοῦ γε καὶ τοῦ παντὸς ἐλλείπω (961)

There is no parallel in tragedy for these variations on the common prose idiom πολλοῦ γε δεῖ,[19] though cf. E. *Tro.* 797.

(k) Asyndeton

Prom. 56, 58, 141, 392, 608, 698, 937, 939 (i.e. eight times), all imperatives; only one of these occurs in lyric (608).[20]

In Aeschylus we find only thirteen examples in dialogue (*Pers.* 426, 463, 683; *Th.* 31, 60, 186; *Ag.* 1669; *Cho.* 289, 779; *Eum.* 124, 139, 180, 801), of which only six are imperative (*Th.* 31; *Ag.* 1669; *Cho.* 779; *Eum.* 139, 180, 801).

In Sophocles and Euripides imperatives in asyndeton in dialogue are more common, e.g. S. *Aj.* 115, 811, 844, 988; E. *Med.* 895, 962, 971. *Prom.* has three imperatives at 58, 392, 937; the only parallel I find in Aeschylus is *Th.* 31f, where the asyndeton is less abrupt. In Sophocles I find e.g. *Aj.* 988, *Tr.* 1255.

Prom.'s impatient, pressing imperatives may simply be due to the context, but in view of their number it may be right to conclude tentatively that they are a distinctive feature of this author's style, a feature which perhaps has more in common with Sophocles than with Aeschylus.[21]

(ℓ) Anadiplosis

Prom. four times in dialogue (266, 274, 338, 999), plus four in lyric (688, 694, 887, 894); in Aeschylus we find no real parallel in dialogue (*Ag.* 973, *Cho.* 246, 652f are all vocative, and quite different; nearest is perhaps *Ag.* 1299); Aristophanes parodies Aeschylus (= fr. 140) at *Birds* 1420, but it is clear from *Frogs* 1352ff that such repetitions were regarded as particularly characteristic of Euripides.[22] Anadiplosis in lyric is quite common in Aeschylus, though he has nothing quite like *Prom.* 887, cf. 894, which reminds us more of e.g. S. *OT* 1210; *Ph.* 135, 688; E. *Alk.* 442, *Pho.* 190. Again, there is nothing very firm to go on, but we seem to have a small unaeschylean feature before us, of a rather rhetorical nature.

(m) οἱ πάντες + *noun*

Prom. 749, 841, 975, cf. 483, 751 (i.e. five instances), as compared with only once the more normal order πάντα τὰ μέλλοντα (*Prom.* 101); Aeschylus never has οἱ πάντες + noun, six times πάντες οἱ, cf. e.g. S. *Ant.* 1023f, E. fr. 733, 1064.4.[23]

We might also note other usages of the article, *Prom.* 94-5 τὸν μυριετῆ χρόνον, 449 τὸν μακρὸν βίον, 538 τὸν μακρὸν τείνειν βίον (cf. Pindar *O.* 2.30; S. *Aj.* 342f, 473, 646; *OT* 518; Ar. *Wasps* 1006; Thuc. 4.117) and 1038 τὴν σοφὴν εὐβουλίαν (cf. E. *Hkd.* 109f), which seem different from anything in Aeschylus.[24]

(n) ἥκω *etc. + direct accusative*

ἥκω *Prom.* 717, 724, 730, 735, 808 (five times); cf. too Π. Λυόμενος fr. 196.1; this construction is never found in Aeschylus (except ? fr. 116.1), who has ἥκω + preposition seven times (cf. fr. 195.2, fr. 199.1); for Sophocles we may note fr. 271.6; for Euripides e.g. *Ba.* 1, *Ion* 5. N.b. too ἔρχομαι + direct acc. *Prom.* 962; in Aeschylus only once (*Th.* 714); ἀφικνέομαι + acc. *Prom.* 709; three times in Aeschylus; εἶμι + acc. and ἐφέρπω + acc. occur once each in Aeschylus. But with seven examples in all, *Prom.* seems unique in tragedy; Aeschylus only has six instances of the construction in six plays, never with ἥκω.

(o) ποινὰς τίνω

Prom. 112, 176, 620; not in Aeschylus (though cf. *Eum.* 268), who uses τίνω or compounds of it twenty times; Sophocles and Euripides often have δίκην τίνω (Sophocles has τίνω etc. eighteen times, Euripides forty times), but the only exact parallel for *Prom.* is Kritias ? fr.5.13 Snell (= Page *GLP* 15), cf. E. *Hks* 755. Aeschylus has plenty of opportunity to use either of these conventional phrases (δίκην/ποινὰς τίνω), especially in the *Oresteia*, but his usage of τίνω is generally bolder.

(p) λόγωι/ἔργωι

Prom. 336, 1080; no true parallel in Aeschylus for this contrast so familiar to later Greek,[25] although *Th.* 847 (if sound) implies it strongly. The prosaic antithesis of *Prom.* suggests a rather self-conscious, perhaps sophistic, mannerism.

(q) References to speech-making [26]

Prom. 46, 505, 610, 641, 827, 833, 870, 875, 949, 975 (ten instances), (cf. too 816f). In Aeschylus we find *Supp.* 273f, 464; *Ag.* 829, 916 (cf. 1112f); *Cho.* 554 (cf. 887); *Eum.* 201, 585, 707; fr. 176 (i.e. nine instances in all); in Sophocles e.g. *Aj.* 1040; *El.* 673, 1335; in Euripides e.g. *Med.* 1351; *Hkd.* 952; *Pho.* 469, 494; *Rhesos* 754, 851.

Prom. with ten or more examples of such self-conscious 'rhetorical' references, shows again, perhaps, the extent of sophistic influence on the play. We note that all Aeschylus' examples are from his latest plays.

(r) The perfect tense

(i) Resultative perfects:[27] Herington outlines some of the problems and uncertainties involved in any attempt to identify every occurrence of this phenomenon, although it is clear enough that a development was taking place in the formation and the usage of the perfect tense during the fifth century. The 'resultative perfect', where the verb is used to describe the effect made on a person or thing in the past which is still true of the present, is not a very common phenomenon at any time. In Aeschylus we might accept about six examples, though only three or four seem at all sure.[28] In *Prom.* Herington accepts at least five examples (211, 446, 586, 740, 821), but only two are beyond dispute (446, 586). In Sophocles there may be about twenty-three, in Euripides rather more, over 200 in Aristophanes; but the problem of definition and classification is insoluble.

If we were sure that we could agree with Herington, that 'by any analysis *Prom.* contains more resultative perfects than any other Aeschylean play, and at least as many as the average extant tragedy of Sophocles', we would find good reason there for placing *Prom.* sometime later than the *Oresteia* (as Herington does), and perhaps later than Aeschylus' lifetime.

(ii) Perfect of -ζω verbs:[29] *Prom.* 211 προὐτεθεσπίκει, 586

γεγυμνάκασιν. There is no other example of a perfect -κα from -ζω verb before Euripides.

(iii) ἐκτημένος: *Prom.* 795[30] (cf. Semonides fr. 13.2; Hdt., Thuc., Plato occasionally). Aeschylus has κεκτημένος at *Supp.* 337, *Ag.* 1051 (cf. *Th.* 1017); so too Sophocles and Euripides often.

(iv) δέδια: *Prom.* 182, 902; not in Aeschylus, who has δέδοικα seven times; Sophocles has δέδια once, δέδοικα twelve times; Euripides never δέδια, δέδοικα thirty times or so; but cf. [Xen.] 'Αθ. πολ.1.11.

(v) ὦπται: *Prom.* 998; not found again before fourth-century prose.

Of these details, (iii), (iv) and (v) may be too small to be in any way significant. But the evidence may be felt to be cumulative, and to amount to a positive indication that the use of the perfect tense in *Prom.* is rather more advanced than it is in Aeschylus.

(s) Reflexive pronoun

The figures for the third person reflexive pronoun in the three tragedians are unremarkable,[31] but for the first and second person they are rather surprising: to *Prom.*'s substantival usage of ἐμαυτόν, σεαυτόν etc. at 68, 309, 336, 344, 374, 438, 474, 508, 708, 748, 965, 1076 (i.e. twelve instances), we can find only two possible Aeschylean parallels, *Cho.* 923 and ?*Pers.* 162. There are forty-seven examples in Sophocles, fifty-eight in Euripides.[32] The adjectival occurrences are less striking: A. *Ag.* 859, 1264, 1323; *Cho.* 229; cf. *Prom.* 776; twenty-seven times in Sophocles, seventeen in Euripides. There is no obvious reason for Aeschylus' apparent reluctance to use ἐμαυτόν, σεαυτόν etc.: it seems simply to be a stylistic quirk, which *Prom.* does not share.

In our second category, details which are too uncertain or rare to bear much weight, we might list the following:

(a) Attraction of relative

Prom. 963, 984 οὐδὲν ὧν ...; Aeschylus never has οὐδὲν ὧν; Sophocles fifteen times, Euripides eleven. The total figures for attraction of any sort are: *Prom.* three; Aeschylus five; Sophocles fifty times (but only four times in *Aj.* and *Ant.* combined: it may be that we see here a chronological development).[33] But two similar examples in *Prom.* within twenty-five lines do not amount to very much.

(b) Article + pronoun

Prom. 249 τὸ ποῖον ... φάρμακον; the article is not found with τίς or ποῖος in Aeschylus; seven times in Sophocles, five or more in Euripides; cf. Aristophanes *Peace* 696, *Clouds* 775, 1270f, *Frogs* 7 etc. One isolated occurrence is not much to go on.

(c) δεῖ *+ accusative and genitive*

Prom. 86 σε δεῖ προμηθέως; the usual construction would be σοι (cf. A. *Ag.* 848); there are no parallels in Aeschylus or Sophocles, but twelve in Euripides.[34]

(d) θέαμα δυσθέατον *(Prom. 69)*[35]

There are no examples in Aeschylus of such an oxymoron with δυσ- adjective; cf. S. *Ant.* 588, 1261, 1276 (and *OT* 1248, *Tr.* 791); Euripides often. Aeschylus has many examples with ἀ- privative, never with δυσ-, unless we accept Hermann's φροιμίοις δυσφροιμίοις at *Ag.* 1216.

(e) ἔα τί χρῆμα *(Prom. 298)*

Nearest in Aeschylus is *Cho.* 10; in Sophocles *Ant.* 1049 (cf. *Aj.* 288, *OT* 1129; *El.* 390; *Ph.* 1231, 1265?); exact parallels at E. *Hipp.* 905, *Hks* 525, *Or.* 1573 (cf. *And.* 896, *Hik.* 92); also Kritias B16.1DK (= fr.1 Snell). τί χρῆμα is very common in Euripides.[36]

(f) Relativum pendens ex πᾶς, ἅπας

Prom. 35, 609, 641, 787 (i.e. four times); not found in Aeschylus; in Sophocles e.g. *Aj.* 1413 (cf. *Aj.* 151, also A. *Th.* 1044); in Euripides e.g. *Med.* 788.

(g) Prophetic present

Prom. 171, 513, 525, 767, 848, 948 (i.e. six instances;[37] in Aeschylus only *Pers.* 585, *Ag.* 126. The frequency of this usage in *Prom.* may be due simply to the many predictions made by Prometheus, with all the quasi-oracular authority inherited from his mother Gaia-Themis.

(h) πέτομαι *etc.*

Prom. 115, 555 προσέπτα, 644 προσέπτατο. Aeschylus only uses forms of ποτάομαι (seven times, including compounds); Sophocles πέτομαι etc. five times (*Aj.* 282, 693; *Ant.* 1307; *OT* 17, 487), only once ποτάομαι (fr. 423.2); Euripides πέτομαι etc. twenty-one times, ποτάομαι seven times.

(i) ἐπεί, *at the start of a narrative rhesis*

Prom. 829; this is characteristic of Euripides[38] but has no parallel in Aeschylus; in Sophocles only *Tr.* 900. One instance does not prove anything, but this may reinforce our feeling that *Prom.* contains an unusual number of rather prosaic turns of phrase.

(j) Sociative dative + αὐτός

Prom. 221, 1047; in Aeschylus only *Th.* 551; in Sophocles only *Aj.* 27, fr. 781.2; about eleven times in Euripides;[39] again too rare to be really significant.

(k) ἀπαλλαγὴ πόνων

The only occurrences in Aeschylus of ἀπαλλάσσω or ἀπαλλαγή with separative genitive, meaning 'release from' are *Ag.* 1, 20; *Eum.* 82f.[40] In *Prom.* we find 316, 470f, 749f, 754, 773. Herington takes this as further evidence of a late Aeschylean date for *Prom.*; but we need only look at e.g. E. *Hkd.* 346, 586, 811; *Hik.* 397, to conclude that there is nothing uniquely Aeschylean about the phrase.

(ℓ) τόλμα *etc.*[41]

In Aeschylus τόλμα, τολμάω are almost invariably accompanied by feelings of disapproval (*Ag.* 1231; *Cho.* 996, 1029; *Cho.* 179; *Ag.* 375; *Cho.* 594; *Eum.* 553; *Th.* 671; *Cho.* 430, 597; *Ag.* 221, 1237); only εὔτολμος *Ag.* 1302 (and ἄτολμος *Cho.* 630?) seem free of this sense.

At *Prom.* 14 and 16, the sense is 'having the heart' to do something necessary but unpleasant. Elsewhere in the play, τολμάω conveys a sense of courage and strength, with associations of approval (235, 299, 331, 381, 999 twice). The same is true of S. *Aj.* and *Ant.* This feature of *Prom.* obviously arises out of the context, as does e.g. the motif of αὐθαδία, not found elsewhere in Aeschylus, but it is interesting to note the similarity in tone of *Prom.* and e.g. S. *Ant.*, where resistance to authority is shown in an increasingly sympathetic light, and the central figure commands our growing respect.[42]

(m) τὸ μὴ οὐ + *infinitive*

Aeschylus and *Prom.* both offer quite regular examples of τὸ μή + infinitive after a main clause denoting prevention or hindering etc.: A. *Pers.* 291; *Ag.* 1589; *Eum.* 219, 691, 940; *Prom.* 235, 865. But Aeschylus offers no parallel to the (again quite regular) use of τὸ μὴ οὐ + infinitive following such a main clause which is itself negative, as at *Prom.* 627, 786, 918, (1056).[43] On the only occasion when Aeschylus has such a negative main clause, at *Ag.* 1170, he apparently prefers to keep τὸ μή.[44] Sophocles usually uses τὸ μὴ οὐ, as at *OT* 283, 1232, *Aj.* 540, 727, though occasionally has τὸ μή (e.g. *OT* 1387). But the uncertainty of the tradition does not allow us to draw any firm conclusions about this delicate problem.[45] (In its usage of τό + infinitive in general, *Prom.* fits with late Aeschylus and with Sophocles, but shows a greater freedom than early Aeschylus.[46] The same is true of the 'noun participle' in *Prom.*[47])

So far we have only looked at details which seem to set *Prom.* apart from the extant work of Aeschylus. There are also, of course, features which fit better with Aeschylus than with Sophocles or Euripides.

(a) Apokope of ἀνα-

This is commoner in Aeschylus than in Sophocles or Euripides. In lyric the practice is quite normal for all three, but Sophocles has only three or four examples in dialogue,[48] whereas Aeschylus has a dozen or so of ἀνα- alone (*Pers.* 163, 807; *Th.* 466, 535; *Ag.* 7, 27, 305, 1180, 1599; *Cho.* 280, 282; *Eum.* 243?). *Prom.* has six examples of ἀνα- (457, 521, 707, 791, 817?, 866; plus 605 in lyric), though three are of ἀντολή, which seems particularly susceptible to this (e.g. E. *Pho.* 504, fr. 482; Homer *Od.* 12.4; A. *Ag.* 7, 1180).

But Euripides seems sufficiently flexible to stop us from regarding Aeschylus' practice as distinctive in this respect: E. *El.* has three probable instances in dialogue (582, 868, 882), *Pho.* perhaps five (489, 504, 744, 1173, 1410, three of them προσαμβάσεις). *Prom.* in fact exceeds all other tragedies in this feature.

(b) πεδάρσιος

Prom. 269, 710, 916; Aeschylus has πεδα- for μετα- three times (*Cho.* 589f, 846, fr. 53); Sophocles never; Euripides *Hks* 819, 873; *Pho.* 1027; *Rhesos* 372. This aeolicism (+ doricism?) is too rare to be helpful.

(c) ματάω

Prom. 57; Aeschylus uses this word twice (*Th.* 37, *Eum.* 142); it does not occur in Sophocles or Euripides.

(d) οὐκ αν ηὔχουν

Prom. 688; cf. A. *Supp.* 330, *Ag.* 506, *Eum.* 561; Sophocles does not use the phrase, but Euripides does at *Hkd.* 931.

The list could be extended with further minor details;[49] but I have not come across any striking syntactical or stylistic peculiarities which link *Prom.* definitely with Aeschylus, certainly nothing to match our first group of unaeschylean features.

But as we might expect, it is with larger features of style that we see the clearest indications that *Prom.* may not be the work of Aeschylus. In general terms, it is fair to say that *Prom.* is 'easier', to translate, to interpret, and to analyse, phrase by phrase, than any of Aeschylus' six undisputed plays. The metaphors are less bold, the word-clusters less dense.[50] More specifically, we can identify particular traits and mannerisms in *Prom.* which seem to be distinctively unaeschylean.[51]

REPETITION[52]

Schmid has collected a remarkable list of passages in *Prom.* in which individual words or phrases are repeated in similar or identical form within the play.[53] These lists are rather indiscriminate, and include some 'repetitions' which hardly qualify as such, but by and large they justify his emphasis on this as an extraordinary feature of the play.

We have already dealt with individual words which occur with particular frequency in *Prom.* We must now consider repeated phrases, bearing in mind that repetition can be of different kinds, and can achieve different effects. Hiltbrunner has studied Aeschylus' use of repeated words and motifs throughout a play or trilogy as an essential contribution to the dramatic and thematic tension, and has suggested that the *Oresteia* marks the highest point in Aeschylus' development, in terms of the extent and subtlety of this technique.[54] But he finds that with *Prom.* the picture is completely different from the other six plays: the repetitions are more numerous, but seem to lack any purpose or pattern. He even denies that we can talk of a 'repetition-*technique*' in *Prom.* at all.[55]

Repetitions within a few lines of each other are not of much significance; they are common in all authors,[56] though the technique of variation is often employed to avoid clumsiness. Many of these repetitions come into the category of 'ring composition', in which *Prom.*'s technique is again unusual, as we shall see.[57] For our present purposes, what is significant is, first, the number of repeated phrases in *Prom.*, and secondly, their apparent pointlessness, in contrast to Aeschylus' 'Wiederholungs- und Motivtechnik'.

The most striking examples cited by Schmid are: 14/39/289; *92f /119/141/304 (cf. 299, 302); 237/306; 144/307; *35/96/149/310/389/ 439/942/955/960; 316/749f/754/471; 259/323/951; 35/186/149f/324/402; 263/330; 347ff/425ff; 376/654; 384/978; 32/396; 118/298/302f; 326/ 339/872; 327/344; 374/392;[58] 7/38/252 (cf. 82, 109f, 254)/107/945; 11/28; 42/178/327; 44/342f; *67/120; *101/265/617 (cf. 913f)/935/ 1040; 116/765; *239/267/507/613f (plus 11, 28, 231ff, 442ff, 476ff, 542)/251ff/469ff; 160f/243f/303; 696f/743f; 870/875; 992/1043; 106/ 197f; 232/668; 500/801; 833/949; 46/610/975; (n.b. too 208, 353, 592, 672 πρὸς βίαν in the same place in the trimeter); 99ff/183f; 194f/255f; 222/736; 249/606; 257/755f; 756/996; 104/377; 513/525; 633/820; 641/701/787; 840/967; 676/812; 214/446/702; 792/810; 112/ 177/620; 476/703/844; 764/909; *83/945; *10/357 (cf. 224, 305, 756, 996); 322/373; 185/577 (never in Aeschylus); 963/984; 85f/733 (cf. 717, 840, 850); 148/426?

We might note too some less striking instances: 338/616; 586f/ 905f; 622/823; 288/302; 309/315 (982, 1000, 1038); 318/329; 342/ 383; 180/311 (318); 262/316; 335f/472ff; 379/1008; 2/270; 84/546; 149ff/162ff; 208/212; 215/240; 705f/789f; 753/833, 1053; 826/842.

Some of these repetitions do serve to keep relevant and important themes constantly in our minds, above all the newness of Zeus' tyranny, the possibility of Prometheus' release, the exposed physical position of Prometheus, and the prospect of Zeus' overthrow: these are marked with asterisks. Yet even here the word-for-word repetition is far more extensive and obvious than is usual for Aeschylus, who prefers more subtle variation of such thematically essential words and phrases. Many of *Prom.*'s repetitions have no such thematic function: they seem merely to be the product of '*ein andrer Stil*'. Even Herington acknowledges that 'there is almost certainly nothing approaching a parallel in tragedy or comedy'.

γνῶμαι

Schmid found *Prom.* slightly richer in *Sentenzen* than Aeschylus' six plays: A. *Pers.* 4, *Th.* 15, *Supp.* 16, *Ag.* 25, *Cho.* 10, *Eum.* 11; *Prom.* 21. The problem of classification is here insoluble, but his findings are more or less borne out by Ahrens,[59] whose figures for 'true' γνῶμαι are: A. *Pers*. 9, *Th*. 19 (+ 3), *Supp*. 30, *Ag*. 50, *Cho*. 20, *Eum*. 22, *Prom*. 28, to which we may add those instances which he classes as '*gnomennahe Aussagen*': A. *Pers*. 4, *Th*. 15 (+ 2), *Supp*. 9, *Ag*. 15, *Cho*. 13, *Eum*. 12, *Prom*. 17. The combined totals produce A. *Pers*. 13, *Th*. 34 (+5), *Supp*. 39, *Ag*. 65, *Cho*. 33, *Eum*. 34; *Prom*. 45, slightly higher than Aeschylus' highest rate (*Prom*. 41 per 1000 lines, A. *Ag*. 39 per 1000).

But much more important than these total figures is Ahrens' judgement on the nature of *Prom*.'s γνῶμαι. A γνώμη is usually introduced, by any author, to express a judgement, and to give to that judgement the weight of tradition or proverbial truth, in the attempt to persuade the listener to agree with the speaker. In Aeschylus the judgement itself (good/bad, profitable/dangerous etc.) is usually expressed indirectly, through a verb, phrase or clause. It is rare to find the more simple and old-fashioned adjective[60] used on its own, like e.g. *Prom*. 17 εὐωριάζειν γὰρ πατρὸς λόγους βαρύ. In *Prom*. we find no less than ten examples: 17 βαρύ, 35 τραχύς, 263 ἐλαφρόν, 385 κέρδιστον, 536 ἡδύ τι, 611 δίκαιον, 698 γλυκύ, 750 κρεῖσσον, 936 σοφοί, 1039 αἰσχρόν (we might add perhaps 49f, 514, 1041f). The only parallels in Aeschylus are: *Th*. 596; *Ag*. 884, 902?, 1331, 1619; *Cho*. 703; *Eum*. 725[61] (i.e. six or seven). *Prom*.'s high number cannot be explained by the context: it seems to reflect an individual idiosyncrasy of style.

Another oddity of *Prom*.'s γνῶμαι, in comparison with those of Aeschylus, is the frequent use of a 'personal' verb (γιγνώσκω, μανθάνω etc.), or of an obvious signpost such as ἐπεί, ὡς etc., to introduce the γνώμη:[62] *Prom*. 186, 328f; 104f, 377f; 888ff, 926f; 385; 611, 637ff (nine times), cf. too *Prom*. 323, 951f; in Aeschylus only *Pers*. 598ff; *Ag*. 884, 1619ff, 1668.[63] The effect is to make the γνώμη more artificial, less well integrated into the speaker's own mode of expression; this self-conscious introduction, like the explicit, adjectival 'judgement', seems to be a stylistic quirk of *Prom*.'s author.

WORDPLAY (POLYPTOTON ETC.)[64]

Schmid classes the frequent occurrence of such phrases as ἄκοντά σ' ἄκων (*Prom*. 19) as Aeschylean. No single term has proved quite satisfactory for covering every form of this stylistic device, but polyptoton will do.[65] Verbal jingles are popular in primitive cult and song, but they are also characteristic of the more sophisticated and self-consciously rhetorical style of Gorgias.[66]

Gygli-Wyss counts ninety-seven examples of polyptoton in Aeschylus (as compared with only sixty in all Homer), of which sixty occur in dialogue; Sophocles has a hundred examples in dialogue, and Euripides' rate appears to be similar (see below). It is difficult to establish an entirely objective criterion of what is and what is not an instance of polyptoton (which we might define loosely as the occurrence close together of words of the same root but different ending), and no two counts would be exactly the same. I have checked Aeschylus' six plays, *Prom.* and E. *Med.*, using the same criteria throughout: I give (a) the occurrences which can, in my view, definitely be called polyptoton (bracketing those examples where more than one word intervenes between the two similar words), and (b) passages in which an element of wordplay is clearly discernible, even though the two words may be too far separated, or too dissimilar, to count strictly as polyptoton.

Prom.: (a) 19, 29, 69f (twice), 92, 192, 218, 230, (244f, twice), 258f, 276, 310, (333), 338f, 342f (twice), 384, 385, 447, 576, 585, 595, 671, 682, 693, 762, 764, 779f, 858, 909, 919, 921, 944, 955, 970, 971f (twice), 977f (twice), 1013, 1020, 1042, (1075f), a total of thirty-nine occurrences.
(b) 37, 72f, 85f, 106, 119f, 127f, 197f, 212f, 238f, 260, 345f, 518f, 588f, 678? (is ἄκρατος ὀργήν a pun on Ἄργος?), 718, 727, 744f, 756f, 765f, 875, 904, 980f?, 986f, 997f = twenty-four.[67]

Combined (a) + (b) = sixty-three.

A. *Pers.:* (a) 24, 151f, (253), 282, 298, 323, 330f, (347), 359, 380, 408, 411, (415), 528, 531, 666, 681, 780, 782, 1041 (twice) = twenty.
(b) 47, 383, 648f, 680, 702, 724f, 759, 792f, 795, 986, 1018f, 1038f = twelve.

Combined (a) + (b) = thirty-two.

Th.:[68] (a) 87, 94, 145, 167, (194), 245f (twice), 261, 340, 347, 352, 353, 406, 451, 458, 505, 509, (526f), 599f, (631), 674f (twice), 675, 721, 851f, (879), 900f (twice), 932f,

961, (971), 974, 983, 993 (and 1005, 1049, 1070f) = thirty-one (plus three).

(b) 100, 124f, 177f, 202, 217, 253f, 262f, 266f, 427f, 481f, 565, 566, 670f, 708f, 800, 803f, 963f (and 1027f, 1044f, 1046f, 1066) = seventeen[69] (plus four).

Combined (a) + (b) = forty-eight (plus seven).

Supp.: (a) (144f), 149, (176), 204, 215f, 226, 227, 396f (3 times), 417f, 447, 449, 451, (512), 524, 525, 526, 626, 627, 842, (921), 951f, 966, 991, 1071 = twenty-four.[70]

(b) 11f, 201, 212f, 230f, 246f, 259, 300f, 306f, 357f, 373f, 375f, 380, 381, 413, 437f, 455f, 506f, 769f, 826, 862, 880f, 919f, 921f, 926f, 957f, 1055, 1056f, 1058 = twenty-eight.

Combined (a) + (b) = fifty-two.

Ag.: (a) 52, 92, 115, 216, 282, 313, 422f, 545, 595, 641, 836, 864f, 1026, 1049, 1110f, 1191, 1212, 1275, 1287, (1307f), 1318, 1339, 1374, 1430, 1461, (1495?), 1562, 1563, 1623 = twenty-nine.

(b) 23, 34f, 39, 240f, 351, 408, 689 (twice), 763ff, 809, 931f, 1052, 1142, 1198, 1302, 1319, 1368f, 1384, 1394, 1396, 1454, 1535f, 1545, 1560, 1651f, 1652f = twenty-five.

Combined (a) + (b) = fifty-four.[71]

Cho.: (a) (60), 89, 107 (twice), 153, 221, 298, 309f, 312f, 354, 461,(twice), 498, 666f, 677, 703, 736, 785, 850, 890, 912f, 1004, (1061) = twenty-one.

(b) 43, 44, 78, 87, 212f, 222f, 234f, 297f, 315, 398, 404f, 434f, 491f, 509f, 527f, 562, 586, 780, 893f, 906f, 910f, 913f, 920f, 922f, 930, 935f, 978f, 987f, 1010, 1027f = thirty.[72]

Combined (a) + (b) = fifty-one.

Eum.: (a) 7f (twice), (71), 145, 411, (435), (468), 503, 515, 530f, 566, 587f, 642, 660, (887), 992, 999, 1012f = seventeen.

(b) 14, 47f, 48f, 94, 143f, 161, 199f, 202f, 227f, 266, 421f, 429f, 432f, 457, 463f, 469f, 471f, 484, 568ff, 586, 602, 603f, 621f, 635f, 638, 653, 655f, 658ff (twice), 687, 688, 689f, 699f, 760f, 822f, 893f, 911f, 1034 = thirty-seven.

Combined (a) + (b) = fifty-four.[73]

In A. *Th.*, *Ag.* and *Cho.* several occurrences are due to the semi-ritual context; their figures for (a) are therefore somewhat larger than we might expect. Yet even so, they fall short of *Prom.*'s figure. So it seems that *Prom.* does contain rather more wordplay than is normal for Aeschylus, particularly of the most simple and obvious type (a): A. *Pers.* 20, *Th.* 31, *Supp.* 24, *Ag.* 29, *Cho.* 21, *Eum.* 17; *Prom.* 39. Many of these in *Prom.* are nothing *more* than playing with words, e.g. 29, 192, 218, 671, 762, 921, 764, 909, 955, 970, 1013, 1042, in contrast to Aeschylus' more pointed use in e.g. *Th.* 340, 347 cf. 505 and 509, 352, 353, 674, 675, 961, 974, to reflect essential motifs of the play; cf. too his technique throughout the *kommos* of *Cho.*

E. *Med.* 1-1080 produces broadly similar figures:

(a) 31, 51, 142, (234f, twice), 288, 321, 333f (twice), 355, 363f, 365, 475, 513, 521, 553, 579, 587, (607f, twice), (626), 656f, (716), 741, (773), 776, 805, 853f, 891, (966), 1009ff (twice), (1041), 1071 = thirty.

(b) 18f, 72f, 298f, 323? (pun on μεν-?), 399f, 419f, 463f (three times), 490, 502f, 602, 669ff (twice), 688, 717, 733f, 782f, 791, 839f, 884f, 889f, 913f, 930, 932f, 1046f, 1067f = twenty-four.

Combined (a) + (b) = fifty-four.

Many of *Med.*'s examples are very obvious and simple (31, 51, 142, 321, 365, 475, 513, 521, 553, 579, 587, 776, 805, 853f, 891), like those of *Prom.*

Although it must be admitted that the difference between *Prom.* and Aeschylus' six plays (and between Aeschylus and E. *Med.*, or even each of Aeschylus' plays) is not easily to be distinguished, to my mind *Prom.*'s high figure for category (a) does seem significant: only *Th.* of Aeschylus' plays comes near it, and we have noted that there are special reasons for this greater use of such phrases, which do not apply to *Prom.* (We have also seen that A. *Th.* is short of instances of (b), so that its combined figure is much lower than *Prom.*'s.) It may be that my criteria of selection are too vague, and that *Prom.*'s category (a) should be smaller, or Aeschylus' larger. If not, we seem to have isolated another stylistic mannerism of *Prom.*, a self-consciousness in the use of assonance and verbal antithesis which we might term 'rhetorical', and consider as another possibly sophistic feature of the play.[74]

THE INTERNAL FORMAL ARRANGEMENT OF SPEECHES

(a) Ring Composition

This apparently easily identifiable and definable phenomenon has been the object of several studies and comments, yet remains rather elusive as a stylometric criterion. Opinions differ as to whether 'framing', or 'ring composition', reflects the natural Greek mode of thought and expression,[75] or whether it reflects more the archaic and formalistic style of early Greek literature (Homer, Hesiod, Aeschylus, Herodotos etc.), which was steadily replaced during the fifth century by more sophisticated and fluent techniques of exposition, narrative, and argument.[76] What cannot be disputed is the fact that some authors use it to a greater extent than others who are nearly contemporary, or whose 'sophistication' cannot be explained on purely chronological grounds (e.g. Herodotos more than Thucydides, Sophocles more than Euripides), and that different authors seem to use it in slightly different ways. So, while we accept the broad similarities between various Greek authors in their use of ring composition, we must look for any significant differences that we can find which we can truly call characteristic of one or other.

Aeschylus is particularly fond of ring composition of the sort described by Garvie,[77] 'the technique by which a speaker returns at the end of his speech, or a section of a speech, to his opening words or thoughts'. This technique of 'framing' may be distinguished from the formulaic division of sections of a speech from each other in the manner of e.g. Hdt. 2.154.5; 1.90 *passim*, and the familiar τοιαῦτα μὲν ταῦτα ... δέ ..., where the anaphora of the previous passage is merely the briefest of recapitulations (sometimes just ταῦτα, οὕτως etc.), and does not echo the opening words of that section. 'Framing', usually in Aeschylus accompanied by verbal parallelism between the beginning and the end of the section, may be thought of as ring composition proper: the speech-division 'formulae' may be more or less close to it according to the extent to which such parallelism is sought. (Thus, for example, S. *El.* 680, 688, 696, 761ff are almost purely formulaic, while 29f/73f, and 288/293, count also as frames.)

The framing technique occurs in Aeschylus as follows:[78]

Pers.: *with verbal parallelism (VP)* 179f/200, 609f/619ff, 603/606, 744/749ff, 753/757f (and cf. 161/245); *without VP* 682/693, 759ff/781, plus the formulaic 361ff/372.

Th.: *with VP* 187f/195, 266/279, 380f/391f (also 1005/1025, 1013f/1020f, 1028/1037); *without VP* 24/27, 487/497ff, 529ff/(549f), plus the formulaic 633/639.

Supp.: *with VP* 254f/259, 260f/268f, 278/290, 407/417, 517/522, 607/621, 710/724f, 991f/1012, 996/1008.

Ag.: *with VP* 1/20, 968/972, 1178/1183, 1184f/1196f, 1580/1603/1611; *with very slight VP* 551/581f, 636/648, 810ff/821ff, 1412ff/1419ff; *without VP* 944ff/956f, plus the formulaic 896/903.

Cho.: *with VP* 2/19, 10ff/20f, 86/100, 87/91f, (525/538), 541/550, 742/765, 749f/762; *without VP* 130f/138ff, 554ff/579ff, and the formulaic 514/522.

Eum.: *with VP* 1/20, 179f/196, 191/197, 235f/241f, 683f/704; *without VP* 681f/707f and the formulaic 436/442, 443f/453.

I have studied two plays of Sophocles, and one of Euripides, for comparison, and have found the following occurrences:

S. *Aj.:* *with VP* 654/690, 845/856f, 961/969, 1073f/1084, 1047f/1062f/1089f, 1334f/1344f; *without VP* 748ff/780ff, 1171f/1180f, plus the formulaic 750/780, 1012/1017.

El.: *with (slight) VP* 254ff/307ff, 341f/365ff, 992ff/1013f, 1126ff/1156ff; *without VP* 359/364, 431/448/461ff, 561f/591, (871ff/916ff/934f), 907f/915, plus the formulaic 29f/73, 35/38, 44/50, 288/293, 295/299, 417/424f, 680/688/696/761ff, 973f/984.

E. *Med.* *with VP* 450/457f, 791/796, 1023/1036ff, (340/355), (not, I think, 788f/806 or 949f/956ff); *without VP* 282f/289ff, 765ff/807ff, 1323ff/1346, plus the formulaic 719f/723, 872/882, 1330/1336.

Aeschylus emerges as the tragedian most fond of the framing technique, not so much in terms of absolute frequency as in the preference for verbal and formal parallelism, sometimes of a closeness unmatched by Sophocles or Euripides (e.g. A. *Supp.* 407/417; *Th.* 380f/391f; *Ag.* 1/20, 1178/1183; *Cho.* 2/19, 87/91f; *Eum.* 683f/704ff). A higher proportion of the examples in Sophocles and Euripides are of the formulaic type. (Of course, in all three tragedians several of the formulaic frames occur when a speaker is reporting another speaker's words, e.g. A. *Pers.* 361/372, *Th.* 633/639 etc.; some such formula is in these cases often almost inevitable, from the context.)

In *Prom.* we find: *with VP* only 870/875f; *without VP* 204ff/214f, 226f/237, (298/302), 309f/315f, 344/374, 645f/655f, 663/669, 824ff/842f, 1014f/1030.

In none of these ten examples is the framing effect at all striking; indeed 298f/302, 309f/315f, 344/374 are hardly frames at all. A high proportion of the frames are of the formulaic type, dividing a speech into ordered parts (226/237, 663/669, 824ff/842f, 1014/1030).[79]

This brings us to our second, closely related object of enquiry:

(b) Rhetorical 'Signpost' Formulae for Speech-Division

Nowhere in *Prom.* do we find a character's whole speech framed in a ring composition (344/374 is the nearest). We find this technique in A. *Pers.* 682/693, 753/757, 759ff/781ff; *Th.* 487/497ff, (1005/1025); *Ag.* 1/20f, 551/581, 944f/956f, 1580/1611; *Cho.* 2/19, 86/100, 514/522, 541/550; *Eum.* 179/196, 236/241f, 436/442, 443/469; also e.g. at S. *El.* 254ff/307ff, 341/365ff, 992ff/1013f; E. *Med.* 765/809f, 1323ff/1346.

Instead, in *Prom.* the formulaic frames tend to divide one part of a character's speech from the next, as formal rhetorical signposts. Sometimes these signposts serve a double function, to round off one section and introduce the next: such transitional formulae occur at 221-7, 271ff, 441-6, 500ff, 740ff, 801ff. Friis Johansen gives parallels in Aeschylus for such formal transitions:[80] *Pers.* 200f; *Supp.* 991, 1009; *Ag.* 829ff, 844, 912f, 950; (*Cho.* 205); *Eum.* 453f, 480ff, 707f; (we might add *Ag.* 598ff, 644ff). But as he observes, the Aeschylean examples 'mark much more important breaks than they do in *Prom.*, while breaks of the same kind as we found in *Prom.* are marked with more discrete means'.[81] The peculiarity of *Prom.*'s transition formulae is that they are so artificial: the transition is usually merely from one item in a continuous narrative to another, whereas Aeschylus tends to use such formulae when a contrast of some sort is intended. Perhaps *Prom.*'s discrepancy is in part to be explained by its content; the scenes do not contain abrupt changes of intention or mood, but tend rather to represent a continuous unfolding of the past or future.

This predilection for rhetorical division of speeches into ordered sections, with introductions and conclusions to each section, can most clearly be seen if we compare the occurrence of such formulae in different plays in tabular form. The table I have drawn up is inevitably too schematic, as it is not always possible to decide for certain whether a phrase should count as a rhetorical 'signpost' formula or as a natural mode of expression, and the table takes no account of subject matter or context. The table is concerned only with speeches of twenty-five lines or more in iambic trimeters. Each speech can obviously only have one introductory formula and one conclusion (though I count A. *Eum.* 1-63 as two speeches, 1-33, 34-63) but can have any number of transitions from topic to topic formally marked with a signpost.

TABLE 10. *Rhetorical 'signpost' formulae*

	INTRODUCTION (= formal ref. to what the speaker intends to say)	*TRANSITION* (= formal marking of the end of one topic or section, and the beginning of another)	*CONCLUSION* (= formal statement that the speech is complete, or final summary of its contents)
A. *Pers.*			
176-214		200f	210ff
302-30			329f
353-432			(429ff)
447-71			470f
480-514			513f
598-622			
759-86			(784ff)
800-42			
Th.			
1-38	1ff		
39-68	39ff		
568-96	568ff		595
597-625			
Supp.			
176-203			
249-73			271
980-1013		991ff	1012

Ag.			
1-39			
281-316			315f
320-50			348
503-37			
551-82			582
587-614		598ff	613f
636-80		644ff	680
810-54	810ff	829ff;843ff	
855-913	855ff		(903)
1256-94			
1372-98	1372f		(1393f)
1577-1611			
Cho.			
124-51		142ff	149ff
183-211			
269-305			
554-84	554	579ff	
734-65			
973-1006		(997)	
Eum.			
1-33	1f	20f	
34-63			
64-93			
443-69	443f	454f	
681-710	681f		707ff
Prom.			
197-241	(197f)	221-7	237ff
340-76			(373f)
436-71		441ff	469ff
476-506	476f	500	505f
640-86	640ff		683
700-41	703ff		740f
786-818	786f	801f	816f
823-76	824ff	842ff	(870) 875f
1007-35	1007	(1014f)	1030ff
S. *Aj.*			
284-330	284		
430-80	430ff	(434,445,450)	480
485-524			
646-92			
748-83	748		780ff
815-65		(831,835 etc.)	864f
992-1039		1021f	1036ff
1052-90		(1062ff)	(1089f)
1226-63			
1266-1315			

El.			
23-76	29		73
254-309		(261,262,266,271)	
341-68			
431-63			
516-51			
558-611	558ff	577;591ff	
634-59	637ff		655ff
680-763	680	688ff;696	761ff
892-919	892		
947-89	947		
1126-70			
E. *Med.*			
1-48			
214-66			
364-409			
465-519	473ff		
522-75	522ff	534f;545ff	
764-810	772f		
869-905			
1019-80			
1136-1230		1222ff	
1323-50			
Rhesos			
105-30			130
284-316	284		314f
393-421	393ff		420f
422-53		432ff	
756-803		800ff	
915-49			948f

TOTALS	*INTRODUCTION*	*TRANSITION*	*CONCLUSION*
A. *Pers.*	0 (out of 8)	1	4(6)
Th.	3 (out of 4)	0	1
Supp.	0 (out of 3)	1	2
Ag.	3 (out of 12)	4	5(7)
Cho.	1 (out of 6)	2(3)	1
Eum.	3 (out of 5)	2	1
Prom.	6(7) (out of 9)	5(6)	8(9)
S. *Aj.*	3 (out of 10)	1(4)	4(5)
El.	6 (out of 11)	4(5)	3
E. *Med.*	3 (out of 10)	3	0
Rhesos	2 (out of 6)	2	4

From Table 10 we observe first, that, as we would expect, the practice of each tragedian is not uniform, even within one play. Aeschylus for instance uses more signpost formulae in *Ag.* than in his other plays, and more in the middle of *Ag.* than at the beginning and end; so too Sophocles uses more in the middle of *El.* than elsewhere. On the whole, it does not seem possible to make any fast distinction between the technique of Aeschylus and Sophocles. On the evidence of *Med.*, Euripides is more sparing than either; *Rhesos* is similar to Aeschylus and Sophocles.

But when we come to consider *Prom.*, it is immediately clear that its speeches contain a markedly higher proportion of these formulae than any other play in the table. Only two of the nine speeches longer than twenty-five lines do not contain a formal introduction; all of them have a formal conclusion (though 373f barely qualifies); i.e. sixteen out of a possible eighteen opening or closing signpost formulae are present, as compared with A. *Pers.* six out of sixteen, *Th.* four out of eight, *Supp.* two out of six, *Ag.* ten out of twenty-four, *Cho.* two out of twelve, *Eum.* four out of ten; S. *Aj.* eight out of twenty-two, *El.* nine out of twenty-two; E. *Med.* three out of twenty; *Rhesos* six out of twelve.

Several more such formulae occur in *Prom.* in shorter speeches. Including these, I find the occurrences of each type to be:

Introduction: 197f, 307f, 476f, 640ff, 703ff, 786ff, 824ff, 1007ff.

Conclusion: 112, 237ff, 373f, 469ff, 505f, 683, 740f, 816f, 875f, 1030ff.

Transition: 221ff, 271ff, 441ff, 500ff, 801f, 842ff.

We should perhaps include too the instances where such formulae are employed for reported speech:[82] 655, 669.

The highest rate of these formulae in Aeschylus occurs in *Ag.*:

Introduction: (266), 810ff, 855ff, 1183ff, 1322f, 1372f, 1402f, 1431.

Conclusion: 312ff, 348f, 582, 613f, 680, 903.

Transition: 598ff, 644ff, 829ff, 950f.

and, after reported speech, 593.

We may compare:

S. *El.*: *Introduction:* 29, 378, (417), 558, 637ff, 680, 892, 947.

Conclusion: 73, 383, 655f, 761ff.

Transition: 261 (+ 262, 266, 271), 424ff, 577ff, 591ff, 688ff, 696, and, with reported speech, 38, 50, 293, 299, 424f, 984.

E. *Med.*: *Introduction:* 473ff, 522ff, 719ff, 772ff, 932ff, 1351ff.

Conclusion: 72f.

Transition: 534ff, 545ff, 790, 1222ff.

and, after reported speech, 882.

If we bear in mind the relative numbers of speeches in these plays, we may tentatively conclude that *Prom.* has more such formulae than Aeschylus (some of whose plays have a much lower rate than *Ag.*), who in turn has slightly more than Sophocles (though I have only studied two of his plays); Euripides seems appreciably lower.[83] As we have already seen, *Prom.*'s formulae are often comparatively pointless and artificial,[84] and seem to reflect a rather formalistic and pedantic technique of speech-division and internal organization that has no real parallel in tragedy. This self-conscious desire for order and symmetry reminds us of other unusual details in the play's structure,[85] and might be termed 'archaic' (though we saw that ring composition and rhetorical 'signposts' continued to be used in later Greek); but it might also be regarded as a sign of self-consciously rhetorical word-arrangement, characteristic of early sophistic style. The presence of several long and potentially monotonous, narrative speeches in *Prom.* may account for the large number of 'signpost' formulae: the author was anxious to break the narrative up into manageable sections (we may compare the technique of S. *El.* 680-763). Aeschylus does not elsewhere display such a concern for the artificial division of continuous narrative as is shown throughout *Prom.*

SENTENCE LENGTH

It has by now been established that one informative and reliable test of authorship can be a statistical study of sentence length,[86] i.e. the number of words per sentence. Unfortunately, its reliability has only really been shown with prose authors, and even here passages of dialogue are liable to be misleading.

I was therefore not very optimistic that such a study of *Prom.* in relation to the three great tragedians would prove very rewarding, and indeed it became clear quite soon that all three are in most respects very similar. I will simply reproduce here the figures which I obtained, without the full discussion of my method and its limitations for Greek tragedy.[87]

Table 11 gives the number of sentences[88] of 1-5 words, of 6-10 words etc., occurring in each play; Table 12 gives the median, first quartile, third quartile, and ninth decile[89] obtained from those figures.

TABLE 11. *Sentence-length distribution*

Words per sent-ence			*Aeschylus*				*TOTAL*		*Sophocles*				*TOTAL*			*Euripides*				*TOTAL*	
	Pers.	*Th.*	*Supp.*	*Ag.*	*Cho.*	*Eum.*	*AESCH.*	*Prom.*	*Aj.*	*Ant.*	*OT*	*Tr.*	*SOPH.*	*Alk.*	*Med.*	*Hipp.*	*Tro.*	*El.*	*Hel.*	*EUR.*	*Rh.*
1–5	13	18	25	39	18	20	133	23	34	25	26	27	112	39	72	41	25	32	58	267	24
6–10	50	54	37	87	52	63	343	63	71	60	46	59	236	87	96	80	69	85	88	505	53
11–15	47	48	35	65	38	42	275	80	84	60	63	66	273	73	83	72	81	59	104	472	55
16–20	26	19	10	35	24	26	140	27	36	35	34	19	124	24	39	28	38	34	42	205	21
21–5	5	12	8	13	8	8	54	10	22	20	12	17	71	13	22	15	15	19	23	107	7
26–30	4	8	3	10	2	7	34	9	10	7	19	16	52	5	11	5	8	9	10	48	3
31–5	3	3	2	4	8	4	24	5	4	3	5	5	17	3	4	4	4	2	5	22	4
36–40	1	1	0	2	1	2	7	1	3	2	3	7	15	2	3	1	1	1	3	11	1
41–5	0	3	0	0	2	0	5	2	2	4	3	5	14	1	0	0	1	1	1	4	1
46–50	1	0	0	1	0	0	2	0	1	0	1	0	2	0	0	0	1	0	1	2	0
51–5	2	0	0	0	0	0	2	0	1	2	0	1	4	0	0	0	0	1	0	1	1
56–60	0	0	0	0	0	0	0	0	0	1	1	0	2	0	0	0	0	0	0	0	0
61–5	0	0	0	0	0	0	0	0	0	0	0	1	1	0	0	0	0	0	1	1	0
TOTALS	152	166	120	256	153	172	1019	220	268	219	213	223	923	247	330	246	243	343	336	1645	170

TABLE 12. *Sentence length*

	MEDIAN	*1ST QUARTILE*	*3RD QUARTILE*	*9TH DECILE*
A. *Pers*	11.4	7.5	15.8	20.8
Th.	11.1	7.2	15.7	24.3
Supp.	9.7	5.7	14.0	20.6
Ag.	10.2	6.4	15.1	21.7
Cho.	10.9	6.9	16.4	23.6
Eum.	10.4	6.8	15.8	22.4
Combined A.	10.6	6.8	15.5	22.4
Prom.	11.5	7.5	15.5	22.5
S. *Aj.*	11.7	7.3	16.7	23.7
Ant.	12.0	7.5	17.8	24.3
OT	12.7	8.0	18.6	27.8
Tr.	11.9	7.4	19.0	29.0
Combined S.	12.1	7.5	17.9	26.4
E. *Alk.*	9.9	6.3	14.1	19.9
Med.	9.8	5.5	14.8	21.6
Hipp.	10.1	6.3	14.4	20.1
Tro.	11.7	7.6	16.0	22.4
El.	10.4	6.7	15.9	22.3
Hel.	11.1	6.5	15.2	22.3
Combined E.	10.5	6.4	14.9	21.5
Rhesos	10.7	6.7	14.6	20.0

We see from the tables that Aeschylus and Euripides are not really distinguishable by these criteria: *Prom.* fits with both. Only in the case of Sophocles do we see a tendency to use more long sentences (over 25 words). I found that within each play there were wide variations between different passages, and clearly the dramatic situation is liable to dictate to an author what style he should use. But the only play which, by my reckoning, emerged as statistically incompatible with Aeschylean authorship was S. *OT*.

The value of this laborious study is therefore largely negative. On this evidence, we can merely say that there is no reason to suppose that Aeschylus could not have written *Prom.* The same is true of Euripides (and the author of *Rhesos*), though not, perhaps, of Sophocles.[90]

SOPHISTIC INFLUENCE[91]

We have already observed *Prom.*'s emphasis on brevity and clarity of speech, its artificial introduction of γνῶμαι and of 'signpost' formulae, which all suggest an unusually self-conscious and rhetorical arrangement of words and speeches: the same was true of the chorus' role in dialogue. And we also find in *Prom.* particular words repeatedly used which seem to be characteristic of that growing interest in man's mind and skills, his social and political development, and the distinction between νόμος and φύσις, λόγος and ἔργον, which we associate with sophistic thought of the mid-fifth century. There is no room here for a full discussion of each term and each idea; nor is it needed, as nobody would deny that *Prom.* is extraordinarily rich in sophistic jargon.[92] But it is interesting to review briefly what we find.

τέχνη (eight times in *Prom.*), εὑρίσκω (seven times), ἐξευρίσκω (four times) are obvious enough words for *Prom.* to use often, in the context of Prometheus' claim to have taught mankind the essential techniques of civilization. More striking are σοφός (four times), σοφιστής (twice, derogatorily), σόφισμα (three times), μανθάνω (twelve), ἐκμανθάνω (five), εὐβουλία (twice), πόρος (three), πόριμος (once), πορεῖν (five), ὠφελεῖν (four), ὠφέλημα (three), which all suggest a strong belief in the mind as the solution to men's problems, and in progress through discovery, a belief which we seem to find most notably in Protagoras (Plato *Prot.* 320cff) and Gorgias

(*Palamedes* 30); cf. too S. *Ant.* 332ff.

ὠφελεῖν occurs first in extant Greek literature at A. *Pers.* 842 (cf. *Cho.* 752); it is not found elsewhere in Aeschylus. ὠφέλεια first occurs in Sophocles, ὠφέλιμος in Thucydides. 'In the classical period the words are mostly used with a rather general and not very concise sense.'[93] During the fifth and fourth centuries, a more specialized meaning develops, to denote the idea of 'benefiting mankind' (corresponding to the notion of εὐεργεσία), and the words become almost technical jargon in the sophistic-philosophical discussion of man's cultural and economic development.[94] In *Prom.*, apart from a few occurrences in the vaguer sense (44, 222, 342), this more specialized meaning is implicit at 251, 501, 507, and 613, and the use of φιλάνθρωπος (11, 28) reminds us of Prometheus' role as εὐεργέτης.

πόρος in the sense 'way out, means, solution' (Italie II), occurs three times in *Prom.*, in Aeschylus only once (*Supp.* 806); in Sophocles never; twelve times in Euripides; cf. Ar. *Knights* 759 parodying *Prom.*?; Plato *Symp.* 203d; Dion. Hal. 7.36. πορέω (*Prom.* 108, 616, 631, 934, 946) only occurs in Aeschylus at *Th.* 738; eight times in Sophocles; never in Euripides (apart from πέπρωται etc.). πόριμος *Prom.* 904; not in Aeschylus or Sophocles; in Euripides only fr. 886.3; (cf. Gorgias *Pal.* 30, which could almost come straight from Prometheus' mouth in *Prom.*).

μηχανή occurs fifteen times in Aeschylus; in Sophocles only four; in Euripides twenty-two times. In *Prom.* it only occurs once (206). But we find μηχάνημα twice (*Prom.* 469, 989); twice in Aeschylus; once in Sophocles; four times in Euripides; and μῆχαρ (*Prom.* 606); three times in Aeschylus; not in Sophocles or Euripides; elsewhere only in Lykophron.

The emphasis on ἐλπίς (*Prom.* 248ff) as man's greatest good is also striking. Although it is contradicted by much sophistic theory, which sees hope as irrational and therefore undesirable,[95] we find a parallel at Antiphon 6.5. But we should perhaps look rather to the Hesiodic account of Pandora's jar. The author of *Prom.* is clearly very familiar with Hesiod, and he is anxious to reinterpret Pandora's gifts in an optimistic way, to correct Hesiod's pessimistic view of man. (Of course Hesiod's account seems itself to be an attempt to reinterpret an older story, and his attitude to ἐλπίς is rather confused.)

Prom. 266 ἑκὼν ἑκὼν ἥμαρτον inevitably reminds us of the 'virtue-knowledge' paradox, familiar to Euripides but not, as far as we can tell, to Aeschylus.

Prom. 317 ἀρχαῖος meaning 'old-fashioned, out of date', reflects a belief in progress that is characteristically sophistic. We may contrast it with the respect for the παλαιοὶ νόμοι/θεοί of *Eum.*, and elsewhere in tragedy. This sense of ἀρχαῖος is not found again in extant Greek before Aristophanes (*Wasps* 1336, *Clouds* 915, 984, 1357, 1469, cf. 821), E. fr. 1088?, and Thucydides (1.71.2, 7.69.2).[96] Similarly Prometheus' sneer at Okeanos' κουφόνους εὐηθία (383) sounds more modern and sophisticated than we might expect from Aeschylus.

The remarkable occurrences of λόγωι/ἔργωι (*Prom.* 336, 1080) have already been discussed. There is no true parallel to this contrast of appearance and reality, expressed in the conventional dative form, before E. *Alk.* 339. In *Prom.* 489f, φύσις in the sense 'true nature' (*indoles*) also puts us in mind of later usage.[97] Elsewhere in Aeschylus, φύσις is used only of physical appearance (*Supp.* 496, *Pers.* 441, *Cho.* 281) or growth (*Ag.* 633).

The contrast πειθώ/βία is implicit in the whole opposition of Prometheus (σοφιστής) to Zeus (τύραννος). This contrast is known to Aeschylus, as well as to later glorifiers of the spoken word. The unsympathetic picture of the tyrant is a commonplace of later political philosophers,[98] and could be taken as another indication of sophistic influence.

Prometheus as the bringer of civilization to man seems to be the invention of the author of *Prom.* Traditionally Prometheus was the giver of fire, and also (in Athens at any rate) the god of potters. But there is no evidence earlier than our play of any belief that he brought such gifts as housebuilding, astronomy, numbers, writing, the use of oxen and horses, sailing, medicine, prophecy, augury, astrology, and mining (*Prom.* 445-506). Prometheus sums up his achievement in such a way (443f, 506) that we cannot fail to appreciate that man's existence is henceforth transformed: he is now civilized, and this civilization is not based solely on material prosperity, but on intelligence and knowledge.

Kleingünther suggests[99] that there is no trace in *Prom.* of any cultural development in human achievements such as is described by the sophists: the new skills are simply the 'gifts' of the philanthropic Titan; Prometheus is the typical πρῶτος εὑρετής, different only in that to him are ascribed *all* inventions (including some usually credited to other gods or heroes, e.g. Hephaistos, Athene, Poseidon, Palamedes). And certainly *Prom.*'s picture of mankind does not suggest that they can achieve much for themselves (cf. 443ff, 547ff); as in the *Hymn* to Hephaistos, they rely on external help.

Yet this may be due simply to the mythological and dramatic setting, which revolves around the individual, Prometheus, just as Plato's Protagoras puts his account of the growth of civilization in mythological terms, again with Prometheus at the centre. Although Prometheus is described as the 'inventor' or 'discoverer' of so many skills, it is also made clear elsewhere (7, 38, 110, 254) that the gift of fire itself leads directly to these further discoveries and developments. Thus Prometheus' traditional gift to man, for which he is so bitterly blamed by Hesiod, is shown to be the source of men's salvation: his φιλανθρωπία goes far beyond this original gift.[100]

It seems to me that Kleingünther's assertion[101] that the *Kulturgeschichte* of *Prom.* 442-506 is radically different from that of later sophistic accounts, is invalid, for two main reasons. First, the very number and extent of the new τέχναι represent such a complete statement of man's development from savagery to civilization as to transform the role of the πρῶτος εὑρετής. He is no mere Triptolemos, or Athene (cf. E. *Tro.* 799ff, 1433); he has shown men πᾶσαι τέχναι, so that they are now safe from extermination at the hand of Zeus (231-6, 248ff), and are the masters of Nature. Their new knowledge is proof of their progress, and a guarantee that it will continue. And secondly, as we have seen, these τέχναι are not simply described as the once-for-all gifts of a benefactor (the mythological explanation), but also as the consequences of the possession of fire (the rational-historical explanation). The account in *Prom.* of man's development has a dramatic function; it is not primarily philosophical or historical. But even within the dramatic/mythological framework, the significance of the name would not be lost: πᾶσαι τέχναι βροτοῖσιν ἐκ ΠΡΟΜΗΘΕΩΣ (504, cf. 85ff).[102]

The presence in *Prom.* of these sophistic preoccupations, rhetoric and cultural history in particular, is due of course to a large extent to the character which the author has chosen to make of Prometheus. Here we are in danger of entering a circular argument. The Prometheus-myth, as presented in our play, incorporates a distinctive and modern (in relation to Aeschylus) interpretation of the world; it is thus not surprising that it contains the sophistic vocabulary, mannerisms and ideas appropriate to that view, which in turn affect our assessment of the action and of the central character. If Aeschylus composed the play, we must suppose that his subject matter affected his style accordingly. We must ask, would he have selected this subject matter unless he had already some familiarity with, and sympathy for, the modern ways of thinking? That Aeschylus had such a familiarity and sympathy is quite possible;[103] but we must acknowledge that in no other play does it so affect the details of his style. We can perhaps trace an interest in verbal persuasion in *Supp.* and *Eum.*, yet there is no trace there of the rhetorical self-consciousness of *Prom.* We can interpret the *Oresteia* in terms of a cultural progress from the old to the new (or as a Herakleitean reconciliation of opposites, a dialectical struggle towards ἀρμονία), yet we do not find the sophistic jargon that surfaces so frequently in *Prom.*

On the evidence of the six undisputed plays, we would not expect to find such strong sophistic influence in an Aeschylean tragedy. Nor would be expect to find it in Athens at all much before 450 B.C. We must conclude, then, either that Aeschylus' original mind (and Sicilian connections?) enabled him to incorporate the new ideas and new turns of phrase in a drama where they would be appropriate, or that another author is responsible for *Prom.* None of the expressions or ideas that we have been looking at would be surprising to find in Euripides. They reflect exactly the new interests and attitudes of Athens in the mid- and late-fifth century, insofar as we can discover them from the (usually hostile) criticism of Aristophanes, Plato, and Xenophon, and from the works of Herodotos, Gorgias, Thucydides, the Presocratics, and Euripides.[104]

OTHER INFLUENCES

We have already seen some possible echoes between *Prom.* and certain fifth-century tragedies,[105] but it must be acknowledged that most of the supposed echoes are probably accidental, and there is no real basis for the belief that *Prom.* has particular similarity to individual plays of Sophocles or Euripides.[106] though we may feel that it has much in common with their early plays as well as with late Aeschylus.[107]

Homeric and Hesiodic influences are of course apparent, but do not help us. Nor do possible echoes from Solon and Bakkhylides. The links between Pindar and *Prom.* have been discussed,[108] and found to be interesting but inconclusive, unless we are impressed by the Sicilian connection.

Three other possible influences, again Sicilian, remain to be discussed: all are often put forward as evidence for Aeschylean authorship of *Prom.*: (a) Empedokles; (b) Pythagoreanism and Orphism; and (c) Epicharmos.[109]

(a) Empedokles

It has plausibly been argued that Aeschylus was aware of, and in some respects influenced by the work of Empedokles, whom he may well have met in Sicily.[110] *Prom.* is also alleged to contain Empedoklean features, notably the four-element theory (*Prom.* 88ff, 1043ff, 1080ff) implicit also in the *Oresteia* (*Cho.* 585ff, *Eum.* 903ff), some verbal echoes, and the choice of 30,000 years' punishment as 'purification'. None of these seems to amount to very much.

There is no real 'theory' of elements in *Prom.*[111] 88ff seems to stem from Homer *Il.* 3.276-8 (Prometheus cannot appeal to Zeus; the sky is the nearest he can go in his call for witnesses, cf. Hom. *Il.* 3.282, *Il.* 16.365; *Od.* 19.540; S. *El.* 86; E. fr. 839, fr. 877); while 1043ff are no more 'Empedoklean' than Solon fr. 13. 18ff West, where the reverse process, calm out of a storm, is described.

The supposed verbal echoes between Empedokles and Aeschylus, and in particular *Prom.*, are far from certain.[112] Many seem purely accidental or negligible (e.g. *Prom.* 27, 376, 654 / Emp. B145.2 DK; *Prom.* 551 / Emp. B122.2, B18; words in -μων, -ειος, -ωμα). More striking is the use of θεμερῶπις (*Prom.* 134 / Emp. B122.2), a word found nowhere else (except Hesychius). Interesting too is the large number of -ωπος words in *Prom.* (253, 356, 364, 498, 568, 667) and Empedokles (B21.6, B2.1); but there are only four instances in Aeschylus (*Ag.* 725, *Cho.* 738, *Eum.* 955, fr. 170.2), and twenty in Euripides.[113]

The 30,000 year punishment mentioned in Πυρφόρος (according to Σ *Prom.* 94) may remind us of Empedokles B115.6.[114] But 30,000 was already a magic number to Hesiod (*WD* 252ff),[115] and in any case *Prom.* is generally less specific, cf. 94, 774.

The case for Empedoklean (and Anaxagorean) influence on Aeschylus is not to be ignored; but it faces considerable chronological objections. Empedokles cannot have been much more than thirty when the *Oresteia* was produced, and we do not hear of Aeschylus visiting Sicily between his first trip and 458 B.C. How could Aeschylus come to be influenced by him in the *Oresteia*? If Aeschylus could feel his influence while remaining in Athens, so could any later dramatist; indeed he might be more likely to absorb it than the aged Aeschylus, and there would be nothing remarkable about any educated Athenian after 450 being familiar with Empedokles' work. I think we may discount this as an argument for Aeschylean authorship.[116]

(b) Pythagoreanism and Orphism[117]

We are told by Cicero that Aeschylus was '*non poeta solum, sed etiam Pythagoreus*', and various hints of this may be found in his work. But there is little that one can grasp firmly and announce, 'This is Pythagorean.' In *Prom.* we may be struck by the importance attached to numbers (459f), but I do not feel that this amounts to an argument either (cf. Stobaios 1.1 p. 15 Wachs., from an unknown tragedian = fr. *adesp.* 470). There is certainly no need to think of a personal acquaintance on the author's part with a Pythagorean sect.

(c) Epicharmos[118]

Another inhabitant of Sicily, he is reported to have been familiar with Aeschylus' work (Σ A. *Eum.* 626), and his parodies may have gone beyond individual words to whole plays (*Persai*, *Thearoi*). There is however no reason to suppose that Epicharmos' Πύρρα ἢ Προμαθεύς owed anything to Aeschylus or to *Prom.* It seems to have dealt with the creation of man, a theme untouched by Aeschylus, as far as we know. The suggestion that some technical peculiarities of *Prom.* may be due to the influence of Epicharmos on Aeschylus,[119] in the last year or two of his life in Sicily, seems to me grotesque.[120]

We may conclude that none of these influences is clearly to be discerned in *Prom.*, and they certainly should not bear any weight in our investigation.

Chapter 10

ALTERNATIVES TO AESCHYLEAN AUTHORSHIP

In Chapter 2 I suggested that the external evidence presented about as good a *prima facie* case for Aeschylean authorship as we would be entitled to expect,[1] but that this evidence alone was far from compelling, and that the final decision would have to be based largely on the play itself. I have now reached the point at which that decision can no longer honestly be avoided.

Had *Prometheus Bound* been newly dug up from the sands of Oxyrhynchus, miraculously intact, but anonymous and lacking any ancient testimony linking it to any particular author, I think it is fair to say that few scholars would regard it as the work of Aeschylus. The metrical technique of the lyrics and anapaests, and of the iambic trimeters,[2] the quantity and context of the actors' anapaests, the irregularities of the stichomythia, the choice of vocabulary, a number of syntactical modernisms, the curious frequency of repetition,[3] and the relative simplicity of the general style, all seem clearly to betray a different hand. The sonorous compound adjectives and rolling three-word trimeters, together with the grand conception of the dramatic action (and perhaps the trilogic form) inevitably remind us of Aeschylus; yet we should find the sophistic elements, the subordinate role of the chorus, and the sometimes rather prosaic[4] and undramatic[5] presentation enough to indicate a date later than 450 B.C.

The choice is not easy. Either Aeschylus wrote a play (or trilogy) in which, for reasons unknown to us,[6] he chose to suppress most of his most distinctive mannerisms and to adopt others not elsewhere observed in his extant work, mannerisms both large and small, conscious and unconscious; or we have to conclude that one of the world's greatest dramas was not written by the dramatic genius to whom it has been almost unanimously ascribed, but by an author whom we are unlikely to be able to identify, and whose name we may never even have heard. In the past, caution and conservatism have prevailed, partly perhaps through a sense of decency;[7]

few scholars have had the confidence to pursue their doubts to the end. But it is now necessary to consider the implications of non-Aeschylean authorship.

Two main questions immediately present themselves: (a) If Aeschylus did not write *Prom.*, who did? (b) If Aeschylus did not write *Prom.*, how and why did it end up in the collection of the seven most popular Aeschylean plays in later antiquity,[8] and why was its authenticity never questioned before this last century? Two subordinate questions also arise: (c) Did Aeschylus write *any* Prometheus-plays (apart from the satyric Πυρκαεύς) and if so, was Λυόμενος one of them? (d) How does our denial of Aeschylean authorship affect the interpretation of the play?[9] It is perhaps easier to answer the first question after dealing with the others.

THE TRADITION

We know that other first-rate tragedians were composing in Athens during the mid-fifth century.[10] Aristophanes' respect for Phrynichos is obvious;[11] Philokles' defeat of Sophocles' *OT* is known, as is Xenokles' of Euripides' Trojan trilogy in 415 B.C.[12] We possess the names, and little more, of a number of tragedians who were probably active between 475 and 413:[13] Phrynichos, Pratinas, Achaios, Akestor, Aristarchos, Aristias, Datis, Euaion, two more Euripides, Euphorion, Gnesippos, Hippias, Ion, Iophon, Kallistratos, Karkinos, Melanthios, Menekrates, Mesatos, Neophron, Nikomachos, Nothippos, Philokles, Polyphrasmon, Theognis, Xenokles, Agathon, Kritias, Meletos (and perhaps Hieronymos, Morsimos, Morychos, Sthenelos). Of these, we are told that Phrynichos won at least two victories, Pratinas[14] one, Achaios one, Aristarchos two, Euphorion probably more than four, Euripides A two, Ion an unknown number, but perhaps several, as he was accepted into the tragic 'canon',[15] Iophon at least one, though detractors claimed that some of his plays were the work of his father,[16] Neophron several? (out of 120 plays), Mesatos between two and four, Philokles at least one, Polyphrasmon at least one, probably two or more,[17] and Xenokles at least one. Agathon, Kritias, and Meletos are perhaps too late to be candidates for authorship of our play; Phrynichos and Pratinas are perhaps too early.

Now it is apparent that *Prom.* did not impress the Athenians in the way that e.g. A. *Niobe*, *Seven against Thebes*, or *Oresteia*[18] did, or E. *Telephos*, *Andromeda*, *Medea*, *Hippolytos* (probably both of them[19]). We find no apparent reference to Δεσμώτης or Λυόμενος before Aristotle,[20] whose comment is unfortunately unintelligible, and may not even refer to our play(s);[21] the first extant author to register his admiration for an Aeschylean Prometheus is Cicero,[22] and he picks on Λυόμενος (indeed Prometheus' reactions to the pain and humiliation of his position in Δεσμώτης would not provide such an impressive example of philosophical endurance). It is fair to say that we have little idea of fifth-century taste in tragedy, apart from the apparently universal popularity of Aeschylus and Sophocles; the changes that took place during the fourth century may have played a major part in deciding which works would survive to be collected by the Alexandrians for their library, and which authors would generally be regarded as most worthy of study.

When Sophocles and Euripides both died within a year of each other, it was natural enough for Aristophanes to base a comedy on the premise that the art of tragedy had died with them. But it would be unwise to conclude from *Frogs* that to fifth-century Athenians the three major tragedians were in a class quite of their own. Aristophanes' own respect for Phrynichos has already been noted,[23] and even in *Frogs* it is recognized that Iophon and Agathon have some claim to the highest rank (71ff). And according to Satyros,[24] Euripides' decision to leave Athens around 410 B.C. was prompted by his resentment of the popularity of his rivals Morsimos, Akestor, Dorilaos, and Melanthios: whether or not this is true, it seemed a possible explanation to later commentators, and Euripides' record in the tragic competitions is not particularly impressive.[25] So it may be that Aristophanes' interest in Euripides' work was occasioned more by his unorthodoxy than by the feeling that he represented an exceptional talent.

But certainly by half-way through the fourth century the three tragedians were firmly established on their own. Herakleides of Pontos, a pupil of Plato, wrote Περὶ τῶν τριῶν τραγῳδοποιῶν;[26] and about the same time (*c.* 350-330 B.C.) Lykourgos apparently tried to establish official texts of their plays, from which producers were not to deviate.[27] We are not told that any other tragedians were so honoured, and we do not know whose plays were revived in the competitions apart from these three: perhaps none were.

The individual whose knowledge and interest in tragedy were most important for posterity was Aristotle. He seems to have been the first to assemble and organize the various records of the dramatic competitions, and his *Didaskaliai* seem to have formed the starting-point for most subsequent scholarship on tragedy and comedy.[28] The precise nature of these *Didaskaliai* is not clear to us; nor is their relationship either to Aristotle's own *Nikai*[29] or to the official inscription set up in Athens around 345 B.C. (now generally known as the *Fasti*[30]) on which are listed, under each archon year, the victorious tribe in the men's and the boys' dithyramb, the choregos and producer of the winning comedy, and the choregos, producer, and (after 449 B.C.) actor of the winning tragedies. This inscription was periodically brought up to date until 305 B.C., and seems to begin with the institution of the choregic system for the competitions around 500 or so.[31] Those pieces of the inscription which survive tally very well with our other sources (*hypotheseis*, Suda, Marmor Parium, etc.), many of which may in any case be dependent on it, and it must be based ultimately on some sort of official fifth- and fourth-century records, as is shown by the formal arrangement, the apparent completeness of the information, and the order in which the names are given.[32] Whether it was copied (or excerpted) from Aristotle's *Didaskaliai* or *Nikai*, or whether both it and he drew directly on the old records, we cannot tell.

Less tenuous seem the links between Aristotle's *Didaskaliai* and the Athenian lists of all the tragedies and comedies performed at the Dionysia and Lenaia, going back at least to the 420s, and perhaps much earlier, which were apparently inscribed on the walls of a building but now survive only in small and tantalizing fragments.[33] We have no idea how complete or accurate the information for the fifth century was, but we should observe that for the similarly comprehensive Roman inscription[34] of the comic playwrights and their productions at the two festivals, which must also be based on an Athenian or Alexandrian original, there are frequent gaps in the knowledge of particular performances. Out of eight fifth-century productions mentioned in the surviving fragments, three refer merely to κωμωιδίαι, without specifying their titles; in another case it is remarked that of all Lysippos' plays, only one is preserved (Βάκχαις· αὗται μόναι σώιζονται[35]). There is no reason to suppose that the details of tragedy were any more complete, and we are forced to conclude that Aristotle and subsequent compilers of *didaskaliai* had no official source for the titles of the plays produced each year in the competitions, but only for the names of their poets or producers.[36] Nor should this surprise us: to the archon, or whoever was responsible for recording the details of the competitions each year in the fifth century,[37] in accordance with normal Athenian concern that public expenditure and achievement should be formally recognized and made known, the particular plays produced were of no more interest than the subjects of the dithyrambs or the costumes of the choruses. We cannot even be certain that the plays were given formal titles for their first performance.[38]

The collection of information recorded in the *Fasti*, or the compilation of chronological lists of victorious poets, tragic and comic, with their records of first, second, third, etc. prizes at each festival, would be simple enough procedures, with the official records to work from; but the amassing of full didaskalic information, as to which four plays each tragedian produced each year, must have been far less straightforward and far more liable to error.

Whence did the author of the *hypothesis* to A. *Pers.* (perhaps Aristophanes of Byzantium[39]) derive his information that ἐπὶ Μένωνος τραγωιδῶν Αἰσχύλος ἐνίκα Φινεῖ Πέρσαις Γλαύκωι Προμηθεῖ? An extant entry in the *Fasti*[40] reads τραγωιδῶν Περικλῆς Χολαρ: ἐχορη Αἰσχύλος ἐδίδασκε, and it is reasonable to conclude that the *hypothesis* is based on this or a similar source: otherwise the retention of τραγωιδῶν would be hard to explain. Similarly the *Fasti* for 459/8 B.C.[41] record ἐπὶ Φιλοκλέους ... τραγωιδῶν Ξενοκλῆς 'Αφιδνα: ἐχορη Αἰσχύλος ἐδίδασκεν, but *hypoth.* A. *Ag.* states ἐδιδάχθη τὸ δρᾶμα ἐπὶ ἄρχοντος Φιλοκλέους 'Ολυμπιάδι $\overline{\pi\eta}$ ἔτει $\overline{\beta}$. πρῶτος Αἰσχύλος 'Αγαμέμνονι Χοηφόροις Εὐμενίσι Πρωτεῖ σατυρικῶι. ἐχορήγει Ξενοκλῆς 'Αφιδναῖος, while for A. *Th.* we are also given details of the rival plays: ἐδιδάχθη ἐπὶ Θεαγενίδου 'Ολυμπιάδι $\overline{o\eta}$. ἐνίκα Αἰσχύλος Λαΐωι Οἰδίποδι "Επτα ἐπὶ Θήβας Σφιγγὶ σατυρικῆι, δεύτερος 'Αριστίας ταῖς τοῦ πατρὸς αὐτοῦ τραγωιδίαις Περσεῖ Ταντάλωι Παλαισταῖς σατύροις, τρίτος Πολυφράσμων Λυκουργείαι τετραλογίαι. In both these examples the record is given in paraphrase and with additions, as it is for example at *hypoth*. E. *Med*. ἐδιδάχθη ἐπὶ Πυθοδώρου ἄρχοντος Ὀλυμπιάδος π̅ζ̅ ἔτει α̅. πρῶτος Εὐφορίων, δεύτερος Σοφοκλῆς, τρίτος Εὐριπίδης Μηδείαι Φιλοκτήτηι Δίκτυι Θερισταῖς σατύροις, and E. *Hipp*. ἐδιδάχθη ἐπὶ Ἐπαμείνονος ἄρχοντος Ὀλυμπιάδι π̅ζ̅ ἔτει δ̅. πρῶτος Εὐριπίδης, δεύτερος Ἰοφῶν, τρίτος Ἴων. Presumably Aelian is drawing from a collection of *hypotheseis* or some similar source for his statement about E. *Tro*.[42] κατὰ τὴν πρώτην καὶ ἐνενηκόστην Ὀλυμπιάδα, καθ' ἣν ἐνίκα Ἐξαίνετος ὁ Ἀκραγαντῖνος στάδιον, ἀντηγωνίσαντο ἀλλήλοις Ξενοκλῆς καὶ Εὐριπίδης. καὶ πρῶτός γε ἦν Ξενοκλῆς, ὅστις ποτὲ οὗτός ἐστιν, Οἰδίποδι καὶ Λυκάονι καὶ Βάκχαις καὶ Ἀθάμαντι σατυρικῶι. τούτου δεύτερος Εὐριπίδης ἦν Ἀλεξάνδρωι καὶ Παλαμήδει καὶ Τρώιασι καὶ Σισύφωι σατυρικῶι.

Whereas *hypoth*. A. *Pers*. resembles the *Fasti* in its arrangement (ἐπὶ Μενωνος τραγωιδῶν ...), the other examples seem to follow a slightly different pattern, with Olympiad and rival competitors included. This may well reflect the arrangement of Aristotle's *Didaskaliai*, but we simply have too little to go on. Similarly, we cannot tell whether the incompleteness of the information (sometimes rival plays are named, sometimes not) stems from the source, from the selectivity of our authorities, or from accidents of transmission. Thus there is insufficient evidence for us to come to any firm conclusions as to the completeness of Aristotle's lists of plays for each year.

In the absence of any authoritative record, Aristotle and his successors must presumably have used all the resources available, victory dedications, family traditions both written and oral from the descendants of the great dramatists, references from historians, comic poets, and storytellers,[43] in their efforts to identify the titles for the various productions. So too, the statement that Aeschylus first competed in 496 B.C.,[44] or that Thespis first produced in about 535,[45] must derive either from private channels or from the scholarly inference of later generations: it is inconceivable that any official record of such details would have been made at the time.[46] Likewise, information about numbers of actors, scene-painting, etc., which was of interest to Aristotle as he traced tragedy to its full realization of its φύσις, must have been available to him only in scattered and possibly unreliable sources, or inferred by him from the texts of the plays themselves.

For our purposes, the important thing is that although it was known which poets won the competitions each year, and perhaps which poets came second and third, probably right back to the beginning of the fifth century, there was nothing like the same degree of certainty concerning the titles of the plays produced by each poet, and nothing like the same completeness in the reconstruction of each year's competition, play by play. We may again surmise that more attention was paid to Aeschylus, Sophocles and Euripides than to the other tragedians of the fifth century, and even here there were clearly gaps in the didaskalic record.[47] We must remember too that no attempt was made by Aristotle or his immediate successors to collect the texts themselves and to identify the particular plays by their first lines. It is not even certain that any distinction was made between different plays with the same name by the same author, though there is some evidence that Aristotle did comment from time to time on possible ambiguities in the record.[48]

Aristotle's researches must at least in part have been connected with his theoretical discussions of poetry, of which we possess only the *Rhetoric* and the fragmentary and enigmatic *Poetics*. In his tantalizingly brief description of the evolution of tragedy at *Poet*. 4.1449a4ff, he only mentions Aeschylus and Sophocles by name, though elsewhere he did apparently refer to Thespis' contribution;[49] and it is noticeable that in his analysis of the aesthetics of tragedy he refers to no fifth-century tragedian apart from Aeschylus, Sophocles, Euripides and Agathon (who really counts as a fourth-century figure). He shows no awareness that tragedians ever composed connected trilogies or tetralogies, and his critical judgements in many respects appear to reflect the standards of the fourth century, in his concern for the different kinds of plot, the emphasis on ἀναγνώρισις, the discussion of the role of choral lyrics, the subordination of μέλος, and the lack of interest in the early form of tragedy.

Aristotle quite frequently refers to specific tragedies or tragedians to exemplify a point he is making. These examples are drawn from Sophocles and Euripides and, to a lesser extent, Aeschylus, and also from Agathon, Theodektes, Karkinos, Chairemon, Antiphon, Dikaiogenes, Astydamas, Polyeides, and Kleophon,[50] all of the fourth century. The conclusion is inescapable that Aristotle knew and cared little about Phrynichos or Pratinas, Ion or Iophon.[51] His pupils, Dikaiarchos, Aristoxenos, and Theophrastos, may have studied fifth-century tragedy,[52] but there is nothing to indicate that they looked far outside the three major tragedians, either.

In short, we have seen nothing to contradict our initial impression that, throughout the fourth century, interest in παλαιαὶ τραγωιδίαι was largely confined to the three. Both in the choice of which plays to produce each year, and in the collection of didaskalic information about past performances, they dominated the field. The families of the poets will have helped to encourage this process; the sons and grandsons of both Sophocles and Euripides were apparently themselves active dramatists,[53] and we may assume that they were concerned that the details of their ancestors' victories, and of course the texts of their plays, should not pass into oblivion.

How were fifth-century plays preserved for posterity?[54] It is hard to imagine that official public texts of any sort were dedicated or registered before the time of Lykourgos. More likely, individual tragedians and their families,[55] and perhaps actors, choregoi, and members of the chorus, retained their own copies and allowed others to have them transcribed more or less informally. The demand would vary from play to play. The theatre-going public[56] would watch generally nine new tragedies at every City Dionysia, plus perhaps a few more at the Lenaia; it might also see revivals at the Rural Dionysia,[57] but it could surely not expect, nor be expected, to be abreast of every new production and familiar with every past one.[58] Probably the first performance was often crucial in deciding the later fate of a play: if it flopped, it would naturally fall into neglect, unless the author saw fit to revise it (e.g. E. *Hipp.*, Aristophanes' *Clouds* etc.[59]). Presumably too some plays were written but never granted a chorus, whether because they were clearly inferior or because their author was not sufficiently well-known.[60]

In the case of Aeschylus a special exception was made: after his death producers could be given a chorus to re-stage one of his tragedies.[61] Yet even here, it is far more likely that the responsibility for obtaining a text and interpreting the play still lay with the producer than that any standard edition existed which was readily accessible to all. We can be fairly confident that producers took some liberties with Aeschylus' plays, in presenting them to an audience accustomed to different styles of acting, music, and staging,[62] and we have no idea who, if anyone, actually verified that the play being produced really was the work of Aeschylus: in the days preceding Aristotle's *Didaskaliai*, what possible means of verification were available, apart from the memories of the older citizens?

The first time that any systematic collection of tragic texts is likely to have been made is during the foundation of the Alexandrian Library of the Mouseion, around 280 B.C.[63] To build up a comprehensive and complete library virtually from scratch was an enormous task, and it appears that, from the start, it was decided to concentrate on certain major authors.[64] In the case of tragedy, the responsibility was given to Alexander of Aitolia.[65] Whether or not the story of the trick by which Ptolemy III obtained the 'original' Athenian texts is true,[66] we need not doubt that the labour and ingenuity required to track down texts of works known only by title or date of performance (from the *didaskaliai* etc.) were considerable, and the process both difficult and lengthy.

The *Pinakes* of Kallimachos are the first known attempt at a more or less complete catalogue of Greek literature,[67] and they seem to have formed one of the main bases for subsequent Alexandrian scholarship. These Πίνακες τῶν ἐν πάσηι παιδείαι διαλαμψάντων καὶ ὧν συνέγραψαν[68] amounted almost to an index of Greek authors and their works in every field, and were apparently published for general consumption; they should be distinguished from the actual catalogues of the Library which must have existed in some form, for the use of the librarians and others who wanted to consult its contents.[69] Thus it may be assumed that the *Pinakes* mentioned many works which the Library did not possess, and that the Library possessed innumerable second-rate works (and duplicate copies) which Kallimachos did not think it worth recording.

We know that Kallimachos and his successors sometimes specified that certain works were not possessed by the Library (οὐ σώιζεται[70]). For the minor tragedians this probably went for quite a sizeable proportion of their work,[71] but for Aeschylus, Sophocles, and Euripides exceptional pains were naturally taken to get as complete a collection as possible. Even so, the author of the catalogue to which the *Life* of Euripides refers has to acknowledge that fourteen of his ninety-two known works are lost.[72] The *Life* of Sophocles states that seventeen of the 130 plays which Aristophanes of Byzantium attributed to Sophocles are spurious, but does not make it clear whether or not this was Aristophanes' own judgement. It is natural to suppose that information concerning performances and titles of plays was more complete for works of the later fifth century than it was for Aeschylus' time, and that the tradition which preserved the texts of Sophocles and Euripides was more reliable than that of their predecessor; it certainly appears that the private reading of books became steadily more common as the century entered its final third.[73] There can be little doubt too that scholarly interest and acumen were directed more vigorously towards the Euripidean corpus than towards the surviving works of Aeschylus.

Whatever the means by which Aeschylus' plays were preserved from the times of their first performances to their arrival and cataloguing in the Library, whether through his family, or through public channels, or through a variety of more or less accidental traditions, it is hard to believe that all the plays which he wrote reached the Library intact. The number of performances recorded in the *didaskaliai* is likely to have exceeded the number of plays in the Library's possession, and so is the number of recorded titles, though we do not know how complete the *didaskaliai* were.[74] It is highly likely too that the scholars of the Library (Alexander of Aitolia, Kallimachos etc.) made active searches for those plays which were not already in their possession, in their attempt to preserve the 'most brilliant'[75] of the classical writers.

The Alexandrians are generally supposed to have established 'canons' of the most important authors in each genre, but the evidence is scanty and often contradictory.[76] The best attested canons are those of the ten Attic orators and the nine lyric poets,[77] but it is far from certain that these were formally established before the turn of the millenium, or that they were due to any individual critic or school of critics. Often different canons seem to have coexisted: thus Demosthenes, Isokrates, Lysias, Aischines, Isaios, and Hypereides were put in a higher bracket than

Antiphon, Andokides, Lykourgos, and Deinarchos;[78] so too Herodotos, Thucydides, and Xenophon were distinguished from Philistos, Theopompos, Ephoros, Anaximenes, Kallisthenes, Hellanikos, and Polybios.[79] There were suggestions that Korinna should be added to the lyric ennead.[80] Amongst the comic poets, Aristophanes, Eupolis, and Kratinos stood out in the first rank, but the degree of prominence given to Krates, Pherekrates, Plato, and (especially) Epicharmos, seems to have varied considerably from critic to critic,[81] while to some only Menander and the New Comedy really counted.[82]

The tragic canon comprised Aeschylus, Sophocles, and Euripides, plus or minus Ion and Achaios.[83] The choice of these two in particular, out of all the tragedians of the fifth and fourth century, is rather curious. According to the Suda, Achaios only won one victory out of perhaps forty-four plays, while Ion may not have written more than a dozen plays all told, and certainly not more than forty.[84] It is very hard to see why these two were selected rather than their contemporaries Iophon and Philokles, for example, or Polyphrasmon and Euphorion, who all apparently had better records at the tragic competition. The answer may well be that the choice reflects the stylistic preference of a particular group of critics, or even possibly the accident of the tradition. Ion was apparently known to the Alexandrians in other capacities than that of tragedian,[85] and it may be that he owed his inclusion to his range of talents as much as to his excellence as a dramatist, although the criticism that he stood in relation to Sophocles as Bakkhylides to Pindar[86] is no mean compliment, and his style was apparently praised for its smooth craftsmanship. But the preference for Ion over, say, Phrynichos, whom Aristophanes clearly rated not far behind Aeschylus in the old school, may simply be due to changing taste or even to inadequate preservation of Phrynichos' work.

In any case, it is not easy to see who would have created this canon of five, or when, and it never established itself as a serious rival to the triad which we know. When Aristophanes of Byzantium came to write his *hypotheseis* to the great tragedies, he confined his attention to the three,[87] and it is natural to suppose that he reflected the general standards of the Alexandrians. It is possible that Kallimachos' Πίνακες picked out five (or three) major figures in tragedy, but there is no evidence for this, and his work seems to have consisted less of evaluation than of organization of existing material. The indications are that some works of minor authors (comedies, tragedies, mimes, orations etc.) continued to be read and copied in Greek Egypt right into the second century A.D.,[88] but that scholarly attention, in the form of ὑπομνήματα and ὑποθέσεις, was devoted largely to the classics. The excerptors, epitomizers, anthologists and lexicographers set to work quite early,[89] and they would tend to preserve the choicest fruits of the lesser-known authors, and thus encourage the neglect of the rest of their work, and it is doubtless through them that such figures as Athenaios and Plutarch satisfied their omnivorous appetites for learning, rather than through first-hand acquaintance with most of the poets whom they quote; often, indeed, we may suspect that they do not even know the author themselves.[90]

Let us then imagine the situation in Alexandria, when Kallimachos came to compile his catalogue of tragedians and their work. Alexander of Aitolia had gathered all the tragic material he could, though with a pronounced emphasis on the classic three. Kallimachos had now to complete the process of arranging this material in accordance with the plays' own super- and subscriptions, with the help of independent information from Aristotle's *Didaskaliai* (and perhaps a few earlier works on tragedy[91]). To his alphabetical list of the known works of each tragedian he would assign the plays that he found; some would doubtless be duplicated in the Library, others missing completely. A large number of plays must have turned up for which there was no corresponding entry in the didaskalic records. In the case of Aeschylus, it seems that there was already some uncertainty as to exactly how many plays he had produced, and this is probably true of Sophocles and Euripides too. In at least one case (A. Αἰτναῖαι), two different plays were contending for one pigeonhole, and one was pronounced spurious, perhaps for the first time in a hundred years or more.[92] In other cases, it is natural to suppose that Kallimachos had to use his common sense - and his poetic sensibility - to put title (and author) to work.[93] Before the Alexandrians, authenticity had not been a matter of much concern,[94] and probably many works survived with no title or author's name attached; others were known by alternative titles, which again might cause confusion.[95]

The *didaskaliai* may have listed a victory (or even second or third place) one year for Αἰσχύλος Προμηθεῖ or Προμηθείαι, apart from the fourth play produced with *Persians* in 472; or there may have been no clue at all as to whether Aeschylus had composed any other plays on this subject. But neither Sophocles nor Euripides was supposed to have composed an entire play on this theme,[96] and, as we have seen, relatively little interest was shown in obtaining the actual works of the other tragedians. Kallimachos found three Prometheus-plays, now known to us as Δεσμώτης, Λυόμενος, and Πυρκαεύς,[97] all of which he attributed to Aeschylus. In the absence of any rivals to the position this attribution was canonized, and remained virtually unchallenged until this century: Kallimachos' οὗ ἡ ἀρχή would ensure 'correct' attribution among his successors.

That Kallimachos did take our play to be the work of Aeschylus is probable, but not quite certain. The style of the *hypothesis* to the play fits the pattern which may go back to Aristophanes of Byzantium (ἡ μὲν σκηνὴ τοῦ δράματος ὑπόκειται ἐν Σκυθίαι ... ὁ δὲ χορὸς συνέστηκεν ἐξ 'Ωκεανίδων νυμφῶν ... κεῖται ἡ μυθοποιία ... etc.)[98] but we cannot be certain that this formula was not imitated, or even invented, by later scholars. But in any case, Aristophanes and his successors concerned themselves only with the three great tragedians,[99] and it is unlikely that *Prom.* could have been unknown to Kallimachos and Aristophanes, yet unquestioningly attributed to Aeschylus by the scholiasts and composer of the *hypothesis*. (It is also unlikely that the play would have arrived in Alexandria for the first time between the composition of the *Pinakes* and that of an Aristophanic *hypothesis*.) Only if we are prepared to accept that the scholia and *hypothesis* to *Prom.* are non-Alexandrian in origin (i.e. Pergamene?, Byzantine?) will it be easy for us to avoid tracing the Aeschylean ascription back to Kallimachos.

We have seen already that the emphasis on the three had resulted since the fourth century in the relative neglect of other fifth-century tragedians, but we must nevertheless acknowledge that Kallimachos had much more material for comparison available to him than we do (including of course Λυόμενος), and might therefore be expected to have been in a much stronger position to judge whether or not

Δεσμώτης was Aeschylean than we are. But at this point we should perhaps review briefly the Alexandrians' record in such matters.

From the earliest days of 'scholarship' the epic attracted the most interest, as one might expect.[100] Homer was regarded as the author of the *Iliad*, and generally of the *Odyssey* too.[101] But the ascription of the 'cyclic' epics was far from certain or consistent.[102] Even in Herodotos' time there was dispute as to the Homeric authorship of the *Kypria*;[103] and later opinions were divided between Homer, Hegesias (or Hegesinos), Kyprias, and Stasinos.[104] The *Aithiopis* (or *Amazonia*) was variously ascribed to Homer and to Arktinos;[105] the *Ilias Mikra* occasionally to Homer, or to Thestorides, Kinaithos, or Diodoros, but most often, from the fifth century onwards, to Lesches;[106] the *Iliou Persis* was given to Homer, to Lesches, and to Arktinos;[107] the *Nostoi* to Homer or to Agias;[108] the *Telegonia* (or *Thesprotis*) to Kinaithos, to Eugammon, even to Mousaios.[109] The Homeric scholia refer frequently to οἱ νεώτεροι,[110] as if more specific identification were impossible. Aristotle speaks confidently of Homer as the author of *Margites*,[111] but distinguishes him from οἱ ἄλλοι ... οἷον ὁ τὰ Κύπρια ποιήσας καὶ τὴν Μικρὰν Ἰλιάδα.[112] Some later scholars apparently rejected *Margites*; but Kallimachos accepted it as the work of Homer.[113] Clearly then there was no reliable evidence to connect the existing poems with the semi-mythical names (Arktinos, Lesches, Homer, etc.) which were traditionally associated with the epic; in some cases elaborate stories were invented to explain the connections between Homer and his 'pupils' or 'rivals'.[114]

With Mousaios and Orpheus the position must have been at least equally chaotic.[115] We have no idea what Kallimachos catalogued under their names, though it does not appear that they received anything like the scholarly attention devoted to the *Iliad* and the *Odyssey* by Zenodotos, Aristarchos, and their successors. Hesiod was given *Works and Days* and *Theogony*, and also the *Catalogues* (sometimes referred to as *Eoai*), the *Shield of Herakles*, *Peirithoos*, and various other works which appear to us to have very little claim to authenticity.[116] The history of the 'Homeric' Hymns is very obscure, but here again it is obvious that the Alexandrians knew little, if anything, more than we do.[117]

As for prose works, which were in most cases far more recent and might therefore be expected to be more reliably transmitted,[118] we know of several mistakes of attribution which strike us as glaringly obvious. The (presumably anonymous, but clearly unxenophontic) 'Αθηναίων Πολιτεία was ascribed to Xenophon.[119] Miscellaneous speeches were given to Demosthenes which he could not possibly have written, and which make no pretence to being his work.[120] In the case of Lysias, who wrote speeches mostly for others to deliver, the position is hopelessly unclear:[121] Dionysios of Halikarnassos knew of 425 speeches ascribed to him, of which he accepted 230;[122] Harpokration cites ninety-five speeches and one epistle, thirty-nine of which he regards as possibly spurious,[123] but Photios suggests that some perfectly genuine speeches were wrongly athetized in antiquity, and therefore lost to posterity.[124] Of the thirty-five works which we possess as the *Corpus Lysiacum* (including the *Erotikos* from Plato's *Phaedrus*), modern scholars show no signs of agreeing how many are truly Lysias'.[125] Similar uncertainty surrounds some of Isokrates' speeches, although here the tradition should have been more secure at least in the years immediately following his death; his students might be expected to keep track of their master's works.[126]

The Alexandrians apparently gave to Plato a collection of *Letters*, of varying quality and credibility,[127] plus such obvious fakes as *Demodocus*, *Axiochus*, *Definitions* etc., and the probably spurious *Hippias A*, *Hipparchus*, *Theages*, *Amatores*, *Minos*, *Eryxias*, *Sisyphus*, *Clitopho*, and the two *Alcibiades*.[128] Here, of course, the excuse for misattribution is easily enough found: we are told that Plato continued to revise his works throughout his life,[129] and this process was probably continued after his death by his pupils in the Academy.[130] The same is true of Aristotle, all of whose published works are lost,[131] and whose surviving writings continue to pose insoluble problems of authenticity.[132]

When we turn to tragedy, the Alexandrians' achievements seem equally unreliable. In the case of Thespis, scholarly ignorance was apparently so great that Herakleides of Pontos was able to pass off his own work as that of the inventor of tragedy.[133] Things may not have been much better for Phrynichos.[134] Of course there was one big difference between the tradition for the tragedies (and comedies) and that for the huge quantities of prose and hexameter verse, viz. the various *didaskaliai* and the other works of Aristotle and his successors on related subjects. But as we have seen, these records were by no means complete or comprehensive, and we should not overestimate the aids available to the early librarians in this field.

Three specific questions concerning the authenticity of tragedies offer us evidence as to the reliability of the tradition:

(1) The Medicean Catalogue of Aeschylus' plays, which presumably goes back to the Alexandrians,[135] records two plays entitled Αἰτναῖαι,[136] described respectively as γνήσιοι and νόθοι. No indication is given as to who athetized the second play, nor on what grounds, though the most natural answer is Kallimachos or a near-contemporary. But the fact that the play was still listed suggests that it had some claim to Aeschylean authorship, whether its antique style or its ascription by others to Aeschylus. In either case, it appears that a play was available to the maker of the Catalogue which some people at one time believed to be the work of Aeschylus, but which he did not. We might ask ourselves what would have happened if the genuine play had not been available: would the other have been questioned?

(2) Three plays are said by the *Life* of Euripides to be spurious: νοθεύεται δὲ τρία, Τέννης, Ῥαδάμανθος, Πειρίθους. Another reference suggests Kritias as the author of *Peirithous*,[137] and clearly by the second century A.D. it was recognized that the problem could not be resolved: with all their records and catalogues, the Alexandrians had left one, perhaps three, plays from the late fifth century under the name of Euripides, which some believed spurious. Perhaps the general eagerness to find Euripidean plays had been too great, and only later had it been found that no corresponding titles could be found in the *didaskaliai* for Euripides, whereas for Kritias a *Peirithous* was known to have been produced. Or perhaps this play was first correctly attributed to Kritias, but as so much more interest was lavished on the three major tragedians, it ended up being included with the works of Euripides. Or perhaps confusion arose because both writers had composed tragedies with these same titles, and nobody was sure which ones these were. This last explanation seems quite probable in the separate case of the *Sisyphos* play(s). The well-known atheistic fragment, cited by

Sextus Empiricus as the work of Kritias, is attributed by Aëtios and others to Euripides' *Sisyphos*;[138] we also learn from Aelian that the fourth play produced by Euripides in 415 B.C. was a satyric *Sisyphos*.[139] In this case too, modern scholars are divided, but the fact remains that, after Kallimachos, it should have been easy to check: he gave, as well as title and author, also the first line (οὗ ἡ ἀρχή ...), so that confusion should not be possible in the future. We must therefore conclude that either Kallimachos failed to mention the plays at all, or his judgement was considered sufficiently fallible for others to challenge it.[140]

(3) The third and most fascinating problem is *Rhesos*.[141] Krates of Mallos, the leading Pergamene scholar of the second century B.C., believed that Euripides produced a play of this name early in his career;[142] there is also little doubt that the play which we possess (with two prologues attached which are now lost)[143] was classified as Euripidean by Kallimachos and accepted as such by the source of the *hypothesis*.[144] Most modern scholars believe that they were mistaken: this should not be forgotten when we consider *Prom.* The evidence for Euripides, and interest in his work, were undoubtedly far greater in the fourth and third centuries B.C. than they were for Aeschylus, and it is reasonable to suppose that the Alexandrians were in a better position to judge in his case than in Aeschylus'. The scholia too register no doubts: we are just told in the *hypothesis* that ἔνιοι νόθον ὑπενόησαν ὡς οὐκ ὂν Εὐριπίδου.

If *Rhesos* is spurious, we must conclude (as most scholars apparently do) that Euripides' play was lost, quite early in its life, and that the Alexandrians in their search for the play which their *didaskaliai* told them was produced by Euripides in his youth, fastened on this (inferior, fourth-century) version of the same story (which was itself already anonymous?), and identified it with the object of their quest; or else they simply came across it somewhere, and in looking for a likely author saw that Euripides had produced a play of that name and gave it to him.

If *Rhesos* is genuinely the work of Euripides, we must accept that the judgement of most modern scholars is wrong,[145] but also that ἔνιοι in antiquity found it impossible either to confirm or quell their suspicions. The authority of Kallimachos (who presumably gave the title, author, and first line as usual) was not regarded as a good enough guarantee of authenticity, if stylistic considerations argued against it.[146]

How can these three examples help us in our enquiry? They show that the Alexandrians had no sure way of determining the authorship of a disputed play, and that even when doubts were expressed a play would tend to be retained among an author's works, rather than to be rejected and classed as anonymous. Thus the 'spurious *Aetnaeans*' did not simply disappear from the catalogue of Aeschylus' plays, any more than e.g. [Dem.] 58 did from Demosthenes' orations. We may assume too that the actual text of the play was also kept with Aeschylus' genuine work, whether or not its spuriousness was indicated in its title or its entry in the Πίνακες. Thus even if uncertainty existed in the mind of Alexander or Kallimachos as to the authorship of a particular tragedy, the tendency would always be for the play itself to continue to be attached to that author, while the grounds for doubt or suspicion, even if recorded, would be liable to pass into oblivion unless rescued by Aristophanes or a later commentator.

Amusing tales are told of forgery and fraudulent deceptions which the Alexandrians failed to spot;[147] many others were doubtless never told because the truth was never revealed. But underlying all these proceedings the principle is clearly to be discerned, that of giving works to well-known authors (or their 'pupils') rather than leaving them unassigned and anonymous - a sort of librarian's *horror vacui* for each work's official entry in the catalogue.

Before we criticize the imperfections of these first Alexandrian scholars too sharply, we should pause to remind ourselves both of the physical conditions of their library, and of the regular practice of author and reader in antiquity, as reflected in their methods of book-production and transmission. Papyrus rolls were not easy to use for reference, especially since no care was taken to mark line numbers, chapters etc., or even to distinguish clearly between verse and prose in the presentation of the text. It seems that most ancient works of literature did not bear formal titles such as we are accustomed to;[148] they were generally known either by their subject matter, e.g. Plato's Σοφιστής (*Pol.* 284B, 286B), or Aristophanes' Ὁ σώφρων χὠ καταπύγων (i.e. his Δαιταλῆς, *Clouds* 529); or by their opening words, e.g. καὶ σπουδαῖα νομίζων (Dem.

Phil. 3, as described in the subscription of Didymos' commentary);[149] or often by both together. Authors sometimes cited their own or other people's works by different names at different times,[150] and alternative titles seem often to have been equally well established: thus to Plato belonged Φαίδων ἢ Περὶ ψυχῆς,[151] Συμπόσιον ἢ Ἐρωτικὸς λόγος,[152] Εὐθύφρων ἢ Περὶ ὁσίου, etc. For tragedy several alternative titles are known, e.g. Aeschylus' Κᾶρες ἢ Εὐρώπη, Σεμέλη ἢ Ὑδροφόροι, Φρύγες ἢ Ἕκτορος Λύτρα (presumably in each case the one identifying the chorus, the other the hero or subject matter of the play), Ἀργὼ ἢ Κωπαστής. For the works of many of the early philosophers, titles were probably only invented several generations after their death: most were simply christened Περὶ φύσεως.[153]

Even less attention was paid to authorship. Here writers would naturally behave differently according to the genre in which they were working. The epic poet was consistently (and notoriously) anonymous; but Hesiod had good reasons for identifying himself in the much more personal *Works and Days*.[154] Such figures as Archilochos, Alkaios, and Solon would often be easy to identify, but Pindar, Bakkhylides, or Simonides might be harder. The historians generally took care to make themselves known in their opening words,[155] and to take responsibility for the veracity (or otherwise) of their accounts; philosophers might be expected to be more subtle, and to let the λόγος speak for itself, but here again their approach would vary from author to author and from work to work, according to the writer's intentions.[156] In every genre, public or private recitation doubtless remained the normal medium through which an author of the sixth or fifth century would present his work,[157] and it is quite uncertain how widespread the practice of solitary reading and private book production may have been even in the second half of the fifth century in Athens.[158]

The tragedians, of course, had one particular public performance in mind, in which originally they participated as actors,[159] and always as producers. Certainly individual tragic poets could win considerable reputations, good or bad, but it is possible that they were given little more credit than their choregos or protagonist (and later even their flute-player),[160] to whose munificence and skill the success of the performance would in no small part be due. (Aristophanes, of course, himself a poet, would be anxious to stress the playwright's role alone.) Once it had been performed, a tragedy would become almost public property, and it seems that the poet's concern to be known as the author of his work was far less evident than it is today.[161]

For these reasons, we may regard it as very likely that a large number of texts were floating around during the fifth and fourth centuries with no title and no author's name attached, and that among them were many tragedies. Even where a super- or subscription had once given that information, it was particularly liable to damage or loss, as the ends of the papyrus would be the first to deteriorate. So we may take it that the Alexandrians were faced with a wide range of anonymous works, in varying degrees of disrepair, obtained from many different cities and through many different channels, and that they would often have very little clue as to the date or the author of the work before them.[162]

It would be far easier to mistake *Prom.* for the work of Aeschylus than it would be to mistake, say, [Dem.] 58, or [Xen.] 'Αθ. Πολ. (especially in an age in which interest in tragic lyrics was small).[163] Many scholars in fact believe that a more obvious mistake *was* made in the case of *Rhesos*. In my opinion, the internal stylistic arguments against the authenticity of *Prom.* are substantially stronger than those against *Rhesos*, and the latter might never have been seriously challenged by modern scholars but for the reference in the hypothesis to ἔνιοι ... It is largely the traditional ascription of *Prom.* to Aeschylus which has weighed against the technical arguments, together with a profound feeling of embarrassment that such a great drama should be denied to such a great dramatist. I think that we should confess that this traditional ascription is not worth very much.

So let us return to our hypothesis, that Kallimachos was faced with an anonymous *Prom.* It does not appear that he interested himself any more than was strictly necessary in problems of authenticity, nor should we expect him to have done so, amid the enormous labour of compiling his lists of each author's tragedies, comedies, epics, mimes, histories, treatises, and miscellaneous poems, a labour which would presumably entail wading through most of the material contained in the Library.[164] Let us agree, therefore, that Kallimachos would probably have had little hesitation in ascribing this play to Aeschylus, rather than to Sophocles or Euripides. Alternatively, he might have come across a play which Alexander (or someone else engaged in the task of unpacking and sorting the huge quantities of incoming material from all over the Greek world, in the early days of the Library) had already marked tentatively as Αἰσχύλου τραγωιδία; again Kallimachos would probably have accepted it without serious question. But in either case, once entered in the *Pinakes* (and perhaps in the Library catalogue too) as Aeschylus' Προμηθεὺς Δεσμώτης οὗ ἡ ἀρχὴ Χθονὸς μὲν ἐς τηλουρόν, the play remained securely entrenched in the tragic corpus, and even went on to displace many genuinely Aeschylean companions in the post-Christian collection of his most popular works. Throughout antiquity, the commentators (who seem in any case to have ignored for the most part questions of trilogic connection)[165] treated it just like any other Aeschylean tragedy, and the chances of its true author being revealed were reduced virtually to nothing.

PROM. AND THE OTHER PROMETHEUS-PLAYS

If we accept that it would have been easy enough for *Prom.* to be thus adopted into the Aeschylean corpus, we must now ask ourselves whether it is not after all possible that Λυόμενος *was* a genuinely Aeschylean play, which drew Δεσμώτης to it as a companion piece, but which was originally quite independent of our play. Perhaps Λυόμενος, a monodrama of Aeschylus, or even possibly a member of a connected trilogy whose other plays were lost or not identified as such, was recorded in the *didaskaliai* simply as Προμηθεύς or Προμήθεια, and duly classified as his by Kallimachos. A second play in the possession of the Library, although not previously attributed to Aeschylus, was clearly not the work of Sophocles or Euripides, seemed old, and dealt with an earlier stage of the same story. And so Kallimachos assigned the two plays adjacent places in his catalogue: this would be because of their titles rather than their continuity of theme,[166] but the effect would be the same. Whether or not Kallimachos himself voiced any doubt as to its authenticity, the play would naturally stay where it was.

In Chapter 2 we saw that, despite certain apparent duplications and contradictions,[167] the two plays seem to fit rather well together, so that in themselves they give rise to no real suspicion.

But we also observed that it seems very hard to reconstruct any plausible outline for a third play on the same theme. Λυόμενος, however we construct it,[168] looks like the end of the story; it also appears to follow directly the action of Δεσμώτης. Thus, if there was a trilogy, Δεσμώτης would have to be the second play. Yet it seems to show signs that it is introducing us to a new situation, as if for the first time.[169]

After all that has been said about 'the trilogy', from Welcker in 1824 to the present, can we really believe after all that Δεσμώτης and Λυόμενος were composed separately and by different authors?[170] The negative answer to this question, which is almost universally given, is based both on the stylistic evidence of the extant fragments of Λυόμενος and on the dramatic content of Δεσμώτης itself. In neither case is the argument wholly compelling.

There are indeed some stylistic similarities between the fragments of Λυόμενος (Aesch. frs. 190-204 (319-339M)) and Δεσμώτης. The overlap of two syllables from one anapaestic metron to the next in fr.192.4;[171] the presence of a 'first-foot anapaest' in iambic trimeters at fr.199.7 (though here our suspicions are aroused by the unaeschylean double-resolution of this line, with νεφέλην and νιφάδι[172]); the use of ἥκω in fr.196;[173] the choice of ἄθλους in fr. 190, a word not found in Aeschylus' six undisputed plays, but favoured by *Prom.*[174] (and used here with ἐποψόμενοι, cf. εἰσοράω, a favourite word in our play);[175] the geographical instructions of frs. 195-9, and the warning of fr.195 (cf. *Prom.* 712, 715, 807); such details are interesting, but far from conclusive.[176]

It cannot be denied that the fragments, and later references by mythographers, reveal a remarkable parallelism between this play and *Prom.* The correspondence between Ge and Okeanos, between Herakles travelling west and Io travelling east, between the chorus of Titans arriving to commiserate with their brother, and the chorus of Okeanids with their brother-in-law, and between the unbinding and binding of the hero, seems unlikely to be purely accidental. Yet, as I remarked in Chapter 2, some of the points of correspondence seem to amount to outright repetition, and it is impossible to judge whether or not they are truly complementary and effective. Reference to the parallel structures of A. *Ag.* and *Cho.* does not help us, although the indications are that the parallels between Δεσμώτης and Λυόμενος are more obvious, indeed crude. We simply have too little to go on to draw any conclusions at all.

There would be no difficulty in reconstructing Λυόμενος as an independent monodrama. The opening scene, with the newly released Titans visiting the chained Prometheus, would require no previous action; indeed it seems that Prometheus did describe his gifts to mankind, presumably as part of an explanation for his predicament (fr.194), an explanation that might seem superfluous after Δεσμώτης. There would be plenty of dramatic action, with the confrontation of Zeus and Prometheus resolved through the revelation of the Thetis-secret (via Ge or Themis and Prometheus himself), and Herakles' shooting of the eagle, culminating in the crowning of Prometheus,[177] and perhaps the institution of the cult of Prometheus and Hephaistos, or of the first Prometheia. There would be nothing in all this that would require Δεσμώτης to precede it.

On the other hand, there are good reasons for concluding that Δεσμώτης was composed with an eye on Λυόμενος. The choice of Okeanos and Io as leading characters, the geographical descriptions, and the lack of final resolution despite frequent references to its possibility or inevitability in the future,[178] cannot all be coincidental. So the crucial question seems really to be this: Is it at all likely that a fifth-century playwright would compose a tragedy so obviously indebted to, or directed towards, the work of a predecessor or contemporary?

To this the answer would appear to be, Yes. Even with the limited information available to us, we can confidently point to specific cases in which dramatists availed themselves of each others' work. Aeschylus' *Persians* was said by Glaukos of Rhegion (*c.* 400 B.C.) to be based on Phrynichos' *Phoinissai*.[179] Euripides apparently modelled his own *Medea* on Neophron's, not only in matters of general organization and plot (e.g. the killing of the children by Medea rather than by the Corinthians, and the arrival of Aigeus in Corinth), but also in details of language.[180] Euripides also directed his *Elektra* unmistakably 'against' Aeschylus' *Choephoroi*, again both in general and in particular detail; Sophocles' *Elektra* is seen by some as a further contribution, or rejoinder, to the 'debate'. (The Gyges-fragment should perhaps be left out of the reckoning, as its date and relation to Herodotos are too uncertain,[181] but Sophocles' adaptation of Hdt.3.119 at *Ant.* 909ff is well-known, and to some critics rather embarrassing.) These examples should not surprise us. Aristotle remarks that a very few myths provide the matter for most of the tragedies known to him,[182] and the surviving titles from the minor tragedians bear this out.[183]

Plagiarism, more or less subtle, is one thing (and a practice common to the theatre in many ages[184]), but the composition of a work which depended on the audience's familiarity with another drama for it to be fully appreciated would be a rather different phenomenon - though Aristophanes' detailed parodies of individual tragic scenes show that even this is by no means out of the question for the Athenian stage.[185] And it should be acknowledged that Δεσμώτης is not so crudely dependent on Λυόμενος as to make no sense on its own: rather it seems to invite us to think about the necessary solution to the conflict, by means of its frequent predictions and explicit accounts of what is to happen. (By contrast, the first two plays of the *Oresteia* contain very few specific statements about what is to follow; Aeschylus prefers to build up the emotional tension by *not* telling us all.) It was not uncommon in Elizabethan times for a playwright to try to emulate the success of a rival, or even of one of his own plays, by modelling a new play quite blatantly on the pattern of a predecessor, or by composing a sequel to a previously self-contained drama.[186] There seems therefore nothing inherently improbable about *Prom.*'s being composed with Λυόμενος in mind, provided that the connections between the two plays do not amount to dependency.

There is nothing in *Prom.* which appears to depend on a sequel for an adequate understanding either of individual passages or of the whole dramatic situation.[187] The entry of Okeanos may be poorly motivated, but it makes no better sense even if it *is* paralleled by the arrival of Ge in an ensuing play; so too, the arrival of Io, which at first seems rather an unexpected intrusion, is shown within *Prom.* itself to be wholly relevant, both to the torment of Prometheus, and to the depiction of the tyrant Zeus. Nor are we left in any great uncertainty as to what will in fact happen in the years to come: the future is rather fully described within the play; Zeus, although threatened with overthrow, will be reconciled with Prometheus; Herakles, descendant of Io, will kill the eagle (which the myth - and the author of Λυόμενος - include as integral to the story, but which the author of *Prom.* introduces almost as an afterthought); Cheiron will surrender his immortality and descend into Hades. The details are left intentionally vague, and thus the tensions remain largely unresolved: we still do not know *how* the reconciliation can take place; the enemies seem too proud and stubborn, the clash too fierce, for any compromise. This lack of resolution is striking, and effective.[188] Was it intended by the author of *Prom.*, or is it a mere accident of transmission? Is *Prom.* 1093 a possible ending for a fifth-century tragic performance?[189] Could so much be left in the air, with the tragic resolution largely unexpressed and merely implicit in the audience's knowledge of other versions of the myth, most notably Λυόμενος? And could *Prom.* be presented as a single drama without any further explanation or mitigation of Zeus' cruel and apparently unjust behaviour towards Prometheus and mankind?

PROM. AS MONODRAMA

Every Athenian in the audience was familiar with Prometheus as a cult-figure and as the patron of the torch-festival.[190] Thus they hardly needed to be told that he had regained his position of respect among the gods. Although Euripides likes to introduce an explicit aetiological connection between the action of his plays and the cults of his own day, this is by no means compulsory procedure for every tragedian: Sophocles, for example, says nothing in *Trachiniai* about Herakles' future role as hero and demigod. Both Sophocles and Euripides give us examples of single plays which intentionally leave loose ends to the story, even when they may themselves have treated later stages of the same myth elsewhere. Thus in *Oedipus at Kolonos* we are told virtually nothing about the consequences of Oedipus' refusal to help Kreon or Polyneikes: it is left to us to supply the details, so familiar from A. *Th.*, S. *Ant.*, E. *Pho.*, etc., and from the epic. In Euripides' *Troiades*, Kassandra's prophecies (353-461) certainly do not look forward to another play, yet are far from straightforward in their relation to what the audience knew from e.g. the *Nostoi*, the *Odyssey*, and the *Oresteia*. Nor does Sophocles' *Elektra* give any indication of what will follow the killing of Klytaimestra and Aigisthos; here, although the audience is inevitably aware of the traditional role of the Erinyes,[191] Sophocles has apparently taken care to confine the scope of his play to the theme of Orestes' and Elektra's revenge, and to ignore its consequences.[192]

This question, whether *Prom.* can be interpreted as a monodrama, or whether it requires a sequel to make dramatic sense, must remain a matter of subjective judgement. (It is also, perhaps, the one question which would justify to the literary critic the whole of this investigation.) To me, the action of *Prom.* seems quite intelligible as it stands. The unresolved tensions contribute effectively to its paradoxical impact. There can be no neat resolution in the conflict between the law of nature and the ingenuity of man, between the demands of political authority and stability, and those of personal loyalty and compassion, between man's greatness and his puniness. The story of Oedipus[193] reveals similar tragic tensions, and his blinding seems scarcely more 'just' than the torture of Prometheus, who at least, like Antigone, did choose to commit the act for which he is punished, in full knowledge of what he was doing and what he would suffer.

Although the ending of *Prom.* would in some respects be the most disturbing conclusion to a monodrama that we would possess, in its explicit portrayal of the tyrannical behaviour of Zeus, we need not interpret this as proof that Zeus must immediately have been shown as a more reasonable or merciful ruler in another play. The closing scene of *Troiades*, itself the last play of a trilogy, again provides an interesting comparison. As Hekabe appeals to Zeus (1288-90) Κρόνιε ... ἀνάξια τᾶς Δαρδάνου γονᾶς τάδ' οἷα πάσχομεν δέδορκας, the chorus can only reply, δέδορκεν, ἁ δὲ μεγαλόπολις ἄπολις ὄλωλεν οὐδ' ἔτ' ἔστι Τροία. The language is even reminiscent of *Prom.* 1093 (also of e.g. 92ff, 141-3, 303-7), and in both plays the will of Zeus, as manifested in the Greek victory at Troy and in Prometheus' torments, seems impossible to explain in terms of what is 'fair' (ἀνάξια, ἔκδικα) to the individuals involved. The final words of S. *Trachiniai*[194] are equally mysterious; we may compare too E. *Hks* 1367ff, or *El.* 1245f, even, in a different mood, the whole *Ion.*

Prometheus Bound is of course a special case, in that the major characters of the myth are themselves divine. Thus Zeus inevitably loses many of his teleological associations - he is greater in degree, but not in kind, than Prometheus, Hephaistos, Okeanos, and Hermes. When Zeus becomes a character in the drama, even though he does not appear before our eyes, the anthropomorphic and less dignified aspects of his personality are naturally exaggerated, as they are in those parts of Homer in which the domestic life of the Olympians is presented. (It is interesting to see what an awkward time Hesiod has when he tries to rescue his Zeus at Mekone from a myth in which he originally cut a slightly ridiculous figure, so as to preserve his reputation for omniscience and justice.)[195] And no more distasteful trio of representatives of Zeus' physical presence could be imagined than Kratos, Bia, and Hermes.

We can think of other divine characters on the fifth-century stage: Apollo in *Eumenides*,[196] Athene in S. *Ajax*, Aphrodite in E. *Hippolytos*, Dionysos in E. *Bacchants* and Aristophanes' *Frogs*; all must be interpreted within their dramatic context. The same must be true of Zeus in *Prom.*, as it is in Aristophanes' *Birds*. He is a participant in the dramatic action, not an object of abstract theological discussion.[197]

In the *Oresteia*, Zeus is frequently linked intimately with the Erinyes, with Moira, and with Dike.[198] In his capacities as ξένιος, ἑρκεῖος, σωτήρ, and τέλειος he becomes, in effect, the personification of the moral, domestic, and political necessity which works throughout the trilogy towards the restoration of a harmonious order in the house of Atreus and the cities of Argos and Athens. In e.g. S. *Oedipus Tyrannos*, it is through the figure of Apollo that Sophocles articulates the peculiar dramatic combination of coincidence and necessity which his play requires; in E. *Hippolytos*, we are introduced to Aphrodite in two different guises, through two different modes, as the petulant personality of the divine frame, and as the natural force of human passion: both modes continue to operate throughout the play. In *Prom.*, such a role for any god, even Zeus, is ruled out by the myth itself; only such powers as the Moirai might be felt to be 'above' or 'behind' the action (cf. *Prom.* 516); even Themis is personally involved, as Prometheus' mother (and perhaps the source of his knowledge about Thetis[199]).

It could be argued, therefore, that there is no need for Zeus to be 'reinstated' after *Prom.* The audience knows how the myth turns out, and perhaps they half-consciously bear Λυόμενος in mind as the astonishing forecast is made (907-40) that Zeus will fall. Thus a balance is struck, between two conflicting logics, the one leading to Zeus' humiliation at the hands of man's champion, the other to the necessary re-establishment of harmony among the new and old gods, symbolized by the sympathy between Prometheus and Hephaistos, and guaranteed by the prophecies concerning Io.

Yet it is surely a sound critical assumption that a work of literature contains within itself all that is required for adequate sense to be made of it, and we cannot deny that *Prom.* as a monodrama would demand more of its audience, in the way of prior mythological and literary knowledge, than we should expect from a playwright of any age. If the play was directed specifically *against* an Aeschylean Λυόμενος, with the intention of challenging or inverting some of that play's main themes, then we possess a most remarkable document of the early 'theatre of ideas'. If it was merely modelled on its predecessor as a convenient point of reference, then the apparent parallels and echoes must be taken as evidence of a certain dramatic clumsiness on the part of its author.

WHO WROTE PROM.?

The true relationship of Δεσμώτης to Λυόμενος could only be more surely established if new fragments of the latter were to come into our possession. For the moment, we can only conclude that, although the balance of probabilities continues to favour the traditional theory of a Prometheus-trilogy, the alternative (two separate plays by different authors) cannot wholly be discounted. In any case, we should not forget our observation of Chapter 2,[200] that even if we do accept *Prom.*'s place within a trilogy, we do not thereby in any way shake the arguments against Aeschylean authorship: instead we may merely conclude that our unknown author wrote a Prometheus-trilogy, presumably consisting of Πυρφόρος, Δεσμώτης, Λυόμενος, plus perhaps a related satyr-play, and that all three plays looked sufficiently like the work of Aeschylus to be classed as his by the Alexandrians. We might even find that the repetitiousness and formalism displayed by Δεσμώτης and Λυόμενος (which would be yet more tiresome if Δεσμώτης was itself the second play and reminding us what took place in the first), suggest a trilogic technique which is rather different from that of Aeschylus: we are again reminded of our author's predilection for rhetorical order and symmetry shown within Δεσμώτης itself.

If we now ask ourselves who this author was, we must recognize from the start that we can do little more than guess. We may make several more or less tentative inferences about him, his style, his date, and his relationship to some of his literary predecessors and contemporaries, but these will all be highly speculative. Nevertheless, it is perhaps worth stating briefly what appear to be his most striking characteristics.

The author of *Prom.* composed his play for an Athenian audience.[201] He was familiar with the early exponents of sophistic rhetoric, and consciously adopted certain features of their technique in organizing his own speeches.[202] He was also perhaps familiar with the teaching of Protagoras, whose myth of the development of culture may have inspired our author's choice of material.[203] He also knew well the work of Aeschylus,[204] and of early Sophocles and Euripides;[205] also of Pindar, and possibly Empedokles and Anaxagoras.[206] His intellectual grasp of fundamental human problems was firmer than his dramatic control of the stage action, though he attempted to compensate for this by lavish use of spectacle and special effects:[207] he was, in fact, a playwright of ideas first, of the stage second - perhaps closer in spirit to Euripides, Marlowe or Shaw than to Sophocles, Shakespeare or Chekhov?[208] His interest in the chorus was small: they were still of course a necessary part of his play, as the conventions demanded, but he was not much concerned to integrate them into the dramatic whole or to give them lengthy or very significant lyric utterances.[209]

We obviously should not draw too many conclusions about the author's own attitudes from the statements of his characters in the play; but we may observe that the ambivalence of forethought and blind hope, of human ingenuity and vulnerability, of the old order confronted with the upstart generation of Zeus, seems to be entirely characteristic of Athenian tragedy of the mid-fifth century. It finds echoes in e.g. A. *Eum.* (old and new), S. *Aj.* and *Ant.* (man's greatness and feebleness), S. *OT* (man's cleverness and ignorance). But any attempt to be more specific in dating the play before or after, say, 440 B.C. would be presumptuous, when we possess so little material, verse or prose, from that precise period.[210]

If we have to pick a name for our author, we could find few objections to any of the following: Polyphrasmon, son of Phrynichos, victor probably twice between 470 and 450, composer of one known trilogy/tetralogy, but unknown to the Suda; Mesatos, victor for the first time shortly after 468, winner of further first prizes, third in ?463 to Aeschylus and Sophocles; Karkinos, father and grandfather of famous tragedians, frequently criticized by Aristophanes, especially for his love of the μηχανή, victor in 446; Philokles, son of Aeschylus' sister, winner of first prize the year that Sophocles produced *OT*, ridiculed by Aristophanes, and by Telekleides for his Aeschylean manner, composer of a *Pandionis* tetralogy; Euphorion, son of Aeschylus, credited with four victories with unproduced plays of his father, victor in 431 over Sophocles and Euripides' *Medea*.

Any others from the list given earlier in the chapter would seem equally possible: virtually nothing is known about any of them; Ion of Chios should perhaps be excepted.[211] The strongest claims could perhaps be made for Euphorion and Philokles: both were first-rate dramatists, both were members of Aeschylus' family, and this might help to explain the mistaken attribution. Nor can we rule out the possibility of multiple authorship, with Euphorion or another member of the family completing a tragedy or trilogy begun by Aeschylus, for production after his death,[212] perhaps even in his name. Further speculation is amusing but pointless: we do not know who wrote *Prometheus Bound* - that is almost all that we can truly say.

Appendix A

METRICAL SYMBOLS AND ABBREVIATIONS

⏑	short syllable
–	long syllable
×	*syllaba anceps*, i.e. syllable of unspecified metrical quantity
‖	pause
= or ~	'responding to', strophe to antistrophe
○	short syllable counted long before pause (*brevis in longo*)
∧	syncopation, i.e. omission of one syllable within the metron
adon.	–⏑⏑–– (adonean)
aeolics	metres of the family to which glyconic, pherecretean, etc. belong[1]
alc. dec.	–⏑⏑–⏑⏑–⏑–– (alcaic decasyllable)
anac. ion.	⏑⏑–⏑–⏑–– (anaclastic ionic, sometimes known as anakreontic)
anap.	⏑⏑– (anapaest); ⏑⏑–⏑⏑– = anapaestic metron
anc.	(*syllaba anceps*), syllable of unspecified metrical quantity
arist.	–⏑⏑–⏑––(aristophanean)
ba.	⏑–– (bacchiac), a syncopated form of iambic metron
brevis in longo	naturally short syllable counted long before pause
cat.	(catalectic), line shortened by omission of final syllable
chor.	–⏑⏑–(choriamb)
cho. dim.	–×–×–⏑⏑–(choriambic dimeter)
cr.	–⏑– (cretic)
D	–⏑⏑–⏑⏑–(hemiepes), an element of dactylo-epitrite[2]
dac.	–⏑⏑ (dactyl)

dac.-ep.	(dactylo-epitrite), a combination of hemiepes, anceps, and cretic
dim.	(dimeter), a colon of two metra
do.	× – – × – (dochmiac)
dodrans	– ⏑ ⏑ – ⏑ – or – ⏑ – ⏑ ⏑ –[3]
e	– ⏑ – (cretic), as an element of dactylo-epitrite[4]
enop.	× – ⏑ ⏑ – ⏑ – – (enoplion)
ex. met.	*(extra metrum)* syllable(s) of exclamation not included in the metrical scheme
glyc.	– × – ⏑ ⏑ – ⏑ – (glyconic)
hem.	– ⏑ ⏑ – ⏑ ⏑ – (hemiepes)
hex. do.	⏑ – ⏑ – ⏑ – (hexasyllabic dochmiac)[5]
hipp.	– × – ⏑ ⏑ – ⏑ – – (hipponactean)
hyp.	– ⏑ – ⏑ – (hypodochmiac), an anaclastic version of ⏑ – – ⏑ – (dochmiac)
ia.	× – ⏑ – (iambic metron), i.e. anceps plus cretic
iambel.	× – ⏑ – × – ⏑ ⏑ – ⏑ ⏑ – (iambelegos)
ibyc.	– ⏑ ⏑ – ⏑ ⏑ – ⏑ – (ibycean)
ion.	⏑ ⏑ – – (ionic)
ithyph.	– ⏑ – ⏑ – – (ithyphallic), cretic plus bacchiac
lek.	– ⏑ – ⏑ – ⏑ – (lekythion), cretic plus iambic
mol.	– – – (molossus), a syncopated form of iambic metron
paroem.	⏑ ⏑ – ⏑ ⏑ – ⏑ ⏑ – – (paroemiac), often clausula to anapaestic dimeters
pher.	– × – ⏑ ⏑ – – (pherecretean)
reiz.	× – ⏑ ⏑ – – (reizianum)
resolution	two short syllables taking the place of one long
sp.	– – (spondee), a syncopated form of cretic
syncopation	(marked ∧), omission of one syllable within the metron
tel.	× – ⏑ ⏑ – ⏑ – (telesillean)
tetr.	(tetrameter), colon of four metra
trim.	(trimeter), colon of three metra
tro.	– ⏑ – × (trochaic metron), cretic plus anceps

For fuller descriptions of these elements see Maas *Greek Metre*, D.S. Raven *Greek metre: an introduction* (London 1962), B. Snell *Griechische Metrik* (second ed., Göttingen 1957), and the relevant sections of Wilamowitz *GV* and Dale *LM*.

Appendix B

PROM. 165f = 184f AND THE CLAUSULAR ITHYPHALLIC

Prom. 165f γέννων οὐδὲ λήξει πρὶν ἂν ἢ κορέσηι κέαρ ... etc.

184f χρή σε τέρμα κέλσαντ' ἐσιδεῖν· ἀκίχητα γάρ ... etc.

These are usually taken as –⏑–⏑––|⏑⏑–⏑⏑–⏑⏑ etc., cr. ba., dactyls. In the strophe this analysis is unobjectionable, but in the antistrophe we do not have proper diaeresis after the ithyphallic clausula –⏑– ⏑––.

Wilamowitz was clearly aware of this problem, and divided –⏑–⏑–|–⏑⏑–⏑⏑–⏑⏑–⏑⏑–⏑⏑ commenting in his edition 'membrum –⏑–⏑– cuius non suppetit explicatio, cf. *Sept.* 783', on which in turn he remarks, 'membrum obscurum ⏑⏑⏑⏑⏑⏑⏑– nec dactylis neque iambis conveniens'. Elsewhere he gives examples of –⏑–⏑– in contexts other than dochmiac (*GV* 406): in cat. tro. (lekythia) E. *IA* 235, 256; in iambics E. *Or.* 991-3 (three consecutive), *Pho.* 1023-5 (three); in dactylo-epitrite as clausula E. *El.* 865-9 (two: or cr. ba. ia.); in iambic (+ do?) context ?S. *OT* 1202-3 (two). But, he concludes, 'Befremdlich steht es *Prom.* 164.' One notes too that in all his examples –⏑–⏑– is followed by diaeresis: here it would not be.[1]

Dale (*LM* 72) says, 'The bacchiac ... is practically never found succeeding an iambic metron of the form × –⏑– or –⏑– except with following Pause' - and cites the only exception she has found, Ar. *Thesm.* 1034-5, a quotation from the *Andromeda*, ⏑–⏑– ⏑–– ––⏑– ⏑–– without pause. But she does not explain how she reconciles this with her colometry of *Prom.* 584 (p.109) or, by implication, *Prom.* 165 (p.67). Possible examples of (×)–⏑– ⏑–– without word-end and possible pause are:

A. *Th.* 735-6 = 743-4[2]

Supp. 88-90 = 93-5: the arrangements of Wilamowitz and Murray are both implausible; better seems

–––⏑⏑–

–⏑– ⏑––

–⏑–⏑⏑– ⏑––‖, the arrangement of Schroeder.

In the antistrophe there is no pause after the bacchiac.

Ag. 197-8 = 210-11, with Blomfield's transposition. (If we retain the MSS order in the antistrophe, we have ––⏑– –⏑– ––⏑– ia. cr. ia., ⏑–⏑– ⏑––⏑⏑– ⏑––‖ ia. hipp. But we are still faced with problems: (1) 'Αργείων must be a cretic cf. E. *Or.* 1247, 1268?; (2) the single ia. before glyconic or hipponactean, while not uncommon in Soph. and Eur.,[3] does not occur in Aesch. An alternative would be to take 198ff as ⏑–⏑–⏑– –⏑⏑– ⏑––, as Denniston does.)[4]

Ag. 223 = 233, a rare form of syncopated trimeter, in purely ia. context.

Ag. 1123 = 1134? (see Fraenkel, Denniston-Page *ad loc.*; also Schroeder, whose analysis ⏑⏑⏑–⏑–|–⏑– –⏑– ⏑––⏑–‖ do. cr. cr. do. seems good to me).

S. *OT* 665-6 = 694-5. (Both str. and ant. are corrupt, but it looks as though we have overlap with σαλεύουσαν; the context is iambic.)

Tr. 888? (The text is uncertain;[5] even if we accept the received text, we could divide with Pohlsander after the ba.)[6]

E. *Alk.* 217 = 231? This could be taken as cr. ba. ia.; but there is a good case to be made for considering –⏑–⏑– to be a colon in its own right, and both Wilamowitz[7] and Dale[8] take these lines as a pair of them. The same applies to E. *El.* 865 = 879, *Pho.* 1023-4 = 1047-9, *Or.* 1382.

Hik. 605-6 = 616-17: no division avoids the overlap in either str. or ant., whether 2ia. / ia. ba. / cr. ba. (Murray), or 3ia. / ba. cr. ba. / (Wilamowitz' analysis[9] ia. sp. / 3ia. ba. is unlikely). Again, the context is purely iambic.

Hel. 201 = 220: (unless we analyse it as –‸– ⏑–⏑–|⏑⏑⏑⏑⏑⏑ –‸–|–⏑– ⏑–⏑–, sp. ia. / ia. sp. / lek., which does not fit very well with the surrounding trochaics).

Hel. 210 = 228 ⏑⏑⏑⏔ ⏑–– –⏑– ⏑–⏑– a certain example, in trochaics.

Pho. 1026 = 1050ff? (Perhaps best arranged × –– –⏑– ⏑–⏑– mol. lek., ⏑–– ⏑⏑⏑– ⏑––‖ ba. cr. ba., giving two unremarkable trimeters.[10] The antistrophe (1050) seems to resist this treatment, as we are left with an elision from one colon to the next, δι' αἱμάτων δ' /ἀμείβει. But the removal of δ' is simple, its intrusion likely enough; we might punctuate after δι' αἱμάτων rather than before.)[11]

Or. 1458ff: whatever the true reading and position for ἄλλος ἄλλοσε, it seems difficult to escape the trimeter ia. ba. ia.

Rhesos 25 = 43: Here we have diaeresis after the ba., but no pause is possible, as the previous colon, and that in the next line, are wholly different (aeolic, dactylic), so that the single ia. at the end of the line would be isolated.

Of this handful of exceptions[12] to the clausular function of (×)–⏑– ⏑––, all are in purely iambic (or trochaic) context, except for A. *Supp.* 88ff, and *Rhesos* 25. So we might modify Dale's 'rule', and say that a few syncopated ia. / tro. cola appear to admit (×)–⏑– ⏑–– without following pause, but elsewhere the ithyphallic is almost invariably clausular. In A. *Supp.* 88ff, this might argue in favour of Murray's colometry rather than Schroeder's, since in Murray's the ba. occurs in the middle of an ia. trim. (cr. ba. cr.). Similarly, in *Rhesos* 25 = 43, the ba. is followed by an ia. metron, before the change of metre.

At *Prom.* 184 there is an abrupt change of metre immediately after the ithyphallic: the ear, after hearing –⏑⏑–⏑⏑– –⏑– ⏑––, is startled by the run-on into a wholly different metre ('rising' dactyls), without the slightest pause. Fraenkel[13] points out that we often find dactyls introduced by one iambic metron with overlap ×–⏑––{⏑⏑–⏑⏑–⏑⏑ etc., often with punctuation after the fifth syllable (e.g. A. *Ag.* 108 = 127, 116 = 135, fr. 132, 238; S. *OT* 175 = 186; E. *Hipp.* 1105 = 1113, fr. 303.4 and cf. *Hks* 895), whereas ×–⏑–{ –⏑⏑–⏑⏑ is comparatively rare (cf. S. *OT* 174, E. *Hipp.* 1147). Here we can only engineer this by dividing

(183) πᾶι ποτε τῶνδε πόνων χρή

σε τέρμα κέλσαντ' ἐσιδεῖν ... etc.

where the colon –⏑⏑–⏑⏑–– is difficult (the last syllable cannot be anceps as it is followed by the anceps of the iambic, and no pause is possible rhetorically), and the lack of word-end at colon-end makes for a very long period without diaeresis.

Emendation does not seem the answer: κέλσαι for κέλσαντ' is easy enough, but we are left with the intractable ἐσιδεῖν.

We are left, then, with the choice between Wilamowitz' –⏑⏑–⏑⏑–| –⏑–⏑–⊥–⏑⏑–⏑⏑–⏑⏑ etc., or –⏑⏑–⏑⏑–‸–⊥⏑–⏑–⊥–⏑⏑–⏑⏑–⏑⏑ etc., or –⏑⏑–⏑⏑–|–⏑–⏑––⊥⏑⏑–⏑⏑–⏑⏑. If Wilamowitz' analysis is correct, it is certainly unique. –⏑–⏑– never occurs elsewhere in a comparable context (always either in dochmiacs or iambics), and never without following word end, unless in a pair (E. *El.* 865). The two alternatives are both also peculiar. The combination of iambic plus dactylic was not uncommon in drama: in Ar. *Frogs* 1261ff 'Euripides' is shown as parodying Aeschylus' lyrics, and this mixture of ia. + dac.(often starting ⏑–⏑– –⏑⏑–⏑⏑ etc.) which Eur. considers ἐκ τῶν κιθαρωιδικῶν[14] νόμων εἰργασμένην was presumably thought characteristic of Aesch. Fraenkel[15] remarks that, 'In the extant plays of Aesch., this triad [*sc. Ag.* 104ff] is the only instance of dactylo-iambics. But there were many more', referring to the *Frogs* passage. In the extant plays, the mixture is much more frequent in Eur.

But nowhere can I find a parallel for a single iambic metron that is rhetorically inseparable both from the preceding and from the succeeding dactyls (as the second analysis above demands): the closest are:

E. *Tro.* 1069 = 1079 –⏑⏑–⏑⏑– ⏖⏑–|–⏑⏑–⏑⏑–⏑⏑–⏑––
Or. 181 = 203 ⏑–⏑⏑–⏑⏑–⏑⏑–⏑⏑–⏑–⏑|–⏑⏑–⏑⏑–⏑⏑–
Hipp. 1109 = 1116 –⏑⏑–⏑⏑|⏑–⏑–|⏑⏑–⏑⏑–⏑⏑

And as we saw, there is no parallel for –⏑– ⏑–– after dac. and leading straight into more (rising) dac. It seems nevertheless that we must accept this analysis, on the slender support of A. *Supp.* 88ff and *Rhesos* 25.

Appendix C

PROM. 571ff AND THE ARISTOPHANEAN (–⏑⏑–⏑––)

571 ἀλλά με τὰν τάλαιναν ἐξ ἐνέρων περῶν κυνηγετεῖ
πλανᾶι τε νῆστιν ἀνὰ τὰν παραλίαν ψάμμον.

This is the received text; most editors read ἀλλ' ἐμὲ and κυναγεῖ, and analyse as –⏑⏑–⏑––‖–⏑⏑–⏑– ⏑––⏑– ⏑–⏑⏑⏑– ⏑⏑⏑–––, i.e. aristophanean and four dochmiacs.[1] After 570, hiatus tells us that we have pause after κεύθει. It is rare, but not unknown, in Aeschylus for the aristophanean –⏑⏑–⏑–– to occur immediately after pause. It is itself always followed by pause, except where it occurs as a pair (e.g. *Ag.* 770-1, 226ff) or as an aeolic colon, akin to enoplion (––⏑⏑–⏑––), in aeolic context. Pause is here confirmed by *brevis in longo* τάλαινᾰ̄ν, though there is no accompanying pause in the sense. (Cf. A. *Supp.* 1062ff, also with no sense-break,[2] lek.//arist.//etc., *Cho.* 459 = 464. 2ia.//arist.// as clausula; S. *El.* 479ff = 495ff is printed by Wilamowitz, Dale, Pearson, etc. as:

⏑–⏑– –⏓‖	ia. sp.
–⏑⏑– ⏑–⏓‖	arist.
–⏑– ⏑–⏑–	lek.

Better surely is

⏑–⏑– –⏓–⏑⏑– ⏑–⏓‖	ia. hipp.
–⏑– ⏑–⏑–	lek.

E. *Alk.* 455 = 466 –⏑⏑–⏑–– is first colon of a strophe, but in aeolic context, *Hipp.* 162 ia. cr. ba.‖–⏑⏑–⏑––|–⏑⏑–⏑⏑–⏑––‖, again aeolic 'dicolon'.) A. *Supp.* 1062 seems to be the only example of an aristophanean preceded by pause, in the middle of a non-aeolic colon.

Aeschylus employs the aristophanean much more freely than Sophocles and Euripides. Counting strophe and antistrophe as one occurrence, the figures are:

Aeschylus 31 times final clausula of strophe, 11 times clausula of period within strophe, 5 times in a pair (i.e. 'aeolic').

Sophocles 9 times final clausula of strophe, 4 times clausula of period, 3 times in a pair.

Euripides 14 times final clausula, 13 times clausula of period, 8 times in a pair (or more).

The aristophanean –⏑⏑–⏑–– is an obviously suitable final clausula for dochmiacs, especially of the –⏑⏑–⏑– form. It is therefore rather surprising to see it here apparently *preceding* a series of dochmiacs, which themselves have no special clausula.

We thus have a combination of rarities, none of them startling in its own right, but cumulatively of some weight, if ἀλλά με τὰν τάλαιναν is to be taken as aristophanean.

(i) Pause demanded by metre after τάλαιναν, which is not suited to the sense.

(ii) –⏑⏑–⏑–– as first colon after a pause, and itself followed by a pause.

(iii) *Brevis in longo* in aristophanean (only, I think, at A. *Pers.* 572, *Ag.* 1531, E. *Alk.* 970 = 980).

(iv) –⏑⏑–⏑–⏒‖ before dochmiacs, in view of its similarity to –⏑⏑–⏑– do.

We should therefore perhaps consider whether ἀλλά με τὰν τάλαιναν may not be a dochmiac, followed by a short. If it is, we are at once plunged into metrical difficulties, from which it seems impossible to save ourselves without some degree of emendation of the text. This would be more distasteful if we did not already have a peculiarity in 572 that has driven most editors, from Hermann onwards, to emend. If we take ἐξ ἐνέρων ... ψάμμον as four dochmiacs, we are faced in the MSS tradition by κυνηγετεῖ πλανᾶι as a dochmiac. Some accept this as an example of 'hexasyllabic' dochmiac.[3] The most popular alternative is to adopt Hermann's κυναγεῖ, which gives ⏑––⏑–, an exemplary do. There are, however, considerable objections to this apparently easy alteration.

(i) Only κυνηγετέω is found in tragedy (S. *Aj.* 5, E. *Hks* 898, *Ion* 1422). Indeed κυνηγέω is not attested before Aristotle (cf. L-S-J *s.v.*).

(ii) κυνηγέω was the later form, and common in later Greek (e.g. Polybios): it would be surprising if scholars or scribes substituted an unfamiliar for a familiar, an archaic for a current word.

If we accept the MSS κυνηγετεῖ we might cast around for a moment to see if an alternative interpretation to hex. do. is possible.

(a) 572 –⏑⏑–⏑– ⏑–⏑– ⏑–⏑– ⏑⏑⏑– ⏑⏑⏑––– do. 2ia. cr. do. is theoretically possible, but the resolved cretic does not seem convincing.

(b) With our suspicions of 571 already aroused, we might consider the idea:

ἀλλά με τὰν τάλαιναν ἐκ νερτέρων	2do.
περῶν κυνηγετεῖ πλανᾶι	2ia.
τε νῆστιν ἀνὰ τὰν παραλίαν ψάμμον	2do.

explaining ἐνέρων either as a gloss for νερτέρων (ἐνέρων is the commoner word, especially in Homer), or as an error arising from the similarity of ΕΝΕΡΩΝ to ΝΕΡΤΕΡΩΝ especially with ΠΕΡΩΝ coming immediately afterwards. The same confusion occurs in the MSS at A. *Pers.* 629.

(c) Keeping the received text, we could take it as

–⏑⏑–⏑– ⏑–⏑⏑–⏑–	do. tel.
⏑–⏑– ⏑–⏑– ⏑⏑⏑– ⏑⏑⏑– –‸–‖	2ia. 2cr. sp.

The telesillean looks a little out of place,[4] and the final spondee is a bit lame, though we could call –⏑⏑–⏑– dodrans rather than dochmiac, to make more congenial company for the telesillean.

(d) We might, with Schroeder, follow Weil and read κἀξ ἐνέρων (cf. S. *Ph.* 624; Theogn. 703), to give –⏑⏑–⏑––|–⏑⏑–|⏑–⏑–|⏑–⏑–| ⏑–⏑⏑⏑– ⏑⏑⏑–––, arist., cho., 2ia., 2do.

I would not defend any of these analyses with any confidence. But on the assumption that κυνηγετεῖ is correct, the 'hexasyllabic' dochmiac would argue against Aeschylean authorship. Conomis cannot find any example in Aesch. of even a probable hex. do. in do. context: his three possible examples (*Supp.* 120 = 131, *Th.* 782 = 789, *Eum.* 159 = 165) are all heavily resolved, and admit alternative interpretations. There are certain examples in Soph. and Eur.[5]

Appendix D

PROM. 580 = 599

580 οἰστρηλάτωι δὲ δείματι δειλαίαν

599 σκιρτημάτων δὲ νήστισιν αἰκείαις

Analysis here is troublesome. Dale[1] divides as × –∪–∪| –∪∪– × –, 'penthemimer' plus dochmiac. This breaks one of the few apparently certain rules that have been discovered for Greek metre: anceps is never preceded by *brevis* or anceps without intervening pause. Thus, while her parallel of S. *OT* 1339 may well be right, × –∪– × –∪–∪– 'penth.' + hypodochmiac, since the first syllable of an hyp. is a true long, × –∪– × × –– × – (penth. + do.) cannot exist. So, too, Stinton's examples[2] do not provide a parallel for *Prom.* 580: only A. *Pers.* 976 has any claim,[3] and there we observe (a) that the context by no means demands a dochmiac (though any other analysis is awkward), (b) that the first five syllables can easily be interpreted as –‸– ∪–– sp. ba., i.e. the last syllable of the penth. can be a true long.

Wilamowitz was clearly aware of this problem, and printed as ––∪– ∪–∪⏒‖––‸– ∪∪∪∪– ∪––‖ 2ia.//mol. ia. ba.// The coincidence of *brevis in longo* in both str. and ant., without any pause in the sense, is very suspicious indeed; so is the subsequent molossus. *Prom.* contains no other molossus, or even spondee, in ia. context. Denniston[4] in fact cites no Aeschylean example of ––‸– as syncopated ia. metron at all (but cf. *Th.* 368?, and *Th.* 346 in dochmiacs). It is much more characteristic of Soph. (cf. *OT* 660; *El.* 160f, 483, 504ff, 849ff; *Tr.* 523ff etc.; also E. *Med.* 204, *Tro.* 579ff, *Pho.* 1021, *Or.* 1305, etc.). Aesch. does not often use even the spondee as a syncopated ia. metron: *Ag.* 160; *Eum.* 382, 987.[5] It is quite common as such in both Soph. and Eur. If Wilamowitz' colometry is correct, we have another unaeschylean element, the trimeter ––‸– ∪∪∪∪– ∪––‖, in itself a rather unlikely looking object.

How else can we account for ––∪–∪–∪∪––– ? The penultimate syllable may be long, or may be anceps or short as δειλαίαν (and even αἰκείαις) can be –⏑– or –––. We might have here a contracted version of the iambelegos, the characteristic colon of dactylo-epitrite, × – ⏑ – × –⏑⏑–⏖–, which we also seemed to discern amid the chaos of 425ff. Against this are: (a) we have no evidence that in ––⏑–⏑ either the first or the fifth syllable is anceps, and we have the additionally unusual feature of *short* before the 'hemiepes'; dac.-ep. strongly favours long anceps; (b) the contraction (–⏑⏑–⏖–) is not very common (cf. A. *Pers*. 568ff, *Supp*. 41; S. *El*. 1082ff, *Tr*. 114, *Ph*. 707ff, *OK* 518; E. *And*. 773, *Rhesos* 535; mostly of the form –––⏑⏑–), and although at S. *El*. 1082ff and A. *Supp*. 41 the combination –––⏑⏑– –⏑–– occurs, the only clearly dac.-ep. cases are E. *And*. 773 = 785 ––⏑⏑–⏑⏑– ––⏑– –––⏑⏑– ––⏑⏑–⏑⏑– etc. and *Rhesos* 535 = 554.

For iambelegos in dochmiac context there are several parallels, all in Euripides: *Alk*. 872; *Hks* 1082ff, 1185ff; *Ion* 768f (685); (*Hel*. 685).

Several of these examples have short anceps. ⏑–⏑⏑–⏑⏑– in do. context is common in Eur. (*Pho*. 119, 350, etc.). A. *Th*. 781ff contains two hemiepe in ia. + do. surroundings that might be taken as do. with irrational anceps –⏑⏑–⏑⏑–: but neither has the slightest hint of dac.-ep. usage, which, as we observed above, is foreign to the extant lyrics of Aeschylus.

Another theoretical possibility is ia. + (dragged?) telesillean, × –⏑– × –⏑⏑– × –. I would prefer the iambelegos interpretation, as a tel. in this context would be unusual,[6] and a 'dragged' tel. unparalleled.

Appendix E

PROM. 691

691 πῆματα λύματα δείματ' ἀμφήκει κέντρωι ψύχειν ψυχὰν ἐμάν
This, the received text, gives –∪∪–∪∪–∪–––––––––––∪–, a very curious assortment of which no metrical sense can be made. The usual solution is, with Hermann, to remove δείματα, explaining it as a gloss. Dawe points out[1] that Q *ante corr.* omitted either λύματα or δείματα, and takes this as a strong argument in favour of the deletion of one or other. Clearly δείματα would be a more likely gloss word than λύματα which, if correct here, has a meaning not exactly paralleled in extant Greek;[2] so that if one must be omitted, it must be δείματα. But there are considerable objections to this solution: (a) δείματα is not a synonym for λύματα, which must mean 'ruin, destruction'; (b) we still have the suspicious ψύχειν in parallel construction to the future μολεῖσθαι after ηὔχουν. This would be easier with ἄν, which might have dropped out (ΑΝΑΜΦΗΚΕΙ); (c) even if the omission of δείματα gives us one familiar form of dochmiac (–∪∪–∪–), the other two that apparently remain are very strange, ––––– (no certain parallel in Aesch. or Soph.[3]), and –––∪– (3 times in Aesch., 9 in Soph., 38 in Eur.). If we insert ἄν before ἀμφήκει and omit ἐμάν we can produce dactylo-anapaests of the form –∪∪–∪∪–∪∪–– etc., which can be made into the required length with the retention of δείματα and the insertion of μοι (glossed by ἐμάν), reading πῆματα λύματα δείματ' ἂν ἀμφήκει κέντρωι ψύχειν μοι ψυχάν = eight anapaests, albeit of an unusual shape.

πῆμᾰτᾰ λῦμᾰτᾰ// = dochmiac might seem a possible solution, followed by δείματ' ἂν ἀμφήκει (–∪∪––– is a form of do. rare in Aesch. but not uncommon in Soph. and Eur.[4]); if ἄν is not inserted, we have –∪∪–∪⏑‖–∪–|––––– –––∪– cr. 2 do., which produces two highly suspect do.'s in succession, as well as leaving the construction harsh. But the pause after λύματα, demanded by *brevis in longo*, is in any case impossible.

ψύχειν ψυχάν is in itself possible: the word-play would be characteristic of tragedy (and for the metaphor cf. A. *Eum.* 161). But it might equally suggest a possible area of corruption, an area that may have grown too wide to be cured. The combination of peculiarities (viz. incomprehensible metre, unusual sense of ξένους, juxtaposition of ψύχειν ψυχάν, and apparent change of construction in the infinitives) is disturbing, and the truth may be unattainable. For this reason, any conclusions on the metre of 691-3 and its significance are likely to be subjective and misleading. We shall therefore draw none.

Appendix F

COMPOUND ADJECTIVES (see p.149 n.6)

Here are listed the figures for the separate categories of Clay (pp. 54-68, 84-99), which I have subsumed into my own category of 'compound adjectives' in ch.8.

		(i) -ης	(ii) -τος	(iii) -τος	(iv) *others*	(v) *Total*
A.	*Pers.*	52	25	23	171	271
	Th.	53	12	27	217	309
	Supp.	66	45	21	207	339
	Ag.	74	56	42	283	455
	Cho.	51	28	22	168	269
	Eum.	44	27	17	172	260
	Prom.	51	39	21	165	276
S.	*Aj.*	45	34	20	146	245
	Ant.	41	25	19	186	271
	OT	40	31	6	156	233
	Tr.	28	28	13	124	193
	El.	40	21	11	132	204
	Ph.	46	10	2	128	186
	OK	49	39	11	207	306
E.	*Alk.*	34	8	4	93	139
	Med.	42	15	0	134	191
	Hkd.	33	5	1	71	110
	Hipp.	36	27	3	144	210
	And.	36	16	6	108	166
	Hek.	27	18	6	114	165
	Hik.	40	9	4	93	146
	Hks	38	22	5	172	237
	Ion	52	35	7	164	258
	Tro.	33	12	6	122	173
	El.	42	12	1	125	180
	IT	34	32	7	164	237
	Hel.	62	28	6	174	270
	Pho.	50	21	8	227	306
	Or.	44	19	5	184	252
	Ba.	17	20	4	157	198
	IA	31	29	7	146	213
	Kyk.	23	9	4	47	83
	Rhes.	29	8	8	114	159

Column (i) stands for compound adj, with suffix -ης (Clay 54-8); (ii) for adj. in -τος, with prefix ἀ-, δυσ-, or εὐ- (63-6); (iii) for adj. in -τος with substantive or verb prefix (66-8); (iv) for 'other' compound adj. (84-9).

Appendix G

THE VOCABULARY STUDIES OF NIEDZBALLA AND PERETTI

Niedzballa listed those words in *Prom.* which do not occur in Aeschylus, according to their grammatical status (nouns, adjectives, etc.), and according to their origin or type (simple/compound, epic, Pindaric, etc.). His total comes to 649 words, Schmid's to 631: my own investigations yield 690. A small part of the discrepancies must be due to inevitable differences of reading; but more important are the differences between our methods.

N. omits adverbs whose adjectival form occurs in Aeschylus, whereas I feel that these qualify as separate words. He also uses the fragments of Aeschylus as well as the extant plays to make up his Aeschylean corpus, whereas I leave them out of the reckoning throughout, since there is no question of our finding out 'Aeschylus' total vocabulary':[1] we want merely a sure and unchanging corpus, and the six plays comprise over nine tenths of Aeschylus' surviving work. The fragments are in some cases satyric; readings are often uncertain, in the absence of a wider context; Aeschylean attribution is frequently dubious.

Even these differences of method do not account for all of the discrepancy: they only apply to 75 words which he omits and I include,[2] and to 28 of his words which I omit, either because they do not occur in Murray's text, or because N. lists two forms of the same word separately.[3] Some twenty-five words remain unaccounted for, and have apparently simply been overlooked by N. So not only does N. fail to provide any comparative figures for the other six plays or for Sophocles or Euripides, but even his figures and lists for *Prom.* are found to be inexact and unsatisfactory.

Unfortunately too, the other detailed study which we might expect to prove useful, and to provide our necessary basis of evidence, that of Peretti,[4] suffers from even more severe limitations. P. starts from N.'s lists, and aims to disprove the thesis that *Prom.*'s *Eigenwörter* are more numerous than we would expect from an Aeschylean play. He lists *Eigenwörter* for A. *Supp.*, *Pers.*, *Cho.*, and *Eum*. (all about the same length as *Prom*.); but his method allows him to distort the picture hopelessly. In looking for *Eigenwörter* in these four plays, he leaves *Prom*. out of Aeschylus' corpus, which means that, whereas *Prom*. was checked against six plays, these four are checked against five: in each of those plays, therefore, the probability that any particular word will be an *Eigenwort* is significantly higher, and it is likely that they will contain significantly more *Eigenwörter* than *Prom*.

Equally misleading is P.'s policy (stated p.177 n.1, p.194 n.1) of omitting verbs whose simple or compound form occurs elsewhere in Aeschylus. P. seems to fall into the trap of supposing that we are trying to discover 'Aeschylus' vocabulary'. Thus, if εἰσαΐσσω occurs at A. *Ag*. 1181(?), ἀναΐσσω at *Ag*. 77 (and *Pers*. 96?), then Aeschylus clearly 'knew' the word ἀΐσσω; it was part of his 'vocabulary'. Therefore we should not class ἀΐσσω (*Prom*. 676, 837), διαΐσσω (*Prom*. 134), or προσαΐσσω (*Prom*. 146) as *Eigenwörter*. This seems to me to be fundamentally mistaken: these are quite separate and different words.[5]

So when P. observes that A. *Supp*. has 521 *Eigenwörter*, *Pers*. 513, *Cho*. 390, *Eum*. 368, *Prom*. 471, and concludes that *Prom*. is in no way exceptional, he is merely finding what he wants to find, because of the way in which he is looking. That is not to say that his figures are worthless; they can still be used as a check for our own investigations. I give an example of the sort of differences which emerge when P.'s method and mine are both applied to the same material, as an indication of the degree of agreement and discrepancy which we should be expecting.

For repeated *Eigenwörter* in *Pers*., P. gives the figure of 55 (excluding proper names); mine is 58.[6] But this apparent closeness is illusory. P. includes words which occur in *Prom*. (πάτρα, ἀράσσω, μύριος, βάθος, ῥεῦμα, τέγγω): these six should be discounted, for the reasons given above. We should also remove from his lists καταφθίω (cf. *Eum*. 727), ναί (cf. *Supp*. 468?), δίψος (*sic*, cf. *Cho*. 756, Italie *s.v.*), ἵππος (which P. counts as a separate feminine noun), and δόκιμος (I count the adverb at 547 as a different word, so it is not repeated). Thus we are left with 44 words on which P. and I agree. The words which P. omits but I include are: αἰνῶς, ἄλαστος, ἄναυς, βαλλήν, θεομήστωρ, ἰωά, ὀᾶ (all in refrain or ritual repetition[7]), ἐκπρεπής (P. reads 184 εὐπρεπής?), ἐφέπω (cf. ἐφέπομαι), κόρυμβος (P. cites only 411, not 659), πόσος (P., rightly perhaps, does not count 292), προσπίτνω (cf. A. *Th.* ποτιπίπτω), ἐχυρός (cf. A. *Ag.* ὀχυρός), and εὐτυχῶς (cf. εὐτυχής), a total of fourteen.

Thus P.'s figure provides a reasonable basis for cautious inference and comparison; he does not seem to be so misleading as to be negligible. I have therefore used his figures and lists as a check on the plays which I have not studied in detail for myself, i.e. A. *Supp.*, *Cho.*, and *Eum.*

Appendix H

EIGENWÖRTER

PROM.

ἄβροτος, ἀγείτων, ἄγναμπτος, ἀγνόρυτος, ἄγρυπνος, ἀδαμάντινος (2), ἀδαμαντόδετος (2), ἀδήριτος, Ἀδράστεια, ἀεικής (4), ἀήσυρος, ἀθέτως, ἀθλεύω, ἆθλος (6), ἀθυμέω, αἰθαλόεις, αἰκεία (3), αἰκίζω (4), αἴκισμα, αἱμύλος, αἰνικτηρίως (2), αἰολόστομος, αἰπυμήτης, αἰπύνωτος, αἵρεσις, αἰσθάνομαι, ἀίσσω (2), ἀιστόω (2), αἰτίαμα (2), Αἰτναῖος, αἰφνίδιος, ἄκεσμα, ἀκηδέω, ἄκικυς, ἀκίχητος, ἀκοή, ἀκοίμητος, ἀκραγής, ἀκρατής, ἀκριβῶς, ἀλατεία, ἀλγίων, ἀλέξημα, ἀλίγκιος, ἀλίστονος, ἀλλάσσω, ἄλυτος, ἀμαλάπτω, ἅμιλλα, ἀμοχθεί, ἀμπλακία, ἀναγγέλλω, ἀναμυχθίζομαι, ἀναύγητος, ἀνεψιός, ἀνηκουστέω, ἀνήροτος, ἀνθεμώδης, ἀνθρακόομαι, ἀνιστορέω, ἄνους, ἀντειπεῖν, ἀντιβαίνω, ἀντισπάω, ἀνωφελής, ἀπάνθρωπος, ἀπαντλέω, ἀπαράμυθος, ἀπέδιλος, ἀπειλή, ἀπενθής, ἀπέραντος, ἀπέχθεια, ἀπιστέω, ἄπλατος, ἀποδύρομαι, ἀποικία, ἀποκλαίω, ἀποκλήιω, ἀποκρύπτω, ἄπορος, ἀποστροφή, ἀποσυλάω, ἀπρόοπτος, Ἀραβία, ἀραρίσκω, ἀρδεύω, ἄρδην, αρδις, ἄρηξις, ἀρθμός, Ἀριμασπός, ἀριστεύω, ἁρμοῖ, ἁρμονία, ἀρχαιοπρεπής, ἄσβεστος, ἀσθενής (3), ἀσμένως, ἀστεργάνωρ, ἀστράπτω, ἀστρογείτων, ἀσχαλάω, ἀταρβής, ἀτέραμνος (2), Ἄτλας (2), αὐθάδης (2), αὐθαδία (5), αὐθάδισμα, αὐλή, αὐλών, ἄυπνος, αὐτόκτιτος, ἀφεγγής, ἄφετος, ἄφοβος, ἀχέτας, ἀχθηδών, ἄχθομαι, ἄχρειος, ἄψορρον, βασιλικός, βούκερως, βούστασις, βουφόνος, βρόντημα, βρώσιμος, Βύβλινος, γαμέτης, γαμφηλαί, γαμψῶνυξ, γάπεδον, γεγωνίσκω, γεγωνῶ (7), γέλασμα, γέννημα, γνάμπτω, γνωρίζω, Γοργόνειος, γοργωπός, γρύψ, γύης (2), γυιοπέδη, γυναικόμιμος, δαιταλεύς, δακρυσίστακτος, [δάμαρ] (3), δαρόν (2), δέλτος, δεσμώτης, δήθεν (2), διάδοχος (2), διαθρύπτομαι, διαίσσω, δίαιτα, διάκονος, διαμφίδιος, διαμυθολογέω, διαρραίω, διαρταμέω, διαστοιχίζομαι, διάστροφος, διαφθορά, δίθηκτος, δίοδος, διορίζω (2), δολιχός, δοτήρ, δουλεύω (2), δρακοντόμαλλος, δρῦς, δυσάλωτος, δυσεκλύτως, δυσεύρετος, δυσκρίτως, δύσλοφος, δύσλυτος, δυσπαραίτητος, δυσπετῶς, δύσπλανος (2), δυστέκμαρτος, Δωδώνη (2), δωρεά (2), δωρέομαι (2), ἔγγονος, ἐγκελεύω, ἐγκονέω, ἐγκρατής, ἕδνα, εἰκῆι (2?), εἰλίσσω (3), εἰσάπαξ, εἰσβάλλω, εἰσοιχνέω, ἑκατογκάρανος, ἐκβροντάω, ἔκγονον, ἐκδιδάσκω (2), ἐκθοινάομαι, ἐκκαλύπτω, ἐκκυλίνδω, ἐκλάμπω, ἔκλυσις, ἐκμοχθέω, ἐκπίπτω (5), ἐκρήγνυμι, ἐκρίπτω, ἐκτήκω, ἐκτροπή, ἐκφυσάω, ἐλαφρός (3), ἐλεινός, ἐλελεῦ (2), ἐλευθεροστομέω, ἐλίγδην, ἐλινύω (2), ἕλιξ, ἐμπλέκω (2), ἐμποδίζω, ἐναντιόομαι, ἐνδείκνυμι, ἐνζεύγνυμι (2), ἐνθένδε, ἔννους, ἔννυχος, ἐνόδιος, ἐντολή, ἐξαιστόω, ἐξαίφνης, ἐξαμαρτάνω (2), ἐξαμύνομαι, ἐξαναζέω, ἐξανίστημι, ἐξαρτύω (2), ἐξελαύνω, ἐξευρίσκω (4), ἐξομματόω, ἐπαιτιάομαι, ἐπαναγκάζω (2), ἐπαναδιπλάζω, ἐπαυρίσκομαι, ἐπαφάω, ἐπαχθής, ἐπεξέρχομαι, ἐπιθωΰσσω (2), ἐπικότως, ἐπιπλήσσω, ἐπιρρίπτω, ἐπιτέλλω, ἐπιτιμητής, ἐπιχαλάω, ἐπιχαρής, ἐπίχειρα, ἔποικος, ἐπόπτης, ἐραστεύω, ἐργάνη, ἐρεθίζω (2), ἐρευνάω, ἐρημία, ἐρρωμένως (2), ἕσπερος, ἔσχατος (3), εὐάγκαλος, εὔβατος, εὔελπις, εὐηθία, εὔκυκλος, εὐμορφία, εὐξύμβλητος, εὐφροσύνη, εὐωριάζω, ἐφημέριος, ἐφήμερος (3), ἑῷος, ζάπυρος, ζεύγλη, ζητέω (3), ἥδομαι, ἠλιθιόω, ἡλιοστιβής, ἤπιος, ἦρ, Ἡσιόνη, ἡσυχάζω, θακέω (2), θαλασσόπλαγκτος, θάλπω (2), θανατόω, θαρσαλέος, θέα, θέαμα (2), θεμερῶπις, Θεμίσκυρα, θεοπρόπος, θέορτος, θεόσυτος (3), Θερμώδων, Θεσπρωτός, θεωρέω, θεωρία, θηλυκτόνος, θηλύνους, θηλύσπορος, θήν, θηράσιμος, θοίνη, θολερός, θράσσω, θρασυσπλάγχνως, θώπτω, ἰάσιμος, ἴδιος (2), Ἰνάχειος (2), Ἰόνιος, ἰότης, ἰπόω, ἰσθμός, ἰσόνειρος, καθορμίζω, καίτοι (4), κακότης, καλλίκαρπος, κάρπιμος, καταβασμός, καταιβάτης, καταμηνύω, κατάπτερος, κατασκέλλομαι, κατοκνέω, κατῶρυξ, Καύκασος (2), κελαινόβρωτος, κενόφρων, κεράννυμι, κεραστίς, κέρδιστος, κερτομέω, Κερχνεία, κηδεύω, κηρόπλαστος, Κιλίκιος, Κιμμερικός, κινάθισμα, κίνυγμα, κιρκόω, Κισθήνη, κίων, κλέπτης, κλοπαῖος, κνεφαῖος, κνῖσα, Κολχίς, κομπέω, κορέννυμι, κουφόνους, κραδαίνω, κράζω, κραιπνόσυτος, κραιπνοφόρος, κρᾶσις, κραταιός, κρήνη, Κρόνιος, κρόταφος, κυκάω, κυκνόμορφος, κυνηγέω, λαβροστομέω, λαβρόσυτος, λάβρως, λαθραίως, λαιός, λαμπρῶς, λατρεία, λατρεύω, λεῖος, λειότης, λεωργός, Λέρνα (2), λευκόπτερος, λίαν (2), λινόπτερος, λιπαρέω (2), λῦμα, λωφάω (3), Μαιωτικός, Μαιῶτις, μαλακογνώμων, μαλθακίζω (2), μᾶσσον, μασχαλιστήρ, μεγαίρω, μεγαλόστονος, μεγαλοσχήμων, μεγαλύνομαι, μεθαρμόζω, μελαμβαθής, μελίγλωσσος, μέμψις, μεταχωρέω, μηδαμῆι, μῆδος, μήνη, μήπω, μητρυιά, μισέω (2), μνῆμα, μνηστήρ, Μολοσσός, μόναρχος, μονόδους, μουνῶψ, μουσομήτωρ, μόχθημα, μυδροκτυπέω, μύκημα, μυριετής, μυριωπός, μύρμηξ, νᾶμα, ναρθηκοπλήρωτος, Νειλῶτις, νεκροδέγμων, νεοζυγής, νηλεῶς, νιφάς, νοσέω (4), νόσημα (3), νότιος, νουθετέω, νυκτίφοιτος, νυκτιφρούρητος, νωθής, ξυλουργία, ὁδηγέω, ὀδμή, ὀδυρμός, ὁθούνεκα, οἰακονόμος, οἴγω, οἶμος (2), οἰστράω, οἰστρήλατος, οἰστροδίνητος, οἰστροπλήξ, οἴω?, ὀκνέω, ὀκρίς, ὀλέκω, ὀλιγοδρανία, Ὄλυμπος, ὁμαλός, ὀμίχλη, ὁμοπάτριος, ὀξύπρωιρος, ὀξύστομος (2), ὀρθόβουλος, ὀρθοστάδην, ὀροθύνω, ὀσφύς, ὀχέω, ὀχλέω, ὀχμάζω (2), παιδιά, παλίμπλαγκτος, παμμήτωρ, πανήμερος, παντελῶς (2), πάντεχνος, παπταίνω (2), παράκοπος, παράκτιος, παράλιος, παραμυθέομαι, παραμυκάομαι, παράορος, παραπαίω, παρασύρω, παρειπεῖν, παρέξειμι, παρθενεύομαι, παρθενία, παρθενών, πέλεια, πελώριος, πέρα (3), πέργαμα, περισσός, περισσόφρων, πετραῖος, πετρηρεφής, πέτρινος, πημαίνω, πημοσύνη, πιστός, πλανάω (4), πλάνη (7), πλάνημα, πλάσσω, πλατύρρους, πλήρης, πλήσιον, πλινθυφής, Πλούτων, ποικιλείμων, πόλος, πολύπλανος, πορεία (3), πορεύομαι, πόριμος, πορπάω, ποτινίσσομαι, προδείκνυμι, προδέρκομαι, προδότης, προθεσπίζω, προθυμέομαι (3), προθυμία, προκήδομαι, Προμηθεύς (18), προοίμιον, προσαίσσω, προσαυαίνω, προσβλέπω, προσδοκητός, πρόσειλος, προσέρπω (2), προσήγορος, προσθροέω, προσλαμβάνω (2), προσμανθάνω, προσπασσαλεύω, προσπέτομαι (3), πρόσπλατος, προσπορπατός, προσχρήιζω (2), πρόσχωμα, προτίθεμαι, προτρέπομαι, προὐξεπίσταμαι (2), προυσελέω, πρόχειρος, πρῶι, πταίω, πτερυγωκής, πτῆσις, Πυθώ, πυρωπός, πωλέομαι, ῥαδινός, ῥαιδίως, ῥαιστήρ, ῥαίω, ῥάκος, ῥαχιά, Ῥέα, ῥητός (2), ῥυθμίζω, σαλεύω, Σαλμυδήσσιος, σαφηνῶς, σεμνόστομος, σεπτός, σιδηρομήτωρ, σιδηροτέκτων, Σικελία, σκεθρῶς (2), σκιρτάω, σκίρτημα (2), σκόπελος, σμερδνός, σόφισμα (3), σοφιστής (2), σπαράσσω, σπορά, σταθευτός, στενάχω, στενόπορος, στενωπός, στερεός, στερρός, στοιχίζω, στρόμβος, στυγάνωρ, στυγητός, συγκαθίστημι, συγκαλυπτέος, συγκαλυπτός, συγκάμνω (2), συγχώννυμι, συλλήβδην, σύμβολος, συμπαραστατέω , συμπονέω, συμπράσσω, σύμφημι, συναίρομαι, συναλγέω, συναμπέχω, συνασχαλάω (3), συνεδρία, συνέχω, συνθάλπω, σύνθεσις, σύνθετος, σύννοια, συνομαίμων, συνταράσσω, σφάκελος (2), σφήν, σφίγγω, σφοδρύνομαι, σφριγάω, σχέτλιος, ταλαίπωρος (3), ταπεινός (2), ταχύπτερος, τεκμαίρω (2), τερμόνιος, τετρασκελής, τηλέπλαγκτος, τηλουρός (2), τινάκτειρα, τινάσσω, Τιτάν (2), τλητός, τραχύτης, τρίγωνος, τρικυμία, τρίμορφος, τρόχις, τροχοδινέομαι, τρύω, τυφλός, ὑμεναιόω, ὕπαρ, ὑπερήφανος, ὑπερμήκης, ὑπέροχος, ὑπέρπικρος, ὑπέρπλουτος, ὑπηρέτης (2), ὑπνοδότης, ὑποβρέμω, ὑποθάλπω, ὑποπτήσσω (2), ὑποστενάζω, ὑποσυρίζω, ὑποτοβέω, ὑψήγορος (2), ὑψηλόκρημνος, ὑψίκρημνος, φανός, φάραγξ (4), φεψαλόω, φθέγμα, φιλάνθρωπος (2), φιλήνιος, φλογωπός (2), φλογώψ, φλοῖσβος, φοῖβος, φοιταλέος, φορητός, Φορκίδες, φρενοπληγής, φρενόπληκτος, φυγγάνω, Χάλυψ (2), χαριτογλωσσέω, χειμάζομαι (2), χερνήτης, χλιδάω (3), χόλος (4), χρησμωιδία, χριστός, χρίω (4), χροία (2), χρυσόρρυτος, ψαίρω, ψάμμος, ψελλός, ψευδηγορέω, ψευδωνύμως, ψύχω, ὠθέω, Ὠκεανός (3), ὠλένη, ὦμος, ὠφέλημα (3).

= 690 or 691 *Eigenwörter*.

A. *PERS*.

ἁβροβάτης, ἁβρόγοος, ἁβροδίαιτος, ἁβροπενθής, ἁβροχίτων, Ἀγαβάτας, ἀγαυός, Ἀγβάτανα (3), ἀγή, ἀγρέτης, Ἀγχάρης, ἀγχίαλος, ἀγχιγείτων, [ἀδείμαντος], Ἀδεύης, ἀείμνηστος, Ἀθαμαντίς, Ἀθῆναι (8), Ἀθηναῖος, ἀθροίζω, αἰάζω, Αἴας (3), Αἰδωνεύς (2), αἱματοσφαγής, αἰνῶς (2), αἰχμάζω, αἰχμήεις, ἀκάκας, ἄκακος (2), ἀκάματος, ἄκμων, ἄκοιτις, ἀκοντιστής, ἄκοσμος, ἀκόσμως (2), ἄλαστος (2), ἁλιβαφής, ἀλίρροθος, ἀλίτυπος, ἀλκίφρων, ἄλλοσε, ἄλμη, Ἄλπιστος, Ἅλυς, ἀμίαντος, Ἀμίστρης, Ἄμιστρις, ἀμμείγνυμι, ἄμπελος, ἀμύσσω (2), ἀμφιβάλλω (2), ἀμφίζευκτος, ἀμφικυκλόομαι, ἀμφιλόγως, Ἀμφιστρεύς, ἄμωμος, ἀναβοάω, ἀνακωκύω, ἀνανδρία, ἀναπομπός, ἀναπτύσσω (2), ἀνάριθμος [*Prom.*], ἀναστρέφω, ἀνατρέπω, ἄναυς, ἀνδροπλήθεια, Ἄνδρος, ἀνθεμουργός, ἀνθίσταμαι [*Prom.*], ἄνιος (6), ἀνοιμώζω, ἀνταλαλάζω, ἀντέχω, ἀντίδουπος (4), ἀντισηκόω, Ἀξιός, ἀπαθής, ἀπαυράω, ἀποθραύω, ἀπολείπω, ἀποπέμπω, ἀπόρθητος, ἀπορρήγνυμι, ἀποσκήπτω, ἀποσφάλλω [*Prom.*], ἄποτμος, ἀποτροπή, ἄπριγδα (4), ἀπρόσοιστος, Ἄραβος, ἀράσσω [*Prom.*] (2), Ἀργήστης, ἄρδω (2), ἀρίδακρυς, ἀριθμός [*Prom.*] (2), Ἀριόμαρδος (3), Ἀρκτεύς (2), Ἀρσάκης, Ἀρσάμης (2), Ἀρτάμης, Ἀρτάσπης, Ἀρταφρένης (3), Ἀρτεμβάρης (3), ἀρτιζυγία, ἀρχέλειος, ἆσθμα, Ἀσία [*Prom.*] (4), Ἀσίας [*Prom.*] (2), Ἀσιατογενής, Ἀσιῆτις, ἀσκέω [*Prom.*], ἄσμενος [*Prom.*], ἀσπαίρω, ἀτάρ [*Prom.*], ἀτέκμαρτος, αὐθημερόν, ἀφάλλομαι, ἄφαρ, ἀφνεός, ἄφωνος, Ἀχελωίδες, ἀχρήματος, Βαβυλών, βάγμα, βάθος [*Prom.*] (2), βάθρον, βαθύβουλος, Βάκτριος (3), βαλλήν (2), βάσκω (2), Βατάνωχος, βιοτή, βοᾶτις, Βοιωτός (2), Βόλβη, βόλος, Βόσπορος [*Prom.*] (2), βρύχιος [*Prom.*], βύσσινος, γενειάς, γέφυρα, γηραλέος, γνάπτω, γυναικοπληθής, Δαδάκης (2), δακνάζομαι, δάκρυμα, Δαρειογενής (2), Δαρεῖος (14), δασμοφορέω, δεκάς, δέος, δέργμα, δέσμωμα, δήν, διαβαίνω, διαβοάω, διαίνω (4), Δίαιξις, διαμυδαλέος, διάπλοος, διαπορθέω, διαπρέπω, διασπαράσσω, διεκπεράω, δίομαι (2), δίοπος, δίπλαξ, δίρρυμος, δίφρος, διχόθεν, δόκιμος, δοκίμως, δόναξ [*Prom.*], δορίκρανος, Δοτάμας, δουρίκλυτος, δράμημα, δρασμός (2), δύρομαι [*Prom.*], δυσαιανής, δύσβατος, δυσβάυκτος, δύσθροος (3), δυσκλεής [*Prom.*], δύσλεκτος, δυσμή, δυσπόλεμος, δυσπόνητος, δυσφρονῶς, Δωρικός, Δωρίς (2), ἐγκατασκήπτω, ἔγχος, εἰρήνη, ἑκατόν, ἐκεῖσε, ἐκθρωίσκω, ἐκμανθάνω [*Prom.*], ἐκπεύθομαι, ἐκπιδύομαι, ἐκπίμπλημι, ἔκπληξις, ἔκπλους (2), ἐκπρεπής (2), ἐκσῳίζομαι (2), ἐκφθίνω (2), ἐκφοβέω, ἐλαιόφυτος, ἐλατήρ, ἐλειοβάτης, ἔλειος, Ἕλλη (4), Ἑλληνίς, Ἑλλήσποντος, ἐμβατεύω, ἐμβολή (4), ἔμβολον, ἐμβριθής, ἔμπειρος, ἐνάλιος, ἐνάλλομαι, ἐνδυναστεύω, ἐνέζομαι, ἔνεροι [*Prom.*], ἔντη, ἔντοσθεν, ἐνύπνιον (2), ἐξαμείβω [*Prom.*], ἐξαναστρέφω, ἐξανθέω, ἐξαποφθείρω, ἐξαρκής, ἐπαναθρῳίσκω, ἐπαναμένω [*Prom.*], ἐπανέρομαι, ἔπαυλος, ἐπεγχωρέω, ἐπευθύνω, ἐπευφημέω, ἐπιβοάω, ἐπιδεσπόζω, ἐπικείρω, ἐπίκουρος, ἐπικύρω, ἐπιρρήγνυμι, ἐπιστενάζω, ἐπιστρατεύω, ἐπιτίμιον, ἐπιφλέγω, ἔποχος (2), ἐρέτης, ἑστιοῦχος, ἑτεραλκής, εὐαγής, εὐαίων, εὔαρκτος, εὐβουλία [*Prom.*], εὐγένεια, εὔδηλος, εὐδόκιμος, εὐειδής, εὐείμων, εὐέξοδος, εὐήρετμος, εὔθυμος, εὐθυντήριος, εὐθύνω [*Prom.*] (2), εὔκοσμος, εὐκτέανος, εὔλογος, εὔμαρις, εὐνάτειρα [*Prom.*], εὐνατήρ, εὐνατήριον, εὔνους, εὐπάτωρ, εὔποτος [*Prom.*], εὐροέω, εὐρύπορος, Εὐρώπη [*Prom.*], εὐσταλής, εὐτάκτως, εὐτλήμων, εὐτυχῶς (2), εὐφεγγής, εὐχείρωτος, εὐψυχία, εὔψυχος, ἐφέπω (2), ἐφέτης, ἐφορμαίνω, ἐφορμάω, ἐχυρός (2), ζαπληθής, ζηλωτός, ζόφος, Ἠδωνίς, ἡλικία, ἡμερολεγδόν, ἡνία [*Prom.*], ἠπειρογενής, ἠχή, ἠχώ [*Prom.*], θαλάσσιος [*Prom.*], θαλασσόπληκτος, θαρσύνω, Θάρυβις (3), θεοβλαβέω, θεοκλυτέω, θεομήστωρ (2), θεότρεπτος, Θεσσαλός, Θῆβαι, θηράω [*Prom.*], θησαυρός (2), θίς, θρηνητήρ, θοῦρος [*Prom.*], θοῶς [*Prom.*], Θρῄκη (2), θυηπόλος, θυμόμαντις, θύννος, ἰά, Ἰάονες (5), ἰαχή, ἰθαιγενής, Ἴκαρος, Ἰμαῖος, ἰός, ἱππεύς, ἱππηλάτης, ἱππιάναξ, ἱππιοχάρμης (2), ἱπποβάτης, ἰσοδαίμων, ἰσόθεος (2), ἰσόρροπος, ἴυγξ, Ἰωά (2), Ἰωνία, κακομέλετος, κακόφατις, καλλίρροος, κασιγνήτη [*Prom.*], κατακρύπτω, κατάρχω, καταυχέω, καταφθείρω (4), κατερείκω, κάτοχος, κενανδρία, κένανδρος, κέρας, Κίλιξ, κλεινός [*Prom.*], κλίνω, κλύδων [*Prom.*], Κνίδος, κοιρανέω [*Prom.*], κολαστής, κολούω, κολπίας, κόρυμβος (2), κραιπνός, κρεοκοπέω, κρηναῖος, κρηπίς, κροκόβαπτος, κρυσταλλοπήξ, κρυφαίως, κύανεος, Κυχρεῖος, κυρίσσω, Κῦρος (2), κῶκυμα (2), κωπήρης, λαοπόρος, λεκτός, λεπτόδομος, Λέσβος, λευκήρης, λευκόπωλος, λιβάς, Λίλαιος (2), λινόδεσμος, λόγχη (3), Λυδός (2), Λυθίμνας, Λυρναῖος, Μαγνητικός, Μᾶγος, μακαρίτας, Μακεδών, μακιστήρ, μακροβίοτος, Μαραθών, Μάραφις,

Μάρδοι, Μάρδος, Μάρδων, Μαριανδυνός, Μασίστρης (2), Μάταλλος, μαχαιροφόρος, Μεγαβάτης (2), μεγάλατος, μεγάλαυχος, μεγαυχής, μέγεθος, μειλικτήριος, μελαγχίτων, μέλι, μέλισσα, μέσακτος, μεσόω, μεταρρυθμίζω, μετάτροπος, μέτωπον, μηδαμά [*Prom.*], μηδέπω [*Prom.*], Μηδικός, Μῆδος (2), Μηλιεύς, μηλοτρόφος, Μητρογαθής, μητρόπολις, μνημονεύω, μόγις [*Prom.*], μολπηδόν, μονάς, μονόζυξ, Μύκονος, μυριάς, μυριόνταρχος, μυριοταγός, Μύσιος (2), μύχιος, μωραίνω, Νάξος, ναός, ναυάγιον, ναύφαρκτος (2), νεοχμός [*Prom.*], νημερτής, νησιῶτις, νουθέτημα, νώνυμος, Ξάνθης, ξανθός, Ξέρξης (17), ὀᾶ (6), ὄδισμα, οἰακοστροφέω, Οἰβάρης, οἰκτρῶς, οἰμωγή, οἰστοδέγμων, ὄπιθεν, ὀρθιάζω, ὀρσολοπέω, ὄρχαμος, οὐδαμῆι [*Prom.*], Πάγγαιος, πάμμεικτος (2), παμμιγής, παμπήδην, παμφαής, πάμφορος, παναίολος, πάνδυρτος (2), πάννυχος, παντάλας, παντarκής, παράγω, παρακαλέω, παραστάτης, Πάρθος, πάροικος, Πάρος, πάτρα [*Prom.*] (2), Πάφος, πεδιήρης, πεζονόμος, πεζός (6), πείθαρχος, πελάγιος (2), Πελάγων, πελάτης, πελειοθρέμμων, πεμπαστής, πεντάκις, πεντήκοντα, πέρας, περίκλυστος (2), πέριξ (2), Πέρσαι (33), περσέπτολις, Περσικός (7), Περσίς (10), περσονομέω, περσονόμος, Πηγαστάγων, πίασμα, πινύσκω, πίστις, Πλαταιαί, πλατύς, πλεκτός [*Prom.*], ποδουχέω, ποιμανόριον, ποιμάνωρ, πολεμοφθόρος, πολέω, πολιαίνομαι, πολύγομφος, πολύδονος [*Prom.*], πολυθρέμμων, πολυναύτης, πολυπενθής, πολύχειρ, πολύχρυσος (4), πορφύρεος, πόσος (2), ποτισαίνω, πραΰνω (2), πρεσβεία, πρόκακος (2), προπίτνω, Προποντίς, πρόρριζος, προσκυνέω [*Prom.*], προσοράω [*Prom.*] (2), προσπίτνω (2), πρόσφθογγος (2), πρόσχωρος, πρωτόμορος, πτήσσω [*Prom.*], πύργινος, πυργοδάικτος, πυργόω, πυρσός, ῥᾶ, ῥαχίζω, ῥεῦμα [*Prom.*] (2), Ῥόδος, ῥοθιάς, ῥόθος (2), ῥόος, ῥῦμα, ῥώμη, σάκτωρ, Σαλαμίς (4), Σάμος, Σάρδεις (2), σαφηνής [*Prom.*] (2), Σεισάμης, Σευάλκης, Σησάμης, Σιληνίαι, σκαλμός, σκεδάννυμι [*Prom.*], σκηπτός, σκηπτουχία, σκληρός, σκύλλω, σμῆνος, Σόλοι, Σοσθάνης, Σοῦσα (4), Σούσας, Σουσιγενής, Σουσίς (2), Σουσισκάνης (2), Σπερχειός, στάγμα, στεναγμός, στενός, στεῦμαι, στημορραγέω, στῖφος (2), στοιχηγορέω, στοῖχος, στόμωμα, στονόεις [*Prom.*], στρατεύομαι, Στρυμόνιος, Στύγιος, στυφελός (2), στύφλος [*Prom.*], σύδην, Συέννεσις, συλάω [*Prom.*], συμβολή, συμμαχέω, συναρπάζω, συνῆλιξ, σύρδην, σφαδάζω, σχεδία, ταγέω, ταγός [*Prom.*] (3), τέγγω [*Prom.*] (3), τέμενος, Τενάγων, τευχηστήρ, τῆλε, Τῆνος, τιάρα, τίλλω, τιμωρία, Τμῶλος, Τόλμος, τόξαρχος, τοξικός, τοξοδάμας (3), τοξόδαμνος, τοξουλκός (2), τοσουτάριθμος, τριακάς, τρίρρυμος, τρίσκαλμος (2), τρισμύριος, τριτόσπορος, τρομέω [*Prom.*], τροπόομαι, τροχήλατος, Τύριος, ὑπαντιάζω (3), ὕπειμι, ὑπεκσῴζω, ὑπέρπολυς, ὑπομιμνήσκω, ὕποχος, ὑπτιόω, Ὑσταίχμας, φάλαρον, Φαρνδάκης (2), Φαρνοῦχος (2), φαύλως, φθάνω, φθίνασμα, φιλόφρων, φιλόχορος, φλαῦρος, Φοίνισσος, Φρύξ, φυγαίχμας, φύλλον, φύρδην, χαλκήρης, χαλκόστομος, χαράσσω, χιλίαρχος, χιλιάς, Χίος, χλιδανός, χρυσεόστολμος, Χρυσεύς, χρυσόγονος, ψάλλω, Ψάμμις, ψυχαγωγός, ὠμοφρόνως, ὠφελέω [*Prom.*]

= 666, of which 56 occur in *Prom.*, = 610 *Eigenwörter.*

A. TH. 1-860, 875-1004

ἀβουλία, ἀγάστονος, ἀγήνωρ, ἀγχίπτολις, Ἄδραστος (2), αἰθέριος [*Prom.*], αἴθων, αἱματηφόρος, αἰνόμορος, ἀκόμπαστος, ἄκομπος, ἀκριτόφυρτος, ἀκρόβολος, ἀκρόπτολις, Ἄκτωρ, ἀλδαίνω [*Prom.*] (2), ἀλεξητήριος, ἀληθεύω, ἀλύω, ἀλφηστής, ἄλως, ἀμάχετος, ἀμβλύνω, ἀμεμφεία, ἀμνήμων, ἀμπυκτήρ, Ἀμφιάρεως, ἀμφιβαίνω, ἀμφίβολος, ἀμφιλέκτως, ἀμφιτειχής, Ἀμφίων, ἀνασχετός [*Prom.*], ἀνατέλλω, ἀναύδητος, ἀνδρεία, ἀνδρηλάτης, ἀνδροκτασιά, ἀνδρόπαις, ἀνδροφόντης, ἄνη, ἄνοια [*Prom.*], ἀντηρέτης (3), ἀντίπαλος [*Prom.*], ἀντιστάτης, ἀντιτάσσω (3), ἀντίτυπος, ἄντλος, ἄξων, ἀπαμβλύνω [*Prom.*], ἀπαρτίζω, ἀπογυμνάζω, ἄποικος, ἀποστέγω, ἀραγμός, ἀργός, Ἀρκάς (2), ἀρματόκτυπος, ἁρπάξανδρος, ἀρτιτρεφής, ἀρτίτροπος, ἀρτίφρων, Ἀστακός, ἀστιβής, ἄστονος, ἀστραπή, ἀστυδρομέομαι, ἀτιμαστήρ, ἀτρύμων, αὐτοδάικτος, αὐτόδηλος, αὐτοκτόνος (2), αὐτοπήμων, αὐτόστονος, αὔω, ἀφανής, Ἀχέρων, ἀψυχία (2), ἄψυχος, βαθύχθων, βακχάω, βαρυδότειρα (2), βλάστημα, βλαχά, βλαψίφρων, Βορραῖος, βουλευτήριος, βρόμος (2), γεγωνός, γένυς, γοργός, γράμμα [*Prom.*] (4), γυμνόω, δαικτήρ, δαιόφρων, δάις, δακρυχέων, δαρόβιος, δατήριος, δατητάς, δηιάλωτος, διαδρομή, διάδρομος, διαλαγχάνω (2), διαλλακτήρ, διαλλάσσω, διαπάλλω, διαπεράω, διαρκέω, διαρροθέω, διατομή, διδυμάνωρ?, δινέω (2), διόδοτος, Διρκαῖος, Δίρκη, διχόφρων, δορίμαργος, δορίπονος (2), δοριτίνακτος, δουλοσύνη, δουλόω, δουρίπληκτος, δοχμόλοφος, δράσιμος, δρέπομαι, δυσευνήτωρ, δυσθέατος [*Prom.*], δυσμόρως, δύσορνις, ἑβδομαγέτας, εἴκασμα, εἰσαμείβω, εἰσθρῴσκω, ἐκδίκως [*Prom.*], ἐκεῖθεν, ἐκεῖθι, ἐκθαμνίζω, ἔκκρουστος, ἐκλαπάζω, ἐκπέρθω [*Prom.*] (2), ἑλικότροχος, ἑλκοποιός, ἐλλείπω [*Prom.*], ἐμβριμάομαι, ἐμποδών [*Prom.*], ἐναίρω, ἐναργῶς, ἐνδατέομαι, ἐνύπνιος, Ἐνυώ, ἐξεύρημα, ἔξηβος, ἔξοδος (3), ἐξοτρύνω, ἐξυπτιάζω, ἔξωθεν (2), ἐπακτός, ἐπαλαλάζω, ἐπεμβαίνω, ἐπεξιακχάζω, ἐπιβούλευσις, ἐπίγονοι, ἐπικηρύσσω, ἐπίλυσις (2), ἐπιμαστίδιος, ἐπίμολος, ἐπιπνέω, ἐπίρροθος, ἐπιρρύομαι, ἐπίσημα, ἐπισπέρχω, ἐπίχαρις, ἐποπτήρ, ἐποτρύνω, ἑπτάπυλος, ἑπτατειχής, ἐρειψίτοιχος, Ἐτεοκλέης (3), Ἐτέοκλος, ἑτερόφωνος, εὐδία, εὔεδρος (2), εὔκηλος, εὐκήλως, εὔκυκλος [*Prom.*], εὐπραξία, εὖρος, εὐτελής, εὐτρεπής, εὐτυκάζομαι, εὐφίλητος, ἐφηβάω, ἐχθρόξενος [*Prom.*] (2), ζεύγλη [*Prom.*], ζέω, ζόη, Ἤλεκτρος, ἡμεροσκόπος, ἡσσάομαι, ἠχήεις?, θαλαμηπόλος, θεμιστός, θεόκλυτος, θεομανής, θεόπτυστος, θεωρίς, θηκτός, θρέμμα, θυμοπληθής, θύραθεν (2), θυστάς, θωρακεῖον, ἴουλος, ἱππικός (4), ἵππιος (2), Ἱππομέδων, ἱππότης, Ἰσμηνός (2), ἰχθυβόλος, Καδμεῖος (6), Καδμογενής, Κάδμος (5), καθυπέρτερος, καινοπηγής, καινοπήμων, κάκη (3), κακόσπλαγχνος, κακουχία, καμψίπους, Καπανεύς (2), καπηλεύω, καταιγίζω, καταλλαγή, κατάρα, κατασθμαίνω, κατασποδέω, κατήγορος, κατοπτήρ, κατόπτης (2), καχλάζω (2), κεραύνιος [*Prom.*], κήδομαι, κηρύκευμα, κινύρομαι, κλαυτός, κλῇθρον, κληρόω, κλῖμαξ, κνημίς, κοιλογάστωρ, κομιστέος, κόμπασμα [*Prom.*] (2), κόναβος, κορκορυγή, κοταίνω, κράνος (2), κρεισσότεκνος, Κρέων, κρίμνημι, κροτησμός, κύβος, κυκλόω (2), κυκλωτός, κυμαίνω, κώδων (2), Λάιος (4), λαΐς, λαοδάμας, Λασθένης, Λατογένεια, λεύκασπις, λευστήρ, λεχαῖος, λιγνύς, λιθάς (2), λίπτομαι (2), λούω?, λόφος (2), λοχαγέτας, μαργάω, μαρμαίρω, μεγαλήγορος, Μεγαρεύς, μεθύστερος, μειξόθροος, μελάγκροκος, μελάναιγις, μελάνδετος, Μελάνιππος, μελεοπαθής, μελεοπόνος, μεταλλακτός, μεταξύ, μνημεῖον, μνήστωρ, μοιράομαι, μοναρχία, μονόμαχος, μυκτηρόκομπος, μωμητός, ναυκληρέω, ναύστολος, νείφω, νέμεσις, νεμέτωρ, νεφέλη, Νήισται, νόμιμος, νυκτηγορέω, νύμφιος, ξηρός, ξυνός, Ὄγκα (3), ὀδύρομαι. οἰακοστρόφος [*Prom.*], Οἰδιπόδης (3), Οἰδίπους (11), οἰκητήρ, Οἰκλείδης, Οἰκλῆς, Οἶνοψ, ὀκριόεις [*Prom.*], ὁμιλητός, Ὁμολωίδες, ὁμόσπλαγχνος, ὁμώνυμος, ὀξύγοος, ὀξυκάρδιος, ὁπλίζω, ὁπλίτης (2), ὄργια, ὀρεσκόος, ὀρκάνη, ὁρμαίνω, ὀροτύπος, ὅτλος, ὅτοβος (3), οὐτιδανός, ὀφέλλω (2), ὄχθη [*Prom.*], πάγχαλκος, πάγχυ, παιδεία, παιδολέτωρ, παιωνίζω, παλαίχθων, παλινστομέω, παμπησία, παναρκής, πανδάκρυτος (2), πανδοκέω, πανομιλεί, πάνοπλος, πανουργία, πανσέληνος, παντευχία, παντοδαπός, πάντρομος, πάντροπος, παράνοια, παραφρονέω, παρβασία, πάρευνος, Παρθενοπαῖος, πάταγος (2), πατροφόνος, πεδιονόμος, πειθαρχία, περίθυμος, περιπίτνω, περιρρήγνυμι, πευθώ, πηδάλιον, πηδάω, πικρόγλωσσος, πικρόκαρπος, πλεκτάνη, ποίφυγμα, πολεμόκραντος, πολύβοτος, Πολυνείκης (3), πολυνεικής, πολύρροθος, πολύφθορος [*Prom.*], Πολυφόντης, πόμπιμος (2), ποντομέδων, ποτάμιος, πρέσβιστος, πρόβλημα

(2), πρόδρομος (2), προϊάπτω, Προιτίδες, Προῖτος, προλέγω [*Prom.*], πρόμαχος (2), προμήτωρ, προπάροιθεν, πρόπρυμνα, προσάμβασις, προσεδαφίζω, προσιζάνω [*Prom.*], προσμηχανάομαι (2), προστατέω, προστέλλομαι, προσφίλεια, προσφιλής, προταρβέω, προῦπτος, πρύμνηθεν, πρυμνόθεν, Πυθικός, πύλωμα (2), πυλωρός, πυργηρέομαι (2), πυργοφύλαξ, πύργωμα (3), πυργῶτις, πυριγενέτης, πύρπνοος [*Prom.*] (2), πυρφορέω, πυρφόρος (2), πύστις, πωλικός, ῥίζωμα, ῥίψοπλος, ῥόθιον [*Prom.*], ῥυσίπολις, ῥύτωρ, σαφήνεια, σείω, σηματουργός, σιδηρονόμος, σιδηρόπληκτος (2), σιδηρόφρων [*Prom.*], σπερχνός, σπουδή (3), στίχες, στόμαργος, στρατόπεδον, συγκαθέλκω, συλλογή, συνάγω (2), συναλλάσσω, συναυλία, συνεισβαίνω, συνίσταμαι (4), συνναίω, συντέλεια, συντυγχάνω, συρίζω [*Prom.*], Σφίγξ, σχέσις, σχῆμα, σχηματίζω, ταγεύω, ταράκτωρ, ταρβόσυνος, ταύρειος, ταυροκτονέω, ταυροσφαγέω, ταφή, ταχύρροθος, τεκνογόνος, τεός [*Prom.*], τευχηστής, Τηθύς [*Prom.*], τιτρώσκω, τρίπαλτος, τρίχαλος, τρίχωμα, τροπαῖον, τροφεῖον, Τυδεύς (4), ὑπέραυχος, Ὑπέρβιος (3), ὑπερδέδοικα, ὑπερφοβέομαι, ὑπέρφρων (2), ὕπτιος, φάντασμα, φείδομαι, φέριστος [*Prom.*], φθονέω [*Prom.*] (2), φιλαίματος, φίλανδρος, φιλογαθής, φιλόθυτος, φιλόπολις, φιλοστόνως, φιμός, φλύω [*Prom.*], φοίτος, φονεύω, φονόρυτος, φρενώλης, φρύαγμα (2), φυλακτέος, φυράω, χαίτωμα, χαλκόδετος, Χάλυβος, χαμάδις, χειροτόνος, χερμάς, χερσαῖος, χνόη (2), χρηματοδαίτας, χρυσοπήληξ, χρυσότευκτος, ψαφαρός, ψευδώνυμος, ὠκύποινος, ὠκύς, ὠλεσίοικος, ὠμοδακής, ὠμόδροπος, ὠμόσιτος.

TH. 861-874
ἀμφιβόλως, Ἀντιγόνη, βαθύκολπος, δυσάδελφος, δυσκέλαδος, ἐπιμέλπω, ἐρατός, Ἰσμήνη, λιγαίνω.

TH. 1005-1078
ἄγοος, ἄθαπτος (2), ἀλλοδαπός, ἀναβάλλω, αὐτόβουλος, διατιμάω, δραστήριος, [ἐμποδών + 1] [*Prom.*], [ἐπακτός + 1], ἐρύκω, [Ἐτεοκλέης + 1], [Καδμεῖος + 5], κατακλύζω, [κοιλογάστωρ + 1], μακρηγορέω, μομφή, μονόκλαυτος, [Οἰδιπόδης + 1], ὀξύμολπος, περισσός [*Prom.*], πετηνός, [Πολυνείκης + 2], προσσέβω, [πρυμνόθεν + 1], συνεπαινέω, συνθάπτω (2), τραχύνω, τυμβοχόος, φθερσιγενής.

In all, 549, of which 33 occur in *Prom.*, = 516 *Eigenwörter*.

S. AJ. 1-1090

ἀγελαῖος, ἀγέλη, ἀγκών, ἁγνίζω, ἀγωνάρχης, ἀγώνιος, ἄδαστος, ἄδηλος, ἄδωρος (2), ἀηδώ, ἀθυμέω [Prom.], Αἰακίδης, ἀίδηλος, αἰκίζω [Prom.] (4), αἱμοβαφής, αἱμύλος [Prom.], αἰνός, αἰπόλιον, αἰπύς, αἵρεσις [Prom.], ἀίσσω [Prom.] (3), ἀιστόω [Prom.], αἰχμαλωτίς, ἄλημα (2), ἀλιάδαι, ἀλίπλαγκτος, ἀλίπληκτος, ἄλκιμος, ἀμενηνός, ἀμπνοή, ἄμυγμα, ἀμφίδρομος, ἀμφίρυτος, ἀμφίστημι, ἀνάλγητος, ἀναπέτομαι, ἀναπνέω, ἀναρίθμητος, ἀναρπάζω, ἀναρρήγνυμι, ἀνατίθημι, ἀνέρομαι, ἀνία (2), ἀνιάω (3), ἀνόητος (2), ἄνους [Prom.], ἄντυξ, ἄοκνος, ἀπαίσσω, ἀπαρνέομαι, ἀπατάω, ἀπαυδάω, ἀπειλή [Prom.], ἀπειρέσιος, ἀπερύκω, ἀπιστέω [Prom.], ἄπλατος [Prom.], ἀποβλάπτω, ἀποδιδράσκω, ἀποκαλέω, ἀπολωβάω, ἄποπτος, ἀπόστροφος, ἄποτος, ἀποψύχω, ἀπρίξ, ἀπωθέω, ἀπωστός, ἀργίπους, ἀριστεία, ἀριστεῖον, ἀριστερός, ἀριστεύω [Prom.], ἀριστόχειρ, ἀρκτέος, ἄρνειος, ἄρρητος (2), ἀρτίως (6), ἄσιτος, ἀσπιστήρ, ἄσπλαγχνος, ἀστεργής, ἀτάλλω, ἀτάρβητος, ἄυπνος [Prom.], αὐτοδαής, αὐτοσφαγής, αὐχενίζω, ἄφοβος [Prom.], ἀφορμάω, ἀφροντίστως, ἀφρόνως, Ἀχίλλειος, Ἀχιλλεύς, ἄψορρον [Prom.], ἀψόφητος, βαρύαλγητος, βαρύψυχος, βάσση, Βοσπόριος, βραδύς (2), βρυχάομαι, γηροβοσκός, γοργῶπις, δειλία (2), δειράς, δεννάζω, δεσμώτης [Prom.], δεσμῶτις, δεύω, δῆλος (2), δημιουργός, δημότης, διαπεραιόω, διαρρήγνυμι, διάστροφος, διαφοιβάζω, δικρατής, διοίγω, διοίχομαι, διοπτεύω, δίπαλτος, διπλάζω, δισσάρχης, διφρευτής, διφρηλατέω, δορίληπτος (2), δουριάλωτος, δρασείω (2), δυσθεράπευτος, δυσκλεία, δυσλόγιστος, δύσμορος (6), δύσοργος, δυσπετής, δυστάλας, δυστράπελος, δυσώνυμος, δωρεά [Prom.], δωρέομαι [Prom.], ἐγκαταζεύγνυμι, ἐγκονέω [Prom.] (2), ἐθελοντής, εἰρεσία, εἰσακούω (2), εἰσβάλλω [Prom.], εἰσέπειτα, εἰσλεύσσω, εἰσπίπτω, ἐκκαλύπτω [Prom.], ἐκνέμω, ἐκπυνθάνομαι, ἐκρήγνυμι [Prom.], Ἕκτωρ (4), ἐκφέρω, ἐκφύω, ἐκχωρέω, ἐλαφηβολία, ἕλιξ [Prom.], ἑλίσσω [Prom.], ἐναλλάσσω (2), ἔναρα, ἐννύχιος, ἐνστάτης, ἐντολή, ἐντρέπομαι, ἐντυγχάνω, Ἐνυάλιος, ἐξαίρω, ἐξαίφνης [Prom.], ἐξαλλάσσω, ἐξανύω (2), ἐξετάζω, ἐξευρίσκω [Prom.], ἐξεφίημι, ἐξίστημι (2), ἐξιχνοσκοπέω, ἐξοιμώζω, ἐξομοίομαι, ἔπαινος, ἐπαίσσω, ἐπάκτιος, ἐπαπειλέω, ἐπεγγελάω (3), ἐπεμπίπτω, ἐπιβουλευτής, ἐπιπλήσσω [Prom.], ἐπισκέπτομαι, ἐπίσκηνος, ἐπίτριπτος, ἐπιχαίρω (2), ἑπτάβοιος, ἔρεβος, Ἐρεχθείδης, Ἐρίβοια, ἐρυστός, ἕσπερος [Prom.] (3), ἔσχατος [Prom.], ἑταιρεία, εὐάνεμος, εὔγνωστος, εὔερος, εὐήμερος, εὐθέως, εὐκάρδιος, εὔκαρπος, εὔκερως (2), εὐνοέω, εὐνομία, εὐνώμας, εὔπειστος, εὔρινος, Εὐρυσάκης (2), εὐσκευέω, ἔφαλος, ἐφήκω, ἐφυβρίζω, ἐχθαρτέος, ἐχθοδοπός, ζαμενής, ζῆλος, ζητέω [*Prom.*] (2), ζητητέος, ζωστήρ, ἥδομαι [*Prom.*] (2), ἡμέριος, ἡνίκα (3), ἠρεμία, θακέω [*Prom.*] (2), θέαμα [*Prom.*], θεατός, Θεστόρειος, θηλύνω, θολερός [*Prom.*], θορυβέω, θόρυβος, ἱδρυτέος, ἱδρώς, Ἰκάριος, ἱπποδέτης, ἱππομανής, ἱππόνωμος, ἰχνεύω, καθυβρίζω, καίτοι [*Prom.*] (5), κακανδρία, κακόθρους, κακοπινής, κακοῦργος, καλλιστεῖον, καρτερέω, κατακτάομαι, καταλλάσσω, καταμελέω (2), καταπεφνέω, κατασπείρω, κατεναρίζω, κατοπτεύω, καχάζω, κεῖθεν (2), κεῖσε, κελαινώπας, κίναδος, κίων [*Prom.*] (2), κληροῦχος, κλισία, κνώδων, Κνώσιος, κοιμίζω (2), κοινόπλους, κολεός, κρημνός, κρήνη [*Prom.*], κριός, κυβερνάω, κυδάζω, Κυλλήνιος, κυνηγετέω [*Prom.*?], κυνηγία, Λαέρτιος, Λάκαινος, Λάρτιος (2), λατρεία [*Prom.*], λεηλατέω, λεία (3), ληθίπονος, λιγυρός, λιθόλευστος, λογίζομαι, λῦμα [*Prom.*], λυμεών, λυπέω (5), λυσσώδης, λώβη (2), λωφάω [*Prom.*], μακραίων, μαλάσσω, μανιάς, μελαίνω, μενοινάω, μεταγιγνώσκω, μήν, μισέω [*Prom.*] (2), μνῆστις (2), μομφή, μῶρος (2), νάπος, ναύλοχος, νεηκονής, νέμος, νεόρραντος (2), νεοσφαγής (2), νεοχάρακτος, νιφοστιβής, νόθος, νοσέω [*Prom.*] (6), νόσημα [*Prom.*], νότος, νύκτωρ (2), ξιφοκτόνος, ξυρέω, ὄγκος, ὁθούνεκα [*Prom.*] (3), οἰοβώτης, οἰχνέω, οἴως, ὀκνέω, Ὀλυμπιάδης, ὁμευνέτις, ὀξύτονος, ὄργανον, ὀρύσσω, ὀρφανιστής, ὀρφανός, ὄρχημα, οὔλιος, ὀφειλέτης, πάγχρυσος, πάθη, παιδεύω, πακτόω, πάνδημος (2), πάνθυτος, παντοῖος, παντουργός, πανύστατον, παπταίνω [*Prom.*], παράκτιος [*Prom.*], παράλιος [*Prom.*], παραλλάξ, πάραλος, παράπληκτος, παραπράσσω, πάραυλος, παρευθύνω, παρήκω, παταγέω, πέλεια [*Prom.*], περιπτυχής (2), περισκελής, περισπερχής, περισσός [*Prom.*], περιφανής, περίφαντος (2), περιφανῶς, περιχαρής, πετραῖος [*Prom.*], πηκτός, πλάσσω [*Prom.*], πλευροκοπέω, πλευρόν, πλήρης [*Prom.*], ποίμνιον, ποίνιμος, πολύκερως, πολύρραφος, πολύτλας, ποντοπόρος, πορευτέος, πόρπαξ, πρίασθαι, πρίω, πρόβλητος, προθυμία [*Prom.*], πρόθυμος, προΐστημι, προσβλέπω [*Prom.*], προσέρπω [*Prom.*], προσκαλέω, πρόσκειμαι, προσλεύσσω (2), προσμολεῖν (2), πρόσοψις, προσπέτομαι [*Prom.*], πυκάζω, πωλοδαμνέω, ῥῆμα, ῥίς, ῥυτήρ, σακεσφόρος, σβέννυμι, σιδηροβρώς, σιδηροκμής, Σισυφίδης, Σκαμάνδριος, σκοτόω, σκύμνος, στερεόφρων, στέφανος, στηρίζω, στιβέω, στοναχή, στρατήγιον, στρατηγίς, συγκαθαρμόζω, συγκάμνω [*Prom.*], συγκαταζεύγνυμι, συγκατακτείνω, συγκομίζω, συμμανθάνω, σύμμεικτος, σύμπας, σύμφημι [*Prom.*], σύναιμος (2), συναλγέω [*Prom.*] (2), συναλλαγή, συναυδάω, σύναυλος, συνδαίζω, σύνδετος (2), συνδέω, σύνεδρος, συνείργω, συνέρχομαι, συνναύτης, σύντροφος (2), σφαγεύς, σφόδρα, σχέτλιος [*Prom.*], ταλαίφρων, τανύπους, Ταυροπόλα, Τέκμησσα (3), Τελαμών (5), Τελαμώνιος, Τελεύτας (2), Τεῦκρος (15), τεχνάομαι, τηλόθεν, τηλωπός, τίσις, τλητός [*Prom.*], τομάω, τομός, τρανής, τρύχω, Τρωιάς (2), τυμβεύω, ὕπαυλος, ὑπεικτέος, ὑπειπεῖν, ὑπερβριθής, ὑποβάλλω, ὑπόβλητος, ὑποδείδω, ὑποζεύγνυμι, ὑποστενάζω [*Prom.*] (2), ὑποτείνω, ὑψικόμπως, φαέθων, φαεννός (2), φατίζω, φευκτός, φθέγμα [*Prom.*], φιλόπονος, φιλοφρόνως, φοινίσσω, φοιτάω, φορβή, φρενοβόρως, φρενόθεν, φρόνιμος, Φρύγιος, φυσάω, φυτεύω, φώνημα, χαλκεύω, χαλκοθώραξ, χαρμονή, χείριος, χειροδάικτος, χειρόπληκτος, χήρα, χιονόκτυπος, χόλος [*Prom.*] (2), χοροποιός, χρήσιμος, χρυσόνωτος, ψάμαθος, ψιθυρός, ὠδίνω, ὠιδή, ὠκύαλος, ὠμόθυμος, ὠμοκρατής, ὠφελήσιμος

= 506, of which 62 or 63 occur in *Prom.*

Appendix J

REPEATED *EIGENWÖRTER*

PROM.

*ἀδαμάντινος (2), ἀδαμαντόδετος (2), ἀεικής (4), ἆθλος (6), αἰκεία (3), *αἰκίζω (4), αἰνικτηρίως (2), ἀίσσω (2), *ἀιστόω (2), *αἰτίαμα (2), ἀσθενής (3), ἀτέραμνος (2), Ἄτλας (2), αὐθάδης (2), αὐθαδία (5), γεγωνῶ (7), γύης (2), δάμαρ? (3), δαρόν (2), δῆθεν (2), διάδοχος (2), *διορίζω (2), δουλεύω (2), δύσπλανος (2), Δωδώνη (2), δωρεά (2), δωρέομαι (2), εἰκῆι (2), εἱλίσσω (3), ἐκδιδάσκω (2), ἐκπίπτω (5), ἐλαφρός (3), (ἐλελεῦ 2), ἐλινύω (2), ἐμπλέκω (2), ἐνζεύγνυμι (2), *ἐξαμαρτάνω (2), ἐξαρτύω (2), ἐξευρίσκω (4), ἐπαναγκάζω (2), ἐπιθωΰσσω (2), ἐρεθίζω (2), *ἐρρωμένως (2), ἔσχατος (3), ἐφήμερος (3), ζητέω (3), *θακέω (2), *θάλπω (2), θέαμα (2), θεόσυτος (3), ἴδιος (2), Ἰνάχειος (2), καίτοι (4), Καύκασος (2), Λέρνα (2), λίαν (2), λιπαρέω (2), λωφάω (3), μαλθακίζω (2), μισέω (2), νοσέω (4), νόσημα (3), οἶμος (2), ὀξύστομος (2), ὀχμάζω (2), παντελῶς (2), παπταίνω (2), πέρα (3), πλανάω (4), πλάνη (7), πορεία (3), προθυμέομαι (3), Προμηθεύς (18), προσέρπω (2), προσλαμβάνω (2), προσπέτομαι (3), προσχρήιζω (2), προὐξεπίσταμαι (2), *ῥητός (2), σκεθρῶς (2), *σκίρτημα (2), σόφισμα (3), σοφιστής (2), συγκάμνω (2), συνασχαλάω (3), σφάκελος (2), ταλαίπωρος (3), ταπεινός (2), τεκμαίρω (2), τηλουρός (2), Τιτάν (2), *ὑπηρέτης (2), ὑποπτήσσω (2), *ὑψήγορος (2), φάραγξ (4), *φιλάνθρωπος (2), φλογωπός (2), Χάλυψ (2), χειμάζομαι (2), *χλιδάω (3), χόλος (4), χρίω (4), χροία (2), Ὠκεανός (3), ὠφέλημα (3).

A. PERS.

Ἀγβάτανα (3), Ἀθῆναι (8), Αἴας (3), Αἰδωνεύς (2), (αἰνῶς 2), (ἄκακος 2), *ἀκόσμως (2), (ἄλαστος 2), *ἀμύσσω (2), *ἀμφιβάλλω (2), *ἀναπτύσσω (2), (ἄναυς 2), ἄνιος? (6), ἀντίδουπος (4), (ἄπριγδα 4), ἄρδω (2), Ἀρίδμαρδος (3), Ἀρκτεύς (2), Ἀρσάμης (2), Ἀρταφρένης (3), Ἀρτεμβάρης (3), Βάκτριος (3), (βάλλην 2), (βάσκω 2), Βοιωτός (2), Δαδάκης (2), Δαρειογενής (2), Δαρεῖος (14), διαίνω (4), (δίομαι 2), *δρασμός (2), δύσθροος (3), Δωρίς (2), *ἔκπλους (2), ἐκπρεπής (2), *ἐκσωίζομαι (2), ἐκφθίνω (2), Ἕλλη (4), ἐμβολή (4), ἐνύπνιον (2), *ἔποχος (2), εὐτυχῶς (2), ἐφέπω (2), *ἔχυρος (2), Θάρυβις (3), (θεομήστωρ 2), θησαυρός (2), Θρήικη (2), Ἰάονες (5), *ἱππιοχάρμης (2), ἰσόθεος (2), (ἰωά 2), καταφθείρω (4), κόρυμβος (2), Κῦρος (2), *κῶκυμα (2), Λίλαιος (2), λόγχη (3), Λυδός (2), Μασίστρης (2), Μεγαβάτης (2), Μῆδος (2), Μύσιος (2), *ναύφαρκτος (2), Ξέρξης (17), ὀᾶ (6), πάμμεικτος (2), *πάνδυρτος (2), πεζός (6), *πελάγιος (2), περίκλυστος (2), *πέριξ (2), Πέρσαι (33), Περσικός (7), Περσίς (10), *πολύχρυσος (4), *πόσος (2), πραΰνω (2), *πρόκακος (2), προσπίτνω (2), πρόσφθογγος (2), *ῥόθος (2), Σαλαμίς (4), Σάρδεις (2), σαφηνής (2), Σοῦσα (4), Σουσίς (2), Σουσισκάνης (2), στῖφος (2), στυφελός (2), τοξοδάμας (3), τοξουλκός (2), τρίσκαλμος (2), ὑπαντιάζω (3), Φαρανδάκης (2), Φαρνοῦχος (2).

A. TH.

Ἄδραστος (2), ἀντηρέτης (3), ἀντιτάσσω (3), Ἀρκάς (2), αὐτοκτόνος (2), ἀψυχία (2), (βαρυδότειρα 2), βρόμος (2), *διαλαγχάνω (2), *δινέω (2), δορίπονος (2), ἔξοδος (3), ἔξωθεν (2), ἐπαλαλάζω (2), (ἐπίλυσις 2), Ἐτεοκλέης (3+1), εὔεδρος (2), θύραθεν (2), ἱππικός (4), *ἵππιος (2), Ἰσμηνός (2), Καδμεῖος (6+5), Κάδμος (5), κάκη (3), Καπανεύς (2), κατόπτης (2), καχλάζω (2), *κράνος (2), κυκλόω (2), *κώδων (2), Λάιος (4), *λιθάς (2), *λίπτομαι (2), *λόφος (2), Ὄγκα (3), Οἰδιπόδης (3+1), Οἰδίπους (11), ὁπλίτης (2), *ὄτοβος (3), *ὀφέλλω (2), πανδάκρυτος (2), πάταγος (2), Πολυνείκης (3+2) πόμπιμος (2), πρόβλημα (2), πρόδρομος (2), *πρόμαχος (2), προσμηχανάομαι (2), πύλωμα (2), πυργηρέομαι (2), πύργωμα (3), *πυρφόρος (2), (σιδηρόπληκτος 2), σπουδή (3), συνάγω (2), συνίσταμαι (4), Τυδεύς (4), Ὑπέρβιος (3), *ὑπέρφρων (2), φρύαγμα (2), χνόη (2),
plus 1005ff *ἄθαπτος (2), ἐπακτός (2), κοιλογάστωρ (2), πρυμνόθεν (2), *συνθάπτω (2).

S. AJ. 1-1090

ἄδωρος (2), αἰκίζω (4), ἀίσσω (3), *ἄλημα (2), *ἀνία (2), ἀνιάω (3), ἀνόητος (2), ἄρρητος (2), ἀρτίως (6), *βραδύς (2), δειλία (2), δῆλος (2), δορίληπτος (2), δρασείω (2), δύσμορος (6), ἐγκονέω (2), εἰσακούω (2), Ἕκτωρ (4), ἐναλλάσσω (2), ἐξανύω (2), ἐξίστημι (2), ἐπεγγελάω (3), ἐπιχαίρω (2), ἕσπερος (3), εὔκερως (2), Εὐρυσάκης (2), ζητέω

(2), ἥδομαι (2), ἡνίκα (3), θακέω (2), καίτοι (5), καταμελέω (2), *κεῖθεν (2), κίων (2), κοιμίζω (2), Λάρτιος (2), λεία (3), λυπέω (5), λώβη (2), μισέω (2), *μνῆστις (2), μῶρος (2), νεόρραντος (2), νεοσφαγής (2), νοσέω (6), νύκτωρ (2), ὁθούνεκα (3), πάνδημος (2), *περιπτυχής (2), περίφαντος (2), προσλεύσσω (2), προσμολεῖν (2), σύναιμος (2), *συναλγέω (2), σύνδετος (2), σύντροφος (2), Τέκμησσα (3), Τελαμών (5), Τελεύτας (2), Τεῦκρος (15), Τρωιάς (2), ὑποστενάζω (2), φαεννός (2), χόλος (2).

Appendix K

REPEATED *EIGENWÖRTER* (FROM PERETTI)

A. SUPP.

ἀγός (2), *αὐτανέψιος (2), ἀφίκτωρ (2), *ἄχορος (2), βούλαρχος (2), βοῦνις (3), διωγμός (2), ἐκδίδωμι (4), ἐξοπλίζω (3), ἐπίπνοια (4), ἐπιχώριος (2), ἑσμός (3), ἐφάπτωρ (3), *ἱκέτις (2), κινητήριος (2), *κοννέω (3), λευκοστεφής (2), *μάρπτις (2), *ὀπώρα (2), πίναξ (2), πόρτις (2), πρόξενος (4), *συγγιγνώσκω (2), σχολάζω (2), ὑψόθεν (2), [δήμιον? (2)].

NOT ὁρίζω, εὐλόγως, κάρβανος, ἀντάω.

A. CHO.

*ἀνοίμωκτος (2), ἀνταποκτείνω (2), ἀπεύχετος (2), *ἀποφθείρω (2), ἀφίστημι (3), γέλως (2), ἔγκοτος (3), *ἐλευθερία (2), ἐξαυδάομαι (2), *ἐπιρροθέω (2), *ἑρκεῖος (3), θρεπτήριος (2), καρανόω (2), κήδειος (3), λυγρός (2), μάομαι (2), μαστός (3), *πιέζω (2), προσφέρω (2), *πυθόχρηστος (2), σκοτεινός (2), συγγίγνομαι (3).

A. EUM.

ἀδικέω (3), ἄμομφος (3), ἀντίκεντρον (2), ἄοινος (2), βουλευτήριον (3), *δέσμιος (3), διαιρέω (3), ἐπικτάομαι (2), *εὐθενέω (3), ἐφέρπω (3), καθιππάζομαι (4), *μητραλοίας (2), μητροκτονέω (3), μητρῷος (4), *μύζω (2), νεβρός (2), ὅρκωμα (2), ποιμαίνω (2), πρεσβῦτις (2), προσέρχομαι (2), προσίκτωρ (2).

NOT ἐπαίτιος.

Appendix L

WORD DISTRIBUTION

One stylistic criterion which has been successful in distinguishing between authors is 'word distribution'. G.U. Yule (*Statistical study* chs. 1, 2, 9) demonstrated that one author may tend to use a wider range of nouns, each used only a few times, than another, who would use each individual noun rather more frequently within his smaller range. If samples of comparable size and character are selected, the 'frequency distribution' of nouns for any author remains fairly constant, and can safely be compared with that for another. (Yule uses this criterion to argue for Thomas a Kempis' authorship of *De Imitatione Christi*, against that of Jean Charlier de Gerson. He also applies it to Bunyan and Macaulay. For further discussion of his method see Williams 32f, 96-104.)

As with sentence-length distribution (pp. 214ff), I had no very high expectations that this method would prove helpful for such a stylized genre as Greek tragedy, but it nevertheless seemed foolish not to find out. I collected on cards all the occurrences of nouns in A. *Th.*, *Ag.*, *Eum.*, S. *Aj.*, *Ant.*, and *Prom.*, and then sorted out (a) the 'frequency distribution', i.e. how many nouns occurred once, how many twice, etc., in each play; (b) the total number of occurrences of nouns, which I then divided by the number of separate nouns, to obtain the 'mean frequency', i.e. the average number of times that any particular noun is used in each play. I also worked out the median, third quartile, and ninth decile (see p. 214 n. 89). In Table 13 I give the frequency distribution of nouns, in Table 14 the total number of occurrences and mean frequency, etc. (In each Table I give also the figures for S. *Aj.* 1-1050, a sample comparable in size to *Prom.*, A. *Th.* and *Eum.*, but rather smaller than A. *Ag.*, S. *Aj.* and *Ant.*)

From Table 13 we observe that *Prom.* has a slightly larger total of separate nouns than any of the other plays, in proportion to their size: *Prom.* 507 in 1,093 lines, *Th.* 491 in 1,077, *Ag.* 750 in 1,673, *Eum.* 472 in 1,047, *Aj.* 484 in 1,419, *Ant.* 510 in 1,352;

TABLE 13. *Noun distribution*

	1	*2*	*3*	*4*	*5*	*6*	*7*	*8*	*9*	*10*	*11*	*12*	*13*	*14*	*15*	*Over 15*	*Total nouns*
Prom	323	70	38	22	13	10	10	4	1	4	3	1	3	1	0	4	507
A. *Th.*	306	77	39	22	10	8	6	3	1	5	2	1	3	2	2	4	491
Ag.	418	146	70	34	19	13	6	7	4	4	4	4	3	2	2	14	750
Eum.	275	97	30	10	13	10	8	6	2	4	1	0	2	2	1	11	472
S. *Aj.*	284	82	41	22	14	11	4	6	3	2	2	0	5	0	0	8	484
Ant.	291	105	39	14	15	9	5	3	5	5	2	2	1	3	2	9	510
[*Aj.* -1050]	262	72	26	14	10	9	8	2	1	1	2	2	0	1	1	5	416

TABLE 14. *Frequency of nouns*

	Total occurrences	*Mean frequency*	*Median*	*Third quartile*	*Ninth decile*
Prom.	1137	2.24	1.3	2.3	4.7
A. *Th.*	1209	2.46	1.3	2.3	4.4
Ag.	1955	2.61	1.4	2.5	4.8
Eum.	1218	2.58	1.3	2.3	5.5
S. *Aj.*	1276	2.64	1.4	2.5	5.0
Ant.	1327	2.60	1.4	2.4	5.2
[*Aj.* -1050]	960	2.31	1.3	2.2	4.5

(*Aj*. 1-1050 has 416). Yet *Prom*. also has rather a small number of nouns used often: the totals for nouns used six times or more are: *Prom*. 41, *Th*. 37, *Ag*. 63, *Eum*. 47, *Aj*. 41, *Ant*. 46, *Aj*. 1-1050 32. This suggests that *Prom*.'s vocabulary is in this respect quite wide in range.

From Table 14 we note that *Prom*.'s figure for occurrences is rather lower than Aeschylus': *Prom*. 1,137, *Th*. 1,209, *Ag*. 1,955, *Eum*. 1,218; i.e. nouns occur slightly less often in *Prom*. than appears normal for Aesch. For Soph., the figures are lower still: *Aj*. 1,276, *Ant*. 1,327 (both longer plays than *Prom*.), *Aj*. 1-1050 960.

We are therefore not surprised to find that *Prom*.'s 'mean frequency' is slightly lower than that of the other plays. In *Prom*., each noun is used, on average, 2.24 times; Aeschylus ranges from 2.46 to 2.61, Sophocles also is close to 2.6, though in the smaller sample of *Aj*. 1-1050 the figure (2.31) is closer to *Prom*. (It may be that the figure for A. *Ag*. is likewise slightly distorted by the play's greater length.)

On the whole, however, more striking than *Prom*.'s minor divergencies from Aeschylus' norm are the general similarities of all the plays. There is really no significant statistical variation from author to author. This is particularly clear from the figures for median, third quartile, and ninth decile. It appears, then, that both Aesch. and Soph. have similar tendencies: in a sample of about 1,000 lines, they both use between 250 and 350 nouns once, and another 150-200 more than once (30-50 of them six times or more). It is possible that further study of the remaining two plays of Aesch., and of more plays of Soph. and Eur., might reveal distinctive differences; but it seems to me more probable that it would not, and I have chosen not to spend more time on this laborious and tiresome work.

In case other students may find the details useful, I append (a) lists of those nouns which occur more than five times in each play, and (b) a list of the number of nouns in each play which do not occur in each of the other plays.

(a) *Nouns occurring six times or more:*

Prom. (6 times): ἆθλος, γένος, ἔργον, μορφή, ποίνη, πόρος, πόταμος, φίλος, χείρ, χρόνος

(7) αἰθήρ, ἀνάγκη, γνώμη, ἥλιος, κέαρ, μῦθος, ὄμμα, πλάνη, τρόπος, τυραννίς
(8) βία, μόχθος, πέτρα, τέχνη
(9) πῦρ
(10) γάμος, παῖς, πημονή, τέρμα
(11) νόσος, πῆμα, χθών, (12) γῆ, (13) βροτός, δεσμός, φρήν, (14) τύχη, (16) πατήρ, (21) πόνος, (28) λόγος, (33) θεός

A.*Th*. (6) αἷμα, ἀλκή, ἀρά, λιτή, μόρος, σάκος, φόνος, φῶς
(7) ἄναξ, μάχη, μήτηρ, ὄμμα, πτόλις, σῆμα
(8) γυνή, πολίτης, φίλος
(9) μάντις
(10) βία, γῆ, φόβος, φρήν, χθών
(11) πατήρ, στρατός, (12) δαίμων, (13) δόμος, δόρυ, λόγος, (14) γένος, πύργος, (15) ἀσπίς, χείρ, (30) πύλη, (48) ἀνήρ, (56) θεός, πόλις

A.*Ag*. (6) ἄχος, γένος, δόρυ, ἦμαρ, κράτος, λάμπας, μάχη, μέρος, ὄνειρον, πέδον, πλοῦτος, τάχος, φῶς
(7) θάνατος, καρδία, κύων, πάθος, φόβος, φόνος
(8) βωμός, ἥλιος, μέλαθρον, μοῖρα, ὕπνος, φάτις, φῶς
(9) βασιλεύς, γλῶσσα, ναῦς, φάος
(10) ἄναξ, ἔργον, πῆμα, χθών
(11) ἄτη, ἐλπίς, πόνος, φίλος, (12) αἷμα, βίος, μόρος, παῖς, (13) γῆ, δαίμων, ὄμμα, (14) δῶμα, πῦρ, (15) οἶκος, στρατός, (16) βροτός, τύχη, (17) πατήρ, χάρις, (18) χρόνος, (19) λόγος, (21) χείρ, (25) φρήν, (26) δίκη, (32) γυνή, πόλις, (38) δόμος, (40) ἀνήρ, (46) θεός

Eum. (6) γένος, ἕδρα, λαός, λάχος, μόρος, νόμος, πούς, στρατός, τόπος, φίλος
(7) ἄνθρωπος, βρέτας, θεά, θρόνος, καρδία, οἶκος, ὅρκος, τέλος
(8) ἀστός, γυνή, κότος, ξένος, πολίτης, ψῆφος
(9) δῶμα, πόνος
(10) παῖς, πρᾶγμα, τιμή, φόνος
(11) δαίμων, (13) φρήν, χείρ, (14) λόγος, χώρα, (15) χρόνος, (16) δόμος, (19) γῆ, μήτηρ, πατήρ, (20) αἷμα, πόλις, (22) βροτός, (23) χθών, (28) ἀνήρ, (33) δίκη, θεός

A.*Aj*. (6) γλῶσσα, δόμος, ναῦς, νόμος, νόσος, νύξ, οἶκος, πάθος, φάτις, φόνος, χάρις
(7) ἡμέρα, ὅπλον, ποίμνη, τάχος

(8) γνώμη, δόρυ, τέκνον, τύχη, φρήν, φῶς

(9) ἄναξ, ἄτη, νεκρός

(10) μήτηρ, ὄμμα

(11) βροτός, πόνος, (13) ἄνθρωπος, γυνή, ἔπος, ἔργον, χρόνος, (18) στρατός, (20) φίλος, (22) πατήρ, (24) παῖς, (25) λόγος, (32) χείρ, (46) θεός, (84) ἀνήρ

Ant. (6) βίος, γένος, γλῶσσα, νόσος, οἰωνός, ὀργή, πρᾶγμα, τύχη, φρόνημα

(7) ἀδελφός, κάρα, μάντις, ὁδός, πῦρ

(8) ἐλπίς, χθών, ψυχή

(9) γνώμη, ἔπος, κέρδος, νέκυς, χρόνος

(10) ἄτη, βροτός, γῆ, μήτηρ, τέκνον

(11) ἄναξ, μόρος, (12) δίκη, νεκρός, (13) λόγος, (14) δόμος, ἔργον, χείρ, (15) τάφος, φίλος, (16) φρήν, (17) γυνή, (18) νόμος, (21) ἄνθρωπος, (23) πατήρ, (29) παῖς, (32) πόλις, (41) θεός, (42) ἀνήρ

(b) *Number of nouns not found in each of the other plays:*

Prom. (507 nouns): 344 not in *Th.*, 256 not in *Ag.*, 325 not in *Eum.*, 302 not in *Aj.*, (324 not in *Aj.* 1-1050), 297 not in *Ant.*

A. *Th.* (491 nouns): 328 not in *Prom.*, 241 not in *Ag.*, 292 not in *Eum.*, 294 not in *Aj.*, (313 not in *Aj.* 1-1050), 277 not in *Ant.*

Ag. (750 nouns): 506 not in *Prom.*, 508 not in *Th.*, 485 not in *Eum.*, 493 not in *Aj.*, (521 not in *Aj.* 1-1050), 478 not in *Ant.*

Eum. (472 nouns): 292 not in *Prom.*, 275 not in *Th.*, 201 not in *Ag.*, 281 not in *Aj.*, (297 not in *Aj.* 1-1050), 276 not in *Ant.*

S. *Aj.* (484 nouns): 276 not in *Prom.*, 287 not in *Th.*, 220 not in *Ag.*, 293 not in *Eum.*, 265 not in *Ant.*

Ant. (510 nouns): 297 not in *Prom.*, 295 not in *Th.*, 230 not in *Ag.*, 337 not in *Eum.*, 290 not in *Aj.*

Aj. 1-1050 (416 nouns): 231 not in *Prom.*, 238 not in *Th.*, 180 not in *Ag.*, 241 not in *Eum.*, 220 not in *Ant.*

There is no apparent difference here between Sophoclean and Aeschylean plays, no indication, for example, that plays from one author will tend to share a common 'vocabulary' of nouns (cf. p. 171).

NOTES

Chapter 1. The problem

1 Mediceus Laurentianus 32.9 (known as M for those plays of Aeschylus, L for those of Sophocles which it contains), of *c.* A.D. 1000. For the state of the text of Aesch. since the tenth century, see esp. Wilamowitz *ed.* v-xxxv, A. Turyn *The ms. tradition of the tragedies of Aesch.* (New York 1943), Fraenkel *A. Ag.* 1-33, Dawe *Coll. and invest.*, and Page's OCT v-xii.

2 *Proleg. zu Aesch.* 6; but cf. already Rossbach-Westphal *Metrik der gr. Dramatiker und Lyriker* 3 (Leipzig 1856) (= *Theorie der mus. Künste der Hellenen* 3.2 (1889) viii, xii). For the history of the problem see further Schmid 1-5, Grossmann 291-5, Zawadzka *Altertum* (1966) 210-23.

3 Since T. Bergk *Philol.* 12 (1857) 579 and *Gr. Literaturgeschichte* 3 (Berlin 1884) 302f; for the whole question, see esp. Wilamowitz *A. Int.* 88-95, Schmid *GGL* 2.215 n.5, and Lloyd-Jones *CQ* 9 (1959) 80ff, with further references.

4 E.g. B. Steusloff *Zeus und die Gottheit des Aesch.* (Progr. Lissa 1867), J. Oberdick *Act. ann. lit. Jena* (1876) n.380, H. Kramer *PV esse fabulam correctam* (diss. Freiburg 1878), A. Röhlecke *Sept. adv. Theb. et PV esse fabulas post Aesch. correctas* (diss. Berlin 1882), T. Heidler *De comp. metrica Prom. fab. Aesch.* (diss. Breslau 1884), E. Bethe *Proleg. Gesch. Theaters* (Leipzig 1896) ch. IX, Wackernagel *Verhandl. versamm. deutsch. Philol.* (1901) 65 and *Stud. zur Gesch. der gr. Perfekts* (Göttingen 1904).

5 So Wackernagel *Verhandl. versamm. deutsch. Philol.* (1901) 65.

6 In the relative obscurity of the *Zeitschrift für das Gymnasialwesen* 65 (1911), in B. Laudien's *Bericht über den zweiten schlesischen wissenschaftlichen Ferienkursus* 164-74.

7 Ever since Welcker's pioneering work *Die aesch. Trilogie Prom.* (Darmstadt 1824).

8 See pp. 10f.

9 Wilamowitz *A. Int.* 114-62, Körte *NJA* (1920) 201-13; see too J. zum Felde *De Aeschyli Prom. quaestiones* (diss. Göttingen 1914).

10 Focke *Hermes* (1930) 259-304.

11 W. von Christ's *Geschichte der gr. Literatur*, revised by W. Schmid (after O. Stählin) (sixth ed., Munich 1912) 1.296.

12 *Untersuchungen zum Gefesselten Prom.* (= *Tüb. Beitr.* 9, Tübingen 1929).

13 See esp. Yorke *CQ* (1936) 116-19, 153f, Robertson *PCPS* (1938) 9f, Stanford *Proc. Irish Acad.* (1938) 229ff, Fitton Brown *JHS* (1959) 52-60, Cataudella *Dioniso* (1963) 5ff, Herington *passim*.

14 In particular, those of Ahrens, Dale, Descroix, Earp, Harrison, Hiltbrunner, Jens, Friis Johansen, Nestle, van Otterlo, Rode, Schein, Taplin, Yorke.

15 Weight of numbers is not a very reliable index, but recent scholars who refuse to sweep the problem under the rug include Lesky *Hist. Gr. Lit.* 254f, Else *Origin and early form of Gr. tragedy* ch. IV n.14, Garvie *A. Supp.* (cf. 'subject index' p. 277 s.v. *Prometheus*), and Page *Aesch. trag.* (OCT) p. 288.

16 Campbell *Soph. and Pol. of Plato* (Oxford 1867) intro., and *Plato's Rep.* (ed. B. Jowett and Campbell, Oxford 1894) 2.46-66, 165-340; W. Lutoslawski *Origin and growth of Plato's logic* (London 1897) and 'Principes de stylométrie' *REG* (1898) 61-81; cf. too H. von Arnim *Zeitschr. f. d. österr. Gymn.* 51 (1900) 481-92 and *Sprachliche Forschungen zur Chron. der platon. Dialoge* (Vienna 1913), W. Dittenberger *Hermes* 16 (1881) 321-45; further literature in Thesleff *Studies in the styles of Plato* 174-88.

17 Thesleff 172; see too H. Cherniss *AJP* 78 (1957) 225-66, H.-J. Horn *Hippias Major* (diss. Köln 1964), and, on the *Seventh Letter*, N. Gulley Fond. Hardt *Entretiens* 18 (1972) 105-43, E. G. Caskey *CP* 69 (1974), with further references.

18 For Lysias, see most recently Dover *Lysias*, T.N. Winter *CJ* 69 (1973) 34-40; for Demosthenes, see Lesky *Hist. Gr. Lit.* 597-612, with refs.; also, for Demosthenes, Isokrates, Aristotle, and other Greek prose authors, cf. Wake *JRStat.Soc.* A120 (1957) 332-46, Morton *JRStat.Soc.* A128 (1965) 169-224.

19 Most scholars clearly regard the play as spurious, but Ritchie's arguments (*Authenticity of the Rhesus of Eur.*), that the play may be an early Euripidean work, are not wholly overturned by Ed. Fraenkel *Gnom.* 37 (1965) 228-41; see Ritchie 362-5 for refs. to earlier literature.

20 The pioneers were G.U. Yule and (for Greek authors) W.C. Wake; cf. too C.B. Williams, A.Q. Morton, for good introductions to some of the methods that have been developed. The bimonthly *Calculi* (published by Dartmouth College, Hanover, NH, U.S.A., at no charge) gives up-to-date information on statistical and computer studies in the Classics. For sensible remarks on the limitations of such studies, see Dover *Lysias* 98-114, Thesleff 8ff.

21 See Appendix L, and ch. 9, pp. 214ff.

22 If it be objected that this means that I have succumbed to the

'biographical fallacy', I can only reply that almost all conjectural reconstructions of the trilogy do in fact start from the *Oresteia* and the other plays of Aesch., and many go further, in incorporating particular Athenian, Aeschylean, or even Sicilian features which might have been appropriate. See also pp. 13ff and 245ff.

23 A few tentative suggestions are made in my final chapter, pp. 248ff.

Chapter 2. External evidence

1 Else *Ar. Poet.* 526ff is sure that our *Prom.* is meant; but even if he is right, Aristotle's examples are not confined to Aesch., here or elsewhere (cf. 1456a1ff).

2 *Frogs* 1026ff (*Pers.*), 1021 (*Th.*), 1276 (*Ag.*), 1126, 1172f (*Cho.*). At least fifteen other plays are confirmed as being Aeschylean by Aristophanes; cf. Wartelle *Hist. du texte d'Esch.* 92f.

3 See Wartelle 95-9 for Plato and Aristotle; also above, pp.230 ff.

4 The Library of the Mouseion was said to contain about half a million books; cf. Schmidt *Die Pinakes des Kallim.* 37, Fraser *Ptol. Alex.* 328f. Over eighty titles of Aeschylean plays are attested in antiquity.

5 See in particular Snell *TrGF* 15 T 1-3 (the *Medea* plays of Eur. and Neophron), 4 T 2 (Aristias and Pratinas), 12 T 1 (Euphorion and Aeschylus), 22 T 1 (Iophon and Sophocles), cf. Σ Ar. *Frogs* 67. See too pp. 236ff.

6 See pp. 234ff.

7 See e.g. Wilamowitz *Einleitung* 121ff, Turner *Athenian books* 16-23; both tend, if anything, to exaggerate the extent of literacy and the circulation of texts in the fifth and early fourth centuries.

8 See further ch. 10 *passim*.

9 Unless, with e.g. Kolisch, Gercke, we believe that *Prom.* 365-74 was interpolated later, after the eruption of 425, or even of 396.

10 Von Mess *Rh.Mus.* (1901) 171.

11 See Solmsen 128ff for Hesiodic influence on *Prom.* - perhaps slightly exaggerated: there were other traditions too; cf. also Grossmann 12-24.

12 For a fuller discussion and different explanation see Focke *Hermes* (1930) 287-93.

13 Most likely perhaps is *Prom.* 127 / S. *Aj.* 228; also n.b. *Prom.* 444 / S. *Ant.* 492 (but cf. S. fr. 104, A. *Ag.* 542). Other possibly significant echoes: *Prom.* 383 / *Ant.* 780; *Prom.* 400f / *Ant.* 527ff; *Prom.* 939 / *Ant.* 768; *Prom.* 92 / *Ant.* 942; *Prom.* 673 / *Aj.* 447 (cf. W. Aly *Rh. Mus.* (1913) 539 n.1 for further echoes *Prom.* / *Aj.*; also Groeneboom on *Prom.* 644); *Prom.* 765f / *OT* 993; *Prom.* 804f / *Tr.* 1095f; *Prom.* 353 / *Ph.* 92; *Prom.* 10, 357 / fr. 320; *Prom.* 589f / *El.* 5 (but cf. A. *Supp.* 17, 573); also *Prom.* 789 / S. fr. 540 from *Triptolemos* of 468 B.C. (cf. Mette *Fr. Trag. Aesch.* 256f).

14 Least improbable are perhaps: *Prom.* 39 / *And.* 985, *Prom.* 505 / fr. 362.5 (but cf. S. *El.* 673, E. *Hek.* 1180). See Schmid 18, Niedzballa 60f; and further O. Krausse *De Eur. Aeschyli instauratore* (diss. Jena 1905).

15 Mullens *CR* (1939) 165f, cf. Schmid *GGL* 282 n.1 (*Hks*); Haines *CR* (1915) 8-10 (*Ant.*).

16 For the attribution of these plays see pp. 240f. The possible echoes are: *Prom.* 126, 428f / Kritias fr. 18.4f DK; *Prom.* 193 / fr. 16.5 DK; *Prom.* 298 / fr. 16.1 DK; *Prom.* 6 / fr. 20 DK; *Prom.* 208 / fr. 16.10 DK; *Prom.* 24 / fr. 19.4 DK; *Prom.* 944 / fr. 19.1 DK (all from *Peirithous*); *Prom.* 923, 1062 / fr. 25.32 DK (*Sisyphos*); (cf. too *Prom.* 385 / fr. 28 DK; *Prom.* 535 / fr. 6.12 DK; *Prom.* 460 / fr. 2.10 DK; *Prom.* 366 / fr. 1.9ff?).

17 Nor do *Prom.* 459 / fr. *adesp.* 470 (cf. E. *Hik.* 201f; *Hymn. Hom.* 20.2f), and *Prom.* 263ff / fr. *adesp.* 342 (cf. Σ Pind. *O.* 6.105 / *Prom.* 1032).

18 E.g. *Prom.* 846ff / A. *Supp.* 42ff, 317; *Prom.* 857 / *Supp.* 223f (but also Hom. *Il.* 22.139f, E. *And.* 1140f, etc.); for parallels between *Prom.* and A. *Th.*, see Groeneboom n.218 on *Prom.* 504, a list comparable to that for *Prom.* / S. *Ant.* or *Prom.* / E. *Hipp.*

19 For Aristophanes' parody of Aesch. see P. Henning *Aristophanis de Aeschyli poesi iudicia* (diss. Leipzig 1878), C.B. Gulick *HSCP* 10 (1899), H.T. Becker *Aisch. in der gr. Komödie* (diss. Darmstadt 1915), A. de Propris *Eschilo visto da Aristofane*, in *Esch. nella critica dei Greci* (Turin 1941); also Schmid 5f, Wartelle 92f.

20 N.b. too the use of σκῆπτρον (*Birds* 1535, 1600; cf. *Prom.* 171, 761). For more detailed argument for extensive use of *Prom.* by Aristophanes in *Birds* and *Ploutos* see J.R. Bacon *CR* (1928) 117-19, J.A. Davison *TAPA* (1949) 66 n.2, Herington *Phoenix* (1963) 236-43. I find many of these supposed echoes very faint, and Herington's suggestion of thematic allusions rather fanciful: I do not think that an audience would make very much of them.

21 The possible parody of Λυόμενος in Kratinos' *Ploutoi* is too uncertain, and too uninformative, to be more than tantalizing: we do not even know the play's date. See Page *GLP* 38, Luppe *WZHalle* (1967) 57-91 for fuller discussion.

22 E.g. resolutions in the iambic trimeter, enjambement, details of structure, syntax and grammar, sophistic influence, etc.; these will all be discussed in the following chapters; see too Herington *passim*.

23 Cf. Engelmann *Jahrb. Deutsch. Arch. Inst.* (1903) 46f, Webster *Monuments* 144f, Bock *Gymn.* (1958) 432f with further literature; also Beazley *ARV* 1122, 1689.

24 Pearson *Frag. Soph.* 1.197-9; the date of the play is not known: it may have been satyric. See now D.F. Sutton *HSCP* 78 (1974) 134f, and R. Carden *Pap. frag. of Soph.* (Berlin 1974) 52-93.

25 Cf. Eckhart *RE* 702-30, with further literature, Séchan *Etudes* 256ff, Terzaghi *Prometeo* 145ff.

26 See A. Furtwängler *Die antiken Gemmen* (Berlin 1900) Tables 37, 40, 41, 45, 46, Terzaghi 151ff, Bapp *Roscher Myth. Lex.* 3093-6.

27 Cf. Athen. 15.674d, [Apollod.] 2.119, Hyginus *Poet. astr.* 2.15; further Kerenyi 121ff.

28 See Eckhart *RE* 719ff.

29 This is not the place to explore all the intricacies of this famous problem. I try here simply to summarize what we know, rather than what we more or less confidently infer, since it seems to me that many of our inferences will depend on our decision as to *Prom.*'s authenticity. See pp. 6f and pp. 245ff.

30 Cf. Σ Pindar *I.* 3.24 ἐν τῆι ἑξῆς ὠιδῆι.

31 A. fr. 196, fr. 199 (cf. Dion. Hal *AR* 1.41, Hyginus *Poet. astr.* 2.6), fr. 200, fr. 201.

32 E.g. [Apollod.] 2.5.11.10, Hyginus *Fab.* 54, Servius on Virgil *Ec.* 6.42.

33 See Mette *Frag. Trag. Aesch.* 256f.

34 Cf. Herington 101f, and further *Phoenix* (1963) 180-97, *TAPA* (1961) 239ff, for more suggested echoes and parallels, as well as common peculiarities of technical detail.

35 Cf. Σ *Prom.* 167, Strabo 15.1.8, 11.5.5, etc., and West on Hesiod *Th.* 522ff.

36 See Wilamowitz *A. Int.* 156f, Bock *Gymn.* (1958) 421 n.119, Groeneboom on *Prom.* 707, etc.

37 Collected by K. Frey (cited by Gercke); Herington *TAPA* (1961) 240f.

38 The chronological problem, how *Prom.*'s thirteen generations (774) can be reconciled with the 30,000 years of Πυρφόρος (Σ *Prom.* 94), need not worry us. The inconsistency would be unremarkable in drama if '30,000 years' was merely a statement

of intention; cf. *Prom*. 94.

39 That he *is* a tyrant, with all the vices traditionally associated with that name in Greek political theory, is beyond dispute; cf. Thomson *ed*. 6ff and *CR* (1929) 3-5, Podlecki 103ff.

40 Other traditions told of Prometheus remaining in perpetual torment, e.g. Hesiod *Th*. 615f, Ap. Rhod. 2.1246ff, 3.851ff, Horace *Od*. 2.13.37, *Epod*. 17.67; see West *Hesiod Th*. p.314 for further references.

41 Σ Ar. *Frogs* 131, Harpokr. s.v. λαμπάς; for the altar cf. Pausanias 1.30.2; further Kraus *RE* 692ff, Kerenyi 57ff.

42 Athen. 15.674d (= Aesch. fr. 202), Hyginus *Poet. astr*. 2.15, Pliny *NH* 33.8, 37.2, Catullus 64.295, Servius on Virgil *Ec*. 6.42; also Kerenyi 121ff.

43 And *Prom*. 1021ff seems to be an attempt to reconcile two well-known versions, (a) Herakles and the eagle, (b) Cheiron and Prometheus' release from Tartaros, more or less in passing, as is often done in single tragedies; cf. [Apollod.] 2.5.11.10, contradicted by Servius on V. *Ec*. 6.42, Hyginus *Fab*. 54.

44 See the further discussion pp. 249ff.

45 We know of no dilogies, unless *hypoth*. A. *Th*. is correct, β̄ 'Αριστίας Περσεῖ Ταντάλωι Παλαισταῖς σατύροις.

46 Pollux 9.156, 10.64. Further citations from a Prometheus-play which is clearly satyric are fr. 206 (Galen) and fr. 207 (Plutarch); cf. too Pap. Oxy. 2245.2 (= fr. 278 L-J). The other two plays produced with *Pers*. in 472 B.C. are likewise missing from the Medicean Catalogue, *Glaukos Potnieus* and *Phineus*; and another eight plays otherwise attested as Aeschylean are not found there, cf. Wartelle 25-34.

47 Αἰτναῖαι has been suggested (Lloyd-Jones *Justice of Zeus* 98 ff), but this is little more than a guess; we must then accept a performance around 470 B.C. in Sicily, with a rather abrupt movement away from Prometheus in the third play.

48 Pohlenz *GT* 33ff establishes once and for all that the epithet does not help us: 'fire-bringer' or 'torch-carrier' are equally possible.

49 Athen. 15.674d.

50 See Servius on Virgil *Ec*. 6.42, Philodemos *De piet*. p.41 Gomperz (= Aesch. fr. 321a M). For interesting but highly speculative suggestions about the trilogy in general and Πυρφόρος in particular as the third play, see Thomson *Aesch. and Athens* 297-324, esp. 315f, Solmsen 146ff, and Herington *Phoenix* (1963) 236ff. There is a tendency among recent scholars to argue, from the *Oresteia*, that Aesch. developed a consistent, 'progressive' world-view, and that his *Prometheia*

shows the evolution of a new and better order out of the old. The argumentation is often circular (the Prometheus- and Danaid-trilogies are used to support the 'progressive' interpretation of Aesch.'s trilogic conception, which is in turn used to 'reconstruct' the two trilogies), and seems to be contradicted by A. *Th.*, the last play of his Theban trilogy, written within ten years of the *Oresteia* and five of the Danaid-trilogy.

51 The tense of δεδέσθαι is immaterial, cf. Pohlenz *GT* 77.

52 See Mette *Verlor. Aisch.*, *passim*, for speculation about further Aeschylean trilogies, much of it unconvincing.

53 Cf. C. Robert *Oidipus* (Berlin 1915) 396ff. G.L. Koniaris *HSCP* 77 (1973) 85-124 denies that Eur.'s Trojan plays are really 'connected'; his arguments do not seem to me to be very strong.

54 *Hypoth.* A. *Th.*

55 Σ Ar. *Birds* 281.

56 Σ Plato *Apol.* 18b, with reference to Aristotle's *Didaskaliai*; cf. W.C. Greene *Scholia Platonica* (Haverford 1938) 420.

57 The evidence, such as it is, for tetralogies/trilogies in the fifth century is conveniently summarized by Pickard-Cambridge *DTC* 60-3, *DFA* 80f.

58 E.g. Herington *Phoenix* (1963) 236ff, Reinhardt *Hermes* (1957) 12-17 and *Eranos-Jahrb.* (1956) 241-83, with ref. to Pap. Heidelberg 185.

59 Cf. Aesch. fr. 369? and Reinhardt *Eranos-Jahrb.* (1956) 261ff, Pearson *Frag. Soph.* 2.135-7. The statement of Σ Pindar *P.* 5.35, that Soph. wrote a *Prometheus*, is generally regarded simply as a misattribution of *Prom.* 86.

60 We might add Ibykos(?), cf. *PMG* 342 = Aelian *NA* 6.51; Akousilaos(?), cf. Σ Hom. *Od.* 10.2; Sappho(?), cf. Servius on Virgil *Ec.* 6.42

61 For good discussions of *Prom.*'s innovations and possible sources see Wilamowitz *A. Int.* 130-45, Reinhardt *Aischylos* 29-53, Solmsen 125-45, Pohlenz *GT* 67-76 (and *Erl.* 30ff), Kraus *RE* 694-701, Grossmann 12-31, 85-102.

62 This seems to me a major argument against the theory that *Prom.* was composed for performance in Sicily. For Prometheus' cult see L.R. Farnell *Cults of the Greek states* (Oxford 1909) 5.378-83, L. Deubner *Attische Feste* (Hildesheim 1959) 211, Bapp *Roscher* 3036.41ff, A. Mommsen *Feste der Stadt Athens* (Leipzig 1898) 324ff.

Chapter 3. The lyric metres

1 The subject of exclamations will be dealt with more fully on 574ff.

2 Wilamowitz *A. Int.* 159, after Headlam *CR* (1898) 189, who also read πέδον.

3 In fact E. *Or.* 177, cited by Wilamowitz as a parallel, has ⏑⏑⏑–⏑⏑⏑; but Conomis *Hermes* (1964) 23 gives eight examples of –⏑⏑–⏑⏑⏑, two certain in Soph., two certain, four more or less probable in Eur.

4 One resolution only, in 116.

5 See Rose *ad loc.*; but his repetition of πόνων ἐμῶν is very feeble.

6 Wilamowitz' parallels of A. *Ag.* 1213ff, 1256, 1315 are considered below.

7 *Hermes Einzelschr.* 5 (1937) 14 fr. 40.

8 Conomis *Hermes* (1964) 23.

9 See Conomis p.25 for occurrences.

10 Stinton *CR* (1965) 142ff suggests that *Prom.* 117 –⏑⏑–⏑⏑ ⏑⏑⏑⏑– is 2 dac. ia., and cites as parallels E. *Hipp.* 1108 = 1116; *And.* 482 = 490; *Ion* 1077 = 1093; *El.* 459 = 471, 711 = 724; *Tro.* 1070 = 1079; S. *Tr.* 825 = 835, as well as Ar. *Lys.* 262f = 277f. I do not think that the Aristophanic display of *Responsionsfreiheit* is a valid criterion for tragedy. It also seems suspicious that only E. *Hipp.* 1108 is confirmed by its antistrophe: all the other examples demand more or less startling freedom of responsion (except E. *Ion* 1076ff, where Stinton scans 1093 ἀθέμιτας). E. *Hipp.* 1108 = 1116 (a) is in dactylic context (and all Stinton's possible examples have dactylic/choriambic/aeolic elements nearby), (b) has diaeresis –⏑⏑–⏑⏑{⏑–⏑–, (c) contains no resolution in the iambic metron. If we were to accept Stinton's theory, that –⏑⏑ –⏑⏑ can somehow correspond to, or equal, ×–⏑–, and that *Prom.* 117 is an example of this, we would have a small but weighty piece of evidence against Aeschylean authorship.

11 See Wilamowitz *A. Int.* 160, Dale *LM* 101. Wilamowitz followed Hermann at *Ag.* 1072, 1080 in reading Ἀπόλλων, Ἀπόλλων, which he cites as parallel to *Prom.* 115. Fraenkel (*Ag.* p.489) argues for Ἄπολλον, but still takes them as bacchiacs ⏑–O‖⏑–O‖ ; Denniston-Page read ὤπολλον, ὤπολλον || ia. cr. ∧ .

12 The similarity is even closer if we take ἆ ἆ ἔα ἔα (*Prom.* 114) as a dochmiac: Kreousa also starts with a dochmiac, half comprised of exclamations.

13 See Fauth 250.

14 Nestle's parallel (*Struktur des Eingangs* 113) of *Pers.* 154f is quite different. There the chorus see Atossa approaching (anapaests 150-4), and then, to start the new episode, address her in trochaic tetrameters. There is no overlap in sense at all.

15 Cf. S.V. Tracy *HSCP* (1971) 59-62, and B.E. Donovan *HSCP* (1973) 125-7.

16 J.C. Merlant *REA* (1957) 275f attempts to read Pythagorean significance into the symmetry of the numbers of lines in each metre: 5-8-13-5-8; 5+8 = 13, and 5:8 almost exactly equals 8:13. I suspect that such subtlety would be missed by an audience - perhaps Merlant would agree with Schmid that *Prom.* was a *Lesestück*?

17 But cf. e.g. Heidler 33f (a pupil of Rossbach); also E. Fraenkel *Kl. Beitr.* 1.389ff, Kraus *Strophengestaltung* 231.

18 *LM* 129.

19 *LM* 129.

20 As Schroeder observes *A. Cantica* 41.

21 Cf. Barrett *E. Hipp.* p. 423.

22 Two textual points affect the metre. (a) In the strophe, line 399 contains –∪∪– more than the corresponding line 408 in the antistrophe. In both lines the sense is complete as they stand. Triclinius (followed by Wilamowitz and others) removed λειβομένα, which cures the metre, though it leaves us with rather a harsh construction, which W. compares to 902 μηδὲ ἔρως ἄφυκτον ὄμμα προσδράκοι με: even so, the internal accusative here does seem unnatural (cf. Barrett on E. *Hipp.* 246). Heath suggested making ῥέος subject, and emending to ἔτεγξε: λειβομένα could be a gloss (it is a common Homeric word). But it is probably simpler to assume that a word has dropped out of the antistrophe. In either case, the character of the metre is unaltered, whichever colometry we adopt: we merely have one choriamb or ionic more or less, ––∪∪–[–∪∪–]–∪∪–– etc. (b) More important metrically is the freedom of responsion that the tradition offers us between δακρυσίστακτον δ' ἀπ' ὄσσων and μεγαλοσχήμονά τ' ἀρχαι-, which gives us either chor.∾ia. (–∪∪––⏑∪––∪∪–) or two sorts of ionic (∪∪––⏑∪––, cf. Ar. *Frogs* 323ff). Dale argues from this passage and from A. *Th.* 723 that such responsion is legitimate in tragic ionics. (By Wilamowitz' colometry A. *Th.*'s apparent lack of responsion coincides with anceps, –∪∪–⏒–∪–. It is possible that the middle syllable of εὐκταῖος is shortened here by a correption similar to that commonly found with e.g. δείλαιος, cf. Jebb on S. *Ant.* 311. Alternatively we could scan ὠμο̄φρων, but the lengthening before φρ would be unusual, and the metre still unsatisfactory.) But in the *Prom.* passage the remedy is so simple and obvious that, as evidence for such a curious freedom, it is almost worthless: if we remove δ', as Triclinius did, all is well.

23 As e.g. Thomson (*ed.* pp.180f) suggests.

24 E.g. *Hek.* 444ff, *Ion* 184ff.

25 E. Fraenkel *Kl. Beitr.* 1.389ff examines *Th.* 720ff closely, and points to the coincidence in strophe and antistrophe of syntactical and metrical cola. He suggests that the same process can be seen in *Prom.* 128ff. Certainly the slight pause before the clausulae (132 = 147, 135 = 151), followed by the syntactically almost self-contained alcaic decasyllable, reminds us of the Aeschylean passage. But this is a tendency by no means confined to Aesch.: one might compare e.g. S. *OK* 1239ff, where the self-contained unit 1244 ––⏑⏑–⏑⏑–⏑––‖ (- alc.dec.) rounds off both metrically and syntactically the two preceding minor periods; cf. too E. *El.* 486. As Fraenkel remarks, 'Man sieht, die Symmetrie von Strophe und Gegenstrophe ist hier [sc. *Prom.* 128ff] weniger streng als in dem Lied der *Sieben*'; and on the general question of strophic correspondence of this sort he adds 'Das Phaenomenon ist nicht auf diese wenige Lieder und überhaupt nicht auf Aischylos beschränkt; es verdient eingehendere Untersuchung.' Cf. W. Kuehn *De vocum sonorumque in strophicis Aeschyli canticis aequabilitate* (diss. Halle 1905), D. Korzeniewski *Gr. Metrik* (Darmstadt 1968) 162-70, and *RhM* 104 (1961) 193-201, 105 (1962) 142-52.

26 In some of these passages, the 'iambic penthemimer' is probable: cf. Ar. *Wasps* 303.

27 But cf. fr. *adesp.* 127, and Pap. Oxy. 1176.38.2, discussed below.

28 Pap. Oxy. 1176.38.2.

29 *De aud. poet.* 13.36c; see Snell *Hermes Einzelschr.* 5 (1937) 20, Page *GLP* 154, Wilamowitz *GV* 328. It may come from E. *Alexandros*, but we cannot be certain that it is by Eur. at all.

30 Snell's and Wilamowitz' efforts to avoid a hemiepes (by scanning πε̄τραν and finding ways to lengthen the last syllable of χρυσήλατον) seem over-zealous. A possible arrangement of the whole fragment would give: 1 ––⏑⏑–⏑⏑– (- D), 2 ⏑–⏑– –⏑⏑– (ia. chor.), 3 –⏑⏑–⏑– (dodrans), 4 –⏑⏑– ⏑–⏑– (chor. ia.), 5 –⏑⏑–⏑– ⏑–⏑⏑–⏒‖ (dodrans reiz.//), 6 ––⏑⏑–⏑⏑–⏑– ⏑–– (- ibyc. ba.), 7 ⏑–⏑– –⏑– (x e e), 8 –⏑⏑–⏑⏑– (D), 9 ––⏑⏑ –⏑⏑– (x D), 10 ⏑–⏑–⏑⏑–⏑–– (x hipp.), [11 ––⏑⏑–⏑–– (enop.)].

31 Fr. *adesp.* 127.

32 Diod. Sic. 16.92.

33 On A. *Eum.* 364. He did not expand his argument beyond 'Aeschyli, ut opinor, fragmentum'.

34 See on Pap. Oxy. 1176 fr. 38 (*Alexandros*?) above; also *Rhesos* 360ff, fr. *adesp.* 127.

35 *Lyric iamb.* 143f.

36 See Appendix B for further discussion of this non-clausular ithyphallic, and possible alternative interpretations.

37 *Lyric iamb.* 124.

38 *Lyric iamb.* 127.

39 Substantial unsyncopated periods also occur at E. *Or.* 1246ff, *Med.* 204ff.

40 E. *Tro.* 1060ff starts with aeolics, though 1066ff is pure iambic with dactylic close.

41 A. *Eum.* 996 −∪∪−∪∪−∪∪−∪−−, as we remarked above, is the only example longer than the alcaic decasyllable.

42 The MSS give a freedom of response between 534 ἀλλά μοι and 543 ἰδίαι, ⏑∪− (see Dale *LM* 188). ∪∪− is found in Pindar (cf. Wilamowitz *GV* 433) occasionally as the first element in a dactylo-epitritic colon, where we would expect −∪−, but never in responsion to −∪−. (Bakkhylides fr. 4 was cited by Wilamowitz as an example of such responsion, but Snell does not think that the two are meant to correspond.) Dale points out (a) that no adequate and convincing emendation, whether of strophe or of antistrophe, has yet been offered; (b) that the existence of ∪∪− in this position in Pindar would be a strange coincidence if this is an accident of the textual tradition; (c) Aristophanes allows similar *Responsionsfreiheit* at *Wasps* 273ff = 281ff; she compares ∪∪−−−∪−∼−∪−∪−∪− to the effect of anaclastic ionics (anakreontics). In view of the lack of a single certain example of such responsion anywhere in dac.-ep., and of the strictness of this rather stately metre, it seems more likely to me that we have a corruption, probably in the antistrophe. Even if the free responsion is genuine, it tells us nothing about its author. In 541 the antistrophe appears to have lost ×−∪−.

43 Dale *LM* 180.

44 I include as 'pure' those with ithyphallic clausula, but otherwise containing only −∪∪−∪∪−, −∪−, and anceps.

45 E. *Ba.* contains three iambelegoi, two of them consecutive.

46 Dale *LM* 104.

47 E. *Hkd.* is the sole exception, though S. *El.* only contains the rather dubiously dac.-ep. 1082ff.

48 Ar. *Frogs* 1264ff. See Appendix B, p.259.

49 See Dawe *Rep. of conjectures* 18, Headlam *CR* (1900) 106.

50 Dale *LM* 168 gives examples.

51 See further Dale *Metrical analyses of tragic choruses*, fasc. 1 (= *BICS* Supp. 21.1, London 1971).

52 Cf. Dale *LM* 159 n.1.

53 *Eur. frag.* ed. C. Austin (Berlin 1968) p.31.60.

54 Cf. Heidler 36 'nusquam [*sc*. in Aeschylo] mixtura talis est'.

55 *Coll. and invest.* 130.

56 See, on the iambics of 566-70, pp.48f.

57 Appendix C, p.261.

58 Conomis *Hermes* (1964) 28ff; see Appendix C.

59 *Lyric iamb.* 125.

60 The occurrences are: A. *Th.* 118 (=?137); *Supp.* 528=535; *Ag.* 369=388, 1487=1511; S. *El.* 163=184, 1276, 1277; *OT* 192=205, 202=215, 865=875, 889=904, 891=905; *Ant.* 592=603; *Tr.* 954=963; *OK* 541=548, 1672=1699; E. *Alk.* 222=234; *Hipp.* 762=775; *And.* 846, 1033=1043; *Hek.* 634=644; *Hks* 112=124; *Ion* 1459, 1463, 1464, 1492, 1493, 1500; *Tro.* 1088=1106, 1290, 1292, 1303=1318; *El.* 1207=1215; *Pho.* 1712, 1738; *Or.* 1371: these are certain; probable are: *Hks* 1056; *Tro.* 1296, 1298, 1316=1332; *Hipp.* 1379. In *Prom.* certain are 566, 568, 570, 690; probable or possible are 567, 903, 905.

61 It is very uncertain whether *Th.* 109ff should respond to 127ff; 137 only responds to 119 after transposition, in Murray's text.

62 Σ τοῖς μήδεσι καὶ βουλεύμασι τῆς Ἥρας.

63 Conomis *Hermes* (1964) 38ff.

64 See Fraenkel *Ag.* p.826 App.E, and Barrett on E. *Hipp.* 760 (pp. 309f and 435). Fraenkel states that 'Aeschylus does not admit the lengthening caused by initial mute and liquid even in the case of "praepositiva"; in this he differs from the other two tragedians.' The only two possible Aeschylean exceptions (apart from *Prom.* 582, where Fraenkel accepts Elmsley's emendation) are *Cho.* 606 τινᾶ πρόνοιαν (where Page's γυνᾶ is accepted by Barrett as 'certain') and *Eum.* 378 ἐπὶ κνέφας, where Fraenkel and Barrett both comment on the dactylic context (i.e. possible imitation of epic usage). Barrett points out that most examples in tragedy are of two words which go very closely together, almost suggesting medial rather than initial lengthening: so at *Prom.* 582 we can compare πυρῑ φλεγέθων (Hom. *Od.* 10.513 etc.).

65 *LM* 108 n.3.

66 See further Fraenkel's note (pp.521f).

67 See Dale *LM* 75 n.1, G. Zuntz *Inquiry into the transmission of the plays of Eur.* (Cambridge 1965) 65f.

68 See Appendix C.

69 Cf. Conomis *Hermes* (1964) 31ff.

70 *Coll. and invest.* 123 n.2.

71 See Fraenkel on *Ag.* 1497.

72 See Dawe *Coll. and invest.* 147

73 Unless we so interpret A. *Supp.* 162ff; cf. *Ag.* 1455ff.

74 E.g. *And.* 863; *Hek.* 186, 1065ff; *Hks* 1206ff; *Ion* 716, 1497ff; *Tro.* 249ff; *El.* 585ff.

75 The reading of 887f = 894f is uncertain, and something is definitely missing from the antistrophe; but the metre is not in doubt.

76 See Dawe *Coll. and invest.* 139.

77 Page retains θεῶν, reads ἔρωι, and analyses as 2 ia. 2 ia. lek. 2 ia.

78 Unless we read (251) τὸ μέλλον<δ'>, and take the bacchiac with what follows, to give a tetrameter.

79 See above on 160ff (pp.35f).

80 Denniston *Lyric iamb.* 121.

81 *Ibid.*

82 I had better define my terms. By 'stanza' I mean usually a strophe, or an epode, or an obviously self-contained astrophic passage of comparable length. At e.g. A. *Ag.* 367ff, I count 367-80 as one stanza, 381-4 as another - otherwise, there are not many places where 'strophe' does not equal 'stanza' by my definition. In Eur. however, the astrophic passages become increasingly difficult to divide; but since almost none of these passages sustain pure iambics for long, this does not affect our argument. By 'purely iambic' I mean 'containing not more than one non-iambic element', be it one aeolic colon, one dochmiac, one hemiepes or short run of dactyls, or one clausular aristophanean or somesuch. I include syncopated and unsyncopated, resolved and unresolved iambics. Several stanzas which one would describe as 'predominately iambic' fail to qualify, in all three authors, especially Aesch.; in *Prom.* cf. 425ff. The length of stanza obviously varies considerably, from four or five short cola (e.g. A. *Pers.* 256, *Th.* 975) to thirteen or more (e.g. E. *And.* 1197, S. *Tr.* 881, A. *Ag.* 975). It might be argued that the tendency towards greater length of stanza in Soph. and Eur. renders the likelihood of a purely

iambic stanza rather smaller, but in fact the length of stanza does not seem to make much difference, as an examination of Soph. and Eur. will show (n.b. E. *Hik.* and *Tro.*); in any case, *Prom.*'s short stanzas would, by this argument, be all the more likely to be 'purely iambic', and the fact that they are not, all the more significant.

83 Many of Eur.'s later plays contain astrophic lyrics which cannot easily be divided into stanzas: thus no exact total of stanzas can be given (nor is it needed). See the previous note.

84 *Prom.* 415ff is the nearest; but it is trochaic rather than iambic, and contains two aeolic cola at the end. There are many examples in Aesch., Soph., and Eur. of stanzas which come closer to qualifying than this.

85 See above on *Prom.* 160ff (pp.35f).

86 See above on *Prom.* 566ff (pp.48f).

87 See above on *Prom.* 160ff (pp.35f), and 901ff (pp.59f).

88 *Lyric iamb.* 123.

89 Denniston does not give the actual numbers of 'spondees' and metra. I find that Aesch. has about 160 unsyncopated dimeters (= 320 metra) in the six plays, and 95 trimeters (= 285 metra).

90 An interesting detail, ignored by Denniston, who would have assumed *Supp.* to be Aesch.'s earliest play: *Pers.* has none, *Th.* only four lyric iambic trimeters (excluding *Th.* 78-107).

91 If we include all the lyric iambics of *Prom.*, syncopated as well as unsyncopated (but excluding ia. + do., ia. among aeolic and other alien cola, and dac.-ep., where the long anceps is almost obligatory), we find sixty-five iambic metra, six with long anceps, i.e. about 9%. Denniston does not give figures for syncopated iambic dimeters or trimeters: clearly e.g. –∪–∪–∪– is much commoner than –∪–––∪–.

92 The totals for Aesch., Soph., and Eur. are taken from Conomis *Hermes* (1964) 23. For *Prom.* I have not included the problematical metron of 576 = 595; although each was clearly once a dochmiac, the form of neither is certain. (See above on 574 ff, pp.49ff.)

93 See the fuller discussions of the relevant details in the analyses of 114ff, 566ff, 574ff, 687ff, 901ff.

94 See Conomis *Hermes* (1964) 28-31.

95 See Appendix C.

96 Conomis *Hermes* (1964) 30 gives as possible Aeschylean examples

Supp. 120, *Th*. 782, *Eum*. 159.

97 S. *Ant*. 1275 = 1299; four times certain in Eur. (Conomis 28-31).

98 See Conomis 31-4.

99 See above on *Prom*. 687ff (p.54).

100 See Conomis 38, who points out that Murray's conjecture at A. *Th*. 84 is impossible. (He does not mention *Prom*. 582.)

101 See Appendix B.

102 A. *Ag*. 104ff, *Pers*. 852-97.

103 See above on 160ff (pp.34f).

104 A. *Cho*. 315ff = 332ff, 466ff = 471ff; cf. *Ag*. 717ff = 727ff.

105 *Supp*. 639ff, 663ff, 684ff; *Ag*. 381ff, 416ff, 452ff.

106 S. *Tr*. 116ff, 633ff, 841ff; *OT* 463ff, 1186ff.

107 Fr. *adesp*. 127; Pap. Oxy. 1176 fr. 38 (E. *Alexandros*?); also *Rhesos* 360ff. See above on *Prom*. 128ff (pp.30ff).

Chapter 4. The recitative anapaests

1 A. *Persae* 284-7.

2 *LM* 49.

3 My labels (taken from Broadhead) are used merely for convenience: they do not represent any attempt at subdivision of the metron.

4 I omit the unique (as far as I know) and suspicious –⏑⏑ ⏑⏑– DA (E. *Tro*. 101?) and ⏑⏑⏑⏑ ⏑⏑– (E. *Hek*. 62?), both accepted by Murray among otherwise unremarkable recitative anapaests.

5 Even A. *Pers*. 10% is explained by the content: nine of the eighteen examples contain proper names, most of them from the impressive list of Persian leaders.

6 *CQ* (1958) 82-9.

7 The same applies to S. *OT* 1310; cf. too Kratinos *Ploutoi* (Page *GLP* 38), esp. line 21.

8 See too Herington 50.

9 Sophocles' ratio is lowered by his practice of having in some passages two consecutive paroemiacs, e.g. *El*. 86ff, *Aj*. 1402 ff, *Tr*. 971ff.

10 The heading 'others' includes all the spondaic forms (i.e. ⏕⏔⏕----‖).

11 For this purpose I mean, by 'diaeresis', with neither overlap nor elision.

12 As for S. *El.* (one diaeresis in seven paroemiacs), we observe: (a) only a very small sample of paroemiacs is available; (b) three of the seven are of the unusual -------‖ form.

Chapter 5. The iambic trimeters

1 The figures in this section are based on Garvie *A. Supp.* 32-6, Ceadel *CQ* (1941) 84, and also Descroix, Zielinski *passim.*

2 As we certainly should; see Ceadel 66ff, Garvie 32f. I omit A. *Th.* 1004ff from that play's figures.

3 See Zielinski, Ceadel *passim.*

4 Cf. Ceadel's table (p.88); Neophron's figure is only 5.0; but the totals are all far too small to be reliable.

5 Two passages contain an exceptionally large number of resolutions, 347-72, 709-35. Schein points out (p.44, cf. p.154 n. 110) that resolutions tend to be more common in long descriptive narratives, partly because such speeches tend to contain more proper names.

6 *A. Supp.* 35; see his Table D.

7 E.g. by Hermann, Westphal, and most scholars concerned with the authenticity of our play. For the sake of convenience I shall continue to use the misleading term 'anapaest' for the irrational resolution of the anceps syllable of the iambic metron.

8 E.g. by Schein in his special appendix on 'the trimeter in *Prom.*'; cf. Ceadel *CQ* (1941) 69.

9 Cf. fr. 109, fr. 274 L-J, fr. 282 L-J (all satyric); fr. 283, fr. 464 are probably not Aeschylean. For A. *Ag.* 1257 see Fraenkel *ad loc.* ἱκέτης and related forms are common at the beginning of the trimeter in all three tragedians, e.g. S. *Aj.* 1172, *OT* 41, *Ph.* 470; E. *Hkd.* 33, 94, 123, 224, 246, 345, 417. It may be that such forms as ἱκτήριος made it easier to accept this licence with this particular stem. (*Pers.* 808, *Th.* 495 should both be taken as ⏑– .)

10 See Zielinski 199ff

11 Suggestions of Epicharmian influence (Herington) seem to me grotesque. It is clear that Epicharmos, like the Athenian comic playwrights, admitted more licences of all sorts than *Prom.*, and did not restrict himself to first-foot anapaests. The same is true of our scanty fragments of Agathon, Achaios

etc.; cf. Caedel *CQ* (1941) 88.

12 *Rh. Mus.* (1886) 261.

13 Kopp *Rh. Mus.* (1886) 378. Soph.'s plays contain substantially more trimeters than Aesch.'s.

14 At *Pers.* 321 the MSS give ὅ τ' ἐσθλὸς Ἀριόμαρδος Σάρδεσι. In *Pers.* 38, 968, Ἀριόμαρδος is –⏑⏑–⏑ ; but in view of the variation of Ἀρτεμβάρης (*Pers.* 302/29, 972), we are entitled to take this name, unfamiliar to Athenian ears, as ⏑⏑⏑–⏑ here. (The text is under suspicion, as Porson's Law is flagrantly disregarded; but there is no reason to doubt that Ἀριόμαρδος is correct.) In A. fr. 356 Εὐβοικόν may be –––, or the play may be satyric: it is not a certain example of 'anapaest'.

15 Yorke *CQ* (1936) 118. The only possible exception is E. *Pho.* 208 in lyrics. Maas' suggestion (*GM* §106) that Ἰόνιος scans here as –⏑–, seems impossible to me. Aesch. always uses the Attic-Ionic Ἰάον- (Ἰων-) form, probably of quite different origin. See the section on prosody, p.83.

16 Cf.above, n.14;also A. *Th.* 488, 547, where either the prosody of Ἱππομέδοντος, Παρθενοπαῖος is altered to ––⏑––, or we have a strange 'anaclastic' metron –⏑⏑– = ⏑–⏑– (cf. Maas *GM* §107). C. Prato's attempt (*SIFC* 33 (1961) 101-13) to defend other 'anapaests' in the tragic trimeter which editors have refused to accept (e.g. *Prom.* 265, 354, 472, 680, 945) totally ignores the problem of diaeresis within such resolutions: only *Prom.* 680 is remotely possible.

17 See Harrison *CQ* (1914) 206-11, Descroix 46-9, Ritchie 274-83.

18 Ritchie, following Descroix, does not include figures for the resolved lines too. I have done this for Aesch. only, and the difference to the overall figure is slight.

19 A. *Cho.* appears to give an exceptional figure for long anceps at 1 and 3 (11.3%: the next highest is *Pers.* with 9.5%); but we find that when we count in the figures for 1, 2, and 3, *Cho.* is unremarkable (25.9%, cf. *Ag.* 25.2%, *Eum.* 26.4%).

20 The figures are based on Descroix, with my own figures for resolved lines added; anceps of uncertain length is counted as short.

21 I.e. 'spondees 3 and 5' plus '3 spondees' in Ritchie's table (p.282).

22 There are too few instances of 'first-foot tribrach' to be worth investigating from this point of view.

23 Cf. Descroix 17ff, Kopp *Rh. Mus.* (1886) 247-65, 376-86, von Mess *Rh. Mus.* (1903) 270ff, Naylor *CQ* (1907) 4ff, Barrett on E. *Hipp.* 760.

24 See Naylor *CQ* (1907) for fuller discussion; also H. Dietz *Rh.Mus* 117 (1974) 202-12.

25 Based on Naylor *CQ* (1907), but omitting *Prom.*'s instances; the figures for Soph. and Eur. also come from him.

26 See Murray *ad loc.*, Blass on A. *Eum.* 186ff, Maas *GM* §130, Herington 35ff. N.b. too *Prom.* 89, where PK read ποντίων τε ῥευμάτων; see Dawe *Coll. and invest.* 105.

27 See Dodds *ad loc.*

28 P.37; his suggestion that *Prom.* here shows an affinity with comic style seems rather desperate.

29 See Descroix 20, Groeneboom on *Prom.* 1023. OncT read ῥάκος μέγα.

30 Cf. Blass *ad loc.*

31 Descroix 23, who has missed this *Prom.* example (and also E. *Alk.* 1108). See too appendix to Jebb S. *Ph.* p.234.

32 Unless we accept Kirchoff's reading at *Supp.* 959, with Page.

33 Cf. Jebb on S. *Ph.* 984.

34 Cf. Schmid 63 for Aeschylean parallels; also Fraenkel on *Ag.* 274.

35 Descroix includes under (2) all lines which have both penth. and hephth.

36 Descroix makes it four; Harrison, whose figures are usually more reliable, corrects it to three in a marginal note to his personal copy of Descroix, now in the Cambridge University Library.

37 Harrison makes *Prom.*'s figure ten, presumably through using a different text.

38 Descroix gives *Ag.* 1256 as a possible example; see Fraenkel *ad loc.* Even if we accept the tradition, we still have a strong break × – ∪ – × – ⁞;this is much less extraordinary than the two *Prom.* examples.

39 Descroix does not distinguish between these examples, which completely disregard the caesura, and such cases as S. *Ant.* 997, *Aj.* 312, E. *Ion* 828?, where alternative caesurae are at hand. Nor does he make clear whether his list is comprehensive for Soph.

40 Descroix also cites A. *Cho.* 660, but this has a perfectly good hephthemimeral caesura.

41 Descroix 284ff.

42 See too the section below on 'word division', pp. 92ff.

43 See Descroix 320, with table.

44 Soph.'s fragments give a figure of only 14.7%.

45 This is discussed more fully in the section on 'word division', pp. 92ff.

46 See Broadhead *ad loc.*, who follows Bothe in emending, for reasons of sense as well as metre. A. *Pers.* is easily the strictest of his plays as far as Porson's Law is concerned, with only two minor infractions.

47 This should be twelve (107, 313, 345, 648, 747, 760, 763, 872, 915, 933, 956, 1027), since Descroix wrongly includes *Prom.* 986 (following Q etc., Triclinius).

48 Descroix 329, who fails to note A. *Cho.* 903.

49 Fraenkel thinks this line corrupt, but the end seems all right.

50 As far as I know, this peculiarity has not been observed before.

51 Including quasi-enclitics, such as γάρ, μέν, δέ etc., and proclitics, as at A. *Supp.* 290, 391, etc.

52 Depending on how we take *Ag.* 1354.

53 We might add *Ag.* 556, though here τί δ' οὐ coheres closely together.

54 Occurrences of truly independent final monosyllables are marked with an asterisk.

55 By 'looking forward', I mean enjambement of the type already discussed.

56 My figures are based on Stanford *CR* (1940) 8; cf. too Descroix 75ff. Stanford includes lines with elided monosyllables, but not lines with the article or καί etc. as a fourth word.

57 See Descroix 76 n.1.

58 'The iambic trim. in Aesch. and Soph.' (diss. Columbia 1967). He includes a short appendix on the authenticity of *Prom.*, but this consists largely of a restatement of earlier attacks (mainly Schmid), which he finds unpersuasive. He does not mention some of his own figures which could be used to argue for Aeschylean authorship, nor others which could be used against it. In this section I point to some of them.

59 I had observed this independently, and found the observation confirmed by Schein's figures (p.70, and nn.154, 155).

60 My figures for E. *Med.* and *Hkd.* are 34% and 36%; see Schein 111.

Prom.'s figure is 29%.

61 Schein 111.

62 Schein 37, and Table 6 (p.113).

63 Schein 41, and Table 18 (p.119).

64 Schein 41, and Table 20 (p.120).

65 Schein Tables 24 and 25 (p.122).

66 Especially in the absence of any figures for Eur., and in view of his decision not to take account of proclitic words inseparable from their surroundings.

67 Harrison *PCPS* (1921) 14f, Yorke *CQ* (1936) 153f, Herington 46ff.

68 So Harrison, Yorke, and Herington, for example.

69 E.g. Kritias (?) fr. 1 (= fr. 19 Snell) 18, 27; Karkinos fr. 8; Dionysios fr. 7; Theodektes fr. 8.1; Chairemon fr. 21.

70 Cf. Ficker *Vers und Satz*, *passim*; also Garvie 37f.

71 These are Ficker's figures; mine tally more or less with his, though overall I count fewer occurrences than he does in each play, e.g. *Pers*. 6.5%, *Supp*. 8.0%, *Prom.* 8.9%. The figures for Soph. and Eur. seem to be similar to *Prom.* (e.g. *Med.* 8.7%) or slightly lower. Ficker suggests (p.134) that *Prom.* displays some unaeschylean features in its handling of ordinary (i.e. non-'Sophoclean') enjambements. He singles out *Prom.* 739f and 648f for their unusual separation of noun and adjective; elsewhere in Aesch.'s enjambements only two positions for noun and adjective in different lines are admitted: either the last word of one line agrees with the first word of the next, or the word following a penthemimeral caesura agrees with the first word of the next line. But I don't think that we can attach much weight to this.

72 *CQ* (1936) 73-9, with corrections on p.192 for his failure to allow for the different numbers of trimeters in each play.

73 Cf. Denniston *CQ* (1936) Table 1 (pp.74f). His distinction between colon and full-stop is basically false; they will vary from editor to editor. So I have only distinguished between 'major' stop (A), i.e. colon, question-mark, and full-stop, and 'minor' stop (B), i.e. comma.

74 Discounting stichomythia, where enjambement is naturally impossible.

75 Denniston *CQ* (1936) 76, who does not include *Prom.* 821; this surely should count, as the comma at the end of 820 is unnecessary.

76 Denniston *CQ* (1936) 192; his further suggestion, 'it is much commoner in Aesch. than in Soph.', is not true, if we remove *Prom.* from the other six plays of Aesch.

77 Major *Prom.* 41, 342, 361, 734, 750, 856, 940; minor 684, 855, 909, 1022.

78 Except perhaps position 9, where Soph. is consistently higher.

79 A. *Pers.* has an unusual figure at position 9 (four; otherwise Aesch. never more than one), and an isolated minor stop at position 11 (where I think we should include *Prom.* 502; see the earlier section on 'Sophoclean enjambement', p.96).But in both cases the numbers are too small to be really significant.

80 *CQ* (1936) 78, his Table 2. His table shows too that in position 6 (i.e. mid-line), *Prom.*'s figure of three is too low for Soph. (lowest *Tr.* seven, *Ant.* eight), but compatible with Aesch. and Eur. (A. *Ag.*'s figure of fourteen, five of them major, is unusually high for Aesch., but not too far from *Cho.* seven, *Pers.* five, in shorter plays.)

81 Obviously 'punctuation' is a modern and subjective criterion, but there is no reason to suppose that Murray punctuated *Prom.* on radically different principles from the other plays in his edition.

82 *CR* (1941) 22ff; cf. too Groeneboom on *Prom.* 263.

83 Table 1, p.39; see his discussion pp.37-40, in which he concludes that '*Prom.* drops completely out of the Aeschylean - and tragic! - pattern.' Herington fails to observe that non-stop lines overall are more common in *Prom.* than in Aesch., which increases the opportunities for non-stop hiatus; but his conclusion seems nevertheless to be justified, even when we allow for this fact.

84 See above on 'enjambement', pp.98ff; also the previous note.

85 Harrison *CR* (1941) 23 reminds us that modern editors are rather sparing of punctuation, as compared with e.g. Porson or Elmsley.

86 Interlinear hiatus seems not uncommon among the minor tragedians, though our material is far too scanty to be reliable; cf. Neophron fr. 2.2, Kritias(?) fr. 1 (= fr. 19 Snell), Agathon fr. 8, Theodektes fr. 1, Karkinos fr. 1, Chairemon fr. 21, etc.

87 Particularly when we read articles which express no doubt as to Aeschylean authorship, yet constantly describe *Prom.* as an exception; this provides a guarantee of objectivity sometimes lacking in this debate.

Chapter 6. Structure and dramatic technique

1 It is argued in ch.7 that it is highly unlikely that a puppet was used to represent Prometheus; in any case the question does not concern us here.

2 Herington 90.

3 Cf. Wilamowitz *A. Int.* 119 'ganz Sophokleisch'.

4 Unless we wish to argue that *Prom.* was written by Aesch. before *Pers.* and Phrynichos' *Phoinissai*. For the whole question see the references in Garvie 121 nn.3 and 4.

5 According to Aristotle, it was as old as Thespis (Themistios *Or.* 26.316d); see Nestle *Struktur des Eingangs*, *passim*.

6 See Garvie 121.

7 Perhaps with a few exceptions: see p. 104n.9.

8 There is no reason why the play should not have started with a prologue, delivered by (say) Hephaistos; Prometheus could have been led on by Kratos and Bia, and then quickly chained to the rock, without any lengthy dialogue.

9 As apparently *Andromeda* did, cf. Σ Ar. *Thesm.* 1065, quoting E. fr. 114 as τοῦ προλόγου τῆς 'Ανδρομέδας εἰσβολή. *Rhesos* is not of much real use to us here, since, apart from the authenticity question, it seems likely that it may once have had a spoken prologue (see Ritchie 101ff). E. *IA* is also problematical, of course: see now B.M.W. Knox *YCS* 22 (1972) 239-61.

10 E.g. *intro.* Σ to S. *Aj.*, Σ S. *El.* 1, Σ *OT* 8, Σ E. *Tro.* 1.

11 *Struktur des Eingangs* 117.

12 See the section on *Prom.*'s stichomythia, pp.136ff.

13 This feature is also emphasized by Unterberger (p.31), who compares the Aeschylean fondness for striking stage effects etc. in *Phrygians* and *Psychostasia*. Schmid, on the other hand, found the details of *Schmiedearbeit* out of place (p.33).

14 See Gollwitzer 67f.

15 See *Life* of Aesch. 6.

16 See Denniston-Page on A. *Ag.* 489ff, and below, p. 321n.107.

17 It is interesting to note that the convention (if there was one, as Nestle maintains) that the prologue be delivered by minor characters, is thus preserved, despite the presence on stage of the hero. Of course our knowledge of the opening scenes of *Niobe* and *Phrygians* is extremely sketchy.

18 See p.107, on the technique of exposition.

19 *Life* of Aesch. 6 Ἀχιλλεὺς ... οὐ φθέγγεται, πλὴν ἐν ἀρχαῖς ὀλίγα πρὸς Ἑρμῆν ἀμοιβαῖα. What does ἐν ἀρχαῖς mean? Is it the very beginning, or merely the opening scene in general? And how much should we understand by ὀλίγα ἀμοιβαῖα?

20 *Prolog und Expositionstechnik* 14.

21 Gollwitzer 19-23, who also observes (5-13) that usually an Aeschylean drama starts after most of the action is already over, so that the play shows only the final process. Though true of *Persians*, I do not think this generalization is of much use. Gollwitzer treats the *Oresteia* as a single unit (showing the 'final process' in the House of Atreus), and ignores the fact that we only possess the final play of Aesch.'s Theban trilogy, which is bound therefore to start after most of the action has taken place (cf. *Eum.*); and since we have little idea what happened in the rest of the *Danaid* trilogy, we are in no position to pass judgement on *Suppliants* on this score. Gollwitzer, who labours under the influence of excessive *Tychoismus*, is really trying to contrast the comparative lack of plot in Aesch.'s plays with its supposedly greater interest for Soph. But if we consider the plot of S. *Aj.*, in comparison with the action which has already taken place before the play starts, I do not think that we can maintain this distinction between Aeschylean and Sophoclean practice.

22 P.92.

23 We saw in ch.3 (pp.23ff) that there is not the remotest parallel in extant tragedy.

24 E.g. Wilamowitz *A. Int.* 160, Thomson (*ed.*) p.141, Unterberger 33; cf. too Tracy *HSCP* (1971) 59-62, Donovan *HSCP* (1973) 125-7.

25 *A. Int.* 159.

26 E.g. Thanatos in E. *Alk.* See on the use of anapaests for actors pp.111ff.

27 The short outbursts of Herakles at S. *Tr.* 1080ff (cited by Wilamowitz) and Elektra at S. *El.* 1160ff are so far removed from our play's formality and symmetry as to be of no use to us either.

28 *A. Int.* 160.

29 Bethe *Proleg. Gesch. Theat.* 164 cites E. *And.* 91-116, *Hek.* 59-97 as parallels to *Prom.*: both are quite different.

30 'Für eine verfeinerte Technik ist das unmöglich' (p.113).

31 See Kranz *Stasimon* 20ff, Nestle 115ff, Ritchie 341ff. For a discussion of different applications of the term 'epirrhema' see Michelini 'Rhesis and dialogue' 154ff.

32 In Aesch. the alternation is usually between iambics and lyrics, but we find actors' anapaests at *Ag*. 1448ff and *Eum*. 916 ff, as at *Prom*. 128ff. Soph. has four examples of anapaests, three of iambics, Eur. four of anapaests, two of iambics; *Rhesos* has anapaests twice, iambics once; cf. Michelini 157ff.

33 *Der Gefesselter Prom*. 38.

34 Nestle 118ff also suggests that the hero was already on stage and was addressed by the chorus in the parodoi of A. *Niobe* and *Phrygians* (add too fr. 131, from *Myrmidons* ?). He considered 'Die Form der Parodos mit einfachen epirrhematischen Schauspieleranapästen ist nicht jünger als *Aj*. und *Alk*.' Kranz argues (pp.48ff) that *Prom*. is more 'advanced' than S. *Ant*. and E. *Alk*., but his approach is too schematic to be convincing.

35 This section owes much to the observations of Kussmahly 8f.

36 It is of course uncertain whether Eur. wrote 1-48, and if so, where it should stand; see Knox *YCS* 22 (1972) 239ff.

37 See Bethe *Proleg. Gesch. Theat*. 172f. Anapaests were often used to accompany movement onto or off the stage or orchestra; so perhaps here too the anapaests accompany the movement of the god onto the theologeion, or of the μηχανή out into view (though the 'marching' rhythm would then have less point).

38 The problems raised by Okeanos' extraordinary aerial entry are discussed in ch.7.

39 The passages are: *Aj*. 200ff, 1402ff; *Ant*. 931ff; *Tr*. 974ff; *El*. 86ff; *Ph*. 144ff, 1409ff, 1445ff; *OK* 1751ff. Of these, *Aj*. 200ff and *Ph*. 144ff are epirrhematic.

40 The passage also bears a strange resemblance to the end of *Prom*.; cf. *Ant*. 937 / *Prom*. 1091, *Ant*. 939 / *Prom*. 1080, *Ant*. 940ff / *Prom*. 1093 (and cf. *Prom*. 92), *Ant*. 943 / *Prom*. 1091. Compare too E. *Med*. 160ff, also in anapaests.

41 The passages are: *Alk*. 29ff, 273ff, 861ff; *Med*. 96ff, 1389ff; *Hipp*. 176ff, 1283ff, 1347ff; *And*. 515ff; *Hek*. 59ff; *Ion* 82ff, 859ff; *Tro*. 98ff, 782ff; *El*. 1292ff; *Or*. 1682ff; *Ba*. 1368ff; *IA* 1ff; *Rhesos* 11ff, 732ff. The epirrhematic passages are *Alk*. 861ff, *And*. 515ff, *Rhesos* 11ff; cf. too the second part of *Med*. 96ff.

42 The scholiast attributes *OT* 1524ff to Oedipus; Ritter *Philol*. (1861) 424, followed by Pearson and others, believes that it should not be there at all, and has displaced the usual anapaestic coda; he is surely right. See now R.D. Dawe *Studies on the text of Sophocles* (Leiden 1973) 1.266-73.

43 Cf. Jebb on S. *OT* 1524ff.

44 Jebb's suggestion (see previous note), that the end of A. *Ag*. is to be explained by its position within the trilogy (i.e.

that no hint of finality is intended, such as is implied by a choral coda), seems rather dubious: *Supp*. and *Cho*. have no hint of finality, despite their choral codas.

45 Had the author not chosen to give his chorus a sudden and quite unexpected injection of courage at 1063ff, he might have allowed them to abandon Prometheus to his fate. He could then have been withdrawn (on the ἐκκύκλημα ?), and the chorus could have remained to give a final statement as he disappeared. The problem of the stage management of this whole final scene is very awkward, and is treated more fully in ch.7.

46 Perhaps the unusual ending of A. *Ag*. has a similar explanation. The chorus have been facing up to Aigisthos' bodyguard, and now the two groups are trooping off, by the different exits. Klytaimestra is left in the middle, vainly trying to bridge the gulf with her final couplet (she has been silent throughout the altercation of 1612-53); cf. Fraenkel pp.803f, who cites a remark of Hermann on similar lines.

47 See ch.7.

48 I find no parallel in Aesch. for a scene involving two or more characters which does not also involve the chorus, whether announcing an incoming character, or participating in the dialogue, or commenting on the scene and its significance as it ends.

49 This is the solution of e.g. Wilamowitz and Pickard-Cambridge; see further ch.7. It is strongly suggested by *Prom*. 272ff.

50 See Deckinger 66, Schmid 6ff (whose criticism of the Okeanos-scene is merciless, and at times exaggerated; but many of his points are valid).

51 Perhaps Groeneboom and Dodds are right to suggest a lacuna after 331.

52 Schmid 7 'Er geht, und alles bleibt beim alten.'

53 See Unterberger 54ff for a good defence of the dramatic function of the scene.

54 Unless we agree with Wilamowitz that the playwright is anxious to introduce Atlas and Typhos at any cost, in which case Okeanos is as good a means as any.

55 Most of what Okeanos says is either virtual repetition of what the chorus have already said (cf. Schmid 10 for a list of repetitions), or gnomic platitude, or offers of help which are never implemented; the excursus on Atlas and Typhos, which an audience familiar with Hesiod would find quite appropriate, is not vital to the drama (though cf. Unterberger 64ff for suggested links with Λυόμενος), but does not seem to me in any way objectionable.

56 Schmid 8.

57 On 'Aeschylean' silences see O. Taplin *HSCP* (1972) 57ff, with whom I agree on most points.

58 P.14.

59 Emendation, such as Gercke's ingenious σφριγᾶν, is not the answer: it would still be unclear what behaviour on Prometheus' part was being referred to. A lacuna before 436 is more likely.

60 Tentatively suggested to me by Prof. D.L. Page.

61 Cf. E. *And.* 117ff, unless the chorus there enter and take up their positions during 91-116.

62 *A. Int.* 122; cf. Groeneboom p.174, Unterberger 69.

63 E.g. Wilamowitz *A. Int.* 158, Mazon *ad loc.*

64 E.g. Wilamowitz *A. Int.* 160, Gollwitzer 67.

65 There 'Euripides' refers to A. *Phrygians* and *Niobe*, where the leading characters each sat in silence, with their faces hidden, while the chorus sang long 'strings of lyrics', and 'the audience sat and wondered when they would say something'. This sounds a very different procedure from *Prom.* 1-87; see Taplin *HSCP* (1972) 58ff. We might bear in mind that Aristophanes does not mention *Prom.* as being remarkable for any Aeschylean silence, though it seems that he was familiar with the play, to judge from *Knights* and *Birds* (see ch.2).

66 The theory that, because Prometheus was represented by a puppet, and only two speaking actors were available, he could not speak until either Kratos or Hephaistos had left the stage, is almost certainly mistaken in both its main assumptions. See ch.7.

67 This seems clear from 35 ὅδε, 74 ὅδε, 84 οὗτος. See further Taplin *HSCP* (1972) 94-6.

68 Cited by Groeneboom as parallel to *Prom.* 436ff.

69 In the section on the Okeanos-scene above, p.115.

70 Deckinger 28, Schmid *GGL* 302.

71 *Th.* 861ff was probably not written by Aeschylus. On *Ag.* 489ff see Denniston-Page *ad loc*; *contra* Taplin *HSCP* (1972) 91.

72 See Deckinger 28, 58ff.

73 For example, Deckinger 160 says that A. *Cho.* 838 is too clumsy for Sophocles. (He does not consider Euripides, however, who provides parallels, e.g. *Med.* 866.)

74 For ἥκω etc. cf. *Pers.* 159ff; *Th.* 39f; *Cho.* 1ff, 658f, 838; *Eum.* 235f, 250f, 397ff, 576ff; and for the chorus (cf. *Prom.* 128ff) *Ag.* 258, *Cho.* 22.

75 E.g. S. *Ant.* 988f, *OT* 512ff; E. *Med.* 214f, 866, *Alk.* 614, etc.; and for the chorus E. *Tro.* 153ff, 176f, *El.* 167ff. Also for departures cf. E. *Alk.* 74, 730, etc.

76 P.92.

77 I suggested earlier (pp.108ff above) that *Prom.* 88-127 should not be considered a monody in the conventional sense of that word; it is almost entirely spoken or recited, not sung, and is of an entirely different character from the passages which will now be considered. Herington does not make this clear, and more or less ignores the problem of Prometheus' soliloquy.

78 Herington must mean only monodies like 566ff, not 114ff; see my previous note.

79 Owen *Date of S. El.* 149-52; see too Barner *Die Monodie* 279f.

80 See Ritchie 339f, Barner 293f.

81 Indeed Ritchie considers only S. *El.* 86-120 (*Klaganapäste*) and *OK* 237-53 to be true monodies.

82 See the discussions of the metre of 566ff and 574ff, pp. 47ff.

83 Cf. Owen 148ff.

84 I do not count *Th.* 875ff or *Supp.* 836ff: in neither case do I think that actors sang.

85 P.339. For a discussion of kommos and epirrhema in early tragedy see further Michelini 155-60.

86 My figure is based on Owen. The passages are: *Aj.* 348-429; *Ant.* 806-82, 1261-1346; *Tr.* 879-95, 1004-43; *OT* 649-86, 1307-66; *El.* (86-120), 121-250, 823-70, 1232-88; *Ph.* 1081-1217; *OK* 176-253, 510-41, 1670-1750.

87 Aesch. does not give Orestes lyrics to express his agitation at *Cho.* 1048ff; but Kassandra is given epirrhematic lyrics for her wild utterances at *Ag.* 1072-1172.

88 See Schmid 73f, Herington 56ff; both are based on Wendel *Gesprächsanrede*.

89 Herington's table (p.57) illustrates the point, which was first noticed by Wendel.

90 P.58.

91 Herington 58, who suggests that this detail is 'engineered ... to fit the unique content and ethos of the play as a whole'.

92 There is only one other example in extant tragedy of such a double address by the proper name alone, cf. Wendel 6.

93 The question of the role of the chorus, and their direct address to Prometheus in their odes, is treated more fully on pp. 128ff.

94 P.74.

95 φίλοι, φίλαι, with or without ὦ, occur eleven times in Aesch.; cf. S. *OT* 1321 ἰὼ φίλος; E. *And*. 1205, *IT* 830, *Tro*. 267, *Rhesos* 367 ὦ φίλος; E. *Med*. 1133 φίλος. Aristophanes never has ὦ φίλος; cf. Pindar *N*. 3.76 χαῖρε φίλος. Aesch. has φίλε, φίλτατε only at *Th*. 159, 677, *Ag*. 1654, *Cho*. 893, 1051.

96 Note for example *Rhesos* 687, 688, 690, 730 (ἴσχε πᾶς etc.); Wendel cites as parallels only S. *Aj*. 1413f, and several instances in Aristophanes (e.g. *Ach*. 204ff). All other tragic examples are in the plural.

97 Wendel 53. Her figures include both dialogue and lyrics, and we should not forget that Aesch. has a greater proportion of lyric than Soph. and Eur.

98 Herington 56.

99 This lack of conventional formulae may be due to a certain extent simply to their inappropriateness to the characters involved in *Prom*.: Prometheus himself is hostile to all except Io and the chorus (to whom he has an unusual relationship); Okeanos (γέρον ?) and Hermes, even Io (τέκνον ?) do not obviously fit such formulae either.

100 So that e.g. E. *Med*. 1-1080 has fifty formulae = 4.6%; S. *Aj*. 1-1092 has forty-seven = 4.3%, both considerably lower than the average for Soph. and Eur.

101 Aesch.'s rate is also lowered by his avoidance of direct address by the chorus in lyrics; as we saw, *Prom*. is in this respect unaeschylean.

102 Again at 763, the chorus use the bare proper name for their final remark.

103 First Westphal in 1869.

104 Largely based on Gercke (p.173); the figures for Eur. are my own.

105 A. *Supp*. has 58 lines of choral anapaests, *Eum*. only 14; thus the difference between their figures for pure lyrics is rather less.

106 P.20 'so musste der Umfang der Chorlieder möglichst gekürzt werden'.

107 Scholars disagree as to Klytaimestra's movements between *Ag.* 40 and 974; cf. Fraenkel and Denniston-Page on 83ff. There is no positive indication that Klytaimestra leaves the stage at all before 974; but see Taplin *HSCP* (1972) 89-94.

108 Cf. too *Niobe* and *Phrygians* ?

109 And of course Io, with her emotional monody 561ff.

110 Unless we merely shrug our shoulders, and plead that we know too little about Aesch. and his style to say *what* we should expect from him. There are obvious objections to the theory that the lack of choral lyrics is due to composition for performance in Sicily, where a chorus might be unequal to a lengthier role: the Athenian choruses were not professional, and if Aesch. could train them, I do not see why he should not train Sicilians who apparently managed to fulfil Pindar's exacting requirements. The Sicilian production is of course no more than conjecture.

111 In ch.3.

112 The structure of the parodos is discussed above, pp.110f.

113 The table is based on that of Kranz (*Stasimon* 124f); as will be seen, his criteria are not wholly consistent or satisfactory.

114 Nine of these occur in his last four plays, *Pho.*, *Or.*, *Ba.*, *IA.*

115 Unless we count the parodos of *Th.*

116 I find it hard to believe that the original form of 425-35 was much like what has come down to us. Apart from the repetition of the Atlas-motif from 347ff, if 425-30 is anywhere near complete it seems incongruously short and isolated in content from the surrounding stanzas, especially its antistrophe (?) 431-5; I cannot think of any other choral passage similar to this in Aesch., or anywhere else in tragedy. Yet the alternative (interpolation) seems equally improbable.

117 Five, if we include the epirrhematic *Ph.* 827ff.

118 E.g. the parodoi of *Pers.*, *Supp.*, *Ag.*

119 In fact, E. *Hek.*, with the chorus in the parodos confined to recitative anapaests, really has only three strophic choral odes in all. *Prom.* 687ff, an isolated, short, astrophic choral ode between two iambic episodes, is rather unusual; but the parallels of A. *Cho.* 152ff, S. *Tr.* 205ff, E. *Hik.* 918ff, *El.* 585ff, *Hipp.* 1268ff seem close enough.

120 Rode's study tends to be a little too rigid in its distinctions and definitions, and to look rather too hard for a uniform development in Aesch.'s style from *Pers.* to the *Oresteia*.

But it is useful for its analyses of what is consistently present - and absent - from Aesch.'s choral lyrics. Rode finds *Prom.*'s style quite different from that of the other six plays; some of his reasons will be found here.

121 See Rode 176ff.

122 *Prom.* 143ff, in epirrhematic exchange, is of course different.

123 E.g. *Pers.* second stasimon, *Supp.* parodos and second stasimon, *Cho.* parodos, etc. (and n.b. p. 124 above). In the first two stasima of *Eum.*, Orestes is referred to in the third person.

124 As quite often in Soph. and Eur., e.g. S. *Aj.* 182ff; E. *Alk.* 435ff, *Hipp.* 141ff, etc.

125 Röhlecke considered only the parodos, 687ff, and 901ff to be genuine; Kranz rejected the second and third stasima, Rose most of the third.

126 The same is true of their metres; see ch.3, esp. pp. 60ff.

127 Recognition of this fact has even led scholars, e.g. Robertson and Dodds, to suggest that Aesch. left *Prom.* uncompleted at his death, and that someone else (e.g. Euphorion) wrote the choral lyrics. If we felt that the choral lyrics were the only major obstacle to the acceptance of Aeschylean authorship, we might find this the best way out.

128 Further figures for Eur., by my calculation, are: *Hipp.* 58½ lines, *And.* 41½, *Hkd.* 46.

129 P.32, with references to previous literature; in greater detail *CR* (1963) 5-7.

130 *CR* (1963) 5-7.

131 But as I argue below, I think that four of these longer speeches should be counted as 'conventional'. The twelve lines *Ag.* 489-500 should perhaps be given to Klytaimestra, and only 501f given to the chorus.

132 Though Herington counts it as 'conventional'.

133 The figures other than for quatrains, for S. *Aj.*, *Ant.*, E. *Alk.*, *Med.*, *Hkd.*, are my own. Unless stated, quatrains are of the 'conventional' type.

134 Herington *CR* (1963) 6.

135 He even suggests that 'the last of them includes a remark 1037f ... which to the present writer ranks among the most pointless ever composed by a Greek playwright'. This is perhaps a little strong.

136 Cf. Rode 202ff, who argues that Aesch. purposely increased the role of the chorus as a character, involving it in the dialogue and action, whereas Soph. and Eur. reverted to the normal, more stylized pattern.

137 Symmetry; the detachment of the chorus from the action of the drama, and the consequent increase in Prometheus' feeling of isolation? (Yet this makes the closing scene, where the chorus suddenly align themselves spiritually and apparently physically with Prometheus, as he is overwhelmed by the elements, all the more unexpected and baffling.)

138 See sections (1), (2) and (3) above.

139 See section (4) above.

140 Cf. 88ff, 133, 573, 583, 1048ff, 1082ff. On the whole problem of the chorus' aerial entry, and of their movement in the final scene, see further ch.7.

141 As it is argued that they must do, in ch.7; cf. too the discussion of the Okeanos-scene, pp.115f.

142 See p.143.

143 The chorus in A. *Th.* also manifest a change of character as the play develops, from timorous, 'feminine' uncertainty to the giving of reasoned and moderate advice. But this change is more gradual, and is dramatically justified, indeed necessary, corresponding as it does to the shift in emphasis from Eteokles' role as protector of the city to that of brother of Polyneikes and victim of the curse of the Labdakids.

144 See ch.7, p.144.

145 A. Gross (1905), W. Jens (1955); the latter concentrates on middle-period Sophocles, and ignores Euripides, yet includes late Soph. as well as Aesch.: thus his title is rather misleading. See too B. Seidensticker in *Die Bauformen der gr. Trag.* (ed. W. Jens, Munich 1971) 183ff.

146 Gross took A. *Supp.* to be the earliest play. Jens took it as the nearest to the *Oresteia*, a conclusion that he reached from his own and Nestle's studies before the publication of Pap. Oxy. 2256 fr. 3.

147 P.33.

148 *Hermes* 32 (1897) 387.

149 See Gross 18, Herington 49f, and the discussion of the prologue, above, p.105.

150 The nearest to a parallel in Aesch. is perhaps *Eum.* 117-28; cf. too *Supp.* 903-8, S. *Aj.* 331-9. All are short and very different from *Prom.* 40ff.

151 Cf. S. *Tr.* 663-71, 738-43; *OT* 99-107, 935-40, 1001-6; *El.* 660-7, 668-73; *OK* 465-73; also *Ph.* 317-31 for 2:3 alternation. Herington compares too Seneca *Oed.* 509-22.

152 *Not* A. *Supp.* 207ff, nor 310ff.

153 E.g. S. *Aj.* 74ff, 735ff, 1044ff; *Ant.* 39ff, 237ff, 401ff, 1095 ff; *OT* 316ff, etc.; though n.b. the symmetry of *Ant.* 724-72.

154 E.g. E. *Med.* 59ff, 746ff, 1009ff, 1121ff.

155 S. *Ant.* 536ff, 724ff; *OT* 549ff; *Tr.* 1120ff; E. *And.* 577ff, 896 ff; *Ion* 256ff; *Tro.* 51ff; *Ba.* 792ff (see Gross 17). There are several more passages where single-line stich. is introduced by just two couplets.

156 See Schmid 39.

157 It seems likely that something is missing before *Prom.* 970: it simply does not make sense as it stands. 'Versum vel gestum Promethei excidisse iudicat Reisig' (Murray), and Prometheus is not free to make much of a 'gestus'. If a single line has dropped out, the transition from two- to one-line stich. is rather more symmetrical.

158 Also cf. S. *Aj.* 1316ff 222211222; *Ant.* 237ff 1321131, 1095ff 31121221; *Tr.* 61ff 312112111221; E. *Med.* 59ff 112112, etc. Eur. is generally more regular than Soph.; *Rhesos* tends to be rather irregular, e.g. 87ff 3121141, 565ff 23111112111232223l, 622ff 233121.

159 P.33.

160 A. *Supp.* 207ff, as arranged by various editors, often gives a similar pattern, with the chorus delivering two consecutive lines. This is neither desirable nor necessary: see Page's arrangement.

161 Although at E. *Eum.* 674 a two-line stich. is interrupted by a single line from Athene, cf. S. *OT* 527. But this interchange between three speakers is hardly long enough to be classed as stichomythia.

162 Pp.87f. He also points to the related technique of Aesch. and Eur., of padding out lines with redundant phrases, merely to preserve the one-line stichomythia, e.g. A. *Cho.* 175, 767; E. *Alk.* 522; *Med.* 678, 693, 701, etc.; so too *Prom.* 763, 765. But Soph. also uses this device, e.g. *OT* 1009, so this does not help us with our authorship problem.

163 *Th.* 806 and 810 by Weil's numeration, 805 and 810 by Murray's. The passage is in something of a mess, but there definitely seems to be one example of this sort of interruption after Οἰδίπου γένος (807/809).

164 The MSS ascribe *Prom.* 255-7 all to the chorus, but it seems

clear that Prometheus must speak 256. See further, on this and similar techniques in Aeschylean stichomythia, S. Ireland *Hermes* 102 (1974) 509-24.

165 *Th.* 961 in a lyric kommos (perhaps not even composed by Aeschylus) is no parallel; there is no need to divide the line.

166 I make the occurrences *Aj.* 8, *OT* 12 (twice double), *Tr.* 5, *El.* 27, *Ph.* 30 (once triple), *OK* 51.

167 See Ritchie 295ff (where unfortunately *Hkd.* appears as NINE instead of NONE): *Alk.* 3 (once double), *Med.* 1, *Hipp.* 4 (once double), *And.* 1, *Hek.* 3, *Hik.* 3, *Hks* 5, *Ion* 1 (but cf. too tro. tetr. 517ff), *El.* 4, *IT* 2, *Hel.* 1, *Pho.* 18, *Or.* 24, *Ba.* 5, *IA* 8.

168 In the discussion of the iambic utterances of the chorus, pp. 130ff.

169 P.77.

170 P.47.

171 For *Rhesos* I make the figures 3a 1b/a 4d.

172 Perhaps we should count *Prom.* 377ff (22212111 etc.) as b/a instead of d, as the single-line part has only one interruption.

173 See pp.130ff.

Chapter 7. Staging

1 Thomson's suggestion that the chorus enter the orchestra during the parodos 'pretending to fly in the dance' is not wholly convincing. 'Symbolical dance' (Thomson *ed.* 143f, citing Ar. *Poet.* 1.1447a) may well have been used to express mood and characterization, but I do not believe in 'a dance conventionally associated with the flight of sea-nymphs on their winged seahorses'; nor would this explain the complete lack of communication between the chorus and Okeanos, and Prometheus' remark 272ff. Nevertheless, we should confess that, for all we know, Thomson could be right: we simply have to rely on our instincts and on the meagre evidence available.

2 See the discussion of this scene on pp.115f.

3 See Ed. Fraenkel *Kl. Beitr.* 1.389ff, Hammond *GRBS* (1972) 423f.

4 Pickard-Cambridge *TDA* 39f, Arnott 76.

5 Wilamowitz suggested (*A. Int.* 117) that the choral lyrics of *Prom.* are 'in ganz ruhigen Rhythmen', and that the chorus must remain by Prometheus' side throughout the play. This is most improbable, and quite pointless. The metre of 128ff, and the other choral metres of *Prom.*, seem just as lively as those of most other tragedies.

6 Cf. Pickard-Cambridge *TDA* 41, Arnott 123ff, esp. 129f.

7 This must be a griffon: cf. Σ 284, also Σ Hom. *Od.* 5.453; both are probably guessing on the basis of the text. A winged horse would hardly be called οἰωνός, and the griffon is the only alternative known to carry passengers; see Orsini 498ff. The ἱππόκαμπος was not winged.

8 Hammond's suggestion (*GRBS* (1972) 423-5), that both the chorus and Okeanos enter at ground level along the *parodos* from behind Prometheus, who is fixed to the πάγος on one side of the orchestra, does not face up to their lack of communication with each other, nor to Okeanos' frequent references to flight.

9 The explanation of Arnott 77f.

10 Cf. Arnott 78, but also Hammond *GRBS* (1972) 444f (and 389-91 for a defence of Pollux's reliability).

11 Arnott 73 gives as virtually certain examples: E. *Hks* 815ff, *Ion* 1549ff, *And.* 1226ff, *El.* 1238ff, *Rhesos* 883ff, plus *Bellerophon*, *Sthenoboia*, and *Andromeda*. Yet in the extant plays only *And.* 1226ff positively demands the μηχανή; cf. too *Med.* 1317ff, *Or.* 1625ff.

12 Apparently Karkinos and his sons (who included Xenokles, another tragedian of some note), were too free with it for Aristophanes' taste; cf. *Peace* 790 with scholia.

13 Nereus sometimes rides a 'hippokampos'; the Nereids ride dolphins; Poseidon sometimes rides in a chariot drawn by winged horses, like Apollo or Helios. Other, non-nautical gods are depicted on griffons (e.g. Apollo, Dionysos), or on winged chairs (e.g. Dionysos, Hephaistos, Triptolemos?).

14 So too Hammond's reconstruction of the *mise-en-scène* of Aeschylean tragedies (*GRBS* (1972) 387ff) is too speculative to provide a real basis for argument. It is indeed interesting that a πάγος features so prominently in A. *Pers.*, *Th.*, and *Supp.*, but his conclusions, based on the archaeological evidence of the theatre itself, are far from certain; and even as late as S. *Ph.* we still find references to such a πάγος, even though, according to Hammond, the actual rock had been removed from the theatre before 420 B.C. In any case, the presence of a πάγος in *Prom.*, and the absence of references to a palace building, tell us nothing: they are demanded by the context, not the stage arrangements.

15 But cf. the discussion of the opening scenes, pp.104f, 117f.

16 See e.g. Wilamowitz *A. Int.* 114f, Stinton *Phoenix* (1974) 262. The third actor was introduced, according to ancient tradition, either by Sophocles (Ar. *Poet.* 4.1448a18, Suda *s.v.* Σοφοκλῆς, *Life* of Soph. 4, Diog. Laert. 3.56) or by Aeschylus (*Life* of Aesch. 15, Cramer *Anec. Par.* 1.19). Cf. Pickard-Cambridge *DFA* 126-31, 137-49, with further literature 330f. The chief obst-

acle to accepting two actors for *Prom.* is the need for some sort of puppet to represent Prometheus himself, into or behind which the actor who played Hephaistos would have to move between 81 and 88.

17 Only at *Ag.* 782-974, *Cho.* 875-930, *Eum.* 566 (or 397)-775, are three speaking actors required.

18 Cf. Pickard-Cambridge *DFA* 145, A.M. Dale *E. Alcestis* (Oxford 1954) xix, Page *E. Med.* xxxi.

19 For the developing sophistication of two- and three-actor dramaturgy see esp. Pickard-Cambridge *DFA* 132-48, Else *Wien. Stud.* 72 (1959) 106 and *Origin and early form of Greek tragedy* 86-100, Garvie 125-40.

Chapter 8. Vocabulary

1 Cf. the introductory remarks of Dover *Lysias* 94ff, Yule 1-9, and Williams 1-20, 64ff.

2 *G&R* (1959) 96ff.

3 Much of the material of this section is based on D.M. Clay's study, which lists the words of each class (e.g. simple nouns in -τηρ, compound verbs in -ιζω etc.), according to whether they occur in all three tragedians, two of the three, or only one. The great limitation of her study is that she does not state in which plays the listed words occur, nor how often they are used. (Nor does her 'analysis' of the lists add much of interest: it often fails even to draw attention to those interesting points which the lists themselves reveal.) So it was necessary, whenever I came across a category in which a difference was observable between Aesch. and Soph. or Eur., or both, to use the lexicons to ascertain the exact occurrence of all the words in her lists. Only then if the figures for each play confirmed that a real difference existed between Aesch. and the others, was it possible to judge where *Prom.* fitted in to the pattern. I have complete lists of the actual words in the relevant categories, but they are too long and uninteresting to be worth including here.

4 For instance, if Aesch. has twenty examples of one type, Soph. and Eur. only about eight each, a figure of four or five for *Prom.* might be due to chance: we might well find that three or four of Soph.'s examples came from one play.

5 Only A. *Ag.* is longer than 1100 lines; of Soph.'s plays, only *Tr.* (1278) is under 1350; so too most of Eur.'s are over 1200. Clay often fails to take this into account in her analysis.

6 Clay divides these into many different categories, and I began my investigation by studying each separately; but it soon became clear that the differences between Aesch. on the one hand and Soph. and Eur. on the other were consistent in the

main categories, and that a cruder generalization was likely to be more useful to us. My figures for compound adjectives therefore combine the four major categories of Clay: (1) compound adj. with suffix -ης (Clay 54-8), (2) in -τος, with prefix ἀ-, δυσ-, or εὐ- (63-6), (3) in -τος with substantive or verb prefix (66-8), (4) 'other' compound adj. (84-99). Although this last category omits a number of small categories treated separately by Clay (69-83), it nevertheless covers the vast majority of the rest of the compound adjectives. (The other small categories were examined too, but most were found to reveal no difference between the tragedians: those that do are considered later.) These four categories cover over 90% of all the compound adjectives of the three tragedians, and I therefore refer to my combined category loosely as 'compound adjectives'. See further Appendix F.

7 As we shall see, we must sometimes be careful to distinguish between *words* and *occurrences*: an author may use one word repeatedly or many words once each; and I have taken care to draw attention to this distinction where it is relevant, e.g. with the adverbs.

8 See above, n.6. I also omit from these combined figures Clay's category 'compound adj. in -τος with prepositional prefixes' (62f). This shows a different trend from the other main categories, and is treated separately later.

9 The figures for each of the four categories of compound adjective making up these totals are given in Appendix F. No obvious differences emerge from them: in each category Aesch. (and *Prom.*) outnumbers Soph. and Eur. One small but interesting detail does emerge, however, from Clay's list of compound adj. in -τος with prepositional prefixes (62f). Here Soph. consistently equals or outnumbers Aesch., whereas in all the other categories he falls short. The figures are: A. *Pers*. 5, *Th*. 3, *Supp*. 0, *Ag*. 13, *Cho*. 5, *Eum*. 9; S. *Aj*. 12, *Ant*. 10, *OT* 4, *Tr*. 11, *El*. 4, *Ph*. 6, *OK* 7; E. *Alk*. 0, *Med*. 3, *Hkd*. 1, *Hipp*. 6, *And*. 9, *Hek*. 8, *Hik*. 0, *Hks* 3, *Ion* 4, *Tro*. 8, *El*. 4, *IT* 5, *Hel*. 2, *Pho*. 5, *Or*. 2, *Ba*. 1, *IA* 5, *Kyk*. 1, *Rhesos* 3; *Prom*. 2. The figures are obviously too small to bear much weight, but it seems that we may consider this a minor detail of Sophoclean style; *Prom*. fits with Aesch. and Eur.

10 (i) Clay 102-4, (ii) Clay 101.

11 Of E. *Med*.'s 86 occurrences, four words account for 49 (κακῶς, καλῶς, ὅμως, οὕτως); the other 37 occurrences are spread over twenty-seven adverbs. Of S. *OT*'s 85 occurrences, 34 come from these same four adverbs, plus another 7 from ἀρτίως; the other 44 occurrences are spread over twenty-five words. By contrast, of A. *Ag*.'s 84 occurrences, only 23 are accounted for by the four most-used adverbs (οὕτως, καλῶς, δικαίως, φίλως), and another forty-six adverbs are used for the other 61 occurrences.

12 Of *Prom*.'s 61 occurrences, 19 are accounted for by four words

(σαφῶς, πάντως, κακῶς, τορῶς).

13 The other three are ὀρθοστάδην, συλλήβδην, ἐλίγδην, which are all unusual words, more original than those generally found in Soph. and Eur.; but cf. E. *Hks* ἐπιρροίβδην, *And.* περισταδόν.

14 This class does not include the common nouns αἷμα, ἅρμα, δῶμα, ἕρμα, ὄνομα, πῆμα, σῆμα, στόμα, σῶμα, χεῖμα, which Clay presumably does not regard as being *suffixed* with -μα. Cf. Buck and Petersen 221, who distinguish between those old words in which the -μα suffix was long-established, and those which were more self-consciously invented (often in Ionic) by the addition of the suffix, to denote 'the result of the action, as opposed to -σις denoting the action itself'.

15 The other figures are *Ag.* 64, *Cho.* 62, *Eum.* 66 per 1000.

16 The other frequencies per 1000 lines are: S. *Aj.* 34, *OT* 42, *Tr.* 38, *Ph.* 41, *OK* 40; E. *Med.* 47, *Hkd.* 38, *Hipp.* 47, *And.* 40, *Hek.* 59, *Hik.* 62, *Hks* 58, *Tro.* 47, *El.* 52, *IT* 67, *Hel.* 57, *Pho.* 65, *Or.* 61, *Ba.* 49, *IA* 56, *Rhesos* 37.

17 The other frequencies for separate words per 1000 lines are: A. *Pers.* 34, *Ag.* 39, *Cho.* 42, *Eum.* 41; S. *Aj.* 23, *OT* 27, *Tr.* 25, *Ph.* 25, *OK* 22; E. *Med.* 20, *Hkd.* 26, *Hipp.* 26, *And.* 26, *Hek.* 30, *Hik.* 42, *Hks* 34, *Ion* 38, *Tro.* 37, *El.* 35, *IT* 34, *Hel.* 31, *Pho.* 36, *Or.* 35, *Ba.* 32, *IA* 31, *Kyk.* 38, *Rhesos* 23.

18 Clay 51; cf. Buck and Petersen 216ff. Clay excludes from this category εὐδαίμων, δυσδαίμων, ἀνθρωποδαίμων, ἰσοδαίμων, ἐχθροδαίμων, on the grounds that they are not suffixed with -μων, but are merely compounds (prefix plus δαίμων). Similarly, she excludes αἵμων, αὐθαίμων, ὁμαίμων, συνομαίμων, ἀναίμων, συναίμων, πολυαίμων, ἀσήμων, on the grounds that the μ is part of the root, so that the suffix is really only -ν. I follow this distinction mainly because it enables us to exclude εὐδαίμων and δυσδαίμων, which are common in all three tragedians and therefore serve to disguise Aesch.'s distinctive preference for the rarer -μων forms. It should be noted, incidentally, that Clay omits τεθριπποβάμων (*Or.* 989) from her list for Eur.

19 E. *Tro.* and *Pho.* each have four in a greater number of lines. We note too that *Prom.* twice has μνήμων, which occurs only once in Soph., never in Eur., to raise its occurrences of -μων adjectives even higher; but cf. the previous note. In the fragments of Soph. we find: ἀμνήμων, ἀγχιτέρμων, ἀφράσμων, σκηπτροβάμων, δυστλήμων, ἀνοικτίρμων; in those of Eur. we find: μονοβάμων, ἀπράγμων.

20 Clay 60f.

21 Clay 60.

22 Clay 118f, 4A and 4B.

23 I have not investigated all of Eur.'s plays, but it is clear

that the high number of -ευω verbs is not due just to the greater bulk of his work; many of them are used repeatedly.

24 Clay 22-6; see too Ernst Fraenkel *Gesch. der gr. Nomina agentis* 2.1ff.

25 See Clay 22ff.

26 Fraenkel and Clay both suggest that -τηρ and -τωρ forms are more common in lyric than in dialogue.

27 Schmid 50 points to *Prom.*'s relative lack of -τηρ and -τωρ forms but gives no figures or comparative information to support his argument.

28 Clay 18.

29 See p.150 n.9.

30 Pp.41-50. Much of his work is based on Niedzballa. As we shall see, his figures are far from being completely reliable; but the overall impression that they give is correct.

31 P.43.

32 Schmid wrongly gives *Eum.* 35%.

33 Schmid 45. My own investigations show that his figures are not always accurate; in fact he underestimates *Prom.*'s figures slightly, and overestimates those of A. *Pers.* and *Th.*

34 I.e. with regard to occurrences of three times or more; with the other figures, some discrepancies are inevitable, but they are unlikely to be significant.

35 We should remind ourselves at this point that he is only dealing with words which occur just in one play; he does not ask how many rare epic words *overall* occur in each play. (In fact, as we shall see, *Prom.* is not unusual in this respect.) Schmid's methods are rightly criticized by Snell *DLZ* (1930) 298-302.

36 P.46; cf. Niedzballa 1-17.

37 He also gives *Pers.* ἀμαλδς, *Ag.* μῆχος, neither of which seems in fact to occur.

38 *DLZ* (1930) 298ff.

39 Some of these are from *GGL* 303 n.1.

40 See Appendix G for a discussion of Niedzballa's and Peretti's studies.

41 See Appendix H for the complete list of words. I chose *Pers.* and *Th.* because they are the same length as *Prom.*, unlike *Ag.*,

and come high in Schmid's figures, unlike *Cho.* and *Eum.*: *Supp.* has several corrupt passages in which it is very uncertain what words are occurring at all, and there is no reason to suppose that its figures would be higher than those of *Pers.* and *Th.* I took S. *Aj.* 1-1090 as a check, of the same size as the other plays. My criterion for selection of a word was generally whether or not it occurred in Murray's OCT, though where there was serious doubt as to whether a word might not occur elsewhere in Aesch.'s plays I did not count it as an *Eigenwort.* I leave the fragments out of the reckoning completely, for reasons given in Appendix G.

42 I have not counted *Th.* 1005-78 as the work of Aesch., as far as comparative Aeschylean material is concerned; i.e. if a word occurs e.g. in A. *Pers.*, and elsewhere only in *Th.* 1005 ff, I include it as an *Eigenwort.* On the other hand, in collecting *Eigenwörter* for A. *Th.* itself, I *have* counted 1005-78, simply in order to make the play similar in length to *Prom.* and *Pers.* The effect will be to increase, if anything, *Th.*'s total of *Eigenwörter*, if these lines were not composed by Aesch.

43 See the complete lists of *Eigenwörter* for each play in Appendix H.

44 The figures for (a), (b), and (c) are given in Table 7.

45 These lists are given in full in Appendix J.

46 With the exception of Ἀθῆναι in A. *Pers.*, which could easily have been used in *Eum.*

47 See e.g. Easterling *Hermes* (1973) 14-34, Schinkel *Wortwiederholung.*

48 Usually the occurrences are only two or three; in one case (*Prom.* αἰκίζω) we have four. The words I have excluded on this criterion are marked with an asterisk in Appendix J.

49 See the complete lists of the words excluded on this criterion, pp.167ff.

50 Here we can use Peretti to inform us about A. *Supp.*, *Cho.*, and *Eum.*, so that we have a fair body of evidence for comparison. See Appendix G.

51 The figures for A. *Th.* include 861-74 and 1005-78; see p.161 n.42. Without these passages, the figures are (in the same order as in the table): 487, 45, 442; 582, 83, 499; 61, 14, 47.

52 As is explained below, the figures for A. *Pers.* are distorted by the frequent use in this play of refrain and ritual repetition; the figures in brackets discount these repetitions, and thus give a fairer picture. In *Prom.* only one *Eigenwort* is thus repeated.

53 See the previous note.

54 *Th.* 170 out of 442, if we exclude 861-74, 1005ff.

55 Not counting 861-74, 1005ff.

56 Niedzballa's claim, that *Prom.*'s *Eigenwörter* contain an exceptional number of epicisms, does not bear the scrutiny of Peretti; nor is it supported by Sideras, nor by a look at the actual lists of *Eigenwörter* (cf. Appendix H).

57 Including 861-74, 1005ff; without them the figures are: 60, 14, 46; 14, 2.

58 See the description of my criteria in selecting 'significant' words, pp.162ff.

59 I do not count words repeated more than twice only in refrain (ἄνιος, διαίνω, ὀᾶ).

60 Except A. *Pers.* Ἀθῆναι; see p.163 n.46. Thus the figure for *Pers.* should really be 37, not 36.

61 See Appendix G.

62 Peretti does not consider A. *Th.* or S. *Aj.*

63 See the discussion of (iv) above, where I state my crude method, viz. to decide whether more than one of the six other plays presented a context in which the word was reasonably likely to appear; if not, I excluded the word.

64 Of these, the least specialized are ἰσόθεος (appropriate to an Oriental despot), πεζός (repeatedly contrasted with the navy), and πάμμεικτος (of the chaos of the battle).

65 Of these, ἱππικός, κυκλόω, πάταγος are borderline cases; but it is clear that ἔξοδος, ἐπακτός and συνίσταμαι all do have specialized senses: 'gate', 'invading', 'meet in combat', cf. L-S-J *s.v.*

66 Some might not agree that αὐθάδης, αὐθαδία, μαλθακίζω, προὐξεπίσταμαι or φλογωπός are too specialized. Other words which might be thought specialized but which I have included as 'significant' are: δωρεά, δωρέομαι (but cf. δῶρον, δίδωμι, both common in Aesch.); σόφισμα, σοφιστής (but cf. S. *Ph.* 14, fr. 820; E. *Hkd.* 993, *Hipp.* 921, fr. 972, *Rhesos* 924; Pindar *O.* 13. 17, *I.* 5.28 - why not Aesch. in the context of Aigisthos and Klytaimestra, or Orestes in *Cho.*?). For ἐξευρίσκω cf. S. *Aj.*, *OT*, etc.

67 Least specialized are ἐπεγγελάω and ἐπιχαίρω, which could both occur elsewhere quite easily, though Aesch.'s six plays do not give many suitable opportunities.

68 We might add ἐπίπνοια, βοῦνις, ἑσμός.

69 Plus perhaps θρεπτήριος.

70 Plus perhaps ἀντίκεντρον, προσίκτωρ.

71 Depending on whether or not we believe that ἄνιος occurs repeatedly in the play, and whether ὀᾶ is specifically Persian, and hence not 'significant'; see the list immediately below. So too *Prom.* δάμαρ may be paralleled in A. *Ag.*

72 ἄνιος may not occur at all: it does not in Page's OCT. διαίνω, ὀᾶ only occur in two separate places; the rest of their repetitions are due to refrain etc.

73 Niedzballa has done much of this work, with little tangible result. The words can be inspected in Appendixes H, J, and K.

74 *Cho.* ἀφίστημι, cf. fr. 12, fr. 80; *Prom.* ἀεικής, cf. Pap. Oxy. 2164 (= fr. 279 L-J); ἆθλος, cf. fr. 312; ἔσχατος cf. fr. 74; (σοφιστής, cf. fr. 314); S. *Aj.* ἡνίκα, cf. fr. 304; λυπέω cf. fr. 266, fr. 310.

75 As I explained earlier, these words were included as *Eigenwörter* for S. *Aj.*, excluded for A. *Pers.* and *Th.*; in this way, each play was measured against a comparable sample of six plays. See the description of my method, pp.162ff.

76 Which common-sense, and the consistency of Aesch.'s figures minus proper names, both indicate that we should.

77 Some of these words will be examined in the following section on individual words.

78 Much of the following material is based on the work of Niedzballa and Schmid, and on Groeneboom's commentary. Further references are given where relevant.

79 Unless at A. *Cho.* 326 it means 'nature', as it does in *Prom.* 80, 190, 315, 378, 678.

80 Cf. the whole ἐπιμαρτυρία of *Prom.* 88-93; see Unterberger 34 n.23.

81 See Schmid 59, Dumortier *Vocab. médical d'Esch.* 29-63, Mielke 96-101.

82 Found only once in Homer, one in *Hymn Merc.*, not in Pindar, once(?) in Bakkhylides.

83 Cf. fr. *adesp.* 519.

84 Herington 72.

85 To prove this would require a large-scale statistical study of all the major Greek authors, which might well be very interesting and rewarding. That it is true of Aesch. emerges from what follows.

86 Musurillo *CP* (1970) 175-7, Herington 63-75; cf. also Denniston *GP passim.*

87 These are quite informative for some prose authors; cf. A.Q. Morton *JRStat Soc* (1965) 184-224.

88 For A. *Th.* I excluded 1005ff.

89 Despite the plethora of brackets and question-marks in Italie, there are few seriously doubtful occurrences, never more than two or three in one play. *Prom.*'s instances are: 42, 60, 73, 77, 162, 248, 254, 256, 258, 268, 307, 335, 379, 481, 518, 622, 631, 696, 700, 746, 768, 774, 776, 871, 904, 931, 953, 961, 982, 985, 1011, 1053, 1058, 1065.

90 Schmid 74, Musurillo *CP* (1970) 176f, Herington 69-72.

91 Pp. 71f.

92 Soph. fr. 253, fr. 503; see Jebb on *Ant.* 673, Denniston *GP* 287.

93 He also mentions a few words which are not really particles, e.g. ναί (three times in *Pers.*, only elsewhere in Aesch. at *Supp.* 468?; not in *Prom.*, five times in Soph., once in E. *Alk.*, eleven times in *Med.*, etc.), and μά (A. *Ag.* once, not elsewhere in Aesch., once each in Soph. and Eur.).

94 Only A. *Th.* δῆτα, μέν, οὐκοῦν, *Supp.* ἦ, *Ag.* καί, *Eum.* γε, καίπερ, plus the examples given by Herington, are in any way remarkable in relation to the rest of Aesch.'s figures, and none of them is at all striking.

95 Only the adjective γεγωνός (*Th.* 443); cf. Fraenkel *Sitzb. Bayr. Akad.* (1957) n.58 = *Kl. Beitr.* 1.290 n.2.

96 Nearest is *Pers.* 479, a polite invitation.

97 Cf. Groeneboom on *Prom.* 563, Phrynichos *Epitome* p.387 Lobeck with note; also Dumortier *Vocab. médical d'Esch.* 70f.

98 Half of them in the fragments.

99 Schmid 72. Aesch. twice has προσδέρκομαι + direct object (*Ag.* 952, *Eum.* 167), which may count as a satisfactory parallel, though this almost equals δέρκομαι πρός + accusative; A. *Ag.* 602, *Eum.* 34 are epexegetic; *Th.* 104 is really internal.

100 See Sideras 111, Niedzballa 50.

101 See Schmid 74 for others.

102 Cf. Chantraine *Glotta* 33 (1954) 31-6.

103 More often in his later plays: *Pers.* once, *Th.* once, *Supp.* twice, *Ag.* six, *Cho.* six, *Eum.* six. See Snell *Philol. Suppl.* 20 (1928) 1-33 for a discussion of the developing sense of δράω.

104 By an anonymous pupil of Groeneboom.

105 Cf. too e.g. νιν A. *Ag.* twelve, *Cho.* fifteen, *Eum.* five, *Th.* seven - but *Pers.* one, *Supp.* two; five times in *Prom.* Further examples in Appendix L.

106 Hiltbrunner 41-3 points out how πλῆθος and πολυ- compounds are repeated in *Pers.* to build up the motif of Persian opulence and abundance. Each play has its own patterns of significant repetitions and motifs; we may compare τύραννος, νέος, ἐκπίπτω in *Prom.* *Prom.*'s fondness for repetition is treated on pp.201f.

107 Further prosaic, even at times colloquial, expressions are pointed out in the following chapter.

Chapter 9. Style and syntax

1 Cf. Kussmahly 13; Niedzballa 53f; Schmid 51.

2 See Sturm 60f.

3 Only three of Eur.'s twelve examples are thus placed; five are in resolution in the trimeter or in crasis, four in anapaests or lyrics. It is interesting that ὅτι = 'because' is differently treated by the tragedians: of Soph.'s five examples, two are lengthened by position in the trimeter, two are in lyrics, one in anapaests; A. *Eum.* 971 (Aesch.'s only instance) is in anapaests; of Eur.'s nineteen instances, four are in lyric, fifteen in resolution in the trimeter. There is thus not one instance of ὅτι = 'because' in σχῆμα Σοφοκλεῖον.

4 Aesch. uses ὡς after verbs of saying/thinking seventeen times, Soph. thirty-four times, Eur. often, *Prom.* six times (not 293).

5 Mommsen *Beiträge zu der Lehre von gr. Präpositionen*; cf. too E. Lalin's not very helpful dissertation.

6 See Mommsen 611. (μετά occurs just once in *Prom.*)

7 Mommsen 3-8 gives figures for other authors. It is interesting to note that e.g. Thucydides (400 μετά + gen. 72 σύν) differs from the non-Attic Herodotos (65 and 72) not only in his marked preference for μετά, but also in the total number of times he uses either (though Hdt. also uses ἅμα in this sense).

8 Mommsen 15-16.

9 Mommsen 19.

10 Mommsen takes this as evidence of a later reworking of *Prom.* (p.21).

11 See Mommsen 611; he gives no figures, and I have worked them out from Italie.

12 Cf. Mommsen 762-4.

13 Cf. ? *Supp.* 551, *Cho.* 415, fr. 72.

14 Homer only has about forty examples, Hesiod about ten, Pindar none.

15 See Groeneboom on *Prom.* 42, Schmid 72. Herington 53-5 rightly points out that *Prom.*'s ellipse of the first person (246) is paralleled in Aeschylus at least five times. But he does not really face up to the lack of a true parallel to the second person (A. *Supp.* 370 is not, I think; cf. C. Guiraud *REG* 76 (1963) p. xii).

16 Cf. Groeneboom on *Prom.* 1001; Schmid 71; Breitenbach 164f; Rappold *Die Gleichnisse*, *passim*.

17 Not *Ag.* 242.

18 Italie AI 2(b), ὡς *in comparatione*.

19 Cf. Kühner-Gerth 2.36, Groeneboom on *Prom.* 961, Niedzballa 51.

20 Schmid 52; Wecklein on *Prom.* 56. Also cf. Bromig 37-9, T. Gollwitzer *De asyndetis Aeschyleis* 394f, Kumaniecki 72-8.

21 We may note too φέρε + imperative *Prom.* 294, 545; not in Aeschylus; cf. Sophocles eight times φέρ' εἰπέ. But Aeschylus has ἄγε/ἄγετε + imperative four times, the same construction, and this does not seem to add up to much.

22 See Breitenbach 217ff for examples. For *Prom.* see Groeneboom on *Prom.* 266, Schmid 53-5, Schinkel 45f, Kumaniecki 67-9.

23 Niedzballa 55. For the singular the figures are unremarkable. See further B.L. Gildersleeve *Syntax of class. Greek* (New York 1911) 2.309-11.

24 Cf. Herington 40f, Stinton *Phoenix* (1974) 260.

25 We find the contrast of word and action (as at Homer *Il.* 9.443) in one form or another at A. *Pers.* 174; *Ag.* 1359, cf. 1250; and the contrast between appearance and reality phrased in other ways at *Th.* 592; *Ag.* 787, 840, 1369; *Cho.* 1053f. (*Prom.* 660, A. *Cho.* 315 are different.) See further Groeneboom on *Prom.* 336, Niedzballa 51, Heinimann 44f.

26 Niedzballa 51f; Schmid 27, 29f; see too my discussion of rhetorical 'signpost' formulae for speech-division, pp.209ff, and A.N. Michelini *Hermes* 102 (1974) 524-39.

27 See Wackernagel, esp. p.11; Niedzballa 52; Schmid 51; Chantraine 119-29; Herington 41-4.

28 Definite are *Th.* 821, *Ag.* 267, *Eum.* 587 (and *Th.* 423?). Less easy to classify are *Supp.* 246, *Eum.* 57. Similarly, of *Prom.*'s

possible examples 51, 211, 740, 821 are in-between cases.

29 See Groeneboom on *Prom.* 211, Wackernagel *Verhandl. versamm. deutsch. Philol.* (1901) 65.

30 Niedzballa 53; Groeneboom on *Prom.* 795; Kühner-Blass 2.468; Sideras 108.

31 See Rappold *Das Reflexivpronomen* 29ff.

32 Rappold 8f.

33 See Foerster 43f; also Groeneboom on *Prom.* 963, Niedzballa 55.

34 Cf. Ritchie 249; also Groeneboom on *Prom.* 86, Schmid 71.

35 See Groeneboom *ad loc.*, Breitenbach 191, 237.

36 Stevens *CQ* (1945) 95-105 considers this another colloquialism, more characteristic of Soph. or Eur. than of Aesch.; cf. *CQ* (1937) 182-91, and below, p. 201 n.51.

37 Cf. Groeneboom on *Prom.* 171; Fraenkel on A. *Ag.* 126.

38 Ritchie 253 cites eleven examples, plus *Rhesos* 762.

39 Mommsen 162f, 611.

40 In other senses cf. A. *Supp.* 339, *Ag.* 1288, *Eum.* 180 (fr. 304. 9?). See Herington 59-60, and *CR* (1964) 239f.

41 Cf. Zawadzka *Eos* (1954) 44-55; her distinction between the 'good' and 'bad' associations of τόλμα is too sharp, but I think her main point is sound.

42 See further the parallels between these two plays cited above (p. 10 n.13); and for the frequent use of αὐθαδία etc. see pp. 186f. Schmid sees in Prometheus' attitude a characteristically sophistic mood of protest; J.A. Davison *TAPA* (1949) 66-93 follows a similar line, but carries it to an absurd degree in attempting to make connections between Zeus and Perikles, Prometheus and Protagoras. For a sensible discussion see further Grossmann 170-80, 301-8.

43 Cf. Wecklein *Stud. zu. Aesch.* 18-20; further Goodwin *MT* §811, A.C. Moorhouse *CQ* 34 (1940) 70ff, Kühner-Gerth 2.218.

44 See Fraenkel and Denniston-Page *ad loc.*

45 Cf. Moorhouse *CQ* (1940) 75f and Fraenkel on *Ag.* 1171.

46 Cf. F. Birklein *Entwickl. Subst. Infin.*, esp. 10-38; also Gildersleeve *TAPA* (1878) 1-19.

47 Cf. S. Ireland *CR* 24 (1974) 2f.

48 Radermacher *Wien. Stud.* 41 (1919) 1-7; it is impossible to be sure about e.g. ἀμμένει/ἀναμένει at E. *And.* 444, *Hek.* 1281, *El.* 1397, and it is therefore dangerous to generalize about Eur.'s frequencies. Apokope of prepositions other than ἀνα- does not help us; it is generally rare, and confined mostly to Aesch., apart from κατθανεῖν and related forms.

49 Commentators on *Prom.* tend naturally to give parallels from Aesch. before any other author; they thus give the possibly false impression that *Prom.* is particularly Aeschylean.

50 I have not carried out a thorough study of the imagery of *Prom.* in relation to that of Aeschylus. Schmid's approach is much too schematic; the study of H. Mielke suggests that quantitative analysis is inconclusive; and neither van Nes nor Dumortier is much use for our purposes. Earp 168f confirms the subjective judgement, that *Prom.*'s metaphors are generally simpler, both in conception and in expression, than Aesch.'s; but I think that more could be done in this area. For the overall impression of simplicity of style in *Prom.* as compared with Aesch., see too Earp *JHS* 65 (1945) 11f, Lesky *Trag. Dichtung der Hell.* 78.

51 It does not seem to me that the findings of Stevens *CQ* (1945) 95-105, concerning colloquialisms in tragedy, really amount to very much, although they lead him to conclude that 'The *PV* in language as in some other respects is marked by certain characteristics not found in the other extant plays of Aesch. In the use of colloquial expressions there is closer approximation to the practice of the later tragedians.' But the only peculiarities which Stevens really identifies in *Prom.* are ὅπως (μή) + fut. indic. (p.100), ἀτάρ, ὡς ... γε = 'for' *Prom.* 77 (p.101), δήπου, εἶέν = 'well, all right' *Prom.* 36 (p.102), and τί οὐ *Prom.* 747 (p.103). If we were to agree with Stevens, we might add these to our list of prosaic features in *Prom.*

52 See Schmid 9-11, 46, 68-71, 74-6, and *GGL* 301; Gollwitzer 44ff, Hiltbrunner *passim* (esp. 75-7); Herington 33-5; Schinkel *passim.*

53 This is a rather different process from the repetition *close together* of particular words, discussed, with regard to Soph., by Easterling *Hermes* (1973) 14-34; see ch.8, p.163.

54 Although his confirmation of the then generally accepted early date of A. *Supp.* leads us to view his 'steady development' theory with reservations.

55 Hiltbrunner 76; Schinkel however does not find *Prom.* to be unaeschylean (169).

56 See Easterling *Hermes* (1973) 14-34, with further references.

57 See pp.207ff.

58 All these, as Schmid points out, involve the Okeanos-scene, which he finds particularly repetitious and offensive.

59 Schmid 63; E. Ahrens *passim*.

60 This is the technique favoured by Homer and Hesiod; see Ahrens 47, 100.

61 Distinctly different are: *Pers*. 690; *Supp*. 190, 386, 437, 485, 514, 973, 998; *Th*. 766; *Ag*. 264, 456, 602, 832, 862, 1365; *Eum*. 218, 233, 262, which are parallel to e.g. *Prom*. 39, 105, 685f.

62 Ahrens 120; cf. the discussion of 'Sophoclean' enjambement above, p.96.

63 A. *Pers*. 818ff, *Supp*. 707ff, 991ff, are less personal and rather different. Aesch. prefers to use more subtle introductions, τεκμήριον, λόγος, etc., e.g. *Th*. 217, 224f; *Supp*. 760f; *Ag*. 264f, 750f; *Cho*. 520f; *Eum*. 432, 447ff, 657ff, 662, etc. See also Ficker 51, for *Prom*.'s redundant 'padding' before γνῶμαι.

64 Cf. Schmid 52f, Sideras 133f; further Gygli-Wyss and Fehling *passim*, Breitenbach 221-6, Schinkel 50-3, Kumaniecki 63-5.

65 See Gygli-Wyss 13ff for a discussion of the definition and history of the term.

66 E. Norden *Die antike Kunstprosa* (Leipzig 1898) 1.25-9, 63-5.

67 *Prom*. 106, 260 are slightly different, and barely merit inclusion; cf. too *Th*. 100, 202, 427f, 566, *Ag*. 39, 1394, *Cho*. 78, 491f, 1010, etc.

68 In A. *Th*. we are particularly conscious of the ritualistic, almost magical, use of wordplay, both in Eteokles' choice of opponents at each gate (e.g. 406, 451, 458, 505, 509, 526f, 631, 674, 675), and in the lament over the brothers (e.g. 932f, 961, 963f, 971, 974, 983, 993); cf. Cameron *TAPA* 101 (1970) 95-118, Schinkel 105ff.

69 Perhaps we should not count 100, 202, 427f, 566, (1066).

70 Of which 524, 525, 526 are all of the ritualistic 'king of kings' type.

71 *Ag*. 67f, 500, 1305 do not seem strong enough to me for inclusion.

72 I do not count *Cho*. 139, 406f.

73 I do not count *Eum*. 34, 140, 679, 798.

74 This fondness for wordplay is quite a different phenomenon from the elements of refrain, repetition, and alliteration so common in the choruses of Aeschylus' plays, but so notably lacking from those of *Prom*.; cf. Kranz *Stasimon* 127ff, Höhlzle *passim*, e.g. p.105 'Klagen und Gebete und deren freiere Nachbildungen sind - ausser im *Prometheus* - in jedem Stück vorhanden.'

We might add this to our collection of unaeschylean aspects of the chorus in *Prom.*, pp.123ff.

75 The view of e.g. Peretti *Gnom.* (1940) 258-68; cf. Fraenkel *A. Ag.* p.551 n.1.

76 As most scholars seem to think, notably H. Fraenkel *NGG* (1924) 97ff, van Otterlo, Friis Johansen 31-48, Wilamowitz *A. Int.* 165 n.1, Garvie 74ff, Lesky *Trag. Dichtung der Hellenen* 92.

77 P.74; cf. Schinkel 90-102.

78 My figures for Aesch. throughout are based on Friis Johansen and Garvie.

79 N.b. too *Prom.* 443ff/469f (which is not quite a true 'frame', since 469f looks forward as well as back), and 476f/500.

80 Pp.48ff.

81 P.51. He considers A. *Eum.* 480ff to be the nearest to *Prom.*, and points out that the *Oresteia* plays are somewhat closer to *Prom.* in this respect than Aesch.'s earlier tragedies.

82 As we remarked above, signpost formulae are to some extent indispensable when speech is reported, to mark the beginning and end of the quotation or paraphrase.

83 E. *Ba.* seems to have almost none. It is interesting to note that *Rhesos* has several: *Introduction* 284, 393ff, (837); *Conclusion* 130, 215, 314ff, 420f, 640f, 948; *Transition* (432ff), (668ff), 800f; after reported speech 300.

84 Schmid 29ff saw in *Prom.* a 'rein formalistischen, spieleristischen Charakter', which greatly offended him. His collection of examples was small, and his search for parallels inefficient; but I think his judgement has some truth. But cf. Grossmann 298-301 for a defence of the dramatic (and Aeschylean) point of such devices in this play.

85 E.g. the epirrhematic parodos, 2:1 stichomythia, choric quatrains, even Prometheus' soliloquy.

86 The simplest introduction and explanation of achievements in this field are to be found in Morton and McLeman 52-64; see further W.C. Wake, C.B. Williams, G.U. Yule, K.J. Dover *Lysias*.

87 In general my methods were those of Yule and Wake, adapted for the requirements of tragedy. S. Ireland's Cambridge dissertation (1972) 'Structure, esp. of sentences in the plays of Aesch., with special ref. to *Prom.*' tends to confirm these conclusions: his Table 15 (p.254) shows no great difference between the lengths of sentence in Aesch., Soph., and Eur. In general, Ireland concludes from his computer study (p.285) that 'the tendency has been for the *Prom.* to associate itself closely with the technique of composition employed in the rest of Aesch.'.

His figures certainly confirm that the plays of Soph. and Eur. seem to have a wider range of 'types of sentence' than *Prom.* or the plays of Aesch. (cf. his p.193); his principles of definition and classification of 'sentence type' are developed from those of T.B.L. Webster *AJP* 62 (1941) 385-415, who appeared to identify certain unaeschylean complications in *Prom.* Yet Ireland himself also reveals other details of *Prom.*'s syntactical structure which do *not* fit squarely with Aesch., e.g. in 'frequency of noun amplification' (Table 13, p.241), where *Prom.* is well below Aesch.'s lowest rate, and 'participles as clause-makers' (243-7, Table 14), where *Prom.* is again lower, close to Soph. and Eur.

88 I simply took as 'sentences' the words occurring in the OCT between one major stop (colon, question-mark, or full-stop) and the next. I only studied those passages in which a speaker had at least eight lines to himself; otherwise, the demands of dialogue necessarily restrict the length of sentences.

89 See Williams 52-63 for a description of the elementary statistical procedures required.

90 I later ran a check which showed that S. *El.* had fewer long sentences than the four Sophoclean plays I first studied; even so, it had more than *Prom.* My conclusions coincide largely with those of Ireland; see above, p. 214 n. 87.

91 Cf. Schmid 75, 92ff; Skard 11-18; Kleingünther 66-90; Herington 94-7; for a sensible overall view see Grossmann 296-308.

92 See e.g. Herington 94.

93 Skard 12.

94 E.g. Prodikos B2.25, 28 DK; Ar. *Frogs* 1030ff; Isokrates *Helen* 67, *Bousiris* 24f, *Nikokles* 30; Strabo (quoting Ephoros) *Geog.* 9.3.11-12; Diodoros; Philo; Galen, etc.

95 See Schmid 95 n.2 for references; cf. too Theognis 1135ff, Herakleitos B 18 DK; also Grossmann 50-69.

96 See Dover on Ar. *Clouds* 821; Herington 95f.

97 Cf. Heinimann 92 n.5.

98 Cf. Thomson *ed.* 6ff and *CR* (1929) 3-5, Podlecki 103ff, Grossmann 170ff.

99 P.78; cf. further Thraede *Reallex. für Antike und Christentum* (Stuttgart 1962) 5.1179ff, *s.v. Erfinder.*

100 It is curious that none of the τέχναι described is closely connected with fire: Prometheus makes no mention of pottery or metal-working, his special provinces in Athens. Perhaps the rest of the trilogy filled this gap; or perhaps the author was anxious to introduce aspects of civilization which were less

obviously associated with Prometheus, so as to underline the pervasive effect of his gift.

101 P.66 n.3.

102 It is particularly interesting for the dramatic effect of the play that Prometheus does not go so far as to claim that he has given men the social virtues: they now possess τέχναι - but perhaps not yet δίκη (cf. Plato *Prot.* 322a-d). Only Zeus can instil that?

103 See e.g. Herington 95ff, Rösler *passim*; also my discussion of the external evidence, pp.9f. Although there are obvious connections between e.g. Empedokles and Gorgias, Herakleitos and Protagoras, it seems best to consider possible scientific-philosophical influences on *Prom.* separately from these sophistic elements; see pp.222f.

104 [Xen.] 'Αθ. πολ. also shows some curious similarities to *Prom.* in its combination of sophistry and archaism, of self-conscious artifice and formal simplicity.

105 In ch.2, pp.10f.

106 E. *Hks* and *Pho.*, for example, offer as many possible parallels as S. *Ant.* or E. *Hipp.*; cf. pp. 10f, and O. Krausse *De Euripide Aeschyli instauratore* (diss. Jena 1905) 58-65, 78-83, 172.

107 Especially in details of their structure; cf. ch. 6 *passim.*

108 Above, pp.9f.

109 I shall not here discuss at length the supposed Sicilian influences on *Prom.*, suggested by Focke, Bock, Herington *et al.* Here I merely summarize the main objections to their arguments; cf. too pp. 13f, on the trilogy.

110 See esp. Bock *Gymn.* (1958) 412ff, Traglia *Studi sulla lingua di Emp.* 40ff, Garvie 49-55, Herington *Phoenix* (1963) 180-97.

111 *Pace* Herington; cf. Burkert *Lore and Science* 231 n.67, 276 on Philolaos and five (?) elements, as in *Prom.*?

112 Cf. Traglia 49ff, Bock *Gymn.* (1958) 413ff, Groeneboom on *Prom.* 134, 551.

113 Cf. Breitenbach 171, Clay 70-84.

114 See Bock 413 n.68, with further literature.

115 See Herington *Phoenix* (1963) n.54; Usener *Rh. Mus.* 58 (1903) 1-47, 161-208, 321-62.

116 For a sober assessment of the influence on Aesch. of Empedokles, Anaxagoras, and Philolaos (and also Herakleitos and Xenophanes), see Rösler *passim.* F.M. Cleve *Giants of presoph.*

Gr. philos. (Hague 1969) 2.332ff argues unconvincingly for an earlier date for Empedokles.

117 See Thomson on *Prom.* 475 (his numeration), Herington 92-4. The two terms, 'Orphic' and 'Pythagorean', are beset with innumerable uncertainties, and we are largely in the dark as to what each would connote in the mid-fifth century at Athens. See esp. Burkert *Lore and Science* 97-120, 277-98, F. Graf *Eleusis und die orph. Dichtung Athens* (Berlin 1974) *passim.*

118 See Focke *Hermes* (1930) 302, Körte *NJA* (1920) 213, Bock *Gymn.* (1958) 417, 439, Herington *TAPA* (1963) 113ff; again, I only summarize my objections.

119 Herington 115-17; also *TAPA* (1963) 113ff.

120 See the discussion of resolutions in p.78 n.11.

Chapter 10. Alternatives to Aeschylean authorship

1 In fact, as we saw (pp.8f), the external evidence for each of the six undisputed plays happens to be considerably stronger.

2 See chs.3, 4, and 5.

3 See chs.6, 8, and 9.

4 E.g. the emphasis on formal arrangement and brevity of speeches, and certain unpoetical turns of phrase; cf. ch.9, esp. pp.191ff, 207ff.

5 Above all, the Okeanos-scene (see ch.6); cf. too the problems of staging (ch.7), and the role of the chorus (ch.6, pp.128ff).

6 Neither old age, nor Sicily, nor the influence of Sophocles seems at all convincing as an explanation; even together they do not add up to much. It would be better simply to confess that we know too little about Aeschylus to offer any explanation at all.

7 See ch.1. If *Prom.* were a worse play, like e.g. *Rhesos*, I am sure that Schmid's arguments would have fallen on more receptive ears.

8 For theories about this collection, compare Wilamowitz *Einleitung* 196-220 with Barrett *E. Hipp.* 50-3. The inclusion of *Rhesos*, and of *A. Supp.* (if this is more than sheer accident), suggests that the taste of the selector(s) was rather different from ours: we might have preferred e.g. Aesch.'s Ὅπλων Κρίσις or Οἰδίπους, Eur.'s Τήλεφος or Ἀνδρόμεδα?

9 This last question is peripheral to the present enquiry, but obviously of great interest in its own right; cf. ch.1, and pp. 245ff.

10 I confine myself here to discussion of dramatic performances: Schmid's suggestion of a *Lesestück*, never intended for the stage, has rightly found no favour; such plays are not attested before the fourth century, and *Prom.* displays an obvious, perhaps excessive, concern for ὄψις.

11 E.g. *Wasps* 219f, *Birds* 748ff, *Thesm.* 164ff, *Frogs* 1298ff; see further (on Phrynichos) Lloyd-Jones *Prob. early trag.* 19-21, 31-3.

12 *Hypoth.* 2 to *OT*; Aelian *Var. hist.* 2.8, who is highly indignant at Euripides' defeat, but at the same time makes it quite clear that he knows nothing at all about Xenokles. Cf. too *hypoth.* E. *Med.*, for Euphorion's defeat of Soph. and Eur. in 431 B.C.

13 See the *testimonia* in Snell *TrGF* 69-188, from which most of the following material is derived.

14 Or his son Aristias; cf. *hypoth.* A. *Th.*

15 But this is uncertain: see pp.234f. For Ion see further T.B.L. Webster *Hermes* 71 (1936) 263ff, F. Jacoby *CQ* 41 (1947) 1ff, and A. von Blumenthal *Ion von Chios* (Stuttgart 1939).

16 E.g. Ar. *Frogs* 71-9 with scholia, Suda *s.v.* Ἰοφῶν; but others apparently credited Iophon with Sophocles' *Antigone* (Σ *Londin.* Dion. Thrax 1.3 p.471 Hilgard).

17 Snell *TrGF* 84.

18 Cf. Aristophanes' parodies and references at *Wasps* 580, *Frogs* 911f, 1018ff, 1123ff; Plut. *Qu. conv.* 7.10.715e (= Gorgias 82B 24 DK); Aristotle *Poet.* 18.1456a17ff; *Life* of Aesch. 6, 19 etc.; also Séchan *Etudes* 86-101. But cf. Schmid 104f, who contends that *Prom. was* popular in the fifth and fourth centuries.

19 Cf. Ar. *Clouds* 922, *Ach.* 430ff, 497ff, *Thesm.* 1008ff, *Frogs* 53, 855, 1471; Aristotle *Poet.* 14.1453b28, 15.1454b1; see Barrett *E. Hipp.* 15ff.

20 *Poet.* 18.1456a3; cf. Else *Ar. Poet.* 326f, 526ff.

21 Else *Ar. Poet.* 526f is confident that he means Δεσμώτης, and that ἐπεισοδιώδης should be read. If so, the manner in which Aristotle refers to the play certainly suggests that he regards it as quite well-known, and the use of the singular (Προμηθεύς) would seem to indicate that he was only familiar with one Prometheus-play, and did not expect such a reference to be ambiguous.

22 *Tusc. disp.* 2.23-5 (= Aesch. fr.193).

23 See p.226 n.11.

24 Pap. Oxy. 1176 fr.39.15.20ff, cited by Snell *TrGF* 48 C18.

25 He won only four victories in his lifetime.

26 Diog. Laert. 5.88, cf. Wehrli *Die Schule des Aristoteles* (second ed., Stuttgart 1967-74) vol.7 fr.179 with commentary; n.b. too fr.170, and Herakleides' Περὶ τῶν παρ' Εὐριπίδηι καὶ Σοφοκλεῖ (fr.180).

27 [Plut.] *Dec. orat. vit.* 841f, cf. *IG* 2.2.240.

28 See Pickard-Cambridge *DFA* 70ff, 103f, Pfeiffer *Hist. class. schol.* 80ff, Jachmann *De Aristotelis didascaliis*, Reisch *RE* 5 *s.v. Didaskaliai* 394-401.

29 Diog. Laert. 5.26; cf. Oellacher *Wien. Stud.* 38 (1916) 81ff, Pickard-Cambridge *DFA* 103 n.3.

30 *IG* 2.2.2318, quoted in full, with discussion, by Pickard-Cambridge *DFA* 101-7; see too A. Wilhelm *Urkunden dramatischer Aufführungen in Athen* (Vienna 1906), Körte *CP* 1 (1906) 391ff, Capps *AJP* 21 (1900) 38ff and *Hesperia* 12 (1943) 1ff, Snell *TrGF* 22ff.

31 Cf. Capps *Hesperia* (1943) 1ff, Pickard-Cambridge *DFA* 102f.

32 The evidence concerning the procedures followed by poet and archon is scanty; but cf. e.g. Ar. *Knights* 513, *Clouds* 530ff, Plato *Symp.* 194, and Jachmann 20ff, Pickard-Cambridge *DFA* 67-71.

33 *IG* 2.2.2319-25, quoted, with discussion, by Pickard-Cambridge *DFA* 107ff; cf. C.A. Ruck *IG 2.2323: the list of the victors in comedies at the Dionysia* (Leiden 1967).

34 *IG* 14.1097ff (Pickard-Cambridge *DFA* 120ff); cf. Capps *CP* 1 (1906) 201ff, Körte *RhM* 60 (1905) 425ff.

35 *IG* 14.1097.9; σῶιαι is an equally possible restoration.

36 The question whether the poet's name or the producer's, when the two were different, appeared in Aristotle's lists, cannot be finally resolved; cf. Jachmann 1ff, Capps *AJP* 28 (1907) 187ff. It seems likely to me that he and his successors were more concerned to identify the actual author, whatever the practice may have been in the fifth century.

37 Jachmann assumes that each eponymous archon, whose responsibility it was to supervise the conduct and expenses of the City Dionysia, maintained an official record of the competitions; but there is virtually no evidence in support of this theory, except the analogy of e.g. the athletic competitions at Olympia and Delphi. (Aristotle was also involved with the records of the Pythian games, cf. Tod *Greek historical inscriptions* (second ed., Oxford 1951) 2.187, Pickard-Cambridge *DFA* 67ff.)

38 See O. Taplin *JHS* 95 (1975) 184-6, with particular reference to the four Prometheus-plays.

39 It is impossible to be certain whether any particular detail of a tragic *hypothesis* is actually the work of Aristophanes. Achelis *Philol.* (1913-14) identifies recurring phrases which may go back to an original Aristophanic pattern, but it would have been possible for this pattern to be imitated by later scholars. Recent discoveries of 'Aristophanic' *hypotheseis* on papyrus suggest that his name was given to at least two quite different types, neither of which may in fact be his work; nevertheless, it remains likely that his versions did form the basis of at least some of our extant prose *hypotheseis*. See further G. Zuntz *The political plays of Euripides* (Manchester 1955) 129-52.

40 *IG* 2.2.2318 col.1, 9-11.

41 *IG* 2.2.2318 col.2, 41-51.

42 Aelian *Var. hist.* 2.8.

43 Including perhaps Ion of Chios' *Epidemiai*, and odd references in dialogues and mimes, such as Plato *Symp.* 194 (on Agathon), or the sources of the stories about Socrates' fondness for Euripidean tragedy, and his behaviour during the performance of Ar. *Clouds* (Aelian *Var. hist.* 2.13, cf. Dover *Ar. Clouds* (Oxford 1968) xxxiii).

44 Suda *s.v.* Αἰσχύλος and Πρατίνας.

45 Suda *s.v.* Θέσπις, and Marmor Parium (Snell *TrGF* 61); cf. Pickard-Cambridge *DTC* 69ff, 294f.

46 No archon would be interested in whether or not this were a dramatist's first performance, or even his first victory. Aeschylus is not supposed to have won his first victory until 486.

47 See above, p.229.

48 Harpokration *s.v.* διδάσκαλος; ὅτι γὰρ Παντακλῆς ποιητὴς δεδήλωκεν Ἀριστοτέλης ἐν ταῖς διδασκαλίαις; Σ Ar. *Birds* 1379 ὁ δὲ Ἀριστοτέλης ἐν ταῖς διδασκαλίαις δύο [sc. Κινησίας] φησὶ γεγονέναι. These remarks show too that Aristotle's investigations extended beyond tragedy and comedy to dithyramb as well.

49 Themistios *Orat.* 26.816d; cf. Pickard-Cambridge *DTC* 78f, Else *Ar. Poet.* 149ff.

50 In the *Poetics*, Aeschylus is mentioned by name three times (4.1449a16, 18.1456a17, 22.1458b20), and his work perhaps once or twice more (18.1456a1ff, cf. 23.1459b5, 24.1460a32); in the *Rhetoric* he is not mentioned at all (though the quotation at 2.10.1388a7 is said by the scholiast to be from Aeschylus). Euripides is mentioned by name nine times in *Poet.*, twenty-one in *Rhet.*, and on several further occasions his plays are clearly quoted or referred to; cf. H. Bonitz *Index Aristotelicus* (= *Aristotelis Opera* ed. Bekker vol. 5 (Berlin 1870, repr. 1961))

p.300. Sophocles is mentioned by name eight times in *Poet.*, nine in *Rhet.*, again with further references to his plays (especially to *OT* in *Poet.*); cf. Bonitz p.689. In *Poet.* and *Rhet.* combined we find the following numbers of references by name to the other tragedians: Agathon 7, Antiphon 3, Astydamas 1, Chairemon 4, Dikaiogenes 1, Karkinos 4, Polyeides 2, Theodektes 7 (plus Kleophon 3, though he may not be a tragedian).

51 None of these is ever mentioned by Aristotle. According to T.W. Organ's *Index to Aristotle* (Princeton 1949), there are in all of Aristotle 32 references to Eur. by name, 20 to Soph., only 5 or 7 to Aesch. (including his opinion on comets 343a1ff, 344b15, if this is indeed the same Aeschylus; cf. too *Hist. an.* 9.633a18, and Aesch.'s alleged disclosure of the mysteries *Eth. Nic.* 3.2.1111a9). There are 10 references to Agathon (cf. *Eth. Nic.* 6.2.1139b10, 6.4.1140a19, *Eth. Eud.* 3.1.1230a1). These figures seem to tally with Bonitz (see previous note) as far as I have checked them.

52 Dikaiarchos wrote Ὁ τῆς Ἑλλάδος βίος (*hypoth.* E. *Med.*), and Περὶ Διονυσιακῶν ἀγώνων (or Περὶ μουσικῶν ἀγώνων); cf. F. Wehrli *Die Schule des Aristoteles* (second ed., Stuttgart 1967-74) vol.1 frs.63, 75, 76. Aristoxenos wrote Περὶ τραγικῆς ὀρχήσεως (Wehrli vol.2 frs.103-12) and, like Herakleides, Περὶ τῶν τραγῳδοποιῶν (Wehrli frs.113-16). Theophrastos wrote Περὶ κωμῳδίας, Περὶ μουσικῆς, Περὶ ποιητικῆς, Πρὸς Αἰσχύλον (Diog. Laert. 5.47ff).

53 Jachmann 32, Snell *TrGF* 208, etc.

54 In general see Wilamowitz *Einleitung* 121ff, Turner *Athenian books*, Alline *Hist. du texte de Platon* 1-64. Similar questions arise with respect to e.g. Pindar's occasional poetry, or the private speeches of the Attic orators.

55 The writing of tragedies seems often to have passed from father to son, like most occupations in archaic and classical Greece; for example, Phrynichos-Polyphrasmon, Pratinas-Aristias, Aeschylus-Euphorion, Karkinos-Xenokles, Sophocles-Iophon, Euripides-Euripides; Philokles was Aeschylus' nephew and Morsimos' father. N.b. too Simonides-Bakkhylides (nephew); cf. Burkert *Mus. Helv.* 29 (1972) for epic 'clans'.

56 For different assessments of the general rate of literacy and literary sophistication we may compare e.g. Ar. *Frogs* 53 and 114, or Plato *Apol.* 26d, with Aristotle *Poet.* 9.1451b26. Turner argues for widespread literacy in Athens in the fifth century, but the evidence is very sketchy; cf. Sedgwick *C&M* (1948) 1-9, Else *Ar. Poet.* 318f, F.D. Harvey *REG* 79 (1966) 585ff. Reading a play on a sea-voyage (*Frogs* 52f) might suggest that private consumption of tragedies in book form was widespread: but it is equally possible that Dionysos' behaviour is intended to strike the audience as unusual in its fanatical devotion to Euripides, even in the most unlikely situations.

57 Cf. Pickard-Cambridge *DFA* 51ff.

58 Cf. Sedgwick *C&M* (1948) 1-9, who concludes 'that the better classes among the audiences at Athens had a good knowledge of select lyric poetry, and considerable familiarity with recent tragedy and certain old favourites among the more ancient; that this familiarity was acquired in social and civic life far more than from books, which at that time must have been rare and expensive, and would not give the music'. The analogy of Shakespearean London may or may not be helpful: some plays made an immediate and lasting reputation for themselves and their authors (e.g. *Tamburlaine* and many of Shakespeare's tragedies and histories); others survive which appear to have attracted no attention at all. Even when a play was popular and highly regarded, its author was not necessarily accorded the same fame: *A Yorkshire Tragedy*, first produced around 1605, was soon afterwards published as a work of Shakespeare, and many others have followed it into the Shakespeare *Apocrypha*; Marlowe's *Doctor Faustus* was successful and frequently performed, yet none of the early editions (1604-16) contain his name on the title page, and all show strong signs of substantial revision and interpolation by later hands. Of course, one fundamental difference remains between Athens and London, that Elizabethan plays were generally purchased and owned by a professional acting company, which would continue to perform them as long as there was a public demand.

59 Cf. Barrett *E. Hipp.* 15-45, Dover *Ar. Clouds* (Oxford 1968) lxxx-xcviii. To judge from Aristophanes, some of Euripides' less successful tragedies still made quite a stir, and they may have continued to be read by an enthusiastic minority.

60 Aristophanes only produced under his own name after he had established himself with Δαιταλῆς and Βαβυλώνιοι, produced by Kallistratos. Most tragedians seem to have been of aristocratic, or at least distinguished, families.

61 It is not clear, from Philostr. *Vit. Apoll.* 6.11, and *Life* of Aesch. 12 (cf. Ar. *Ach.* 9ff, *Frogs* 866ff), whether a single play or a trilogy was normally revived on these occasions, nor whether the revival competed with the new productions of that year. In the fourth century, a separate category of 'old tragedies' was established, and plays of Sophocles and Euripides, and perhaps others, were revived; cf. Pickard-Cambridge *DFA* 99f, 108f.

62 Otherwise Lykourgos' edict would have had no point, and we would have no explanation for the numerous interpolations in our surviving tragic texts, ranging from single lines to wholesale rewriting or revision (as in the cases of A. *Th.* and E. *Pho.* and *IA*.).

63 In general see Pfeiffer *Hist. class. schol.* 96ff, Fraser *Ptol. Alex.* 1.312-35, with notes, Wartelle *Hist. du texte d'Esch.* 135-42, 325-36.

64 The title of Kallimachos' *Pinakes* might suggest this (see the following paragraph); it is echoed in Cramer *Anec. Par.* 4.195

Πίναξ τῶν ἐν ῥητορικῆι διαπρεψάντων etc. (The so-called 'canons' are dealt with on pp.234f.) In any case it would have been both pointless and impossible to try to include the whole of Greek literature, ancient and modern, however ambitious the royal librarians may have been.

65 According to Tzetzes *In Aristoph. proem.* 1.19 (= *CGF* p.19 Kaibel): cf. Pfeiffer *Hist. class. schol.* 105ff.

66 Galen *In Hipp. epidem. 3 comm.* 2.4.

67 See Schmidt *Pinakes des Kallim.*, Pfeiffer *Callim.* 344-50 and *Hist. class. schol.* 127ff, Fraser *Ptol. Alex.* 1.452f, Regenbogen *RE s.v. Pinax* 1455ff.

68 Cf. Pfeiffer *Callim.* 344; for their arrangement and aim, see esp. Schmidt *Pinakes des Kallim.* 49-70 (followed by Pfeiffer), Fraser *Ptol. Alex.* 2.654 n.42.

69 Cf. Fraser *Ptol. Alex.* 1.325-30, 453, and n.51 with refs.

70 Cf. *hypoth.* E. *Med.*, *hypoth.* Ar. *Ach.*, *Life* of Eur.; see too Pfeiffer *Hist. class. schol.* 288.

71 Papyrus finds confirm that Aesch., Soph., and Eur. continued to attract most of the interest in fifth-century tragedy throughout antiquity, and there is no other way to account for the paucity of references even to the names of plays by their contemporaries, let alone quotations from them, in all our sources from the third century B.C. onward; cf. Wartelle 316-36, R.A. Pack *The Greek and Latin literary texts from Greco-Roman Egypt* (second ed., Ann Arbor 1965), W.H. Willis 'A census of the literary papyri from Egypt' *GRBS* 9 (1968) 205-41. From Willis' Table VII, we see that for Aesch. twenty-eight papyri have been published, for Eur. seventy-five, for Soph. twenty. Aesch.'s relatively high figure seems to be due largely to the discovery of a batch of second-century A.D. plays and *hypotheseis* from Oxyrhynchus (Pap. Oxy. 18.2159ff = Pack 20, 21, 26-8, 33, 36, 42, 44, and Pap. Oxy. 20.2245ff = Pack 24, 25, 30, 37, 38, 40, 41, 43, 45-9); apart from this collection, only three Aeschylean papyri have turned up, whereas the Sophoclean and Euripidean fragments are spread over the whole period 300 B.C. - A.D. 700. For tragic *adespota*, the figure of thirty-seven (only three later than A.D. 300) seems quite high: but it may of course include some Sophoclean and Euripidean fragments from unknown plays; most of the rest are likely to be later than the fifth century in origin. The taste of the Roman tragedians of the Republic confined itself almost exclusively to the three, just as that of the comic poets concentrated on Menander, Diphilos, and Philemon; Aristarchos, of the late fifth century, was occasionally selected for translation or imitation (cf. Plautus *Poen.* 1, *Gloss. Latin.* 1.568), and Alexis and Poseidippos received some attention, but the Romans do not seem to have had a very wide range of their works to draw from; see further H.D. Jocelyn *Ennius* (Cambridge 1967) 3-12, 43-7, Wartelle 201ff.

72 The source of this catalogue is likely to be, at least in origin, Alexandrian, and presumably no later than about A.D. 100, by which time many of Eur.'s plays were dropping out of circulation completely. But at no time can the number of his plays have been very precisely known, since some were never produced at Athens, and would thus not be included in the *didaskaliai* (e.g. *Andromache* and *Archelaos*), while others were apparently regarded with suspicion as not being his work (e.g. *Rhesos*, *Peirithous*, etc.; see pp.240f). Similar uncertainty surrounds the correct number of Aeschylus' plays, and the Medicean *Catalogue*; see p.240.

73 See T. Birt *Das antike Buchwesen* (Berlin 1882) 430ff, Turner 18ff, F.D. Harvey *REG* 79 (1966) 585-635.

74 See pp.228ff.

75 Cf. p.233 n.64.

76 The only explicit versions of most of these selections occur in very late sources, Montfaucon *Codex Coislinianus* 387, Cramer *Anec. Par.* 4.195-7, Tzetzes *Proleg. in Lyc.* 256 M, etc.; some of the lists (e.g. of grammarians) include names from the sixth century A.D. See G. Steffen *De canone qui dicitur Aristophanis et Aristarchi* (diss. Leipzig 1876), J. Brzoska *De canone decem oratorum atticorum* (diss. Warsaw 1883), F. Susemihl *Gesch. der gr. Lit. in der Alexandrinerzeit* (Leipzig 1891) 1.444ff. The most useful general discussion is O. Kroehnert *Canonesne poetarum scriptorum artificum per antiquitatem fuerunt?* (diss. Königsberg 1897), which contains the texts of the Montfaucon and Cramer codices; cf. too Pfeiffer *Hist. class. schol.* 203ff, Fraser *Ptol. Alex.* 1.456, Radermacher *RE s.v. Kanon.*

77 Brzoska (see previous note) argues that the decad of orators was first established in Pergamum during the late second century B.C., to reinforce the supremacy of the Atticists over the Asiatics, and duly received in Rome during the first century B.C. Yet Cicero shows no sign of being aware of any such formal canon, and it is not certain that it existed much, if at all, earlier than Quintilian; cf. A.E. Douglas *Mnem.* 4 (1956) 30ff (*contra* J. Cousin *Etudes sur Quintilian* 1 (Paris 1936) 546ff). The lyric poets are more uniformly attested from an earlier date, e.g. *Anth. Pal.* 9.184, 9.571, though Quintilian 10.1.61-4 only refers to three, plus Pindar in a class of his own.

78 Cf. Dion. Hal. *De orat. ant.* 1.451, *De Isaeo* 19.625ff, *De Din.* 1.629, etc., Cicero *De orat.* 2.93, 3.28, 3.71, etc., *Brut.* 32 ff, 285, 289ff, etc. (But elsewhere Cicero gives a decad of ten early orators: Solon, Peisistratos, Kleisthenes, Themistokles, Perikles, Kleon, Alkibiades, Kritias, Theramenes, Thucydides (*Brut.* 27ff); cf. Quintilian 3.1.8ff Empedokles, Korax, Teisias, Gorgias, Thrasymachos, Prodikos, Protagoras, Euathlos, Hippias, Alkidamas; also Panaitios' judgement (Plut. *Dem.* 13.4) οὐκ ἐν τῶι κατὰ Μοιροκλέα καὶ Πολύευκτον καὶ Ὑπερείδην ἀριθμῶι τῶν ῥητόρων, ἀλλ' ἄνω μετὰ Κίμωνος καὶ Θουκυδίδου καὶ Περικλέ-

ους, ἄξιος ἦν τίθεσθαι.)

79 Cramer *Anec. Par.* 4.197 (cf. 4.195); clearly this decad at least is fairly late, and not Alexandrian in origin. So too, we find ten 'Socratici' in Diog. Laert. 2.47, of whom, apart from Plato, Xenophon, and Antisthenes, only four are counted as 'important', Aischines, Phaidon, Eukleides, and Aristippos. Panaitios would only accept Plato, Xenophon, Antisthenes, and Aischines as definitely genuine (Diog. Laert. 2.64). The list of selected φιλόσοφοι in Cramer *Anec. Par.* 4.197 separates Plato and Aristotle from all their successors, who form a most unlikely crew.

80 Cf. Anon. in Pindar (*ed.* Boeckh) 2.7-8 τινὲς δὲ καὶ τὴν Κόρινναν. The lyric ennead may be said in a sense to predate the Alexandrians, since it was presumably based on the number of the Muses; the librarians merely reflected the received opinion. If Korinna was a near-contemporary of Pindar, her poetry seems to have remained almost completely unknown until the third century B.C.; alternatively, it was only then that she composed it. See D.L. Page *Corinna* (*Soc. Prom. Hell. Stud., suppl. pap.* 6 (1953)) 65ff, K. Latte *Eranos* 53 (1955) 57-67, D.A. Campbell *Greek lyric poetry* (London 1967) 408-10. The analogy of the Alexandrian Pleiad is obvious enough, as is that of the ancient 'seven wise men': in neither case need one think of a formal 'canon'.

81 Even in the fifth century cf. Ar. *Knights* 518ff, 526, 537; Aristotle *Poet.* 5.1449b; Cramer *Anec. Par.* 4.196; Horace *Sat.* 1.4, etc.

82 Cf. A. Dain *Maia* 15 (1963) 278ff, T.B.L. Webster *AJA* 66 (1962) 333ff.

83 Cramer *Anec. Par.* 4.196.

84 Suda *s.v.* Ἀχαιος, Ἴων; cf. Snell *TrGF* 95ff.

85 His Ἐπιδημίαι and Τριαγμός (prose works) were both known by later generations, and the latter received some attention from Kallimachos (fr.449 Pf.). Of his plays, the satyric Ὀμφάλη is the most often mentioned (cf. Athen. 14.634, 10.436f); similarly there is some evidence that Achaios was best known for his satyr-plays (cf. Sutton *HSCP* 78 (1974) 116f).

86 [Longinus] Περὶ ὕψους 33.5.

87 Cf. *hypoth.* A. *Eum.* παρ' οὐδετέρωι κεῖται ἡ μυθοποιία, *hypoth. Prom.*, E. *Alk.*, *Med.*, etc., and Achelis *Philol.* (1914) 150. (For Aristophanes' relation to the 'Aristophanic' *hypotheseis*, see p. 229 n.39.) Aristarchos and Didymos are each supposed by some to have written commentaries on Ion's Ὀμφάλη (cf. Athen. 14.634), and in the second century B.C. Baton wrote Περὶ Ἴωνος τοῦ ποιητοῦ (Athen. 10.436), but their work made little impression on later generations of scholars and readers; cf. Pfeiffer *Hist. class. schol.* 223, 277.

88 Cf. Willis *GRBS* 9 (1968) 205-41, Pack nos. 1699-1738; of course some of these may come from lost plays of Soph. and Eur., but we should not push this argument too far: nobody has suggested that either of them wrote the Gyges-fragment (Pap. Oxy. 23. 2382). For an interesting analysis of the reading tastes of Greek Egypt as reflected in papyrus-finds (which are admittedly fortuitous, and possibly unrepresentative), see C.H. Roberts *Mus. Helv.* 10 (1953) 264-79, who confirms that Euripides, Menander, and Demosthenes continue to be preeminent, but that other less predictable authors do crop up until the second and third centuries A.D.

89 Aristophanes of Byzantium epitomized Aristotle's *Hist. an.*, and his *hypotheseis* seem to represent a very condensed example of the same sort of thing. The *Garland* of Meleager belongs to about 90 B.C., and it is by no means the earliest representative of its kind: for poetic anthologies of the Ptolemaic period see Pack nos. 1568, 1569, 1573-7, 1579, 1580, 1593-5, 1600-3, 1605, 1607, 1612, 1621.

90 Cf. H. Schäpfer *Plutarch und die klass. Dichter* (diss. Zurich 1950) 8-10, 42-56, W.C. Helmbold and E.N. O'Neil *Plutarch's quotations* (= *Philol. monogr.* 19, Baltimore 1959). For a favourable assessment of Plutarch's first-hand knowledge of Aesch., see Wartelle 236-51; yet even he concludes that Plutarch may never have read the *Oresteia*.

91 For example the work(s) in which Gorgias referred to A. *Th.* and put forward his theory of ἀπάτη (cf. Plut. *De aud. poet.* 15d, *De glor. Ath.* 348c, T.G. Rosenmeyer *AJP* 76 (1955) 225ff); Sophocles' Περὶ τοῦ χοροῦ (cf. Athen. 13.603ff); Glaukos of Rhegion's Περὶ Αἰσχύλου μύθων (cf. *hypoth.* A. *Pers.*) and Περὶ τῶν ἀρχαίων ποιητῶν καὶ μουσικῶν (Plut. *De mus.* 1132e, cf. 1133f); Herakleides of Pontos' Περὶ τῶν τριῶν τραγωιδοποιῶν; and of course Aristotle's work had been supplemented by that of Dikaiarchos, Aristoxenos, and Theophrastos (see p.232 n.52).

92 See p.240.

93 See p.244 n.164 for Kallimachos' judgements on problems of authenticity.

94 See e.g. Dover *Lysias* 23ff, and above, pp.238ff.

95 Cf. W. Hippenstiel *De Graecorum tragicorum principum fabularum nominibus* (diss. Marburg 1887) 12ff, Nachmanson *Der gr. Buchtitel, passim. Prom.* could equally well have been called Ὠκεανίδες; perhaps it owes its present title to the summary in the *hypothesis*, τὸ δὲ κεφαλαῖον αὐτοῦ ἐστι Προμηθέως δέσις?

96 Cf. *hypoth. Prom.* κεῖται ἡ μυθοποιία ἐν παρεκβάσει παρὰ Σοφοκλεῖ ἐν Κολχίσι, παρὰ δ' Εὐριπίδηι ὅλως οὐ κεῖται.

97 Either Πυρφόρος did not survive, or it was identical with Πυρκαεύς, or it did make its way into the collection of Aeschylus' plays, only to lapse quickly into obscurity.

98 Cf. Achelis *Philol.* (1913-14).

99 Cf. *hypoth.* A. *Eum.* 3-4 παρ' οὐδετέρωι κεῖται ἡ μυθοποιία, *hypoth. Prom.* 6-7, *hypoth.* E. *Alk.*, *Med.*, *Pho.*, *Ba.*, S. *Ant.*, *Ph.*; see Achelis *Philol.* (1914) 148f.

100 See Pfeiffer *Hist. class. schol.* 103ff. Such interest is evident as early as the sixth century B.C., e.g. in Xenophanes, and then among the sophists; cf. too Plato *Ion*. Even Aristotle traces the origins of tragedy and comedy back to Homer.

101 The χωρίζοντες first appear around Aristotle's time; cf. J.W. Kohl *De chorizontibus* (diss. Darmstadt 1917) 19f. They never became dominant in antiquity.

102 See the *testimonia* in Bethe *Homer: Kyklos* 149-98.

103 Hdt. 2.117 ... δηλοῖ ὅτι οὐκ Ὁμήρου τὰ Κύπρια ἔπεά ἐστι ἀλλ' ἄλλου τινός, cf. 4.32.

104 E.g. Athen. 8.334bc, 15.682de, Suda *s.v.* Ὅμηρος; cf. Bethe 152ff.

105 Eusebius *Chron.* 4, Proklos *Chrest.* 2 (Jahn-Michaelis *Gr. Bild.* p.111), cf. Athen. 7.277d; see Bethe 167f.

106 Cf. Aristotle *Poet.* 23.1459a30, Σ E. *Tro.* 822, Σ Pind. *N.* 6.85, Σ Lykophron 344, Pausanias 10.25.9, etc.; Bethe 169ff.

107 Pausanias 10.25.5, Eusebius *Chron.* 4, Proklos *Chrest.* 2 (J-M p.112); Bethe 179f.

108 Proklos *Chrest.* 2 (J-M p.112); Bethe 184.

109 Eusebius *Chron.* 4; but cf. *Chron.* 53, Clem. *Strom* . 6.2.25.2; Bethe 187ff.

110 E.g. Σ *Il.* 1.59, 1.71, etc.; Apollodoros (?) uses the same term to refer to the unknown author of *Meropis* (Pap. Colon. inv. 5604.2.9ff, 33ff). cf. A. Henrichs *Cron. Ercol.* 5 (1975) 23 and n.109);it goes back as far as Aristarchos, and perhaps further.

111 *Poet.* 4.1448b34ff.

112 *Poet.* 23.1459a30.

113 Cf. e.g. Σ *Londin.* Dion. Thrax (= Cramer *Anec. Ox.* 4.315f38), Suda *s.v.* Πίγρης, Clem. *Strom.* 1.4.1, etc. (for rejection of Homeric authorship); *contra*, Aristotle *Eth. Nic.* 6.1141a12 and Eustratios *ad loc.* (ed. Heylbut p.320), μνημονεύει δ' αὐτῆς (sc. *Margites*) οὐ μόνον Ἀριστοτέλης ... ἀλλὰ καὶ Ἀρχίλοχος (fr. 303 W) καὶ Κρατῖνος (fr. 332 Kock) καὶ Καλλίμαχος (fr. 397 Pf.) ἐν τῶι ἐπιγράμματι, καὶ μαρτυροῦσιν εἶναι Ὁμήρου τὸ ποίημα. Cf. also [Plato] *Alc.* 2.147b.

114 E.g. Aelian *Var. hist.* 9.15, Tzetzes *Chiliad* 13.636ff, and such

concoctions as the *Contest between Hesiod and Homer*.

115 Aristotle apparently considered at least some of the alleged work of Orpheus to be spurious; cf. Ar. fr. 7 Rose (Cic. *De nat. deor.* 1.38.107). For 'Orphic' poetry in general, see F. Graf *Eleusis und die orphische Dichtung Athens* (Berlin 1974) *passim*.

116 See the *testimonia* in Merkelbach-West *Fragmenta Hesiodea* (Oxford 1967). Pausanias 9.31.4-5 remarks that Βοιωτῶν ... (some) λέγουσιν ὡς ἄλλο Ἡσίοδος ποιήσειεν οὐδὲν ἢ τὰ Ἔργα. According to *hypoth.* Hes. *Sh. Her.*, ὑπώπτευκε δ' Ἀριστοφάνης ὡς οὐκ οὖσαν αὐτὴν Ἡσιόδου ἀλλ' ἑτέρου τινός; cf. Quint. 1.1.15.

117 The title of *Hymn* 3 is given in M as τοῦ αὐτοῦ Ὁμήρου ὕμνοι [*sic*] εἰς Ἀπόλλωνα, in DL as Ὁμήρου ὕμνος, εἰς Ἀπόλλωνα etc.; cf. Allen and Sikes *ad loc.*

118 Demosthenes, for example, died less than fifty years before the founding of the Alexandrian Library, Plato and Isokrates less than seventy years; Aeschylus had been dead nearly two hundred years.

119 Xenophon was one of the select prose authors at Alexandria, both as historian and as philosopher, it seems. The first recorded doubts of his authorship of Ἀθ.πολ. are those of Demetrios of Magnesia, of the first century B.C. (Diog. Laert. 2. 57). Pollux and Stobaios both quote from it as a work of Xenophon, and it is virtually certain that it was catalogued as his in the Library; otherwise it would presumably have perished. See further E. Kalinka *Die pseudox.* Ἀθ.πολ. (Leipzig 1913), esp. 19f, H. Frisch *The constitution of the Athenians* (Copenhagen 1942) 41-184, and G.W. Bowersock Ps. Xen. *Constitution of the Athenians* (= *suppl.* to Xen. *Scripta minora* vol.7 ed. Marchant, Loeb Class. Lib., Harvard 1968) 461ff, with further literature.

120 Most notably [Dem.] 58, which refers repeatedly to Demosthenes in the third person. Modern scholars are far from agreement about the authenticity of several Demosthenic speeches, and so apparently were ancient; the *hypotheseis* sometimes record doubt, but their sources cannot be determined (e.g. *hypoth.* [Dem.] 17, 24, 42, 58, 59); style seems to be their main criterion, but it is rather crudely applied: e.g. 17 ... τῶι Ὑπερείδου χαρακτῆρι μᾶλλον προσχωρεῖ, 59 καὶ τοῦτον τὸν λόγον οὐκ οἴονται Δημοσθένους εἶναι, ὕπτιον ὄντα καὶ πολλαχῆι τῆς τοῦ ῥήτορος δυνάμεως ἐνδεέστερον; cf. *hypoth. Rhesos* τὸν γὰρ Σοφόκλειον μᾶλλον ὑποφαίνει χαρακτῆρα.

121 Compare Dover *Lysias* with T.N. Winter 'On the corpus of Lysias' *CJ* 69 (1973) 34-40.

122 D.H. *De Lys.* 17; cf. [Plut.] *Dec. orat. vit.* 836a.

123 Harpokration *Lexicon in dec. orat. Att.*; cf. Winter *CJ* (1973) 34 n.2.

124 Photios 262 (p.489 Bekker).

125 Dover is sceptical about almost all of them; Winter is more confident that many are authentic.

126 But Dion. Hal. *De Isoc.* 18 (weighing Aristotle's testimony against that of Aphareus, Isokrates' stepson) should warn us against being too confident about this.

127 Only the *Seventh* and *Eighth Letters* now find many defenders: see (in support of Platonic authorship) L. Brandwood *RELO* 4 (1969) 1-25, G. Morrow *Plato's epistles* (New York 1962) 3-11; P. Deane *Mind* 82 (1973) 113-17, and (against it) L. Edelstein *Plato's Seventh Letter* (Leiden 1966), M. Levinson, A.Q. Morton, A.D. Winspear *Mind* 77 (1968) 309-25, N. Gulley in Fond. Hardt *Entretiens* 18 (1972), W.G. Caskey *CP* 69 (1974) 220-7; further literature in Caskey.

128 See Alline 36ff, Thesleff 11-25, with further literature.

129 Dion. Hal. *De comp. verb.* 208f; cf. Plato *Theaet.* 143ac and Anon. *In Plat. Theaet.* (*Berlin. Klass.-texte* ed. Diels-Schubart (1905) 3.28ff.

130 Cf. Alline 34-64.

131 Cf. Diog. Laert. 5.22ff, Rose *Ar. frag.*, etc.

132 See e.g. Wake *JRStat Soc* (1957) 332ff, J. Burnet *The Ethics of Ar.* (London 1900) xiff.

133 Diog. Laert. 5.92; cf. Pickard-Cambridge *DTC* 69ff. We are reminded of the success of Alberti, the Italian humanist of the early fifteenth century, in having his comedy *Philodoxeus* accepted in the highest circles as an authentic product of Republican Rome; it was more than ten years before he acknowledged his own authorship, and only in the nineteenth century did it become widely accepted; cf. M. Herrick *Italian comedy in the Renaissance* (Urbana 1960) 17.

134 Cf. Pickard-Cambridge *DTC* 63ff, Lloyd-Jones *Prob. early trag.*; his lyrics seem to have been better known than the rest of his plays, to judge from e.g. Plut. *Qu. conv.* 732f, Suda *s.v.* Φρύνιχος, [Ar.] *Probl.* 920a11, Athen. 1.22a; cf. Sedgwick *C&M* (1948) 5f for fifth-century enthusiasm too. As a result, we may have a rather distorted impression of his dramatic technique.

135 The alternatives do not seem very likely: Pergamum? Athens? Byzantium?

136 Or Αἶτναι.

137 Athen. 11.496a ... μνημονεύει αὐτῶν καὶ ὁ τὸν Πειρίθουν γράψας εἶτε Κριτίας ἐστὶν ἢ Εὐριπίδης ... None of the other ancient citations, quotations, or *hypotheseis* from any of the three

plays express any doubt but that Eur. is the author; nor does Satyros (frs. 37, 39 von Arnim). The evidence is conveniently assembled in Snell *TrGF* 170-80; cf. too Wilamowitz *Analecta Eur.* (Berlin 1875) 161ff, Page *GLP* 120ff, A. Dihle *Hermes* (forthcoming).

138 Sext. Emp. *Adv. math.* 9.54, Aët. *Plac.* 1.7 (*Doxogr.* p.298 Diels = Plut. *Plac.* 880e). Cf. Snell *TrGF* 170f, 180-2.

139 Aelian *Var. hist.* 2.8.

140 That his opinions were often challenged or supplemented cannot be doubted; for example, Aristophanes wrote Πρὸς τοὺς Καλλιμάχου Πίνακας (Athen. 9.408f, Et. Magn. 672.29; cf. too Athen. 8.336e, Dion. Hal. *De Din.* 1 (630), 11 (669)). See further, p.244 n.164.

141 See esp. Ritchie, and the review by Ed. Fraenkel *Gnom.* 37 (1965) 228ff.

142 Σ *Rhesos* 528 Κράτης ἀγνοεῖν φησὶ τὸν Εὐριπίδην τὴν περὶ τὰ μετάρσια θεωρίαν διὰ τὸ νέον ἔτι εἶναι ὅτε τὸν 'Ρῆσον ἐδίδασκε: Ritchie 18f, 53f.

143 Ritchie 29ff.

144 The play possesses an 'Aristophanic' *hyothesis* (cf. Achelis *Philol.* (1914) 152); none of the scholia express the slightest doubt that Eur. is the author; and the play (rather surprisingly, to our taste) made its way into the selection of Eur.'s ten most popular plays sometime after A.D. 100; see further Ritchie 4-59.

145 This is likely enough: let us never forget the lesson of Pap. Oxy. 2256 fr. 3 for the dating of A. *Supp.*; n.b. too the complete disagreement of modern scholars as to the date, even within fifty years, of the Gyges-fragment.

146 The reason given in antiquity for doubting Euripidean authorship seems very flimsy: the alleged Σοφοκλεῖος χαρακτὴρ is not apparent to us (*hypoth. Rhesos*; cf. *hypoth.* [Dem.] 17 etc., and p.239 n.120 above).

147 Galen *De libr.* 2.91 Marquardt; Dion. Hal. *De Isoc.* 1.85.13ff; Lucian *Ver. hist.* 2.24, etc., cf. Nachmanson 36. There was much money to be made in the sale of 'ancient' texts, both in Ptolemaic Egypt (and Pergamum), and in Imperial Rome; cf. J.E. G. Zetzel *HSCP* 77 (1973) 240-3.

148 See Nachmanson *passim*.

149 *Berliner Klass.-texte* 1. p.36.11 Διδύμου περὶ Δημοσθένους $\overline{κη}$ Φιλιππικῶν $\overline{γθ}$ πολλῶν ὦ ἄνδρες 'Αθηναῖοι $\overline{ι}$ καὶ σπουδαῖα νομίζων $\overline{ια}$ ὅτι μὲν ὦ ἄνδρες 'Αθηναῖοι Φίλιππος $\overline{ιβ}$ περὶ μὲν τοῦ παρόντος, cf. Nachmanson 43.

150 Nachmanson 9ff; the casual reference to Aristotle's Λόγοι περὶ

τῆς πρώτης φιλοσοφίας as Τὰ μέτα τὰ φυσικά produced some peculiar consequences; cf. Wackernagel *Vorles. über Syntax* 2.247 for other words coined on this false analogy.

151 E.g. [Plato] *Thirteenth Letter* 363a, Kallim. *Epigr.* 23.

152 Cf. Aristotle *Pol.* 1.4.1262b11; also Proklos *Comm. in Rep.* (1 pp.8f Kroll).

153 Herakleitos' work was also apparently called Μοῦσαι, perhaps from its dedication (Diog. Laert. 9.12); cf. Nachmanson 5ff.

154 N.b. in particular *WD* 633ff, 648ff, and the attitude shown throughout towards his brother Perses.

155 Hdt. 1.1 Ἡροδότου Ἀλικαρνησσέος ἱστορίης ἀπόδεξις ἥδε ..., Thuc. 1.1 Θουκυδίδης Ἀθηναῖος ξυνέγραψε (n.b. too the subtitles τῶι πολέμωι ... τῶιδε ὃν Θουκυδίδης ξυνέγραψεν (2.103.2, 3.116.3, 4.135.2), which serve perhaps to mark the end of a book-roll); Hekataios *FGH* 1 F1 Ἑκαταῖος Μιλήσιος ὧδε μυθεῖται· τάδε γράφω, ὥς μοι δοκεῖ ἀληθέα εἶναι; cf. Dio Prus. 53.9 (2. 112 von Arnim).

156 Thus Herakleitos or Empedokles, for instance, appears more personal in his presentation than Parmenides or Protagoras. The Σωκρατικοὶ Λόγοι which were composed in the early fourth century by Antisthenes, Aischines, Xenophon, Plato, etc., allowed a nice blend of dialectic and biography: the contrast with e.g. the *Seventh Letter*, or Aristotle's extant esoteric writings, is striking. The Pythagoreans provide a good example of total disregard for historical authenticity in favour of a higher truth.

157 Plato's *Prot.*, *Gorg.*, *Phaedr.*, etc., although themselves literary works, serve to underline the public nature of fifth-century sophistic activity; Socrates' failure to write any formal philosophical work only represents an extreme example of this general tendency to prefer the spoken word.

158 I think Turner exaggerates the extent of literacy in Athens at this time. The main basis for Wilamowitz' belief that the tragic texts themselves were the source of a flourishing book trade seems to be Aristophanes (see above, p. 232 n.56); his theory (*Einleitung* 121-30) has been widely accepted, but the evidence is very thin; cf. Sedgwick *C&M* (1948) 1-9.

159 This is frequently attested of Thespis (e.g. Marmor Parium on 534 B.C., Plut. *Solon* 29, Suda *s.v.* Θέσπις; cf. Athen. 1.22a), and it is argued by Else *Hermes* 85 (1957) 19-46 that the poet was his own protagonist right up until the institution of the actors' competition in 449 B.C.

160 Cf. Athen 14.617b (quoting Pratinas fr. 1), and Pickard-Cambridge *DTC* 17ff; here the reference is probably to dithyramb, where the music played an even greater role, or perhaps to satyric drama, but Aristophanes' literary criticisms constantly

remind us that the musical and choreographical elements of tragedy made at least as great an impression as the purely verbal. As for the fame of the choregos, the analogies of Greek athletics (in which the owner, not the driver of the chariot and horses, received the public acclaim), and of Roman festivals, are borne out by the emphasis found in the orators and elsewhere on *choregia*. So too, in a modern film or TV drama, the writer of the screenplay rarely receives as much attention as the actors and director.

161 A similar lack of concern is evident in the early printed books, in which the author's name is often not even included on the title-page. In the case of religious or semi-religious pseudepigraphy (e.g. the synoptic gospels, or Pythagorean and Orphic writings), the motives for ascribing one's work to a revered master are obvious enough; cf. Fondation Hardt *Entretiens* 18 (1972) *passim*. But this is rather different from the mere lack of concern apparently demonstrated by many ancient authors. In the area of drama, for instance, there was no particular reason for the authors of the Roman *Octavia* or the Elizabethan *Edward III* to remain anonymous: they seem simply to have found no reason to flaunt their names abroad. For fifth-century Athens, we can trace the growth of individual self-consciousness, giving rise to the greater desire for personal recognition, in the portraiture and victory *stelai*: at first rigidly stylized and conventional, they gradually begin to reflect the personalities and idiosyncracies of their subjects.

162 Similar problems confronted Cicero and his successors, e.g. *De Orat*. 2.93, *Brut*. 27, 44 (on the authenticity of alleged orations of Perikles; cf. Quint. 3.1.12, 12.2.22, Plut. *Per*. 8), *Brut*. 61-2, 99, 205 (concerning more recent Roman authors). See further A.E. Douglas *Cicero Brutus* (Oxford 1966) *ad loc*. and intro. xlv-lii.

163 The texts of Menander, and even of Ar. *Ploutos*, merely indicate χοροῦ at the point at which a musical interlude interrupted the dialogue; so too, a third-century B.C. papyrus of E. *Hipp*. (Pap. Sorbonne 2252) omits choral passages completely. It is almost certain that Hellenistic tragedians continued the practice already found in Agathon (Ar. *Poet*. 18.1456a29), of limiting the chorus to irrelevancies and ἐμβόλιμα; cf. Else *Ar. Poet*. 554ff. It is noticeable that Aristotle pays much less attention to μελοποιία than Plato does (e.g. in his educational programme in *Rep*.); and we cannot even be sure that Aristophanes of Byzantium, who first arranged the choral lyrics of tragedy according to their metrical cola, knew much more about the nature of Aeschylean song and dance than we do. Certainly the metrical analyses of Hephaistion (*c*. A.D. 150) seem pretty crude, and if they go back to any Alexandrian theories of metrics they do not suggest that these were very advanced.

164 Ancient references to Kallimachos' *Echtheitskritik* are few (cf. Schmidt *Pinakes des Kallim*. 91-8, Dover *Lysias* 23ff): only frs. 437, 442, 444, 445, 446, 449, 451 Pf. mention Kallim.

as having passed judgement on particular works, and of these frs. 437, 444, 445, and 446 do not involve any 'criticism - Kallim. may merely have given the works to the different authors without comment, and without being aware of any problem. Only fr. 442 Pf. (= Diog. Laert. 9.23) ... οἱ δὲ Πυθαγόραν. Καλλίμαχος δέ φησι μὴ εἶναι αὐτοῦ τὸ ποίημα, fr. 449 (= Harpokr. *s.v.* Ἴων, on the Τριαγμός; cf. *FGH* 392 F 24 with commentary, Burkert *Lore and science* 129 n.50, A. von Blumenthal *Ion von Chios* (Stuttgart 1939) fr. 1, fr. 24) ὅπερ Καλλίμαχος ἀντιλέγεσθαί φησιν ..., and fr. 451 (= Σ Eur. *And.* 445) ὁ δὲ Καλλίμαχος ἐπιγραφῆναί φησι τῆι τραγωιδίαι Δημοκράτην, imply a positive choice on Kallim.'s part *not* to give a work to an author who had some claim. In none of these instances does he appear to have examined the problem very thoroughly, nor would the choice have been at all difficult. For discussion of the size and organization of the Library in the third century B.C., see Schmidt *Pinakes des Kallim.* 29-45, Fraser *Ptol. Alex.* 1.320ff, Regenbogen *RE s.v. Pinax* 1418ff.

165 There is no reference in all the tragic scholia or *hypotheseis* to a τριλογία (but cf. Ar. *Frogs* 1155 and Σ *Frogs* 1124); nor do the old scholia to A. *Ag.*, *Cho.*, and *Eum.* show any awareness that the plays were performed together. The terms τριλογία and τετραλογία were probably coined to describe the Alexandrian groupings of Platonic dialogues and of Attic orations; cf. Alline 84-6, 112-24, Pfeiffer *Hist. class. schol.* 196f. The alphabetical cataloguing of plays would tend to encourage their separation; cf. ch.2, pp.15f.

166 It seems that Kallimachos' Πίνακες were probably alphabetical, within their different categories (epic, tragedy, history, etc.); cf. the Medicean *Catalogue* of Aesch.'s plays, and Schmidt *Pinakes des Kallim.* 46-66.

167 See pp.13ff.

168 See ch.2, on the trilogy, pp.14f.

169 Above all, Prom. 1-38, 193-258, 347-76, 442-506.

170 As both Gercke and Schmid concluded; Herington (123ff) regards Schmid's arguments here as 'grotesque', and takes the unity of Δεσμώτης and Λυόμενος as certain; but cf. now O. Taplin *JHS* 95 (1975) 184-6, who argues from the titles of the plays that they did not form a trilogy: if it was the Alexandrians who first gave distinguishing epithets to plays of the same name (e.g. Τύραννος and ὁ ἐν Κολῶνωι for the two Sophoclean Oedipus-plays, etc.), then these three plays must each hitherto have been known simply as Προμηθεύς, a situation unparalleled for any known trilogy.

171 Cf. ch.4, pp.70f.

172 Cf. ch.5, pp.76f.

173 Cf. ch.9, p.195.

174 Cf. ch.8, p.170.

175 Arrian reads ἐσοψόμενοι in quoting this passage.

176 See Herington *Phoenix* (1963) for further suggested parallels between the larger aspects of the two plays, based mainly on Ar. *Birds*.

177 Athen. 15.674d (= Aesch. fr. 202) Αἰσχύλος δ' ἐν τῶι Λυομένωι Προμηθεῖ σαφῶς φησιν ὅτι ἐπὶ τιμῆι τοῦ Προμηθέως τὸν στέφανον περιτίθεμεν τῆι κεφαλῆι ἀντίποινα τοῦ ἐκείνου δεσμοῦ.

178 See Unterberger *passim*, who rightly stresses the importance of these references to the future and to Zeus' youth and the newness of the tyranny.

179 *Hypoth.* A. *Pers.*; see further Lloyd-Jones *Prob. early trag.*

180 Cf. E.A. Thompson *CQ* 38 (1944) 10-14, and Page *E. Medea* xxx-xxxvi.

181 Suggested dates range from *c.* 500 B.C. to *c.* 300 B.C.; for good discussions see D.L. Page *A new chapter in the history of Greek tragedy* (Cambridge 1951), Lloyd-Jones *Prob. early trag.* 24-30 (both for an early date), and A. Lesky *Hermes* 81 (1953) 1-10, K. Latte *Eranos* 48 (1950) 136 (arguing for the Hellenistic period).

182 *Poet.* 9.1451b26, 13.1453a18.

183 There are no less than eight known Oedipus-plays from the fifth and fourth centuries, not counting those of Aesch., Soph., and Eur.; so too we find several *Alkmaions*, *Orestes*, etc.; cf. Else *Ar. Poet.* 391ff.

184 The Roman theatre is the most obvious example; but many Elizabethan dramatists stole shamelessly from each other. One conspicuous example is Robert Greene, who accused Shakespeare ('an upstart crow beautified with our feathers') of dependency on the work of others for his own glory (whether as actor of their plays, or as plagiarizer in his own compositions is not clear: the former seems more likely), but who himself wrote *Alphonsus, King of Aragon* in an attempt to cash in on the enormous popularity of *Tamburlaine*. Cf. too the anonymous *True tragedy of Richard III*, *King Leir*, *The taming of a shrew*, *The troublesome reign of King John*, *The famous victories of Henry V*, and the presumed *Ur-Hamlet*: for none of these is the precise relationship to Shakespeare established. Further references in T.P. Logan and D.S. Smith (edd.) *The predecessors of Shakespeare* (Univ. Nebraska 1973) 161ff. At a more subtle level, we could compare Marlowe's 'adaptation' of *Aeneid IV* in *Dido, Queen of Carthage*, which includes direct quotations from Virgil and presupposes the audience's familiarity with the original, or Dryden's version of Shakespeare's play about Antony and Cleopatra, *All for love*; his *Troylus and Cressida* is again quite a different sort of adaptation.

185 Cf. e.g. the *Dionysalexandros* and *Ploutoi* of Kratinos, and perhaps Hermippos' *Europe*?

186 Marlowe's second part to *Tamburlaine*, and the second and third parts of Shakespeare's *Henry VI*, are examples of the latter; each in turn found a number of imitators (cf.n.184 above).

187 *Prom.* 331 may possibly provide a sole exception, but cannot bear the weight of any argument.

188 It was this, and the defiant independence of the humanitarian hero, which appealed so much to Shelley and Goethe: man had outgrown the need for god, and god could now be replaced. It has not always been possible to exclude all traces of this Romantic view from discussions of *Prom.*, and the results have been sometimes rather confusing.

189 Schmid could not believe that an archon of the fifth century would have granted a chorus to such a play: hence his theory of a *Lesedrama*.

190 See ch.2, pp.14ff.

191 This had been a regular feature of the myth at least since Stesichoros, and had apparently made a great impression on the theatre-going public (cf. *Life* of Aesch. 9 τινὲς δὲ φασὶν ἐν τῆι ἐπιδείξει τῶν Εὐμενίδων σποράδην εἰσαγαγόντα τὸν χορὸν τοσοῦτον ἐκπλῆξαι τὸν δῆμον ὥστε τὰ μὲν νήπια ἐκφῦξαι, τὰ δὲ ἔμβρυα ἐξαμβλωθῆναι).

192 J.T. Sheppard's attempt to deny this, recently revived by J.H. Kells *Sophocles Electra* (Cambridge 1973) 1-12, flies in the face of all the evidence of the play itself, and has rightly found few followers.

193 The story, i.e. the raw material of myth, is open to many different presentations and interpretations, but Sophocles' *OT* undeniably remains the most famous, the most harrowing, and (by most definitions of the term) the most tragic, of all. The multiplicity of explanations, condemnations, and justifications of the 'morality' of the play correspond in many respects to those offered for *Prom.*

194 1264ff αἴρετ', ὀπαδοί, /μεγάλην μὲν ἐμοὶ/τούτων θέμενοι/ συγγνωμοσύνην, /μεγάλην δὲ θεῶν/ἀγνωμοσύνην/εἰδότες ἔργων τῶν/ πρασσομένων, /οἳ φύσαντες/καὶ κληιζόμενοι/πατέρες τοιαῦτ'/ ἐφορῶσι πάθη ... κοὐδὲν τούτων/ὅ τι μὴ Ζεύς. Speaker and authenticity are both uncertain; cf. pp.113f.

195 The vase-painters did not shrink from depicting Zeus in pursuit of mortal women; and Xenophanes clearly regarded many poetical representations of him as demeaning and degrading.

196 Cf. Reinhardt's remarks on the almost comic nature of the trial scene in this play (*Aischylos* 144ff).

197 The literature on Aeschylean religion and theodicy is voluminous; it has abated slightly over the last few years, as critics have accepted that a dramatist's treatment of moral 'problems' is essentially different from a philosopher's, or even a gnomic poet's. The 'problem' of Zeus, Dike, and revenge in the *Oresteia* is 'answered' in dramatic terms, as is that of the ghost and revenge in *Hamlet* (cf. E. Prosser *Hamlet and revenge* (Stanford 1951) *passim*), or of love vs duty in *Antony and Cleopatra*.

198 See e.g. W. Kaufmann-Bühler *Begriff und Funktion der Dike* (Heidelberg 1951).

199 Cf. Pindar *I.* 8.30ff.

200 See pp.16f.

201 The subject-matter itself argues strongly for this; cf. ch.2, pp.14f.

202 Cf. ch.9, esp. pp.207ff.

203 Cf. Plato *Prot.* 320ff.

204 Cf. pp. 9f (three-word trimeters), pp.149ff (compound adjectives), pp. 200f, and the frequent parallels cited by the commentators.

205 Cf. the parallels referred to in ch.2, pp.10f.

206 Cf. ch.2, pp. 9f (Pindar), ch.9, p.222 (Empedokles etc.).

207 Cf. ch.7.

208 These trios may seem glib or silly, but it is hard to pin down more precisely the nature of the surface clarity of *Prom.*'s *rheseis*, and the simplicity of the odes, than by such subjective comparisons.

209 Cf. ch.6, pp.123ff.

210 Between 458 (*Oresteia*) and 431 (*Medea*) we possess only one drama, the atypical *Alkestis*, unless *Rhesos* or S. *Aj.*, *Ant.*, or *Tr.* are to be dated to this period. From the prose writers, Herodotos must have been in the process of composition during the 440s, and so perhaps was the author of the Ἀθ.πολ.; otherwise we have no Athenian literature except fragments.

211 What we know of his style would not fit *Prom.*; and see p.235 n.85.

212 As E.R. Dodds had suggested (*Ancient concept of progress* 26ff). This might seem to bring us full circle back to the revision-theory of Westphal and the nineteenth century (see ch.1); but the difference is important: whoever was responsible for *Prom.* as we know it did not simply alter a complete Aeschylean play

to suit his own (and his audience's) requirements; he composed a unified and independent drama of his own, even if it was built around an Aeschylean skeleton. The play is essentially his, not Aeschylus'.

Appendix A. Metrical symbols and abbreviations

1 See e.g. Dale *LM* 131ff, 216.

2 Cf. Dale *LM* 178-80 for a description of this system of notation, which was established by Maas.

3 Cf. Dale *LM* 139.

4 Dale *LM* 179, cf. 177.

5 Cf. Dale *LM* 115, Conomis *Hermes* (1964) 28ff.

Appendix B. Prom. 165f = 184f and the clausular ithyphallic

1 For –⏑–⏑– in lyric iambic contexts see too Dale *LM* 114f.

2 The MSS reading of this strophe gives (QTr) ⏑–⏑– –⏑– –⏑⏑– –⏑–⏑ –⏑⏑–⏑̱–. If this were retained (instead of introducing Hermann's γαῖα), and δ' removed from 744, we should have: ⏑–⏑– –⏑– –⏑⏑– –⏑–× ‖ (ia. cr. chor. tro.//; n.b. rhetorical pause in both str. and ant.), followed by καὶ χθονία κόνις ∼ αἰῶν' ἐς τρίτον (or αἰῶ δ' ἐς τρίτον (Tucker)) –⏑̱⏑̱–⏑– (dochmiac), and then ⏑–⏑– –⏑–⏑–⏑– etc. (ia. lek.). The dochmiac would be rather lonely (though this play rarely goes for long without dochmiacs occurring; cf. 888ff, 937ff), and the trochaic metron 736 slightly unusual; but cf. S. *Ph*. 1181.

3 See Denniston *Lyric iamb*. 133.

4 *Lyric iamb*. 129, with possible parallels for ⏑–⏑–⏑–.

5 ματαία seems wrong: it is a curious term of address for a chorus to direct to a sympathetic character at this point (cf. 863). ἐπεῖδες ματαίαν τάνδ' ὕβριν;, with μάταιος in the sense 'profane' (L-S-J *s.v.* II, cf. A. *Eum*. 337) might be better, but the trimeter form 2 ba. cr. (or ia.) is very rare (Denniston 126 gives only E. *El*. 1190).

6 See too Pohlsander's remarks on S. *El*. 1273 and *Tr*. 888f.

7 *GV* 534.

8 *LM* 114.

9 *GV* 159f.

10 See Denniston *Lyric iamb*. 124 for the freedom of responsion of the first syllable.

11 The continuation is metrically uncertain: Murray's colometry demands the coincidence of four *breves in longo* (1028, 1029, 1052, 1053); Wilamowitz' πνῖγος (*GV* 177) might be preferable. In either case, the ithyphallic is not affected.

12 I reject A. *Ag.* 374, *Supp.* 136=147, *Cho.* 78; S. *OK* 1725=1739; E. *Pho.* 685ff.

13 *Rh. Mus.* (1917) 334.

14 Cf. Wilamowitz *Timotheus. Die Perser* (Leipzig 1903) 103.

15 *A. Ag.* p.58.

Appendix C. Prom. 571ff and the aristophanean

1 So Wilamowitz, Murray, Page.

2 Though in the antistrophe a pause would be quite natural.

3 See Conomis *Hermes* (1964) 28ff.

4 But see Appendix D, p.265.

5 *Hermes* (1964) 28ff.

Appendix D. Prom. 580 = 599

1 *LM* 108.

2 *CR* (1965) 145f.

3 Stinton's analysis of E. *IT* 828f demands a *brevis in longo* which is, according to Conomis *Hermes* (1964) 45, impossible. *Prom.* 575 νόμο̊ν˙// however, before punctuation, is not unusual.

4 *Lyric iamb.* 125.

5 A. *Pers.* 282 (2 ia. ba. cr., ––––⏑– , chor. cr. ba.) seems to give a molossus as an iambic metron, but is emended by Hermann, Broadhead, *et al.*; *Ag.* 146 παιᾶνα// is scanned by Denniston-Page as ⏑–– (bacchiac), cf. Bakkhylides 17 (16).129.

6 Cf. E. *Hks* 880ff, after 2cr. 7do. 2ba., 3ia. –⏑⏑–⏑–⏑–⏑–⏑⏑––; and 1069, after 4do. 4(ia. ba.), ⏑–⏑⏑–⏑–⏑⏑–⏑⏑– ; *Hek.* 1091 ff 2do. 3ia. ⏑–⏑–⏑–⏑⏑–⏑– ⏑–⏑– –⏑–⏑⏑–⏑– (i.e. ia. tel. ia. glyc.); and see too *And.* 841ff, 861f, *Alk.* 400, *Ion* 499ff, 1448ff, *Tro.* 313f, *Hel.* 657, 680f, 688, *Or.* 1246, *Ba.* 1174.

Appendix E. Prom. 691

1 *Coll. and inv.* 134.

2 See L-S-J *s.v.* λῦμα; but cf. E. *Tro.* 591, and λύμη.

3 Conomis *Hermes* (1964) 25f.

4 Conomis *Hermes* (1964) 23, 26.

Appendix G. The vocabulary studies of Niedzballa and Peretti

1 Any newly discovered play of Aeschylus would immediately present us with hundreds of words previously not thought to belong to his 'vocabulary': see the introductory remarks to ch.8.

2 Thus N. does not list e.g. δαρόν (cf. δαρός *Supp.* 516), ἀσμένως (cf. ἄσμενος *Pers.* 736), λαμπρῶς (cf. λαμπρός *Pers.* 504, four times in *Ag.*, etc.); nor ἆθλος (fr. 312.2), διορίζω (fr. 182. 2), ἔσχατος (fr. 74.2), etc.

3 E.g. θῶκος? (cf. θᾶκος), ἐπαοιδή (cf. ἐπωιδή), κράτιστος (cf. κρείσσων), φέρτερος (cf. φέριστος), Χάλυψ and Χάλυβες, ἐκπίτνω and ἐκπίπτω, etc.

4 'Observazione sulla lingua del Prom.' *Stud. Ital.* (1927) 165-231.

5 Nobody would suggest that anyone who used the word 'object' must therefore have also in his vocabulary such words as 'project', 'reject', 'interject', etc.

6 The words are listed in Appendix J; see too pp.166ff.

7 See pp.162f.

BIBLIOGRAPHY

I TEXTS AND EDITIONS

For Aeschylus, unless I specify otherwise, I have used the Oxford Classical Text (OCT) of G. Murray (second ed., Oxford 1955)

For Sophocles, the OCT of A.C. Pearson (Oxford 1924)

For Euripides, the OCT of G. Murray (Oxford 1902-9)

I also refer at times to the following:

U. von Wilamowitz-Moellendorff *Aeschylus Tragoediae* (Berlin 1914)

P. Mazon *Eschyle* vol.1 (Budé, Paris 1920)

D.L. Page *Aeschyli Tragoediae* (Oxford 1972)

For the fragments of the tragedians, I use A. Nauck *Tragicorum Graecorum Fragmenta* (second ed., Leipzig 1889)

I also refer at times to the following:

For Aeschylus: [M] H.J. Mette *Die Fragmente der Tragödien des Aischylos* (Berlin 1959)

[L-J] H. Lloyd-Jones *Appendix* to H.W. Smyth *Aeschylus* vol.II (Loeb Classical Library, Harvard 1963)

For Sophocles: [P] A.C. Pearson *The fragments of Sophocles* (Cambridge 1917)

For *Prometheus Bound*, I refer to the following editions:

N. Wecklein *Aeschylus Prometheus* (tr. F.D. Allen, Boston 1893)

E.E. Sikes and S.J.B.W. Willson *Aeschylus: Prometheus Vinctus* (London 1908)

P. Groeneboom *Aeschylus' Prometheus* (Groningen 1928, repr. Amsterdam 1966)

G. Thomson *Aeschylus: The Prometheus Bound* (Cambridge 1932)

H.J. Rose *A commentary on the surviving plays of Aeschylus* (Amsterdam 1957)

Other Greek authors, unless I indicate otherwise, are cited according to the relevant OCT.

II ABBREVIATIONS

DK H. Diels *Die Fragmente der Vorsokratiker* (fifth ed., revised by W. Kranz, Berlin 1934-7)

FGH F. Jacoby *Die Fragmente der griechischen Historiker* (Berlin 1923-)

IG *Inscriptiones Graecae* (Berlin 1873-)

L-S-J H.G. Liddell and R. Scott *A Greek-English Lexicon* (ninth ed., revised by H. Stuart Jones, Oxford 1940)

PMG D.L. Page *Poetae Melici Graeci* (Oxford 1962)

RE Paulys *Realencyclopädie der classischen Altertumswissenschaft* (new ed., Stuttgart 1893-)

TrGF B. Snell *Tragicorum Graecorum Fragmenta*, vol.I (Göttingen 1971)

Abbreviations of periodicals generally follow the practice of *L'Année philologique* or of O. Laistner *Internationale Titelabkürzungen* (Osnabrück 1970).

III BOOKS AND ARTICLES WHICH HAVE HELPED ME IN MY INVESTIGATIONS; MOST OF THEM ARE REFERRED TO AT THE RELEVANT POINT IN THE TEXT

Achelis, T.O.H. 'De Aristophanis Byzantii argumentis fabularum' *Philol.* 72 (1913) 414ff, 518ff, and 73 (1914) 122ff

Adams, S.M. 'The four elements in *PV*' *CP* 28 (1933) 97-103

Ahrens, E. *Gnomen in griechischer Dichtung* (diss. Halle 1937)

Allen, J.T. and Italie, G. *A concordance to Euripides* (Berkeley 1954)

Alline, H. *Histoire du texte de Platon* (Paris 1915)

Aly, W. *De Aeschyli copia verborum capita selecta* (Berlin 1906)

Arnott, P. *Greek scenic conventions in the fifth century* (Oxford 1962)

Barner, W. 'Die Monodie', in *Die Bauformen der griechischen Tragödie* (ed. W. Jens, Munich 1971)

Barrett, W.S. *Euripides Hippolytos* (Oxford 1964)

Beazley, J.D. *Attic red-figure vase-painters* (Oxford 1942) [*ARV*]

Becker, H.T. *Aischylos in der griechischen Komödie* (diss. Darmstadt 1914)

Bergson, L. *L'épithète ornamentale dans Eschyle, Sophocle, et Euripide* (diss. Upsala 1956)

Bethe, E. *Prolegomena zur Geschichte des Theaters im Althertum* (Leipzig 1896)

Bethe, E. *Homer, Band* II, *Teil* II: *Kyklos* (Leipzig 1929)

Bock, M. 'Aischylos und Akragas' *Gymnasium* 65 (1958) 402-50

Breitenbach, W. *Untersuchungen zur Sprache der Euripideischen Lyrik* (Stuttgart 1934, repr. Hildesheim 1967)

Broadhead, H.D. *The Persae of Aeschylus* (Cambridge 1960)

Bromig, G. *De asyndeti natura et apud Aeschylum usu* (diss. Aschendorff 1879)

Buck, C.D. and Petersen, W. *A reverse index of Greek nouns and adjectives* (Chicago 1944)

Burkert, W. *Lore and science in ancient Pythagoreanism* (tr. E.L. Minar, Jr, Harvard 1972)

Cataudella, Q. 'Eschilo in Sicilia' *Dioniso* 37 (1963) 5-24

Ceadel, E.B. 'Resolved feet in the trimeters of Euripides' *CQ* 35 (1941) 66-89

Chantraine, P. *Histoire du parfait grec* (Paris 1927)

Clay, D.M. *A formal analysis of the vocabularies of Aeschylus, Sophocles, and Euripides* (Minneapolis and Athens 1958, 1960)

Coman, J. *L'authenticité du Promethée enchaîné* (Bucharest 1943)

Conomis, N.C. 'The dochmiacs of Greek drama' *Hermes* 92 (1964) 23-50

Dale, A.M. *The lyric metres of Greek drama* (second ed., Cambridge 1968)

Davison, J.A. 'The date of the *Prometheia*' *TAPA* 80 (1949) 66-93

Dawe, R.D. *The collation and investigation of manuscripts of Aeschylus* (Cambridge 1964)

Dawe, R.D. *Repertory of conjectures on Aeschylus* (Leiden 1965)

Deckinger, H. *Die Darstellung der persönlichen Motive beim Aischylos und Sophokles* (diss. Leipzig 1911)

Denniston, J.D. 'Lyric iambics in Greek drama', in *Greek poetry and life*: essays presented to Gilbert Murray (Oxford 1936)

Denniston, J.D. 'Pauses in the tragic senarius' *CQ* 30 (1936) 73-9, 192

Denniston, J.D. *The Greek particles* (second ed., Oxford 1954) [*GP*]

Denniston, J.D. *Aeschylus Agamemnon* (with D.L. Page, Oxford 1957)

Descroix, J. *Le trimètre iambique* (Macon 1931)

Deubner, L. *Attische Feste* (Hildesheim 1959)

Dodds, E.R. 'The *PV* and the progress of scholarship', in *The ancient concept of progress* (Oxford 1973)

Donovan, B.E. '*Prometheus Bound* 114-117 reconsidered' *HSCP* 77 (1973) 125-7

Dover, K.J. *Lysias and the corpus Lysiacum* (Berkeley 1970)

Dumortier, J. *Le vocabulaire médical d'Eschyle et les écrits hippocratiques* (Paris 1935)

Dumortier, J. *Les images dans la poésie d'Eschyle* (Paris 1935)

Duysinx, F. 'Les passages lyriques dans le *Promethée enchaîné* d'Eschyle' *AC* 34 (1965) 47-83

Earp, F.R. *The style of Aeschylus* (Cambridge 1948)

Easterling, P.E. 'Repetition in Sophocles' *Hermes* 101 (1973) 14-34

Eckhart, L. *s.v. Prometheus* [*RE*] (1957) 702-30

Eitrem, S. 'De Prometheo' *Eranos* 44 (1946) 14-19

Ellendt, F. *Lexicon Sophocleum* (second ed., Berlin 1872)

Else, G.F. *Aristotle's Poetics: the argument* (Harvard 1957)

Else, G.F. *The origin and early form of Greek tragedy* (New York 1972)

Engelmann, R. 'Die Io-sage' *Jahrb. Deutsch. Arch. Inst.* 18 (1903) 37-58

Farnell, L.R. *The cults of the Greek states* (Oxford 1909)

Farnell, L.R. 'The paradox of the *PV*' *JHS* 53 (1933) 40-50

Fauth, E. *Ueber Beziehung zwischen Rhythmos, Inhalt, und Aktion in den Cantica des griechischen Dramas* (diss. Göttingen 1953)

Felde, J. zum *De Aeschyli Prometheo quaestiones* (diss. Göttingen 1914)

Fehling, D. *Die Wiederholungsfiguren und ihr Gebrauch bei den Griechen vor Gorgias* (Berlin 1969)

Ficker, W. *Vers und Satz im Dialog des Aischylos* (diss. Leipzig 1935)

Fitton Brown, A.D. 'Prometheia' *JHS* 79 (1959) 52-60

Focke, F. 'Aischylos' *Prometheus*' *Hermes* 65 (1930) 259-304

Foerster, F. *De attractionis usu Aeschyleo* (diss. Breslau 1866)

Fowler, B.H. 'The imagery of the *Prometheus Bound*' *AJP* 78 (1957) 173-84

Fraenkel, Eduard 'Lyrische Daktylen' *RhMus* 72 (1917) 161-97, 321-52

Fraenkel, Eduard *Aeschylus Agamemnon* (Oxford 1950)

Fraenkel, Eduard 'Der Einzug des Chors im *Prometheus*' *ASNP* 23 (1954) = *Kleine Beiträge* (Rome 1964) 1.389ff

Fraenkel, Ernst *Geschichte der griechischen Nomina agentis* (Strasburg 1910)

Fraenkel, H. 'Eine Stileigenheit der frühgriechischen Literatur' *NGG* (1924) 97ff

Fraser, P.M. *Ptolemaic Alexandria* (Oxford 1972)

Garvie, A.F. *Aeschylus' Supplices: play and trilogy* (Cambridge 1969)

Garzya, A. 'Le tragique du Promethée enchaîné d'Eschyle' *Mnemosyne* 18 (1965) 113-25

Gercke, A. in 'Bericht über d. zweiten schles. wiss. Ferienkursus von B. Laudien' *Zeitschr. für Gymnasialwesen* 65 (1911) 164-74

Gladigow, B. 'Aischylos und Heraklit' *AGPh* 44 (1962) 225-39

Golden, L. *In praise of Prometheus* (N. Carolina 1966)

Gollwitzer, I. *Die Prolog und Expositionstechnik der griechischen Tragödie mit besonder Berücksichtigung des Euripides* (diss. Munich 1937)

Goodwin, W.W. *Syntax of the moods and tenses of the Greek verb* (revised ed., Boston 1896) [*MT*]

Grene, D. 'Prometheus Bound' *CP* 35 (1940) 22-38

Gross, A. *Die Stichomythie in der griechischen Tragödie und Komödie* (Berlin 1905)

G. Grossmann *Promethie und Orestie* (Heidelberg 1970)

Gygli-Wyss, B. *Das nominale Polyptoton im älteren Griechisch* (Göttingen 1966)

Haines, C.R. 'Note on the parallelism between the *PV* and the *Antigone* of Sophocles' *CR* 29 (1915) 8-10

Hammond, N.G.L. 'The conditions of dramatic production to the death of Aeschylus' *GRBS* 13 (1972) 387-450

Harrison, E. 'Verseweight' *CQ* 8 (1914) 206-11

Harrison, E. 'Aeschylus *Sophokleizon*' *PCPS* (1921) 14-15

Harrison, E. 'Interlinear hiatus in Greek tragic trimeters' *CR* 55 (1941) 22-5, and 57 (1943) 61-3

Heidler, T. *De compositione metrica Promethei fabulae aeschyleae* (diss. Breslau 1887)

Heinimann, F. *Nomos und Physis* (Basel 1945)

Herington, C.J. *The author of the Prometheus Bound* (Austin and London 1970)

Herington, C.J. 'Aeschylus *Prometheus Unbound* fr. 193' *TAPA* 92 (1961) 239-50

Herington, C.J. 'A unique technical feature of the *Prometheus Bound*' *CR* 13 (1963) 5-7

Herington, C.J. 'Some evidence for a late dating of the *Prometheus Bound*' *CR* 14 (1964) 239-40

Herington, C.J. 'The influence of Old Comedy on Aeschylus' later trilogies' *TAPA* 94 (1963) 113-25

Herington, C.J. 'A study in the *Prometheia*' *Phoenix* 17 (1963) 180-97, 236-43

Herington, C.J. 'Aeschylus: the last phase' *Arion* 4 (1965) 387-403

Herington, C.J. 'Aeschylus in Sicily' *JHS* 87 (1967) 74-85

Hermann, J.G.J. *De Prometheo Aeschyleo* (Leipzig 1846) = *Opuscula* (Leipzig 1827-77) 8.144ff

Hiltbrunner, O. *Wiederholungs- und Motivtechnik bei Aischylos* (Bern 1950)

Höhlzle, R. *Zum Aufbau der lyrischen Partien des Aischylos* (diss. Freiburg 1934)

Hoppin, J.H. 'Argos, Io, and the *Prometheia* of Aeschylus' *HSCP* 12 (1901) 335-45

Huddilston, J.H. *Greek tragedy in the light of vase paintings* (London 1898)

Ireland, S. 'Noun participles in Aeschylus' *CR* 24 (1974) 2-3

Ireland, S. 'Structure, especially of sentences in the plays of Aeschylus, with special reference to the *PV*' (diss. Cambridge 1971, unpublished)

Italie, G. *Index Aeschyleus* (second ed., Leiden 1964)

Jachmann, G. *De Aristotelis didascaliis* (Göttingen 1909)

Jens, W. *Die Stichomythie in der frühen griechischen Tragödie* (Munich 1955)

Jens, W. 'Strukturgesetze der frühen griechischen Tragödie' *Stud. Gen.* 8 (1955) 246-53

Johansen, H.Friis 'Sentence structure in Aeschylus' *Suppliants*' *C&M* 15 (1954) 1-59

Johnson, R. 'The Promethean commonplace' *JWI* 25 (1962) 9-17

Jones, H.J.F. *On Aristotle and Greek tragedy* (London 1962)

Kamerbeek, J. 'Sophocle et Heraclite' in *Studia Vollgraf* (Amsterdam 1948)

Kerenyi, K. *Prometheus: archetypal image of human existence* (London 1963)

Keseling, P. 'Aischylos' *Gefesselter Prometheus* in Platon's *Protagoras* und *Gorgias*' *PhW* 50 (1930) 1469-72

Kiefer, K. *Körperlicher Schmerz auf der attischen Bühne* (diss. Heidelberg 1908)

Kleingünther, A. *Protos heuretes* (*Philol. Suppl.* 26, 1933)

Knox, B.M.W. *The heroic temper* (Berkeley 1964)

Kolisch, A. 'Ueber den *Prometheus* des Aischylos' *Philol.* 41 (1882) 227-41

Kopp, A. 'Ueber *positio debilis*' *RhMus* 41 (1886) 247-65, 376-86

Körte, A. 'Das Prometheus-Problem' *NJA* 45 (1920) 201-13

Kramer, H. *PV esse fabulam correctam* (diss. Freiburg 1878)

Kranz, W. *Stasimon* (Berlin 1933)

Kraus, W. *s.v. Prometheus* [*RE*] (1957) 653-702

Kraus, W. *Strophengestaltung in der griechischen Tragödie* (Vienna 1957)

Krausse, O. *De Euripide Aeschyli instauratore* (diss. Jena 1905)

Krischer, T. *Das Problem der trilogischen Komposition und die dramaturgische Entwicklung der attischen Tragödie* (diss. Frankfurt 1960)

Kühner - Blass: R. Kühner *Ausführliche Grammatik der griechischen Sprache*, I *Teil* (third ed., revised by F. Blass, Hanover 1890-2)

Kühner - Gerth: R. Kühner *Ausführliche Grammatik der griechischen Sprache* II *Teil* (third ed., revised by B. Gerth, Hanover 1898-1904)

Kumaniecki, C.F. *De elecutionis Aeschyleae natura = Archivum Filologiczne* 12 (Cracow 1935)

Kussmahly, F. *Beobachtungen zum Prometheus des Aischylos = Progr. des Sophien-Realgymn.* 95 (Berlin 1888)

Lalin, E. *De praepositionum usu apud Aeschylum* (Upsala 1885)

Leo, F. *Der Monolog im Drama* (Göttingen 1908)

Lesky, A. *History of Greek Literature* (tr. J. Willis and C. de Heer, London 1966)

Lesky, A. *Die tragische Dichtung der Hellenen* (Göttingen 1956)

Lloyd-Jones, H. 'Zeus in Aeschylus' *JHS* 76 (1956) 55-67

Lloyd-Jones, H. 'Problems of early tragedy', in *Estudios sobre la tragedia griega* (Madrid 1966)

Lloyd-Jones, H. *The justice of Zeus* (Berkeley 1971)

Long, H.S. 'Notes on Aeschylus' *Prometheus Bound*' *PAPS* 102 (1958) 229-80

Luppe, W. 'Die Papyrosfragmente der *Plutoi* des Kratinos' *WZHalle* 16 (1967) 57-91

Maas, P. *Greek metre* (tr. H. Lloyd-Jones, Oxford 1962)

Méautis, G. *L'authenticité et la date du Promethée enchaîné* (Geneva 1960)

Mess, A. von 'Der Typhonmythos bei Aischylos' *RhMus* 56 (1901) 167-72

Mess, A. von 'Zur Positionsdehnung vor *Muta cum liquida*' *RhMus* 58 (1903) 270-93

Mette, H.J. *Die Fragmente der Tragödien des Aischylos* (Berlin 1959)

Mette, H.J. *Der verlorene Aischylos* (Berlin 1963)

Michelini, A.N. 'Rhesis and dialogue: evidence in the *Persians* for the form of early tragedy' (diss. Harvard 1971, unpublished)

Mielke, H. *Die Bildersprache des Aischylos* (diss. Breslau 1934)

Moeller, H. *Untersuchungen zum Desmotes des Aischylos* (diss. Greifswald 1936)

Mommsen, Tycho *Beiträge zu der Lehre von griechischen Präpositionen* (Berlin 1895)

Morton, A.Q. 'The authorship of Greek prose' *Journ. Royal Stat. Soc.* A 128 (1965) 169-224; cf. 229-31 (criticism by G. Herden)

Morton, A.Q. and McLeman, J. *Paul, the man and the myth* (London 1966)

Mullens, H.G. 'Date and stage arrangements of the *Prometheia*' *G&R* 8 (1939) 160-71

Mullens, H.G. '*Hercules Furens* and *PV*' *CR* 53 (1939) 165-6

Münscher, K. 'Der Bau der Lieder des Aischylos' *Hermes* 59 (1924) 204-32

Myres, J.L. 'The wanderings of Io' *CR* 60 (1946) 2-4

Nachmanson, E. *Der griechische Buchtitel* (Göteborg 1941, repr. Darmstadt 1969)

Naylor, H.D. 'Doubtful syllables in iambic senarii' *CQ* 1 (1907) 4-9

Nes, D. van *Die maritime Bildersprache des Aischylos* (Groningen 1963)

Nestle, W. *Die Struktur des Eingangs in der attischen Tragödie (Tüb. Beitr.* 10, Tübingen 1930)

Niedzballa, F. *De copia verborum et elocutione Promethei Vincti* (diss. Breslau 1913)

Orsini, P. 'Observations sur la mise en scène du *Prométhée enchaîné*' in *Mélanges O. Navarre* (Toulouse 1935)

Otterlo, W.A.A. van *Beschouwingen over het archaische Element in den Stijl van Aeschylus* (Utrecht 1937)

Otterlo, W.A.A. van *Untersuchungen über Begriff, Anwendung und Entstehung der griechischen Ringcomposition* (= *Med. Ned. Akad. Wet.* 7, Amsterdam 1944)

Owen, A.S. 'The date of the *Electra* of Sophocles', in *Greek poetry and life*: essays presented to Gilbert Murray (Oxford 1936)

Page, D.L. *Euripides Medea* (Oxford 1938)

Page, D.L. *Greek literary papyri* I (Loeb Classical Library, London 1942) [*GLP*]

Peretti, A. 'Observazione sulla lingua del *Prometeo* Eschileo' *Stud. Ital.* 5 (1927) 165-231

Peretti, A. *Epirrema e tragedia* (Florence 1939)

Peretti, A. Review of van Otterlo *Stijl van Aeschylus*, *Gnom.* 16 (1940) 258-68

Peretti, A. 'Zeus und Prometheus bei Aischylos' *Antike* 20 (1944) 1-39

Pfeiffer, R. *Callimachus* (Oxford 1949)

Pfeiffer, R. *History of classical scholarship* (Oxford 1968)

Pickard-Cambridge, A.W. *Dithyramb, tragedy and comedy* (second ed., revised by T.B.L. Webster, Oxford 1962) [*DTC*]

Pickard-Cambridge, A.W. *The dramatic festivals of Athens* (second ed., revised by J. Gould and D.M. Lewis, Oxford 1968) [*DFA*]

Pickard-Cambridge, A.W. *The theatre of Dionysus at Athens* (Oxford 1956) [*TDA*]

Platnauer, M. 'Prodelision in Greek drama' *CQ* 10 (1960) 140-4

Podlecki, A.J. *The political background of Aeschylean tragedy* (Michigan 1966)

Poetscher, W. 'Die Funktion der Anapästpartien in den Tragödien des Aischylos' *Eranos* 57 (1959) 79-98

Pohlenz, M. *Die griechische Tragödie* (second ed., Göttingen 1954)

Pohlenz, M. *Die griechische Tragödie: Erläuterungen* (Göttingen 1954)

Pohlsander, H.A. *Metrical studies in the lyrics of Sophocles* (Leiden 1964)

Radermacher, L. '*Apokope* der Präpositionen im Dialog der attischen Tragödie' *Wien. Stud.* 41 (1919) 1-8

Rappold, J. *Das Reflexivpronomen bei Aischylos, Sophokles, und Euripides* (Klagenfurt 1873)

Rappold, J. *Die Gleichnisse bei Aischylos, Sophokles, und Euripides* (= *Progr. Klagenfurter Staatsgymn.* 1876-8) (Leipzig 1887)

Reinach, S. *Répertoire des vases peints grecs et étrusques* (Paris 1899)

Reinhardt, K. *Aischylos als Regisseur und Theologe* (Berne 1949)

Reinhardt, K. 'Prometheus' *Eranos-Jahrbuch* 25 (1956) 241-83

Reinhardt, K. 'Vorschlage zum neuen Aischylos' *Hermes* 85 (1957) 1-17, 123-6

Ribbeck, O. *Qua Aeschylus arte in Prometheo fabula diverbia composuerit* (Berne 1859)

Richardson, L.J.D. 'Further remarks on an epic idiom in Aeschylus' *Eranos* 55 (1957) 1-6

Ritchie, W. *The authenticity of the Rhesus of Euripides* (Cambridge 1964)

Robertson, D.S. 'On the chronology of Aeschylus' *PCPS* (1938) 9-10

Robertson, D.S. 'Prometheus and Chiron' *JHS* 71 (1951) 150-5

Robertson, H.G. 'Legal expressions and ideas of justice in Aeschylus' *CP* 34 (1939) 209-19

Rode, J. *Untersuchungen zur Form des aischyleischen Chorliedes* (diss. Tübingen 1966)

Röhlecke, A. *Septem adv. Theb. et PV esse fabulas post Aeschylum correctas* (diss. Berlin 1882)

Rombaut, L. *Het Prometheus-problem* (diss. Gand. 1935) [*non vidi*]

Rose, H.J. 'On an epic idiom in Aeschylus' *Eranos* 45 (1947) 88-99, 46 (1948) 72

Rösler, W. *Reflexe vorsokratischen Denkens bei Aischylos* (*Beitr. klass. Phil.* 37, Meisenheim 1970)

Schadewaldt, W. *Monolog und Selbstgespräch* (Berlin 1926)

Schein, S.L. 'The iambic trimeter in Aeschylus and Sophocles' (diss. Columbia Univ., New York 1967, unpublished)

Schinkel, K. *Die Wortwiederholung beim Aeschylus* (diss. Tübingen 1972)

Schmid, W. *Untersuchungen zum Gefesselten Prometheus* (*Tüb. Beitr.* 9, Tübingen 1929) [Schmid]

Schmid, W. *Geschichte der griechischen Literatur* I.3 (Munich 1940) [*GGL*]

Schmid, W. 'Epikritisches zum *Gefesselten Prometheus*' *PhW* 51 (1931) 218-23

Schmidt, F. *Die Pinakes des Kallimachos* (*Klassisch-Philologische Studien* 1, ed. F. Jacoby, Berlin 1922)

Schroeder, O. *Aeschyli Cantica* (Leipzig 1909)

Séchan, L. *Etudes sur la tragédie grecque* (Paris 1926, repr. Paris 1967)

Séchan, L. *Le mythe de Prométhée* (Paris 1951)

Sedgwick, W.B. 'The *Frogs* and the audience' *C&M* 9 (1948) 1-9

Seewald, J. *Untersuchungen zu Stil und Komposition der aischyleischen Tragödie* (Greifswald 1936)

Sideras, A. *Aeschylus Homericus* (Göttingen 1971)

Skard, E. 'A remark on *Prom.* 613' *Symb. Oslo.* 27 (1949) 11-18

Smith, G. 'On verbal repetition in Aeschylus', in *Studies in honour of B.L. Ullman*, ed. L.B. Lawler (Missouri 1960)

Smyth, H.Weir 'Notes on the anapaests of Aeschylus' *HSCP* 7 (1896) 139-65

Snell, B. *Aischylos und das Handeln im Drama* (*Philol. Suppl.* 21.1, 1928)

Snell, B. (Review of Schmid) *DLZ* 51 (1930) 298-302

Snell, B. *Euripides Alexandros* (*Hermes Einzelschr.* 5, Berlin 1937)

Snell, B. *Tragicorum Graecorum Fragmenta vol.* I (Göttingen 1971) [*TrGF*]

Solmsen, F. *Hesiod and Aeschylus* (Cornell 1949)

Stanford, W.B. 'Traces of Sicilian influence in Aeschylus' *Proc. Irish Acad.* 44 (1938) 229-40

Stanford, W.B. 'Three-word iambic trimeters' *CR* 54 (1940) 8-10

Stanford, W.B. *Aeschylus in his style* (Dublin 1942)

Stevens, P.T. 'Colloquial expressions in Aeschylus and Sophocles' *CR* 39 (1945) 95-105

Stinton, T.C.W. 'Two rare verse forms' *CR* 15 (1965) 142-6

Stinton, T.C.W. (Review of Herington) *Phoenix* 28 (1974) 258-64

Stoessl, F. *Die Trilogie des Aischylos* (Baden bei Wien 1937)

Sturm, J. *Geschichtliche Entwicklung der Constructionen mit prin* (= Schanz *Beitr. zur histor. Syntax der gr. Sprache* 3, Würzburg 1882)

Taplin, O. 'Aeschylean silences and silences in Aeschylus' *HSCP* 76 (1972) 57-97

Terzaghi, N. *Prometeo* (Florence 1966)

Tetsall, R.G. 'Violence on the Greek stage' *Euphrosyne* 1 (1957) 213-16

Thesleff, H. *Studies in the styles of Plato* (*Acta philos. Fennica* 20, Helsinki 1967)

Thomson, G. 'Zeus *tyrannos*' *CR* 43 (1929) 3-5

Thomson, G. *Aeschylus and Athens* (third ed., London 1966)

Thomson, J.A.K. 'The religious background of the *PV*' *HSCP* 31 (1920) 1-37

Todd, O.J. 'The character of Zeus in Aeschylus' *Prometheus Bound*' *CQ* 19 (1925) 61-8

Tracy, S.V. 'Prometheus Bound 114-117' *HSCP* 75 (1971) 59-62

Traglia, A. *Studi sulla lingua di Empedocle* (Bari 1952)

Turner, E.G. *Athenian books in the fifth and fourth centuries B.C.* (London 1952)

Uhlmann, N. 'Zum Prometheusproblem' *ZG* n.s. 7 (1919) 329-32

Unterberger, R. *Der Gefesselter Prometheus des Aischylos* (*Tüb. Beitr.* 45, Tübingen 1968)

Vandvik, E. *The Prometheus of Hesiod and Aeschylus* (Oslo 1943)

Wackernagel, J. 'Sprachgeschichtliches zum *Prometheus*' *Verhandl. des versamm. deutsch. Philol.* 46 (1901) 65

Wackernagel, J. *Studien zum griechischen Perfektum* (Göttingen 1904, = *Kl. Schr.* 2.1000-21)

Wake, W.C. 'Sentence length distributions of Greek authors' *Journ. Royal Stat. Soc.* A 120 (1957) 332-46

Wartelle, A. *Histoire du texte d'Eschyle dans l'antiquité* (Paris 1971)

Webster, T.B.L. 'A study of Greek sentence construction' *AJP* 62 (1941) 385-415

Webster, T.B.L. *Greek theatre production* (London 1956)

Webster, T.B.L. *Monuments illustrating tragedy and satyr play* (second ed., *BICS* 20, London 1967)

Wecklein, N. *Studien zu Aeschylus* (Berlin 1872)

Welcker, F.G. *Die aeschyleische Trilogie Prometheus* (Darmstadt 1824)

Wendel, T. *Die Gesprächsanrede im griechischen Drama der Blütezeit* (*Tüb. Beitr.* 6, Tübingen 1929)

West, M.L. *Hesiod Theogony* (Oxford 1966)

Westphal, R. *Prolegomena zu Aeschylus* (Leipzig 1869)

Wilamowitz-Moellendorff, U. von. *Einleitung in die griechische Tragödie* (= *Euripides Herakles*, vol. I, second ed., Berlin 1895)

Wilamowitz-Moellendorff, U. von *Aischylos Interpretationen* (Berlin 1914, repr. 1966) [*A. Int.*]

Wilamowitz-Moellendorff, U. von *Griechische Verskunst* (Berlin 1921) [*GV*]

Williams, C.B. *Style and vocabulary* (London 1970)

Yorke, E.C. 'Trisyllabic feet in the dialogue of Aeschylus' *CQ* 30 (1936) 116-19

Yorke, E.C. 'The date of the *PV*' *CQ* 30 (1936) 153-4

Young, D. 'Miltonic light on Professor Denys Page's Homeric theory' *G&R* 6 (1959) 96-108

Yule, G.U. 'On sentence length as a statistical characteristic of style in prose' *Biometrika* 30 (1939) 363-90

Yule, G.U. *The statistical study of literary vocabulary* (Cambridge 1944)

Zawadzka, I. '*Tolma*' *Eos* 54 (1964) 44-55

Zawadzka, I. 'Die Echtheit des *Gefesselten Prometheus*' *Altertum* 12 (1966) 210-23

Zielinski, T. *Tragodumenon libri tres* (Cracow 1925)

The recent Kiel *Habilitationschrift* of E. Lefèvre was unfortunately not available to me.

INDEXES

SUBJECT INDEX

INDEX OF GREEK WORDS DISCUSSED

INDEX OF PASSAGES CITED

Prometheus Bound

Prometheus Bound (cont.)

Prometheus Bound (cont.)

Choephoroi (cont.)

Eumenides

Herakleidai

Herakles

Hiketides

Hippolytos

Oed. at Kolonos (cont.)

Oed. Tyrannos

Philoktetes

THUCYDIDES

TZETZES

In Aristoph. proem.

Chiliad

Proleg. in Lyc.